"This handbook covers just about every question that Christians will encounter in engaging skeptics about the truth of Christianity. Comprehensive in scope, evidential in perspective, and authored by some of the most influential apologists, this anthology will prove an indispensable resource for those who would defend the faith."

—William A. Dembski
author of *The Design Inference* and other books on intelligent design

"*The Harvest Handbook of Apologetics* is a book that is sorely needed in this day when so few have undertaken the apologetic task that is so needed in the church. May our Lord be pleased to use it to his honor and glory, for never has the case for the truthfulness of our Lord and his word been so abundant in its sources and verification."

—Walter C. Kaiser Jr.
President Emeritus,
Gordon-Conwell Theological Seminary

"It is a joy to commend this book which features some of the world's top apologists, addressing the most relevant apologetic issues of our time. Readers will find the book immensely helpful."

—Ron Rhodes
president, Reasoning from the Scriptures Ministries

"Dr. Joseph Holden has amassed an impressive group of scholars for *The Harvest Handbook of Apologetics* to affirm the truths of the Christian religion and to defend against alternative religious viewpoints. An amazing group of well-known scholars and apologists cover the majority of the areas of apologetic concerns, such as the matter of apologetic approaches, the nature and existence of God, the historical nature and reliability of the Bible, the historical truth about Jesus, and alternatives to Christianity. An added feature is a look at key apologists of the past. I highly recommend this book."

—H. Wayne House
Distinguished Research Professor of Theology, Law, and Culture,
Faith International University and Faith Seminary

The

HARVEST HANDBOOK™ OF APOLOGETICS

JOSEPH M. HOLDEN
GENERAL EDITOR

HARVEST HOUSE PUBLISHERS
EUGENE, OREGON

Cover by Darren Welch Design

Cover photo © Renata Sedmakova / Shutterstock

The Harvest Handbook™ of Apologetics
Copyright © 2018 Joseph M. Holden
Published by Harvest House Publishers
Eugene, Oregon 97408
www.harvesthousepublishers.com

ISBN 978-0-7369-7428-8 (hardcover)
ISBN 978-0-7369-7429-5 (eBook)

Library of Congress Cataloging-in-Publication Data

Names: Holden, Joseph M., editor.
Title: The Harvest handbook of apologetics / Joseph M. Holden, general editor.
Description: Eugene, Oregon : Harvest House Publishers, 2018.
Identifiers: LCCN 2017059565 (print) | LCCN 2018019804 (ebook) | ISBN
   9780736974295 (ebook) | ISBN 9780736974288 (hardcover)
Subjects: LCSH: Apologetics.
Classification: LCC BT1103 (ebook) | LCC BT1103 .H375 2018 (print) | DDC
   202--dc23
LC record available at https://lccn.loc.gov/2017059565

Printed in the United States of America

18 19 20 21 22 23 24 25 26 / Bang-SK / 10 9 8 7 6 5 4 3 2 1

*To my teacher of apologetics, who loved me as a son,
inspired me to learn, and mentored me to serve,
Dr. Norman Geisler.*

Joseph M. Holden

Acknowledgments

In a work like this one, which bears the mark of so many skilled individuals, it is difficult to adequately acknowledge everyone involved. We are deeply grateful to the team of distinguished contributors who caught the vision of this book. Without their generous giving of labor and scholarly expertise, this project would have never made it to the press.

In addition, the tireless effort, skill, and vision of the editorial team of Steve Miller, Terry Glaspey, and President Bob Hawkins Jr. of Harvest House Publishers has done a masterful job in ensuring the many essays of this work speak to the needs of the reader. Their personal professionalism, attention to detail, and care for their authors have truly made publishing an enjoyable experience.

For their patience and encouragement throughout the writing of the book, it is my pleasure to acknowledge the staff, administration, and colleagues of Veritas International University. A special word of appreciation is due to Deborah DeLargy for her organizational assistance, and to Denise Ostermann for her constant encouragement and support throughout the project.

Thank you, Theresa, my dear wife of 20 years, for patiently allowing me to edit, type, and research nightly, and for displaying a servant's heart and angelic faithfulness, without which this book would not be possible!

Most of all, I would like to honor and give thanks to our Lord Jesus Christ for the opportunity and privilege to equip others to share and defend the faith. I am truly undeserving and humbled!

We sincerely desire this work will glorify God and equip the next generation to share the gospel and defend the historic Christian faith.

Contents

Contributors

Randy Alcorn, MA, DMin (Hon.)
Founder and director of Eternal Perspective Ministries (www.epm.org), Gresham, OR

Thomas W. Baker, PhD
Associate Professor of Theology and Apologetics, Veritas International University, Santa Ana, CA

J. Thomas Bridges, PhD
Academic Dean and Assistant Professor of Philosophy, Southern Evangelical Seminary, Charlotte, NC

Christopher P. Burke, LLM, MA(c), JD
Attorney at Law, Professor of Apologetics and Law, Veritas International University, Santa Ana, CA

Dillon Burroughs, PhD
Senior Fellow and Director of Publications, Ankerberg Theological Research Institute

Assistant Professor of Divinity, Liberty University, Lynchburg, VA

Steven Collins, PhD
Professor of Archaeology and Biblical History, Veritas International University, Santa Ana, CA

Dean of College of Archaeology at Trinity Southwest University, Albuquerque, NM

Natasha Crain, MBA, CCA (Apologetics)
Author and speaker on Christian parenting

Writer of popular parenting blog at www.christianmomthoughts.com

Don Deal, PhD(c)
Director of Research and Development, Norm Geisler International Ministries, Indian Trail, NC

David R.C. Deane, BEng, MA(c)
Graduate student in apologetics, Veritas International University, Santa Ana, CA

Engineering contractor for the Royal Australian Air Force, Australia

William A. Dembski, PhD, PhD
Former Senior Fellow at Discovery Institute's Center for Science and Culture, Seattle, WA

Educational technology entrepreneur

Miguel Angel Endara, PhD
Academic Dean, Professor of Philosophy and Religion, Veritas International University, Santa Ana, CA

F. David Farnell, PhD
Senior Professor of New Testament, The Master's Seminary, Sun Valley, CA

Adjunct Professor of New Testament, Veritas International University, Santa Ana, CA

Phil Fernandes, PhD
Professor of apologetics and theology, Director of Doctor of Ministry in Apologetics program, Veritas International University, Santa Ana, CA

President of Institute of Biblical Defense, Bremerton, WA

David Geisler, DMin
President of Norman Geisler International Ministries, Indian Trail, NC

Adjunct Professor at Southern Evangelical Seminary, Charlotte, NC

Norman L. Geisler, PhD
Chancellor, Occupant of the Dr. Norman L. Geisler Chair of Christian Apologetics, Distinguished Professor of Theology and Apologetics, Veritas International University, Santa Ana, CA

Distinguished Senior Professor of Theology and Apologetics at Southern Evangelical Seminary, Charlotte, NC

Terry Glaspey, MA

Independent scholar and author of numerous books, including the award-winning *75 Masterpieces Every Christian Should Know, Not a Tame Lion: The Spiritual Legacy of C.S. Lewis*, and *The Prayers of Jane Austen*

Guillermo Gonzalez, PhD

Astronomer, coauthor (with Jay Wesley Richards) of *The Privileged Planet: How Our Place in the Cosmos Is Designed for Discovery* (2004)

Gary R. Habermas, PhD

Distinguished Research Professor of Apologetics and Philosophy, Liberty University, Lynchburg, VA

David Haines, PhD

Associate Professor of Philosophy and Religion, Veritas International University, Santa Ana, CA

Philosopher and pastor in Québec, Association Axiome, Canada

Mark H. Hanna, PhD

Professor of Philosophy and Religion, Veritas International University, Santa Ana, CA

Author of *Biblical Christianity: Truth or Delusion?*

Christopher Travis Haun, MA(c)

Graduate student in apologetics, Veritas International University, Santa Ana, CA

Author and speaker

Edward E. Hindson, DMin, PhD

Founding Dean of The Rawlings School of Divinity, Distinguished Professor of Religion, Liberty University, Lynchburg, VA

Adjunct Professor of Biblical Studies and Religion, Veritas International University, Santa Ana, CA

Joseph M. Holden, PhD

President, Professor of Theology and Apologetics, Veritas International University, Santa Ana, CA

H. Wayne House, JD, ThD

Distinguished Research Professor of Theology, Law, and Culture, Faith Evangelical College and Seminary, Tacoma, WA

Adjunct Professor of Biblical Studies and Apologetics, Veritas International University, Santa Ana, CA

Richard G. Howe, PhD

Emeritus Professor of Philosophy and Apologetics, Southern Evangelical Seminary, Charlotte, NC

Brian Janeway, PhD

Professor of Archaeology and Biblical History, Veritas International University, Santa Ana, CA

Clay Jones, DMin

Associate Professor of Christian Apologetics, Biola University, La Mirada, CA

Walter C. Kaiser Jr., PhD

President Emeritus, Gordon-Conwell Theological Seminary, Hamilton, MA

Casey Luskin, MS, JD

Cofounder of the Intelligent Design and Evolution Awareness Center, Moraga, CA

Ralph E. MacKenzie, MA

Author, Emeritus Professor of Church History and Systematic Theology

Josh McDowell, MDiv

Founder of Josh McDowell Ministry, author, speaker, and apologist, Plano, TX

Sean McDowell, PhD

Author, speaker and apologist, assistant professor at Biola University, La Mirada, CA

Stephen C. Meyer, PhD

Senior fellow and director of Discovery Institute's Center for Science and Culture, Seattle, WA

Terry L. Miethe, PhD, PhD, DPhil (Oxon. Cand.)

Professor, Tennessee State University, Nashville, TN

John Warwick Montgomery, LLD, DTheol, PhD

Director of the International Academy of Apologetics, Evangelism and Human Rights, Strasbourg, France

Terry Mortenson, PhD

Historian of geology, author, speaker, and researcher with Answers in Genesis, Petersburg, KY

William E. Nix, PhD

Professor of Historical and Theological Studies, Veritas International University, Santa Ana, CA

Denise Ostermann, PhD

Emeritus Professor of Clinical Psychology, Biola University, Rosemead School of Psychology, La Mirada, CA

Douglas E. Potter, DMin

Assistant Professor of Theology and Apologetics, Southern Evangelical Seminary, Charlotte, NC

J. Randall Price, PhD

Distinguished Research Professor, curator of the Liberty Biblical Museum at Liberty University, Lynchburg, VA

Adjunct Professor of Archaeology and Apologetics, Veritas International University, Santa Ana, CA

Ron Rhodes, ThD

President of Reasoning from the Scriptures Ministries, Frisco, TX

Adjunct Professor of Theology and Apologetics, Veritas International University, Santa Ana, CA

J.C. Sanford, PhD

Geneticist, Courtesy Associate Professor, Cornell University, Ithaca, NY

Benjamin C.F. Shaw, MAR, PhD (ABD)

His PhD dissertation is on specific research regarding the subject of Jesus's resurrection. He has published a number of articles in a variety of journals (*Philosophia Christi*, *Christian Research Journal*, and elsewhere) and has also presented his research at conferences like the Evangelical Theological Society and Ratio Christi. He has been Gary R. Habermas's research assistant since 2013.

Jay H. Smith, PhD

International director of Pfander Center for Apologetics, London, England

Adjunct Professor of Islamic Studies, Veritas International University, Santa Ana, CA

Don Stewart, MA

Author, speaker, and founding director of Educating Our World

Cohost of *Pastor's Perspective* radio program (KWVE 107.9 FM), Santa Ana, CA

Patty Tunnicliffe, MA

Author, Bible teacher, and conference speaker (Islam), Santa Barbara, CA

Edwin M. Yamauchi, PhD

Professor Emeritus of History, Miami University, Oxford, OH

Patrick Zukeran, ThM, DMin

Author, speaker, apologist; president and founder of Evidence and Answers apologetics ministry

Foreword

Ravi Zacharias

The story is told of two Australian sailors who staggered out of a London pub into a dense fog looking around for help. As they steadied themselves, they saw a man walking into the pub—but evidently missed the military medals flashing on his uniform. One sailor shouted out to him, "Say, Mate, do you know where we are?" The officer, not impressed with this casual way of being addressed, snarled back, "Do you men know who I am?" The sailors looked at each other and one said to the other, "We're really in a mess now. We don't know where we are, and he doesn't know who he is."

As witty as the scene may be, it is an illustrative reminder of where postmodern thinking has landed us. From the days of a rugged rationalism and journeying through logical positivism or empiricism, through the challenges of existentialism, we have arrived at a postmodern view of life that in effect returns to "man being the measure of all things" without pausing to ask, "Which man?" Hence, we have entered the treacherous terrain of skepticism of truth, meaning, and certainty.

More than ever now, questions rise and answers seem vacuous. The truth is that without an ultimate frame of reference, we don't know who we are in essence or where we are in the grand scheme of life. And yet whatever our station in life or perspective, each of us has a worldview, whether we recognize it or not. A worldview basically offers answers to four haunting questions: origin, meaning, morality, and destiny. In attempting to answer these questions, it is imperative that the answers be correspondingly true on particular questions and, as a whole, all answers put together must be coherent. Correspondence and coherence are existentially and logically needed if one is to be legitimately persuaded.

The field of apologetics deals with the hard questions posed to the Christian faith. Having had deep questions myself, I listen carefully to the questions raised. Indeed, we must always bear in mind that behind every question is a questioner. So, answering difficult questions is not merely a theoretical exercise. It has personal ramifications for all of us. The convergence of intellectual and existential struggles drives a person to a brutal honesty in the questions they have, whether about God's existence or His goodness. In fact, Jesus consistently drove this home. His one-on-one conversations were remarkably personal and left the questioner looking into his or her own heart and its spiritual condition.

Whether you are a Christian or a skeptic, the formidable volume you hold in your hands offers rational and existentially compelling answers to the very questions of life, from the question of origin to the question of meaning. An incredible array of scholars has contributed to this work, and I am honored to write the foreword. From my professors Norman Geisler, John Warwick Montgomery, and Walter Kaiser to fellow apologists Josh McDowell and Gary Habermas—so many of these authors have shaped my own thinking and touched my life deeply. To read what they have to say is to find answers that go deep and motivations that are real. Having such an array of scholars in one volume is not merely a feast for the mind; it is energy for the soul. After four decades of traveling the globe, I have sensed how real these questions are across every culture. This is true especially for the young. "Why?" is not just a toddler's response out of curiosity; it is also a mature mind's genuine pursuit to find life meaningful and significant.

The Harvest Handbook of Apologetics is a rich and unparalleled resource that will challenge you to examine your own beliefs with candor and in the light of counter-perspectives. I commend this volume to you with great appreciation for the labor and time involved in producing it. You will refer to it time and again and make it a companion for life. The writers here are among the best in this discipline and will add to your thinking in enriching ways. As Augustine heard the words "Take and read," he took the Word of God and read. This volume takes those biblical truths and presents a brilliant defense in response to the legitimate questions in pursuit of the truth. "Take and read."

—**Ravi Zacharias**
author and speaker

Preface

The Battle for Hearts and Minds

At the dawn of the twenty-first century, challenges to the Christian worldview have increased in both intensity and sophistication, challenging even the brightest among us. The skeptic's sharp criticism of Scripture, disbelief in God, promotion of postmodernism, and the social progressive's relentless push for special rights have created a formidable beachhead in the war of ideas. Collectively, these critical notions have spawned numerous questions and arguments that have been weaponized by our critics to bludgeon the very foundations of Christianity.

Make no mistake, this war has been raging for centuries, and has now reached a fever pitch, especially within academic institutions as well as the media. Their relentless pursuit has always been for hearts and minds. In the past, their tactics were to push tolerance and a progressive social agenda, to create an ever-widening divide between conservatives and liberal, left and right, and Christian and secular.

Today we are experiencing a change in tactics from skeptics who seek to take the moral high ground and from social progressives who are intolerant of all conservative speech not in alignment with their ideals.

The cry for "tolerance" is no longer needed because the culture they sought to establish in the previous decades has been realized and fully tolerated by America's institutions. Now, the threats of lawsuits and violence are marshaled against those who offer morally conservative voices that threaten the recently established successes of the left.

Instead of responding in like kind, Christians recognize that in order to change our world, we must prayerfully change hearts and minds (2 Corinthians 10:3-6) by presenting Christ, recognizing that the most difficult things to overcome are ideological in nature.

The current environment has made it necessary to double down our efforts in equipping the church, as well as informing seekers of truth from outside the Christian faith to intelligently wrestle with (Jude 3, "*contend* for the faith") and respond to the crucial issues confronting our world today.

C.S. Lewis recognized what is at stake in the battle of ideas when he insightfully reminded Christian leaders of their responsibility to defend the faith:

> To be ignorant and simple now—not to be able to meet the enemies on their

own ground—would be to throw down our weapons, and to betray our uneducated brethren who have, under God, no defence but us against the intellectual attacks of the heathen. Good philosophy must exist, if for no other reason, because bad philosophy needs to be answered.[1]

Lewis's words reflect the spirit in which every chapter of this book was written. Each distinguished contributor is a scholar in their respective field and has followed in a long tradition of church leaders who took seriously the biblical command to defend the faith (1 Peter 3:15-16). Our goal is to equip you to make a difference in the marketplace of ideas, as well as broaden your toolkit for evangelism and responding to crucial questions that have the potential to change lives.

Each of the following 75 chapters have been carefully crafted using nontechnical language with a view toward not only answering a medley of important questions confronting believers today, but to serve as food for nourishing the soul. Because of the varied challenges confronting the Christian worldview, our team of esteemed contributors were hand picked from a wide variety of disciplines, including science, philosophy, theology, apologetics, psychology, engineering, and law. Each essay is designed for learning, offering you useful content to employ in your apologetic evangelism.

What is more, it is our desire that you grow in both your relationship with Christ and your courage to offer fresh insight in a winsome and humble manner during your interaction with others. The final goal of this work is twofold: (1) to equip the church body to engage culture for Christ, and (2) the salvation of the lost. Our prayer is that you will have a life-changing experience with truth as you journey through this book!

In a world of doctrinal decay and the ever-present lure to compromise biblical truth, we would do well to remind ourselves of the eccentric, uncompromising, camel-hair-wearing desert preacher John the Baptist. The church needs more uncompromising leaders, faithful believers, and steadfast voices clothed in camel hair!

—Joseph M. Holden, PhD
President, Veritas International University
General Editor

Part One

QUESTIONS ABOUT APOLOGETICS AND TRUTH

What Is Apologetics and
Why Do We Need It?

Norman L. Geisler

Since the beginning of the church in the first century AD, the Christian worldview has been challenged at every turn. The earliest attacks often came from the Roman government, which sought to discover any hint of treasonous activity among the "strange" ideas and practices of the faithful. While other theological assaults emerged from the Jewish religious leaders (Pharisees), both kinds of challenges would often lead to persecution.

As the church spread throughout Asia Minor (Turkey) and Europe, it came into contact with rival religious belief systems such as emperor worship, the Roman mystery cults, polytheism, and the cult of Artemis (Acts 19:28) along with their magical incantation formulas known as the *Ephesia Grammata*. Christians were pressed to defend the faith and develop an apologetic response that could both clearly distinguish Christianity from the cults and withstand severe counterargument. Among these early apologists were the apostle Paul (Philippians 1:7, 17), Justin Martyr, Irenaeus, Tertullian, and eventually Augustine.

However, as Christianity grew over the next few centuries, while at the same time clarifying its doctrines, it would be challenged with more sophisticated ideas emerging from Gnosticism (believed the creator god of the Old Testament is evil, matter is impure, and wrote false accounts of Christ), Arianism (Jesus did not have a divine nature), and from other heretics on the fringes of the church (e.g., the teachings of Cerinthus, Valentinus, Arius, Eutychius, and Nestorius). Because Christianity grew up in this intellectually challenging environment of Hellenistic philosophy and Roman religious practice, believers understood the need to defend, clarify, and present the gospel in understandable terms.

Today, the Christian worldview remains under attack on an industrial scale as the world searches for meaning and significance. These assaults come primarily through print publications, entertainment media, false religious movements, and in academic instruction, and they originate from various sources such as atheists, skeptics, critical theologians, proponents of evolutionary theory, and from liberal progressives seeking to advance their social agenda of abortion and gay rights. If there was ever a time to defend the faith, that time is now!

Apologetics is the discipline that deals with a rational defense of the Christian faith whether the challenges comes from inside or outside the church. The word *apologetics* comes from the Greek word *apologia* (1 Peter 3:15), which means to give a reason or defense. Thankfully, in last few decades, we have experienced a resurgence of lay interest and scholarship in the area of apologetics, as this book will attest. Therefore, the church finds itself in a much healthier position now than it was 50 years ago to defend against its modern critics and to provide more powerful counterarguments.

The Purpose of Apologetics

As it has from the beginning, apologetics serves both an offensive and defensive purpose. Offensively, it builds a case for the Christian faith, which is accomplished through 12 basic premises:[1]

1. Truth about reality is knowable.

2. Opposites cannot both be true.

3. It is true that the theistic God exists.

4. Miracles are possible.

5. Miracles performed in connection with a truth claim confirm the truth of God through a messenger of God.

6. The New Testament documents are reliable (textually and historically).[2]

7. As witnessed in the New Testament, Jesus claimed to be God.

8. Jesus's claim to be God was proven by a unique convergence of miracles (e.g., resurrection).

9. Therefore, Jesus was God in human flesh.

10. Whatever Jesus (who is God) affirmed as true, is true.

11. Jesus affirmed that the Bible is the Word of God.

12. Therefore, it is true that the Bible is the Word of God, and whatever is opposed to any biblical truth is false.

Offensively, apologetics answers the crucial question, Why is Christianity true? To fully answer this question, it is important to cover all the points listed above, which are addressed throughout this book.

Defensively, apologetics answers any sincere objection or question about the Christian faith.[3] For example, when objections arise to the existence of God, it is important to first explain the absolute nature of truth. Likewise, when someone asks questions about the resurrection, the answer needs to include mention of the reliability of the New Testament. To put it another way, apologetics is pre-evangelism. That is to say, it is done *before* evangelism *if needed* or when an objection or question is raised.

Why Apologetics Is Necessary

There are many good reasons why we need apologetics. First, God commands the use of apologetics. Second, reason demands a defense. Third, the world needs apologetics. Finally, results confirm the success of apologetics. Let's examine each in order.

God Commands the Use of Apologetics. Throughout the Bible there are verses that emphasize engaging in apologetics. Over and over again the Scriptures exhort believers to defend the faith (Jude 3). The apostle Peter wrote, "In your hearts honor Christ the Lord as holy, always being prepared to make a defense to anyone who asks you for a reason for the hope that is in you; yet do it with gentleness and respect" (1 Peter 3:15).

This verse communicates several important points. First, it's our duty to *be prepared* in case a defense of the faith is necessary. We might never need to use apologetics, but being prepared to do the work of an apologist is a biblical command for all Christians. As a representative for Christ, a Christian is adequately prepared not only to understanding various arguments, but is also eagerly looking for opportunities to share the truth of Christ with others.

Second, we are to *give a reason* to those who ask questions (cf. Colossians 4:5-6). Not every conversation with unbelievers requires an apologetic response or pre-evangelism, but when necessary, the Christian apologist should possess the ability and desire to give others an answer.

Finally, 1 Peter 3:15 addresses the special place we ought to have for Christ in our hearts and lives in doing apologetics. Those who follow Christ should routinely "destroy arguments and every lofty opinion raised against the knowledge of God, and take every thought captive to obey Christ" (2 Corinthians 10:5). Scripture clearly encourages us to address our own doubts as well as the faulty ideas that prevent others from knowing Christ as their Savior and the Bible as the Word of God. This is the essence and goal of apologetics.

The apostle Paul clearly stated that his mission was the "defense and confirmation of the gospel" (Philippians 1:7), and he reiterated in verse 16, "I am put here for the defense of the gospel." Some are hesitant to defend the faith because they believe they are not *gifted* as an apologist. However, we must recognize that though we may not feel gifted in this endeavor, we are certainly called by Scripture to do the *work* of an apologist. The half brother of Jesus (Jude) said, "Beloved, although I was very eager to write to you about our common salvation, I found it necessary to write appealing to you to contend for the faith that was once for all delivered to the saints" (Jude 3). Jude was concerned about those in the church who had been ravished by false teachers, encouraging them to defend what had been revealed to them through Christ—to the point of *agony*. Jude also addressed our demeanor when defending the faith when he wrote, "Have mercy on those who doubt" (verse 22). Apologetics, then, is a form of compassion.

Moreover, the pastoral epistles make clear that Christian leaders in the church should demonstrate knowledge of evidence that supports the Christian worldview. Titus said, "He must hold firm to the trustworthy word as taught, so that he may be able to give instruction in sound doctrine and also to rebuke those who contradict it" (Titus 1:9). Paul said, "The Lord's servant must not be quarrelsome but kind to everyone, able to teach, patiently enduring evil, correcting his opponents with gentleness. God may perhaps grant them repentance leading to a knowledge of the truth" (2 Timothy 2:24-25). The Bible has much to say about patience. This is particularly important when doing apologetics because we are all prone to losing patience with unbelievers. We need to remember our ultimate goal is to help them understand the significance of the gospel message of Christ's death and resurrection.

Indeed, the exhortation to use reason is

part of the greatest command. For Jesus said, "You shall love the Lord your God with all your heart and with all your soul and *with all your mind*. This is the great and first commandment" (Matthew 22:37-38, emphasis added).

Logic Requires a Defense. In the beginning, God created us in His image; this included the power of reason (Genesis 1:27), which distinguishes human beings from animals (Jude 10). Throughout Scripture, we are encouraged to use reason (Isaiah 1:18) in order to discover truth (1 John 4:6), to discern what is moral and immoral (Hebrews 5:14), and to learn the difference between a true and false prophet (Deuteronomy 18:19-22).

A fundamental principle of reason is that we should have sufficient grounds for what we believe. An unjustified belief is just that— *unjustified*! Being created rational creatures and not "unreasoning animals" (Jude 10), we are expected to use the reason God gave us. In doing so, we fulfill part of the greatest command, which includes loving God with all of our minds (Matthew 22:36-37).

Unbelievers Need Apologetics. The world may have good questions, but Christians have good answers. However, many people refuse to believe without some evidence, as indeed they should. It makes sense that if God created us with the power of reason, we should think and behave in a rational manner. He desires us to seek and evaluate the evidence prior to taking a step of faith (John 3:12; Romans 1:4). Some have suggested that seeking facts destroys faith. It does not. Any rational person will consider the evidence prior to taking a step of faith. Not to do so is both dangerous and irresponsible. For example, no one dives headlong into a swimming pool before verifying the pool is full of water. To put it another way, no one comes

to faith in Christ because it is *contradictory* or *irrational*! Rather, we serve Christ because it is reasonable (Romans 12:1).

Further, the intellectual assent *that* something is true or exists is prior to belief *in* (volitional trust of the heart) something. Evidence and reason are important to establish belief *that* something is true. It is reasonable to assume unbelievers will want good reason to believe *that* Jesus is the Savior of the world prior to placing trust *in* Him.

Results Confirm Apologetics

There is a common misnomer among many Christians that apologetics never helps bring anyone to Christ. This is a serious misrepresentation of the facts.

The Results of Investigation and Reason. The great medieval theologian Augustine wrote about several significant rational turning points in his life before he came to Christ.[4] First, he reasoned his way out of Manichaean dualism. To Augustine, a significant turning point in his change was the success of a young Christian debater of Manicheans named Helpidius. Second, Augustine reasoned his way out of total skepticism by seeing the self-defeating nature of it, since Augustine would have to be *certain* of his skepticism. The only way he could be true to his total skepticism was to be skeptical of his skepticism. Third, were it not for studying Plotinus (AD 204–270), Augustine informs us that he would not even be able to conceive of a spiritual being, let alone believe in one.

Another success story is Simon Greenleaf, professor of law at Harvard, who is widely credited for writing the book on legal evidence. He was challenged by students to apply the rules of legal evidence to the New Testament to see if its testimony would stand up in court. The result was a book titled *The*

Testimony of the Evangelists,[5] in which he expressed his confidence in the basic documents and truths of the Christian faith.

In addition, Frank Morrison, an unbelieving attorney, set out to disprove Christianity by showing the resurrection never occurred. The quest ended with his conversion and a book titled *Who Moved the Stone?*[6] Ironically, the first chapter of his book was titled "The Book That Refused to Be Written"!

The Results of Debates. Many people have been led toward Christ as a result of debates we have had with atheists and skeptics. After debating then-University of California, Berkeley philosopher Michael Scriven on "Is Christianity Credible?" the University of Calgary audience voted three to one in favor of Christianity. The campus newspaper report read: "Atheist Fails to Convert Campus Christians"!

Following a debate on the rationality of belief in Christianity with the head of the philosophy department at the University of Miami, the Christian student leaders held a follow-up meeting. The atheist professor attended and expressed doubts about his view stated at the debate. It was reported that some 14 people who had attended the debate made decisions for Christ!

After a debate on the Moonie religion at Northwestern University in Evanston, Illinois, a young woman who was a follower of Moonie asked some questions about Christianity. I could see that she had been convinced that the Unification Church was not teaching the truth. After talking with her briefly, I introduced her to a female seminary student who led her to Christ.

While sharing the gospel with Don Bly, he informed us that he was an atheist. After reasoning with him from atheism to open-minded agnosticism, he agreed to read Frank Morrison's book. The evidence for Christ's resurrection convinced him, and we had the privilege of leading him to Christ. He has subsequently raised his family for Christ and became a leader in a church south of St. Louis.

The Results of Reading. Over the years, I have received numerous letters and reports of people who have been converted to belief that God exists or to belief in Christ after reading books on apologetics. God uses argumentative reasoning as an instrument to bring people toward God and to Christ.

One of the world's most notorious atheists, Antony Flew, changed his mind about God and wrote, "Nor do I claim to have had any personal experience of God or any experience that may be called supernatural or miraculous. In short, my discovery of the divine has been a pilgrimage of reason and not of faith."[7]

Noted former atheist Francis Collins said, "After twenty-eight years as a believer, the Moral Law still stands out for me as the strongest signpost to God. More than that, it points to a God who cares about human beings, and a God who is infinitely good and holy."[8]

A college student wrote, "God sent me your book *I Don't Have Enough Faith to Be an Atheist*[9]…I opened the book thinking I would rip it apart with my superior viewpoint, and about one-quarter of the way through I ended up apologizing to God and accepting him into my heart. I have since grown exponentially in Christ, and I thought I would thank you for your inspiring book."

Ready with an Answer

Christianity must be defended against attacks from within by cults and heresies, and from without by skeptics and other religions. We have a reasonable faith, and the Bible has commanded that we give reasons for it. As perhaps the greatest apologist of the twentieth century, C.S. Lewis, said: "Good philosophy must exist, if for no other reason, because bad philosophy needs to be answered."[10]

To be certain, utilizing apologetics helps the skeptic to recognize that it takes more faith to reject Christ than it does to receive Him!

What About a Short History of Apologetics?

John Warwick Montgomery

The history of the defence of the Christian faith is coterminous with the history of Christianity itself.[1] This is the case because Christianity, unlike religions of the East, such as Buddhism and Hinduism, is non-syncretic: Christianity asserts that religious truth can ultimately be found only in Jesus Christ and Christian revelation (John 14:6; Acts 4:12). From this it follows that religious claims contradicting Christian faith cannot be true and must be opposed, and negative criticisms of the truth of the Christian position must be answered.

Covenant theology bifurcates the history of salvation, treating it in terms of Old Testament or Covenant, and New Testament. Dispensationalists prefer to divide salvation history into numerous epochs, often seven in number. We shall try to satisfy both! The major divide in the history of apologetics occurs at the time of the 18th century so-called "Enlightenment," when secular thinkers such as Thomas Paine endeavoured to replace the "Book of Scripture" with the "Book of Nature"; subsequently, apologetics followed a very different path from that of the preceding centuries. Prior to that massive ideological divide, Christianity had occupied stage centre in Western intellectual history; afterwards, it found itself relegated to the wings.

But the expanse of apologetic history from biblical times to the 21st century can also be discussed in terms of seven epochs or styles of defence, and we shall briefly comment on each of them in turn: (1) Apologetics in the Bible itself; (2) Patristic defence of the faith; (3) Medieval apologetics; (4) Renaissance and Reformation; (5) Apologetics at the zenith of the "classical Christian era"; (6) Response to the Enlightenment in the 18th and 19th centuries; (7) Apologetics today. In our final section, we shall have opportunity to reflect on the weaknesses of the apologetic situation in today's church.

Apologetics in the Bible

Charles Finney was supposed to have downgraded apologetic argument by remarking: "Defend the Bible? How would you defend a lion? Let it out of its cage and it'll defend itself!" But, in point of fact, the Bible, unlike the Qur'an and the "holy books" of other religions, does not expect its readers to accept its revelational character simply because the text claims to be true. In the Old Testament, Elijah competes with the false prophets of Baal, and the superior miraculous demonstration by the power of the God of Israel wins the day (I Kings 18). In the Gospels, Jesus makes the truth of his entire ministry depend on a single sign—that of his resurrection from the dead (Matthew 12:39-40). In the Epistles, not only is Christ's physical resurrection asserted, but the Apostle is concerned as well to provide a list of eyewitnesses to the risen Christ (1 Corinthians 15:4-8).

The biblical apologetic focuses in four areas, and these are subsequently employed throughout Christian history: *miracle, fulfilled prophecy, natural revelation,* and *personal experience* (what the philosophers term "subjective immediacy"). Three caveats: (1) natural revelation (proofs of God from nature), though present in the Bible (e.g., Psalm 19:1), is the least emphasised apologetic; (2) personal experience never "floats free": the subjective is always grounded in one or more of the objective areas of proof—generally miracle and prophecy; (3) occasionally, a "double-barreled" argument is made through *miracle* being the object of *prophecy,* as in the case of the Virgin Birth of our Lord (Isaiah 7:14; Matthew 1; Luke 1–2).

Since the biblical plan of salvation centres on God's revealing himself in real history, through prophets, priests, and finally by the incarnation of his eternal Son, Jesus Christ, the biblical apologetic is essentially one of asserting and demonstrating the *factual* nature of the events recounted. The Apostle is willing to make the entire truth of the faith turn on the reality of Jesus's resurrection (1 Corinthians 15:17-20). The case for biblical truth, then, connects with the nature

of Christianity as "historical religion": it is in principle falsifiable—and, in this case, verifiable—thereby removing Christianity from the analytical philosophers' category of a meaningless metaphysical claim and placing it in the realm of the empirical and the synthetic, along with historical events in general.

Patristic Apologetics

The church fathers closest to the New Testament understandably followed its apologetic lead: prophecy and miracle were their preferred arguments. The earliest of them (Irenaeus, for example) favoured the prophecies of the Old Testament fulfilled in Christ, since in his time the gospel was being proclaimed and defended "to the Jew first." Moreover, the Gnostic heretics employed pseudo-miracles (sherbet in Eucharistic wine!), but had no fulfilled prophecies to support their views. As Christian evangelism reached a predominately Gentile audience, miracle evidence came to the fore. Eusebius of Caesarea, in his *Ecclesiastical History,* employs a testimonial argument in support of Christ's miraculous resurrection from the dead, sarcastically asking whether it would be reasonable to suppose that the Apostles, had they known that Jesus did not rise from the dead, would have lost all they had and ultimately been martyred whilst maintaining that he *had* in fact conquered death. Tertullian's oft-quoted phrase, *"Credo quia absurdum,"* rather than being an invitation to irrationality, expressed the belief that the Christian gospel was almost too good to be true—as the children in C.S. Lewis's Narnian chronicles would later discover.

The bridge between the Patristic and medieval worlds was Augustine of Hippo. He was converted from neo-Platonism to Christianity and offered an apologetic of a

Platonic nature to the intellectuals of his time, convinced as they were that Plato was the summation of classical philosophy. For Plato, one must rationally (and for neo-Platonists, rationally *and* spiritually) rise from the world of phenomena to the world of ideas/ideals—of which the highest expression is the Good, the True, and the Beautiful. Augustine identified that realm with the God of the Bible. He also, in his *Confessions*, made a compelling argument from personal experience: "Thou hast made us for thyself, O God, and our hearts are restless until they rest in thee." In the 20th century, Edward John Carnell would expand on this in his axiological apologetic, *A Philosophy of the Christian Religion*.

Medieval Defense of the Faith

Theodore Abu Qurra, an Eastern theologian (9th century), set forth an apologetic parable demonstrating comprehension of the apologetic task well in advance of his time; it raises the critical question as to how one can test multiple revelation claims (in his case, Islam vs. Christianity). For Abu Qurra, one asks each religion what it says of God, what it says of sin, and what sort of remedy it offers for the human condition—thereby demonstrating the superiority of Christianity.[2]

Although a primitive form of the ontological argument for God's existence can be found in St. Augustine, St. Anselm of Canterbury provided its classic formulation in the 11th century. The argument purports to prove God's existence from the concept of God itself: God is "than which no greater can be conceived"; he must therefore have all properties; and since *existence* is a property, God exists! The argument rests on the idealistic assumption that ideas have reality untouched by the phenomenal world

(so rational idealists have been somewhat comfortable with it), but the overwhelming fallacy in the argument is simply that "existence" is not a property alongside other properties; *existence* is the name we give to something that in fact has properties. To determine whether a something (God?) exists, we need to investigate the empirical evidences of its/his reality.[3] Thus the far better Christian argument is that "God was in Christ, reconciling the world unto himself" (2 Corinthians 5:19). This critique having been offered, it is worth noting that neo-Orthodox theologian Karl Barth (*Anselm: Fides Quaerens Intellectum*) was quite wrong that Anselm was not trying to do apologetics but was simply preaching to the converted.[4]

The most influential medieval apologist of Western Christendom was its most influential theologian: Thomas Aquinas. Though probably having never met a pagan, he wrote his *Summa contra Gentiles* ("Summation against the pagans"). By his time—the 13th century—Aristotle had replaced Plato as the most favoured classical philosopher, so Aquinas developed his apologetic along Aristotelian lines. He took over Aristotle's traditional proofs for God's existence, and argued that they can establish a foundation of Reason upon which Faith can operate. This stress on the Aristotelian proofs would have a tremendous influence on all subsequent Christian apologetics.

Contemporaneous with Aquinas was Ramon Lull (or Lullius), a Catalonian who is considered to be the first European missionary to the Moslems. Lull was a philosopher, but not a scholastic in the Aristotelian tradition. He developed an original "method" for the conversion of the infidel through the combining of theological and philosophical concepts and the illustrative use of rotating, interlocking disks. He now figures in the pre-history of the modern computer.[5] Lull also practiced literary apologetics by way of his apologetic novel, *Blanquerna.*

Renaissance and Reformation

By the time of the Italian Renaissance (15th–16th centuries), the world was opening up to exploration and Plato had returned to philosophical prominence. Thus the apologists of that era directed their efforts to adventurous thinkers committed to a Platonic view of the world. Thomas More, in his *Utopia,* well illustrates this. The Utopians pray each night that "if there is a better and truer faith, may God bring it to us." More's explorers reach Utopia and present the Christian religion as that better faith. The Utopians, in seeking the Good, the True, and the Beautiful, accept the God of Christian revelation.

The Protestant Reformers were not concerned with apologetics as such; they had more than enough to do cleaning up the theology of the medieval church. But their work had much indirect value for apologetics. Thus, Luther's insistence on *sola Scriptura* and thoroughgoing christocentricity were healthy counteractives to medieval Aristotelian/Thomistic emphases.[6] And when the Roman Catholic opponents of the Reformation argued that the Bible is an obscure book, requiring the Roman Church to interpret it, Protestants such as Andreas Althamer produced books defending the clarity ("perspicuity") and non-contradictory nature of the teachings of Holy Scripture. Such writings are the forerunners of modern treatises that deal with and refute claims to alleged errors and contradictions in the Bible.

17th Century Apologetics

This was the last century of "old Western man"—the last century when Christian thought dominated the intellectual landscape of the West. It was the era of "system"—Protestant systematic theology, the musical summation of the Western musical tradition in the labours of Lutheran J.S. Bach, the literary summation in Milton's Paradise Lost, the architectural summation in Wren's magnificent churches constructed after London's Great Fire of 1666.

As for apologetics, Hugo Grotius, the father of international law, published in 1622 his *De Veritate religionis Christianae* ("On the truth of the Christian Religion"). This seminal work was widely translated and in print until the 19th century. It sets forth a modern, historical apologetic for the soundness of Jesus's claims in the New Testament.

Even more famous and influential was the apologetic work of Blaise Pascal, a Roman Catholic but a follower of the Port Royal, Jansenist movement, which was regarded by its conservative Catholic enemies as tantamount to Protestantism—owing to its great appreciation for St. Augustine and central stress on salvation by grace through faith. Pascal's posthumously collected *Pensées* ("Thoughts") offer a powerful apologetic for the truth of biblical revelation and the saving work of Christ. His "wager" (even if Christianity were false, in accepting it you would be better off, for you would obtain the best ethic and the best human example—Jesus) was not intended as the totality of his apologetic (as his philosophical critics generally maintain, in order to make it appear silly), but only as a device for getting the unbeliever's attention. Having been struck by the force of the wager, the unbeliever would then have powerful reason to examine the full gamut of evidence for the faith and thereby come to see that the probabilities are overwhelmingly in favour of Christian commitment.[7]

The Great Divide and Its Apologetic Aftermath

The 18th century was characterised politically by the French and American Revolutions and ideologically by Deism: the belief that one could and should dispense with the "revealed" religion of historic Christianity, contaminated by superstition (blood sacrifice, miracles, etc.) and substitute a "religion of Nature," focusing on a God of immutable natural law and morality.[8] "Enlightenment" philosophers included Immanuel Kant, who claimed that the traditional proofs of God's existence were inadequate and that only an absolute ethic could be established (the "categorical imperative"); Gotthold Ephraim Lessing, who dug his "Ditch" between absolute, philosophical truth on the one hand, and what he considered the inadequacies of history (including biblical history) on the other; and David Hume, who claimed that, owing to "uniform experience," miracles could always be rejected out of hand, since it would always be more miraculous if the witness were telling the truth than that the miracle actually happened.

These attacks were devastating and historic Christianity lost much intellectual ground as a result of them. The identification of the churches with the privileges of monarchy and the Old Régime only made matters worse. But apologists for the faith heroically entered the fray.

In the 18th century itself, William Paley (*Natural Theology; Evidences*) argued for the soundness of the biblical witness—both as to God's hand in nature and as to the soundness of the New Testament portrait of Jesus;[9] and

Thomas Sherlock pointed out, in his legally orientated work *The Tryal of the Witnesses of the Resurrection of Jesus,* that people of the 1st century were as capable as those of his own "enlightened" time to distinguish between a dead body and a live one—and that the case for Jesus's resurrection could not therefore be dismissed philosophically.[10]

The most famous defence of faith in the 18th century was Bishop Butler's *Analogy of Religion,* which attempted to convince the Deist using his own reasoning: The Scriptural teaching, said Butler, was directly *analogous* to the work of God in nature—and since the Deist accepted the latter, he had no ground for rejecting the former. Examples: nature displays seeds falling into the ground and dying, followed by life again every spring, and Scripture presents the crucifixion followed by the resurrection; human society survives only because each person acts for others by doing work the other cannot do, and Scripture makes divine substitution the key to salvation.

The 19th century dealt a further, perhaps even more crushing, blow to the faith. With the publication of Darwin's *Origin of Species* in 1859, even the Deist's God of Nature could be discarded: natural selection could allegedly account for all development. Defenders of the faith offered two very different apologetic approaches to this incipient atheism that culminated, at the end of century, in Nietzsche's famous declaration that "God is dead."

The great Roman Catholic (former Anglican) apologist John Henry Newman doggedly fought the revelational battle on epistemological and historical grounds (*Essays on Miracles; Grammar of Assent*): He refined the notion of historical probability with his concept of the *illative sense*: when "congeries" (concatenations) of facts inexorably point to the same conclusion—as in the testimonies to the resurrection of Christ—they raise the level of the argument to a practical certainty and cannot rationally be dismissed.

Lay philosopher and theologian Søren Kierkegaard, the father of existentialism, took an inner route: for him, "truth is subjectivity." As finite creatures, we cannot, à la Hegel and German idealistic philosophy, discover the "essence" of things; we can only experience our own "existence"—which, owing to the fall, is *Angst* and estrangement without Christ. But his successor existentialists in the 20th century (Heidegger, Sartre), left with only their own subjectivity, did not find Christ, but a valueless, atheistic world, both microcosmically and macrocosmically. By discounting the value of probability and historical reasoning to vindicate Christian revelation, Kierkegaard ended up substituting an unstable, subjective experientialism for the objectivist *hubris* of the unbelieving philosophers he opposed. Modern evangelicalism has frequently made the same mistake.

Apologetics Today

In the early decades of the 20th century, what appeared to be a powerful case against all metaphysical and religious thinking appeared on the scene. This stemmed from Ludwig Wittgenstein's *Tractatus Logico-Philosophicus* and from the so-called Vienna Circle of analytical philosophers and logical positivists. They argued that truth claims, including metaphysical and religious views, were meaningless unless they could be verified. Many theologians and most metaphysicians tried to counter this position by discounting the need for verification (a Pyrrhic victory if there ever was one!). In point of fact, as this essayist has maintained in his

major work (*Tractatus Logico-Theologicus*[11]), whereas secular metaphysical systems and virtually all non-Christian religions do in fact entirely lack testability, Christian faith alone offers the solid, empirical, historical evidence of its truth by way of the case for Jesus Christ.

The 20th century and the onset of the 21st have been marked by a number of influential Christian apologists and by several apologetic schools of thought.

Needless to say, the liberal churches did not carry on apologetic activity, since inherent to theological liberalism has always been an accommodating of the faith to secular ideology rather than a defending of it over against secularism (cf. liberal theologian Willard L. Sperry's *"Yes, But"—the Bankruptcy of Apologetics*). The Scopes evolution trial drove many American evangelicals into a radical separation from mainline intellectual life and therefore from apologetic activity: the only choice they saw was to pluck "brands from the burning" through revival campaigns and personal testimony. But even the twelve popular paperbound volumes that introduced the term "fundamentalist" into the language (*The Fundamentals*, 1910) contained fine apologetic defences of historic Christianity by such notables as James Orr and B.B. Warfield.

Warfield, as a Princeton Theological Seminary professor, commanded great respect. His defence of scriptural inerrancy (*The Inspiration and Authority of the Bible*) had immense impact, especially in Reformed theological circles. Later, this would be blunted by the Westminster Theological Seminary theologian Cornelius Van Til, who criticised Warfield's evidential argumentation as not being sufficiently Calvinistic—since it did not insist on starting from the presupposition of the truth of the faith and God's sovereignty, above and beyond evidential considerations.

In the 1940s, Moody Bible Institute instructor and Bible commentator Wilbur M. Smith wrote his book *Therefore Stand: A Plea for a Vigorous Apologetic*. Essentially a work of historical apologetics, this book had wide influence: its author could be trusted as not being a closet intellectual or one critical of the evangelical lifestyle. *Therefore Stand* remains a classic, demonstrating on every page the wide learning of the preeminent theological bibliographer of 20th century evangelicalism.

Smith would later accept a chair at the newly founded Fuller Theological Seminary. There (before Fuller gave up its inerrancy position), apologist Edward John Carnell produced exceedingly important works: *An Introduction to Christian Apologetics* and *A Philosophy of the Christian Religion*. The *Introduction* endeavours, without success, to combine a Van Tilian presuppositionalism with E.S. Brightman's truth test of "systematic consistency" (a true assertion must be logically consistent and must also fit the facts of the external world)—but the second part of the book contains masterful responses to a host of common objections to biblical religion: the problem of evil, evolutionary theory, anti-miraculous views, etc.

The mid-20th century was also marked by the writings of the most influential of all English-language apologists of the time: C.S. Lewis. To apply the terminology of William James, Lewis successfully practised both "toughminded" and "tenderminded" apologetics. His broadcast talks (later combined under the title *Mere Christianity*) brought many to the faith in England: My Cornell professor, the late literary critic David Daiches, remarked that more had been converted through Lewis than in the British revival campaigns of Billy Graham! *Miracles*

dealt with Hume's attempt to short-circuit historical investigation through philosophical speculation;[12] *The Problem of Pain* was a superb popular justification of the God of the Bible against the standard argument that an all-powerful and loving God could not exist in the face of the evils of the world. On the tenderminded front, Lewis's science-fiction trilogy (*Out of the Silent Planet, Perelandra, That Hideous Strength*) and his Narnian chronicles brought many who were indifferent to traditional apologetics to see the truth of the faith on the level of "deep myth."[13]

A number of "schools" of apologetics came into existence in the latter years of the 20th century and continue to influence the intellectual climate. We have mentioned above the *presuppositionalist* approach. Its major representatives have been philosopher Gordon Clark and theologian Cornelius Van Til; its epicentre is the Westminster Theological Seminary (Philadelphia) and its advocates include John Frame and the late Greg Bahnsen. Though there are important differences among these thinkers, they are all convinced that, owing to the fall of man, facts cannot be used to convince unbelievers of Christian truth: As Van Til put it: "All is yellow to the jaundiced eye." Generally (but not in every case) this presuppositionalism is combined with an ultra-Calvinist understanding of predestination.

Philosopher Alvin Plantinga's "Reformed epistemology" can be regarded as a variant of the presuppositionalist position. For Plantinga, historical argumentation is necessarily inadequate and no demonstration that Christianity is true will succeed with the unbeliever: The apologetic task cannot go beyond showing that Christian theism is a legitimate option, plausible and "warranted"—unable to be discounted epistemologically. This position has been severely critiqued for its weakness by non-presuppositionalists[14]—and by presuppositionalists of the stricter variety as well.[15] But Plantinga's *God and Other Minds* is one of the best treatments of the problem of evil, and, almost single-handedly, he has been responsible for making Christian thinking respectable in secular philosophical circles in America.[16]

Over against presuppositionalism are the *evidentialists* and the self-styled *classical apologists*. Evidentialists hold that the fall, though certainly keeping sinful man from reentering Eden by human effort or will, did not destroy his capacity to distinguish fact from non-fact, even in the religious realm (when God calls to Adam in the garden after he has eaten the forbidden fruit, Adam can still recognise God's voice). The apologetic task consists, then, of marshalling the full panoply of factual evidence to show that Christianity is true and its rivals false. Among prominent evidentialists are the author of this article; Gary Habermas; and the many advocates of the "Intelligent Design" movement (the most important being William Dembski).

"Classical" apologists, such as Norman Geisler, R.C. Sproul, and William Lane Craig, insist that, prior to making a factual, historical case for Jesus Christ, one must establish God's existence—generally using the classical, Aristotelian proofs, or sophisticated variants on those proofs (such as Craig's favourite, the medieval, Arabic *kalam* cosmological argument). Evidentialists almost invariably take the christocentric route, focusing their apologetic on the case for Jesus Christ and especially His resurrection—and approaching issues of God's existence by way of the incarnate Christ (Jesus to Philip: "he who has seen me has seen the Father"—John 14:8-9).

As Edward John Carnell once remarked,

"There are as many apologetics as there are facts in the world." One should therefore expect specialised apologetic approaches in particular factual areas. Intelligent Design is such an approach—focusing on scientific fact. Other examples include *literary apologetics,* as exemplified by G.K. Chesterton, the Inklings (C.S. Lewis, J.R.R. Tolkien, Charles Williams), and contemporary literary scholars such as Gene Edward Veith;[17] and *juridical* (or *legal*) *apologetics,* where the sophisticated evidential techniques of the law are applied to the collection and interpretation of evidence in behalf of the faith. Historical representatives of legal apologetics would certainly include Thomas Sherlock (*The Tryal of the Witnesses of the Resurrection of Jesus*) and Simon Greenleaf (*The Testimony of the Evangelists*[18]); contemporary work in the field has been carried out by the author of this article, and by others such as Craig Parton and Ross Clifford. A recent survey of the area is William P. Broughton's *The Historical Development of Legal Apologetics, with an Emphasis on the Resurrection.*[19]

And there are what might be termed non-apologetic apologists, such as Regent College's John G. Stackhouse (*Humble Apologetics: Defending the Faith To-day*). Stackhouse is highly critical of the kind of decisiveness represented by the title of Josh McDowell's influential book of popular apologetics, *Evidence That Demands a Verdict,* as well as aggressive attempts to defend the faith through public debates with unbelievers (he particularly dislikes William Lane Craig). Stackhouse seems to favour a postmodernist style of non-confrontation: the building of relationships with unbelievers rather than argumentation.[20]

How effective is the contemporary Christian apologetic? In spite of fine examples, there is much room for improvement. Here are three serious difficulties, as the present essayist sees them:

1. A continuing, virtually endemic disinterest on the part of many evangelical denominations, pastors, and laymen for the kind of rigorous academic study apologetics demands—and a corresponding preference for non-intellectual, subjective religiosity ("the devotional life"), group activities within the church ("fellowship"), and church-growth activism ("mega-churchism"). This may appear on the surface as spirituality, but it is just the opposite— since it leaves the seeking unbeliever without an adequate witness.

2. The self-defeating nature of presuppositional and "humble" apologetic approaches. In the Apostolic witness of the New Testament (Paul on the Areopagus, for example), the Christian starts from a common ground with the unbeliever, moving him or her to the cross of Christ. One does not argue that the non-Christian's worldview is utterly inadequate and that only by starting from the Christian presupposition can any proper knowledge be arrived at. And the Apostles certainly did not fear confrontation or insist first on establishing personal "relationships" before the case for Christianity could be made. Our modern secular world is much like the pagan world of the Apostles, and it would behove us to

consider seriously their defence of the faith as the proper model for ours.

3. Overemphasis on issues of God's existence rather than on the case for incarnation. We have seen how, owing to Aquinas's baptism of the traditional Aristotelian proofs for God's existence, these proofs became central to Roman Catholic apologetics and to much of Protestant defences of the faith during and even after the 18th-century "Enlightenment." We are not questioning the underlying logic of these proofs, but we are questioning the emphasis placed upon them. Salvation does not depend on believing in God: Scripture tells us that "the devils also believe, and tremble" (James 2:19). Salvation requires coming to terms with Jesus Christ—as the only Saviour from sin, death, and the devil. Thus the Christian apologetic needs to be, root and branch, an apologetic for Jesus Christ—not a disguised exercise in the philosophy of religion.[21]

The history of apologetics is really a special case of the history of evangelism. And the more secular the modern world becomes, the more important it is. If we neglect to answer the legitimate intellectual concerns of the unbelievers of our time, we are admitting that we do not really care about their eternal destiny. Apologetics does not save; only Jesus Christ is able to do that. But apologetics can—and should—serve as a John the Baptist, making the paths straight, facilitating routes to the cross of Christ.

What Are Some Apologetic Approaches?

H. Wayne House

Most Christians understand that there is a need to defend the Christian faith from counterarguments that are critical to its tenets of faith and basis for existence. Certainly, much of the world is without a presentation of the gospel and in need of a clear understanding of the message of Christ. In presenting the gospel, the evangelist has a duty to be prepared to demonstrate why the claims of Christianity are true and worthy of being embraced, rather than the claims of others. This gives rise to the need for Christian apologetics, and the question of how best to set forth the truth of the Christian proclamation.

The Importance of Method in Apologetic Practice

Consequently, the concern of this chapter is not to outline a defense of the doctrines of Christianity, but to present the different approaches that Christians have utilized in setting forth and defending Christian truth, as well as highlighting the underlying distinct theological ideas and emphases apologists place within their method.

Though Christian apologists are united on the essentials of the faith, there are differences among them on a variety of issues relating to their methodology. For example, they differ in several areas, such as whether there is a shared common ground set of ideas between the Christian and the non-Christian to utilize in their case for Christianity; whether arguments for God's existence are adequate or even necessary to convince an unbeliever of the truth of Christianity; whether one should emphasize the crucial role worldviews play in the interpretation of Christian evidence; whether tangible and material evidence presented through discoveries of archaeology and history is sufficient to convince the skeptic; and whether the gospel is sufficient apart from other apologetic arguments. There is also the perennial argument between role of faith and reason (see the chapter "What Is the Relationship Between Faith and Reason?").

What is more, the divisions between apologetic methodologies also relate to each one's perspective on the use and limits of the two ways in which God has revealed

Himself—that is, in nature (general revelation) and in Scripture (special revelation). This perspective will form the apologist's view on the nature and capacity of humans to respond to these means of revelation.

Generally, there are four recognized methods[1] that are utilized to defend the faith, which include: (1) classical, (2) evidential, (3) presuppositional, and (4) the fideist approach, though most apologists identify with one of the first three, or overlap at certain points. In analyzing these different approaches, it is important to remember the caution issued by Norman Geisler: namely, that there is no universal way in which we can categorize each of these views with their variations.[2]

The Four Types of Apologetic Systems

Classical Apologetics. The classical method of apologetics is usually developed through a three-step approach (for a more detailed response, see the chapter "What Is the Overall Apologetic Task?"). First, the classical apologist recognizes the crucial role that one's worldviews play in coloring (interpreting) the data and material evidence. For example, because atheists do not believe in God, they would not believe it possible to have a Son of God (since there is no God in the first place). Therefore, by addressing worldview considerations in the first step, such as the undeniable first principles of philosophy (or reality), like the laws of logic, personal existence (your own being), knowledge, and the nature of truth.

Once the basic fundamental principles of one's worldview are established, the second step sets forth various arguments for the existence of God and the possibility of miracles. According to the classical apologist,

because evidence does not come with a set of instruction manuals telling how to interpret the data, the first two steps are crucial to preparing the individual's worldview to correctly make sense of the material evidence in the final step.

In the third step, the apologist argues from empirical (what can be seen with the naked eye) and historical evidence that the Bible is authentic, historically reliable, inspired, and is a trustworthy record of miracles and the physical resurrection of Christ.

The classical apologist believes that the person whom he addresses is capable of understanding rational arguments in spite of being a sinner, and that the Spirit of God uses such argumentation and evidence to apply the gospel to the individual.

An example of this three-step method of argument is found in classical apologist Norman Geisler's work *Baker Encyclopedia of Christian Apologetics*. He sets forth a 12-point argument, starting with undeniable first principles such as personal existence, truth, and logic.[3] Each proposition of the argument both depends on the former proposition and logically leads to the next proposition. The argument concludes with the premise that "the Bible is the Word of God and whatever is opposed to any biblical truth is false."

To summarize, if truth is knowable, and a theistic God exists, then miracles are possible (which are acts of God confirming the message of God). And if this is so, then the message of the New Testament is historically reliable, and because the New Testament says Jesus is the Son of God as was confirmed by His resurrection from the dead, then Jesus is God. Thus, the Bible is the Word of God because Christ (who is God) affirmed it. If all of this is true, then orthodox Christianity is true. Therefore, since anything opposed to truth is false, anything opposed to the Bible must also be false—thus Christianity is true.

To be clear, the classical view sees great importance in offering evidence, which should be presented. However, if there are chronic rejections of the material and Christ, one must do pre-evangelism to discover if there is a worldview problem hindering a proper interpretation of the evidence. If the individual possesses a theistic worldview but is not a Christian, it may be appropriate to start with the evidence. The classical approach has served the body of Christ well through the centuries and has been extremely useful in combating the philosophical arguments against the Christian worldview.

The classical view has been criticized because its opponents believe it is inappropriate to attempt to understand the infinite God through human logic (Isaiah 55:8-9). Classical apologists respond by saying that it is certainly true that God's ways are *beyond* human reason (meaning we cannot fully understand His ways); nonetheless, they are not *contrary* to human reason (we can grasp some of His ways without contradiction—Isaiah 1:18; 1 Timothy 6:20).

Some well-known modern classical apologists include Norman Geisler (*Christian Apologetics*), R.C. Sproul (*Classical Apologetics*), William Lane Craig (*Reasonable Faith*), and J.P. Moreland (*Scaling the Secular City*).

Evidential Apologetics. Unlike the deductive approach (in which the conclusion is based on logical premises) to apologetics that we have seen in the classical view, evidentialism is *inductive* (visual and tangible) in nature.[4] This method defends and corroborates Christian truth by following historical evidence discovered through investigating what the evidentialists aver to

be the facts of the matter. Whereas the classical apologist begins with logical arguments before any experience, the evidentialists, in the words of Bernard Ramm,[5] look to three kinds of factual data. The first relates to material facts that are found in historical events, documents, and archaeological artifacts. The second relates to events or phenomena that may be considered supernatural in nature. Third are experiential facts, such as individual and social phenomena.

It is important to remember that evidentialists do not reject logical argument per se, nor do they reject arguments for the existence of God, but only the *overemphasis* that may be placed upon them. Accordingly, our focus should be on demonstrating the incarnation of Christ and those issues that relate to Christ, including demonstrating the trustworthiness of the biblical text. That is to say, our apologetic should be Christocentric. Therefore, logic should be used in analyzing evidences that support the Christian position. Evidentialists argue that one needs to offer reasons why the Christian viewpoint is consistent with truth. Those who hold this position will focus on the source documents that present issues relating to the historicity of the biblical text, its reliability, and particularly the questions surrounding the incarnation, birth, life, death, and the bodily resurrection of Christ. Evidential apologetics has served the church well, with some Christians seeing an overlap between the classical and evidential approaches.

Some of the most recognizable evidential apologists of our time include John Warwick Montgomery (director of the International Academy of Apologetics, Evangelism, and Human Rights in Strasbourg, France), Josh McDowell (*Evidence That Demands a Verdict*), Gary Habermas (*The Historical Jesus:*

Ancient Evidence for the Life of Christ), and Don Stewart (*10 Reasons to Trust the Bible*).

In agreement with the classical approach, the evidentialist believes that unregenerate skeptics have the ability to understand rational arguments and truths, yet due to the sinfulness of the mind, emotions, and will, those who are unregenerate distort the truth and will not embrace the truth of God. Ultimately, a proclamation of the gospel is necessary to bring the non-Christian to Christ.

Presuppositional Apologetics. The presuppositional approach is the position advocated by some within Reformed theological circles. Cornelius Van Til, a professor at Westminster Seminary in Philadelphia, was the most noted advocate earlier in the twentieth century.[6] Later presuppositionalists were Greg Bahnsen and Rousas J. Rushdoony. Each of these theologians and philosophers believed that because humans are fallen and sinful creatures, they are not able to understand spiritual truth about God. Consequently, presuppositionalists do not believe that there is any common ground between the regenerated and the unregenerated, so that logic and rational arguments are ineffective. According to this view, because humans are totally depraved, with sin having corrupted their minds, emotions, and wills, they are unable to understand or receive God's truth as revealed in nature and Scripture. Essentially, presuppositionalism argues that the unbeliever's worldview is inadequate and that only when one first assumes Christian presuppositions (of God and the Scriptures) can any appropriate knowledge be obtained. The believer, in contrast, is able to understand the truth of God because of the work of the Spirit in creating faith in the nonbeliever.

Fideist Approach. The fideist approach to apologetics is distinct from the other methods discussed above. This is so because no rational justification or evidence is needed for a defense. One only needs to engage the unregenerate from Scripture and allow your own life to be an example. For the fideist, Christianity is viewed as being above reason. To be clear, this is not saying that Christian ideas are irrational. Rather, they are beyond the reach of human reason. There is the perception that, from a negative standpoint, that rational arguments are insufficient and that a faith experience is all that is necessary for answering the challenges of the unconverted. Most would classify individuals such as Soren Kierkegaard, Karl Barth, and Donald Bloesch as fideists.

Those who oppose fideism argue that the biblical text supports the use of reason (Isaiah 1:18; 1 Peter 3:15) with regard to spiritual issues, and that it is not possible to believe in God without first believing that He exists (Hebrews 11:6). The fideist perspective is also viewed as contradictory because reason is used to argue that one should not believe in reason to defend Christianity. Predictably, the fideist would respond that God, not reason, is the basis for salvation, and that only a witness to the heart of the human by the Spirit can bring a regenerate person to belief.

Argument for an Integrated Apologetic Methodology (Apostle Paul)

With regard to the classical, evidential, and presuppositional approaches, one must realize that these are not new ways to look at a presentation or defense of the Christian faith. Aspects of these ideas and approaches are found in the biblical authors and the early church fathers. Even the Greek philosophers argued with each other about the value of using deduction and induction in one's arguments, as well as the difference between arguing from innate first principles (ideas such as logic, truth, personal existence) deductively to construct a worldview, or whether to construct the worldview inductively piece by piece.[7]

Though presuppositionalists say that the unbeliever will not come to belief in Christ based on rational arguments or evidences found in science, history, or other proofs from inductive investigation, few would say that an unsaved person is incapable of accepting the existence of God. Furthermore, few would claim that an unbeliever would necessarily reject facts of history, science, or even miracles. Presuppositionalists only say that none of this will cause a person to believe in Jesus.

On the other hand, evidentialists—and even classical apologists—believe that though one can make a case for Christianity from proofs that can be understood by non-Christians, they also agree that these proofs alone will not cause a person to embrace Jesus; the work of the Holy Spirit in moving the unregenerate toward belief in the gospel is necessary.[8]

In evaluating the three major apologetic positions, namely, classical apologetics, evidential apologetics, and presuppositional apologetics, it seems clear that there are areas of agreement. That is to say, adherents to all three positions accept that no logical or evidential argument could bring a person to faith in Jesus apart from the special work of the Holy Spirit in the heart. In addition, all agree that the unbeliever must recognize the existence of God and also his own sinful condition. Calvin rightly said,

Our wisdom, in so far as it ought to be deemed true and solid wisdom, consists almost entirely of two parts: the knowledge of God and the knowledge of ourselves. But as these are connected together by many ties, it is not easy to determine which of the two precedes, and gives birth to the other.[9]

Calvin sensed the manner in which the effort to bring men to a saving knowledge of God is found within the New Testament itself. When one studies the ministry of the apostle Paul in his efforts to bring others to faith in the Messiah, we discover that his approach, in some sense, includes a combination of these methods.[10]

For example, Paul believed that the person without the Spirit of God could still know certain things about God (Roman 1:19-21). This included an acknowledgment of what God has revealed, His attributes and His divine nature. Because unbelievers possess this knowledge, they are without excuse. But Christians like Paul are not the only ones who understand this recognition of deity on the part of all. One may find quotes from Xenophon (Xen. Mem. 1.iv.c. 3), Plato (Plat. Tim. Loc. c. 5), Cicero (Cic. Disp. Tusc. 1.I.c.26), Maximus (Max. Tyr. Diss. 38), and many others that indicate all humanity knows of God, and persons such as those listed may even have been philosophers from whom Paul developed some of his terminology. They speak of God's invisible nature, that all see Him, that He has divine power, and that all humans acknowledge the existence of God.

Paul's address at the Areopagus (Mars Hill, Acts 17:22-34) combines these elements—his address was well organized and well reasoned. First, he treated his audience with respect, even using the same phrase as Socrates in the *Apology*, "men of Athens," though we should not understand him to be patronizing them, for that was forbidden before the Areopagus. Second, he started with an idea and used literary sources (Epimenides and Aratas, Acts 17:28) that they could understand and largely agree with, though he invested their terms with fuller meaning from the Christian worldview. Moses, in the creation account in Genesis 1, did much the same by using contemporary Canaanite terminology, though he invested his language with correct theological perspective. Christians rightly understood Paul's

method here: "it wraps universal truth in the language and idiom of the day, culminating in a uniquely Christian expression of biblical revelation, and inviting the listeners to a higher metaphysical ground."[11]

Paul moved his unregenerate hearers from creation and took them to the requirement of repentance and essential message of the gospel, the resurrection of Jesus. We should follow Paul as an example in blending the various approaches so that by some means we might lead others to repentance.

4

What Is the Overall Apologetic Task?

Don Deal and Joseph M. Holden

The ultimate goal of every Christian is to give a clear answer or defense (*apologia*) to anyone who asks about the Christian faith (1 Peter 3:15). In addition, because apologetics exists to aid and serve the gospel, this goal also involves presenting a positive case for Christianity, in much the same way that a lawyer argues his case in a courtroom. The process of achieving this goal is known collectively as the "apologetic task."

From a classical point of view, accomplishing this task involves building an argument from the ground up in three successive steps. These foundational steps, in logical order, include: (1) philosophical foundation, (2) theological foundation, and (3) evidential foundation (some combine steps 1 and 2 together under one heading as worldview considerations). Each step of the task treats various issues crucial to offering both a defense of and a convincing case for Christianity.

To be clear, this is not a particular argument we are after here, but an attempt to consider the big-picture progression of ideas and the crucial issues that support the overall argument for Christianity itself. Arriving at incorrect conclusions for any one of these topics below may hinder a person's understanding and receiving of the gospel. The following chart illustrates the progression of the steps and the topics involved.

THE APOLOGETIC TASK		
STEP 1 **Philosophical Foundation** (first principles are undeniable)	**STEP 2** **Theological Foundation**	**STEP 3** **Evidential Foundation**
• Is truth absolute and knowable? • Laws of logic? • Is there objective meaning? • Does something exist?	• Does God exist? • Are miracles possible? • If God, why evil?	• Are the New Testament documents reliable? • Is the New Testament historically reliable? • Is Jesus God? • Did Jesus rise from the dead?

Step 1: Philosophical Foundation

The first point to recognize in our apologetic task is that not everyone holds the same worldview (the lens through which a person interprets reality). Some have claimed there are as many worldviews as there are people in the world! That is to say, each person has a set of glasses through which he or she makes sense of their life, data, and experiences. Sometimes this is why it is a challenge to get others to intellectually understand the gospel message. Everyone relies on his or her own assumptions, whether right or wrong, to help make sense of the world. Therefore, Steps 1 and 2 address the unbeliever's worldview.

This difficulty led Francis Schaeffer to coin the term *pre-evangelism* to refer to the work that needs to be done with regard to an unbeliever's worldview prior to receiving the gospel. To be clear, we always want to give the simple gospel message first! However, when objections arise and a chronic refusal to receive Christ occurs, there may be worldview obstacles that are hindering that person's understanding of what he might think is possible or intelligible. At this point, it is best to discern what exactly is hindering their progress towards Jesus. Most often, unbelievers go wrong in at least one of the three steps. Ultimately, we want to be sure their worldview is not holding back faith in Christ because of misunderstandings or incorrect conclusions. Steps 1 and 2 of the task are designed to address these issues. These include topics relating to the nature and knowability of truth (absolute or relative?), the laws of logic (rules of thought?), reality/being (does something exist?), logic (rules of thought?), and meaning (objective or cultural?).

The answers to these crucial issues can make a big difference in helping an unbeliever be able to accept what is true when it comes to considering Christianity. For example, if a person views truth as relative, then any reference to the gospel "truth" would seem like nonsense (or at least be viewed as having equal status with other mutually exclusive views) because you are merely stating your personal *opinion*.

Moreover, any absolute truth claims you may utter to a relativist will fall on deaf ears because the notion of absolutes (i.e., true for all people, at all times, in all places) is nonsense to him. Given that perspective, it would seem impossible for an unbeliever to ever receive your case for Christianity as "the truth."

To be effective, it is best to treat the problem issues first, thus removing (with the help of the Holy Spirit) intellectual obstacles to faith (2 Corinthians 10:4-5). For instance, to remove the obstacle of absolute truth, you need only to explain that truth is *undeniable*, meaning that when a person tries to deny truth he actually affirms it. The same is undeniably true with logic, knowledge, meaning, absolutes, and other first principles in Step 1 that form the bedrock to any worldview. Any attempt to altogether deny or relativize the topics in Step 1 is tantamount to affirming them. That is, to claim that "Logic doesn't exist" uses logic to deny logic! And the statement "There is no meaning" is itself a meaningful statement! Likewise, to deny your own existence implies your very existence, because you would have to exist in order to deny your existence—*hence something undeniably exists*. The next logical question, then, is this: "How did we get here?"

By helping the lost sort out the most fundamental issues in their worldview, you are clearing an intellectual pathway to faith in

Christ and a proper interpretation of the evidence in Step 3. After demonstrating that the basic philosophical topics in Step 1 are undeniable, you can then move on to the theological foundation of one's worldview (Step 2).

Step 2: Theological Foundation

It is important to deal with Step 1 prior to Step 2, for only then can you make use of the undeniable tenets such as truth, logic, knowledge, meaning, and being.

Step 2 addresses questions relating to (1) God's existence, (2) the possibility of miracles, and (3) the problem of evil. Answering each question in this section has the potential for a broad life-changing impact, which is why we call these "macro issues." The logic behind this step is to help the lost sort through questions pertaining to God with a view toward helping them interpret the tangible evidence presented in Step 3 (evidential foundation), thus hopefully drawing them closer to receiving Christ as Savior.

To begin, acknowledging God's existence is critical to eventually receiving Christ. To offer Christ as the "Son of God" in Step 3 presupposes there is a real God who has a Son. It would make no sense to speak of the Son of God if God did not exist. The same fate is true for the Word of God (Bible), acts of God (miracles), and the people of God (church). Christianity would utterly break down if God did not exist, nor would Christianity be convincing in the mind of the skeptic!

Traditionally, the material world has offered strong support for the existence of God. Paul asserted in Romans 1:19-20 that we can know something about God through His creation. This has fostered various arguments for His existence. Among them are the cosmological argument (reasons from

the universe as an effect to a First Cause), teleological argument (reasons from design in the universe to a Designer), moral argument (reasons from moral law to a moral Legislator or Lawgiver), the argument from motion (reasons from motion in the universe to a First Mover), and the anthropological argument (reasons from intelligent beings to an Intelligent Cause). Christians recognize God as the cause responsible for all the effects seen in creation.

Following closely on the matter of God's existence comes the question of miracles—namely, whether a supernatural event could occur in a world governed by the regular laws of nature. This question has an immediate bearing on the believability of numerous supernatural events mentioned in Scripture, including the incarnation and the crowning proof of Christianity, *the physical resurrection of Christ.* Furthermore, the importance of miracles, signs, and wonders rests in the purpose they serve as direct confirmations of God's message (Acts 2:22; Hebrews 2:3-4).

Some have a difficult time believing in miracles because they assume the laws of nature (such as gravity, strong and weak nuclear forces, etc.) are regular, fixed, and cannot be violated (e.g., David Hume, Immanuel Kant, Benedict de Spinoza). In the past, some have viewed these laws as *mandating* the way the universe *must unalterably* operate at all times. If this is the case, then miracles are closed off from our world, which is seen to act like a rigid machine. However, for Christians, a better way to understand the laws of nature is to recognize that they are flexible and merely descriptive of the way the universe usually or normally operates.[1] If that is true, then it would be possible for miracles to occur as *exceptions* to the laws of nature (not violations of).

And if God does in fact exist, then miracles (acts) of God are possible. There is no reason to doubt the possibility of miracles if there is a God who can act.

Within Step 2, an additional sticking point often surfaces in the mind of the skeptic—namely, the problem of evil, which is generally addressed as a subset under God's existence, known as *theodicy*. Though there are many challenging questions relating to the matter of evil, the most fundamental objection is this: "If God is good and loving, why does He allow evil to occur?" This question implies that God is to blame for evil, and that He is not as good or loving as He claims to be.

Christians have traditionally pointed out that God gave humans free will, and thus He took a risk—He knew that evil could arise through the misuse of free will. As for why God permitted evil, the answer to the question may be surprisingly simple. Perhaps God allowed evil to occur for the same reason good and loving parents allow their young children to play outside knowing the risks involved, such as the possibility of injury. The alternative is to not allow children to play at all so that injury cannot occur. What kind of life would that be for the child? That would probably foster more psychological evils as a result!

To put it another way, it is likely that God made evil possible by giving free will, but people make evil actual by misusing that freedom. In this case, God is only the indirect cause of evil, whereas we are the direct and immediate cause of evil through our choices. If that's true, then blaming God for evil would be like blaming Henry Ford for all auto accidents!

But why does God allow evil to continue today? Its allowance would seem to portray God as lacking the power (impotent) or desire (malevolent indifference) to eliminate evil. However, because evil emerges from a misuse of free choice, the only way to stop its occurrence among free creatures would be to remove freedom. This remedy would indeed remove evil, but it would also abolish the possibility of salvation, since it too is gained by freely receiving Christ. It seems best to allow evil and salvation (good) to coexist until God sorts it out in the future. It is better that evil exists and some people are being saved, than no evil existing and nobody being saved.

Using the problem of evil as an argument against God is dangerous for the skeptic, since, ironically, this problem can turn into an argument in favor of God's existence. No one could claim that something is evil if they had no absolute standard of good to measure it by. To put it another way, as former atheist C.S. Lewis said in his book *Mere Christianity*, you cannot call a line crooked unless you have, at the same time, an absolute standard (of a straight line) to measure it by. That is to say, no one can claim the world is *getting worse* if they do not have an absolute moral standard beyond the world of what is *best*.

Step 3: Evidential Foundation

The final step in clearing away obstacles to faith and presenting a clear case for Christianity involves evaluating tangible evidence. Evidence shows tangible consistency between the Bible and the real world, offering empirical support of the tenets of faith. However, many Christians become frustrated when the evidence itself does not convince a skeptic. At this point, more often than not, we recognize that there are deeper issues at play in how skeptics *interpret* the evidence. Atheists, pantheists, and Christian theists clearly arrive at different conclusions after viewing the same data. This is because evidence does not come with instructions on how to interpret the evidence. Interpretation is provided by one's worldview (which is why Steps 1 and 2 are crucial).

We are fortunate to live in an era in which there is an abundance of evidence to support Christianity, Jesus, and the Scriptures. The important topics in Step 3 are (1) the *textual* reliability of the New Testament, (2) the *historical* reliability of the New Testament, (3) the deity of Christ, and (4) His physical resurrection from the dead.[2]

Though there are fuller explanations of these four topics in the chapters of this work, let's take a brief look at the different kinds of evidence so we can understand how they flow with our three-step process.

The *textual* reliability of the New Testament is overwhelming! A key factor in determining whether Christianity is true is evaluating whether the biblical manuscripts are an accurate representation of the original texts. How can we know that an ancient document has been transmitted or copied accurately? In simple terms, scholars analyze two important clues: (1) the number of manuscripts available (more copies to compare to arrive at what the original text said), and (2) the dates of the manuscripts (the earlier the better, which means less chance for myth and embellishment to enter the text).

For example, scholars today have about 1,850 manuscript copies of Homer's *Iliad*, with a gap of about 400-500 years between the original composition and our oldest copy. Many other works from ancient history, such as Plato and Aristotle's, have not fared better, often having more than a 1,000-year gap between the original and the oldest existing copy, with less than two dozen manuscripts of each.

So how does the New Testament stack up in this ancient competition? We have nearly 30,000 New Testament manuscripts in various languages (versions). Of these, more than 5,800 are in the Greek language, with the oldest verified copy (fragment) of a New Testament document from the Gospel of John, with a gap of fewer than 50 years from the original composition.[3] No other ancient text comes close to the quantity or early dates of New Testament manuscripts.

Based on comparisons of the many manuscripts accompanied by early dates, scholars have estimated that the New Testament documents have been copied with about 99.5+ percent accuracy to the original. Thus, we have more copies of the New Testament, and they are closer timewise to the original Bible than any other ancient document is to their original work, and copied at the greatest percentage of accuracy.[4] This makes it relatively easy to render the Scriptures in the English language as a faithful representation of the original Bible.

The *historical* reliability of the New Testament is equally impressive. Archaeological and historical data have collected an impressive array of finds in the last one hundred years. To date, nearly 100 people mentioned in the Old and New Testaments have been confirmed through historical and archaeological sources.[5] Even Jesus of Nazareth is attested to in nearly a dozen nonbiblical literary sources, often written by unbelievers. This evidence includes the controversial James Ossuary (an ossuary is a small stone box in which the bones of the deceased were placed) bearing the names of Jesus, James, and Joseph.[6]

What is more, dozens of geographical markers in the Bible have been identified; including the Temple Mount area, pools of

Bethesda (John 5) and Siloam (John 9), and many other locations.[7] This is remarkable in spite of the fact that only 1 percent of all the sites in the Holy Land have been excavated!

The *deity of Christ* (incarnation) is an important topic in Step 3. Throughout the Gospels, Jesus said and did things that are only appropriate for God to say and do. For example, Jesus forgave sins and described Himself in unmistakable terms of deity (John 8:58; cf. Exodus 3:14). In Scripture, the titles used of Jehovah are also applied to Christ, and He received worship from His followers.[8]

Christ's status as the incarnated God-man (Greek, *theanthropos*—John 1:14) is crucial to apologetics, since He uniquely possessed two distinct natures (divine and human) in one person (the Son). This uniquely qualified Jesus to be the perfect human offering for the sins of the world (representing mankind, the offender). He also had a divine nature, making it possible for Him to remove sin, serve as a mediator, and live as the very expression of God Himself. Therefore, any sound defense of the faith should be Christocentric.

In addition, Christians have long recognized the *physical resurrection* of Christ as the central miracle claim in the New Testament. It has been said that the resurrection is the capstone in the arch of Christianity; if it is removed, all else crumbles. There are several lines of evidence that support the resurrection as historical fact. They include:

1. Jesus's burial tomb was found empty.

2. Jesus was seen by 500 witnesses, most of which (at least 250) were still alive when Paul wrote 1 Corinthians 15:1-7.

3. Jesus offered Himself to be touched, and was seen on several occasions

after the resurrection, including by the apostles (Luke 24; John 20–21).

4. Mary encountered the resurrected Lord at the tomb (John 20).

5. The apostles' lives were changed. They were transformed from cowards into lions for their faith and message, eventually being martyred for their faith.

6. The lives of some of Jesus's critics were changed. Saul (also known as Paul) and James, the brother of Jesus, were known skeptics of Jesus during His lifetime. After Jesus's death, they became leaders of the new church.[9] People will die for what they believe is true, not for what they know is false.

7. Something radical occurred to immediately change the long-standing dietary restrictions (kosher to nonkosher) and worship habits (Saturday to Sunday) of the apostles and early Jewish followers of Christ. The resurrection is the best explanation for this and other facts relating to the Christian faith.[10]

A Strong Case

Each of the three steps contribute toward forming the foundations of the overall argument for Christianity that takes into consideration the role that worldviews play in the evaluation and interpretation of evidence. Though much more could be said regarding the case for Christianity, this volume offers an excellent panorama of the crucial questions and answers relating to this topic.[11] The evidence that supports the Christian faith is solid; what remains is conveying the information in an understandable way so as to maximize its impact on the skeptical mind. Recognizing the important role of a person's worldview in the interpretation process will ensure the evangelist's flexibility to engage in pre-evangelism when needed. The overall case for Christianity is strong, not because there are some two billion professing Christians (and growing) in the world today, but because it corresponds to reality!

What Is the Relationship Between Faith and Reason?

Mark M. Hanna

Some of the most intense debates between Christians and secularists often concern the relationship between faith and reason. These discussions are focused on discovering whether faith is subordinate to reason or vice versa, and whether the two are mutually exclusive. To be certain, understanding the relationship between these two critical domains will have an enormous impact on how some justify their faith, or whether they approach life with blind faith. Answers to these questions will contribute to our understanding of how God reaches rational people.

The Importance of Definitions

At the root of many disagreements about the relationship of faith to reason is the more fundamental problem of conflicting (and inaccurate) *definitions* of one or both of the terms. To rightly understand this crucial relationship requires a correct understanding of the respective definitions.

Critics of Christianity generally view faith and reason as foes, since critics are inclined to define *faith* as gullibility, by which they mean that faith is either believing something without reason and evidence or believing something against reason and evidence. Richard Dawkins, a proponent of evolutionary biology and an outspoken opponent of Christianity, is a prime example of this. He categorically states that "faith is belief in spite of, even perhaps because of, the lack of evidence."[1]

This view of faith is called fideism (blind faith); to attribute it to biblical Christianity is to indulge in rank caricature. Fideists are also caught in a dilemma, for they invariably seek to justify their antireason position by appealing to reason. If no rational justification is offered to support fideism, it would appear fideism is left rationally unjustified.

Some fideists claim that reason itself is ultimately based on faith, arguing that one can use reason only if he trusts reason—that is, he must have faith that reason is a reliable tool for acquiring knowledge. But this argument undermines his claim, for one cannot have faith in reason unless he first uses reason to distinguish faith *from* reason. What is more, the argument does not solve the problem—it simply postpones it, for there would still need to be a rational justification for why the fideist has faith that reason is a reliable tool.

Reason must also be used to distinguish truth from error, reality from appearance, and good from evil—distinctions essential for the decisions and actions that humans make innumerable times a day. When it comes to answering questions about ultimate reality, however, reason is not self-sufficient, but requires divine revelation. Apart from the Bible, we are left with nothing but speculation about the nature and destiny of human beings.

Nevertheless, certain aspects of reason are universal and absolute, such as the basic principles of logic, without which no valid thinking and interpreting can be done. An adequate definition of reason must recognize both its objective and subjective aspects. Reason is often confused with merely a subjective reasoning process. Without the objective aspect, however, it would be impossible to attain true knowledge about anything.

The Bible's Opposition to Blind Faith

The apostle Paul summed up the biblical case against fideism in a crystal-clear directive: "Test everything; hold fast what is good" (1 Thessalonians 5:21) and to avoid "contradictions" (Greek, *antithesis*) (1 Timothy 6:20). Christians are not to be credulous, but rather to be discerning with their critical faculties, well-honed and informed by Scripture (1 John 4:1). A careful reading of the Bible, from Genesis to Revelation, demonstrates an overarching concern for truth and genuine knowledge. It is replete with warnings against falsehood and ignorance.

Reason Is Essential to Biblical Faith

Faith is always directed into something or someone—that is, faith always has an object.

The crucial question is whether that object has the credentials to justify our trust (cf. Acts 1:3; 2:22). One cannot discover trustworthiness without using reason.

An example of the unbreakable connection between faith and reason is seen in John 14:11, where Christ said, "Believe me that I am in the Father and the Father is in me, or else believe on account of the works themselves." He appealed to two reasons as the basis for trusting in Him and His claims: the unique authority of His character and life, and the divine miracles that He performed. If one reasons properly from the uniqueness of Christ's moral character and the empirical evidence of His miraculous works—especially His resurrection—he will be led to the conclusion that Christ's claims to be the Messiah and the Son of God are true and justified (John 14:1,6,11; 20:31; Romans 1:4).

What Faith Is Not

One can often arrive at a better understanding of a term by contrasting it with what it is not. Nowhere in the Bible is faith contrasted with reason; on the contrary, the Bible always implicitly or explicitly unites them. There are three main contrasts clearly indicated in Scripture.

1. *Faith is contrasted with sight:* "We walk by faith, not by sight" (2 Corinthians 5:7). Neither in this verse nor in any other passage does Scripture make faith and reason mutually exclusive.

2. *Faith is contrasted with works* (Romans 3:27; Galatians 3:2; Ephesians 2:8-9). This contrast pertains to salvation, which cannot be earned by any deeds we perform. An important sequence is found

in Christ's reference to the person who hears the gospel and brings forth good fruit that results from a transformed life. First, such a person *understands* the good news of Christ, and then he *believes* it. Subsequently, his faith is demonstrated in his changed character and deeds (Matthew 13:23).

3. *Faith is contrasted with mere assent* (Matthew 13:20-21; John 2:23-25; 1 Corinthians 15:2; Galatians 5:6; Ephesians 2:10; James 2:14-26; cf. James 2:19). Of course, intellectual assent is an essential part of genuine faith, but it is not the entirety of it. In Romans 10:9-10, the metaphor of the heart includes the capacity to believe, and that capacity necessarily involves reason, for without some clear understanding of what one should believe, there can be no genuine faith.

What Faith Is

Much misunderstanding of faith has resulted from a failure to distinguish its various uses in the Bible. Consider the distinctions between five major uses listed below.

1. The set of distinctive doctrines: In several biblical passages, reference is made to "the faith," a shorthand way of designating *the set of distinctive doctrines* that define biblical Christianity: "Contend for the faith that was once for all delivered to the saints" (Jude 3).

2. Reliance on evidences as support: Some biblical passages use the word "faith" to indicate *reliance on evidences that serve to justify or support the truth*

(John 5:36; 10:37-38; 14:11; Acts 2:32; 1 Corinthians 15:3-17; 2 Peter 1:16-18; 1 John 1:1-3).

3. Faith is also used to refer to *belief in the doctrinal truths* that constitute the distinctives of biblical Christianity (John 20:31; also see John 6:69; 8:46).

4. Numerous biblical passages use "faith" to mean *wholehearted trust* in God or Christ (John 1:12; also see John 3:16,18,36; 14:1; Acts 16:31).

5. "Faith" is often used to connote a *twofold reference, indicating both its objective and subjective aspects*: "Now faith is the assurance of things hoped for, the conviction of things not seen" (Hebrews 11:1). This verse is often taken out of context and misunderstood as a reference to a purely subjective state. But as one reads its context in the entire eleventh chapter of Hebrews, it becomes clear that verse 1 includes both the subjective state of believing and the objective reality of divine revelation (verse 3). Indeed, all of the many heroes of faith mentioned in the chapter subjectively relied on the objective words of God.

The Foolishness of Misplaced Faith

There are general uses of *faith* outside of the Bible that should be distinguished from these five biblical uses. All human beings have faith in a generic sense, for everyone trusts in others and believes a variety of things only read or heard from others.

The similarity between this generic faith and the unique faith referred to in Scripture is formal in that both involve a subjective state of believing and an object of that belief. The object of biblical faith is the true and living God and His revelation, whereas the objects of generic faith are very diverse. In fact, the objects of generic faith can include untrustworthy people and false claims.

Because it is impossible for God to lie (Hebrews 6:18), He alone is worthy of total trust and commitment. A person who places unqualified confidence in himself or in other humans is foolish (Proverbs 28:26; Jeremiah 17:5). Ultimately, confidence should be placed in God alone (Matthew 4:10).

Defining Reason

Like the word *faith*, the term *reason* is used in multiple ways to express a variety of meanings. But it is crucial to understand that reason is a God-given capacity to seek the truth and to acquire genuine knowledge. It is a tool for engaging in careful reasoning, such as drawing sound conclusions from true premises.

But rational deliberation is not possible unless we are free to follow the evidence where it leads. Where determinism completely reigns, there are only causes and no reasons. Advocates of materialistic naturalism (antisupernaturalism) think everything is the deterministic result of blind, impersonal physical causes. Biblical theism, however, accounts for both reason and freedom.

Reason also includes another function that is often overlooked. It is appropriately called *rational insight*. This is the ability to grasp and understand a variety of general principles and truths that are not derived from sensory perceptions of physical objects. The basic laws of logic (such as the law of noncontradiction) and of rational inference (such as the process of deduction and induction) are among these principles.

The Effects of Sin on the Mind

In view of the fact that we are fallen creatures who live in a fallen world, some might think that I have painted a far too rosy picture of reason. The term *fallen* refers to sin and its damaging consequences, which affect our ability to act properly and think correctly. Scripture leaves no doubt that sin distorts our thinking as well as our attitudes, motives, and actions.

Although sin corrupts the whole person, it does not destroy all capacity to reason, nor does it have any effect on the objective standards of rationality. Without these standards remaining intact along with some capacity to reason, human life would not be possible. They are also essential for human responsibility.

God's reality and ultimacy are displayed in the created order, and despite sin's effects, which incites humans to suppress awareness of this fact, their willful rebellion against God incurs guilt (Romans 1:18-23). The sinful desire for complete autonomy is at the root of mankind's attempt to entirely eliminate the thought of God from their minds (Romans 1:28).

Even when faith in God is absent, reason and conscience continue to testify to His reality (Romans 2:1-4,14-15). Scripture unambiguously shows that reason is an ally of faith in various ways (Isaiah 1:18). This inseparable relationship between reason and faith is emphasized in 1 Peter 3:15: "Always [be] prepared to make a defense to anyone who asks you for a *reason* for the hope that is in you." The clear implication is that we have solid reasons for the truth of the Christian faith, and these reasons cannot be dissolved into the relativity of human subjectivity. The reasons are there for anyone who seeks to be objective and honest with the evidence.

We find many examples of the apostle Paul using reason to defend the gospel (Acts 17:2; 18:4,19; 19:8-9). That this was his consistent practice is affirmed in Acts 17:2, stating that his custom was to *reason* with others as he sought to *persuade* them of the truth of the gospel. Of course, no one can come to genuine faith without the Holy Spirit (1 Corinthians 12:3) and the proclamation of the gospel (Romans 10:14), but, like Paul, we can use reason and evidence in our endeavors to bring people to Christ.

What is more, despite sin's effects on the mind, faith and reason have their respective roles. Prior to salvation, reason must be used to evaluate and discern whether the Bible is true. Once this decision is made in the affirmative, faith is then placed in Scripture's message and in Christ. After trust is placed in the Bible, the believer then brings his reason *under* the authority of Scripture. This is not mindless obedience, for the logical categories (laws of logic) are still very active and in play in our rational faculties, even when reading Scripture.

Reason Is a Friend of Faith

It is important to emphasize that *reason cannot save anyone*! Salvation is a gift obtained only through placing faith in Christ. This salvific trust is a *reasonable faith*. The Holy Spirit can use good reason as an instrument to reach unbelievers. The answer to our key question is clear: Reason is not a foe but a friend of faith. Faith and reason are both gifts from God. Like many of His gifts, they can be misused, but when used properly, they lead to Christ, who is the source of reason (*Logos*—John 1:1) and "the way, and the truth, and the life" (John 14:6).

Although the following directive is from a different context, it is apropos of the biblical relation between faith and reason: "What therefore God has joined together, let not man separate" (Matthew 19:6).

What Is Truth?

Richard G. Howe

Pontius Pilate's question to Jesus, "What is truth?" echoes louder today than ever before. Each of us has an expectation of truth telling, especially concerning crucial information coming from our doctor, lawyer, spouse, clergy, business partners, government officials, and others. This expectation should not change when we approach spiritual matters that have temporal and eternal significance. Due to the influences that bad philosophies and alternative religions have on our society, defending the faith now requires that we refresh ourselves and others on what it means for something to be true.

Distinguishing Theories of Truth and Tests for Truth

To ask, "What is truth?" is to address the issues of *theories* (or models) of truth and *tests* for truth. We will distinguish them here and reserve discussing tests for truth in the next chapter, "How Can We Know Truth?"

In distinction, *how someone knows* whether a statement is true is one's *test* for truth. To put it another way, a test for truth is how one *discovers* whether a statement is true. By contrast, a theory of truth is how one *defines* the terms *true* and *truth*. It is the difference between *defining* truth and *discovering* truth.

Theories of Truth

Correspondence Theory of Truth. Not all theories of truth are created equal. While there are several theories of truth that present themselves in our day, only the correspondence theory of truth is the way truth really is. This theory says that *truth is correspondence to reality*, which is to say, a statement is true inasmuch as it aligns with or is in accord with what is actually the case. Thus, the statement "It is raining" would be a true statement if it is in fact raining in reality and would be a false statement if it were in fact not raining in reality. Aristotle summarized it this way: "To say of what is, that it is not, or of what is not, that it is, is false, while to say of what is, that it is and of what is not, that it is not, is true."[1]

The statement "It is raining" can be qualified in a number of ways. It could be raining in one place and not raining in another. Further, it could be raining in one place right now and not raining in the same place sometime later. In fact, there are a number of ways a statement can correspond to reality.

One can use literal language, allegory, metaphor, simile, analogy, symbols, hyperbole, phenomenal language, informal language, synecdoche, or metonymy.[2] The key here is that the correspondence theory of truth does not say that a statement is true only when it corresponds literally. It is true that "the eyes of the LORD run to and fro throughout the whole earth" (2 Chronicles 16:9) even though God does not literally have eyes.

Pragmatic Theory of Truth. Other theories have adversely affected how some understand truth. These inadequate theories have sometimes hampered people's ability to grasp reality with what they say. One inadequate theory of truth that is increasing in popularity in our culture is the pragmatic theory of truth. The pragmatic theory says that a statement is true inasmuch as it works or is practical. The pragmatic theory gives rise to the notion that something can be "true for you but not true for me." The mistake of deciding by pragmatism what is true (or even godly) is as ancient as the Old Testament Israelites.

When God, through the prophet Jeremiah, told the Israelites to stop their abominable practices of burning incense to the "queen of heaven" and pouring out drink offerings to her, their defense of their actions is telling. They said in response to Jeremiah:

> We will do everything that we have vowed, make offerings to the queen of heaven and pour out drink offerings to her, as we did, both we and our fathers, our kings and our officials, in the cities of Judah and in the streets of Jerusalem. For then we had plenty of food, and prospered, and saw no disaster. But since we left off making offerings to the queen of heaven and pouring out drink offerings to her, we have lacked

everything and have been consumed by the sword and by famine (Jeremiah 44:17-18).

Sadly, they made their decision regarding what was true about reality based on the immediate practical results that followed and not on what God had told them through His prophet. Clearly, such pragmatism is inadequate to connect us with the truth about reality. What is more, one cannot even define the pragmatic theory of truth without utilizing the correspondence theory. This is evident when one observes how the advocate of the pragmatic theory would defend his position. Namely, he would find it impossible to avoid saying what the pragmatic theory *is*. But in doing so, he would be saying that his definition of the pragmatic theory *corresponds* to what the pragmatic theory is! Thus, he needs the correspondence theory of truth to define the pragmatic theory of truth.

Functional Theory of Truth. Another theory of truth, sometimes encountered in compromised views on the inerrancy of the Bible, is the functional theory of truth.[3] The functional theory says that a statement is true inasmuch as it fulfills the purpose or function that is intended by the one making the statement. This is also known as the intentional theory of truth. It allows for a compromised view of biblical inerrancy (i.e., the Bible has no errors) by saying that a statement in the Bible might be factually false, but nevertheless serves a certain purpose or function. This approach is what allowed Daniel Fuller to maintain that the Bible is "true" even when (in his estimation) the Bible is wrong about, for example, the mustard seed:

> Although the mustard seed is not really the smallest of all seeds, yet Jesus referred to it as such because...to have gone

contrary to their mind on what was the smallest seed would have so diverted their attention from the knowledge that would bring salvation to their souls that they might well have failed to hear these all-important revelational truths.[4]

Thus, for Fuller, because the Bible's "truth" lies in its purpose or intention, it can seemingly get the facts wrong and still fulfill that purpose or intention.[5] One problem with this is that Fuller's claim that "the mustard seed is not really the smallest of all seeds" only makes sense with the correspondence theory of truth. But with this tacit acknowledgment of the correspondence theory, there is no need to employ a different theory of truth to exonerate the Bible as being true or authoritative while stating factual errors.[6]

In contrast to the functional or intentional theory of truth, the correspondence theory of truth rightly recognizes that the Bible is true in everything it affirms or teaches precisely because the Bible tells us what really is the case. When we defend Christianity as being true, we want to make sure that our hearers understand that we mean that Christianity corresponds to reality.

How Can We Know Truth?

Richard G. Howe

Throughout the centuries there have been many formidable attempts—such as skepticism (David Hume) and agnosticism (Immanuel Kant)—to define the process, parameters, and limits of the human knowing process. Unfortunately, each has led to conclusions that have effectively separated the knower from the thing known (reality). The ability to know the truth is essential to apprehending knowledge of God (Romans 1:19-21), the gospel (Romans 10:9-10), and comprehending the rich nuggets mined from the words of Scripture, which bring real freedom. This is made clear by Jesus's words, "You will know the truth, and the truth will set you free" (John 8:32). What is more, if Jesus is "the truth" incarnate (John 14:6) who perfectly corresponds to the Father (John 1:18; 14:9), our knowing the truth has personal and spiritual implications that go far beyond an intellectual exercise to a life-changing experience (John 4:24; 17:3).

In the last chapter we distinguished theories (or models) of truth from tests for truth. We examined and defended the correspondence theory of truth (i.e., statements/truth claims must correspond to reality) against other theories of what truth is. Here we will address how truth is known by reviewing the *tests* for truth.

Tests for Truth

Language and Logic. There are at least two things that all tests for truth have in common—*language* and *logic*.

Pertaining to language, we talk (to ourselves or to others) about the truth that we have confirmed, including how we confirmed it, utilizing categories (subjects and predicates) and copulas (words that link subjects and predicates, such as the word *is*).[1] With the influence of philosophers such as Ludwig Wittgenstein or A.J. Ayer and philosophies such as logical positivism, deconstructionism, and postmodernism, understanding how truth and language relate, together with how (or whether) each of them relates to reality, is of increasing importance in defending the truth of Christianity.[2]

Regarding logic, we realize that truth claims cannot conflict with each other.[3] Since the ancient Greeks, Western thinking has recognized that all thinking is governed by fundamental "laws" of logic arising from our grasp of reality. The most basic law is the law of noncontradiction. It says that contradictory statements cannot both be true at the same time and in the same sense or false at the same time and in the same sense.[4] Thus, if one test seems to yield one conclusion and a different test seems to yield the opposite conclusion, we know that one of the conclusions has to be false—one of the conclusions does not correspond to reality. This tells us that one of the tests is flawed either within it or in how we applied it.[5]

Kinds of Tests. Tests for truth will often differ according to the kind of thing about which a statement is made or a question is asked. Different aspects of reality require different methods of inquiry and tools of analysis. For example, testing a statement about mathematics requires methods of inquiry and tools of analysis appropriate to the mathematical aspects of reality. Testing a statement about history requires methods of inquiry and tools of analysis appropriate to the historical aspects of reality. Testing a statement about a natural science (like chemistry or biology) requires methods of inquiry and tools of analysis appropriate to the physical aspects of reality.

In each case, the key is coming to understand and appreciate these different methods and tools. Sometimes it is easy to see which methods and tools are suitable for a given statement. No one would try to use a calculator to settle a dispute about history, or a microscope to count the moons of Jupiter.

Sometimes, however, knowing which methods and tools should be used on a question can be challenging. There is the danger that one's assumptions or worldview can interfere with applying the right test. For example, though we know from the testimony of the New Testament that Isaiah wrote the entire book of Isaiah, it has become popular in certain circles of contemporary biblical criticism to say that someone other than Isaiah wrote chapters 40–66 of Isaiah much later.[6] Their argument is that the latter half of the book of Isaiah mentions Cyrus, king of Persia (Isaiah 44:28; 45:1), who lived around two centuries after Isaiah.

What the critics seldom acknowledge is their assumption that Isaiah could not have known the future. While they couch their arguments in the categories of history, literature, and language, the real issue is one of philosophy (does God exist?) and theology (does God reveal the future to His prophets?). They miss the truth of the unity of Isaiah because their assumptions drive them to look in the wrong direction for the proper test for the truth of the matter. Knowing how to test a truth claim requires understanding the kind of statement being made or the kind of question being asked.

Knowing the Truth About Reality. The quest and discovery of truth is really a quest for a discovery of knowledge. Most commonly today in philosophy, one finds the term *knowledge* defined in three ways. First, knowledge can be a skill. One might say that he knows Italian or that he knows karate. Second, knowledge can be acquaintance. When one says he knows his friend, he is saying that he is acquainted with him. Third, knowledge can be about the truth-value of propositions. Thus, if one knows that 2 + 2 = 4, one knows this as a truth. It is this third definition about which much of contemporary philosophy is concerned. This option, according to the standard view, is what concerns truth.

What is missing from these options is the classical understanding of knowledge one finds from Aristotle through Aquinas and with certain contemporary Aristotelian/Thomistic (or classical) philosophers today.[7]

While this is not the place for an in-depth treatment of epistemology (the philosophy of knowledge), a few observations are in order. First, the classical tradition maintains that all knowledge begins in the senses (known as empiricism).[8] Empiricism says we can know reality by what we see, hear, taste, touch, and smell.[9] It comes in two forms. The more familiar and contemporary version is often associated with the hard sciences, which generally has the consequence of concluding that nothing exists beyond the physical world.[10]

Second, because of the influences of modern philosophy, philosophers have lost the means of accounting for the knower's connection with the known, or with reality. Such a connection must be at the level of reality (i.e., being) itself. For example, some philosophers argue that we only directly know the ideas in our minds *about* the external world and not the things themselves in the world.[11] However, if this were the case, there would be no way to stave off skepticism, as the history of philosophy clearly demonstrates.[12]

The only way to account for the fact that the knower truly knows the things in the world is for those things to somehow be *in* the intellect of the knower. Only then will there be no gap between the knower and the known and, thus, there will be no conditions that would necessarily give rise to skepticism. For example, how can a tree be in the intellect of the one knowing the tree? Since it is by the intellect of the knower that the knower knows reality, there must be something "intelligible" in the things of the sensible world that allows them to be knowable. This "something" is its Form or (in certain contexts) its essence. The Form is that metaphysical aspect of a thing by virtue of which a thing is the kind of thing it is. For

instance, the Form "tree" is what makes all trees to be trees. The Form "human" is what makes all humans to be humans.

The importance of understanding things this way can be seen in the Nuremberg trials, which were held immediately after World War II. The justices of the trials were from the Soviet Union, France, the United Kingdom, and the United States. The Nazi defendants could not be tried on the basis of these countries' laws because they were not citizens of those countries. Further, the Nazi defendants could not be tried on the basis of the laws of Germany because they hadn't broken any of Germany's laws. Hitler had made sure that the constitution and laws of Germany were in place for the final solution to the Jewish question. The basis upon which the Nazi defendants were tried, then, gave rise to an expression that is still in use today: They were said to have committed *crimes against humanity*.

But, one must ask, exactly what is "humanity"? Is humanity real in any sense of the term *real*? If one says no, then how could the Nazi defendants have committed crimes against it? If humanity is real, exactly what is its nature? Is humanity male or female, black or white or some other race, tall or short, young or old, sick or well?

In fact, humanity is none of these things. It is what philosophers call a universal. It is that metaphysical aspect of (in this case) a human being that makes one a human. In each human, our humanity (or human nature) is particular, possessing the characteristics of an individual (male or female, young or old, etc.). But through experiencing a sufficient number of human beings, the intellect of a knower is able to abstract that metaphysical aspect (the Form) and know it as a universal. The metaphysical aspect that is able to make the individual human being a human is simultaneously able to exist in the intellect of a knower. Thus, the reality of the individual is *in* the knower, making the knowledge of things in reality possible. Because there is this metaphysical aspect to physical objects that makes these objects knowable to knowers by way of the intellect, we are able to know the world that God has created.

Remaining Confident in Truth Itself

The ability to know and apprehend truth is crucial to the apologetic endeavor of sharing the gospel and defending the faith. Unfortunately, the innate human potential to know and understand God's truth has fallen on hard times with the rise of modern philosophy, skepticism, agnosticism, and postmodernism. However, there is no need to abandon confidence in the knowing process or in truth itself, because God has secured access for everyone to knowledge and truth through the things He has made (Romans 1:19-21).

What Is Conversational Apologetics?

David Geisler

Christian apologist Ravi Zacharias said it best: "There is just enough of the modern worldview left so that reason still has a point of entry. But we have to use this knowledge wisely. We cannot give an overdose of argumentation."[1] If for no other reason, this understanding alone should cause us to rethink how we use apologetics today. Perhaps what is needed is an apologetic that is more conversational.

To fully embrace this suggestion, it is helpful to remember two points. First, the coupling of apologetics with evangelism was a normal practice in the New Testament. Christians appealed to evidence, and this was done by both Jesus and His disciples in their witness to others.[2] Second, approaches today that separate the two domains seem to carry with them some kind of limitation. Relying on a mere proclamation of "the facts supporting the gospel" yields a much shorter shelf life in today's market of effective evangelism.[3] Why? Because so many people in our culture have rejected a knowable reality, a belief in absolute truth, as well as a traditional Judeo-Christian morality. In the minds of many, because there is no overarching truth to embrace, *our evangelistic persuasion*

is prohibited! Therefore, a direct apologetic approach may not always be fruitful in today's culture. Penetrating this modern barrier may require that our approach be more interactive, and thus more conversational.

Broadening Our Understanding to Widen Our Impact

The traditional apologetic paradigm taught that we merely start with answering the skeptics' questions *if asked* (1 Peter 3:15). The problem is that many people today are not even inclined to ask questions with religious implications. In fact, I have discovered that many skeptics and atheists are very comfortable with living their lives in a certain way and have no desire to change. Some, if directly confronted with Christian values, are hostile. Even having a civil discussion on political topics is highly problematic because that often carries ethical implications! So our thinking needs to be realigned as to what it means, in a practical sense, to do apologetics in today's world. Doing apologetics must involve more than just being ready to give an answer to those who question what we believe and why.

To widen our impact and fully appreciate what is involved in using apologetics in our evangelism, I suggest we use Jesus's parable of the four soils as a backdrop (Matthew 13:19-23).

Why consider these verses? We must cultivate good soil in the lives of our nonbelieving friends, because our apologetic responsibilities do not merely rest in just giving an answer (Matthew 13:23). Even if they stop asking us questions, we are still responsible to cultivate good soil in their lives, which involves helping others to see the distortions with their own perspectives.[4]

What makes some of today's evangelistic approaches so ineffective?[5] Far too often we fail to recognize the need for cultivating good soil in the lives of others. Our attempt to plant the seeds of the gospel before we take the time to cultivate (do apologetics) in the lives of others may be shortsighted and ineffective. Our apologetic goal should be to discover how best to cultivate good soil in the lives of our nonbelieving friends. Only then may we see the maximum impact from our apologetic efforts. Helping others see their distorted perspectives in different areas can play a large part in aiding them to see that the foundation upon which they have built their life is not strong enough to support them. Only then might some be more open to considering a different perspective.

Over the years, I have discovered at least three areas of distortions that make our apologetic task more daunting. These include distortions that people have concerning *themselves, Jesus Christ,* and *God the Father.* For example, there are some young people today who do not believe in an afterlife and are fully convinced their bodies will merely dissolve into the ground after their life is over. Therefore, they have difficulty seeing the need

for a Savior. If existence ends at the grave, there is no Creator that we are accountable to in this life, much less after death.

The task of cultivating good soil may be even more urgent today than many Christians realize. Yes, we need to cultivate good soil to reach the indifferent, skeptical, or hostile with the claims of Christ. However, we may also need to reach those who worship with us on Sunday! No longer can we assume that everyone within a Sunday congregation holds to a Christian worldview similar to that which was more widespread a few decades ago, when secular Western society was still influenced by a Judeo-Christian mindset.[6] Today, many in our churches have far more trouble believing in a God who expects us to live according to a certain moral standard and to whom we will give an account someday. What is more, they may even have difficulty accepting that some things can only be one way, or exclusive!

A More Indirect Approach

Getting unbelievers to see the problems with their current perspective can be challenging. For example, conversations with unbelieving friends that involve religious or ethical themes may raise red flags in their minds. It is not uncommon for them to become combative in their dialogue. That's why there is great wisdom in developing approaches that help others to see the truth for themselves rather than trying to tell them directly what is wrong with their beliefs. Jesus and His disciples understood that using reason, evidence, and well-placed questions could be helpful. One good method I have learned over the years is to ask thought-provoking questions that allow others to form the right answers in their own minds!

For example, many people today say it

does not matter what you believe as long as you are sincere. Now, it is doubtful that they apply this principle consistently to all their beliefs. But rather than argue and tell them they are wrong, it would be more helpful if you help them to surface this truth for themselves. Consider asking a hypothetical question, such as, "What if your best friend told you that his religious commitment to his guru requires him to pour gasoline over his head, light a match, and burn himself to death?" Then ask, "Do you think it matters what your friend believes?" You can go another step further and ask, "Would you try to rescue your friend if he were on fire, even if he had instructed you not to intervene?"

Those who are honest will admit that being a good friend would compel them to try to rescue their friend, even if that friend issued a strong protest. By using this indirect questioning approach, you can get others to discover the truth for themselves and admit that it does matter what you believe about certain things.[7]

In suggesting a more indirect apologetic approach, I am not saying you should cease the use of other methods. In the New Testament, we see that Jesus and His disciples employed different approaches at different times, with some being direct and others indirect. Though the direct methods can be beneficial at times, in today's moral climate, a more indirect questioning approach (i.e., using apologetics to cultivate evangelism) may be more fruitful—especially if the individual is open to the Holy Spirit's work in their life.

To help nonbelievers recognize their distortions and inconsistencies is an important part of our apologetic and evangelistic task. Yet people prefer to live in a persuasion-free environment, and this includes their interactions on social media.[8] In order to be more effective, our apologetic approach needs to be more conversational.

Strengthening the Conversational Approach

If we are going to ask the right kind of question, *we need to know more about the beliefs of those we are trying to reach.* This entails more apologetic study, especially about other religious beliefs and practices. The more you know, the more effective your approach will be. This knowledge will give you greater insight into what issues you should focus your attention on as you dialogue with others.

An effective conversational apologetic approach implies that we know more than merely which questions *to ask.* We also need to know *how to ask* these questions and carefully discern which ones *not to ask.* It may take some practice to learn how to juggle these concerns and communicate in just the right way.[9] We should realize that when we ask the right kinds of questions in just the right way, we are essentially holding up a mirror that helps others to see their own worldview in a more accurate light.

To illustrate, here are a few examples. On one occasion while traveling by plane, I had a spiritual conversation with a secular Muslim. I intentionally avoided questions that might land me in prison in some parts of the world. For example, I steered away from questions that would have disparaged the name of Muhammad. I tried to come up with questions that would avoid certain cultural and religious landmines, yet would help him think more deeply about his worldview. I asked, "Do you understand, from a Muslim point of view, why we Christians seem a little confused about Islam?" This question prompted the opportunity to point to statements in the Qur'an concerning Jesus that suggest He was more than just a prophet (consider Surahs 2:253; 4:171; 5:75; 19:19-21). I attempted to get him to think a bit more deeply about Jesus than he ever had before. This question and others like it were designed to help him take one step closer to the truth about Jesus.

On another occasion I asked a man from China (who considered himself an atheist), "Would you agree, at minimum, that there is more evidence now for intelligent design than, say, twenty to thirty years ago?" To my surprise, he answered, "Well, maybe." My hope was to get him to realize that if we do have an intelligent Creator who created all of us, then it is not out of the realm of possibility that we are in some way accountable to this Creator! If I could get him to this point, it might be easier for me to build a bridge to the gospel. If he had been my neighbor, I might have been able to lay down further apologetic planks in future conversations that would have taken him closer to the cross.[10] Even many nonbelievers are willing to admit they do not measure up to their own personal moral standard for life. We can form this statement into a question and ask, "Do you see how it may be possible that God's standard is higher than our own?"

So why are questions so helpful? David Reed, an ex-Mormon, insightfully points out, "A person can close his ears to facts he does not want to hear, but if a pointed question causes him to form the answer in his own mind, he cannot escape the conclusion—because it's a conclusion that he reached himself."[11]

Jesus and the disciples utilized questions when they conversed with others. Questions are beneficial not only because they place the hearer in the role of a teacher and participant, but also because they help the other person to relax enough to discover the truth on their own. Jesus did exactly that when He spoke to the rich young ruler in Matthew 19:16-22. He asked, "Why do you ask me about what is good?" (verse 17). He wanted this young man to understand the discrepancies in his own beliefs and come to the right conclusion. Specifically, Christ desired the young man to realize that his excessive love for his personal wealth exceeded his love and commitment to the "good" teacher, Jesus. He did not tell this to the rich young ruler directly because He knew human nature and realized there are times when it is important for people to see the truth for themselves. In the end, the young ruler's sorrow was a result of realizing that his life and words did not line up with each other, thus setting up a confrontation between his priorities and his worldview.

Keeping the Conversation Going

To use apologetics more effectively, we all should consider taking steps toward joining apologetics with evangelism. To accomplish this task, our apologetic may be more productive by using an *indirect* and *conversational* approach. Choosing the right kind of questions, asked in just the right way (as well as questions *not* to ask), will increase the likelihood that others will want to continue the conversation.

May God give all of us wisdom to make our apologetic approach more conversational in the days ahead! In doing this, we will become more like the men of Issachar, who understood the times (1 Chronicles 12:32) in which they lived and knew what they ought to do.

How Can We Make Apologetics Culturally Relevant?

Miguel Angel Endara

At the dawn of our twenty-first century, the popular culture in the United States increasingly sees interpretations of truth, goodness, beauty, knowledge (what we can know), and what exists in terms of the dichotomy of left and right, progressive and conservative.[1] Our culture's interpretative grid consists of this ever-widening chasm of political categories in which the individual must adhere to the views of the dominant majority (or loudest voice) lest he is called a bigot, hater, or worse.

In this cultural context, many understand orthodox Christian views as stemming from the unpopular "right" and, as a result, these are eschewed or disparaged. How, then, can we defend and promulgate the truths of Christianity? In other words, how can we make apologetics culturally relevant?

In what follows, I explain how we may apply classical rhetoric to our politically dichotomous society, through the research of moral psychology, to construct a culturally relevant apologetic.

Lessons from Aristotle: Classical Rhetoric

It is well accepted that we humans are not just rational or merely emotional beings; we are both. This implies that the best type of persuasive apologetic appeal to others is one that engages both reason and emotion, the mind and the heart. More than 2,300 years ago, the Greek philosopher Aristotle wrote a treatise dedicated to understanding persuasion that involved the heart and mind, titled *Rhetoric*. According to Aristotle, the term *rhetoric* refers to "the faculty of observing in any given case the available means of persuasion."[2] *Rhetoric*, which I will call *classical rhetoric* to distinguish it from our current negative understanding of the term, is the art of persuasion, though not through deceptive means.

According to Aristotle and other classical rhetoricians, the best way to persuade someone is to adopt a tripartite or three-pronged approach that includes *ethos*, *logos*, and *pathos*. That is, the speaker or writer must appeal to (1) the way the audience perceives the communicator's trustworthiness (*ethos*), (2) the intellect of the audience (*logos*), and (3) the emotions (*pathos*) of the audience. This way, the appeal has a much greater chance of persuasive success.

Before we can apply this technique, however, we must understand our culture. We must ask ourselves: How can we couch the veracity of orthodox Christian doctrine and practice using *ethos*, *logos*, and *pathos* in our politically driven culture to invest it with relevance?

This chapter presents one possible method taken from the field of moral psychology. This method may help us to construct apologetic appeals to social progressives who oftentimes vilify Christian doctrine and practice. Beyond this, there are many other methods and people with other types of worldviews for which we must construct other types of apologetic appeals.

Lessons from Jonathan Haidt: Moral Psychology

According to moral psychologist Jonathan Haidt, one reason for the political and religious divide that we currently experience in today's society is due to the different sets of *moral foundations* to which people of the different sides of the political divide adhere.[3] Though Haidt defines *moral foundations* as universal matrices of cognitive moral modules constructed by culture, we may understand these more simply as cultural sets of moral values or ideals.[4]

According to Haidt, social conservatives have a wider moral foundation than social progressives in that they ground morality, almost equally, on the ideals of *care*, *liberty*, *fairness*, *loyalty*, *authority*, and *sanctity*.[5] On the other hand, social progressives ground morality mostly on *care*, *liberty*, and *fairness*.[6]

In other words, progressives promote empathy and solidarity with those who are oppressed (*care*). For them, the practice of social justice (*fairness*) and the observance of the "rights" of others (*liberty*) are most important. We can agree that these are all wonderful ideals. However, social progressives lack, according to Haidt, a strong moral sense of *loyalty*, *authority*, and *sanctity*. For example, progressives are usually not patriotic (*loyalty* and *authority*), they do not adhere to any established religion (*loyalty* and *authority*), and they do not consider their body or anything else to be holy (*sanctity*).

If Haidt's research is accurate, it should make a world of difference regarding our apologetic toward social progressives. For instance, though we place great significance in our sense of loyalty to Christ, participation in the church, and in the authority of the Bible, our apologetic must not begin with these points if we want to influence secular social progressives. Also, we will not get very far if we begin with an appeal to the sanctity of the human fetus or sex. We must structure our initial apologetic around the moral foundations of those to whom it is directed. That is, it is wise to use classical rhetoric along with the social progressive moral foundations as common ground from where we may begin our apologetic. In Acts 17:22-33, the apostle Paul began his preaching at the Areopagus by starting on common ground.[7]

Examples of Apologetic Appeals

How, specifically, can we use classical rhetoric together with the findings of moral psychology to come up with apologetic appeals to social progressives that do not compromise orthodox Christian doctrine? Below are two personal examples of how I have attempted to do this.

Example 1: An Apologetic Approach to Pro-Choice Social Progressives

I once wrote a pro-life article in which I decided to employ rhetorical techniques in accord with Haidt's research. Here is how I began the article:

> The Western World has a long and lamentable history of denigrating and oppressing people. At sundry times and places non-Greeks were "barbarians," the indigenous people of the New World were "savages" and Jews and people of color were sub-human. We've come a long way from these clear cases of prejudice and dehumanization. But, just how far have we come? Do we still unjustly deny "rights" and autonomy to others? Do we still oppress the innocent? The answer is, lamentably, yes. We still do this, but in the worst possible way, we denigrate and dehumanize the smallest and weakest amongst us, those who cannot speak for themselves.

I then identify who I am speaking about—human embryos—and give an argument for the humanity and personhood of embryos.

My appeal, then, began with *pathos*, an appeal to the emotions. But not just any emotions. I appealed to the *pathos* of social progressives by reminding them that we should be most concerned (*care*) about those who are the weakest amongst us and not allow others to mistreat them (*fairness*). This appeal of *pathos* also included *ethos* in that I attempted to establish solidarity with social progressives by implying the following, "You can trust me, for I am just like you in that I have great concern for those who are weak, innocent, and oppressed." Last, I appealed to *logos* through my philosophical arguments

for the humanity and personhood of the human embryo.

Example 2: An Apologetic Approach to Latino Leftists

I come from a large extended Latino family. Many of my family members who are second- and third-generation immigrants have adopted social progressive values while retaining some traditional Latino values, such as the significance of maintaining close familial bonds.

A couple of brothers, who are close family members, grew up wearing Che Guevara T-shirts and criticizing nonprogressive legislation. On the other hand, these brothers are amongst the most affectionate and caring members of my large family. Though political leftists, familial bonds are still sacred to them. These brothers, who are agnostic, used to challenge my Christian beliefs. Considering (1) their political views, (2) their recognition of the significance of loving familial bonds, and (3) the fact that I have not made any progress with appeals to pure *logos*, I came up with an apologetic that, roughly, began as follows:

> Let us not think of God as a distant and despotic tyrant who looks forward to sending us lightning bolts from heaven if we break His prohibitions. This is not the Christian God. Instead, God, our heavenly Father, loves us and calls us back from our wayward ways to be reconciled with Him so that we may join His family fold and be called His sons and daughters. Indeed, God loves us with an everlasting love that transcends the here and now; it transcends our fleeting material existence. Imagine how beautiful it will be for the Father to someday gather us into the eternal family that includes those

family members of ours who have responded affirmatively to God's call. Because of this unfathomable love for us the Father made this possible by sending His only begotten Son, Jesus, as a sacrifice on our behalf and for our reconciliation to Him...

Notice that though these two brothers are agnostic, I appealed to the moral foundation of *care* by explaining that God loves us to the point that He sent His Son Jesus to be sacrificed for us. Also, I appealed to their recognition of the importance of familial love by using terms such as *Father*, *Son*, *family*, and *children*. My appeal had *ethos*, for I come from the same family tree as they do, and they know that I too believe in the significance of familial bonds. Further, I appealed to *pathos* by explaining to them that God loves them and wants to bring them into His familial fold. In this case, I left *logos* out until they asked me questions in response to my explanation.

Evaluating the Classical Rhetorical-Moral Psychological Apologetic Appeal

In my two examples, notice that though classical rhetoric was employed, it was not deceitful, nor did it compromise the Christian message in any way. Further, in my appeals to *pathos,* I did not commit the appeal to emotion fallacy, the error in reasoning

committed when one gives an emotional appeal as if it was a reason for a position. My appeals to *pathos* strictly regarded explanations. They were not arguments. Classical rhetoric helped me to structure and focus on particular truths of the Christian faith, thereby creating an apologetic on what I identified to be common ground.

In addition to learning from classical rhetoric and moral psychology, we must remember that we are not only emotional and rational beings, we are also spiritual beings. That is, we are influenced by spiritual forces, as Ephesians 6:12 reminds us: "We do not wrestle against flesh and blood, but against the rulers, against the authorities, against the cosmic powers over this present darkness, against the spiritual forces of evil in the heavenly places."

Ephesians 6:12 applies to all cultures at all times and in all places, so it also applies to ours. Nonbelievers, as persons, are not our enemies. Our enemies are the spiritual forces of evil that have taken captive their hearts and minds. That is why we must bathe the preparation of our apologetic in prayer, and we must deliver it with gentleness and respect, as urged in 1 Peter 3:15.

Let us, then, pray to the Father, through the Son, in the power of the Holy Spirit, to help us to construct a rhetorically and culturally relevant apologetic that employs knowledge of cultural assumptions wisely and lovingly.

10

What Is the Holy Spirit's Role in Apologetics?

Ed Hindson

Christians have long recognized that the Holy Spirit convicts, converts, and convinces unbelievers of the truth "because the Spirit is the truth" (1 John 5:6). In addition, Jesus said of the Holy Spirit, "When he comes, he will convict the world concerning sin and righteousness and judgment" (John 16:8). The Holy Spirit is essential for the effective use of apologetic information toward persuading unbelievers or strengthening believers. What is more, the Holy Spirit's role is *necessary* for apologetics to be utilized in evangelism to the lost, the discipleship of believers, and in defending against false teachings. Norman Geisler states, "There is no contradiction between reason and evidence on the one hand and the work of the Holy Spirit on the other."[1]

The Holy Spirit, Apologetics, and Evangelism

One important role of apologetics is evangelism. First Peter 3:15 notes, "Always [be] prepared to make a defense to anyone who asks you for a reason for the hope that is in you; yet do it with gentleness and respect."

Peter's mention of "anyone" includes unbelievers. Moreover, the following verse also includes unbelievers by referring to "those who revile your good behavior in Christ" (verse 16). The apostle Peter taught believers to use apologetic methods to persuade unbelievers toward faith in Christ, and did so by complementing communication with a life of conviction. Believers are to have "good behavior" that reflects a life changed by Christ.

There are three important aspects of evangelism that are dependent upon the power of the Holy Spirit.

First, the *godly lifestyle* of the believer is dependent upon the Holy Spirit. Second Peter 1:3 states, "His divine power has granted to us all things that pertain to life and godliness, through the knowledge of him who called us to his own glory and excellence." Believers are given many commands to obey; yet the ability to fulfill these commands is based on the divine power of God living in and through the believer.

Second, the ability to effectively share the *gospel message* with unbelievers is dependent upon the Holy Spirit. The Great Commission teaches believers to make disciples of all nations by going, baptizing, and teaching others the good news of Jesus as Lord (Matthew 28:18-20). Though any person can read the words of the New Testament, the Holy Spirit is necessary to effectively bring the gospel message to an unbeliever who will hear, believe, and receive that message. In Romans 10:14-15, Paul noted, "How then will they call on him in whom they have not believed? And how are they to believe in him of whom they have never heard? And how are they to hear without someone preaching? And how are they to preach unless they are sent? As it is written, 'How beautiful are the feet of those who preach the good news!'" God's Spirit calls the person who shares the gospel message, sends that person to others who have yet to hear, and empowers the message communicated and draws unbelievers to come to faith in Christ (John 6:65).

Third, the *positive acceptance* of the gospel message by an unbeliever is dependent upon the Holy Spirit. Both the sender and the receiver of the gospel message require God's Spirit at work within them for the evangelistic efforts of an apologist to be effective. The Holy Spirit's role in apologetics was clearly seen on the Day of Pentecost in Acts 2. After being empowered by the Holy Spirit, the apostle Peter defended Jesus as the Messiah, resulting in 3,000 people believing and being baptized (Acts 2:41). Throughout the book of Acts the Holy Spirit filled believers with the power to speak God's message with boldness (Acts 4:8,31) and led them to evangelize the lost (Acts 8:29,40).

Speaking the Truth in Love

A second role in which apologetics is dependent upon the Holy Spirit is found in Ephesians 4:15: "Speaking the truth in love, we are to grow up in every way into him who is the head, into Christ." Francis Schaeffer said, "Biblical orthodoxy without compassion is surely the ugliest thing in the world."[2] An apologist is called to speak God's truth with God's love. Doing so is a sign of maturity. However, to speak in love requires the work of the Holy Spirit, because love is a fruit of the Spirit (Galatians 5:22-23). Furthermore, God is love, and love comes from God (1 John 4:8). Thus, the person who desires to speak the truth in love must trust in God's Spirit to effectively accomplish this aspect of sharing truth.

Love also stands at the heart of the Christian message. Jesus taught that the greatest commandments are to love God completely and to love your neighbor as yourself (Matthew 22:34-40). Jesus demonstrated such love through His life and teachings. He further called His disciples to follow His example. The apostle Paul utilized this approach, calling his readers to "be imitators of me, as I am of Christ" (1 Corinthians 11:1).

There is another way in which we are dependent upon the Holy Spirit to do apologetics and to help us speak the truth in love—He *gives us love* for other people. It is easy to argue with someone we do not love. However, God's love compels us to lovingly persuade those who have yet to believe the good news of Jesus. This motivation can drive us toward devoted prayer, personal holiness, committed study of accurate sources, and a diligent pursuit of opportunities to discuss and defend Christian beliefs to evangelize unbelievers and edify believers.

Moreover, our dependence upon the Holy Spirit when defending the faith also involves the *uniqueness* of Christian love. Other religious movements often seek to promote their beliefs as a means of gaining favor or securing their salvation by their good works. In Christianity, our love for others is based on God's love for us. Therefore, it is unselfish, directed at others, and focused on the enrichment of others. With God's Spirit at work in and through the life of the apologist, this love is offered through friendship, discussion, debate, and other means to help the life of the lost person. Even in cases in which the unbeliever remains unpersuaded, the believer maintains unconditional love, knowing that the Holy Spirit must do His work to bring change into the heart of the unbeliever. Ultimately, it is He alone who illuminates the mind, confirms the truth, and changes the unbeliever's heart (1 Corinthians 2:14-15). Thus, no one comes to faith in Christ apart from the gracious work of the Holy Spirit.

Apologetics with Gentleness and Respect

Another important aspect of apologetics is to persuade others "with gentleness and respect" (1 Peter 3:15). To be gentle and show respect requires the believer to be dependent upon the Holy Spirit. Gentleness is also a fruit of the Spirit (Galatians 5:23). Jesus served as one who was "gentle and lowly in heart" (Matthew 11:29; see also 21:5). Paul wrote with humility and gentleness when he corrected believers in Corinth (2 Corinthians 10:1).

Throughout Scripture, living with gentleness toward others stands as a clear calling for every believer. Philippians 4:5 calls believers to "let your gentleness be evident to all" (NIV). God's chosen people are to show "gentleness and patience" (Colossians 3:12), while church leaders are to be "not violent, but gentle" and "to be gentle toward everyone" (1 Timothy 3:3;

6:11; Titus 3:2). Wives are likewise called to have a gentle spirit (1 Peter 3:4). The context of each of these passages toward believers includes a close walk with God and living by the power of His Spirit.

Respect also is an important trait for all believers, and it requires dependence upon the Holy Spirit. Believers are to respect everyone (1 Peter 2:17) and show respect to governing authorities (Romans 13:7). Wives are called to respect their husband (Ephesians 5:33), husbands are to respect their wives (1 Peter 3:7), slaves were to respect their master (Ephesians 6:5; 1 Timothy 6:1). The daily life of the believer is to win the "respect of outsiders" (1 Thessalonians 4:12 NIV). Further, church elders are to be respectable and manage their family "in a manner worthy of full respect" (1 Timothy 3:4 NIV). Likewise, deacons and their families are to be "worthy of respect" (1 Timothy 3:8,11 NIV).

In apologetics, showing respect for unbelievers and their beliefs and backgrounds can often remove barriers to sharing the gospel. For example, rather than disrespecting a Buddhist's belief in reincarnation, a respectful apologist can instead discuss what evidence exists for reincarnation. He or she might also help the adherent better understand the historical origin of this belief. A conversation may then lead toward the biblical discussion of eternal life and the need for faith in Jesus Christ to receive it. The goal, in this context, would be to help the person understand there is one life and then judgment (Hebrews 9:27), while respectfully appealing to the opportunity to obtain through Jesus an eternal life better than reincarnation (Ephesians 2:8-9).

Addressing False Teachings

In Titus 1:9, the apostle Paul instructed that a church elder "must hold firmly to the trustworthy message as it has been taught, so that he can encourage others by sound doctrine and refute those who oppose it." Jude verse 3 adds, "I was very eager to write to you about the salvation we share, I felt compelled to write and urge you to contend for the faith that was once for all entrusted to God's holy people." The Christian faith includes both a *positive* communication of the gospel and a *defense* against inaccurate teachings. Jude felt "compelled" by the Holy Spirit to address certain false teachings, leaving an example for believers today.

In Titus 1:9, the New Testament Greek word translated "sound" (*hugiainō*)—in reference to sound doctrine—can also be translated "healthy." Certain teachings are unhealthy and inaccurate, requiring a response from the apologist. Those gifted in teaching by God's Spirit can often most effectively address such errors. However, all believers are called to "be steadfast" and "stand firm" in the faith (1 Corinthians 15:58; 16:13). Addressing false teachings involves both the intellect and the heart. The believer is called to present accurate beliefs or ideas regarding God, yet a spiritual side also exists. Paul addressed this in Ephesians 6:10-20, noting the need to wear "the whole armor of God" (verse 13).

Part of this spiritual armor includes "the sword of the Spirit" (verse 17). Paul refers to this spiritual sword as the Word of God. In this context, a direct association is made between the Holy Spirit and Scripture working together to respond to false teachings. Powerful examples of this method are found in the New Testament. Jesus responded to the three temptations of Satan in the wilderness by appealing to Scripture (Matthew 4:1-11; Luke 4:1-13). Matthew's Gospel frequently cited Old Testament passages in support of

its accounts, a method followed to various degrees by the other Gospel writers. The apostle Paul also frequently cited from the Old Testament to support his teachings, as did James, Jude, and the author of Hebrews. In fact, a compelling case can be made that every New Testament author strongly utilized the Old Testament in their writings.

A further aspect of addressing false teachings through the Holy Spirit is *prayer*. In Colossians 4:3-4, Paul wrote, "At the same time, pray also for us, that God may open to us a door for the word, to declare the mystery of Christ, on account of which I am in prison—that I may make it clear, which is how I ought to speak." He clearly relied on the Holy Spirit's power, his own prayers, and the prayers of other believers to strengthen his apologetics arguments. This was true both when he communicated Christ to unbelievers and he addressed false teachings. James 1:5-8 also addresses the need for believers to pray for wisdom when it is lacking, trusting the Lord to provide it. Prayer appeals for the spiritual power necessary for effective apologetics in all areas in which wisdom is needed, both in presenting and defending the gospel message.

In John 14:16-17, Jesus told His followers, "I will ask the Father, and he will give you another Helper, to be with you forever, even the Spirit of truth." Followers of Christ receive the Holy Spirit as an ongoing helper and advocate. He is the Spirit of truth that empowers the life and communications of the apologist. *Reasoning alone saves no one apart from the work of the Holy Spirit.* He alone prompts people to believe in God's saving truth, and He alone enlightens the unbeliever's mind to understand the evidence of His truth.

Part Two

QUESTIONS ABOUT GOD

Why Does God Seem "Hidden"?

Natasha Crain

This chapter begins a section examining various evidences and arguments for the existence of God. But the very fact that we must discuss these issues betrays a philosophical and theological problem people have struggled with for hundreds of years: *God does not make His existence undeniably obvious.* If He did, these chapters would not be necessary; God's existence would be a foregone conclusion. Yet that is far from the case. Atheists often claim there is *no* relevant evidence for God's existence and promptly dismiss any such discussions. Christians and other theists believe God has revealed Himself sufficiently for belief, but often still long to know why God has not revealed Himself *more.*

Before looking at the evidences and arguments for God's existence, therefore, it is helpful to have a framework for considering *why* God would be hidden enough to warrant those discussions in the first place. We will start by considering the most basic question of all.

Is There *Any* Evidence of God's Existence?

When my daughter was a toddler, she gleefully informed me one day that she had been hiding a tiny toy car in her room that she had found at the park. She was extraordinarily proud of herself when she came to me and said, "It's been there for days and you never even guessed where it was!" Her obvious logic fail was that I did not know I *should* be looking for a toy car in her room. She thought it was hidden; I had no reason to think it even existed.

Many atheists feel this way about God. They say there is *no* evidence of His existence and no valid reason to go looking for Him; those who "find" God are just engaging in wishful thinking. In other words, God is not hidden at all—He just does not exist. For example, atheist author Dan Barker says, "I am an atheist because there is no evidence for the existence of God. That should be all that needs to be said about it: no evidence, no belief."[1] Best-selling atheist author Richard Dawkins says, "Faith is the great cop-out, the great excuse to evade the need to think and evaluate evidence. Faith is belief in spite of, even perhaps because of, the lack of evidence."[2] Barker and Dawkins, like many atheists, state this supposed lack of evidence as a universally acknowledged fact and go on to claim that theists are unreasonable for believing in God anyway. It is critical to understand, however, that this is *not* a universally acknowledged fact. Neither theists nor atheists are willing to believe in something without evidence. Theists believe there *is* evidence for God's existence (even if He is somewhat hidden) and believe *because* of it, not in spite of lacking it.

How can people draw such vastly different conclusions? That is just the nature of any kind of evidence. Evidence itself does not say anything—all evidence requires human interpretation. And because evidence requires human interpretation, there will always be differing conclusions, depending on a person's available information, life experiences, and motivations. Therefore, as you consider the evidences and arguments in the following chapters, it's vital to bear in mind that just because God has not made His existence undeniably obvious, it does not necessitate the common atheistic conclusion that He has given us *no* evidence. Theists and atheists simply disagree over the *interpretation* of the evidence.

Is There *Enough* Evidence of God's Existence?

Rather than say there is no evidence for God, many people say the evidence is not strong enough. *Enough*, however, is a highly subjective quantity. What might be enough for one person to believe in God might not feel like enough for another person. For example, consider this wish list from one atheist blogger:

If I saw an unambiguous message from God, I would be persuaded of his existence. If I saw writing suddenly appear in the sky, in letters a hundred feet high, saying "I Am God, I Exist, Here Is What I Want You To Do"—and if

that writing were seen by every human being, written in whatever language they understand, comprehended in the same way by everyone who saw it—I would be persuaded that God existed.[3]

Although I personally do not need God to skywrite in order to persuade me of His existence, I can certainly relate to the desire for that kind of revelation. If we were honest, many of us would love to encounter God in such a direct way. But when God does not reveal Himself, as we would personally like, it does not logically follow that there is not enough evidence to conclude He exists. Rather, there are two questions we should ask ourselves.

First, is our standard of proof reasonable? The blogger I just quoted is looking for absolute certainty. Yet if we applied a similar criterion to anything else in life, there is little we would be able to claim we know. We lack that kind of undeniable evidence for many things. Do we have undeniable evidence, for example, that Abraham Lincoln existed? No, but we all assume he did based on the preponderance of evidence. We should not *necessarily* expect that the evidence for God's existence would be different (more on that shortly).

Second, what is the best explanation for the evidence we *do* have—things like the origin of the universe, the complexity of life, and our innate moral knowledge? The importance of this question cannot be overstated. To see why, consider for a moment how you would respond if you discovered one evening that someone broke into your house and stole everything. You have no idea who would have done this—there are no *obvious* suspects. The police arrive, and after finding out there is no undeniable evidence of who committed the crime, they wish you luck and leave. Is that what you would expect them to do?

Of course not! Maybe no one left a clear note confessing he did it, but you would still expect the police to look at the evidence that *does* exist and create a suspect profile accordingly. The question would not be what kinds of evidence the police would *like* to have, but rather what is the best explanation for the evidence they *do* have. Similarly, we can draw up our own list of evidence we wish God would give us, but that is neither here nor there. We are not absolved from the need to draw conclusions about the evidence we have just because we wish the evidence were different. Our subjective standards can be a poor guide to determining what is true.

But Why *Wouldn't* God Make Himself More Obvious?

While it is not logical to conclude God does not exist simply because He has not made Himself known according to every person's subjective wishes, it is reasonable to ask *why* God would not reveal Himself in more obvious ways. We may not have undeniable evidence that Abraham Lincoln existed, but Lincoln's existence also does not have immediate bearing on our lives. If God is perfectly loving and good, it seems He would make His existence so obvious that no one could deny it—especially when people long to encounter Him more directly.

The force of this question is compounded by two biblical truths: (1) God wants "all people to be saved and to come to the knowledge of the truth" (1 Timothy 2:4) and (2) Jesus is the only path to salvation (John 14:6). If our belief and trust in Jesus has eternal consequences, why would

God remain hidden—even a little? This tension was powerfully stated by the atheist German philosopher Friedrich Nietzsche (1844–1900):

> A god who is all-knowing and all-powerful and who does not even make sure his creatures understand his intention—could that be a god of goodness? Who allows countless doubts and dubieties to persist, for thousands of years, as though the salvation of mankind were unaffected by them, and who on the other hand holds out the prospect of frightful consequences if any mistake is made as to the nature of truth?[4]

While we can only ever have a limited understanding of why God has chosen to reveal Himself in certain ways, at certain times, and in certain amounts, philosophers have long identified at least one possible reason that God may choose to remain as hidden as He does: to preserve our free will.

Generally speaking, free will is our ability to make choices without external coercion. If God wanted us to genuinely love Him, it was necessary to create us with some degree of free will. Otherwise, we would be nothing more than robots, lacking the ability to have a genuine relationship with our Creator. This fact has bearing on the question of God's hiddenness. If God revealed Himself in an undeniable way, He would effectively be taking away our freedom to seek and love Him. Rather than coerce us into belief and trust, He gives us the space to either genuinely pursue or avoid Him. Christian philosopher Blaise Pascal (1623–1662) put it this way:

> Willing to appear openly to those who seek him with all their heart, and to be hidden from those who flee from him with all their heart, God so regulates

the knowledge of himself that he has given indications of himself, which are visible to those who seek him and not to those who do not seek him. There is enough light for those to see who only desire to see, and enough obscurity for those who have a contrary disposition.[5]

Importantly—especially as it relates to Nietzsche's concern—the Bible says that when we do seek God, we will find Him (Deuteronomy 4:29). While God might not reveal Himself in the undeniable ways many would prefer, this verse implies that God has revealed Himself in *sufficient* ways for allowing genuine seekers to find Him. From a Christian perspective, that includes general revelation (knowledge of God through natural means, such as the observation of nature, philosophy, and reasoning) and special revelation (knowledge of God through supernatural means, such as the Bible and the person of Jesus Christ).

What About Those Who Say They *Cannot* Find God?

But what about those who *do not* find God, even when they say they look? Does their unbelief seem to contradict Deuteronomy 4:29? The answer is in Romans 1:18-20—all people know God exists, but some suppress the truth:

The wrath of God is revealed from heaven against all ungodliness and unrighteousness of men, who by their unrighteousness suppress the truth. For what can be known about God is plain to them, because God has shown it to them. For his invisible attributes, namely, his eternal power and divine nature, have been clearly perceived, ever since the creation of the world, in the things that have been made. So they are without excuse.

While we are never in a position to identify why a given person claims to not believe in God, we know from the Bible that some people will not put their faith in God no matter *how* much He reveals. The Israelites, for example, witnessed the kinds of supernatural events that many today would yearn to experience, but that did not result in their unwavering belief and trust in God (for reference, see the entire Old Testament). In the New Testament, we read of how Jesus performed miraculous signs but there were still people who chose not to believe (John 12:37). If God skywrote today, you could bet that many would still deny His existence. Clearly, faith in God is a matter of both the heart and mind—regardless of *how* hidden He may seem at any given time.

What Are the Classical Proofs
for God's Existence?

Richard G. Howe

Before the onset of Christianity, and subsequently throughout Christian history, a number of proofs have arisen regarding the existence of God. To be *classical* means that an argument utilizes philosophical categories and concepts found in the philosophy of the ancient Greeks and improved upon by Christian philosophers.[1] The classical proofs stand in contrast to the more popular, contemporary arguments for God's existence.[2] Further, because philosophy in general, and Greek philosophy in particular, is relatively unknown by the average person, the popular, contemporary arguments (culling as they do from the more familiar categories and data of modern science) generally resonate with people more so than do the classical proofs.[3]

Classical Proofs

Broadly speaking, both contemporary and classical arguments for God's existence fall within three categories: (1) arguments for God as the cause of the existence of the universe (cosmological arguments), (2) arguments for God as the cause of the design or purpose of the universe (teleological arguments), and (3) arguments for God as the cause of human morality (moral arguments). Let's review them in order.

Cosmological Arguments

There are different versions of the cosmological argument. One of the most important differences between the classical cosmological argument and the contemporary arguments is that the contemporary arguments aim to show that God is the cause of the universe coming into existence a finite time ago.[4] In contrast, the argument from the medieval philosopher Thomas Aquinas (c. 1225–1274) demonstrates that God is the cause of the *current* existing of the universe.[5]

The Kalam Cosmological Argument. The kalam cosmological argument appeals to the latest findings in science to show that the universe had a beginning a finite time ago in the big bang.[6] The argument says (1) the universe began to exist; (2) whatever begins to exist must have a cause; (3) therefore, the universe has a cause. In defense of the first premise, contemporary scientific data are marshalled regarding the big bang theory, the expansion of the universe, and the second law of thermodynamics.

In the big bang theory, scientists maintain that the universe began in a colossal explosion a finite time ago. The significance of this is that since the universe has not existed from eternity, it must have come into existence in the finite past. The expansion of the universe says that every object in the universe is moving away from every other object such that even space itself is expanding. The significance of this is that the universe could not have been expanding from eternity; otherwise, it would be infinitely dispersed (which it is not). Therefore, the universe came into existence a finite time ago. The second law of thermodynamics says that all isolated systems will tend toward a state of maximum disorder (entropy). In an isolated system, the amount of energy available to do work decreases and becomes uniform. This amounts to saying that the universe is "running down" (much like the batteries of a flashlight left on for an extended period of time). The significance of this is that the universe could not have been running down from eternity; otherwise, it would have run down by now—which it has not. Therefore, the universe came into existence a finite time ago.

Since the universe came into existence and because whatever comes into existence must have a cause, based on the law of causality, then the universe must have had a cause. Since this cause created matter, it must be immaterial. Since this cause created time, it must be timeless. Since this cause created space, it must be spaceless. For if any of these finite conditions (space, time, and matter) were part of the cause, it would be tantamount to saying the cause caused itself to be, which is absurd, for this would require the cause to exist prior to causing its own existence. Since this cause created the universe, it must be of unimaginable power. Because the effect of this cause (the universe) has not existed forever with the cause, this cause must have willed it to exist, which means it is personal. Thus, we have an immaterial, timeless, spaceless, personal cause of unimaginable power. Many people recognize this cause as God.

A Cosmological Argument of Thomas Aquinas. Many people probably would not think in terms of something needing a cause of its *current* existing. Consider this as an analogy of how Aquinas understood existence (or existing).[7] Suppose you saw a giant ten-foot glass ball in front of a local business. You might ask where it came from. If you were told that it was a promotional tool celebrating the grand opening of the business and that the glass ball had been manufactured at a local glass factory, you no doubt would find this explanation satisfactory.

Now suppose that you began to hear music playing. Most likely you would not ask (as you did about the glass ball) where the music *came from*. Instead, you would ask where the music *is* coming from. This is because you realize that music exists as music only as long as it is being caused to be music. As soon as the cause of the music stops causing the music, the music ceases to exist. For Aquinas, the existence of all created, finite things was like the music. Existence (or existing) is an *act*. It is something that essences *do*.[8] You can find in his (and others') writings the expression "the act of existence."

How does this notion of existence fit into an argument for God's existence? Consider yourself as a human being. Your essence (or nature) is what makes you a human. Your existence is what makes you a being. Now, whatever is true of you is true of you either by virtue of your essence or not. For example, the fact that you have rationality is because you are a human. It is part of your essence as a human to have rationality.

But consider the fact that you are reading this chapter. Is the reason you are reading this because you are a human? Is it part of your essence as a human to be reading this book? The answer is no; otherwise, those who are not reading this article would not be human. However, you can easily account for why you are reading this chapter even though it is not part of your essence to do so. You are reading this chapter because you are causing yourself to read this book.

Now consider the fact that you exist. Is the reason you exist because you are a human? Is it part of your essence to exist? The answer, again, is no; otherwise, you would have always existed.[9] If not, then what is causing your *current* existing (like the current existing of the music)? You cannot be the cause of your own existing, or you would then have to exist (as a cause) before you exist, which is impossible. This ultimately leads to the conclusion that the only way to account for your existing is that you are being caused to exist by something whose very essence *is* existence itself. As Aquinas remarked in another context: "All men know this to be God."[10]

Teleological Arguments

The term *teleological* comes from the Greek word *telos*, meaning "end" or "goal" or "purpose." In contemporary apologetics, the term more often used is *design*. However, the classical teleological argument differs markedly from the contemporary design arguments (see the chapter "What Is the Scientific Case for Intelligent Design?"). In these design arguments, the appeal is made to various scientific aspects of the universe,

such as fine-tuning,[11] irreducible complexity,[12] and information theory[13] to argue for an intelligent designer of the universe.[14]

In the classical teleological argument, given in the fifth of Aquinas's famous "Five Ways" (his five arguments for God's existence in his *Summa Theologiae*), the focus is not on these physical aspects of biological life forms. Instead, it is on the metaphysical aspects of such living beings, particularly final causality.[15] What does all this mean? In classical thought, there are four kinds of causes.[16] Consider the example of making a chair out of wood. The material cause is that *out of which* an effect is—i.e., what it is made of, namely, wood. The formal cause is that *which* an effect is—i.e., its form, structure, or nature, such as chair-ness. The efficient cause is that *by which* an effect is—i.e., who or what produced the chair, namely, the carpenter. The final cause of the chair is that *for which* an effect is—i.e., why it was built, such as to sit on.

The teleological argument says that because all things aim toward their destiny (acorns grow into oak trees, zygotes grow into adult humans), unless hampered by an external impediment, there must be someone who is directing things to their telos. Why? Thomist philosophers (philosophers who follow the philosophy of Thomas Aquinas, who followed, for the most part, the philosophy of Aristotle) offer several reasons. First, the end goal (e.g., the oak tree for the acorn) is the cause (i.e., the final cause) of the acorn moving toward becoming a full-grown oak tree. But something cannot move invariably toward its destiny if it does not have a mind, because aiming toward a purpose can only be done by intelligence. This intelligence we call *God*.[17]

Second, how can the full-grown oak tree

be a cause of anything if it does not actually exist in the acorn? To be sure, it exists potentially, but a thing that exists only potentially cannot itself be a cause. If the final cause does not actually exist in the acorn, the only place it can exist is in an intellect. The explanation is that God, having the purpose or goal or *telos* of the acorn "in His mind," so to speak, moves all things toward their appropriate destiny analogous to how the house "exists" in the intellect of the architect/carpenter who builds it. The "final cause" of the oak tree is in the mind of God as its Maker.

Moral Arguments

As with both the cosmological and teleological arguments, the moral argument in the classical tradition differs in important ways from the popular, contemporary moral argument, which says that if God does not exist, then objective moral values do not exist. But objective moral values do exist. Therefore, God exists.[18]

In the classical tradition, the issue of human morality is called *natural law theory* and is a subset of the broader issue of law, both of which are nested in a context of specific philosophical notions regarding natures (or essences), teleology, goodness as such, moral goodness in particular, the relationship of being and goodness and more.[19]

Natural law theory focuses on how it is that human beings, unique among God's creatures on earth (having as we do rationality and free will), intersect with God's superintendence of all of His creation. Minerals, plants, and animals conduct themselves according to the laws of the physical world (minerals, plants, and animals), with a modicum of life that requires the intake of nutrients for growth (plants and animals), and with sensory faculties like seeing or hearing (animals).

God sovereignly manages the affairs of all of His creation. He aims His creation toward its proper goal or end. Physical forces and elements always behave the way God has created them to behave. Plant seeds always grow toward the specific kind of plant they are unless impeded by some outside force. Animals always grow and behave the way God has created them to. They all obey God's will without knowing they are doing so. God has created them to be and do in accordance with their natures. They never fail to do so. This end or goal toward which all things aim is called *good*.[20]

Human beings are unique among God's sensible creatures. Unlike minerals, plants, and animals, humans have rationality and free will. We are able to choose in accordance with or in violation of our natures. Just as God has created the acorn such that, because of its nature, it will grow up to be an oak tree, God has created humans with a nature that aims us at being the kind of creatures God intends us to be. Being created in His image, God intends for us to be holy as He is holy (Matthew 5:48; Romans 6:19; 2 Corinthians 7:1; Hebrews 12:10). But unlike the acorn, humans can freely choose to disobey God's will. Doing so is called *sin*. Sin does violence to what God intents as our good (i.e., our *telos*). The capacity to choose for or against God's good for us is what makes our actions moral. This is why no action of an animal is a moral action.

A Classical Moral Argument. How does this give us a classical moral argument for God's existence? Notice what the classical approach does not argue. The popular, contemporary moral argument says that God is necessary for morality's objectivity. But in the classical tradition, morality's objectivity arises initially from the fact that the moral good for a human being is to be the kind of being a human ought to be by virtue of human nature. The good of any being is to gain the perfections (i.e., to progress toward its end or *telos*) it ought to have by virtue of its nature.[21] A human ought to have certain perfections because of what it means to *be* a human. Thus, it is not the objectivity of morality that is in question. What is in question is how the elements constituting human morality point to God as the *ultimate* explanation for human morality.

But can we know what we ought to be by virtue of our human nature? There are two sources. First, there is a general source based upon God's general revelation. That is, God has revealed truths through His creation that are knowable by reason (as opposed to faith).[22] Second, God has also spoken through His special revelation—what we know as the Bible. So, while natural law can tell us that murder is wrong, Jesus expanded upon this (external) moral truth to tell us that even being angry (internal) without a cause is also wrong (Matthew 5:22). While the data of special revelation can very well convict the unbeliever (Romans 10:17), as a general rule, no human being (saved or lost) misses out on the data of general revelation.

The classical moral argument, then, can take that which is known about morality and demonstrate what must be true about reality to account for morality. Having identified this, those same aspects can be "rearranged" to formulate a classical cosmological argument like the one laid out above. Human morality concerns itself with human teleology, which is to say, human good. But what is good for a human arises from the fact that human beings have natures or essences. This also points to final causality and efficient causality. Human nature (or essence) can be distinguished from a given human's existence. But anything that has existence, yet whose existence is not because of its nature or essence, can only have existence because it is being given existence (i.e., caused) by something whose essence is existence itself. And all people know this to be God.

A Witness That Always Speaks to Us

The existence of God is crucial to the Christian apologetic. For if God does not exist, there cannot be a Son of God (Jesus), acts of God (miracles), salvation offered by God, or the Word of God (Bible). To be certain, God gave us a general witness of Himself in creation, and a particular witness in the nature (or essence) of reality. This witness is both intelligible and accessible, always speaking to us of the eternal God who is.

What Are Some Other Arguments for God's Existence?

Thomas W. Baker

From the early church onward, Christians have produced many rational and philosophical arguments for God's existence as they reflected upon the world. This should not be surprising given the testimony of Romans 1:20, which reads, "His invisible attributes, namely, his eternal power and divine nature, have been clearly perceived, ever since the creation of the world, in the things that have been made. So they are without excuse."

In this chapter, we will review some additional arguments that bear a strong witness to God. They will come primarily from Thomas Aquinas (c. 1225–1274), who was not only one of the most prolific Christian authors in history, but someone who gave an abundance of arguments for God. In the previous chapter we looked at the classical forms of the cosmological, teleological, and moral arguments; in this chapter, the goal is to present three additional arguments that may not be as familiar.

Arguments for God's Existence

Argument from Motion

While several have provided an argument from motion for a first unmoved mover, perhaps the best of these is found in Aquinas's *Summa Theologiae*, popularly known as the first of his Five Ways and discussed in more length in his *Summa contra Gentiles*.[1] The argument is summarized as follows:

1. It is evident to our senses that in the world some things are in motion.

2. Everything put in motion is put in motion by a mover.

3. There cannot be an infinite regress of movers going backward. If there is no first mover, there can be no subsequent motion.

4. Therefore, there is a first unmoved mover; this is God.

Let us take a closer look at each part of the argument.

1. *It is evident to our senses that in the world some things are in motion.* Aquinas strategically started from motion observed in the world all around us. Local physical motion is the most obvious, as when you move from place to place, but motion can also apply to quantities or qualities, as when a plant grows larger or an apple becomes more red.

2. *Everything put in motion is put in motion by a mover.* This should not be surprising, for every change needs a changer, and every effect needs a cause. When some potential to move is put into motion, then that potential has been actualized. Prior to this, it only had the potential (what can be) and needed another mover to bring about the change in motion.

Something cannot be potentially moving and actually moving in the same respect. It is either one or the other. The consequences are that a potential cannot actualize itself. There has to be something outside that potential, a mover that is already actualized—that is, already existing. Even with created composite self-movers such as animals and humans, one part moves another, for no part can move itself. For example, the will moves the nerves, the nerves fire the muscles, which moves the leg, which moves the body, etc. Even the cognitive and volitional faculties of thinking or willing have not always existed, for something prior to them needed to bring those faculties from mere potentiality to actuality.

In addition, the potential of something limits what kind of change is possible. For example, a block of stone has the potential to be a statue, but not the potential to be an actual person. A gallon-sized jug has the potential to hold one gallon of liquid, and once that jug is full, then that potential

has been actualized and no more potential remains for additional liquid. Things in the natural world vary in their mixture of potentiality and actuality. Some things have more potential for motion or change than other things.

3. *There cannot be an infinite regress of movers going backward. If there is no first mover, there can be no subsequent motion.* If every potential to move or change needed something actual, and if what was actual at one time was in potential, then it also needed something prior that was actual, and so on. Aquinas reasons that this cannot go on infinitely backward (infinite regress). Each potential that has been actualized required something prior to bring about the change. If something went infinitely backward, then it would not have a beginning, as you cannot reach the edge of an infinite. Aquinas emphasized that there has to be a first mover to get the motion started. If there is no first actualizer, there can be no subsequent motion.

Some have been confused on how this might relate to Newton's first law, which says, "Every body perseveres in its state of being at rest or of moving uniformly straight forward, except insofar as it is compelled to change its state by forces impressed."[2] That is, a body that is at rest or in motion tends to stay in that state unless acted on by another. However, this does not negatively affect the basic principle of Aquinas's first way. For whatever is moved is moved by another, and whatever is changed needs a changer, just as every effect needs a cause. Newton's law in fact supports that there needs to be something to cause the body to change from a state of rest to a state of motion or vice versa. Aquinas's argument does not conflict with this, as his argument was interested in what brought about the first motion. The alternative is that there is eternal motion, but that cannot be, as there cannot be an infinite regress of prior changes. Nor can there be some reciprocal or cyclical eternal causality, such as one thing, B1, causes another, B2, which in turn causes a change back on B1 infinitely backward. There still needs to be an accounting of the first movement, since motion, as a series of changes, cannot go back infinitely. If it did, then the infinite number of changes could not be crossed to arrive at the present and current change. Hence, an infinite regress is impossible.

4. *Therefore, there is a first unmoved mover; this is God.* Tracing the motion to its source, Aquinas arrived at a first unmoved mover that is needed to account for all subsequent motion. This is God. God has no beginning, and nothing else actualized Him. God has always existed (Psalm 90:2). Neither can God change, for He has no potential to change (Malachi 3:6). Therefore, God is pure actuality and the first unmoved mover. God is the great "I am" (Exodus 3:14), who gave motion to everything else.

Argument from Contingency

Another argument provided by Aquinas in *Summa Theologiae* Ia.2.3 is known as his third way. It was an argument from contingency to necessity.

1. Contingent (dependent) beings exist (e.g., I am a contingent being).

2. A contingent being needs a cause for its existence.

3. An infinite regress (going backward infinitely) of contingent causes is impossible.

4. Neither can one contingent being cause another contingent being.

5. Therefore, there must be a Necessary Being that is the cause of every contingent being. This is God.

This is a shortened and slightly reformulated form of the argument. To understand the connection further, let us go through each part of the argument.

1. *Contingent beings exist (e.g., I am a contingent being).* In nature we find beings that begin and cease to exist; these are known as possible or contingent beings. These are not self-existent beings. In other words, they do not have existence by nature, for if they did, then they would have always existed. Human beings are an example of a contingent being. We do not have existence by nature and have not always existed. Our existence is dependent upon another, and this cannot be our parents. Our parents are only the instrumental cause (i.e., the instrument through which) of our becoming, but not the cause sustaining us in existence. Why? Every effect needs a cause, and if you remove the cause, then the effect does not follow. If our parents were the primary single cause, then when they died, we (the effect) would cease also. But when parents die, their children remain. The same is true of the blacksmith with his hammer, for he is only the cause of the becoming of horseshoes. When the blacksmith passes away, the horseshoes remain. This is because there is another cause sustaining them in their being.

2. *A contingent being needs a cause for its existence.* A contingent (dependent) being is a being that came to be, and can cease to be. Whatever begins to exist does so only through what already exists. Consequently, a contingent being needs a cause for its existence. It cannot cause itself, for then it would be prior to itself, which is absurd. Something else had to bring it into existence.

3. *An infinite regress of contingent causes is*

impossible. There cannot be an infinite regress, because an infinite cannot be crossed—that is, you cannot get to the other side of it. Moreover, adding more contingent beings to the series does not get rid of the contingency, because the whole thing is still contingent, and needs a cause for its existence.

4. *Neither can one contingent being cause another contingent being.* Consequently, a contingent being cannot be the primary cause of another contingent being to exist, for a being cannot give what it does not have essentially. If a being is contingent, then it does not have its own existence to give. Imagine several people lined up to pay for admission tickets at the entrance of a movie theatre. When the cashier asks the first person for money, that person—and all the others—points to the person behind him and says, "My friend will pay." Then the last person in line becomes exasperated and says, "I don't have any money." None of the people earlier in line have money to give, just as none of the prior contingent beings have existence of their own to give. Here's another way to think about this: If only contingent beings existed, then there would be nothing to explain or be the ground of their existence. Simply adding more contingent beings never provides the basis for existence.

5. *Therefore, there must be a Necessary Being that is the cause of every contingent being. This is God.* The fact that some contingent beings exist means that something must have always existed, for if there ever was a time when there was *absolutely* nothing, then there would have always been nothing. Consequently, there must be a Necessary Being whose essence it is to exist and is the primary cause of existence for all contingent beings. This is God. The question for the atheist is this: Why is there something in existence

rather than nothing at all? The reason is that there is a God who brought all things into being. Stated in terms of dependency for the universe, the sequence would look something like this:[3]

1. Every part of the universe is dependent.

2. If every part is dependent, then the whole universe must also be dependent.

3. Therefore, the whole universe is dependent for existence right now on some independent being—namely, God.

Adding more dependent (or contingent) beings can never remove the dependency. You have to continue back to something that is necessary, something whose nature it is to exist. This is God. In theology proper (the study of God's attributes), the term *aseity* (Latin, "of oneself") is used to denote this most amazing truth that God is self-existent (Genesis 1:1; Exodus 3:14; Psalm 90:2; John 1:1; Romans 11:36; Colossians 1:17).

Argument from Perfection

In his fourth way, Aquinas provided an argument from the gradations of things to a most perfect being (*Summa Theologiae* Ia.2.3), as did an earlier theologian by the name of Anselm of Canterbury (1033–1109) in his *Monologium.*[4] Taking the best of these both produces the following argument for God's perfection:

1. We observe that some beings are more nearly perfect than others.

2. The cause of this perfection is either one or many.

3. If there were many, there would be

no way to compare their perfection, but some things are more perfect than others.

4. Moreover, things cannot be more or less perfect unless there is one wholly perfect source and standard for comparison.

5. Therefore, there must be a most perfect being who is the source of all perfections. This is God.

Several points can be made about each premise.

1. *We observe that some beings are more nearly perfect than others.* As we live, we make comparisons every day with regard to the objects around us to determine what to buy or sell, whom to marry, and so on. And when we do, we find that some things are more or less perfect, noble, true, or good than others.

2. *The cause of this perfection is either one or many.* When thinking about what causes these perfections, it seems natural to inquire whether one or more things cause them. The other option is to say there were no causes, which is impossible given that an effect cannot arise without a cause (the law of causality). All perfections in contingent beings need a cause, a source from which they came.

3. *If there were many, there would be no way to compare their perfection, but some things are more perfect than others.* When we are unable to easily compare things in a practical way, we say, "It is like comparing apples and oranges." Yet Aquinas was not referring to practical or utilitarian comparisons. As we compare things, especially across categories, we may begin to realize that we are comparing them at a more fundamental level. Aquinas was referring to a comparison

of their *quality of being* because trueness, nobility, goodness, beauty, and perfection transcend physical and material categories.

For example, a man approaches these qualities of being more than a stone, and a being that has intelligence is better than a being that does not. So regardless of type, the thing that approaches perfection will exhibit more of these transcendent qualities. Another way to think about this is to imagine the result if perfections were removed. If you remove all the perfections from something, what are you left with? You would be left with nothing (nonbeing). If you have a totally moth-eaten shirt, you have no shirt at all. However, if you remove all the imperfections of something, what are you left with? You are left with something perfect (being). Therefore, when a thing is more perfect, it approaches the perfection of the pureness of being itself (pure actuality).

4. *Moreover, things cannot be more or less perfect unless there is one wholly perfect source and standard for comparison.* Observing that some things are better than others requires an objective standard by which to make the comparison—just as that which is hotter than another more nearly approaches that which is hottest. In terms of causation, an effect derives its perfection from its cause, for an effect cannot be greater than its cause. A cause cannot give what it does not have, but what it does have can be given to the effect. Hence, if some effects are more perfect than others, then they must be caused by a source of perfection.

5. *Therefore, there must be a most perfect being who is the source of all perfections.* This is God. As Aquinas eloquently stated in his fourth way, there needs to be a perfect being who is the source of all perfections (Matthew 5:48):

So that there is something which is truest, something best, something noblest and, consequently, something which is uttermost being; for those things that are greatest in truth are greatest in being…Therefore there must also be something which is to all beings the cause of their being, goodness, and every other perfection; and this we call God.[5]

The Value of Knowing the Arguments for God's Existence

There are many arguments for God available in the sources written across the ages of church history. This brief treatment is only a tiny fraction of what has been written on the subject. I would encourage you to explore the other arguments more fully, as they can be edifying and can contribute to strengthening your faith. They can also be strategically used when you share your faith, as you are likely to encounter questions or alternative viewpoints regarding God's existence. By becoming familiar with the various rational arguments, you can use them to remove objections others may have toward the gospel. This does not necessarily mean quoting the arguments mechanically in their raw form. Instead, it means knowing the essence and truth of the arguments, then utilizing them strategically in conversational language.

If God Exists, Why Is There Evil?

Clay Jones

Evil surrounds us and sooner or later *always* kills us. Earthquakes, fires, cancers, strokes, dementias, rapes, tortures, murder, and countless other tragedies happen all over the earth every single day. The monotony and inescapable effects of evil weigh heavily on all of us, causing people to ask this crucial question: If God exists, why is there evil?

There are four big-picture points we need to keep in mind if we are going to understand why God allows evil. First, we need to understand the origin of natural evil. Second, we need to comprehend the origin and extent of human evil. Third, we need to grasp the nature and value of free will. Fourth, we need to be aware of how God will resolve evil in eternity. Of course, all of these issues merit greater explanation, and I have written on them at length elsewhere.[1]

The Origin of Natural Evil

To understand the origin of natural evil, we must take the book of Genesis seriously. In Genesis 1, we are told that God created the first man and the first woman and placed them in a garden. Genesis 2:16-17 says that "the LORD God commanded the man, 'You are free to eat from any tree in the garden; but you must not eat from the tree of the knowledge of good and evil, for when you eat from it you will certainly die'" (NIV). Here, Adam and Eve, our first and original parents, were given the option to obey or disobey God, and the penalty for disobedience was clear: death.

Adam and Eve rebelled against God and ate from that tree anyway, and we've been attending funerals ever since. In response to their rebellion, the Lord did the following:

First, to the woman God said, "I will surely multiply your pain in childbearing; in pain you shall bring forth children. Your desire shall be contrary to your husband, but he shall rule over you" (Genesis 3:16). So there were two consequences: The first was that childbearing would be very painful (that probably includes everything related to childbearing, such as female reproductive problems). The second was that the husband would now rule the woman. A husband *ruling* over his wife was not a part of God's original plan, and the world has since witnessed many men treating women harshly and unjustly.

Second, in verse 17, the Lord told the man, "Cursed is the ground because of you."

Romans 8:20-21 explains that creation was "subjected to futility" and is now in "bondage to corruption." Thus, natural evil entered the world because God cursed the earth in response to Adam's sin. In fact, what harmful mold, decay, disease, and so on and on, cannot have ensued from God looking at planet Earth and saying, "I curse you"? There is something desperately wrong with our world, and that is because God cursed it.

Third, in Genesis 3:22-24, the Lord banished the man and his wife from the Garden of Eden, thus removing them from the rejuvenating power of the tree of life, and so all humans began to die. Taken together, these things are the origin of natural evil, which was the result of Adam and Eve's free choice to sin. All natural evil, therefore, is in one way or another related to sin.[2]

Sometimes people object that God should have created someone else who would not have sinned. That is exactly what God did: Jesus was born in the likeness of human flesh yet kept all of God's commands perfectly, including death on the cross. And by trusting in Jesus's giving His life for us, we can be saved from our sinful condition. First Corinthians 15:22,45 says that "for as in Adam all die, so also in Christ shall all be made alive…'The first man Adam became a living being'; the last Adam became a life-giving spirit." And what kind of life does Jesus give? Eternal life!

The Origin and Extent of Human Evil

Adam and Eve used their free will to disobey God, thus plunging us into a world of sorrow, sickness, and death. But that is not all that resulted: They also lost their proper relationship with God and their natures were corrupted. We read in Genesis 3:8 that after they sinned, they "hid themselves from the presence of the LORD God." And then in that fallen state, they had children. Thus Adam and Eve, our first and original parents, passed on to us their corrupted natures. In other words, we are the *sexual reproductions* of Adam and Eve. Adam and Eve could not reproduce beings greater than themselves. They could only give birth to fallen humans estranged from God.

Hence Jesus said in John 3:6, "That which is born of the flesh is flesh, and that which is born of the Spirit is spirit." Therefore, all of us are born, in a very real sense, Adams and Eves. We inherited their natures. In fact, we received our souls from Adam and Eve. Further, we received our consciousness from Adam and Eve. Consequently, until a human is born again, he or she is Adamic flesh that needs to be born from above (John 3:3,7; 1 Peter 1:23). This is called the doctrine of original sin, and it explains why people do so many evil things.

There is something terribly wrong with humankind that is best explained by the fact that our natures were corrupted by the sin of Adam and Eve—the original sin. The human propensity for evil could be illustrated in many ways, but I will use only one example—genocide. Every genocide researcher I have ever read (and I have read a lot of them)—and even every genocide survivor I have ever read—agrees that it is the average member of a population that commits genocide. In *Ordinary Men: Reserve Police Battalion 101 and the Final Solution in Poland,* genocide researcher Christopher Browning concluded, "I could have been the killer or the evader—both were humans."[3] Similarly, sociologist Harald Welzer wrote,

> We are left then with the most discomforting of all realities—ordinary,

"normal" people committing acts of extraordinary evil. This reality is difficult to admit, to understand, to absorb…As we look at the perpetrators of genocide and mass killing, we need no longer ask who these people are. We know who they are. They are you and I.[4]

Hannah Arendt concluded of Auschwitz administrator Adolf Eichmann that the trouble with him was that "so many were like him, neither perverted nor sadistic, that they were, and still are, terribly and terrifyingly normal."[5] Even Auschwitz survivor Elie Wiesel concluded, "Deep down…man is not only executioner, not only victim, not only spectator; he is all three at once."[6]

Like it or not, we were all born Auschwitz-enabled. As Christian philosopher Alvin Plantinga put it, "The doctrine of original sin has been verified in the wars, cruelty, and general hatefulness that have characterized human history from its very inception to the present."[7] Even atheist Michael Ruse agrees: "I think Christianity is spot on about original sin—how could one think otherwise, when the world's most civilized and advanced people (the people of Beethoven, Goethe, Kant) embraced that slime-ball Hitler and participated in the Holocaust?"[8]

With these truths in view, perhaps Scripture makes more sense when it says in Romans 3, "There is no one who does good, not even one. Their throats are open graves…Their mouths are full of cursing… Their feet are swift to shed blood."[9] Indeed, *nothing* illustrates humanity's "feet" being "swift to shed blood" like genocide. This is all a horrifying revelation, and indeed, without Christ, I do not know how one could find an affirmative meaning in life. Once we truly understand the depths of human

evil, then the question changes from "Why does God allow evil?" to "Why does God allow humans?" Or, "Why does God allow humans with free will?"

Free Will and Its Value

Free will is the ability to do other than what you do. For example, people can choose between the mundane (such as whether they are going to have Neapolitan ice cream or chocolate) or the morally significant (such as whether or not they are going to remain an alcoholic). If you are going to let your daughter exercise her free will, you cannot give her permission to go out with the boy down the street and then chain her to a heavy kitchen appliance. Similarly, for God to give Adam and Eve free will *required* that God give them the ability to rebel against Him. This is as logical as it gets.

Some have argued, however, that if this evil is the price of free will, then God should not have given us free will in the first place. But would you want to be around only *things* without free will—call them robots or androids or whatever—things that are no more than lifelike, life-size Chatty Cathy dolls that are programmed to say "I love you"? The Lord desires relationship with real beings who can make real decisions and have real desires—and so do we! But that means, for all their flaws, that we must endure the good and the bad from real humans.

In this tragedy of human death and sin, God is doing something wonderful. Both our present knowledge of the horrors of human sinfulness and our further education at the judgment will prepare us to inherit God's kingdom, where we will regard sin as beneath us. This knowledge prepares us for when God sets us free in His kingdom to do what *we want to do*. We will *not* want to sin because we have already learned the knowledge of good and evil here and we will be further informed on the horror of sin at the judgment. Also, in heaven, there will be no world or devil to tempt us. Our lustful, Adamic flesh will be transformed, hell will be an eternal reminder to free beings of the horror of rebellion, and we will live by sight. Again, however, the key point is that we are learning here on earth the horror of rebellion against God.

How God Will Resolve Evil in Eternity

Eternity relates to our suffering here because eternity will dwarf our suffering to insignificance. Our sufferings here will be diminished by the eternal glory that awaits us for three reasons.

First, we Christians will get it *all*, as in we will get *everything*. Consider 1 Corinthians 3:21-23: "So then, no more boasting about human leaders! All things are yours, whether Paul or Apollos or Cephas or the world or life or death or the present or the future—all are yours, and you are of Christ, and Christ is of God" (NIV). "All things" are ours! Similarly, Jesus said in Luke 12:32: "Fear not, little flock, for it is your Father's good pleasure to give you the kingdom." He's going to "give" us the kingdom—not just let us visit it.

Second, not only do we get it all, we get it all forever. Remember, God's promise to the Christian is "eternal life." In fact, the most famous verse in the Bible, John 3:16, ends with "should not perish but have eternal life." (See also Matthew 25:46; John 3:36; 5:24;

6:40; Acts 13:48; Romans 2:7; 6:23; 1 John 5:13.)

Third, forever we will enjoy the Creator of the universe—the King of kings and Lord of lords—and forever we will enjoy other Christians. The Lord is supremely accomplished, supremely beautiful, supremely knowledgeable (in fact, by definition He is omniscient), and supremely powerful (by definition He is omnipotent). And we are told, "God is love" (1 John 4:8). It is not that love is a character quality that God possesses, but that love is God's very nature. Contrary to the popular image of heaven being about sitting on a cloud, sporting flightless wings, and forever strumming a harp, the afterlife is most often compared to a banquet (Isaiah 25:6; Mark 14:25; Revelation 19:9), and we are going to feast like that with each other forever!

Consider 2 Corinthians 4:16-18: "We do not lose heart. Though our outer self is wasting away, our inner self is being renewed day by day. For this light momentary affliction is preparing for us an eternal weight of glory beyond all comparison, as we look not to the things that are seen but to the things that are unseen. For the things that are seen are transient, but the things that are unseen are eternal." When Paul wrote "beyond all comparison," he was not speaking metaphorically. Even a full human lifetime of suffering here is dwarfed to insignificance by eternity. The Lord is giving all things to those who trust Him, and He is giving them all things forever and ever!

Canaanites, Crusades, and Catastrophes—Is God a Moral Monster?

Douglas E. Potter

A common charge leveled against Christianity is this: How can the God of the Bible be a God of love while ordering the destruction of an entire race of people? Apparently God did not hesitate when He laid down these rules of military engagement:

> In the cities of these peoples that the Lord your God is giving you for an inheritance, you shall *save alive nothing that breathes, but you shall devote them to complete destruction,* the Hittites and the Amorites, the Canaanites and the Perizzites, the Hivites and the Jebusites, as the Lord your God has commanded (Deuteronomy 20:16-17, emphasis added).

This command was not a one-time occurrence:

> Thus says the Lord of hosts…Now go and strike Amalek and devote to destruction all that they have. Do not spare them, but *kill both man and woman, child and infant,* ox and sheep, camel and donkey (1 Samuel 15:2-3, emphasis added).

From here, critics quickly move to the Crusades (1095–1291). How can anyone embrace a religion in which its adherents, for hundreds of years, periodically waged wars in which innocent people were killed in the name of God?

We are also reminded that not all evil can be blamed on sin and free will. Does God not control the entire universe—even its natural laws and all that happens on the earth? Yet God allows natural disasters such as earthquakes, hurricanes, and tsunamis. Over the centuries, these have killed millions of innocent men, women, and children. How can God be loving and stand by idly during these natural catastrophes?

Collectively, these concerns cause many to wonder whether God could be a moral monster. Though a serious charge, it is not without an answer.

Why the Command Against the Canaanites?

The Canaanites were people groups who occupied the Promised Land (Canaan) before the Israelites entered under the command of Joshua.[1] These people are known from archaeology and ancient texts to have participated in the most horrific sins, including idolatry, brutal killings (Deuteronomy 25:17-18), self-mutilation, homosexuality, cultic prostitution, incest, bestiality (sex with animals), and child sacrifice by fire (Leviticus 18:21).[2] Leviticus explains,

> You shall keep my statutes and my rules and do none of these abominations, either the native or the stranger who sojourns among you (for the people of the land, who were before you, did all of these abominations, so that the land became unclean), lest the land vomit you out when you make it unclean, as it vomited out the nation that was before you. For everyone who does any of these abominations, the persons who do them shall be cut off from among their people. So keep my charge never to practice any of these abominable customs that were practiced before you, and never to make yourselves unclean by them: I am the LORD your God (Leviticus 18:26-30).

Given the judgment and mercy of God revealed in the Old Testament, we should not be surprised that God would use the Israelites to execute His judgment on such evil. In Noah's day, God used a flood to destroy everyone on the earth, including women and children, except those in the Ark (Genesis 6). He judged Sodom and Gomorrah by raining down fire from heaven (Genesis 19:24-25). In these instances, God gave a period of

warning, calling people to repentance. Noah, for example, preached for 120 years.

This was true about the Canaanites as well. Through Rahab's confession (Joshua 2:10-14) we know the Canaanites had heard about the one true God, His deliverance of the Israelites from Egypt, and what happened to rulers who opposed God's people. We also know that God waited 430 years before bringing judgment upon the Canaanites. In Genesis 15:16 God spoke of the iniquity of these people as not yet being complete, which implies He was waiting for them to repent.

God gave two reasons for the invasion commanded against the Canaanites. First, it would serve as judgment on the wickedness of the people; and second, it would allow the Israelites to enter the land God had promised to them. Deuteronomy 9:5 says,

> Not because of your righteousness or the uprightness of your heart are you going in to possess their land, but because of the wickedness of these nations the LORD your God is driving them out from before you, and that he may confirm the word that the LORD swore to your fathers, to Abraham, to Isaac, and to Jacob.

God is merciful toward the nations who repent and turn from their wicked ways (Jeremiah 18:7-8). Jonah, who preached to the inhabitants of Nineveh, saw this when they repented. But because God is holy and just, He must judge the wicked. The Canaanites stood in the way of God's plan to bring the Savior into the world through His people (Genesis 12:3; 22:17-18). Hence, the motivation was not ethnic hatred or genocide, but hating and removing sin. The Israelites were not immune from judgment against their own sin. God's judgment for sin fell on His own people as well as on other nations (Romans 2).

In addition, God's commands against specific wicked nations are not universal commands for all times, peoples, and places. Some battle rules that were given by God involved exceptions for the innocent. These commands, known as "ban" (Hebrew, *hērem*), mean "forced dedication" and are quite limited when applied to military campaigns (Joshua 6:17; 1 Samuel 15:3,20). Not every battle Israel fought fit this category; some were defensive (Exodus 17:8; Numbers 21:1,21-32; Deuteronomy 3:1). Other times, the Israelites were prohibited from conquering bordering nations (Deuteronomy 2:9,19), and restrictions were placed on whom they could kill and how captives could be treated (Deuteronomy 21:10-14).

What About Women and Children?

To answer this, some suggest that others gave the commands and then later attributed them to God. But this would entail that whatever a prophet and the Bible affirms is met with suspicion. However, this is impossible given the inspiration and inerrancy of Scripture, not to mention Jesus's own view of inspiration.[3] Others have tried to see God's command to kill every living thing as an exaggeration intended to build military confidence rather than a command to be followed with exactness.[4] But if God *did* intend these commands to be followed, it is hard to see how they would be stated any differently.[5]

A better approach appeals to the absolutely unique divine nature of God and His judgments. God is good, or more precisely, He is unchanging moral perfection and not a changing moral creature. Our moral nature

is analogous only to God's. Therefore, it is a mistake to think that God needs moral improvement or even justification.[6] If we do that, then we are not thinking about God biblically or with correct theology.

We must remember that God is sovereign, all-knowing, and all-powerful. He is the Creator and sustainer of all life. God decides when, where, and how everyone is born and dies. We are all sinners by birth (Psalm 51); all humanity, every person, is guilty before God. Theologically, it is safe to say any children who die before they have reached the age of accountability will go to heaven.[7]

God is merciful in the act of bringing people into the world and merciful when removing them from the world. What *wouldn't* be merciful is if God were to completely annihilate people from existing. God is known to take the lives of His own people to judge disobedience (Numbers 16:31-33). Even for Christians today, sin can lead to judgment and death (1 John 5:16). In the future, God will again—in righteousness—judge and make war (Revelation 19:11-15).

God must have a good reason behind the commands that were issued without exception. Sometimes a surgeon must remove good tissue to prevent the reoccurrence of a deadly infection. Gleason Archer explains the consequences of not following God's command:

> In every case the baneful infection of degenerate idolatry and moral depravity had to be removed before Israel could safely settle down in those regions and set up a monotheistic law-governed commonwealth as a testimony for the one true God…The failure to carry through completely the policy of the extermination of the heathen in the Land of Promise later

led to the moral and religious downfall of the Twelve Tribes in the days of the Judges.[8]

Ultimately—and this was no surprise to God—the Israelites failed to carry out the command (Numbers 31:1-18). It is conceivable that some noncombatants decided, in the years prior to the invasions, to leave or perhaps escape during actual battles. Some cities, such as Jericho and Ai, were thought to be military forts with few noncombatants. God always provided deliverance for the repentant. We must also assume that for those who stayed, their future was hopeless in this life, and the Israelites followed God's battle command to the best of their ability.

How Can God Violate His Own Command Not to Murder?

It is commonly assumed that whatever is morally wrong for humans is also wrong for God. But this is not always the case. God does not operate as a moral creature in the world. As Creator, He is the author of the story, not simply another character in His creation. He is absolute goodness, and there is no external moral law imposing upon Him. All of His will and actions are in accord with and flow from His absolutely good, infinite, and morally perfect divine nature. Whereas Muslims believe that because Allah wills something it necessarily makes it good (known as *voluntarism*), Christians believe God's all-good nature ensures that God can only will good (known as *essentialism*).

God, by issuing the order to wipe out the Canaanites, was superseding other moral commands He had given to the Israelites, such as "You should not murder" (Exodus 20:13), a command that was always in place. But only God can command to kill, and the Israelites,

in this context, were to obey the higher command.[9] As William Greene observed, this is not "doing evil that good might come…It is rather doing good in spite of certain necessary evil consequences." Greene further insightfully remarked, "Objection to the fate of these nations, therefore, is really an objection to the highest manifestation of the grace of God. He commanded the Canaanites to be destroyed that the Savior of the world might be revealed."[10]

Because we do not create being (that is, people), nor do we hold them in existence, it is wrong for us to kill an innocent person. Only God can make a rational moral creature in His image and likeness (Genesis 1:27). When God kills, it is not murder, because He alone is able to bring people into and take people out of the world. That is to say, God is the only one who holds the "pink slip" to life. People are not extinguished out of existence when they die; they remain in existence by God's conserving causality, even if they are no longer in this world. Only God can give life and take life (Job 1:18-22; John 5:28-29).

Were the Crusades a Just War?

Regarding the divine sanction of some wars mentioned in the Bible, it is impossible to extend these commands from God beyond the period of Israel's theocracy. Yet war is a reality of our fallen human condition. Though Jesus said there would be wars and rumors of wars (Matthew 24:6), the Bible does support the idea of a just war.[11] But this does not mean that everything that happens in a war is just. It does mean the use of force by one nation against another is sometimes necessary, especially to protect the innocent or punish the guilty.

In the past, some historians ignored or distorted the context and motives for the Crusades. Rodney Stark's reassessment provides a needed correction:

> The Crusades were precipitated by Islamic provocations: by centuries of bloody attempts to colonize the West and by sudden new attacks on Christian pilgrims and holy places. Although the Crusades were initiated by a plea from the pope, this had nothing to do with hopes of converting Islam…The crusader kingdoms that they established in the Holy Land, and that stood for nearly two centuries, were not colonies sustained by local exactions; rather, they required immense subsidies from Europe.[12]

Most crusaders were spiritually motivated and wanted to liberate the Holy Land. However, sometimes armies were hard to control during this brutal and bloody period. Massacres occurred on both sides. Noncombatant Jews, Muslims, and Christians were slaughtered. Christian leaders condemned this and attempted to save lives even at risk of their own.[13] But it should be noted that the crusaders also followed the accepted rules of warfare for that time. They offered cities under siege a chance to surrender. Even under Christian occupation, Muslims were tolerated, and no effort was made to convert them.[14] This is in strong contrast to the "choices" that were offered to people under Muslim occupation during this time, which were conversion, oppression, and in some cases death.

When Christian atrocities occurred during the Crusades, those involved were not following Christ's example. By contrast, the bloody advances of Islam followed the example of Muhammad.

Is Religion the Cause of War?

There is no doubt religion has had a role in causing some wars. Religion, however, is also used as a cover for power and ethnic hatred. It is incorrect to blame religion as the cause of all or even most wars, or at least more than other reasons such as the millions of deaths associated with secular ideologies.[15] A more important question to ask is this: Is violence or war consistent with the teaching of a faith? Christ's ethical teaching is unparalleled among other religions. Jesus taught, "I say to you, love your enemies and pray for those who persecute you" (Matthew 5:44). Jesus refused to spread the gospel by force (Matthew 26:52). He told disciples to buy a sword for defensive purposes (Luke 22:36-38). Christianity, even as acknowledged by its critics, has always been a significant source of social good.[16] Certainly Christians, other religions, and nations should promote peace, but they also have a moral right to defend themselves and the innocent. It is wrong not to resist evil. Sometimes military action is the only way to stop the advance of evil.

Is God Responsible for Natural Catastrophes?

Evil perpetrated by humans can be explained by free choice. However, suffering caused by catastrophes or natural evil cannot be explained by this means. According to some critics, if God created and controls nature, then He must be responsible for natural evil.

God created a material world that is materially interdependent and seems random at times. The plant wilts for lack of water. The lion eats the lamb to survive. Higher forms of life are dependent on lower forms. Even natural disasters have important good byproducts. Wind and rain are required for plant life, but can also produce tornados and floods. Hurricanes, tsunamis, and earthquakes also have good environmental byproducts. Even human health is dependent upon the regularity of natural processes. If we do not care for our bodies, our health declines. If we cannot get food to the masses, starvation ensues. Only humans reflect on the natural world, often finding our environment a hostile place.

Norman Geisler says, "God is the author of everything, including evil, in the sense that He *permits* it, but not in the sense that He *produces* it. Evil happens in His *permissive* will, but He does not promote evil in His *perfect* will. God allows evil yet does not encourage it."[17] These are subtle but important distinctions.

Therefore, God is not the *direct* cause of natural evil suffered by humans. All such evil is a byproduct of the good material world God created (Genesis 1:31). Only when humans are harmed is there serious concern about a natural catastrophe. According to the creation account, God provided a world that needs to be subdued and ruled by humans (Genesis 1:28). The hostility of the natural world is linked to human rebellion, as well as spiritual creatures (Genesis 3) who are also active in the world.

Why Doesn't God Intervene?

According to the Bible and human history, God has intervened, miraculously and naturally, to alter evil consequences. Those who feel God should do this more often must realize that God alone is in the position to know how much is permissible. Indeed, even we can understand that the regularity of nature is necessary to preserve human free choice. If nature were unpredictable or God frequently altered nature's regularity, free will would be curtailed. If such were the case, not only would moral decisions and responsibility be impossible, but also all learning would become meaningless. Hence, it would not be a world worthy of rational creatures.

We know some natural evil produces pain, but we morally improve through pain, trials, and tribulation (2 Corinthians 1:3-9; James 1:2-4). Love and compassion are displayed in us as we help those in need. C.S. Lewis wrote, "God whispers to us in our pleasures, speaks in our conscience, but shouts in our pain; it is his megaphone to rouse a deaf world."[18] Because God is all-good and all-knowing, only He must have a reason for allowing any natural evil, because ultimately, He can use it to produce a better world.

This may not yet be the best world achievable. But given the infinite goodness of God and a finite interdependent world, it is necessary for sustaining human free will. As Geisler puts it, "This world is only the best way possible to the best world achievable."[19]

Toward a Fuller Understanding

One of the most important things both the critic and the Christian can do is explore what the Bible teaches about God's nature, as well as compatible reasons for God's existence and nature.[20] Nothing can be compared to God, who said through Isaiah, "To whom will you liken me and make me equal, and compare me, that we may be alike?" (Isaiah 46:5). He said,

I am the LORD, and there is no other, besides me there is no God...I am the LORD, and there is no other. I form light and create darkness; I make well-being and create calamity; I am the LORD, who does all these things (Isaiah 45:5-7).

God must be trusted even when things happen that do not make sense to us. We may not always know the purposes of God, but we can rest assured His purposes are good. The Bible directs us away from thinking about God as a moral creature (Numbers 23:19). God is absolute goodness and sovereign over everything, as well as the actions of humans in the world and nature itself. His mercy is unending and judgments are flawless. This may help us to see that God's infinite transcendence means He does not operate like the creature. He is a category by Himself, which makes Him nothing like a moral monster.

16

How Can a Loving God
Send People to Hell?

Douglas E. Potter

Among seekers and skeptics, and even some Christians, the attempt to reconcile a loving God with eternal punishment in hell can generate passionate feelings that challenge any rational discussion about the issue.

Many consider eternal punishment as incompatible with the idea of a loving God, and as Bertrand Russell once said, the mere threat of hell seems cruel and inhumane.[1] Even within the church, the very existence or duration of hell are being challenged. But if there is no hell, then we have no reason to spread the gospel, and we can give up on the assurance that justice will be served against those who have committed evil in this life. As Jesus taught (Matthew 10:28), why fear God and be saved if there is no everlasting hell?

While defending the faith, Christians should expect challenges to the reality and justice of hell. Unfortunately, to accommodate their own thinking on the subject, some have mistakenly either changed the nature of hell or changed the nature of God as taught in the Bible. Norman Geisler acknowledges the tendency for Christians to sweep under

the carpet the inconvenient truths about hell: "We can tell ourselves that it would be wonderful if there were no hell or no final day of judgment at which we will be held accountable for all our deeds, but we shouldn't fail to note that all of this is exactly what we naturally want to be true."[2] To avoid this crucial subject—or alter the biblical descriptions of it—is to ignore the clear teachings of Scripture about God's justice and the need for the gospel.

What Does the Bible
Teach About Hell?

The reality of hell can be defended from the Bible and good reason, drawing upon passages in both Old and New Testaments, as well as reviewing the teachings of Jesus. What is more, the reason for eternal punishment is also grounded in God's nature, which includes love and justice for all people.

Psalm 9:17 says, "The wicked shall return to Sheol, all the nations that forget God." The term *Sheol* is used for both the grave and the place where the wicked go after they die.

The Old Testament describes human

beings as a material body united with an immaterial soul (Genesis 2:7). At death, the immortal soul is separated from the body (Genesis 3:19). Therefore, a resurrection is required to reunite soul and body. Such is anticipated for both the saved and the lost (cf. John 5:28-29). Daniel 12:2 reads, "Many of those who sleep in the dust of the earth shall awake, some to everlasting life, and some to shame and everlasting contempt." Note that both receive an *everlasting* resurrection with differing results—"life" versus "contempt."

In the New Testament, the apostle Paul said, "They will suffer the punishment of eternal destruction, away from the presence of the Lord and from the glory of his might" (2 Thessalonians 1:9). Some have suggested that "destruction" entails annihilation or the cessation of existence. However, this is unwarranted given the Bible's entire teaching on hell, especially Jesus's teaching (see below). In Scripture, "destruction" is often used to refer to the ruin of some nature or function rather than the concept of annihilation. The apostle Paul used this same term ("destruction") for physical death (1 Corinthians 10:9-10), but held to the soul's continued existence in the afterlife. In addition, the term "destruction" is used with the modifying word "eternal" to reveal the *duration* of the destruction. This language eliminates the possibility of destruction being a single action with no duration.[3]

The book of Hebrews asserts, "It is appointed for man to die once, and after that comes judgment" (9:27). Revelation describes this judgment for unbelievers:

I saw a great white throne and him who was seated on it. From his presence earth and sky fled away, and no place was found for them. And I saw the dead, great and small, standing before the throne, and books were opened. Then another book was opened, which is the book of life. And the dead were judged by what was written in the books, according to what they had done. And the sea gave up the dead who were in it, Death and Hades gave up the dead who were in them, and they were judged, each one of them, according to what they had done. Then Death and Hades were thrown into the lake of fire. This is the second death, the lake of fire. And if anyone's name was not found written in the book of life, he was thrown into the lake of fire (Revelation 20:11-15).

Whatever one may personally think about hell, these descriptions should leave no doubt that the Bible affirms the existence of such a place and condition. It serves at least two purposes: First, hell separates the unredeemed, in accordance with their decision, from God (and the redeemed) forever. Certainly, God would not be considered just or loving if He forced unbelievers, against their will, into heaven. Second, hell is a place of *eternal* punishment for those who have sinned against an *eternal* God—that is, the punishment fits the crime.

What Did Jesus Teach About Hell?

Some do not realize Jesus spoke more about hell than anyone else in the Bible.[4] He warned in Matthew 10:28, "Do not fear those who kill the body but cannot kill the soul. Rather fear him who can destroy both soul and body in hell" (cf. Luke 12:5). Jesus also spoke of the time when He will "say to those on his left, 'Depart from me, you cursed, into the eternal fire prepared for the devil and his angels'" (Matthew 25:41). He even told an interesting story about a sickly beggar, Lazarus, and a wealthy man.

> There was a rich man who was clothed in purple and fine linen and who feasted sumptuously every day. And at his gate was laid a poor man named Lazarus, covered with sores, who desired to be fed with what fell from the rich man's table. Moreover, even the dogs came and licked his sores. The poor man died and was carried by the angels to Abraham's side. The rich man also died and was buried, and in Hades, being in torment, he lifted up his eyes and saw Abraham far off and Lazarus at his side. And he called out, "Father Abraham, have mercy on me, and send Lazarus to dip the end of his finger in water and cool my tongue, for I am in anguish in this flame" (Luke 16:19-24).

Charles Ryrie offered insights into this story: "Clearly the account teaches some important facts about death and hell: (a) there is conscious existence after death; (b) hell is a real place of torment; (c) there is no second chance after death; and (d) the dead cannot communicate with the living."[5] The teaching of the Bible—and of Jesus— clearly presents the reality and eternal nature of hell.

Is God's Justice and Love Compatible with Hell?

The Bible says God is love (1 John 4:16). He is also completely just and righteous (Isaiah 30:18). Good reason, as well as the Bible, recognizes that perfect justice is not always achieved in this world (Psalm 73:3). Dictators who murder millions and even common

criminals sometimes go unpunished here on earth. Yet God promises that everyone will receive justice in the afterlife. If this were not the case, then God has no final victory over evil and cannot bring justice to the world, and He certainly would not be in sovereign control of everything (1 Corinthians 15:24-28).

James 2:10 says, "Whoever keeps the whole law but fails in one point has become guilty of all of it." There is a standard of moral perfection that no one can measure up to on their own (Romans 3:23). God, because He is a perfect being, cannot approvingly tolerate or overlook moral imperfection or sin. Therefore, God's holy justice *requires* a separation from unrepentant sinful creatures. Some might see this as cruel and inconsistent with God's nature. However, God will not violate individual human freedom; it is preserved by His providence and guaranteed by His infinite love. That is to say, God's love forbids Him to force anyone to love Him. As Norman Geisler states, "Forced love is a contradiction in terms."[6] C.S. Lewis recognized this as well—he said, "The Irresistible and the Indisputable are the two weapons which the very nature of his scheme forbids him to use. Merely to override a human will… would be for Him useless. He cannot ravish. He can only woo."[7]

Those who decide not to love God must be given what they want. Though God desires all be saved and that none perish (2 Peter 3:9), if people rebel against God's light, they have chosen darkness; if they reject God's offer to be with them for eternity, they will be separated from Him for eternity; if they refuse God's offer of eternal bliss, they will experience eternal torment. To not honor human freedom violates human dignity and would not be loving. Lewis insightfully remarked,

"There are only two kinds of people in the end: those who say to God, 'Thy will be done,' and those to whom God says, in the end, 'Thy will be done.' All that are in Hell, choose it."[8]

The Nature of Hell

While the Bible uses metaphors to describe hell, this does not mean hell itself is metaphorical (i.e., not real). According to the collective descriptions found in Scripture, hell is a horrifying reality with sobering implications. These metaphors teach us that hell "is like being left outside in darkness; a wandering star, waterless cloud, a perpetually burning dump, a bottomless pit, an everlasting prison, place of anguish and regret."[9] Hell is most often characterized by real fire because we understand the misery and pain of burning.

Despite the metaphorical descriptions, hell is not a fictional place. The kingdom of heaven is also spoken of in stories using metaphors (Matthew 13). Hell is described with the same words of duration (eternal or everlasting) that are used to describe eternal life. Hell is described as *eternal* punishment and *eternal* fire.[10] Revelation 20:10 mention the fate of the devil and false prophet: "They will be *tormented* day and night forever and ever" (emphasis added). Furthermore, Jesus said the lost would face the same eternal destination as the devil (Matthew 25:41).

What is more, many have misunderstood the nature of hell's punishment as *torture*. It is important to recognize there is a real difference between *torture* and the Bible's usage of the word *torment* to describe the punishment of hell. Essentially, torture is pain inflicted against one's will by external causes, but torment is pain inflicted in accord with one's will by internal causes (e.g., never-ending regret, spiritual thirst without remedy, sadness, depression due to awareness of your condition, darkness, emotional and spiritual pain, etc.).

Unbelievers often respond, "But I don't want to experience those horrible conditions, nor did I ask for them. Thus, God should honor my freedom, which rejects hell." Certainly no rational person would "want" to experience these conditions. However, just as an alcoholic does not "want" cirrhosis of the liver but has willed the condition by his *decision* to drink, those in hell willed their condition (state of being) by their *decision* to reject Christ and the salvation He offers.

C.S. Lewis, in his book *The Problem of Pain*, characterized the unbeliever's decision to be in hell by saying that "the doors to hell are locked on the inside."[11] He further said, "To be 'cured' against one's will...is to be put on a level with those who have not yet reached the age of reason or those who never will; to be classed with infants, imbeciles, and domestic animals."[12]

What About Annihilationism?

Some teach that those in hell will be annihilated—that is, they will cease to exist. However, this is contrary to the language and teaching of the Bible, which depicts hell as conscious torment "day and night forever and ever" (Revelation 20:10). Annihilationism is contrary to an all-loving God. For God to annihilate people created in His image is unloving. What father would kill his children just because they choose to go against their father's will? God allows us to choose our own way, even if it is against His will. It is always better to exist than to not exist. It is an act of God's mercy and love to keep His rational creatures from nonexistence. The conscious torment of the lost in hell preserves human dignity; honors personal decisions; and manifests the goodness, love, and justice of God.

One searches in vain for any mention in the Bible that hell is temporary. As others have noted, the language knife cuts both ways. If we give up the *everlasting* torment of hell, then we must also dismiss the *everlasting* happiness of heaven, for the same word is used of both domains.[13] And there is no good reason to think the Bible teaches that humans, saved or lost, cease to exist at any point after death.[14]

Conclusion

The death of Christ on the cross certainly affirms the reality of hell, for if there is no hell, Jesus's coming to earth was unnecessary. Why suffer death on a cross to pay the penalty for sin? If there is no hell, the good news of salvation from hell is empty. If this is the case, Christ's life, substitutionary death, and resurrection on our behalf are robbed of any eternal significance.

After death, everyone meets his or her intended end, which is God (Philippians 2:10). Those who believe the gospel are forgiven of their sins and are given a new birth. Upon death, their human nature (including the body) will be glorified and freely fixed toward the enjoyment of God. Those who reject the gospel, in accord with their own choice, will be turned away from the enjoyment of God and justly punished for their sins.

According to the Bible, these are the only two destinies of all human creatures.

Part Three

QUESTIONS ABOUT JESUS

Who Is Jesus?

Josh McDowell

A prophet. An insightful teacher. A noble martyr. A delusional fool. A cult leader. Who really was the first-century rabbi who went by the name of Jesus of Nazareth?

As a skeptical university student, I scoffed at the notion that Jesus was anything other than an ancient religious leader. He was simply a man who may have had some good teachings, but He certainly was not God. In my opinion, weak-minded people had built an entire religion around him. And I was not buying into it.

A few Christians on my university campus challenged me to make a vigorous, intellectual examination of the core claims about Jesus Christ—that He is the Son of God, that He inhabited a human body and lived among real men and women, that He died a sacrificial death for the sins of humanity, that He was buried and was bodily resurrected, and that He is alive today and offers eternal life to all who trust in Him as their Savior and Lord.

I accepted their challenge, in part out of pride to prove them wrong. I suspected that if Jesus could be proven to be a fraud, the whole of Christianity would crumble. Why? Because Jesus's claim to be the Savior of the world was exclusive. In fact, He made that truth central to all He said and did. Prove He was not the Son of God, and you simply do not have Christianity.

Much of the Christian faith is based on Jesus, as God's Son, being the perfect and sinless sacrifice for sin. It is crucial that this claim be true, because only as the Son of God could He solve the problem of sin and death. He made believing in Him as deity the pivotal point. Jesus told skeptics, "You are from below; I am from above. You are of this world; I am not of this world. I told you that you would die in your sins, for unless you believe that I am he you will die in your sins" (John 8:23-24). Later He added, "I am the way, and the truth, and the life. No one comes to the Father except through me" (John 14:6). So if Jesus was not the true Son of God, then His offer of salvation was a sham and a lie. It is absolutely vital that His claim to deity be valid if people are to trust Him to be their salvation.

What I discovered in my attempt to prove Christians wrong ended up leading me to Jesus as Savior. I came to realize there was a wealth of evidence to support placing my faith in Jesus as God's Son and the giver of eternal life. This evidence not only provides each of us with an intelligent faith, but also gives us greater confidence to share our faith with others.

Jesus Fulfilled Messianic Prophecies

In the first century, God gave John the Baptist a clear sign or evidence to identify Jesus as God's Son. John saw Jesus coming toward him the day after he baptized Him and said,

> "Look! The Lamb of God who takes away the sin of the world! He is the one I was talking about when I said, 'A man is coming after me who is far greater than I am, for he existed long before me.' I did not recognize him as the Messiah, but I have been baptizing with water so that he might be revealed to Israel." Then John testified, "I saw the Holy Spirit descending like a dove from heaven and resting upon him. I didn't know he was the one, but when God sent me to baptize with water, he told me, 'The one on whom you see the Spirit descend and rest is the one who will baptize with the Holy Spirit.' I saw this happen to Jesus, so I testify that he is the Chosen One of God" (John 1:29-34 NLT).

Just as God gave John a way to identify Jesus as "the Chosen One of God," He has also given us clear and indisputable means to identify His Son through what are called *messianic prophecies*. These are a clear means of knowing with certainty that we can be forgiven by God and have eternal life—because Jesus Christ is God's Chosen One to be our perfect sacrifice for sin.

Messianic Prophecies Fulfilled in One Person

Imagine agreeing over the phone to meet a distant business acquaintance—someone

you've never met in person—at a large business convention.

"How will I know you?" you ask.

"Well," your associate says, "I'll be carrying a briefcase."

"That helps," you reply, "but there will probably be a lot of people carrying briefcases. What color is yours?"

"Black."

"That might narrow it down some," you say, "but not enough."

"I'm a redhead," your associate offers.

"That helps," you answer. *Redhead carrying a black briefcase. Still might not be specific enough.* "What will you be wearing?"

"A blue blazer. How's that?"

"That's better. But just to be sure, can you wear red tennis shoes?"

"Very funny," your associate replies. "I'll just make sure I'm wearing a name tag with my name in big, bold letters."

"That should do it," you answer. *I'll just look for a redhead carrying a black briefcase and wearing a blue blazer with a name tag.* "I should be able to recognize you from a distance, and your name on the tag will seal it."

Identifying the Deity

Now imagine God, several millennia ago, devising the plan to send His only Son to earth to be born as a human infant. If we could have spoken down the corridors of time, we might have asked, "How will we know Him? How will we recognize Him as the Messiah, the holy Lamb of God—Your acceptable sacrifice for sin?"

God might have responded, "I will cause Him to be born as an Israelite, a descendant of Abraham" (Genesis 22:18).

"But," we might have protested, "Abraham's descendants will be as numerous as the stars!"

"Then I will narrow it down to only

half of Abraham's lineage, and make Him a descendant of Isaac, not Ishmael" (Genesis 21:12; Luke 3:23-34).

"That will help, but isn't that still a lot of people?"

"Let Him be born from Jacob's line, thus eliminating half of Isaac's lineage" (Numbers 24:17; Luke 3:23-34).

"But—"

"I will be more specific. Jacob will have twelve sons; I will bring forth the Messiah from the tribe of Judah" (Genesis 49:10; Luke 3:23-33).

"Won't that still be a lot of people? We still might not recognize Him when he comes."

"Don't worry! Look for Him in the family line of Jesse [Isaiah 11:1; Luke 3:23-32]. *And* from the house and lineage of Jesse's youngest son, David [Jeremiah 23:5; Luke 3:23-31]. And then I will tell you *where* He will be born: Bethlehem, a tiny town in the area called Judah [Micah 5:2; Matthew 2:1]."

"But how will we know which person born there is Your Son?"

"He will be preceded by a messenger who will prepare the way and announce His advent [Isaiah 40:3; Matthew 3:1-2]. He will begin His ministry in Galilee [Isaiah 9:1; Matthew 4:12-17] and will teach in parables [Psalm 78:2; Matthew 13:34-35], performing many miracles [Isaiah 35:5-6; Matthew 9:35]."

"Okay, that should help a lot."

"Wait," God might have responded, "I'm just getting warmed up. He will ride into the city of Jerusalem on a donkey [Zechariah 9:9; Matthew 21:2; Luke 19:35-37] and will appear suddenly and forcefully at the temple courts and zealously 'clean house' [Psalm 69:9; Malachi 3:1; John 2:15-16]. In fact, in *one day* I will fulfill no fewer than *twenty-nine* specific prophecies spoken at least five hundred years before His birth."

1. He will be betrayed by a friend (Psalm 41:9; Matthew 26:49).

2. The price of His betrayal will be 30 pieces of silver (Zechariah 11:12; Matthew 26:15).

3. His betrayal money will be cast to the floor of My temple (Zechariah 11:13; Matthew 27:5).

4. His betrayal money will be used to buy the potter's field (Zechariah 11:13; Matthew 27:7).

5. He will be forsaken and deserted by His disciples (Zechariah 13:7; Mark 14:50).

6. He will be accused by false witnesses (Psalm 35:11; Matthew 26:59-60).

7. He will be silent before His accusers (Isaiah 53:7; Matthew 27:12).

8. He will be wounded and bruised (Isaiah 53:5; Matthew 27:26).

9. He will be hated without a cause (Psalm 69:4; John 15:25).

10. He will be struck and spit on (Isaiah 50:6; Matthew 26:67).

11. He will be mocked, ridiculed, and rejected (Isaiah 53:3; Matthew 27:27-31; John 7:5,48).

12. He will collapse from weakness (Psalm 109:24-25; Luke 23:26).

13. He will be taunted with specific words (Psalm 22:6-8; Matthew 27:39-43).

14. People will shake their heads at Him (Psalm 109:25; Matthew 27:39).

15. People will stare at Him (Psalm 22:17; Luke 23:35).

16. He will be executed among sinners (Isaiah 53:12; Matthew 27:38).

17. His hands and feet will be pierced (Psalm 22:16; Luke 23:33).

18. He will pray for His persecutors (Isaiah 53:12; Luke 23:34).

19. His friends and family will stand afar off and watch (Psalm 38:11; Luke 23:49).

20. His garments will be divided up and awarded by the casting of lots (Psalm 22:18; John 19:23-24).

21. He will thirst (Psalm 69:21; John 19:28).

22. He will be given gall and vinegar (Psalm 69:21; Matthew 27:34).

23. He will commit Himself to God (Psalm 31:5; Luke 23:46).

24. His bones will be left unbroken (Psalm 34:20; John 19:33).

25. His heart will rupture (Psalm 22:14; John 19:34).

26. His side will be pierced (Zechariah 12:10; John 19:34).

27. Darkness will come over the land at midday (Amos 8:9; Matthew 27:45).

28. He will be buried in a rich man's tomb (Isaiah 53:9; Matthew 27:57-60).

29. He will die 483 years after the declaration of Artaxerxes to rebuild the temple in 444 BC (Daniel 9:24).

"As a final testimony, on the third day after His death, He will be raised from the dead [Psalm 16:10; Acts 2:31], ascend to heaven [Psalm 68:18; Acts 1:9], and be seated at the right hand of God in full majesty and authority [Psalm 110:1; Hebrews 1:3]."

What extraordinary lengths God went to help us identify and recognize His only begotten Son! Jesus fulfilled 60 major Old Testament prophecies (with about 270 additional ramifications)—all of which were made more than 400 years before His birth. This makes a compelling case for Jesus being the one and only person who "takes away the sin of the world" (John 1:29).

The Probability Factor

Of course Jesus was not the only Jew to be born into the tribe of Judah, in the city of Bethlehem, and buried in a rich man's tomb. Is it possible that the details of Jesus's life just *happened* to coincide with all those Old Testament prophecies?

To answer that question, we can turn to the science of statistics and probabilities. Professor Peter W. Stoner, in an analysis that was carefully reviewed and pronounced to be sound by the American Scientific Affiliation, states that the probability of just *eight* prophecies being fulfilled in one person is 1 in 10^{17} (that is, 1 in 100,000,000,000,000,000).[1]

To get a better idea of the magnitude of that number, assume you were to take 100,000,000,000,000,000 silver dollars and spread them across the state of Texas. That many silver dollars would not only cover the entire state, but would cover it two feet deep! Then take one more silver dollar, mark it with a red X, toss it into that pile, and stir the whole pile thoroughly.

Then blindfold yourself and, starting at El Paso on the western border, walk the length and breadth of that enormous state— from Amarillo in the panhandle to Laredo on the Rio Grande all the way to Galveston on the Gulf of Mexico. As you do so, you're allowed to pick up just one silver dollar out of that enormous two-foot-deep pile. What are the chances that you would have picked the coin marked with the red X? *The same as one person fulfilling just eight messianic prophecies in his lifetime.*[2]

In other words, it is nearly nonsensical to imagine that eight Old Testament prophecies about the Messiah could have come true in any one man by chance—let alone the 60 major prophecies that were fulfilled in Jesus of Nazareth. Unless, of course, He *is* (as He Himself claimed) "the glory of the Father's one and only Son" (John 1:14 NLT).

God gave us these prophecies so we could be confident in the truth that Jesus truly is God's perfect atonement for our sins. Because of Christ's death on the cross, we can be saved from and forgiven of our sins, gain a relationship with God, and enjoy life forever with God. The apostle Peter said, "There is salvation in no one else! God has given no other name under heaven by which we must be saved" (Acts 4:12 NLT).

Messianic prophecies make a compelling case for placing our faith in Jesus as God's Son. Yet there is also compelling logic.

The Trilemma: Lord, Liar, or Lunatic?

Some say Jesus Christ's claim to deity is not all that important. They suggest it is the *teachings* of Jesus that are more significant—love your neighbor, feed the hungry, make this planet a better place, and so on. They

point to Jesus as a great moral teacher and discount His claim to deity. But anyone who said the things that Jesus said about Himself could not merely be a great moral teacher. C.S. Lewis, who was once an agnostic, understood this issue clearly. He wrote:

> I am trying here to prevent anyone saying the really foolish thing that people often say about Him: "I'm ready to accept Jesus as a great moral teacher, but I don't accept His claim to be God." That is the one thing we must not say. A man who was merely a man and said the sort of things Jesus said would not be a great moral teacher. He would either be a lunatic—on a level with the man who says he is a poached egg—or else he would be the Devil of Hell. You must make your choice. Either this man was, and is, the Son of God: or else a madman or something worse.

Then Lewis added:

> You can shut Him up for a fool, you can spit at Him and kill Him as a demon, or you can fall at His feet and call Him Lord and God. But let us not come up with any patronizing nonsense about His being a great human teacher. He has not left that open to us. He did not intend to.[3]

Jesus's claim to be God leaves us with two alternatives: either His claim is true, or it is false. And if His claim is false, we are left with two further options (see diagram).

JESUS CLAIMS TO BE GOD[4]

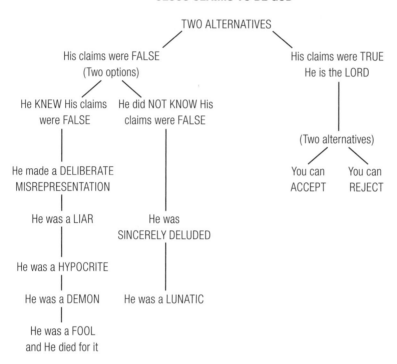

TWO ALTERNATIVES

His claims were FALSE
(Two options)

His claims were TRUE
He is the LORD

He KNEW His claims
were FALSE

He did NOT KNOW His
claims were FALSE

(Two alternatives)

He made a DELIBERATE
MISREPRESENTATION

You can
ACCEPT

You can
REJECT

He was a LIAR

He was
SINCERELY DELUDED

He was a HYPOCRITE

He was a DEMON

He was a LUNATIC

He was a FOOL
and He died for it

First, let us consider the alternative that Jesus's claim to be God was false. This would give us two options: He either knew His claim was false, or He didn't know it was false. *Was Jesus a Liar?* If, when Jesus made His claims, He knew that He was not God, then He was lying and deliberately deceiving His followers. And if He was a liar, then He was also a hypocrite because He taught others to be honest whatever the cost. Worse than that, if He was lying, He was a demon because He told others to trust Him for their eternal destiny. If He couldn't back up His claims and knew it, then He was unspeakably evil for deceiving His followers with such a false hope. Last, He would also be a fool because His claim to be God led to His crucifixion— a claim He could have backed away from to save Himself even at the last minute.

How could Jesus ever be considered a great moral teacher if He wasn't deity? This means He would have knowingly misled people about the most important point of His teachings—that He was the Son of God.

But to conclude that Jesus was a deliberate liar doesn't harmonize with what we know either of Him or of the results of His life and teachings. Wherever Jesus has been proclaimed, we have seen lives changed for the good, nations changed for the better, thieves become honest, alcoholics become sober, hateful individuals become channels of love, and unjust persons embrace justice.

Consider William Lecky, one of Great Britain's most noted historians. Although he was a fierce opponent of organized Christianity, he was able to see the effect true Christianity had on the world. He wrote:

It was reserved for Christianity to present to the world an ideal which through all the changes of eighteen centuries has inspired the hearts of men with an impassioned love; has shown itself capable of acting on all ages, nations, temperaments, and conditions; has been not only the highest pattern of virtue, but the strongest incentive to its practice…The simple record of these three short years of active life has done more to regenerate and soften mankind than all the disquisitions of philosophers and all the exhortations of moralists.[5]

Was Jesus a Lunatic? If we find it inconceivable that Jesus was a liar, then couldn't He have mistakenly thought Himself to be God? After all, it's possible to be both sincere and wrong. But we must remember that for someone to mistakenly think Himself God—especially in the context of a fiercely monotheistic culture like Judaism—and tell others that their eternal destiny depended on believing in Him is no small matter. Is it possible that Jesus Christ was a lunatic—that He was deranged?

Today we would treat someone who believes Himself to be God the same way we would treat someone who believes he is Napoleon. We would see him as deluded and self-deceived. We would lock him up so he wouldn't hurt himself or anyone else. Yet in Jesus we don't observe the abnormalities and imbalance that go along with such derangement. If He was insane, His poise and composure were nothing short of amazing.

Eminent psychiatric pioneers Arthur Noyes and Lawrence Kolb, in their *Modern Clinical Psychiatry* text, describe a schizophrenic as a person who is more autistic than realistic. The schizophrenic desires to escape from reality. Let's face it: For a mere man to claim to be God would certainly be a retreat from reality.

However, in light of all that we know about Jesus, it's hard to imagine He was mentally disturbed. He spoke the most profound words ever recorded. His instructions have liberated many people from mental bondage. Clark Pinnock, professor emeritus of systematic theology at McMaster Divinity College, asked, "Was he deluded about his greatness, a paranoid, an unintentional deceiver, a schizophrenic? Again, the skill and depth of his teaching support the case only for his total mental soundness. If only we were as sane as he!"[6]

Psychologist Gary R. Collins explains that Jesus

> was loving but didn't let his compassion immobilize him; he didn't have a bloated ego, even though he was often surrounded by adoring crowds; he maintained balance despite an often demanding lifestyle; he always knew what he was doing and where he was going; he cared deeply about people, including women and children, who weren't seen as important back then; he was able to accept people while not merely winking at their sin; he responded to individuals based on where they were at and what they uniquely needed. All in all, I just don't see signs that Jesus was suffering from any known mental illness…He was much healthier than anyone else I know—including me![7]

Was Jesus Lord? As we can see, it would be very difficult for anyone to conclude that Jesus was a liar or a lunatic. The only remaining alternative is that He was—and is—the Christ, the Son of God, as He claimed. Yet in spite of the logic and evidence, many people still cannot bring themselves to accept this conclusion.

In his book *The Da Vinci Code,* Dan Brown claims, "By officially endorsing Jesus as the Son of God, Constantine turned Jesus into a Deity who existed beyond the scope of the human world, an entity whose power was unchallengeable."[8] The novel propagates the idea that Christ's deity was invented at the Council of Nicaea. This, however, is not accurate.

The New Testament itself provides the earliest evidence for the belief that Jesus is divine. These documents were composed in the first century AD, which means they predate the Council of Nicaea by more than two centuries. While different people wrote the New Testament books for a variety of purposes, one unmistakable theme all the books share is that Christ is God.

The ante-Nicene fathers were early Christian writers who lived after the close of the New Testament period (c. 100), yet before the Council of Nicaea (325). They provide additional support that Jesus was considered divine long before the Council of Nicaea. They include men such as Justin Martyr, Ignatius, and Irenaeus. There is no doubt that they understood Jesus to be divine. Consider some statements from their ancient works:

> Ignatius of Antioch (AD 110): "God incarnate...God Himself appearing in the form of man."[9]

> Justin Martyr (AD 100–165): "Being the First-begotten Word of God, is even God."[10]

> Irenaeus (AD 177): "The Father is God and the Son is God; for He who is born of God is God."[11]

The issue with regard to whether Jesus was a liar, lunatic, or Lord is not, Which answer is possible? Obviously all three are possible. Rather, the question is, Which is most probable? We cannot, as so many people want to do, put Jesus on the shelf merely as a great moral teacher or a prophet. Those are not valid options. Either He was a liar, a lunatic, or He is Lord and God. We must make a choice. Our decision about Jesus must be more than an idle intellectual exercise. As the apostle John wrote, "These are written so that you may believe that Jesus is the Christ, the Son of God, and that by believing you may have life in his name" (John 20:31).

Jesus *Did* Claim to Be God

There are some today who say Jesus never really claimed to be the Son of God—He only said He was the Son of man, and did not make a claim to deity. But these people are mistaken. Jesus *did* claim to be the Son of God. He made His identity central to His message.

According to the New Testament record, Jesus repeatedly made it clear that He was the unique Son of God, an assertion that did not go unnoticed by the religious leaders of His day. In fact, that claim was the very reason they tried to discredit Him and, eventually, the reason they put Him to death: "The Jewish leaders tried all the harder to find a way to kill him. For he not only broke the Sabbath, he called God his Father, thereby making himself equal to God" (John 5:18 NLT).

On more than one occasion, Jesus's clear assertion of His own deity caused the Jews to want to stone Him. On one occasion, when He told the Jewish leaders, "Your father Abraham rejoiced as he looked forward to my coming. He saw it and was glad," His listeners became indignant: "'You aren't even fifty years old. How can you say you have seen Abraham?'" (John 8:56-57 NLT).

"'Very truly I tell you,' Jesus answered, 'before Abraham was born, I am!' At this, they picked up stones to stone him, but Jesus hid himself, slipping away from the temple grounds" (John 8:56-59 NIV). On another occasion, when Jesus said that He was one with the Father, the Jewish leaders again picked up stones to kill Him (see John 10:30-31).

When Jesus asked why they wanted to kill Him, they retorted, "For blasphemy, because you, being a man, make yourself God" (John 10:33).

Yet another time, Jesus told a paralyzed man, "Son, your sins are forgiven" and again the religious leaders reacted with outrage. "Why does this man speak like that? He is blaspheming! Who can forgive sins but God alone?" (Mark 2:5-7).

In the final days prior to His death, Jesus made it clear—even to the Sanhedrin (the Jewish high council)—just who He was: "The high priest asked him, 'Are you the Messiah, the Son of the Blessed One?' Jesus said, 'I AM…'" In response to the proclamation, the "high priest tore his clothing to show his horror and said, 'Why do we need other witnesses? You have all heard his blasphemy. What is your verdict?' 'Guilty!' they all cried. 'He deserves to die!'" (Mark 14:61-64 NLT).

All that Jesus said and did pointed to His identity as deity and the Messiah, and all of it pointed to the purpose for which He came to earth. If He is not who He claimed to be, then His teachings are either the rantings of a lunatic who sincerely *thought* He was God (but was not), or the words of a liar who *knew* He was not God (but said He was).

But we can be confident in the truth that He is Lord! He is the incarnate Son of the one

and only God of the universe, the one who said, "I am the LORD, and there is no other" and "You shall have no other gods before me" (Isaiah 45:6; Exodus 20:3).

Given the three options considered above, it is fully reasonable to conclude that Jesus is Lord. Yet the solid reasoning and abundance of evidence is only the beginning. What is so amazing is the relevance of Jesus being God's gift to us.

Personally Relevant: God's Heart Behind the Gift of His Son

Sin may have started with the first couple, but we all are at fault. Scripture says, "When Adam sinned, sin entered the world. Adam's sin brought death, so death spread to everyone, for everyone sinned" (Romans 5:12 NLT). Our sin is a rejection of God and His ways. Yet His response to a rebellious human race is profound, beyond our understanding.

When humans sinned, was God vindictive? In anger, was He not justified to reject them? Would He forever cast them from His presence?

But instead of vindictive anger, God felt grief and sadness. From one generation after another His cherished humans lived a life of sin and rebellion. This "broke his heart" (Genesis 6:6 NLT).

Imagine God as He watched in grief and sadness as the people He created fell into sin. Today, we inhabit the very world where He and the first human couple once walked in perfect relationship. And from the moment we were conceived, our sin separated us from the life that is found in Him. From the start, we were sinners. And instead of rejecting us, He reached out to us in spite of our sin. He longed to relate to you and me and those around us as intimately as He once did to them. He wanted to take pleasure in us. He wanted to see in our eyes the delight that only His life and love can bring. But that was not possible because of sin. While His heart loved us without condition, His holiness could not embrace our life of selfishness. For each of us followed in Adam and Eve's footsteps, becoming God's enemy by repeatedly and selfishly choosing our own sinful ways instead of His holy ways.

So what did God do? He took the initiative. We were the ones who desperately needed Him, but we didn't seek Him out. We were the ones who should have been crying out for help. Yet the all-sufficient Lord, who "has no needs...[but] gives life and breath to everything, and...satisfies every need" *wanted you and me* (Acts 17:25). We rejected Him, yet He still accepted us. He wanted to relate to us—to enjoy and delight and take pleasure in a personal relationship with us. He wanted to complete our joy.

So God entered our world and set into motion a plan that would cancel the curse of sin and death. He "became flesh and dwelt among us" (John 1:14). "Because God's children are human beings—made of flesh and blood—the Son also became flesh and blood. For only as a human being could he die, and only by dying could he break the power of the devil, who had the power of death" (Hebrews 2:14 NLT). Only the Son of the living God could wrench the power of death out of the hand of our archenemy, Satan, so that God could be reconnected to His children in personal, one-on-one relationships.

When God came to us in human form, He was saying, "You may have turned away from Me, but I'm not turning away from you. You are so important to Me that I will go to extraordinary lengths to have a personal relationship with you. I'll enter your world and become human like you to save you from death and eternal aloneness without Me." When it came to restoring His relationships with humans, God did not merely send a prophet or even an angel to declare His truth of salvation; He sent the ultimate gift—His only Son!

Is There Evidence That Jesus Really Existed?

Gary R. Habermas and Benjamin C.F. Shaw

Other essays in this volume defend the reliability and inspiration of the canonical Old and New Testament books. Here we inquire as to what additional data from the New Testament era may inform us about the life of Jesus even if we were limited to using only the available non-Christian and Christian sources outside the Bible.

What information concerning Jesus is reported in sources outside of the Bible? Non-Christian sources have made some surprising comments regarding Him and the earliest Christians. Christian writers have also provided valuable insights into how they viewed Jesus as the early church developed. This chapter will provide some of the more important historical references to Jesus from sources outside the New Testament, all from within several decades after Jesus's death.[1]

Before looking at these nonbiblical texts, it is important to place them in perspective, especially because some popular skeptics think that *only* nonbiblical references are useful in such an effort as ours. Such a view is seriously mistaken. The vast, almost unanimous view among critical *scholars* across a wide theological spectrum, including atheists and other unbelievers, is that both New Testament and non-New Testament sources provide valuable information about Jesus.

In fact, the New Testament sources are considered by historians to be extremely important. The agnostic New Testament scholar Bart Ehrman writes, "Whatever one thinks of them as inspired scripture, they can be seen and used as *significant historical sources*."[2] Thus, the sources discussed in this chapter should be understood as evidence that complements the New Testament accounts.

Non-Christian Sources (AD 90–125)

The first group of writings will come from three non-Christian sources. The first two sources are from historians, one Roman and one Jewish. Each source only briefly discusses Jesus, as there was no attempt to provide comprehensive biographical details.

Tacitus (Roman Historian). Cornelius

Tacitus (c. AD 55–120) was an important Roman historian. His writings provide valuable information regarding a number of Roman emperors. Relevant for our purposes is Tacitus's comments in *Annals* 15.44, written around AD 115. While describing the great fire that occurred in Rome during Nero's reign (AD 54–68), Tacitus mentioned both Jesus and Christians. He wrote:

> Consequently, to get rid of the report, Nero fastened the guilt and inflicted the most exquisite tortures on a class hated for their abominations, called Christians by the populace. Christus, from whom the name had its origin, suffered the extreme penalty during the reign of Tiberius at the hands of one of our procurators, Pontius Pilatus, and a most mischievous superstition, thus checked for the moment, again broke out not only in Judaea, the first source of the evil, but even in Rome, where all things hideous and shameful from every part of the world find their centre [sic] and become popular.[3]

Tacitus's comments provide us with a number of important details about Jesus. (1) Christus (from the Latin) was the founder of the Christians, and (2) Pontius Pilatus (again Latin), a Roman procurator, put Christus to death (3) by the most "extreme penalty" (4) while Tiberius was the emperor. (5) His death temporarily stopped the movement, (6) but it "again broke out" (7) in Judaea and (8) eventually in Rome.

These eight facts described by Tacitus align nicely with the New Testament accounts of Jesus. Tacitus apparently did not think very kindly of Christians; he saw them as holding an evil and "most mischievous superstition." Nevertheless,

due to the treatment endured by the early Christians, Tacitus seemed to pity them as having suffered due to the gluttony of "one man's cruelty." This early Christian suffering may have moved Tacitus such that, even though he disagreed with these believers, he included their sad story in his account of the fire at Rome.

Josephus (Jewish Historian). Flavius Josephus (c. AD 37–97) was different from Tacitus in a number of ways. Josephus was, like Paul, a Pharisee. Unlike Paul, he participated in the Jewish revolt against the Romans (AD 67–70). Josephus was eventually captured, but was able to make some significant political inroads with the future Roman emperor, Vespasian. As a result, Josephus was a Jew working with the Romans so he could produce a number of different works.

The writings of present value for this chapter come from his *Antiquities*. In this work, Josephus mentioned Jesus and James, the brother of Jesus, as well as John the Baptist. Regarding Jesus, Josephus wrote,

> Now, there was about this Jesus, a wise man, *if it be lawful to call him a man,* for he was a doer of wonderful works—a teacher of such men as receive the truth with pleasure. He drew over to him both many of the Jews, and many of the Gentiles. *He was [the] Christ;* and when Pilate, at the suggestion of the principal men amongst us, had condemned him to the cross, those that loved him at the first did not forsake him, *for he appeared to them alive again the third day, as the divine prophets had foretold these things and ten thousand other wonderful things concerning him;* and the tribe of Christians, so named from him, are not extinct at this day.[4]

The majority of commentators believe that the italicized words above are likely Christian interpolations (i.e., additions to the original). Part of the reason for this is because Origen, an early Christian scholar, said that Josephus did not believe Jesus was the Messiah.[5] There is no need to enter further into the debate regarding the authenticity of the passage. For our purposes, we will follow the conclusion held by many scholars. As stated by ancient historian Edwin Yamauchi, "the passage has an authentic core but also includes Christian insertions."[6] James Charlesworth agrees: "We can now be as certain as historical research will presently allow that Josephus did refer to Jesus," and in the process provided "corroboration of the Gospel account."[7]

Much like Tacitus above, several facts are provided by this brief comment even when we exclude the italicized portions. Josephus corroborated that Jesus was (1) a wise teacher, (2) did marvelous deeds, (3) had Jewish and Gentile followers, and (4) was condemned by Pilate to crucifixion (5) at the instigation of the Jews, but (6) His followers continued after His death and (7) were called Christians. We can add from Josephus's other texts that (8) Jesus was considered by some to be the Messiah (9) and had a brother named James.[8]

Ancient Christian Sources: Non-New Testament AD 90–125

We will now turn to two Christian non-New Testament sources. These are some of the earliest Christian writings we possess outside of the New Testament. They date from the end of the first century to the beginning of the second century.

Clement of Rome. Clement of Rome wrote a letter to the Corinthian church that is commonly thought to be the earliest Christian writing outside of the New Testament, being dated to approximately AD 95 or even earlier. In this epistle, Clement wrote to the Corinthians and responded to various issues, including providing some information about Jesus:

> The apostles have preached the Gospel to us from the Lord Jesus Christ; Jesus Christ [has done so] from God. Christ therefore was sent forth by God, and the apostles by Christ. Both of these appointments, then, were made in an orderly way, according to the will of God. Having therefore received their orders, and being fully assured by the resurrection of our Lord Jesus Christ, and established in the word of God, with full assurance of the Holy Ghost, they went forth proclaiming that the kingdom of God was at hand. And thus preaching through countries and cities, they appointed the first-fruits, having proved them by the Spirit, to be bishops and deacons of those who should afterwards believe.[9]

In this passage, Clement described that (1) the good news of the kingdom of God was central to the Christian message; (2) the gospel was given to the apostles directly by Jesus; (3) Jesus's resurrection confirmed the truthfulness of these teachings (4) as did the additional confirmation of Scripture. (5) The apostles were provided with assurance by Jesus's resurrection and Scripture as they proclaimed the good news. (6) The apostles appointed bishops and deacons to minister to future believers.

Ignatius of Antioch. Ignatius was the bishop of Antioch and a leader in the early church. He was condemned to die in Rome for being a Christian. While being escorted to Rome he wrote seven letters, six of them to churches and one to an individual (Polycarp). These letters were written around AD 110–115 and discuss a number of different topics and contain several historical references to Jesus.

While we recommend reading all of Ignatius's letters, due to space limitations, we will cite only one here. In his epistle *Trallians*, Ignatius stated,

> Jesus Christ, who was descended from David, and was also of Mary; who was truly born, and did eat and drink. He was truly persecuted under Pontius Pilate; He was truly crucified, and [truly] died…He was also truly raised from the dead, His Father quickening Him, even as after the same manner His father will so raise up us who believe in Him by Christ Jesus.[10]

Ignatius's purpose here was to respond to Gnostics who typically denied the aspects of Jesus's corporeality. In doing so, Ignatius affirmed that Jesus (1) was of the lineage of David and (2) born of Mary. (3) Thus, He really lived, ate, and drank before (4) being crucified under Pontius Pilate. (5) God raised Him from the dead and (6) will similarly raise believers.

The Contribution Made by Multiple Sources

In this essay we investigated four early sources for the historicity of Jesus, two each from both unbelievers and believers. Our goal was to briefly introduce some historical claims made about Jesus from outside of Scripture.

As a side note not to be forgotten, skeptical New Testament scholars (such as major atheists, agnostics, and other non-Christian thinkers) also hold that many additional comments and New Testament sources provide significant texts for understanding Jesus. For example, of the 13 epistles that bear Paul's name, Ehrman states that contemporary scholars grant that seven of these texts were written by Paul: Romans, 1 and 2 Corinthians, Galatians, Philippians, 1 Thessalonians, and Philemon. As such, these seven "undisputed" works may be cited, investigated, and employed as authoritative when it comes to providing an understanding of what early Christians knew and believed about Jesus.[11]

In addition, many other individual New Testament texts, including dozens of early creedal passages, provide many more pieces of historical information regarding Jesus Christ. This is especially the case when even a small number of these minimal facts alone indicate that the heart of the gospel message is true.[12]

But even just the four sources mentioned here provide helpful corroboration of particular facts taught in the New Testament accounts. Brought together, the available sources contribute much more than is often realized concerning the historical Jesus.

Are the Gospel Accounts Reliable?

F. David Farnell

The answer to this question is an unqualified yes! Most recognize that the Gospels comprise a truly unique treasure bequeathed as an enduring testimony from the first-century church to the rest of mankind. This testimony has left an unfailing historical record that God loved the whole world and demonstrated that love by sending His Son to save mankind from alienation from Him (John 3:16-18).

Matthew, Luke, Mark, and John are unique historical accounts set apart from other ancient historical writings. No other ancient account is like them or comparable. As a result, some scholars describe the Gospels using the Latin words *sui generis* ("unique"). How so? Today, classical scholars recognize that ancient historians of the past, especially during the Greek era, often admitted to writing history that they were not eyewitnesses to (Thucydides, Plutarch).[1] In addition, none of them were completely accurate in the details they reported. Indeed, they even acknowledged that in writing their records they often invented speeches and created details about the characters to make them larger than life. No ancient historical account has compared to the accurate record that the Gospel writers

left as a witness to Jesus's life as they were empowered by God's Spirit of truth.

The Testimony of the Very Early Church

Many factors affirm the absolute reliability of the Gospels. The consistent testimony of the early church stands as a firm, inviolable witness to the absolute truthfulness, accuracy, and reliability of the 27 New Testament books, including the four Gospels. What is more, the testimony of the early church stands in direct contrast to the negative criticism of the Gospels that developed so much later during the eighteenth and subsequent centuries. Those who lived closest to the time of Jesus knew with certainty of the assuredness of the Gospel record. What can we learn from this early Christian testimony?

First, the four canonical Gospels—Matthew, Mark, Luke, and John—were *unanimously* affirmed by the earliest orthodox (or "catholic") Christian communities throughout the Roman Empire. Wherever Christianity had spread, the Gospels were never doubted in any way.[2] The first great church historian, Eusebius (ca. AD 260–341), as well as many other very early church fathers, left us a valuable record about the genuineness of the Gospels from which the church derives its information. Eusebius called the four canonical Gospels "the holy four Gospels" that were never once doubted by the orthodox church as coming from the apostles whose names they bore.[3] The early fathers knew that the Gospel of Matthew was written by Levi the tax collector;[4] that Mark, the companion and interpreter of Peter, took Peter's preaching and made it into the Gospel that bears Mark's name; that Luke, Paul's personal traveling companion as seen in the "we" sections of Acts (Acts 16:10-18), composed a two-part series known as Luke-Acts (Luke 1:1-4);[5] and that John the apostle wrote the Gospel that bears his name.[6] Eusebius told us that an unbroken chain of custody in the early church, consisting of orthodox bishops throughout the entire Roman world, from the first to the fourth centuries AD, affirmed these four Gospels, and *only* these four Gospels, as genuinely from the men whose names they bore.

Second, from the earliest times (AD 125), while anonymous in their text, the Gospels bore titles on all their manuscripts: "The Gospel according to Matthew," "The Gospel According to Mark," "The Gospel According to Luke," "The Gospel According to John." No other names ever appeared on any of the manuscripts. From the earliest beginnings, the orthodox church was extremely careful to guard these four Gospels as the only true and authoritative witnesses to Jesus's life. They firmly rejected all other gospels as false. The earliest church fathers authoritatively quoted only the four Gospels, demonstrating their unwavering belief in the full trustworthiness and accuracy of these records of Jesus's life. The early church knew with certainty that they were written testimonies that came from the first-century disciples of Jesus.

Third, the early fathers left a clear record of the chronological order in which the Gospels were written. Clement of Alexandria (AD 150–215) wrote that the Gospels with genealogies (Matthew and Luke) were written before the Gospels without (Mark and John).[7] They tell us always, and without fail, that Matthew was written first. Moreover, Irenaeus tells us that John the apostle wrote his Gospel last. So the chronological order of the Gospels is Matthew, then Luke, then Mark, then finally John.[8]

Finally, and most importantly, the summary impact of the certain testimony of the early church as it testified to the canonical Gospels cannot be overstated. Matthew, Luke, Mark, John were written either by direct apostolic eyewitnesses (Matthew, John) or based on apostolic eyewitness testimony (Mark was based on Peter's preaching, and Luke [Luke 1:1-4] gathered his information by interviewing eyewitnesses and traveling with Paul [Acts]). When a Christian reads these four Gospels, he or she is literally "sitting at the feet" of Jesus, as well as listening to eyewitness reports of men and women who knew Him directly and intimately, and accompanied Him from His birth (Matthew 1-3; Luke 1-3) through His ministry (Matthew 4–27; Luke 3–23; Mark 1–15; John 1–19) to His resurrection and ascension to heaven (Matthew 28; Luke 24; Mark 16; John 20–21; Acts 1).

The Testimony of the Gospels Themselves

When the Gospels are examined, one can readily see the eyewitness elements in them that affirm their reliability. Luke said that he interviewed many eyewitnesses of Jesus's life. One must read the opening verses of his Gospel (Luke 1:1-4), which indicate his reliance on eyewitness accounts:

Inasmuch as many have undertaken to compile a narrative of the things that have been accomplished among us, just as those who from the beginning were eyewitnesses and ministers of the word have delivered them to us, it seemed good to me also, having followed all things closely for some time past, to write an orderly account for you, most excellent Theophilus, that you may have certainty concerning the things you have been taught.

From Luke, Christians can learn how "closely" the gospel writers "followed" Jesus's life "from the beginning" supported by firsthand "eyewitnesses." In Acts, Luke accompanied Paul on his missionary journeys as the "we sections" (see above) indicate, making Luke an eyewitness. Interestingly, Luke was a physician. Because of his education and the fact his kind of work required attention to detail, he would likely have been a good researcher worthy of conducting a careful investigation. Matthew was a trained tax collector, and this required him to be a keeper of records. Thus he would have been well qualified to be the first writer selected to testify about the promised Jewish Messiah.

In John, we learn of firsthand details about Jesus's life that are not recorded in the other Gospels, making John's account 92 percent unique. Furthermore, John was mindful of the smallest details regarding people, times, numbers, and places, which could only come from direct eyewitness experience. He knew the very hour ("the tenth hour"—John 1:39) that Jesus's disciples accompanied Him to his house. He knew when Judas slipped out of the last supper with Jesus (John 13:30) to accomplish his betrayal. John even remembered how many fish were caught when Jesus, after His

resurrection, told the disciples to cast their nets into the Sea of Galilee (153! —John 21:11).

John also knew the very thoughts and feelings of the apostles (2:11,17,22; 4:27; 6:19,60; 12:16; 13:22,28; 20:9; 21:12). He knew how his fishing partner, Peter, would die—Jesus told them the details in a personal conversation during breakfast by the Sea of Galilee (John 21:18-19). Throughout his Gospel and epistles, John used "we" many times to inform the reader of his personal witness to the life of Jesus (for example, John 1:14—"we have seen his glory"; 1 John 1:1-3—"from the beginning," "we have heard"; "we have seen with our eyes"; "we looked upon"; "[we] have touched with our hands"). What is more, he spoke of "testimony" and "witness" throughout his Gospel, which carries the ring of authority and truth, giving the reader confidence in the truthfulness of his documented record of Jesus's life (John 19:35).

John's use of descriptive words and details reveals that he was intimately acquainted with the life of Christ. For example, he was acquainted with Jewish feasts, such as Passover (2:13,23; 6:4; 11:55; 12:1; 18:28), the Feast of Tabernacles (7:2), and the Feast of Dedication (Hanukkah—10:22). John was acquainted with various Jewish customs, such as how water pots were to be arranged (2:1-10) and procedures for burial of the dead (11:38,44; 19:40). He was well aware of the negative feelings that existed between the Jews and the Samaritans (4:9).

Concerning geographical details, John recorded the depth and exact location of Jacob's well (4:11) and distinguished Bethany (2 miles east of Jerusalem) from "Bethany across the Jordan" (21 miles east of Jerusalem—1:28; 11:18).

We learn from the Gospels that Peter and John, along with James, were the three disciples closest to Jesus. They were privileged to witness Jesus's radiant transfiguration (Matthew 17:1-8; Luke 8:51). This witness continued among all the apostles, from the beginning of Jesus's ministry (His baptism) to the very day when He was resurrected and ascended to heaven (Acts 1:21-22). In 2 Peter 1:16-17, we learn that Peter boldly rejected myth and proclaimed his role as an eyewitness, stating,

> We did not follow cleverly devised myths when we made known to you the power and coming of our Lord Jesus Christ, but we were eyewitnesses of his majesty. For when he received honor and glory from God the Father, and the voice was borne to him by the Majestic Glory, "This is my beloved Son, with whom I am well pleased."

Often ancient historians of the Greco-Roman tradition were prone to invent tales or myths about a major person's life, but Peter firmly distanced himself from such ancient practices in the course of writing his accounts, declaring the eyewitness status of those who produced the Gospels.

The Testimony of Jesus Christ as to the Certain Reliability of the Eyewitnesses Who Wrote the Gospels

The accuracy and reliability of the Gospels are, most importantly, anchored to the certainty of the promises Jesus made to those who were eyewitnesses of His life and teaching. In John 14:26, Jesus promised the Gospel writers, "The Helper, the Holy Spirit, whom the Father will send in my name, he will teach you all things and bring to your remembrance all that I have said to you."

From this verse we learn that the writers of the Gospels would have the Spirit of God to empower, energize, and bring to memory everything Jesus taught them. Jesus said,

> When the Spirit of truth comes, he will guide you into all the truth, for he will not speak on his own authority, but whatever he hears he will speak, and he will declare to you the things that are to come. He will glorify me, for he will take what is mine and declare it to you. All that the Father has is mine; therefore I said that he will take what is mine and declare it to you (John 16:13-15).

Here we read a direct promise from Jesus that the eyewitness accounts recorded by those who wrote the Gospels would not be based on mere human recollections, but that they would receive the miraculous ability to remember "all the truth." The power of God guided, controlled, and governed these eyewitnesses as they composed Matthew, Luke, Mark, and John. Indeed, because God's Spirit is "the Spirit of truth" (John 16:13; 1 John 4:6), the Gospels stand as unique eyewitness accounts that are considered inerrant (without error) as well as reliable (John 10:35).

As Hebrews 6:18 reminds us, "It is impossible for God to lie, we who have fled for refuge...have strong encouragement to hold fast to the hope set before us." Because the Gospels record our hope in Jesus, they give us the promised "strong encouragement." And because the Gospels foundationally rest in the nature of God Himself, they are not only reliable, they originated from and are sustained in their certainty by the living God Himself.

Moreover, not even the most cunning nonhuman intelligence created in the history of the universe (known variously as Satan, the

Adversary, Lucifer the "god of light" or the "illumined one," and the devil) has never been able to defeat or destroy God's Word, though he has often tried, nor will he ever be able to do so. Why? The Gospels demonstrate the supernatural intelligence of the living God Himself, who is actively sustaining His Word. Although copies of the Gospels have been destroyed through the ages, they are still here in abundance. Though the apostles were killed, the records they wrote have endured.

One promise given by Jesus deserves special mention here. In Matthew 24:35, He said, "Heaven and earth will pass away, but My words will not pass away." The earth and all its records will one day be gone, but not Jesus's words. While mere human accounts will decay and disappear, the Gospels are a unique genre and will stand forever, for their existence stands on a central promise from Jesus as well as the unfailing power of the Spirit of God, the Spirit of truth Himself.

Are the Gospels reliable? With absolute certainty, yes!

Conclusion

The Gospels offer an accurate and reliable portrait of Christ, and that's because they were "breathed out by God" (2 Timothy 3:16). As such, they are a reflection of God's character, which serves as a guarantee of the Gospel's truthfulness. To put it another way, whatever the Bible says, God says! This means the Bible carries the authority of God Himself. Therefore, any assault on the Bible by critics is essentially an attack on the authority of the Father, who gave it; on the testimony of the Son, who confirmed it; and on the ministry of the Holy Spirit, who inspired it.

Because the Word of God is "living and active," and can act as a critic of "the thoughts and intentions of the heart" (Hebrews 4:12), it is the only book possessing the ability to read you as you read it with an open heart and mind.

What About the Alternative "Gospels"?

H. Wayne House

For most of church history, Christians have been aware of only four canonical Gospels—Matthew, Mark, Luke, and John. But this was not always so. The Gospels, which were written by the apostles or their companions in the ministry, such as Luke and Mark, were written in the decades immediately following the life, death and resurrection of Jesus. Though some modern Christians and scholars believe the early writers were rather ignorant and illiterate, that is not the case for several reasons.

Those who wrote the first-century Gospels possessed confidence when it came to composing letters and treatises in the Greek language. For example, Luke was a companion of the apostle Paul, and as an educated physician, he was capable of producing a carefully written and researched portrait of Jesus known as the Gospel of Luke.

Matthew was a tax collector. This would have required him to be conversant in different languages, possess mathematical skills, and most likely be capable of communicating in written form.

The other apostles, even being "uneducated" (Acts 4:13), would have maintained acceptable reading and writing capabilities

that would have enabled them to write letters to the Christian communities. Some have supposed that the statement in Acts 4:13 means they were unable to communicate in written form. However, the text speaks of no such incapacity, but more precisely of not having rabbinic training.[1]

Matthew, Mark, and Luke were likely written somewhere from AD 40 to 70, and John was probably composed in the late 80s, or early 90s. The early Christians who heard or read the Gospels depended on writings that were based on eyewitness testimonies. Even though the four books did not identify the authors who wrote them, the recipients of these works were well aware from whom they came.

This stands in contrast to the so-called (noncanonical) gospels of the second century, which were often titled using the names of famous individuals from the first century. This was done in attempts to bolster the street credibility of these alternative works. But the early Christians would not likely have been fooled into receiving these works. The authentic canonical Gospels of the first century never had any difficulty with being received by the people of God because of their authenticity and their direct connection with the eyewitnesses. But this does not mean that the early Christians were not careful with regard to what they accepted as the Word of God. Some books, like 2 Peter and Revelation, were available for a number of years before they were widely accepted.

What Is the Origin of the Alternative Gospels?

Whereas Matthew, Mark, Luke, and John were written during the first century, the alternative gospels were not written until the first half of the second century. Though these works bore the names of well-known individuals from the first-century, they originated much too late to have been written by eyewitnesses of the life and resurrection of Jesus. Not only did they lack eyewitnesses, but the authors were not able to interview eyewitnesses, as Luke did for his Gospel.

We have no knowledge of who wrote these alternative gospels, but we do know that these works originated in communities in Egypt, where false doctrine and heresy were prevalent.

Though heretics in Egypt received the alternative gospels, they never gained traction in the rest of the Christian world. Strangely, modern scholars have given them far more credence than even those individuals who were influenced by the orthodox fathers of the Christian church.

The Theology of the Alternative Gospels

What is Gnosticism? To understand why the majority of the church rejected the alternative gospels, we first need to know the dominant theology of those who composed these writings. Because of the media publicity in recent years, many Christians who

are not involved in biblical scholarship have become more familiar with the terms *Gnostic* and *Gnosticism*, but know little of the beliefs of this philosophy. *Gnostic* comes from the Greek word *gnosis*, which means "knowledge." Gnostics were those who sought hidden knowledge—they believed they were a select group of individuals who had achieved levels of special knowledge not yet attained by others who identified with Christ.

During the first half of the first century, in the city of Alexandria, Egypt, a neoclassical Renaissance had begun in Greek language, literature, and culture. Alexandria became the "new" hub of learning much like Athens had been previously. It was the place where important people would come to learn and do research in the vast Alexandrian library. Among them was a Jew by the name of Philo, a contemporary of the apostle Paul. Philo, who imbibed in Greek philosophy, began reinterpreting the Hebrew Scriptures for the Greek-speaking Jews (Hellenists), which filled the cultural demand for retelling the old stories in new and fanciful ways. In doing this, he sought to gain respectability for the Hebrew stories by allegorizing the various accounts recorded in the Greek Old Testament, such as the story of creation, or the exploits of Samson, or the laws given to the Israelites. After Philo, this style of reinterpreting the Hebrew stories as myths would eventually come to full bloom during the second century under Gnosticism.

The influence of Greek philosophy in the development of Gnosticism. Not only was Greek philosophy influential with regard to how some people interpreted Scripture, but also how they viewed the world and humanity. A significant part of Gnostic thought was to view God, the world, matter and spirit, in a much different way. Generally, Gnostics believed that the material world was impure, and by contrast, the spiritual and immaterial were pure. This perspective on the nature of physical and nonphysical reality led to a new view of creation and ethics.

Unlike the biblical model of creation, in which an immaterial deity identified as Yahweh created the physical universe out of nothing, Gnostics believed that the physical world was created by an evil god. While the creative act originated in the God who is pure spirit, the physical world was made through a cadre of increasingly less pure beings (including the one identified as an evil god). Thus Gnosticism held to a different view of creation and the nature of matter and spirit, as well as an ethical teaching that ran counter to Christianity. Because matter was said to be evil and spirit was said to be good, Gnostics had difficulty with the idea that Jesus was God in human flesh.

Attempts to influence orthodox Christianity. Most scholars believe Gnosticism began in earnest by the second century, most likely after the time of the final destruction of the Jewish people under Hadrian in AD 135.[2] Some have thought that Gnosticism originated during the time of the apostles and the writing of the New Testament, but this is very unlikely.[3] However, there is no question that various strains of thought from the Greek and the Eastern worlds found their way into Gnosticism during the second century. Among these influences were Platonic (Plato's) philosophy (which emerged in first-century Alexandria), the stories of the Jews and early Christians, and Zoroastrian dualism from Persia.

The Gnostics attempted to draw Christians away from sound doctrine and the church. One way they did this was through the writing of "gospels" about Jesus that

were supposedly composed by first-century apostles such as Peter, James, and Thomas. These alternative gospels, however, were not written during the lifetimes of these individuals, but much later. Furthermore, these alternative gospels did not speak about Jesus in a manner that reflected the Jewish community and the Hebrew faith depicted in the four authentic Gospels. Rather, they created a uniquely Gnostic Jesus, which was largely rejected by the church.

To some Gnostics, Jesus was seen as a spirit (since matter was impure) sent from the ultimate deity to save humanity by providing special knowledge about salvation. To accomplish this, it was necessary for Jesus to *appear* to be human (known as docetism, from the Greek word *dokein* meaning "to seem" or "to appear") and share this spiritual knowledge with His disciples, rather than have them express faith in Him. According to Gnostic thought, Jesus never became truly human. Some of these ideas were already developing by the end of the first century, but it wasn't until later that they became a tenet of the Gnostic belief system.

Of course, one who has read the Gospel of John (John 1:1,14), as well as John's epistles, would immediately recognize the human Jesus and reject these Gnostic heresies. In addition, John clearly condemned in the strongest terms (e.g., "spirit of antichrist") those who made the claim that Jesus did not come in the flesh (1 John 4:1-4; 2 John 7). Paul's teaching on faith also stood in contrast to the Gnostic view of salvation by special knowledge (Romans 10:9-10).

The Gnostic Gospels

Space limitations permit only a brief mention of the various Gnostic gospels, which were written from approximately AD 120–180.

Though the Gnostic gospels have some similarities to the New Testament Gospels, none of the writers were companions (or eyewitnesses) of those who were the original recipients of the apostolic message. The general opinion of scholars who study these alternative gospels is that there are no *copies* that date into the second century, and the original compositions date from generally the middle of the second century onward.[4]

The Gospel According to Thomas. Possibly the most famous of the alternative gospels is the Gospel of Thomas, which was discovered at Nag Hammadi in Egypt.[5] This work is composed of 114 short sayings attributed to Jesus, and probably dates from about AD 140[6] to 180.[7] There is debate among scholars whether this is truly a Gnostic work, or whether it merely shares aspects of mystical thinking that were present in the first century and were later absorbed into second-century Gnosticism. Even though Thomas contains heretical teaching, it also seems to borrow from the first century New Testament Gospels,[8] though presenting them through Gnostic filters. It also contains references to books that are known to have originated during the second century.[9]

Gospel According to Philip. This is not really a gospel, but a collection of short portions from other Gnostic writers. It summarizes the thinking of some of the disciples of the Gnostic named Valentinus, and was most likely written during the second half of the third century AD.[10] This work also contains a fragmented but seemingly significant statement on page 63 of codex 2, lines 32 through 36: "The companion of the [...] Mary Magdalene [...] her more than [...] kiss her [...] on her [...]." The suggestion has been made that the restored text would read, "the companion of the [Savior is] Mary

Magdalene. [But Christ loved] her more than [all] the disciples [and used to] kiss her [often] on her [...]."[11]

Craig Evans notes that some scholars believe the text indicates that He kissed Mary on her lips, but other words are also possible. Moreover, were these events to have occurred, they should be seen in light of Middle Eastern culture, in which a kiss would have been more a statement of respect and honor than an indication of a romantic relationship.[12]

Gospel According to Mary [Magdalene]. This work is one of the more familiar of the Nag Hammadi gospels because of its use by the novelist Dan Brown in the *Da Vinci Code.* According to Brown's novel, Mary was allegedly the wife of Jesus, and this gospel includes additional information. The pertinent verse reads "Peter says to Mary, 'Sister, we know that you are much loved by the Savior, as no other woman. Therefore tell us what words of the Savior you know, what we have not heard'" (6:1-2). In this text, as well as the remainder of the book, the focus is upon Mary being received by Jesus as a disciple, not a lover.[13]

Gospel of Truth. According to the majority of scholars, this text is a translation of a Greek original, and the Coptic copy was carelessly transmitted with many scribal errors. This includes individual letters written or erased over, omitted letters inserted above the line of the text or in the margins, and an omitted phrase that is found at the bottom of the page.[14]

There was no title to the book in the manuscript, but modern scholars have used the title *Gospel of Truth,*[15] although Jacqueline A. Williams suggests that it is reasonable to have been its actual title.[16]

This gospel may be the one spoken of by Irenaeus in his *Adversus Haeresis* ("Against

Heresies") when he said that the Valentinians used a "Gospel of Truth" that was different from the canonical Gospels.[17] The author of the *Gospel of Truth* developed a complex and often confusing discussion of the various levels of reality that began from the unbegotten Father through the Son from the Father, explaining how the Son represents the Father to bring persons to knowledge of the Father.[18] This is characteristic of much Gnostic thought, which understands salvation not as faith in Christ, but as gaining secret knowledge.

Additional Gospels. There are several more Gnostic gospels, including *The Apocryphon of John*, *The Apocryphon of James*, *The Gospel of Nicodemus*, the *Gospel of the Egyptians*, and the *Lost Gospel of Peter*. Each gospel has unique features, but they share in common a late date, seeking to borrow in various ways from the first-century authentic Gospels. What all these works share in common is an attempt to promote another gospel.

Greater Appreciation for the True Gospels

There has been much attention given to these writings discovered in the sands of Egypt, but not because they help us to understand more about Jesus or the beginning of the Christian church. Rather, their intrigue comes from offering a different look at the person of Christ and a new perspective on salvation, the nature of the universe, and ethical teachings.

None of these books were authored by the person whose name appears on them, and they say little—in some cases, nothing at all—about the historical life of Christ. They only seek to provide additional or alternative sayings of Christ. The Christian who has not had exposure to these books has lost little, if anything.

On the positive side, these works give us a much greater appreciation for the authentic Scriptures of the New Testament, which were written with careful attention to historical detail and spiritual truth!

21

How Do We Know That Jesus Is God?

Ron Rhodes

Christians who are interested in apologetics must have a firm grasp of not only the positive arguments *for* the deity of Christ, but also be able to answer objections *against* Jesus's deity. In this chapter, we will address both.

Arguments That Demonstrate Christ's Deity

Jesus Is Yahweh. Yahweh is an Old Testament term for God meaning "LORD." A comparison of Old Testament verses about Yahweh with New Testament verses about Jesus points to Jesus's identity as Yahweh. In Isaiah 40:3, for example, we read a prophecy of Jesus: "In the wilderness prepare the way of the LORD; make straight in the desert a highway for our God." "LORD" here is literally "Yahweh," just as "God" is literally "Elohim." Jesus is the Yahweh/Elohim of Isaiah 40:3 (see Mark 1:2-4).

In Isaiah 44:24 Yahweh asserts: "I am the LORD, who made all things, who alone stretched out the heavens, who spread out the earth by myself." In the New Testament, however, Christ is presented as the Creator of "all things" (John 1:3; Colossians 1:16). Christ, as the Creator, is Yahweh, just as the Father

is Yahweh. Creation is "from" the Father, but "through" Jesus Christ (1 Corinthians 8:6), and both persons are identified as Yahweh in Scripture. (Such verses are obviously supportive of the doctrine of the Trinity.)

Isaiah witnessed the divine glory of Yahweh in Isaiah 6:1-5. He spoke of Yahweh "sitting upon a throne, high and lifted up" (verse 1). Later, the apostle John—under the inspiration of the Holy Spirit—wrote that Isaiah "saw Christ's glory" (John 12:41 NET Bible). Yahweh's glory and Jesus's glory are hereby equated.

In Zechariah 12:10, Yahweh spoke prophetically: "When they look on me, on him whom they have pierced, they shall mourn for him." Though Yahweh was speaking, this is clearly a reference to Christ's future crucifixion. Jesus is described as the one they have "pierced" by the apostle John in Revelation 1:7. (See also Isaiah 44:6 compared with Revelation 1:17; Isaiah 60:19-20 compared with Revelation 21:23; Isaiah 43:11 compared with Titus 2:13.)

Jesus Has the Names and Titles of God. In addition to the above evidences that Jesus is Yahweh or Lord, Jesus in John 8:58 informed some Jews, "Truly, truly, I say to you, before Abraham was, I am." The Jews immediately picked up stones with the intention of killing Jesus, for they understood He was identifying Himself as Yahweh—the "I AM" of Exodus 3:14. Jesus is Lord.

Likewise, Jesus is identified as Elohim in Isaiah 9:6 (the Messiah is "Mighty God") and Isaiah 40:3 ("make straight in the desert a highway *for our God*"). Elohim literally means "strong one" or "mighty God," and its plural ending (*im* in Hebrew) indicates fullness of power. It is a common name for God in the Old Testament. Jesus is God.

Further, Jesus is identified as *Theos*, a common New Testament Greek word translated "God." It corresponds to the Old Testament Elohim. Jesus is recognized as *Theos* by doubting Thomas (John 20:28), a jailer (Acts 16:31-34), the apostle Paul (Titus 2:13), and Peter (1 Peter 1:1). The heavenly Father even said to Jesus, "Your throne, O God [*Theos*], is forever and ever" (Hebrews 1:8).

Jesus is also identified as *Kurios*, a common New Testament Greek term for "Lord." It is equivalent to the Old Testament Yahweh. The apostle Paul wrote that Christ was given a name above every name, "that at the name of Jesus every knee should bow...and every tongue confess that Jesus Christ *is Lord* [*Kurios*]" (Philippians 2:9-11). Paul, an Old Testament scholar par excellence, was alluding to Isaiah 45:22-24: "I am God, and there is no other...To me every knee shall bow, every tongue shall swear allegiance." Jesus is Lord.

Jesus Has the Attributes of God. For example, Jesus is eternal. John 1:1 affirms, "In the beginning was the Word, and the Word was with God, and the Word was God." The word "was" is an imperfect tense, indicating continuous, ongoing existence. When the time-space universe first came into being, Christ already existed as God.

Jesus is also self-existent. As the Creator of all things (John 1:3), Christ Himself must be *un*created. Because He is "before all things" (Colossians 1:17), He does not depend on anyone or anything outside Himself for His existence.

Jesus is omnipresent. He promised His disciples "where two or three are gathered in my name, there am I among them" (Matthew 18:20). The only way He could be simultaneously present with believers worldwide is if He is omnipresent. Likewise, after commissioning the disciples to bring the gospel to all nations, Jesus assured them, "I am with you always, to the end of the age" (Matthew 28:20). The only way Christ could do this is if He were everywhere present (Ephesians 1:23; 4:10; Colossians 3:11). (Note: The fact that Christ, as God, is everywhere present does not contradict the concept that He also has locality as a human. Christ, in the incarnation, is fully God and fully human.)

Jesus is omniscient. His disciples acknowledged, "Now we know that you know all things" (John 16:30; see also 21:17). Jesus knew the future (John 11:11; 18:4) and knew specific details about what would happen (Matthew 21:2-4). He knew from a distance that Lazarus had died (John 11:14). He knows the Father as the Father knows Him (John 7:29; 8:55; 10:15; 17:25).

Jesus is omnipotent. Christ created the entire universe (Colossians 1:16) and sustains it by His power (Colossians 1:17). In the Gospels we read that He exercised power over nature (Luke 8:25), over physical diseases (Mark 1:29-31), over demonic spirits (Mark 1:32-34), and even over death (John 11:1-44).

In Keeping with His Divine Attributes, Jesus Did What Only God Can Do. Only God can be the Creator (Isaiah 44:24), and yet Jesus is the Creator (John 1:3; Colossians

1:16). Only God can be the Savior (Isaiah 43:11), and yet Jesus is our "great God and Savior" (Titus 2:13). Only God can forgive sin (Isaiah 43:25), and yet Jesus forgives sin (Mark 2:5,7).

The Old Testament teaches that only God is the giver of life (Deuteronomy 32:39; 1 Samuel 2:6; Psalm 119). Yet Jesus claims this power for Himself: "As the Father raises the dead and gives them life, so also the Son gives life to whom he will" (John 5:21).

Jesus's miracles provide further evidence of His divine identity. In the Gospel of John, Jesus's miracles are often called "signs." These signs always *signify* something—in this case, that Jesus is the prophesied divine Messiah. Among the more notable signs performed by Jesus were changing water into wine (John 2:7-8), calming a stormy sea (Matthew 8:26; Mark 4:39; Luke 8:24), feeding 5,000 men and their families (Matthew 14:19; Mark 6:41; Luke 9:16; John 6:11), walking on water (Matthew 14:25; Mark 6:48; John 6:19), and raising Lazarus from the dead (John 11:43-44).

Jesus Accepted Worship as God. The New Testament demonstrates that while holy men refused worship (Acts 14:15), as did angels (Revelation 22:8-9), Jesus accepted worship on numerous occasions, in perfect keeping with His claim to be God. Jesus accepted worship from Thomas (John 20:28), the angels (Hebrews 1:6), some wise men (Matthew 2:11), a leper (Matthew 8:2), a ruler (Matthew 9:18), a blind man (John 9:38), an anonymous woman (Matthew 15:25), Mary Magdalene (Matthew 28:9), and the disciples (Matthew 28:17).

Scripture is consistent on the fact that *only God* can be worshipped. Exodus 34:14 tell us: "You shall worship no other god, for the LORD, whose name is Jealous, is a jealous God" (see also Deuteronomy 6:13; Matthew

4:10). The fact that Jesus accepted worship on numerous occasions testifies to His identity as God.

Others Recognized Jesus as God. Thomas saw the wounds of the resurrected Christ and cried out, "My Lord and my God!" (John 20:28). Paul made reference to "Christ, who is God over all" (Romans 9:5). He referred to Jesus as the one in whom "the whole fullness of deity dwells bodily" (Colossians 2:9). In Titus, Jesus is recognized as "our great God and Savior" (2:13). The heavenly Father's words to the Son are recorded in Hebrews: "Your throne, O God, is forever and ever" (1:8).

Early followers of Christ recognized His deity. Ignatius, who died by AD 116, wrote of "the blood of God" in chapter 1 of his *Letter to the Ephesians.* Mathetes, a disciple of the apostles who died AD 130, wrote of Christ as King, God, man, and Savior. Justin Martyr, who wrote about AD 138–165, referred to Christ as the one "who is Himself this God begotten of the Father" (*Dialogue with Trypho,* ch. 61). Melito of Sardis, who died AD 180, said of the crucifixion "God is murdered." Irenaeus (AD 120–202) wrote in *Against Heresies,* "Jesus is Himself in His own right...God, and Lord."

Jesus's Deity Was Evident in His Teachings. The teachings of Jesus were always presented as being ultimate and final. Jesus never wavered in this. He unflinchingly placed His teachings above those of Moses and the Jewish prophets. He always spoke in His own authority. He never said, "Thus says the LORD..." as did the Jewish prophets; He always said, "Truly, truly, I say to you..."

Jesus never retracted anything He said, never guessed or spoke with uncertainty, never made revisions, never contradicted Himself, and never apologized for what He said. He boldly asserted that "heaven and earth will pass away, but my words will not pass away" (Mark 13:31).

One cannot read the New Testament Gospels long before recognizing that Jesus regarded Himself and His message as inseparable. The reason His teachings had authority was because of His identity as God. The *words of Jesus* were the *words of God* (John 6:35; 7:37-38; 10:10; 14:27; Matthew 11:28).

Answering Objections to Christ's Deity

Not surprisingly, cults that deny Jesus is God cite Bible verses that they believe indicate Jesus is lesser than the Father. In each case, they misinterpret the verse in question. Following is a brief sampling of how to answer such cultic misinterpretations:

While John 3:16 makes reference to Jesus as the Son of God, this title indicates not inferiority, but that Jesus has the *same divine nature* as the Father (John 5:18 makes this clear). Among the ancients, "Son of..." often indicated "Same nature as..."

While John 14:28 quotes Jesus as saying the Father was greater than Him, He was speaking *positionally*—that is, the Father was in heavenly glory, while Jesus was on earth, soon to be crucified.

While Colossians 1:15 calls Jesus the "firstborn [Greek, *prototokos*] of all creation," this phrase indicates not that Jesus was created, but rather that He was *preeminent*. Jesus was presented as preeminent over creation (verse 15) because He *created* the creation (verse 16) and *sustains* the creation (verse 17). This is confirmed by recognizing that others in the Old Testament, such as Israel (Exodus 4:22), David (Psalm 89:27), and Ephraim (Jeremiah 31:9), were described as "firstborn" despite the fact that chronologically, other nations were older than Israel, and David

and Ephraim had older brothers. In this context, "firstborn" does not always mean first created, but more appropriately refers to preeminence—in the case of Colossians 1:15, *Christ's* preeminence.

While Mark 13:32 indicates Jesus did not know the hour of His return, Jesus was speaking only from His finite human nature. Christ in His divine nature is omniscient (Matthew 11:27; 17:27; Luke 5:4,6; John 7:29; 8:55; 10:15; 16:30; 17:25; 21:6-11,17). While fulfilling His messianic mission on earth, Jesus voluntarily chose not to use some of His divine attributes on some occasions (Philippians 2:5-11).

While 1 Corinthians 11:3 says, "the head of Christ is God," and in John 14:28 Jesus said, "The Father is greater than I," these passages speak only of the Father's authority over Jesus. The 1 Corinthians verse indicates that just as a husband is *functionally* the head of the wife even though both are equally human (Genesis 1:26-28), so the Father is functionally the head of Christ even though both are equally divine (John 10:30).

In John, the Son was simply referring to the Father's greater *office*, much like the difference between the offices occupied by the president and vice president. The president is greater than the vice president in terms of office, but they are equal in nature—they are both human. The same is true between the Father and the Son.

While Revelation 3:14 says that Jesus was the "beginning of God's creation," the Greek word for "beginning" (*arche*) carries the idea of *beginner*—that is, Jesus *created* God's creation (see John 1:3; Colossians 1:16).

It is clear to the impartial observer that Scripture—properly interpreted in context—always points to the absolute and unqualified deity of Jesus Christ. *Jesus is God!*

Is There Evidence That Jesus Rose from the Dead?

Gary R. Habermas and Benjamin C.F. Shaw

The late eminent New Testament scholar Raymond Brown argued that the most prominent view in New Testament Christological studies at the end of the twentieth century was that of moderate conservatism. If Brown is correct that this position (moderate conservatism) is "the most agreed upon scholarly approach to Christology,"[1] it may likewise provide a hint regarding what seems to be a recent positive shift toward a more open view of the resurrection of Jesus.[2]

What accounts for these recent, major research trends? It seems that at least two developments have contributed significantly to the more positive historical outlook today regarding the New Testament text in general and its historical portions in particular. Playing the key roles in these studies pertaining to both Christology as well as to the historicity of Jesus's resurrection appearances are two recent developments: the application of the historical criteria of authenticity, and the critical recognition of the historical role played by the early New Testament creedal passages.

This essay addresses these two recent trends and the data they contribute to resurrection studies, in addition to providing an overview of the Minimal Facts Argument for Jesus's resurrection.

The Historical Criteria of Authenticity

First, over the past century, historians have been developing and clarifying various tools that help them to assess whether or not an event has occurred in the past. Among the most important has been the use of historical "criteria" in evaluating reported historical events (and sayings). These criteria function like proverbs that guide historians rather than merely inputting data into a mathematical-like formula in order to tabulate whether or not an event is historical.

While there is still some debate regarding the use of the historical criteria, it is important to note that these criteria can only be used to add to the probability that an event has occurred. For example, if a reported event meets the criteria of multiple independent attestation (meaning that it is attested to by a number of different and independent sources), then this can *add* to the likelihood of the event having occurred. In general, the greater the number of criteria that are met regarding an event, then the greater the probability that the event occurred.

In the same way that everyday tools like hammers and saws have limitations, so too the historical criteria have limitations as tools for historians and for further application by New Testament scholars. If an event fails to meet some of the criteria, then *it does not follow* that the event is therefore nonhistorical. Trying to use historical criteria for a negative conclusion would be an inappropriate use of the tool—much like trying to use a hammer to saw a piece of wood. The hammer is the wrong tool for the job. The late New Testament scholar Ben Meyer provided a nice summary of the value of historical criteria: "[T]heir presence positively tells in favor of historicity, but their absence does not positively tell against historicity."[3] The criteria, then, are among both the historians' as well as the New Testament scholars' tools that can add to the confidence level for whether or not an event occurred.

As will be shown in more detail below, the use of historical criteria has led to an increasing affirmation of the events surrounding Jesus's resurrection. Many of the minimal historical facts surrounding this event meet the standards of multiple criteria. Among the most popular principles for application to the resurrection appearance accounts are the two criteria of early and eyewitness sources, along with multiple independent attestation, and embarrassment. The application of these and occasionally other criteria has led a number of critical scholars from a wide variety of theological backgrounds to affirm the historicity of particular events.

Early New Testament Creeds

Second, early New Testament preliterary or creedal material[4] provides another significant reason for the move toward more conservative views of the resurrection data. Perhaps the most helpful way to introduce these almost always brief texts is to say that creeds are basically the answer to this question, What was the theme of the earliest apostolic preaching prior to the appearance of the very first New Testament writings? The answer is that these traditions filled that role, encapsulating the earliest statements of fundamental strata on which the church is based, even for that majority of early believers who were illiterate but could certainly memorize or sing these messages.

This oral material took various forms such as hymns (Philippians 2:3-11), sermon summaries (drawn from texts like Acts 2:14-39; 4:8-12), or creedal statements and affirmations of the central doctrinal components of the Christian faith (chiefly 1 Corinthians 15:3ff.[5]). These are crucially important building blocks because these creedal passages *pre*date the writings in which they are presently located. Some are pre-Pauline, meaning that they date from prior to Paul's conversion! Hence, these texts were foundational. By studying them, we are hearing the earliest Christian gospel message![6]

Ironically, it was scholars who often assumed skeptical positions regarding the New Testament who brought these creeds to light decades ago. These scholars held that the canonical texts were preserved to meet the existential needs or desires of various Christian communities, whether or not Jesus actually taught these things. They said this concern took a priority over the value of preserving the historical material. New Testament scholar Darrell Bock writes that these opponents "argued that the [oral] tradition was influenced more by a concern for the life setting (*Sitz im Leben*) of the community to which the tradition was directed than for the setting of the event in Jesus' life."[7] These earlier researchers operated upon skeptical assumptions regarding these writings and sought to "get behind" the texts to whatever authentic historical material may lie behind it.

However, these presuppositions backfired in the sense of the scholars' realization that their assuming an unreliable transmission of tradition caused them to acknowledge the confirmed presence of formal, memorized oral traditions that are less susceptible to such bending of the tradition, potentially providing early historical material that existed prior to the writings themselves. So these snippets of the initial proclamations had opened a window into the early content of the Christian message years before it was first written.

Skeptics have recognized this as well, and they now readily concede the importance of the oral formulas. The agnostic Bart Ehrman, for example, writes, "The value of being able to isolate preliterary traditions is that they give us access to what Christians were believing and how they were extolling God and Christ *before* our earliest surviving writings."[8] Jewish New Testament researcher Pinchas Lapide even affirmed that Jesus *was* actually resurrected from the dead and argued that some of these oral traditions, such as stated in 1 Corinthians 15:3ff., could be traced back to the actual eyewitnesses of these events.[9]

Thus, as some critics sought to find the historical material that lurked behind the text, they helped discern various oral traditions that were previously embedded in the texts! These oral formulas have provided scholars with initial information regarding the views of the earliest Christians. These texts have also contributed a line of evidence that argues against the critics' own assumptions that the New Testament writers freely created stories based upon their needs. Instead, this process indicated that believers were careful to preserve the oral traditions that were being passed down to them.[10]

The Resurrection of Jesus: The Minimal Facts Argument

These two developments over recent decades—the criteria of authenticity and the realizations regarding the early creedal texts embedded in the New Testament books—have helped immensely in the study of Jesus's resurrection. Each, in its own way, has gone further in helping to establish the historicity of this event.

While defending an aspect of the more traditional reliability argument, Lydia McGrew recently made a laudatory comment regarding the Minimal Facts Argument. Appreciating it in part, McGrew noted the "near-exclusive use in Christian apologetic circles" of this argument in recent years.[11] Why is this argument so popular of late?

The Minimal Facts Argument is built on two prerequisites: (1) No historical data are employed unless they are supported by several strong arguments each. (2) As a result, virtually all critical New Testament scholars (including even atheistic, agnostic, and other non-Christian researchers) agree with the historicity of each fact. Of these two criteria, it should be noted that the first one is *by far* the more crucial of the two.[12]

Over the years, Habermas has used anywhere from three to eight minimal facts, with the number varying because it is somewhat arbitrary in the sense that virtually no scholar allows *only* this abbreviated number. Of late, six facts have been the usual quantity.

Employing just six of these facts we would include (1) Jesus's death by crucifixion, (2) that the disciples had real experiences that they thought were appearances of the risen Jesus, and (3) that the resurrection event was proclaimed a very short time after the crucifixion. Further, (4) Jesus's disciples were transformed by these experiences, even to the point of being willing to die specifically for this resurrection message. Last, (5) James the brother of Jesus and (6) Paul (Saul of Tarsus) were converted by experiences that they likewise thought were resurrection appearances of Jesus.

A recent count of this research determined that there is a minimum of eight to thirteen arguments of various sorts for each of these six historical facts. These "backup" evidences are of varying strengths, though they draw heavily from both the historical criteria of authenticity as well as the creedal data mentioned earlier.

Most commonly used from the criteria of authenticity are the tests already mentioned: the early and eyewitness sources; along with multiple attestation of sources; plus embarrassing features, such as women being the chief witnesses to Jesus's crucifixion, His burial, and His resurrection appearances. From the creeds, by far the primary emphasis is on 1 Corinthians 15:3-8. Additional reasons further support these six facts as well.

When the entire list of supportive arguments is posted, it is far more apparent why virtually all critical scholars endorse these six facts with very little dispute. But the account does not end there. In turn, this combined case is capable of doing three things: (1) the strongest evidences favoring Jesus's resurrection are provided from these data; (2) they also offer the most crucial refutations of the major naturalistic hypotheses in opposition to this event; (3) plus, these prior two tactics may be carried out with just this minimal foundation, making this maneuver much more concise and easy to handle. Perhaps that is why McGrew attested that the Minimal Facts Argument's "widespread use may be in part a result of the fact that it provides a straightforward template for a debate format."[13]

In addition, this approach provides a grounding from these historical facts that supplies a foundation for the center of Christian theology; such as the gospel message itself. Finally, these facts also provide bridges to Christian ministry and practice.[14] All in all, this is a remarkable amount of uses for a brief, concentrated historical argument.

Did Christianity Copy Earlier Pagan Resurrection Stories?

Edwin M. Yamauchi

In antiquity, people of the Near Eastern and Greco-Roman worlds believed in life after death, generally as bodiless souls or spirits.[1] In certain Jewish circles later associated with the Pharisees, a belief in the resurrection of the body after death developed.[2] To be certain, the resurrection of Jesus Christ is the essential core of Christianity.

But some have maintained that the resurrection of Christ is patterned after the prototype of Near Eastern "dying and rising gods." Others have argued that Paul's interpretation of baptism as an initiation rite, which united believers with the risen Christ, was influenced by Greco-Roman mystery religions.[3]

Dying and Rising Vegetation Gods

The theory that there was a widespread worship of a dying and rising god—Tammuz in Mesopotamia, Adonis in Syria, Attis in Asia Minor, and Osiris in Egypt—was propounded by Sir James Frazer, who gathered a mass of parallels in part IV of his monumental work *The Golden Bough* (1906, reprinted in 1961).[4] Frazer regarded the name Adonis (Semitic *Adon,* meaning "Lord") to be a title for the Mesopotamian Tammuz. In addition, German scholars such as Otto Pfleiderer and Richard Reitzenstein drew explicit comparisons between these "dying and rising gods" and the resurrection of Christ. Reitzenstein's influential work, *Die hellenistischen Mysterienreligionen* (1910), which was not translated into English until 1978, argued that Paul was profoundly influenced by Egyptian and Phrygian mystery religions.[5] Scholars like Reitzenstein and Wilhelm Bousset, who were members of the *Religionsgeschichtliche Schule* ("History of Religions School"), exerted a profound influence on the leading German New Testament scholar Rudolf Bultmann, who, in writing about Paul's understanding of baptism, stated: "The meaning of the latter is to impart to the initiates a share of the fate of the cult-deity who has suffered death and reawakened to life, such as Attis, Adonis, or Osiris."[6]

In the 1930s, three influential French scholars, M. Goguel, C. Guignebert, and A. Loisy, also interpreted Christianity as a syncretistic religion formed under the influence of Hellenistic mystery religions. According to Loisy, Christ was "a saviour-god, after the manner of an Osiris, an Attis, a Mithra…Like Adonis, Osiris, and Attis he had died a violent death, and like them he had returned to life…"[7]

Many who little realize its fragile foundations have adopted this view. For instance, Hugh Schonfield has declared, "The revelations of Frazer in *The Golden Bough* had not got through to the masses…Christians remained related under the skin to the devotees of Adonis and Osiris, Dionysus and Mithras."[8] Furthermore, John H. Randall, emeritus professor of philosophy at Columbia University, has asserted, "Christianity, at the hands of Paul, became a mystical system of redemption, much like the cult of Isis, and the other sacramental or mystery religions of the day."[9] Timothy Freke and Peter Gandy allege, "Jesus is Osiris-Dionysus thinly disguised as the Jewish Messiah in order to make the Pagan Mysteries accessible to Jews."[10] What is more, Roland Guy Bonnel and Vincent Arieh Tobin, in comparing Christ and Osiris, state: "In particular the concept of a god who dies and rises again was widespread over the area for many centuries before the advent of Christianity."[11] They conclude, "With such parallels it is difficult to avoid the conclusion that some form of influence must have been exercised by the Egyptian myth on the development of the Christian tradition."[12] The explanation of the Christian resurrection by such a comparative-religions approach has even been reflected in official Soviet propaganda.[13]

A reexamination of the sources used to support the theory of a mythical origin of Christ's resurrection reveals that the evidences are far from satisfactory and that the parallels are quite superficial.

Dumuzi (Tammuz)

The Sumerian name *Dumuzi* means "the Good Son" (in Akkadian language the name is Tammuz). There were two Sumerian kings called Dumuzi listed in the King List (Sumer is ancient southern Iraq), leading some scholars to think that one of these kings may have been deified. It is noteworthy that early Sumerian kings played the role of Dumuzi in a *hieros gamos* "sacred marriage" with a cultic prostitute on New Year's Day.[14]

As a god, Dumuzi was primarily a shepherd. The view of Thorkild Jacobsen that he also represented the power of the date and of the grain has been disputed.[15]

The primary rituals first attested at Mari (eighteenth century BC) concerned the death and disappearance of Dumuzi/Tammuz. These were held in midsummer, coinciding with the diminution of milk from goats and sheep at that season.[16] (The Jewish month Tammuz corresponds to July.)

Scholars had assumed a resurrection of the god by the goddess (Sumerian Inanna is the same as the Akkadian Ishtar) even though the end of both the Sumerian and the Akkadian texts of the myth of "The Descent of Inanna (Ishtar)" had not been preserved.[17] In 1960, Samuel N. Kramer published a new poem, "The Death of Dumuzi," which proves conclusively that instead of rescuing Dumuzi from the underworld, Inanna sent him there as her substitute.[18] According to Bendt Alster, "The question whether or not Dumuzi rose from the realms of the dead is perhaps best answered with the claim that since this was not celebrated in a cultic festival, it did not play any significant role in the literature."[19] The last lines of the preserved Akkadian text of "The Descent of Ishtar" do speak of Tammuz "coming up" with mourners. This is not a reference to his resurrection, but to the common belief that the shades will arise to partake of funerary offerings: "The dead shall come up and smell the incense offerings."[20] A line in a fragmentary and obscure text is the only positive evidence that, after being sent to the underworld, Dumuzi may have had his sister, Geshtinanna, take his place for half the year.[21]

In the Old Testament, there is one reference to Tammuz: "Then he brought me to the entrance of the north gate of the house of the Lord, and behold, there sat women weeping for Tammuz" (Ezekiel 8:14). Origen's identification of Tammuz with Adonis was incorporated into the Vulgate: "Adonidem." According to Jerome, Hadrian desecrated the cave in Bethlehem associated with Jesus's birth by building a shrine for Tammuz-Adonis.

Adonis

Adonis was the handsome youth beloved of Aphrodite, who was killed by a boar. The hero was transformed into a bright red anemone flower. His premature death was lamented by women in Athens, who planted "gardens of Adonis" with fast-growing vegetation that was placed on rooftops. This vegetation wilted in a week in the hot summer, signifying the death of vegetation (Aristophanes, *Lysistrata* 708-39).[22] Theocritus, in his Idyll 15, described a ceremony lamenting Adonis's death. This was held at the palace of Ptolemy II (c. 250 BC) at Alexandria. At the end of the festival, the image of Adonis was cast into the sea.

Tryggve N.D. Mettinger reports: "As far as I can find, there is nothing in the Greek rites for Adonis that implies a celebration of his resurrection."[23] P. Lambrechts has shown that there is no trace of a resurrection in the early texts or pictorial representations of Adonis; the four texts that speak of his resurrection

are quite late, dating from the second to the fourth centuries AD.[24] The earliest is Lucian's *De Syria Dea* ("The Syrian Goddess"), which dates from the second century AD. Lucian declared: "As a memorial of his suffering each year they beat their breasts, mourn, and celebrate…but then, on the next day, they proclaim that he lives and send him into the air."[25] Lucian also reports, "There are some inhabitants of Byblos who say that the Egyptian Osiris is buried among them and that all the laments and the rites are performed not for Adonis but for Osiris."[26] Lambrechts and other scholars have suggested that the so-called "resurrection" of Adonis was due to the influence of Osiris (see below).

Baal

After the publication of the important Ugaritic texts (1400–1200 BC) from Ras Shamra in Syria, some scholars applied Frazer's category of "dying and rising gods" to Baal, the leading god in the pantheon.[27] Though fragmentary, the Baal epic relates how the god Mot ("Death") caused the death and disappearance of Baal, which resulted in drought and famine for seven years. Then his sister Anat vanquished Death, and Baal and fertility revived again. Baal was not a vegetation deity but a storm god. His myth may indeed be an example of a "dying and rising" god, but one that does not correspond with an annual cycle. There is, however, a noticeable lack of any indication that such a myth had any ritual significance. Mark S. Smith comments, "To my mind, it is especially striking that the rich indigenous corpus of Ugaritic ritual texts does not contain a single indication of the death and rising of Baal."[28]

Attis

Attis was the consort of the mother goddess (*magna mater*) Cybele of Anatolia.[29]

Their cult was never popular in Greece, but when Hannibal of Carthage invaded Italy in 218 BC and kept defeating Roman armies, the Sibylline Oracle advised the Romans to invite Cybele to Rome. Her cult object, a black meteorite stone, was housed in a temple on the Palatine Hill.

According to myth, Cybele, in a jealous rage, rendered Attis mad, which resulted in his emasculating himself. His priests, the *galli*, were eunuchs. Romans were not allowed to join the cult until 102 BC.

The festivities of the cult, the *Megalensia*, were held in March. They included a procession of galli, who whipped themselves to the accompaniment of drums and cymbals as they mourned the death of Attis. The *Hilaria*, a joyful celebration of the hero's "resurrection," is not attested before the middle of the second century AD.[30]

The *taurobolium* was a bloody rite associated with the worship of Attis (and of Mithras), in which a bull was slaughtered on a grating over an initiate in a pit below, drenching him with blood. This was suggested by Reitzenstein as the basis of the Christian's redemption by blood and Paul's imagery in Romans 6 of the believer's death and resurrection. Günter Wagner points out how anachronistic such comparisons are:

> The taurobolium in the Attis cult is first attested in the time of Antoninus Pius for A.D. 160. As far as we can see at present it only became a personal consecration at the beginning of the third century A.D. The idea of a rebirth through the instrumentality of the taurobolium only emerges in isolated instances towards the end of the fourth century A.D.; it is not originally associated with this blood-bath.[31]

By the fourth century AD, Christianity may have influenced some mystery religions. Bruce Metzger, in an important essay, notes:

> Thus, for example, one must doubtless interpret the change in the efficacy attributed to the rite of the taurobolium. In competing with Christianity, which promised eternal life to its adherents, the cult of Cybele officially or unofficially raised the efficacy of the blood bath from twenty years to eternity.[32]

Osiris

Osiris was the most important Egyptian god concerned with the cult of the dead. Frazer had conceived of him as a vegetation god, but his myth has been shown to have developed from royal ideology.[33] From the Egyptian texts themselves there are but scattered allusions to his myth from the Old Kingdom (c. 2500 BC) Pyramid Texts,[34] and the Middle Kingdom (c. 2000 BC) Coffin Texts.[35] The Book of the Dead, which was developed in the New Kingdom (c. 1500 BC), contained scores of spells to enable the deceased to become divine.[36] From the New Kingdom we have the great Osiris Hymn (c. 1500 BC), which is "the fullest account" in Egyptian texts extant.[37] The most complete and coherent account of the myth is narrated by a Greek writer from the Roman period, Plutarch (AD 50–129).[38]

According to the myth, Seth tricked his brother Osiris into climbing inside a beautiful chest, which he then tossed into the Nile River. One might assume that Osiris drowned, though no text explicitly states this. In any case, the chest eventually washed up on the shore at Byblos in Phoenicia, where Isis, his sister and wife, discovered it after a long search. She brought it back to

Egypt and revived Osiris by magic. But then Seth killed Osiris and cut his corpse into 14 parts and scattered them throughout Egypt. Isis was able to collect all the parts except for his reproductive organ, which had been swallowed by a fish. She fashioned a substitute organ, had intimate relations with the reconstructed Osiris, and bore a son, Horus, whom she secretly raised in the delta until he grew to maturity and was able to defeat Seth in a series of contests. Dramatic festivals and rites were held to commemorate the god's death, dismemberment, and resuscitation.[39]

Henceforth, Horus became the god of the living, while Osiris became the god of the dead. Pharaohs were identified with Horus while alive, and with Osiris when dead. Osiris is almost always depicted in a mummiform image seated on his throne. Therefore, while Osiris was resuscitated, he was not in the end "resurrected." Mark S. Smith concludes, "With no resurrection or rising for Osiris, a major cornerstone of Frazer's theory fails in the face of primary evidence."[40]

It is a cardinal misconception to equate the Egyptian view of the afterlife with the "resurrection" of Hebrew-Christian traditions. In order to achieve immortality, the Egyptian had to fulfill three conditions: (1) His body had to be preserved, hence mummification. (2) Nourishment had to be provided either by the actual offering of daily bread and beer, or by the magical depiction of food on the walls of the tomb. (3) Magical spells had to be provided for the deceased.[41] Moreover, the Egyptian did not rise from the dead; separate entities of his personality such as his *ba* and his *ka* continued to hover about his body.[42] Ancient Egyptians did aspire to be identified with Osiris, and to obtain an afterlife with him as his followers.[43]

Mithras

The Persian god Mithras became the focus of a Roman mystery religion known as Mithraism.[44] This became popular among merchants and soldiers who spread this faith to the far ends of the Roman Empire, even to Hadrian's Wall in northern England. While predominantly male, the sect may not have been exclusively so, as there are some patristic (church fathers) references to female members.[45]

There are incidental references in Christian and pagan writings, but there are no detailed expositions of Mithraic doctrines. There are more than 3,000 dedicatory inscriptions and artistic monuments.[46] The Mithraists worshipped in mithraea—small, underground cave-like structures with benches along the walls. The central image was the tauroctony, Mithras stabbing a bull, which has been interpreted along astrological lines, as have a number of attendant images. More than 500 of these tauroctonies have been uncovered. One of the earliest, now in the Cincinnati Art Museum, dates to AD 160–170, while the mithraea all date to the second or third century AD.[47]

The church fathers were well aware of Mithras and his followers. Justin Martyr (c. 100–165), the first great apologist, who recorded that Jesus was born in a cave, knew that the Mithraists worship in a cave-like structure (*Dialogue with Trypho* 78). Their cultic banquets he considered a demonic imitation of the Eucharist (*First Apology* 66). Tertullian of Carthage (c. 160–220) spoke of their initiation "deep in a cavern" (*De corona* 15). He recorded that their followers placed a mark on their foreheads (*De praescriptione haereticorum* 40). Origen (c. 185–254) and Jerome (c. 345–419) both know about the seven grades of their initiation.

Where and when Mithraism developed has been a matter of scholarly debate. The great Belgian scholar Franz Cumont, at the beginning of the twentieth-century, believed that Persian traditions were transmitted through the magi to Anatolia, where the mysteries were developed in the pre-Christian period. He relied in part on a report in Plutarch (c. AD 60–129) that the Cilician pirates Pompey defeated in 65 BC were followers of Mithraic mysteries. But the reliability of this report has been questioned due to the lack of any archaeological or inscriptional evidence for the mysteries in the first century BC,[48] and Cumont's theory has been abandoned.[49]

The scholarly consensus today is that Mithraism arose as a Roman phenomenon late in the first century AD at the earliest. The first literary reference to a Mithraic myth is Statius (AD 80). It is highly significant that mithraea have not been discovered at the sites of Pompeii and Herculaneum, which were buried by the eruption of Vesuvius in AD 79, whereas 14 mithraea have been found at Ostia.[50]

Roger Beck, who has proposed a Commagenian origin of Mithraism, speculates that the court astronomer Tiberius Claudius Balbillus (d. 79), who had ties with Commagene, may have supplied the astrological lore so central to Mithraism.[51] The earliest dated inscription is a dedication by a Roman soldier at Nida in Germany, dated c. AD 90.[52]

Given the relatively late formation of Mithraism, there is no possibility that this mystery religion could have influenced nascent Christianity, nor is there any evidence that it did so later. After a thorough survey of the evidence, Gary Lease concludes, "To be specific, it is clear that the few scattered remarks in Christian polemical literature against Mithraism, together with the scanty archaeological remains of the Mithraic religion, simply do not bear out a direct influence of the one religion upon the other."[53]

Today there are popular books and Internet sites that make unfounded comparisons between Mithras and Christ. For example, Tom Harpur alleges,

> The birth of the Persian sun god, Mithras, also was held to have occurred in a cave at the winter solstice…His birthday was celebrated on December 25. Mithraism, a contemporary and keen rival of early Christianity, had a Eucharist-type meal, observed Sunday as its sacred day, had its major festival at Easter (when Mithras' resurrection was celebrated), and featured miracles, twelve disciples, and a virgin birth.[54]

These descriptions are "modern myths."

The reference to December 25 as the *dies natalis Soli Invicti* (the birthday of the Unconquerable Sun) refers to the emperor Aurelian's dedication to his god, the Sol Invictus, and not to Mithras, who was sometimes addressed with this title and who was associated with the sun. As Halsberghe pointed out in his monograph, these were two distinct deities.[55] Christians at first celebrated Jesus's birth on January 6, as some Eastern Christians still do. The earliest reference to December 25 as Christ's birthday was recorded in AD 336, the year before Constantine's death.

Mithras was not born in a cave. He is most often shown emerging from a rock.[56] There is simply no evidence for Mithras's virgin birth, his 12 disciples, or his resurrection in Mithraic texts and monuments.[57] These are fabrics of a modern myth.

An Abandoned Paradigm

James Frazer was a distinguished classical scholar, but he was not a specialist in Near

Eastern languages. Scholars of comparative religions have abandoned his paradigm of "dying and rising gods." Even such a confirmed skeptic as Robert M. Price dismisses it as "the older, untenable theory that Jesus' resurrection was derived from vegetarian cults centering on mythical dying-and-rising deities like Adonis, Sandan, or Attis."[58]

Mettinger, who does believe that there were indeed pre-Christian dying and rising gods in the Levant, such as Baal, concludes, "There is, as far as I am aware, no *prima facie* evidence that the death and resurrection of Jesus is a mythological construct, drawing on the myths and rites of the dying and rising gods of the surrounding world."[59]

Why Is It Important That Jesus Rose from the Dead?

Phil Fernandes

While many claim to be Christian, not everyone understands the importance of Christ's resurrection. As we will see, the resurrection of Jesus is not an insignificant footnote to the gospel, it is a vital piece of the good news of salvation.

An excellent case for His resurrection has already been presented by Gary Habermas in a previous chapter, as well as in Edwin Yamauchi's formidable defense of the historically unique nature of Christ's resurrection in contrast to the "dying and rising gods" tradition. In this chapter, we will review ten reasons that Christ's resurrection from the grave is so important, and consider why this is the greatest event in human history.

Man's Greatest Enemy— Death—Must Be Defeated

If mankind is to have any hope, his greatest enemy—death—must be defeated. Blaise Pascal, the seventeenth-century philosopher and mathematician, painted a vivid picture of the human dilemma when he wrote:

Imagine a number of men in chains, all under sentence of death, some of whom are each day butchered in the sight of the others; those remaining see their own condition in that of their fellows, and looking at each other with grief and despair await their turn. This is an image of the human condition.[1]

Pascal understood that death was mankind's greatest enemy. If it could not be defeated, then there is no hope for any of us. As a response to this malady, some have resorted to wallowing in despair or diverting attention to self-amusement. But, the wise man, said Pascal, will wager his life on God and seek deliverance from this enemy!

Only in Christianity does God become a man, die for our sins, and rise bodily from the grave to conquer death for all of us. If Jesus of Nazareth did not physically rise from the grave, then human history is one cruel joke. Everyone is born into this world and then they die—death apparently wins in the end. However, if through the resurrection Jesus has conquered the grave, then death has been defeated, giving mankind a unique living hope for life beyond the grave.

Jesus Rose to Validate His Claims: He Is God, Savior, and Messiah

Christ's resurrection is confirmation His bold claims are true. As this work has shown, Jesus revealed Himself to be God incarnate—the Son who became a man (John 5:17-18; 8:23-24; 58-59; 10:30-33; 17:5). In addition, He also presented Himself as the Savior of mankind (Matthew 11:28; Mark 10:45; Luke 19:10; John 3:16-18; 11:25-26; 14:6) and the Jewish Messiah, the one anointed by God the Father to rescue Israel from her enemies (Matthew 16:15-17; Mark 14:61-64; John 4:25-26). To seek confirmation of these claims is only natural, for the bodily resurrection provided the crucial evidence needed to validate His message (Matthew 12:38-40; John 2:18-22; Acts 2:22; Romans 1:4; Hebrews 2:3-4). After all, if Jesus had not risen from the dead, why should anyone believe His promise of eternal life?

Jesus Rose to Fulfill Old Testament Messianic Prophecies

The apostle Paul explained to his readers that Jesus rose from the dead on the third day in accordance with the Old Testament Scriptures (1 Corinthians 15:4). Jesus said, "Everything written about me in the Law of Moses and the Prophets and the Psalms must be fulfilled...Thus it is written, that the Christ should suffer and on the third day rise from the dead" (Luke 24:44-46). Therefore, He had to rise from the dead on the third day if He truly was the Jewish Messiah who came to fulfill the Old Testament prophecies.

Of note are the several allusions to Christ's resurrection in the Old Testament. The prophet Isaiah spoke about the Messiah (the suffering servant) who would die for the sins of His people. Yet Isaiah predicted that, after the Messiah's death, God would "prolong his days" (Isaiah 53:10). This clearly means that the Messiah must come back to life after His substitutionary death for the sins of His people.

What is more, King David said that God would not allow His Holy One's body to see decay or corruption (Psalm 16:10). This strongly implies that if the Messiah dies, He must rise before His body begins to show outward signs of decay (which usually begins on the fourth day—John 11:38-39). Many Bible scholars believe Hosea 6:2 is a clue that the Messiah would rise from the dead on the third day. Moreover, Jesus interpreted Jonah's being swallowed by a fish and remaining there for three days and three nights as a foreshadowing of His own bodily resurrection (Jonah 1:17; Matthew 12:38-40).

It was important for Jesus to rise from the dead to fulfill Old Testament prophecies concerning the resurrection of the Messiah. That is to say, if Jesus had not risen from the dead, then He would not have been the Jewish Messiah.

Jesus Rose to Show Us That the Father Accepted His Sacrifice for Our Sins

The Messiah's resurrection shows that God the Father accepted Jesus's sacrifice on the cross as a worthy offering for the sins of mankind. Had God allowed Jesus's corpse to decay in the tomb, we would have had no way of knowing, in an empirically verifiable manner, that Jesus's sacrifice for our sins was accepted by the Father. Paul said that because Jesus was "obedient to the point of death, even death on a cross," God "highly exalted him and bestowed on him the name that is above every name" (Philippians 2:8-9).

It is inconceivable that the Father would have accepted Jesus's sacrifice as atonement for man's sins, and exalted Him, without having raised Him from the dead. Christ's resurrection is a clear sign that God the Father not only raised Him from the dead, but that His sacrifice was approved by the one who sent Him (Acts 17:30-31).

Jesus's Resurrection Confirms Christian Truth

Jesus's bodily resurrection from the grave is the crowning proof that Christianity is true. According to the apostle Paul, if Jesus had not risen, then Christianity is an empty belief system; we are still dead in our sins, our preaching of the gospel is a waste of time (1 Corinthians 15:14,17), and we are without hope (verse 32). Christians have long recognized that the faith stands or falls on the historical reality of the crucified Christ emerging alive from the tomb. This well-attested event is the keystone in the arch of Christianity. If it is removed, all else crumbles.

Jesus's Resurrection Guarantees Our Future Resurrection

The risen Christ is the only guarantee believers have that they will be raised immortal. Paul explained that Jesus is the "firstfruits" from the dead, the guarantee that all true believers will be raised immortal in their own body (1 Corinthians 15:20, 35-58; Philippians 3:21). The apostle also considered Jesus's resurrection, and the future resurrection of all believers, as a "package deal" (1 Corinthians 15:12-17). That is to say, if Christ is not risen, then the church will not be raised. Likewise, if the church will not be raised, then Christ was not raised. However, Christ did in fact emerge from the tomb alive, making eternal life possible (physically and spiritually) for all people (1 Corinthians 15:20).

Christ's resurrection is God's pledge that He will someday raise us believers from the dead—giving us total victory over the grave (Romans 8:11; 1 Corinthians 15:55; Philippians 3:20-21).

Jesus's Resurrection Gives Meaning to Our Work

Because of Christ's resurrection, we can have confidence that the work we do in God's kingdom is not in vain or a waste of our time (1 Corinthians 15:58). When no one is watching, or when our Christian duties become difficult, we might wonder whether our acts of Christian service really mean anything. However, because Jesus rose, our work carries meaning and great significance. God will reward us in the afterlife for our faithful service for His kingdom and His glory.

Jesus's Resurrection Gives Us Peace and Hope

Jesus conquered death! Knowing this fact calms our fears and gives us a future hope and comfort. That is to say, the historically verifiable resurrection should give us *confidence* of life after death—it should *overcome* our fear of death. This realization kept Peter and Paul in confident peace, without fear, when facing death (Philippians 1:19-26; 2 Timothy 4:6-8; 2 Peter 1:12-15), as it did Stephen the martyr (Acts 8:54-60).

Jesus's resurrection should also give us a sense of comforting optimism in the midst of our sufferings.[2] Paul was not ashamed of suffering for what he believed, because he knew the risen Christ was able to guard him until he entered the Lord's presence (2 Timothy 1:11-12). It is always painful when a loved one dies, but there is great comfort in knowing the story is not over. Paul stated, "We do not want you to be uninformed, brothers, about those who are asleep, that you may not grieve as others do who have no hope. For since we believe that Jesus died and rose again, even so, through Jesus, God will bring with him those who have fallen asleep" (1 Thessalonians 4:13-14). In the midst of our fears, pain, and suffering, we can trust in the Lord Jesus, the one who died for our sins and rose to conquer the grave.

Jesus's Resurrection Shows Us the Power of God at Work in Us

The same power that God the Father displayed when He raised Jesus from the dead is at work in us (Ephesians 1:19-20).

Often, believers feel powerless to make a difference when it comes to serving the Lord and impacting our world for God's glory. Understanding the resurrection reminds us that God's power can be unleashed in our lives as we humbly serve our King. This powerful fact changes our focus from dwelling on our finite limitations and bleak circumstances to marveling over how big our God is. We must remember that our God is all-powerful—He is the God who raises the dead, He is the God who raised Jesus, He is the God of the possible that works in us to do great things for His kingdom and His glory. This is the resurrected life in Christ!

Jesus's Resurrection Is Essential to Salvation and a Test for Sound Doctrine

Finally, the resurrection is important because it is an essential belief for Christians. Paul wrote that in order to be saved, we must acknowledge with our mouths that Jesus is Lord (i.e., Yahweh) and believe in our hearts that God raised Him from the dead (Romans 10:9). Alternatively, if Jesus did not rise from the dead, He could not be our Savior, thus leaving us without hope or confidence in eternal life (1 Corinthians 15:14,17).

Furthermore, by including the bodily resurrection of Christ as an essential aspect of the gospel, it provides us the theological criteria for discovering who is saved and for discerning truth from error (1 John 4:2; 2 John 7). Universally speaking, *only* Christianity holds that God sent His Son in the *flesh* (John 1:14), to die on the cross for our sins in the *flesh*, rise from the dead in the *flesh*, ascend to heaven in the *flesh*, and currently reside at the right hand of the Father in the *flesh*!

To sum up the matter, the believer's identity is so joined to Christ's resurrection that when the church ceases to preach and believe the resurrection, the church ceases to be the church (Acts 2:42; Romans 4:25).

How Did Jesus Use Apologetics?

Patrick Zukeran

Because Jesus made extraordinary claims about Himself, including His claim to be the Son of God, apologetics was an essential part of His ministry. He did not ask or expect people to simply offer blind faith based on His unique message alone. He, more than anyone else, understood that if His words were to have the desired force and effect on His hearers, He would need to offer compelling reasons and actions in their support.

From the Scriptures we recognize that God is a rational being (Isaiah 1:18), and humans who are made in His image are naturally inclined to look for reasons and evidence before making a decision. God has never called on anyone to make an unthoughtful and unreasoned decision about eternity. To be sure, there is a real difference between a leap of faith in the dark (existentialism), and a step of faith in the light (realism). Jesus encouraged the latter. Throughout His ministry, as we shall see, Jesus provided persuasive reasons and evidence to confirm His claims. Jesus is the greatest apologist who ever lived, providing a model for all disciples to follow. His apologetics included the use of reason, witnesses, miracles, prophecy, and His resurrection.

Jesus's Use of Different Apologetic Approaches

Jesus's Apologetic Use of Reason

Jesus was a master logician who presented irrefutable rational arguments that baffled His opponents. God is a rational being, and creatures created in His image are designed to use their senses and reason to discover and discern truth from error. We are created to know and live according to truth (John 8:32; 17:17). Reason is even operative before the gospel, for one must be able to think logically and coherently to understand the message. Reason is also fundamental to communication. Although fallen in sin, people still possess the capacity to reason and discover truth (Romans 1:18-20) and avoid contradictions (1 Timothy 6:20). Throughout His ministry, Jesus employed sound logic in His teachings, discourses, and actions.

Philosopher Dallas Willard said, "He [Jesus] constantly uses the power of logical insight to enable people to come to the truth about themselves and about God from the inside of their own heart and mind. Quite certainly it also played a role in his own growth in 'wisdom.'"[1]

Although Jesus did not articulate the

undeniable first principles of logic, He certainly understood them and used them. Jesus applied the Law of Identity (A is A). In Matthew 5:37, Jesus said, "Let your 'Yes' be 'Yes,' and your 'No,' 'No.'" Jesus applied the Law of Noncontradiction (A is not non-A). This is seen when Jesus contrasted true teachers from false teachers in Matthew 7:15 and 24:24. Jesus applied the Law of the Excluded Middle (either A or non-A). In Matthew 12:30, Jesus said, "He who is not with me is against Me." Jesus always employed the basic laws of reasoning throughout His discourses.

When the Pharisees confronted Jesus, He used many forms of reasoned arguments to answer their challenges. In Matthew 12:22-28, Jesus responded to the charge of demonic empowerment with a reductio ad absurdum argument—that is, showing that if their premise was true, it led to a contradictory or absurd conclusion. Jesus was challenged for healing on the Sabbath (Matthew 12:9-14). He responded with an a fortiori argument. This is an argument from lesser to greater force, or what applies in a less important situation applies in a more important situation, often with greater implications.[2] If the people believed they should rescue a sheep on the Sabbath, how much more should Jesus rescue a man from sickness? In Matthew 22:15-22, the Pharisees attempted to corner Jesus with a seemingly inescapable dilemma regarding whether or not to pay taxes. Facing two unacceptable options, Jesus skillfully avoided the horns of a dilemma. Presented with two unacceptable choices, He went to a third option. After asking about whose image and inscription appeared on the coin, Jesus insightfully replied, "Render therefore to Caesar the things that are Caesar's, and to God the things that are God's" (verse 21).

Jesus's skill in presenting sound arguments is summed up in Matthew 22:46, which states, "No one was able to answer him a word, nor from that day on did anyone dare question him anymore." Jesus proved to be the greatest thinker who used the laws of logic to present truth, demolish arguments, and expose error.

Jesus's Apologetic Use of Witnesses

The Jewish law requires two or three witnesses to verify one's claims (Deuteronomy 19:15). Knowing this, on several occasions, Jesus pointed to the testimony of witnesses to confirm His message. A prime example occurred in John 5 after Jesus healed the lame man at the Pool of Bethesda. An interrogation by the Pharisees followed because Jesus had healed on the Sabbath, thus violating Jewish tradition. What transpired provides one of Jesus's finest discourses defending His claim to be the Son of God. In this discussion, Jesus presented a convincing argument using the testimony of witnesses.

Like a defense lawyer, Jesus presented five witnesses who authenticated His actions. His first witness was John the Baptist, a recognized prophet of their time (John 5:33). The second witness was His miracles (verse 36). His third witness was God the Father (verse 37). His fourth witness was the Scriptures (verse 39). His final witness was Moses, the greatest prophet of Israel (verse 46). Here, Jesus exceeded the minimal requirement of two or three witnesses, and brought five very powerful witnesses to the stand.

Jesus used the testimony of witnesses again in John 8. After declaring He was the "light of the world" (verse 12), Jesus defended His claim by presenting four witnesses. The first was Jesus Himself (verse 14), then the testimony of the Father (verse 19), and finally the testimony of Abraham, the father of the nation (verse 56). His final witness is Jesus's own sinless life (verses 41,46). As a masterful lawyer would do in any courtroom, Jesus provided expert witnesses to defend His claims.

Jesus's Apologetic Use of Miracles

God confirmed His message and messengers with miracles, which are special acts of God that interrupt the normal course of events and confirm the Word of God through a messenger of God.[3] Through His miracles, Jesus demonstrated authority over every realm of creation, authority exclusive to God alone. Norman Geisler states that Jesus's power over the cosmos was seen by the fact that He manifested control over every category of the cosmos as listed by the famous Greek philosopher Aristotle in his *Categories*.[4]

Note Jesus's power over…

- substance (what?)—turning water into wine

- quantity (how much?)—feeding of 5,000

- quality (what kind?)—blind man gains quality of sight

- relation (to what?)—raising Lazarus from relationship

- space (where?)—healing nobleman's son from a distance

- time (when?)—healing an invalid of 38 years

- position (on what?)—walking on water, an unnatural position

- action (from what?)—His victorious death

- passion (on what?)—His triumphant resurrection

- state or habit (under what condition?)—catching a draught of fish

The Jews should have realized that Jesus possessed the authority of God. Several recognized this, including Nicodemus (John 3:2) and the disciples (John 2:11). Jesus often pointed to His miracles as evidence and expected the Jews to make the connection (Matthew 11:20-23; John 10:25,38). No other religious leader has demonstrated the kind of authority Jesus exhibited over creation.

Jesus's Apologetic Use of Prophecy

Only God, who is eternal, can repeatedly predict future events with 100 percent accuracy. In Isaiah 46:9-11, God declared,

> I am God, and there is no other; I am God, and there is none like Me, declaring the end from the beginning, and from ancient times things not yet done, saying, "My counsel shall stand, and I will do all my pleasure…I have spoken it; I will also bring it to pass; I have purposed it; I will also do it."

Jesus has a unique prophetic legacy that no other religious leader can match. J. Barton Payne's *Encyclopedia of Biblical Prophecy* records 127 prophecies regarding the life of Christ.[5]

These prophecies include:

- Prophecies regarding His lineage and birth

  Descendant of Abraham (Genesis 22:18)

  Tribe of Judah (Genesis 49:10)

  Descendant of King David (Isaiah 11:1)

  Place of birth, Bethlehem (Micah 5:2)

- Prophecies regarding His ministry

    Ministry preceded by a messenger (Isaiah 40:3, Malachi 3:1)

    Ministry begins in Galilee (Isaiah 9:1)

    Ministry of miracles (Isaiah 35:5-6)

- Prophecies regarding His death

    Rejected by His own people (Isaiah 53:3)

    Betrayed by a friend (Psalm 41:9)

    Sold for 30 pieces of silver (Zechariah 11:12)

    Hands and feet pierced (Psalm 22:16)

    Crucified with thieves (Isaiah 53:12)

    Garments parted and lots cast (Psalm 22:18)

    Bones not broken (Psalm 34:20)

    Buried in a rich man's tomb (Isaiah 53:9)

    Exact date of death predicted (Daniel 9)

- The Word of God will abide forever (Matthew 5:18)

- The apostles will be persecuted (Matthew 10:17-23)

- His words will abide forever (Matthew 24:35; Mark 13:31)

- Jesus will die and rise three days later (Matthew 12:40)

- The kingdom of heaven will experience great growth (Matthew 13:31-32)

- The church will never be destroyed (Matthew 16:18)

- Jerusalem will reject Jesus and become desolate (Matthew 23:37-38)

- Jerusalem temple will be destroyed (Matthew 24:2)

- Mary's act of anointing Jesus will be remembered throughout the ages (Matthew 26:13)

- The Holy Spirit would come upon the disciples (John 15:15-26; 16:5-15)

- The disciples will do greater works than Jesus (John 14:12)

- John will live to an old age (John 21:18)

Jesus pointed to the Old Testament prophecies of the Messiah that He fulfilled as evidence He was the long-awaited Messiah.

Not only did Jesus fulfill many prophecies, He made predictions of future events, with some being fulfilled during His lifetime. Moreover, Payne documents that Matthew recorded 58 predictions and Mark recorded 47. In Luke there are more than 40. In John, of the 45 predictions, Jesus made most of them. Some of Jesus's prophecies include:

Jesus stated, "Now I have told you before it comes, that when it does come to pass, you may believe" (John 15:29). Jesus not only fulfilled dozens of Old Testament prophecies, but also proclaimed His own prophecies regarding future events. This legacy of fulfilled prophecy is unrivaled and further upholds Christ's claims of deity.

Jesus's Apologetic Use of the Resurrection

The resurrection was the ultimate proof of Christ's deity. On several occasions Jesus prophesied His own death and resurrection (Matthew 12:40; 17:23; Mark 14:58; John 2:19). God alone is the author and giver of life. Therefore, Jesus predicting and accomplishing His own resurrection from the dead conclusively confirmed His claim as the Son of God.

Jesus's resurrection fulfilled Old Testament messianic prophecies. Psalm 16:10 states, "You will not leave my soul in Sheol, nor will you allow your Holy One to see corruption." The Messiah would not remain in the grave, nor would His body suffer the decay of death.

Isaiah 53:8-10 states, "He was cut off from the land of the living; for the transgressions of My people He was stricken. And they made His grave with the wicked—but with the rich at His death…When You make His soul an offering for sin, He shall see His seed, He shall prolong His days, and the pleasure of the LORD shall prosper in His hand" (NKJV).

The phrase "cut off from the land of the living" means the Messiah would be killed. But the following phrase, "He shall see His seed, He shall prolong His days," indicates He would be resurrected to see His descendants. The passage also states the death and resurrection of the Messiah will fulfill the requirements of the Old Testament law. Jesus the sinless Son of God was the only one who could meet God's holy requirements; therefore, He is the only Savior for mankind.

Jesus's resurrection affirms Jesus words, "I am the resurrection and the life" (John 11:25). He is the source of life. The Bible also states that God is the source of life. Only God has the ability to create and restore life. That Jesus raised Himself from the dead demonstrates that He has the authority of God.

The Most Effective Defender of the Faith

In the Gospels, we see clear examples of how Jesus used apologetics. He employed reason, evidence, the testimony of witnesses, miracles, prophecy, and His resurrection. It is important to recognize that Jesus did not present a formal apologetics system per se, but from what we gather from Scripture, His method was consistent with the classical and evidential apologetic approaches.

Jesus was not only the world's greatest teacher, He was the most effective defender of the Faith who ever lived. Time and again He offered compelling reasons and evidence as He defended His claims to be the Son of God. His life and ministry serve as a model for every believer as we seek to do the work of an apologist in a lost and searching world.

Part Four

QUESTIONS ABOUT THE BIBLE

26

Are the Old Testament Manuscripts Reliable?

Walter C. Kaiser Jr.

A total of 39 books comprise what we today call the Old Testament. These books were written over a period of nearly a millennium, from 1400 BC to 400 BC. This raises a crucial question: How did we get these 39 books? And are they trustworthy in their claim to be the Word from God?

How Did We Get the Old Testament?

These 39 books came to us just as Hebrews 1:1 explained: "God, who at various times and in various ways spoke in time past to the fathers by the prophets..." Hence, the "various times" covered the extended period from Moses's day and the next 1,000 years until the last book of the Old Testament was completed—the book of Chronicles.[1]

Likewise, the many or "various ways" can be seen in everything from God speaking "face to face" (i.e., He spoke directly) to Moses in Numbers 12:6-8; or to various psalmists, such as King David in inspired lyrics; or through prophets by means of visions, dreams, and the revelation of His word.

Moreover, in what is considered by many the oldest book of the Bible, Job, God spoke with Job about pain and suffering in light of His goodness and power. Subsequently, the rest of the 38 books that form what is known as the Old Testament followed the book of Job.

Did the Old Testament Writers Use Any Sources?

In the composition of the earlier part of the divine revelation, we should not be startled by the fact that God also had His writers of Scripture employ sources as they wrote. For example, Luke 1:1-4 acknowledged that Luke used numerous sources that were available to him as he wrote the narrative of the life and times of Jesus of Nazareth.

However, there are two exceptional instances when we are expressly taught that the inspired record in Scripture came directly from the very "finger" of God, as Moses carefully taught us: "When the LORD finished speaking to Moses on Mount Sinai, he gave him two tablets of the covenant law, the tablets of stone inscribed by the finger of God" (Exodus 31:18 NIV).

And in another place the Lord taught:

> These are the commandments the LORD proclaimed in a loud voice to your whole assembly there on the mountain from out of the fire, the cloud and the deep darkness; and he added nothing more. Then he wrote them on two stone tablets and gave them to me (Deuteronomy 5:22 NIV).

Israel understood that the Ten Commandments represented the very words of God to the people, for they commented: "The LORD our God has shown us his glory and his majesty, and we have heard his voice from the fire" (verse 24).

The second exceptional time was when the Lord communicated in a direct way in the book of Daniel. This happened when God wrote His message directly on the wall of Babylonian King Belshazzar's banquet hall: "Suddenly the fingers of a human hand appeared and wrote on the plaster of the wall...The king watched the hand as it wrote. His face turned pale and he was so frightened that his legs became weak and his knees were knocking" (Daniel 5:5-6 NIV).

Because this pagan king had not humbled his heart before God or honored Him, his days would come to an end, as this message indicated, and the Babylonian kingdom cease to exist!

Can We Show the Claims for Divine Authority Are Accurate and Reliable?

So far we have addressed the fact that God employed many different *ways* at many different *times* to announce His word to mortals on earth. But that does not address the question of how reliable those claims were. Moreover, the transmission of the text

in the Old Testament across three millennia is another cause for deep concern if we are going to talk about the text's reliability. It leads to questions like, Who wrote these texts? Who copied them? What methods did they use to ensure the integrity of what they wrote by hand-copying accurately the wording that was in the original autograph (i.e., first document that came from the hand of the author)?

To begin answering these kinds of questions, we must recognize the limitations placed on scholars 70 years ago, prior to more recent discoveries. At that time there were only three sources of comparison: (1) the Samaritan Pentateuch, (2) the Greek Septuagint, and (3) the Nash Papyrus dating from around AD 1000. However, with the sensational discovery of the Dead Sea Scrolls in 1946–47, our evidence improved by leaping in time from around AD 1000 to, in some cases, the third century BC (much closer to the original documents of the Old Testament). This was based on some 900 exemplars of Hebrew biblical texts of the Old Testament ranging from AD 50 to 250 BC.

Even more fascinating was the discovery of a tiny silver scroll just south of Jerusalem, alongside the Valley of Hinnom, that contained the Aaronic Benediction from Numbers 6:24-26 and dated to the mid-seventh or sixth century BC. The scroll was written in a Proto-Canaanite (or Paleo-Hebrew) script and worn around the neck as an amulet roll in the form of a typical signet seal.[2] The Hebrew text inscribed on this roll was practically word for word the same as what had been transmitted from Moses's day up until our day in the twenty-first century!

In the book of Isaiah found among the Dead Sea Scrolls, we have another remarkable example of the purity of transmission through the centuries. It represents an unbelievably perfect state of preservation from an eighth-century autograph (original) to our present day. Interestingly, in the entire Isaiah manuscript of 66 chapters, it was discovered that a mere three Hebrew words exhibited a different spelling from that found in our present-day copies. This is a fascinating confirmation of accurate hand-copying of a biblical book containing some 100 or more pages of Hebrew text! While this was our best exemplar (compared to other Hebrew texts that had more variations), it is still extremely remarkable the way this text has been accurately passed down to us—*a level of accuracy unrivaled in documents from ancient history*!

Who or What Criteria Decided What Books Could Be Included in Scripture?

One of the most popular bits of misinformation that has been all too frequently affirmed by many scholars these past two centuries is that a group of rabbinic scholars attended a Jewish council held in Jamnia (AD 90, also known as Jabneh), Israel, to decide which books should be included in the Old Testament.[3] At the council, Rabbi Johanan ben Zakkai, who had earlier escaped from the siege of Jerusalem, was granted permission to set up a school that functioned like the Sanhedrin. But three caveats must be noted regarding the action this school took on two books of the Old Testament, Ecclesiastes and Song of Solomon: (1) its deliberations had no binding authority; (2) only the books of Ecclesiastes and Song of Solomon were discussed, though nothing was concluded about their canonicity because their discussion centered only on their interpretation; and (3) the books this council recognized as canonical (authoritative) in subsequent actions were

the same as those found in the works of the secular Jewish historian Josephus, as well as those in our present Bibles. Jack Lewis commented on this long history of misinformation when he wrote, "It would appear that the frequently made assertion that a binding decision was made at Jabneh [also Jamnia] covering all Scripture is conjectural at best."[4]

It is worthy of note that there was a continuous chain of commendations of their predecessors' contribution to Scripture. For example, 1 Chronicles 29:29 states that the history of David was written in the books of the prophets Samuel, Nathan, and Gad. This was followed by another such notice in 2 Chronicles 9:29 that the history of Solomon was written by the prophets Nathan, Ahijah and Iddo. Likewise, the work of King Rehoboam was written by the prophets Shemaiah and Iddo (2 Chronicles 12:15), while the history of King Ahijah was written by the prophet Iddo (2 Chronicles 13:22). This veritable link of verses in Chronicles[5] shows that the prophets passed the baton from one to the other, thus setting forth a steady stream of historical events and theology. As such, it also meant that there was a progressive recognition of what was an authoritative word from God.

But there is more! In Daniel 9:2, the prophet Daniel explained that Jeremiah's prophecy (Jeremiah 25:11-12), which was written only 100 years earlier, was both the "word of the LORD" and were a part of the "Scriptures" (NIV). In addition, Daniel cited Jeremiah in this text when he predicted that the captivity of the Jewish people would last 70 years. Daniel read that the 70 years was about to come to an end, and he expected God to be true to His word and deliver Israel from captivity.

Likewise, the prophet Jeremiah treated

the prophecy of Micah in the same way, for even though Micah had preceded Jeremiah by 125 years; Jeremiah announced that Micah's prediction that Jerusalem would be plowed like a field would be fulfilled (cf. Jeremiah 26:18; Micah 3:12). Thus, once again, a later prophet certified the truthfulness and reliability of what an earlier prophet had said in Scripture, and in some cases was able to witness the actual fulfillment of that prediction, thereby guaranteeing its divine origin!

The Threefold Division of the Canon

Both the historian of the Jewish people, Josephus, and Jesus Himself used the threefold division of the Old Testament: the "law of Moses and the Prophets and the Psalms" (Luke 24:44). While there were also other references to a different summary of the Old Testament as containing only two divisions, usually "the Law and the Prophets" (Luke 16:16-17; see also Matthew 5:17), there seemed to be a wider use of the threefold division. For example, the noncanonical and apocryphal book of Ecclesiasticus appealed to the same threefold division of the Old Testament in its prologue in 132 BC. The significance of this trifold division is that it allows researchers to project the concept of the present canon of the Old Testament back to the second century BC. Thus, along with the progressive recognition of what books were authoritative, as shown in the prophets' chain of references, here would be another, even if there were a later formalization of the same canonical concept.

In addition, Moses laid up the books he had written before the Lord in the tabernacle (Deuteronomy 31:26), with Joshua doing the same thing (Joshua 24:26). Later, the prophet Samuel wrote "the rights and duties

of kingship" on a scroll and he too deposited them "before the Lord" (1 Samuel 10:25). Thus, the placing of these writings before the Lord (in the temple) indicated the enormous regard and reverence they had for the Scriptures. Namely, they viewed them as being from God, and being fully trustworthy and reliable.

Jesus's View of the Old Testament

There can be no doubt that Jesus pointed to this same set of 39 books as being the inspired body of authoritative teachings from the Father. While Jesus boldly spoke of the temple being destroyed (a site the Jewish people held in highest regard), He did not treat the 39 books of the Old Testament in the same way. Instead, He declared, "These are the very Scriptures that testify about me" (John 5:39 NIV).

If some are still doubtful as to just what books Jesus's affirmation included, then the answer is found in Matthew 23:35 with its parallel in Luke 11:51. In these two passages, Jesus showed what He meant by the "Scriptures"—namely, the identical 39 books we have today as the Old Testament. He did this by pointing to the two texts just mentioned to "all the righteous blood that has been shed on earth, from the blood of righteous Abel to the blood of Zechariah son of Berekiah, whom you [Jews] murdered between the temple and the altar" (NIV). The reference to Abel comes from the Genesis record, the first book in the Old Testament canon. But the mention of Zechariah is not a reference to the prophet who wrote a book by that name, but to a Zechariah killed near the temple (2 Chronicles 24:20-22). Given that the order of the 39 books of the Old Testament runs from Genesis to the last book in the Jewish order of the books (1 and 2 Chronicles), Jesus was pointing to the very same canon we possess today—even though today, the books are in a different order. Thus Jesus pointed to the first and the last murders recounted in the Old Testament.

The Old Testament was given by the inspiration of our Lord, and it is still useful for teaching, rebuke, correction, and even the way of salvation (2 Timothy 3:15-17). The text is fully reliable and accurate in all its details.

How Do the Dead Sea Scrolls Show the Reliability of the Old Testament Text?

J. Randall Price

Written in the three languages of Scripture (Hebrew, Aramaic, and Greek), the Dead Sea Scrolls represent a collection of at least 1,000 manuscripts dating from 250 BC–AD 68. However, some of these, written by Jews, are from the later period of the Jewish revolts against Roman occupation (AD 68–73, and 132–135). The earliest of these documents were written and/or preserved by the members of a Jewish sect that established a community (Qumran) by the Dead Sea during the late Second Temple period (c. 100 BC–AD 70).

These ancient manuscripts, written on either parchment (animal hide) or papyrus (plant used as an early form of paper), are comprised of Jewish literature: two-thirds are nonbiblical texts (Apocrypha, Pseudepigrapha) and sectarian texts (personal letters, deeds, community documents and commentaries on biblical texts), and one-third are biblical texts (Old Testament). Among these caches, there were unique scrolls that predated the Qumran sect and had a quasi-scriptural authority (Temple Scroll, *11Q19*) and one, a treasure map, engraved entirely on copper (Copper Scroll, *3Q15*). Only a few of the scrolls (Great Isaiah Scroll, Temple Scroll, Copper Scroll) are complete, and all are damaged.

The vast majority of the documents found in the 11 caves known to have contained scrolls are fragmentary (between 25,000-50,000 small pieces). Remarkably, scholars have spent more than 50 years piecing together these fragments in order to study and publish their contents.[1]

What Is the Significance of the Dead Sea Scrolls?

The Dead Sea Scrolls were discovered in the Land of Israel, and at the time they were found, they were the first known documents from the Second Temple period. They are uniquely important to those who study this period and especially to students of the Bible (both the Old and New Testaments). This can be seen by the fact that the scrolls cover a transitional period in Jewish history from the time of the Maccabean rule through the Roman occupation. This period of time includes the life of Jesus, the formation of the church, the writing of much of the New Testament, as well as the turbulent period of the second century, during which there were Jewish revolts and exiles (events that sharpened the divide between Jews and Christians).

Interestingly, the scrolls provide previously unknown information about historical figures, political situations, and legal, religious, and social practices only dimly echoed in the much later rabbinic writings (Talmud, Mishnah).[2] They also give new insights into the languages spoken by Jesus and His disciples, as well as the cultural conditions and conflicts that produced Jesus's parabolic method of teaching. In addition, much is learned about His debates with so-called establishment Judaism,[3] as well as the religious background of issues addressed in the Pauline letters.[4] Of particular importance is their contribution to our understanding of the messianic and eschatological beliefs of Jews during this period.[5] The scrolls show us that the developed messianic interpretations found in the New Testament were not the unique provenance of early Jewish Christianity, but the shared interpretation of Jews whose expectations were centered on the prophetic revelation of the Old Testament.

Moreover, the scrolls also provide a pre-Masoretic body of texts that can be compared with other existing texts, such as the Septuagint (LXX, the Greek translation of the Hebrew Scriptures) and the Samaritan Pentateuch. What is more, the Dead Sea Scrolls offer material necessary for an accurate understanding of the transmission of the Hebrew text and for modern translations of the Bible.

What Old Testament Books Were Found Among the Dead Sea Scrolls?

The biblical texts represent the oldest known portions of the Old Testament and contain every book of the Old Testament except the book of Esther (although it is reflected in other writings among the scrolls). There are no New Testament manuscripts among the Dead Sea Scrolls because most of the New Testament was written toward the end of the time of the community's existence. Moreover, because Jewish Christians do not appear to have been a part of the community, it should not be expected that the New Testament would have been distributed to this strictly Jewish sect. The chart on the next page shows the number of manuscripts of each book of the Old Testament discovered until today.[6]

Biblical Manuscripts Represented in the Dead Sea Scrolls		
Canonical Books	Old Testament Book	Number
Torah	Genesis	25
	Exodus	20
	Leviticus	19
	Numbers	11
	Deuteronomy	39
Prophets	Joshua	2
	Judges	3
	1-2 Samuel	4
	1-2 Kings	3
	Isaiah	22
	Jeremiah	7
	Ezekiel	6
	12 minor prophets	10
Writings	Psalms	40
	Proverbs	2
	Job	6
	Song of Songs	4
	Lamentations	4
	Ecclesiastes	2
	Ruth	4
	Daniel	10
	Ezra	1
	Nehemiah	1
	1-2 Chronicles	1
Total		246
Adjusted		238
*Totals adjusted to read 8 less because some scrolls preserve parts of 2-3 books.		

This chart indicates which books of the Bible were considered the most popular among the Dead Sea Scrolls—namely the books of the law, the Psalms, and the prophets. Among the books of the law, the book of Deuteronomy has the most copies; Isaiah and Daniel stand out among the prophets, and Psalms among the Writings. It is interesting that Deuteronomy was also one of the books most cited by Jesus, and that the

Psalms, Isaiah, and Daniel played an important role in Jesus's messianic teaching as well as in the rest of the New Testament's defense and explanation of the messianic program.

How Were the Dead Sea Scrolls Preserved?

The Dead Sea Scrolls were placed in sealed ceramic jars and stored within caves near the community's settlement, today called the site of Qumran, situated on the northwestern shore of the Dead Sea, about 19 miles from Jerusalem. Scrolls from the later period of the Jewish revolts come from regional caves stretching some 33 miles southward from Qumran to Masada (particularly Wadi Murabba'at, Nahal Hever, En-Gedi, and Masada). For the Qumran community, the purposeful hiding of these scrolls may have been simply to preserve them, as suggested by God's direction to the prophet Jeremiah (Jeremiah 32:14). However, the revolt period scrolls were left behind in caves that were used as hiding places by soldiers and as living quarters.

Two types of caves were used for the storage of the scrolls: (1) man-made marl caves surrounding and in the sides of the broad plateau upon which the community's buildings were situated, and (2) natural fault caves located in the limestone cliffs that line the western shore of the Dead Sea. These cave repositories often had rock-cut niches where the jars containing the scrolls were stored.

The Qumran sect may have gained a reputation as caretakers of valuable documents, and it is possible that people from Jerusalem, Jericho, and other nearby cities brought their scrolls to the community for safekeeping. Most likely, many of these scrolls were removed before the Roman army invaded area and destroyed Qumran, but it is believed that others could not be removed due to their remote location and the sudden nature of the Roman attack, and thus they remained in these caves until modern times.

While there are some ancient accounts of biblical scrolls being found in this area, the discovery of these texts is best known from Bedouin (local nomadic Arab shepherds) looters who found jars in some of the caves from the late 1940s–1950s and subsequently sold the contents on the black market. In 1993, the Israel Antiquities Authority launched Operation Scroll and sent hundreds of archaeologists throughout the Judean Desert to locate and identify caves that had the potential to house scrolls. Though these caves were numbered and survey trenches were made in many of them, no excavations were carried out at the time.

In 2017, Operation Scroll was renewed with the excavation of one cave south of Qumran—a cave that was revealed to have contained as many as seven jars that once contained scrolls. Although these scrolls had been removed in antiquity, the discovery provided evidence that many more discoveries await further excavation of the nearly 300 caves in the region.[7] Therefore, it is possible that our knowledge of Scripture, as based on the scrolls, has only just begun!

The Dead Sea Scrolls and Biblical Reliability

There is little doubt the Dead Sea Scrolls constitute the most important manuscript discovery of all time. Their significance lies in their antiquity, their preservation of the biblical text and related Jewish literature, and their description of a Jewish sect that was unknown before their discovery. The scrolls are of great value and significance when it comes to confirming the reliability of the biblical text and examining the transmission of the text so we can better understand textual variants (small differences) that support a more accurate translation and understanding of the text.

Statement of the Divine Origin and Authority of the Biblical Text

While some scholars debate whether Second Temple Judaism recognized a canon (open or closed), the Qumran sect seems to have had an understanding of which books they accepted as Scripture (of divine origin), and which they did not (of human origin). They used the Paleo-Hebrew script (used before the Babylonian exile) for the name of God (YHWH) in the biblical texts, indicating that these texts were accorded greater sanctity and therefore greater authority.[8] This agrees with Jesus's use of only the *authoritative* biblical texts from the three divisions of the Hebrew Bible (Matthew 5:17; 7:12; 22:40; 25:56; Luke 1:70; 16:16,29,31; 18:31; 24:27,44; John 1:45). Importantly, the fact that fragments of every book in our present Old Testament canon existed at Qumran before its destruction by the Roman army in AD 68 reveals recognition of the canonical books from ancient times. This recognition was then passed on to the medieval scribes who produced the Masoretic Text (the traditional biblical text of Judaism).

Evidence of the Careful Transmission of the Biblical Text

The Dead Sea Scrolls also allow us to see how well the scribes preserved the text for us. Until their discovery, our oldest version of the Hebrew text was that compiled by Aaron ben Moses ben Asher in the tenth

century AD.[9] Our modern-language Old Testaments were translated from these late medieval manuscripts. This tenth-century text was compiled by Jewish rabbinic scribes called the Masoretes (from the Hebrew word *masora*, meaning "tradition"). Their text has come to be the received or traditional text of Judaism, known as the Masoretic Text.

As old as this text may seem, it is still more than 1,000 years removed from the last of the original texts of Scripture penned by the prophets. This huge gap of time in which there were no Hebrew witnesses to the transmission of the text (with the exception of some verses of the Ten Commandments preserved in the second century BC Nash Papyrus) left a doubt as to the accuracy of the Masoretic Text, since it was compiled from these older yet unverifiable texts. It seemed possible that scribes working from fading manuscripts in which many letters look alike, and having poor illumination and no eyeglasses, could have made mistakes in the course of copying the biblical texts, and that these errors could have passed on to the Masoretic Text from which our Bibles were translated. After all, the Septuagint and other versions demonstrated that significant variants existed from the Masoretic Text. How could it ever be proven that what we have now is what they had then? How could we know if our own Bible text was reliable?

Remarkably, the discovery of biblical texts in Cave 1 at Qumran, and especially the Great Isaiah Scroll (*1QIsaa*), made it possible to finally answer this question. The book of Isaiah is one of the longest books in the Old Testament (66 chapters) and this copy was dated to 125 BC (although its use as a well-marked study copy can push the date of its text back at least another 100 years). With the discovery of the Great Isaiah

Scroll, scholars now possess the oldest and most complete copy of a book of the Bible from this lost period before the Masoretes. In addition, its text could be compared to the much later Masoretic Text from which our Bibles were translated. The result of the comparison between these texts revealed an almost 95 percent level of agreement, with the variations coming from spelling differences and some significant variants (more in *1QIsaa* than *1QIsab*). This high percentage of agreement was more or less the same for the other fragments of the biblical books found in other caves, especially Cave 4, which provided the greatest number of manuscripts.

From this new knowledge of the text, based on analyses of the scrolls, which reveal a conservative scribal tendency to follow the exemplar in both text and form,[10] we can approach our own translations with greater confidence. We can know the Jewish scribes did a careful job of transmitting the text through time.[11] And most importantly, we can also see that the remarkable consonance with the Masoretic Text indicates that it is a stable text that could serve as a *textus receptus* (traditional text) for Judaism and as the basis for authoritative translation into other languages.

Textual Criticism with the Dead Sea Scrolls Restores Greater Accuracy

While an examination of the biblical text is known as textual criticism, it is necessary to discover certain details about how various texts relate and compare to each other. This helps scholars to have a more accurate reading, translation (into modern languages), and restoration of the original Bible.

Even though there was essential agreement between the Dead Sea Scrolls and the Masoretic Text, there were significant variants (small differences) in the Dead Sea Scroll texts that have proved important to textual critics (those who seek to restore the original text). The Great Isaiah Scroll alone had 200 variants,[12] some important to Christian scholars because they are related to messianic interpretation. Having this wealth of textual evidence from different texts (many of which informed the Masoretes in their compilation of a standard text) has allowed scholars to weigh the evidence of these texts as compared to other known texts of the time (e.g., the Greek Septuagint and the Samaritan Pentateuch). This has also enabled textual critics to offer their verdict as to which reading of a particular text was closest to the original.

A comparison of these variants with Old Testament citations in the New Testament has been extremely helpful in confirming the source of the citations.[13] Also, the vocabulary and doctrine of the sectarian (nonbiblical) scrolls, set in a time parallel to the advent of Jesus, as well as the events recorded in the Gospels and the writing of most of the New Testament, reveal that terms and religious concepts once thought unique to the New Testament were in fact in common use in the first century.[14] As a result of this new knowledge, since 1950, every translation of the Bible has utilized this textual evidence in their translation work.[15]

Conclusion

The Dead Sea Scrolls offer evidence to address other apologetic concerns in the Old Testament. These include the unity of the book of Isaiah, the date of the book of Daniel,[16] and recognizing that the scrolls are vital for biblical research, exegesis, and apologetics. This has been forcefully stated by Emanuel Tov:

> When we collect data of this kind we realize that the Scrolls do make a

difference and they should be taken into consideration, not only in the study of textual criticism but also in the [area of] exegesis, [for] in that area there too the knowledge of the Scrolls is an absolute requirement for anyone studying the Bible critically.[17]

Today, as the search for additional scrolls in the caves around Qumran is underway, new discoveries of manuscripts may be made with the promise of an even greater witness to the reliability of the Old Testament.

28

Does Archaeology Confirm the Historical Reliability of the Old Testament?

Steven Collins[1]

The first 75 years of the twentieth century were heady times for biblical archaeology. Scholars like Nelson Glueck, John Garstang, W.F. Albright, and G. Ernest Wright were practically household names. Indeed, they were some of the greatest minds in the discipline of Ancient Near East archaeology, which also happened to believe in the historical reliability of the Old Testament. For them, the Bronze and Iron Ages of Mesopotamia, Egypt, and the Levant were the stage upon which the stories of Abraham, Isaac, Jacob, Joseph, Moses, Joshua, David, and Solomon played out. Bible scholars quoted them prolifically in support of the historical accuracy of Old Testament narratives. It seemed as if every turn of the spade brought to light a new archaeological find supporting or illuminating Scripture. However, the glory days of biblical archaeology did not last.

The Rise of the Archaeological Minimalists

In the last quarter of the twentieth century and the first decade of the new millennium,

a new generation of archaeologists arose to challenge long-held beliefs in the historical value of the Hebrew Scriptures. They repudiated the once-dominant Albright—and those holding similar positive views of the Bible—as biased. The older, more conservative archaeologists were accused of digging with a biblical agenda, and the younger scholars wanted no part of it. "Archaeology for archaeology's sake"—this was the new paradigm. For Israel Finkelstein and his cadre of like-minded[2] archaeologists, the Old Testament held little or no value in fashioning a history of the Ancient Near East. Finkelstein's approach was made clear when he wrote, "[The] combination of archaeological and historical research demonstrates that the biblical account of the Conquest and occupation of Canaan [by the Israelites] is entirely divorced from historical reality."[3] Niels Peter Lemche also weighed in: "The patriarchal narratives are…fiction, not reality. That world does not represent a real world. It stands outside the usual representation of time and space. As a matter of fact…neither the narratives nor their world can be dated to any precise period."[4]

The minimalists have used archaeology to "disprove" the Bible whenever they saw an opportunity (a minimalist is one who sees little, if any, historical value in the Old Testament books, while a maximalist is one who sees most or all Old Testament books as historically reliable).[5] Joseph Holden and Norman Geisler, in their recent work *The Popular Handbook of Archaeology and the Bible*, correctly summarize the minimalist position—and why it is shortsighted—when they write,

> Minimalists have led a campaign among professional archaeologists to abandon the term *biblical archaeology* altogether…Their contempt for any title associated with the Bible appears to be driven by its [i.e., biblical archaeology's] perceived association to biased research, antiquated methodology, rigid ideology, lack of objectivity, and contempt for the scientific method. (However, this notion seems to be shortsighted since it requires archaeologists to discriminate against the Bible as a valid primary source document originating from the ancient Near-Eastern world.)[6]

However, by the year 2000, the vast majority in the archaeological community declared the death of *biblical* archaeology. The tide had turned. Or so it seemed!

The Resurgence of Biblical Archaeology

The battle between the minimalists and maximalists was under way. Biblical archaeologists, underfunded and marginalized, were at a distinct disadvantage. But *facts* and *opinions*

are two different things, and the minimalists were, in reality, short on facts. Admittedly, the archaeology of Albright and Wright had its flaws. But in their enthusiasm, some of the anti-Bible crowd was becoming embroiled in disputes with fellow minimalists. While every self-assured minimalist was certain that the books of the Pentateuch (Torah) were myth and fiction, some, like William G. Dever,[7] were not quite ready to deny the historicity of kings David and Solomon and later Old Testament figures and events—and for good reason. While most minimalists had relegated David to the realm of fable, the discovery of an Iron Age stela fragment (written stone monument) bearing the phrase "house [dynasty] of David" at Tel Dan in northern Israel reduced that notion to an absurdity.[8] During the first decade of the twenty first-century, minimalism began to unravel.

Attacking the minimalists head-on was renowned Ancient Near East scholar Kenneth A. Kitchen.[9] In his 2003 work *On the Reliability of the Old Testament*,[10] Kitchen demonstrated that minimalist objections to biblical historicity amounted to nothing more than straw-man arguments bereft of factual data. In his inimitable style, Kitchen observed that

> increasingly extreme views about the Old Testament writings have been trumpeted loudly and proclaimed ever more widely and stridently; in the service of these views, all manner of gross misinterpretations of original, first-hand documentary data from the Ancient Near East itself are now being shot forth in turn, to prop up these extreme stances on the Old Testament, regardless of the real facts of the case... And so, we must firmly say to philosophical cranks (politically correct,

postmodernist, or whatever else)—
"Your fantasy agendas are irrelevant in
and to the real world, both of today
and of all preceding time back into
remotest antiquity. Get real or (alas!)
get lost!"[11]

If the minimalists were right in believing
that the books of the Hebrew Scriptures were
mostly religious propaganda written by Iron
Age 2 (c. 1000–332 BC) Israelite and Judahite priests, then those portions of the Old
Testament that, on face value, belong to the
Middle Bronze Age (c. 2100–1600 BC), Late
Bronze Age (c. 1600–1200 BC), and Iron
Age 1 (c. 1200–1000 BC) should be loaded
with Iron Age 2 *anachronisms* (i.e., historical
features that do not fit the time period). They
are not! In fact, the first seven Old Testament
books—from Genesis through Judges—are
authentic to their Ancient Near East contexts in every detail. Even a small sampling
of these historical and cultural minutiae[12] is
impressive:

- Genesis 10 correctly identifies the
  Fertile Crescent—the geographical
  arc formed by Mesopotamia, the
  Levant, and Egypt—as the cradle of
  civilization.[13]

- Abraham's *covenants* with Yahweh
  (Genesis 15; 17) and Abimelech
  (Genesis 21) match the unique structure of Middle Bronze Age treaties
  and contracts, not those of earlier or
  later periods.[14]

- The Mosaic law code conforms to
  the distinctive configuration of
  Hittite treaties and contracts of the
  Late Bronze Age, and no other time
  frame.[15]

- Joseph was sold into slavery for *20*

shekels of silver (Genesis 37)—the
going price of a slave during the
Middle Bronze Age.[16]

- Egypt's mighty eighteenth dynasty
  collapsed as a result of the exodus
  events: the ten plagues, the plunder-
  ing of Egyptian wealth, the loss of a
  large labor force, the decimation of
  its northern military forces, and the
  loss of the Pharaoh himself—Tuthmosis IV. This was the *only dynastic
  collapse* in Egypt during the entire
  Late Bronze Age. It is exactly what
  one would predict if the events of the
  exodus had truly happened![17]

- The exodus itinerary (Numbers
  33) tracks along a trade route well
  attested from Egyptian map lists of
  the Late Bronze Age, including the
  same towns and places along that
  route.[18]

- According to the Mosaic law, the cost
  to replace a slave was *30 shekels* of
  silver (Exodus 21)—the average price
  of a slave during the Late Bronze
  Age. Even the subtle inflation curve
  is preserved from the time of Joseph
  to Moses![19]

- Yahweh required *literacy* of Israel
  (Deuteronomy 27), in preparation
  for which the Semitic alphabet was
  invented in Egypt during the centuries when the Israelites sojourned
  there, and that *same alphabet* chronologically followed the Israelites
  into the Sinai wilderness, and into
  Canaan, tracing their biblical presence in these locations.[20]

- Bronze Age Canaanite religious
  practices are detailed in Genesis

through Joshua. Not only do the Mosaic narratives accurately depict the gods, goddesses, and cult practices of Canaan, but also the books of Joshua and Judges reveal how the Israelites rebelled against Yahweh to embrace these pagan beliefs. All of this is confirmed dramatically in the archaeological record.[21]

- Joshua conquered an *Egyptian-less* Canaan, precisely at the right historical moment—in the midst of the eighteenth dynasty's collapse and withdrawal from Canaan as a result of the exodus events. The first half of the Late Bronze Age (c. 1550–1400 BC) saw the Egyptian domination of the Levant (Canaan and Syria). But none of the promises of Yahweh to give this land to Israel ever mention Egyptians in Canaan, and neither are Egyptian troops mentioned in Joshua's campaigns. It is no coincidence that in the decades following the death of Pharaoh Tuthmosis IV—during whose short reign the terrible exodus events had decimated his land—Egypt withdrew from its Asiatic territories (the Levant), leaving Joshua to take the Promised Land with no threat of Egyptian interference or retaliation![22]

- Joshua took Jericho in the mid-fourteenth century BC, 40 years after the death of the exodus Pharaoh, Tuthmosis IV. It is an archaeological fact that there was no Late Bronze Age occupation at Jericho *before* or *after* the fourteenth century (the 1300s) BC. Thus, *only* the fortified fourteenth-century Jericho could

have been the city of Rahab. Talk about historical precision![23]

- The Merneptah Stela (c. 1210 BC) confirms that Israel was well enough established in Canaan to be recognized by Pharaoh Merneptah as one of the perennial enemies (nine bows) of Egypt. On this stela, Israel is designated (by a linguistic symbol) as a "people," not a nation with a king—which is spot on![24]

- The phrase "smite with the *edge* of the sword" is an idiom derived from the single-edged, curved battle axes of the Middle and Late Bronze Ages, the final form of which was the elegant sickle-sword (so called because it was shaped like a sickle with the cutting edge on the outer curve). These were hacking (smiting) swords with no thrust-point, and only a single sharpened edge. Thus, to "smite with the edge [*singular*] of the sword" was an apt description of this class of weaponry. By the end of Iron Age 1 (c. 1000 BC; the beginning of king David's rule) the sickle-sword was all but extinct. After 1000 BC swords were straight, pointed, and double-edged. It is no coincidence that this "smiting" idiom appears 24 times in the "Bronze Age Scriptures" (Genesis through Judges), but trails off thereafter. The use of the idiom died out after its namesake sickle sword disappeared from history.[25]

- Homer's *Iliad* (lines 10-446) confirms the authenticity of an Aegean-style ritual sequence enacted by the Philistines in 1 Samuel 5–6. Not so coincidentally, the Philistines are known to be the descendants of the Mycenaean Greeks.[26]

These historical and cultural synchronisms (i.e., historical features that match the biblical text)—and there are hundreds more!—are proof positive that the events in Genesis through Judges actually happened during the historical/archaeological periods to which they are assigned via the face-value chronologies of the books themselves. *These ancient details were unknown in the culture of late Iron Age Israelite and Judahite priests!*

Why is this important to know? Simply for this reason: If, as liberal scholars insist, the first seven books of the Old Testament were concocted during the tenth to fifth centuries BC (Iron Age 2), then they, somehow, miraculously managed to record accurate historical and cultural data from the distant past that would have been entirely unknown and unavailable to them. But there were no "James Micheners" during Iron Age 2! The stories of Abraham, Isaac, Jacob, and Joseph have "Middle Bronze Age" written all over them. The accounts of the exodus, the giving of the Mosaic law, and the conquest of Canaan are saturated with Late Bronze Age details, as are the books of Judges, Ruth, and Job, which also spill over into the early part of the Iron Age. I refer to these books collectively as the "Bronze Age Bible" for good reason: *They were written mostly during the Bronze Age.*

But the "Iron Age Bible"—as I like to call the balance of the Old Testament—is likewise loaded with historical and cultural specifics, many of which are organically linked to persons, places, events, and objects from the Ancient Near East. What follows is a mere sampling of these:

- The mini-empire of David and Solomon filled precisely the territory *not* taken up by the known surrounding kingdoms. We would predict the existence of a nation the very size of Israel even if the Old Testament did not exist.[27]

- A fragment of Aramean text—the Tel Dan Inscription—mentions the "house [dynasty] of David" (Hebrew, *bytdvd*), and an Egyptian inscription refers to the "heights of David" (the central highland location of Hebron and Jerusalem, two of David's capital city sites), confirming that King David was a historical figure. The Mesha Stela (tenth century BC), which mentions the Israelite king Omri, may also refer to the House of David (*bytd--*).[28]

- After the death of Solomon, Shoshenq I—biblical Shishak (1 Kings 11; 2 Chronicles 12)—plundered Jerusalem's palace and temple. According to Egyptian records, Shoshenq died just one year later. His son Osorkon I, after ruling barely three years, made spectacular gifts to the gods of Egypt, including more than 383 tons of silver and gold. At this rather "depressed" time in Egypt's history, where did all this wealth come from? It likely came from Solomon's treasures brought back to Egypt by Osorkon I's father![29]

- The Prism of Sennacherib (aka Taylor Prism) records an Assyrian version of Sennacherib's siege of 46 fortified Judean cities, including Jerusalem under Hezekiah (2 Kings 18:13–19:36; Isaiah 36:1-37; 37). In this account of his third campaign (701 BC), Sennacherib describes his victories over several Levantine kingdoms, after which he encountered the Egyptian army. The Egyptian commander is not identified in Sennacherib's *Annals*, but he *is* identified in the Old Testament as Tirhakah (2 Kings 19:9; Isaiah 37:9), a Nubian ruler who later became Pharaoh Taharqa of Egypt (690–664 BC).[30]

• The *Nabonidus Cylinder* sets the record straight on the accuracy of Daniel by confirming that Nabonidus's son, Belshazzar, was in fact, the last ruling monarch in Babylon the night it fell to the Medo-Persians.[31]

The Discovery of the City of Sodom

While the examples above—and hundreds like them!—make a substantial case for the historical authenticity of the Old Testament, one of the most powerful confirmations of its historicity is the recent discovery and excavation of the infamous city of Sodom (Tall el-Hammam, also spelled Tall al-Hammām; "tall," "tell," or "tel" refers to a mound of ancient ruins).[32] By applying the primary biblical text (Genesis 13:1-12) for the location of Sodom and the cities of the Jordan "plain" (Hebrew is *kikkar* of the Jordan; *kikkar* = "circle" or "disk"; thus, Jordan Disk), we successfully located a previously unknown Bronze Age city-state (a large, fortified urban center with many satellite towns, villages, and hamlets under its control) along the eastern edge of the well-watered Jordan Disk, about eight miles northeast of the Dead Sea. It was *exactly* where Genesis 13 locates it—north of the Dead Sea, east of the Jordan

River, and visible from the area of Bethel and Ai. Not only Sodom (Tall el-Hammam), but also Gomorrah (Tall Kufrayn), Admah (Tall Nimrin), and Zeboiim (in Hebrew, a plural indicating two sister cities: Tall Bleibel and Tall Mustah) are lined up in south-to-north order along the eastern Jordan Valley trade route leading up to Laish/Lasha (Tel Dan), just as described in Genesis 10.[33]

The heavily fortified core city—Sodom itself—is located at the Tall el-Hammam excavation site. We (Trinity Southwest University and Veritas International University) are currently well into our second decade of excavating this fantastic archaeological site. We now know that it was the *largest continuously occupied city* in the southern Levant (Israel and Jordan) during the Bronze Age, and it had many towns and villages under its control (Genesis 10; 13–19). Its 100-acre occupational footprint includes massive defensive ramparts and city walls, towers, a monumental gateway, waterworks, residential areas, a huge temple complex, palace(s), and administrative buildings. Its 2,000-year history as a city-state lasted through the Early Bronze and Intermediate Bronze Ages (Genesis 10) and most of the Middle Bronze Age (the time of Abraham). The horrific terminal destruction stratum at Tall el-Hammam confirms that, toward the end of the Middle Bronze Age, "burning stones and fire from Yahweh out of the heavens" obliterated Sodom and "all the land of the Kikkar" (Genesis 19:24-28)—a cosmic airburst that destroyed an entire millennia-old civilization literally in the blink of an eye.[34] Indeed, this well-watered landscape, thus destroyed, lay barren without agriculture or settlements for the next 700 years!

While the vast majority of scholars have traditionally insisted that the story of Sodom and Gomorrah is nothing but fiction, the overwhelming archaeological evidence demonstrates that not only did Sodom and the cities of the Kikkar exist, but that they were, in fact, wiped out in a manner mirroring the precise language of Genesis 19.

With no fear of contradiction, we can safely conclude, on the basis of archaeological evidence alone, that the Old Testament remains the finest collection of historical/geographical texts surviving from Ancient Near East antiquity. Nothing compares to it!

It is appropriate to allow professor Kitchen the final word:

> The theories current in Old Testament studies, however brilliantly conceived and elaborated, were mainly established in a vacuum with little or no reference to the Ancient Near East, and initially too often in accordance with *a priori* philosophical and literary principles. It is solely because the data from the Ancient Near East coincide so much better with the existing observable structure of Old Testament history, literature and religion than with the theoretical reconstructions, that we are compelled—as happens in Ancient Oriental studies—to question or even to abandon such theories regardless of their popularity. *Facts not votes determine the truth* [emphasis added].[35]

Were the New Testament Manuscripts Copied Accurately?

Don Stewart and Joseph M. Holden

Because scholars do not possess the original writings of the New Testament (known as *autographs*), we must ask: How accurate are the manuscript *copies* (*apographs*)? For if the copies do not reflect the original writings of Scripture, we would have no idea what the original texts said. Because there were no copy machines available in ancient times, the tedious transmission process had to be accomplished by the scribe's own hand. Hence, copies were called "manual-scripts" or *manuscripts*.

As modern scholars conduct a careful analysis of the manuscript copies, it is obvious that the New Testament text contains minor scribal "mistakes." This has led some to erroneously assume the Bible is not inspired or inerrant in all that it states, claims, teaches, and implies. This false assumption emerges from the notion that all New Testament *copies* produced through the centuries must be exact replicas of the original text. That is to say, with regard to the time when the New Testament was originally written until the time the printing press was invented, some have demanded that the scribes copy the text 100 percent accurately, or it cannot be considered inspired

or inerrant. They conclude that because the scribes fell short of perfect transmission, an inspired and inerrant Bible is impossible. However, there are several reasons Christians believe the New Testament manuscripts were copied accurately (despite minor scribal mistakes) and why it can still be considered the inspired and inerrant Word of God.

To understand this issue better, we should familiarize ourselves with the process Bible scholars undertake in their effort to reconstruct the original text. Scholars diligently work like forensic scientists analyzing a crime scene, carefully examining the evidence left behind so they can reconstruct what originally happened. Similarly, by evaluating and comparing the textual evidence (known as *textual criticism*), scholars can then work backward to establish what was originally written. Our English Bible is the culmination of this textual investigation.

Examining the Textual Evidence

There are three main areas of textual evidence to consider when answering the question of whether the New Testament manuscripts were copied accurately: (1) the number of Greek manuscripts, (2) the dating of the manuscripts, and (3) the textual accuracy of the manuscript copies.

The Number of Greek Manuscripts

The New Testament possesses the highest number of manuscripts of any book from the ancient world (prior to AD 350). To better understand the scope of the numbers involved, as of 2017, the Institute for New Testament Textual Research, located at the University of Munster in Germany, currently lists the official number at 5,856 partial and complete manuscript copies written in the Greek language.[1] These include handwritten copies of the New Testament papyri, parchment and lectionaries. If we add to this number more than 18,000 New Testament manuscripts written in other languages (translations) besides Greek, the overall count swells to nearly 24,000 New Testament manuscripts! Because the versions are in a different language from the original Greek, they are not as valuable as the Greek manuscripts in reconstructing the text. However, they are still important witnesses to the text's reliability and transmission.

We can appreciate the robust number of New Testament manuscripts by comparing it with the number of manuscripts available for other works from the ancient world. For example, the second-most-supported work behind the New Testament is Homer's well-known poem *Iliad*, with more than 1,900 manuscripts.[2] Ancient literature was rarely translated into another language—with the New Testament being an important exception. From the very beginning, Christian missionaries, in their attempts to spread the gospel, translated the New Testament into the various languages of the people they

encountered. These translations, some made as early as the middle of the second century, give us an important witness to the text of that time.

The greater number of manuscripts available gives scholars added confidence when it comes to reconstructing the original New Testament text, for it offers a textual "checks and balances" when comparing and contrasting the various manuscripts. For example, if one manuscript is missing a passage of Scripture, a scholar needs only to consult the numerous other copies. Alternatively, if any ancient work were to come down to us in only one copy, there would be nothing with which to compare that copy. In such a case, there would be no way of knowing whether the scribe was incompetent, for the text could not be checked against another copy.

Additional witnesses to the accuracy of the New Testament text, which are among the Greek manuscripts, are the *lectionaries*. The church followed the custom of the Jewish synagogue, which had a fixed portion of the law and the prophets read each Sabbath. In the same manner, Christians developed the practice of reading a fixed portion of the gospels and the New Testament letters every Sunday (and on holy days). These fixed portions are known as lectionaries. Surviving fragments of lectionaries come from as early as the sixth century AD, while complete manuscripts are dated from as early as the eighth century. Interestingly, the more than 2,400 copies of lectionaries that still exist reveal greater care in their transmission than other biblical manuscripts.

Because we possess so many manuscripts (from various sources and geographical areas), scholars can have confidence the original biblical text has been well preserved. Consequently, translators never have to rely on blind guesses when determining what the text originally said. The text has come down to us in an accurate manner, with nothing lost in its transmission.

The Early Manuscript Dates

The amount of time that has passed between the original manuscripts and the earliest copies available is a crucial element of determining the accuracy of transmission. The time span between the date the work was originally completed and the earliest existing copy available to us is significant. Usually, the shorter the time span, the more dependable the copy. The longer the interval between the original and the copy, the more room there is for errors, embellishments, and distortions to creep in as the text is copied and recopied.

Fortunately, this time span for the New Testament manuscripts is relatively short, with the earliest manuscript copies currently ranging from 30-300 years from the original texts. In our modern culture, 30-300 years seems like a long time, but for historians of ancient literature, it is like yesterday!

The earliest New Testament manuscript fragment we possess today, the John Rylands Fragment (also called P52), contains a small portion of John 18. Most scholars date the fragment anywhere from AD 117–135, which, at its earliest, is only about 30 years removed from the original writing of the Gospel of John. The entire New Testament text is accounted for in manuscript form within 300 years of the original writing (cf. Chester Beatty Collection, Bodmer Collection, Codex Sinaiticus and Codex Vaticanus).

Christians can truly appreciate the excellent position the New Testament occupies regarding the early dates. For the best writings of the ancient Greeks—such as Plato, Aristotle, Herodotus, Thucydides, and Homer—the time span between the original writings and the earliest copies is often more than 1,000 years. In most cases, only 5 to 20 manuscripts support these ancient non-Christian works. In the case of Homer's *Iliad*, the time span is about 400 years, and, as mentioned earlier, is supported by nearly 2,000 manuscripts.

A comparison with other literary works from the ancient world reveals a growing number of New Testament documents and their early dates, as well as the increasing number of manuscripts from the ancient world.

Biblical Manuscripts Compared to Selected Ancient Sources					
Author	Ancient Source	Date of Original	Earliest Manuscript	Gap from Original	Manuscript Copies
Plato	Dialogues/ Tetralogies	4th cent. BC	3rd cent. BC	c. 150 years	c. 210-240
Homer	Iliad	9th cent. BC	c. 400–415 BC	c. 450 years	c. 1800+
Herodotus	History	5th cent. BC	2nd–1st cent. BC	c. 450 years	c. 100+
Thucydides	History of the Peloponnesian War	5th cent. BC	3rd cent BC	c. 200 years	c. 185
Demosthenes	Orations/ Speeches	4th cent. BC	1st cent. BC	c. 300 years	c. 440+
Aristophanes	Assorted works	448–385 BC	AD 900	c. 1,300 years	10
Sophocles	Plays	5th cent. BC?	3rd cent. BC	c. 200 years	c. 220+
Julius Caesar	The Gallic Wars	58–44 BC	9th cent. AD	c. 900 years	c. 250
Tacitus	Annals of Imperial Rome	AD 58-120	9th–11th cent. AD	c. 800–1000 years	c. 33+
Suetonius	The Twelve Caesars	AD 118–120	9th cent. AD	c. 800 years	c. 8+
Pliny, the Elder	Natural History	1st cent. AD	5th /14th–15th cent. AD	c. 400–1500 years	c. 200
Greek New Testament Manuscripts		AD 45–100	AD 117–325	30–300 years	5,856
Non-Greek New Testament manuscripts (translations)					18,000+
Total New Testament manuscripts					c. 24,000
Old Testament scrolls and codices (in various collections)					c. 42,000
Total biblical manuscripts					c. 66,000+

Source: Adapted and updated from H. Wayne House and Joseph M. Holden, *Charts of Apologetics and Christian Evidences* (Grand Rapids, MI: Zondervan, 2006), Chart 43.

John Warwick Montgomery comments on the strong bibliographical standing the New Testament enjoys when he says, "To be skeptical of the resultant text of the New Testament books is to allow all of classical antiquity to slip into obscurity, for no documents of the ancient period are as well attested bibliographically as the New Testament."[3]

Another early witness to the accuracy of the New Testament text comes from the prolific writings (of more than one million quotations of Scripture) of the early church fathers. For example, seven letters have survived that were written by Ignatius (AD 70–110), and nearly every book of the Bible (except 2 John and Jude) was quoted by AD 110 by only three church fathers—Ignatius, Clement of Rome, and Polycarp. In those seven letters, Ignatius quoted from 18 different books of the New Testament. Every time he cited Scripture, we can observe the Greek text he was using. Consequently, the early fathers provide us with an excellent early witness to the text. For this reason their prolific writings remain an important witness to the New Testament.

The number of quotations from the church fathers is so overwhelming that if every other source for the New Testament (Greek manuscripts and versions) were destroyed, the vast majority of the New Testament text could be reconstructed! Because of this, any impartial person cannot help but be impressed with their abundant testimony. To dismiss these areas of support would be self-defeating, for it would mean that every extrabiblical ancient work considered "reliable" by secular scholars—all of which are based on lesser evidence—would need to be brought into question.

Accurate Transmission and Variant Readings

When a manuscript(s) differs in wording from the base text, the result is known as a "variant reading." Because of the innumerable times the New Testament has been copied over the last 2,000 years, these variants have crept into the text. Some scholars estimate that 400,000 or more of these variants (errors) exist in the New Testament text. However, using the word *error* to describe these deviations from the original text can give the wrong idea and is often misleading. Technically speaking, any deviation from the base accepted text is an error, but the kinds of "errors" represented in the New Testament text are not errors of historical, geographical, spiritual, or scientific fact. Instead, they are rather trivial. Therefore, the term "variant(s)" has been employed by scholars to avoid this confusion, since misspellings, omissions, differing word orders, updated words (substitution), and additions are much different in nature than errors of fact that would threaten biblical inerrancy or the truth value of the message.

There is no doubt that the scribes who copied the texts introduced changes. These scribal changes can be broken down into two basic types: unintentional and intentional. The greatest numbers of variant readings found in the New Testament manuscripts are *unintentional* variants. They could creep into the text through fatigue or through faulty sight, hearing, writing, memory, or judgment on the part of the scribe. Despite these variants, Daniel Wallace of the Center for the Study of New Testament Manuscripts writes, "It is quite true that (virtually) no viable variants are major threats to inerrancy…"[4]

Other variations came about intentionally, as New Testament Greek scholar J. Harold Greenlee notes.

> These comprise a significant, although a much less numerous, group of errors than the unintentional changes. They

derive for the most part from attempts by scribes to improve the text in various ways. Few indeed are the evidences that heretical or destructive variants have been deliberately introduced into the mss [manuscripts].[5]

Thus, the intentional variations, for the most part, were the work of scribes attempting to make the text more readable, not change the meaning. This is the important difference between updating the text (editing) and altering its meaning (redaction). The late Princetonian scholar and renowned authority on New Testament textual criticism Bruce Metzger expands upon the intentional variations. He writes,

> Other divergences in wording arose from deliberate attempts to smooth out grammatical or stylistic harshness, or to eliminate real or imagined obscurities of meaning in the text. Sometimes a copyist would add what seemed to him to be a more appropriate word or form, perhaps derived from a parallel passage.[6]

The charge that is often made, without qualification—especially by New Testament scholar Bart Ehrman—is that copyists radically changed the substance of the text. Again, the facts speak otherwise, as Michael Holmes explains: "Occasionally the text was altered for doctrinal reasons. Orthodox and heretics alike leveled this charge against their opponents, though the surviving evidence suggests the charge was more frequent than the reality."[7] The amount of intentional variation to the text was minimal. The text was carefully copied, and discerning Christians, who were dispersed throughout the entire Roman Empire, would have made it difficult for malicious changes to be introduced.

There is simply no evidence of widespread altering of the text for doctrinal reasons. Furthermore, the variant readings, whether intentional or unintentional, exist in only a very limited portion of the New Testament.

Two of the greatest textual scholars who ever lived, Brooke Foss Westcott and Fenton John Anthony Hort, had this to say concerning the amount of variation in the New Testament manuscripts: "If comparative trivialities, such as changes of order, the insertion or omission of an article with proper names, and the like, are set aside, the words in our opinion still subject to doubt can hardly amount to more than a thousandth part of the whole New Testament."[8]

B.B. Warfield made a similar assertion when he wrote, "[The New Testament] has been transmitted to us with no, or next to no, variation; and even in the most corrupt form in which it has ever appeared, to use the oft-quoted words of Richard Bentley, 'The real text of the sacred writers is competently exact.'"[9] Textual criticism experts Maurice A. Robinson and William G. Pierpont note the following situation in which we find the text of the New Testament:

> For over four-fifths of the New Testament, the Greek text is considered 100% certain, regardless of which textype might be favored by any critic. This undisputed bulk of the text reflects a common pre-existing archetype (the autograph), which has universal critical acceptance. Note...that most of the variant readings found in manuscripts of other textypes are trivial or untranslatable. Only about 400-600 variant readings seriously affect the translational sense of any passage in the entire New Testament.[10]

Therefore, when all the variants of the New Testament are considered, we are dealing with only 400 to 600 variants that have any effect on the translation of the text.

What is more, church historian Phillip Schaff estimated that of the 400 variants that have affected the sense of the passages in the New Testament, only 50 of these are important.[11] Facts like this led textual scholars Kurt and Barbara Aland to make the following observation concerning the text of the New Testament:

> On the whole, it must be admitted that…New Testament specialists… not to mention laypersons, tend to be fascinated by differences and to forget how many of them are due to chance or normal scribal tendencies, and how rarely significant variants occur— yielding to the common danger of failing to see the forest for the trees.[12]

Whatever manuscript tradition we use as the basis for a given translation, the outcome will be substantially the same because the text is basically the same. Whether one prefers to use the Byzantine text type, which is found in the greatest number of manuscripts, or the Alexandrian text type, which has fewer but older manuscripts, the final result will be more or less the same. They all tell the same story! That is to say, the words (*verba*) may vary slightly, but the voice or meaning (*vox*) is the same. For example, consider the following illustration that describes the relationship between variant words and meaning:

1. YOU HAVE WON TEN MILLION DOLLARS

2. THOU **HAST WON** TEN MILLION DOLLARS [Notice the King James bias here]

3. Y'ALL **HAVE WON** $10,000,000 [Notice the Southern bias here]

Observe that of the 28 letters in line 2, only 5 of them [in bold] are the same in line 3. That is, about 19 percent of the letters are the same. Yet, despite the bias, the message is 100 percent identical! The lines are different in form but not in content. Likewise, even with the many differences in the New Testament variants, *100 percent of the message comes through.*[13]

This is a powerful illustration of why we can acknowledge that our manuscript copies contain variants and yet, at the same time, we can state with confidence that the Bible is inerrant. In other words, the words may change slightly, but the meaning is still the same. The voice of God is heard loud and clear in the text! This is seen in the Gospel of Matthew, where the author cited and made allusions to the Old Testament more than 100 times. Even in places where loose paraphrases were used, we can still recognize those allusions as Scripture.

Despite these variants, scholars have recognized the great accuracy with which the New Testament manuscripts were copied. Metzger claimed that the Hindu Mahabharata was copied at about 90 percent accuracy and Homer's *Iliad* at about 95 percent accuracy.[14] As noted in the illustration above, if 90-95 percent accuracy is achieved in the transmission process, it would be more than enough to communicate 100 percent of the original meaning of the text. Other notable Bible scholars, such as Ezra Abbot, figured the copies of the New Testament manuscripts are 99.75 percent accurate.[15] Westcott and Hort calculated the New Testament's accuracy at 98.33 percent by asserting that only one-sixteenth of variants rise above the level of trivialities.[16] Greek scholar A.T. Robertson places the transmission rate at 99.9 percent accurate, believing only a thousandth part of the New Testament text was of any real concern.[17] Even New Testament critic Ehrman, writes, in his *Misquoting Jesus*, "Most of the changes found in our early Christian manuscripts have nothing to do with theology or ideology."[18]

Confidence in the Research Results

Based on the various kinds of evidence, it is clear that great care was taken to accurately copy the Greek manuscripts. Thus we can be confident that the text of the New Testament, as it stands today, is essentially the same text that was originally written by the authors of Scripture. Without any doubt, the quantity of New Testament manuscripts, the dates from the original manuscripts to the earliest copies available, and quality of the copies of the New Testament manuscripts all serve as undeniable and powerful witnesses to the accurate preservation of God's inspired and inerrant Word.

Is the Qur'an's Text More Reliable
Than the Biblical Text?

Jay H. Smith

In the previous chapters we have looked at the reliability of the Old and New Testament texts and found them to be quite trustworthy. We now move our attention to a third text within the Abrahamic religious tradition, that of the Qur'an (or Koran), the scripture of Islam.

Before exploring whether it is reliable, we need to consider what Muslims claim concerning the text of the Qur'an, and then ascertain whether it actually meets those claims. This will reveal to us whether the Qur'an can be deemed reliable or not. The Qur'an is a much newer book (only about 1,400 years old) than both the Old and New Testaments, and thus would not qualify as an "ancient" document as are the biblical texts. Because it originated much later, Muslims should have no difficulty producing full and complete original texts for each of its 114 Surahs (or books/chapters).

Muslims claim that the Qur'an has always existed, preserved on eternal tablets that reside in heaven (Surah 85:22), and sent to earth piecemeal via the angel Gabriel to Muhammad from AD 610–632.[1] They claim that the text Muhammad received is identical with the text that can be read in today's Arabic Qur'an. What is more, they maintain that it is the only scripture that is still "preserved to the present time in its exact original form"[2]—that not a chapter, nor a verse, "nor a word,"[3] nor "even a letter,"[4] nor a "diacritical mark,"[5] nor a "dot,"[6] "not even a jot or tittle"[7] has been changed since it was written down by the third caliph, Caliph Uthman, around AD 652.

Thus, it is a text that is eternal, sent down to Muhammad over a period of 22 years and completed by Uthman 20 years after Muhammad's death, and unchanged over the last 1,400 years. These are enormous claims.

Muslims have set the bar so high concerning the Qur'an that it is rather easy to test their claims about it. All we need to do is ask them to provide just one complete manuscript of the Qur'an from the mid-seventh century (i.e., the time of Caliph Uthman in AD 652) that is unchanged. In other words, it is exactly the same as the present canonized Hafs Qur'an used by the majority of Muslims today. The problem is, they cannot do that.

What Kinds of Problems Are at Issue?

Manuscript Problems

Two leading Turkish Qur'anic scholars, Dr. Tayyar Altıkulaç and professor Dr. Ekmeleddin İhsanoğlu, the only Muslim scholars who have been permitted complete access to review and research the six oldest Qur'anic manuscripts,[8] agree with the consensus of Western scholars who state that none of these manuscripts are from the time of Uthman,[9] nor are they from the seventh century.[10] Though these earliest manuscripts were compiled in the early to mid-eighth century,[11] they do not agree entirely with each other.[12] Nor are any of them complete or uniform. In some cases they contain thousands of manuscript variants when compared with the current canonized Hafs Qur'an that is so popular today.[13]

Furthermore, recent research on these six manuscripts by Dr. Dan Brubaker (research done for his doctoral thesis)[14] proved that there are thousands of *intentional* human changes to these manuscripts, including later insertions, erasures, erasures overwritten, overwriting without erasures, tapings, selective coverings, as well as selective coverings overwritten.[15] These changes are not limited to simple diacritical marks[16] or vowel changes,[17] as many Muslims suggest, but include a manipulation of the *Rasm* itself (i.e., the original consonantal text), which would alter the meanings of the words. These alterations are found not only in manuscripts that are written in the eighth century, but continue to be observed in manuscripts dating from the ninth and tenth centuries as well. This suggests that there was an intentional process of standardizing the Qur'anic text for more than 200 years after the Qur'an was supposed to have been written down.

This now leads us to address the issue of *when* the Qur'an, which is currently in use today, finally received its canonization in its final form.

Canonical Problems

This is an issue that Muslims rarely talk about, with very good reason. The official and canonical Hafs Qur'an, which is popular in most Muslim countries, was compiled by a group of scholars at Al-Azhar University in Cairo, Egypt, in 1924—less than 100 years ago!

From what early Qur'anic manuscript was it derived? We know the manuscript could not have been the Topkapi, nor the Sammarqand, nor the Ma'il, nor the Petropolitanus, nor the Husaini, nor even the more recently discovered Sana'a manuscript, for all of these are incomplete and have hundreds and even thousands of variants when compared to the 1924 Hafs text. So what manuscript did these scholars use?

The name attributed to this canonical Qur'an gives us a clue—it was supposedly taken from the text of a certain person named Hafs (who died in AD 805). He was a student of Abu Bakr Aseem (died AD 778), who in turn was the student of Abu Abd ar Rahman (died AD 690); all of whom lived in the city of Kufa. Yet notice the dates of their deaths. Hafs would have been working on his manuscript more than 170 years after the Qur'an was written. Hafs wrote his text nearly 200 years after Muhammad died, and he did so in a city hundreds of miles away.

Moreover, we do not have the original Hafs manuscript. All we possess today is what was attributed to him by the Al-Azhar scholars in 1924. Keep in mind that he had died more than a thousand years previous!

Uniformity Problems

There is another difficulty: Hafs was not the only differing text that existed in the eighth and ninth centuries. Scholars today are scouring the Arabic-speaking world and are collecting currently published Arabic Qur'ans in Middle Eastern marketplaces, all of which differ from the canonical Hafs Qur'an. Dr. Bernie Power in Melbourne has collected 17 different Arabic Qur'ans, while a London colleague, Hatun Tash, has amalgamated 31 differing Arabic Qur'ans.[18]

Hatun, along with native Arabic speakers and teachers in London, have had time to look at only 23 of these Qur'ans, which were compiled in five cities (Mecca, Medina, Damascus, Kufa, and Basra). Yet up to this point, they have been able to tabulate a total of 56,664 differences between these 23 Qur'ans.

Muslims are quick to respond that these differences are nothing more than minor changes, known as *Ahruf,* or *Qira'at,* derived from trivial dialectical variations, yet the meanings remain unchanged. Hatun and her team have disputed that argument and have recently filmed the variants and released them on the Pfanderfilms YouTube site,[19] proving that for more than 1,000 years Muslims have known about these changes, many of which contain not only grammatical mistakes[20] and changes in meaning,[21] but in some cases theological differences.[22]

Is the Qur'an's Text Reliable?

Just how reliable, then, is the Qur'an? Because of its relatively younger age of origin, Muslims should have no problem producing not only an original but also a complete and unchanged manuscript from the mid seventh century. Yet they cannot.

Instead, we have found that the earliest six manuscripts are not from the seventh century at all, but began to appear in the eighth century.

In addition, they are incomplete, and they disagree with each other and with the canonical Hafs text—in some cases containing thousands of variants. Even more damaging is the fact that 2,200 consonantal changes have been recorded so far, some of which continue into the tenth century. We now are told that this intentional manipulation continued up until 1924, when a specific text was finally canonized at the Al-Azhar University.

In addition, we now know that this canonical Qur'an has no original manuscript to support it. Rather, it is attributed to a Qur'anic student named Hafs, who died more than 170 years after Muhammad died. Beyond the Hafs reading of the Qur'an are another 30 derivatives of the Qur'an written by Qur'anic students around the same era. These disagree with each other more than 56,000 times. So why did the Al-Azhar scholars choose Hafs reading over the other 30? We have not been given an answer.

So the question still stands: How reliable is today's Qur'an? With no extant original manuscript available, and given the fact that the earliest manuscripts disagree with one another and with the Qur'an used today, how can anyone say the text of the Qur'an is reliable?

In conclusion, clearly the modern Qur'an is not eternal, nor was it sent down to a man named Muhammad, nor was it completed during the time of Uthman, though it has been changed. These facts prove the Qur'an is, in fact, a document created by men who, over a period of more than 1,000 years, changed, accreted, and deleted the text. This demonstrates that it is not a scripture from an infinite and omnipotent God, but a handwritten book created and altered by finite and erring men.

Does Archaeology Confirm the Historical Reliability of the New Testament?

Brian Janeway

For more than three centuries, the New Testament has come under attack from critics (such as Benedict de Spinoza, Julius Wellhausen, D.F. Strauss, James Frazer, the Jesus Seminar, and others) who have concluded that the Bible is the product of myth, embellishment, or biased stories emerging from the fertile imagination of the authors' minds.

Correspondingly, however, the past two centuries have witnessed the rise of biblical archaeology that has been diligently applied, like a forensic science, in excavating ancient remains throughout the Middle East and Europe. As a result, many thousands of artifacts have been unearthed from the ruins that either directly or indirectly relate to the stories of the Bible. These discoveries have been subjected to modern analysis and have revealed that the New Testament was framed in an authentic first-century historical context.[1]

Recent analysis of the material has contributed to our knowledge of the customs, culture, practices, events, people, and places of the New Testament. Collectively, the vast amount of data has strengthened our understanding in several areas relating to apologetics and the New Testament. What is more, these discoveries have greatly limited the critical theories that portray the New Testament as historical fiction or myth.

People of the New Testament

Archaeologists and historians have succeeded in identifying nearly 100 persons mentioned in the Bible, more than 30 of which are mentioned in the New Testament. The following chart lists some of these individuals and their corresponding discovery in non-Christian sources. Recently published research has also expanded the number of political figures known (and those related to them) from ancient secular sources.[2]

New Testament Persons Cited in Ancient Non-Christian Sources

Person	Scripture	Source
Herod Agrippa I and II	Acts 12; 23:35 Acts 25:13-26; 26	Philo, Josephus Coin inscriptions Nabatean inscription Beirut Museum inscription
Ananias (high priest)	Acts 23:2; 24:1	Josephus
Annas (high priest)	Luke 3:2; John 18:13, 24 Acts 4:6	Josephus
Herod Antipas	Matthew 14:1-6 Mark 6:14-22 Luke 3:1 Acts 4:27; 13:1	Josephus Coin inscriptions that read "Herod the Tetrarch"
Herod Archelaus	Matthew 2:22	Josephus
King Aretas IV (Damascus)	2 Corinthians 11:32	Josephus Madaba map inscription Coins with Aretas's bust
Caesar Augustus (Octavius)	Luke 2:1	Priene inscription announcing birthday; Coin inscriptions Funerary inscription (*Res Gestae Divi Augusti*)
Bernice	Acts 25:13-15	Josephus Suetonius Beirut Museum inscription
Caiaphas (high priest)	Matthew 26:57 John 18:13-14, 24	Josephus Ossuary inscription
Emperor Claudius	Acts 11:28; 18:2	Josephus Suetonius Tacitus Coin inscriptions
Drusilla	Acts 24:24	Josephus Suetonius
Erastus	Romans 16:13-23; 2 Timothy 4:20	Erastus inscription at Corinth

New Testament Persons Cited in Ancient Non-Christian Sources		
Person	Scripture	Source
Marcus Antonius Felix	Acts 23:23–24:27	Josephus Suetonius Tacitus
Porcius Festus	Acts 24:27; 25; 26:24, 32	Josephus
Gallio	Acts 18:12-17	Gallio inscription at Delphi Pliny the Younger Suetonius
Gamaliel	Acts 5:34; 22:3	Josephus Jewish Mishna Talmud

King Herod (Judea)	Matthew 2:1-22; Luke 1:5	Josephus
		Tacitus
		Coin inscriptions
		Herod's tomb at the Herodium
		Latin wine jug inscription
		Herodian architecture
		    (i.e., Temple Mount, Masada,
		    Macherus, Herodium, etc.)

Herodias	Matthew 14:3; Mark 6:17	Josephus
James (son of Mary)	Acts 15; epistle of James	James Ossuary
James (son of Zebedee)	Matthew 4:21; 10:2; Mark 5:37	Josephus
Jesus (of Nazareth)	Gospels	Josephus Tacitus Sutonius Pliny the Younger Lucian Babylonian Talmud Mara Bar Serapion Teledoth Jesu James Ossuary inscription Megiddo mosaic floor inscription Alexamenos Graffito (picture)

New Testament Persons Cited in Ancient Non-Christian Sources		
Person	Scripture	Source
John the Baptist	Matthew 3:1-13; Luke 1:7-39	Josephus Baptismal site (and steps) in Jordan at Jordan River John the Baptist cave (TBD)
Joseph (adoptive father of Jesus)	Matthew 1:20	James Ossuary
Judas the Galilean	Acts 5:37	Josephus
Lysanias	Luke 3:1	Josephus Stone inscription at Abila (northern Morocco)
Herod Philip I (of Iturea)	Luke 3:1	Josephus
Herod Philip II (of Galilee)	Matthew 14:3; Mark 6:17; Luke 3:19	Josephus Coin inscriptions
Pontius Pilate	Matthew 27 Luke 23:6 John 18:25–19:30	Josephus Tacitus Philo Coins minted during his reign Pilate dedication stone inscription
Quirinius (Publius Sulpicius)	Luke 2:2	Josephus Tacitus Res Gestae inscription at Antioch Pisidia
Salome ("daughter of Herodias")	Matthew 14:6	Josephus
Sergius Paulus	Acts 13:7	Two stone inscriptions (Cyprus and Rome) L. Sergius Paulus inscription (Pisidian Antioch, Turkey)
Theudas	Acts 5:36	Josephus

New Testament Persons Cited in Ancient Non-Christian Sources		
Person	**Scripture**	**Source**
Caesar Tiberius	Luke 3:1	Josephus
		Tacitus
		Suetonius
		Marcus Velleius Paterculus
		Coin inscriptions
		Mentioned on Pilate dedication stone (Caesarea)

© Joseph M. Holden, 2013, 2018, adapted from Joseph M. Holden and Norman L. Geisler, *The Popular Handbook of Archaeology and the Bible: Discoveries That Confirm the Reliability of Scripture* (Eugene, OR: Harvest House, 2013), 303-305

The Remains of Luke

In addition to the individuals mentioned above, recent studies have revealed interesting information about the apostle Paul's travel companion, Luke.

Several years ago, an intensive investigation of human remains purported to be those of Luke (author of the third Gospel and the book of Acts) were undertaken by an international team of more than 30 experts from various disciplines.[3] The *New York Times*, in an article titled "Body of St. Luke Gains Credibility" (October 16, 2001), summarized the results of the research.[4]

According to the early church historian Eusebius, Luke was a native of Antioch. He was a physician by trade, and his high level of education is evidenced in the elevated style of Greek found in his writings. His claim to be writing actual history, his accurate use of ancient titles and names, and his Gospel's many correspondences with extrabiblical historical sources and archaeology testify to his credibility and fidelity as an eyewitness historian of the early church. Several so-called "we passages" in Acts support the notion that he was a companion to Paul during his travels.

Second Timothy 4:11 again places Luke in the company of Paul—"Luke alone is with me"—when the apostle was imprisoned in Rome near the end of his life. Following Paul's execution, Luke is believed to have continued preaching the gospel in the regions of Italy, Galatia, Dalmatia, and Macedon. Eastern tradition holds that Luke died at the age of 84 in Thebes, Greece, early in the second century. Interestingly, the city today contains an Attic-style (Greek) sarcophagus quarried from local stone, empty of the presumed human remains of the evangelist.[5]

Following Luke's initial burial in Thebes, his remains were transferred to Constantinople to the Church of the Holy Apostles in the year AD 357 during the reign of the Emperor Constantius, according to both Procopius and St. Jerome. There is some disagreement in the sources about where the remains were taken next, some suggesting that his relics were transferred for safekeeping during the Iconoclastic (Greek meaning "image breaking") period, which swept across the Eastern church during the eighth and ninth centuries.[6]

Eventually the remains made their way to Padua, Italy, at an unspecified time before AD 1177, when the Benedictine monks of

St. Justina discovered a leaden casket on April 14, 1117—a date that is commemorated to this day in the city. An affidavit describes several objects found in or around the coffin. They included an image of three calves' heads (the ancient symbol of Luke), an eight-armed cross stamped on the exterior of the casket, and a marble tablet bearing the inscription "S.L. Evang." In AD 1313, the remains were placed in a marble sarcophagus, and in the year 1562, the sepulcher was put on permanent exhibition in the just-completed Basilica of St. Justina, where it continues to reside today.

The results of the scientific investigation on Luke's reputed remains were quite revealing. Signs of osteoporosis and severe arthritis of the spine were present in the skeletal remains, which indicated the remains came from a man about 163 cm tall (5'4"), who was between 75 and 85 years of age at the time of death. Two teeth were subjected to DNA analysis, and the results were compared to those of modern populations of Greeks, Turks, and north Syrian Arabic speakers, the latter of which reside in the vicinity of ancient Antioch, Luke's hometown. A Greek origin for the remains was ruled out, with the closest parallel being to the Syrian group. Radiocarbon dating suggested a date between the second and fourth centuries AD.[7]

Several additional lines of evidence lend strong support for the authenticity of the remains:[8]

1. The pelvis had fused with the coffin itself, indicating their contemporaneity, and the coffin also contained pollen of Greek pine found only in that region.

2. Two small lead tablets found with the coffin state that the remains are those of Luke. Linguistically, both tablets date prior to the fourth century.

3. An eight-armed cross on one side of the casket is a fusion of the Greek cross and the St. Anthony cross specific to usage in charnal houses of the second and third centuries.

4. The leaden coffin fits into the empty chamber of the marble sarcophagus in Thebes, which itself stylistically dates to the second and third century, specific to the Attica region of Greece.

Modern science is incapable of giving total certainty regarding the authenticity of the remains. But the various lines of archaeological data, combined with a reliable history of veneration, offer as much proof as is possible for such ancient relics (see my articles detailing research on the tomb of the apostle Paul and the martyrium of the apostle Philip).[9]

Indeed, the more archaeology uncovers, the more Scripture is upheld through the evidence of material culture, something for which we can all feel blessed and fortified.

Locations of the New Testament

Of the nearly 6,000 sites located in Bible lands, only a few hundred have been excavated. Even so, archaeology has revealed that many of the cities mentioned in the New Testament were described in an authentic geographical context. Locations such as Jerusalem, Philippi, Caesarea, Capernaum, Thessalonica, Athens, Ephesus, and many more cities have been excavated sufficiently to corroborate their New Testament descriptions.[10] In addition, various geographical features described in Scripture—such as lakes, hills, valleys, mountains, seas, and rivers—are confirmed to have been recorded accurately, and in some cases have helped archaeologists locate biblical cities. To be certain, the writers of the New Testament always used real geography to provide the setting for the narratives they present. Because the cumulative amount of information confirmed about various locations in the New Testament dwarfs the space allowed in this chapter, I will mention just two specific recent discoveries that correspond to the New Testament record.[11]

The Pool of Bethesda. John 5 recounts Jesus's miraculous healing of a man who had been lame for 38 years. The pool was described as having five porticos, and was the scene of multitudes of the sick and suffering, who would lounge about waiting for a divine stirring of the waters. The individual first into the pool at such time was believed to be cured. This corresponds well to the Aramaic meaning of the name as "house of mercy" or "place of flowing water."

First uncovered in the 1880s approximately 100 meters north of the Temple Mount, the pool was found to consist of a rectangular basin with a wall dividing it into two sections, thus making it a five-sided pool, precisely as described by John. Due to its importance to early Christians, a Byzantine church was constructed over its eastern end, and a Crusader chapel was later erected over the central wall.

Recent investigations at the site by Ronny Reich and Eli Shukron have established it as a large public Jewish ritual bath known as a *mikveh*.[12] Shimon Gibson has demonstrated the ritual nature of the complex on the basis of monumental stairs that extend across the entire width of the southern pool, which would otherwise waste valuable capacity if it

had functioned simply as a cistern or reservoir. Moreover, the staircase has three wide sets of stairs and landings to accommodate a maximum number of bathers.[13]

The northern pool functioned as an *otzer*, or reserve pool for the *mikveh*. Being naturally fed and then collected, it subsequently flowed into the *mikveh* and thereby satisfied Jewish purity laws. Such water was required to be "given by the hand of God," by way of rainwater, a stream, or a river (Mishnah, *Mikva'ot* 6.8). Beginning in the second century BC, ritual purity laws that had been confined to the clergy were broadly applied to all people, particularly when they were present in Jerusalem. Though small *mikva'ot* can be found in private residences, large ritual pools were now required to accommodate the crowds who participated in the three great pilgrimage festivals (Pesach or Passover, Sukkot or Tabernacles, and Shavuot or Weeks). Today, the pool can be seen at the Church of St. Anne, several hundred feet inside Stephen's Gate.[14]

The Pool of Siloam. The Pool of Bethesda and the Pool of Siloam constitute the two largest *mikva'ot* ever found in Jerusalem. Curiously, they are mentioned only in John's Gospel, indicating the apostle's intimate and detailed knowledge of the city. But before we address the Siloam Pool of Jesus's day, we should clarify that there are actually three such pools by that name. The earliest one dates to the reign of King Hezekiah, who constructed his famous tunnel to secure the water source of the Gihon Spring from attack by Assyrian King Sennacherib in 710 BC (2 Kings 20:20; 2 Chronicles 32:2-4). The latest Pool of Siloam is visible today at the exit of Hezekiah's Tunnel. But this was constructed during the Byzantine period (fifth century AD), long after Jesus's time.

The scene of Jesus's healing of the blind man (John 9:6-12) was only recently discovered in 2004 during a construction project at the southern end of the City of David, just southeast of the Byzantine pool described above. What began with the uncovering of two stone steps subsequently revealed a monumental trapezoidal-shaped pool measuring 225 feet long. With features not unlike those of the Pool of Bethesda, this pool also functioned as a *mikveh* during the Second Temple period.[15] In addition, archaeology has further confirmed that ancient Jerusalem was filled with such ritual pools during the time of Christ.[16]

The discoveries of the Pools of Bethesda and Siloam reveal striking confirmation of biblical events and details long since buried in 2,000 years of accumulated debris.

Conclusion

The historical importance of the New Testament narratives cannot be overstated, for Christianity's foundational doctrines often flow out of the events recorded in the text (Romans 4:25). Ultimately, if the crucifixion and resurrection did not occur as actual historical events, then we do not receive the spiritual benefit of the forgiveness of sins or salvation (cf. John 3:12; Romans 4:25). As we have seen, archaeological evidence continues to conclusively demonstrate that the New Testament writers were historically accurate. Attempts to dismiss the New Testament as myth or fiction can no longer be maintained without strong counterargument in view of the ever-increasing body of information unearthed from the rubble of the ancient Near East and Europe. Christian believers can rest assured that their faith in Christ is well grounded in history, which firmly reflects the truth of the historic Christian faith.

32

What Is the Internal Evidence for the Historical Reliability of the New Testament?

H. Wayne House

Until the Enlightenment (1688–1800), the concerted opinion of the Christian church—with few disagreements—was that the Bible was a book inspired by God. As such, the biblical text represented true events, persons, and geographical and historical particulars, and provided a revelation from God regarding His will and His plan for humanity. With the emergence of the Enlightenment, however, there arose a number of people who denied the foregoing and asserted that the biblical text was merely a human work. According to these thinkers, human reason is the means by which all forms of human knowledge should be evaluated. Thus, the Bible was subjected to the same criterion.

Since that time, the number of negative biblical critics has increased, particularly in academia, so that both Christian scholars and the general Christian public have been subjected to ridicule because of their stand that the Word of God is infallible. In addition, Scripture itself has come under intense rationalistic criticism.

In contrast to this critical approach, conservative scholars have argued that an antisupernaturalistic (i.e., disbelief in miracles) approach to biblical studies does not demand a rejection of the historical and moral information that we discover in the study of the biblical text. Moreover, there is no compelling reason to accept the view that the biblical stories, and other information within the text, are inaccurate representations of what they claim. What is more, there is simply no reason to doubt that the various books of the New Testament were written by anyone other than those who were associated with Jesus, or who were protégés of these men.

Consequently, it is reasonable and consistent with historical research that the writings of the New Testament date within the first century of the Christian era. The authors, for the most part, were witnesses of all those things that are found within the Gospels, or were associates with those individuals who wrote the Gospels and the epistles of the New Testament.

In adopting this position, conservative biblical scholars are not simply embracing the accuracy of the New Testament from only a religious faith standpoint, for the writings themselves reveal the marks of historically reliable composition, unlike the second-century compositions not written by eyewitnesses (e.g., the Gnostic gospels). When those who personally witnessed the words and events recorded in the New Testament were no longer present to provide corrections, it would have been relatively easy for anonymous sources to write revised accounts of Christ that introduced mythical elements that have no historical basis.

In addition, the attempts of many to pit various texts of the New Testament, particularly the Gospel accounts, against one another are not found to be credible.

There are essentially three ways that the writings of the New Testament, or any historical work, are studied: (1) the *bibliographical test*, which speaks to questions regarding the quantity, quality, and dating of the biblical manuscripts; (2) the *external test*, which examines the evidence found *outside* the New Testament in disciplines such as ancient books, archaeology, or in studies of historical literature; and (3) the *internal test*, through which we can discover the accuracy of the biblical writings by an internal study of its contents. Our purpose in this chapter is to review the *internal* evidence that demonstrates the reliability of the New Testament.

Internal Support for the Reliability of the New Testament

Now let us turn our attention to some considerations regarding the central focus of the New Testament: our Lord and Savior, Jesus the Messiah. Christ's authority provides a foundation and a standard by which we can evaluate the apostolic writings—namely, the Gospels, Acts, the epistles, and Revelation.

Jesus as the Authority for the New Testament. I should point out that this inherence to the canonical Scriptures comes not from adherence to sentimental reliance on some emotional experience, but rather on the acceptance that Jesus stands as the authority of the unique nature of the Hebrew and Greek Scriptures. The apostle John said as much when he spoke to Jesus these words, "Now you are speaking plainly and not using figurative speech! Now we know that you know all things and do not need anyone to question you; this is why we believe that you came from God" (John 16:29-30). We see, then, that Jesus Himself *is* the authority over the nature of the Word of God, and not those scholars who subjected the text to the minutia of critical analysis in hope of finding fault with its truth.

We know that Jesus never wrote any books of the New Testament, but He did indicate in John 14 and 16 that the Spirit of God, when He came, would remind His disciples of the words that Jesus spoke, and they would be led by that same Spirit into the truths that would be explained afterward. Following the Last Supper with His disciples, Jesus spoke these words: "The Helper, the Holy Spirit, whom the Father will send in my name, he will teach you all things and bring to your remembrance all that I have said to you" (John 14:26), and "When the Spirit of truth comes, he will guide you into all the truth, for he will not speak on his own authority, but whatever he hears he will speak, and he will declare to you the things that are to come" (John 16:13).

Not only were the words and understanding of truth to be given to them by the

Holy Spirit, but even those words they spoke before others were to be directed by the Spirit of the Father (Matthew 10:19-20; cf. Luke 12:11-12).

In line with these promises of the Lord, it is significant that we see the church being built upon the teachings of the apostles (Acts 2:42). The continued reading of Acts demonstrates that the apostolic teaching and preaching served as the foundation for the early church. Consistent with this, Paul's statement in Ephesians 2:20 is significant, where he mentions that the church is built "on the foundation of the apostles and prophets, Christ Jesus Himself being the cornerstone." As Norman Geisler and William Nix observed, "Thus, the New Testament is the only primary source for study of the Spirit-directed teaching of the apostles, which teaching was promised by Christ in the Gospels."[1]

The Gospels. The importance of the Gospel accounts cannot be overstated, for they are the only reliable record of the churches' knowledge of Jesus and His teaching, other than a few short statements by the apostle Paul. In view of this, it is not unexpected that critical scholars would attack these four records of the life and teachings of Christ, questioning whether they have provided much, if any, of the actual words of Jesus. For example, the highly publicized Jesus Seminar came to the conclusion—through their subjective method of deciding which words in the Gospels are actually the authentic words of Jesus—that 82 percent of His words were inauthentic!

According to the Jesus Seminar, many of the most well-known words of Jesus were not uttered by Him. Among the "discredited" words are the Sermon on the Mount, the commissioning of the 12 apostles in Matthew 10, the parables of Matthew 13, and the Olivet Discourse.

It is necessary to repudiate the careless methodology of the members of the Jesus Seminar in favor of the historical accuracy of the Gospel accounts. These records by the apostles, or their helpers, are not merely biographical sketches of Jesus, but an effort to present to their recipients the evidence that Jesus was in fact the one prophesied from God in the Old Testament. The words and miracles of Jesus surprised and amazed the disciples as much as the people to whom Jesus spoke. They all knew He was special, a prophet from God, and toward the end of His life, and particularly after the resurrection, they came to the realization that He was indeed God in the flesh.

The Book of Acts. The book of Acts, penned by the physician Luke, a companion of Paul the apostle, has had a rocky road among critical scholars. In spite of this, Acts has been vindicated by information confirmed by external evidence from archaeology.

Luke followed a meticulous approach in his work, giving considerable detail of persons, events, places, customs, religious practices, among other information. This reveals him to have been a very careful historical scholar.[2] He was well adapted to dealing with facts and their interaction with the Mediterranean world. Even as Luke has been vindicated by external evidence, the book itself has been used by archaeologists to assist them in their quest for access and accuracy in their own work.

The Epistles and the Revelation. The letters of the New Testament (written by the apostles Paul, Peter, John, and the half-brothers of Jesus, James and Jude) and the Revelation of John are consistent with the form of letter writing used during the first century.

Furthermore, John's Revelation tells us not only about the churches of Asia Minor and the second coming of Jesus, but also aspects of prophecy and apocalyptic writing that was known for hundreds of years in the Jewish community.

Key Questions About Reliability

When viewing the internal evidence for the New Testament, there are considerations that we must take into account in determining whether the books are historically reliable. There are four questions that will guide our evaluation: (1) Are the books written by either eyewitnesses of the events about which they speak, or by someone who wrote on behalf of an eyewitness? (2) Do these written accounts contain contradictions, so as to disqualify them as a reliable guide to the words and events that they speak? (3) Do the New Testament books contain lies such that the information and guidance within them should not be taken at face value? (4) Does the New Testament contain myths, even if those who wrote them believe them to have been true? Were the writers truly eyewitnesses who recorded what they observed and participated in, or were they merely passing along stories they received from others far removed from the original setting of which they speak? The following addresses these four considerations.

When was the New Testament written? Our primary concern about the dating of the New Testament books relates to whether they were written at a time appropriate to when individuals who actually were eyewitnesses could speak of the events they recorded. Or at least, like Luke, who investigated the facts that were passed along to him by eyewitnesses.

If the writers were providing information decades after the events took place, then we would have no certitude that what was recorded is truly historical in nature. Fortunately, there is a plenty of evidence that the writers of the New Testament were involved with the events they described. This is true for a number of reasons, such as the considerable number of persons mentioned in the writings, and the close connection of these persons with the events recorded—this gives the writings a ring of authenticity. Richard Bauckham, in his book *Jesus and the Eyewitnesses*, provides a long list of individuals both by name and activity found within the Gospels. What is more, the accuracy of these names is consistent with the cultural setting. Oftentimes, obscure individuals are left in the background, but there is considerable discussion of the event in which they are mentioned. This is very unlikely in a made-up account.[3]

The writings of the church fathers make it clear that some of them, as third-generation Christians, were familiar with some of the individuals who are mentioned in the biblical text. Men such as Papias and Polycarp spoke of the days of the apostles with intimate knowledge, for they were connected to those who were closest to the writings of the New Testament.

In addition, there is ample evidence that the Gospels were written in the middle portion of the first century, certainly before the destruction of Jerusalem in AD 70, except for the Gospel of John. The same is true about Paul's letters, which were written around AD 48–65. The New Testament authors demonstrated considerable knowledge of the environs of Jerusalem, which would not have been possible for a writer whose sole experience of Jerusalem took place after the city's destruction. The New Testament writers were familiar with names, historical events, and spoke with intimacy of the time they spent with Jesus.

Several passages in the Gospels and elsewhere reveal that the individuals who penned the New Testament either were eyewitnesses of all that had happened, or were close to these eyewitnesses. Most notable are the words of the physician Luke, who said,

> Many have undertaken to compile a narrative about the events that have been accomplished among us, just as those who from the beginning were eyewitnesses and ministers of the word have delivered them to us. It seemed good to me also, having followed all things closely for some time past, to write an orderly account for you, most excellent Theophilus (Luke 1:1-3).

And the apostle John wrote, "That which we have seen and heard we proclaim also to you, so that you too may have fellowship with us; and indeed our fellowship is with the Father and with his Son Jesus Christ" (1 John 1:3).

The writings of the New Testament circulated among the very people and within the environment in which the New Testament events reportedly took place, meaning that many people, if they had wanted to, could have provided counter-testimony that would have invalidated the claims being made by the authors. However, no significant attempt was made in that era to refute the claims that appear in the New Testament.

Does the New Testament have contradictions?[4] One common charge made against the New Testament books, especially the Gospels, is that they contain statements that contradict one another. Much of this criticism is uninformed, since the objectors do not distinguish between *different* and *contradictory* statements. A contradiction is a violation of true opposites, in which both cannot be true in the same way and at the same time. A difference is when the two accounts provide particulars that are not identical and may simply supplement each other. If one Gospel account were to say that Jesus was born in Bethlehem, and another were to say He was born in Nazareth, that would be a contradiction. But to provide information in one account that isn't present in the other accounts, or is not included in the same way, is not contradictory. It's possible to have witnesses offer differing details about a traffic accident, or during a trial in a court of law, without those details posing a problem to the big-picture eyewitness testimony.

Does the New Testament contain lies? It is commonly stated that the early preachers of the gospel intentionally misrepresented the facts regarding Jesus and the particulars about His life. Such an assertion needs a rebuttal, for several reasons.

The sermons and miracles of Jesus are broadly attested. Moreover, the apostles, who gave their lives for the gospel message, boldly proclaimed Christ's death and resurrection. It would have taken little effort by the rulers of the Jews to silence the apostles once and for all. Produce Jesus's dead body, and the apostles would have been silenced. But that didn't happen. And the apostles, including Paul, made it clear that the gospel proclamation (Greek, *kerygma*) had traveled broadly by the time he made his appeal before King Agrippa II: "The king knows about these things, and to him I speak boldly. For I am persuaded that none of these things has escaped his notice, for this has not been done in a corner" (Acts 26:26).

Later, Paul stated clearly his enthusiasm for preaching this same gospel in Rome (Romans 1:15-16). None of the apostles were timid about sharing the gospel, and in fact, they suffered much for their boldness. Some claim the apostles were delusional, but that would mean they had suffered and died for a lie. People do not die for what they know to be false!

Does the New Testament contain myths? This question deals with whether the true stories passed down by the apostles gradually became myths that included miraculous deeds, claims of deity, and the resurrection of Christ. It is claimed by some that what was originally the insignificant life of a young Jewish rabbi (Jesus) allegedly grew into a magnificent story of a God among men—a God who suffered, died, and rose from the dead. However, mere myths would not have caused the ire the Jewish leaders or Roman officials expressed in response to the preaching of the apostles.

The claim of exaggerated stories has little support and may be the weakest of all the objections to the historicity of Christ and the reliability of the New Testament text. We do not find in the New Testament the kinds of exaggerated and fanciful statements about Jesus that are observed in the Gnostic literature from Egypt. Rather, the text reads quite historically, with many details and connections that are accurate fits for the setting of the story. It is well known that it takes many years, particularly in an ancient Middle Eastern setting, for a text to evolve from truth to myth.

The true facts of Christ's life were too well known in the Judean setting, and the first-century Jews in Israel were not given to

propagating myths. In fact, the apostle Peter spoke directly against this charge: "We did not follow cleverly devised myths when we made known to you the power and coming of our Lord Jesus Christ, but we were eyewitnesses of his majesty" (1 Peter 1:16).

A Trustworthy New Testament

There is simply too much literary and internal evidence available for anyone to maintain the notion that the New Testament cannot be trusted. Among them are the many instances of "counterproductive features" (i.e., incidents in the storyline that seem to work counter to the message of Christ or to portray Jesus and the disciples in an unflattering light) that bear the marks of a trustworthy document. These include Jesus's first postresurrection appearance to Mary, who as a first-century *woman* had no substantial rights of testimony; the account of Peter, who said he would die for Jesus then ended up denying the Lord three times; the fact one of Christ's chosen apostles, Judas, would betray Him; the doubt that came over Thomas; the fearful disciples hiding from the religious leaders; the slow understanding of the disciples; the plotting and scheming by selfish Christians (Ananias and Sapphira) to lie and hide money for themselves; and the embarrassing torture and death of the self-proclaimed Son of God at the hands of His enemies. These unflattering markers reflect the authors' desire to tell the truth rather than try to look good in the eyes of the reader and promote a lie.

The objections raised by critics do not stand up to a serious scrutiny of the internal evidence. They say their arguments emerge from textual difficulties, but in reality their arguments against the New Testament come about as a result of their rejection of miracles and the divine inspiration of Scripture. This rejection of the supernatural eliminates their ability to view the New Testament as historically reliable. Despite these critical efforts, the evidence is overwhelmingly in support of a trustworthy New Testament that is worthy of our faith!

33

Are There Contradictions in the Bible?

Norman L. Geisler

Critics claim the Bible is filled with errors and contradictions. However, through the ages, orthodox Christians have claimed that the Bible is without error in the original text, also known as the *autographs*. For example, Augustine wisely noted, "If we are perplexed by any apparent contradiction in Scripture, it is not allowable to say, 'The author of this book is mistaken'; but either the manuscript is faulty, or the translation is wrong, or you have not understood."[1] Though difficulties remain with our interpretation of some passages of Scripture, it is remarkable that not one error has ever been demonstrated to have extended to the original text of the Bible.

Why the Bible Cannot Err

The Christian argument for an errorless (inerrant) Bible can be put in this logical form:

1. God cannot err.

2. The Bible is the Word of God.

3. Therefore, the Bible cannot err.

Logically, the argument is valid. If the premises are true, the conclusion is also true. Let's review each of the argument's premises.

God Cannot Err

If the theistic God exists, then the first premise is true. An infinitely perfect, all-knowing God cannot make a mistake. Scripture testifies to this, declaring emphatically that "it is impossible for God to lie" (Hebrews 6:18). Paul said of God that He "never lies" (Titus 1:2), and John wrote that God is truth (John 14:6). In addition, Jesus said to the Father, "Your word is truth" (John 17:17), and the psalmist exclaimed, "The sum of your word is truth" (Psalm 119:160).

The Bible Is the Word of God

Jesus, who is the Son of God, referred to the Old Testament as the "word of God," which "cannot be broken" (John 10:35)—meaning the Bible does not have the potential to fail. It is infallible. In Matthew 5:18 Jesus said, "Until heaven and earth pass away, not an iota, not a dot, will pass from the Law until all is accomplished." Paul added, "All Scripture is breathed out by God" (2 Timothy 3:16). The Scriptures came "from the mouth of God" (Matthew 4:4), although human authors recorded the messages: "No prophecy was ever produced by the will of man, but men spoke from God as they were carried along by the Holy Spirit" (2 Peter 1:21).

Therefore, the Bible Cannot Err

If God cannot err, and if the Bible is from the mouth of God, then the Bible cannot err. God has spoken, and He has not stuttered. The God of truth has given us the Word of truth, and it does not contain any untruth. The Bible is the unerring Word of God. This is not to say that there are no difficult texts in our Bibles. But God's people can approach those texts with confidence, knowing that there are no actual *errors*; God did not err.[2]

If Inspired, Then Inerrant

Inerrancy is a logical result of inspiration. *Inerrancy* means "wholly true and without error." And what God "breathed out" (inspired—Greek, *theopneustos*) must be wholly true (inerrant). Because *truth* is that which corresponds to reality (i.e., telling it like it is), *error* is what does not correspond to reality. Nothing mistaken can be true, regardless of the author's intention. Otherwise, every sincere utterance ever made is true, even those that are grossly mistaken.

Some argue that the Bible cannot be inerrant and use this faulty reasoning to reach their conclusion:

1. The Bible is a human book.

2. Humans err.

3. Therefore, the Bible errs.

The fallacy of this reasoning can be seen from a similar argument:

1. Jesus was a human being.

2. Human beings sin.

3. Therefore, Jesus sinned.

We can readily see that this conclusion is wrong. Scripture says Jesus was "without sin" (Hebrews 4:15; see also 2 Corinthians 5:21; 2 Peter 1:19; 2 John 2:1; 3:3). In what way, then, is the above argument wrong?

The mistake is the assumption that Jesus was simply human. Certainly, mere human beings do sin. But Jesus was not *merely* a human being; He was also God. Likewise, the Bible is not *merely* a human book; it is also the Word of God. Like Jesus, it has divine elements that negate the statement that anything human errs. Both are divine and cannot have error. There can no more be an error in God's written Word than there was a sin in God's living Word (Jesus). Besides, human beings do not *always* err, but only sometimes.

What About Errors Related to Science and History?

Some say Scripture can be trusted on matters of faith and morals, but it is not always correct on scientific and historical matters. They say, "Rely on the Bible in the spiritual domain, but not in the scientific domain."

If true, this would render the Bible ineffective as a divine authority because the historical and scientific statements in Scripture are inextricably interwoven with the doctrinal and spiritual truths (cf. Romans 4:25). One cannot separate the spiritual truth of Christ's resurrection from the fact that His body permanently and physically vacated the tomb and walked among the people (Matthew 28:6; 1 Corinthians 15:13-19).

Jesus often directly compared Old Testament events with important spiritual truths. He related His death and resurrection to Jonah and the great fish (Matthew 12:40), and He compared the world conditions at the time of His second coming to the conditions at the time of Noah and the flood

(Matthew 24:37-39). Both the occasion and the manner of comparison make it clear that Jesus was affirming the historicity of those Old Testament events. Jesus asserted to Nicodemus, "If I have told you earthly things and you do not believe, how can you believe if I tell you heavenly things?" (John 3:12). The corollary to this statement is that if the Bible does not speak truthfully about the physical world, it cannot be trusted when it speaks about the spiritual world. The two are intimately related.

Inspiration includes not only all that the Bible explicitly *teaches*, but everything the Bible *touches*. This is true of history, science, and mathematics—whatever the Bible declares is true, whether it is a major point or a minor one. The Bible is God's Word, and God does not deviate from the truth. All the parts are as true as the whole they comprise.[3]

Bible Difficulties

Mistakes come not in the revelation of God, but in the misunderstanding of man. With the exception of scribal errors and extraneous changes that crept into the manuscript copies over the centuries, all the critics' allegations of error in the Bible are based on errors of their own. Appealing to one or more of the following categories can solve most Bible difficulties.

Difficulties Should Promote Continued Research. No informed person would claim to be able to fully explain all Bible difficulties. However, it is a mistake for the critic to assume that the unexplained cannot be explained. When a scientist comes upon an anomaly in nature, he does not give up doing further scientific exploration. Rather, the unexplained motivates further study. Likewise, when something in the Bible is encountered for which no explanation is

known, the student continues to do research, looking out for the means to discover an answer.

Approaching the Bible with the Presumption of Innocence. Many critics assume the Bible is wrong until proven right. However, like an American citizen charged with an offense, the Bible should be read with at least the same presumption of accuracy given to other works of literature that claim to be nonfiction. This is the way we approach all human communications. If we didn't, life would not be possible. Imagine assuming that all food packages are mislabeled. The Bible, like any other book, should be presumed to be giving us the author's message, experience, and what was heard. Negative critics begin with the opposite presumption. Little wonder they conclude that the Bible is riddled with errors!

Understanding Changing Interpretations and Unchanging Revelation. While the Bible is infallible, human interpretations are not. Even though God's Word is perfect (Psalm 19:7), as long as imperfect human beings exist, there will be misinterpretations of God's Word and false views about His world. In view of this, people should not be hasty in assuming that a dominant assumption in science is the final word. Today's scientists consider some of yesterday's irrefutable "laws" to be errors. So contradictions between popular opinions in science and widely accepted interpretations of the Bible can be expected. But this falls short of proving there is a real contradiction in Scripture.

Context! Context! Context! The most common mistake of all Bible interpreters is that of reading a text outside its proper context. As the adage goes, "A text out of context is a pretext." One can prove anything from the Bible using this mistaken procedure. For example, the Bible says, "There is no God"

(Psalm 14:1). Of course, the context is that "*the fool* says in his heart, 'There is no God'" (emphasis mine).

Some passages in the Bible are difficult to understand because their meaning is obscure. This is usually because a key word in the text is used only once or rarely, making it difficult to know what the author was saying unless it can be inferred from the context. At other times, the words are clear but the meaning is not evident because we are missing background information that the first readers had.

Using Clarity to Solve Obscurity. When we are not sure of a difficult passage, we should not build a doctrine around it. The rule of thumb is, "The main things are the plain things, and the plain things are the main things." This is called the *perspicuity* (clarity) of Scripture. If something is important, it is clearly taught and probably in more than one place. When a given passage is not clear, we should never conclude that it means something that is opposed to another plain teaching of Scripture.

The Bible Was Written by Humans for Humans. Except for small sections such as the Ten Commandments, which were "written with the finger of God" (Exodus 31:18), the Bible was not verbally dictated. The writers were not secretaries of the Holy Spirit. They were human composers who employed their own literary styles and idiosyncrasies. These human authors sometimes used human sources for their material (Joshua 10:13; Acts 17:28). In fact, every book of the Bible is the composition of a human writer. The Bible also manifests different human literary styles and human thought patterns, including memory lapses (1 Corinthians 1:14-16) and emotions (Galatians 4:14). The Bible discloses specific human interests.

Like Christ, the Bible has a human element, yet is without error. Forgetting the humanity of Scripture can lead to falsely impugning its integrity by expecting a level of expression higher than that which is customary to a human document.

False Assumptions About Historical Reporting. Critics often jump to the conclusion that a partial report is false. However, this is not so. If it were, most of what has ever been said would be false, since seldom does time or space permit an absolutely complete report. Occasionally, biblical writers express the same thing in different ways, or at least from different viewpoints, at different times, stressing different things. Hence, inspiration does not exclude a diversity of expression. The four Gospels will relate the same stories—often the same incidents—in different ways to different groups of people and sometimes even quote the same sayings with different words.

Paraphrasing and Indirect Quotes of the Old Testament. Critics often point to variations in the New Testament use of Old Testament Scriptures as a proof of error. They forget that such citations need not be exact quotations. Sometimes direct quotations are used, and other times, indirect quotations. It is perfectly acceptable, literarily speaking, to give the essence of a statement without using precisely the same words. The same meaning can be conveyed without using the exact same verbal expressions.

Seek Plausible Explanations to Explain Divergent Accounts. The fact that two or more accounts of the same event differ does not mean they are mutually exclusive. Matthew 28:5 says there was one angel at the tomb after the resurrection, whereas John informs us there were two (20:12). That does not mean these are contradictory reports. An infallible mathematical rule easily explains this problem: Where there are two, there is always one. Matthew did not say there was *only* one angel. It is also possible there was one angel at the tomb at one point on this confusing morning, and two angels at another point. In addition, Matthew may have been referring only to the one angel who *spoke*, while John mentioned the two angels he *saw*. One has to add the word "only" to Matthew's account before it would contradict John's.

The Bible Records the Good, the Bad, and the Ugly. It is a mistake to assume that everything contained in the Bible is commended by the Bible. The whole Bible is true (John 17:17), but it records some lies—for example, Satan's lie in the Garden of Eden (Genesis 3:4) and Rehab's lie at Jericho (Joshua 2:4). Inspiration encompasses the Bible fully in the sense that it records accurately and truthfully even the lies and errors of sinful beings. The truth of Scripture is found in what the Bible reveals, not in everything it records. Unless this distinction is held, it may be incorrectly concluded that the Bible teaches immorality because it narrates David's sin (2 Samuel 11:4), that it promotes polygamy because it records Solomon's many wives (1 Kings 11:3), or that it affirms atheism because it quotes the fool as saying, "There is no God" (Psalm 14:1).

The Bible is Prescientific. For Scripture to be true doesn't mean it must use scholarly, technical, or so-called scientific language. The Bible is written for the common person of every generation, and it, therefore, uses common, everyday language. The use of observational, nonscientific language is not unscientific, it is merely prescientific. The Scriptures were written in ancient times by ancient standards, and it would be anachronistic to superimpose modern scientific standards upon them. However, it is no more unscientific to speak of the sun "stand[ing] still" (Joshua 10:12) than to refer to "the sunrise" (Joshua 1:16). Today, meteorologists still use the terms *sunrise* and *sunset*.

The Bible Uses Paraphrases, Round Numbers and Literary Devices. Matthew's Gospel offers many paraphrases and allusions to Old Testament passages. As with all communication, the Bible uses human language to convey meaning. A paraphrase may not be an exact duplication of a quote, but it is sufficient for communicating the meaning. When we recognize that there are many ways to convey meaning, the difficulty of paraphrases evaporates.

What is more, as in everyday speech, the Bible uses round numbers (see Joshua 3:4). It refers to diameter as being about one-third of the circumference (1 Kings 7:23; 2 Chronicles 4:2). This, of course, is only an approximation. In today's technological society it may be considered imprecise to speak of 3.14159265 as 3, but it is not incorrect.

Human language is not limited to only one mode of expression. So there is no reason to suppose that only one literary genre was used in a divinely inspired Book. The Bible uses a number of literary styles and devices: Whole books are written as poetry (e.g., Psalms). The Synoptic Gospels feature parables. In Galatians 4, Paul utilized an allegory. The New Testament abounds with metaphors (2 Corinthians 3:2-3), similes (Matthew 20:1), hyperbole (John 21:25), and even poetic figures (Job 41:1). Jesus employed satire (Matthew 19:24). Figures of speech are common throughout the Bible.

It is not a mistake for a biblical writer to use a figure of speech, but it *is* a mistake for a reader to take a figure of speech literally. Obviously, when the Bible speaks of the believer resting under the shadow of God's "wings" (Psalm 36:7), it does not mean that God is a feathered bird. When the Bible says, "Awake! Why are you sleeping, O Lord?" (Psalm 44:23), it is not saying God actually sleeps. Rather, it refers to God being roused to action.

The Original Text Is Inerrant. Genuine mistakes have been found—in *copies* of Bible text made hundreds of years after the autographs. God only uttered the original text of Scripture, not the copies. Therefore, only the original text is without error. Inspiration of the original does not guarantee that every copy is without error, especially in copies made from copies made from copies made from copies. Therefore, we are to expect that minor scribal copy errors can make their ways into the manuscript copies over time.

The Bible Uses General and Universal Statements. Critics often jump to the mistaken conclusion that unqualified statements admit no exceptions. They seize upon verses that offer general truths and then point with glee to obvious exceptions. Yet such statements are intended to be generalizations. The book of Proverbs has many generalizations. Proverbial sayings, by their very nature, offer general guidance, not universal assurance. They are rules for life, but rules that admit exceptions.

Progressive Revelation Does Not Mean Mistaken Revelation. God does not reveal everything at once, nor does He lay down the same conditions for every period of history. Some later revelations supersede His earlier statements. Bible critics sometimes confuse a change in revelation with a mistake. But such change is progressive revelation, with each command suited to the circumstance.

God tested the human race by forbidding Adam and Eve to eat of a specific tree in the garden of Eden (Genesis 2:16-17). This command is no longer in effect. Under the Mosaic law, God commanded that animals be sacrificed for sin. However, because Christ offered the perfect and final sacrifice for sin (Hebrews 10:11-14), this Old Testament command is no longer in effect. There is no contradiction between the former and latter commands.

Of course, God cannot change commands that have to do with His unchangeable nature (Malachi 3:6). For example, because God is love (1 John 4:16), He cannot command that we hate Him or each other. Nor can He command what is logically impossible (e.g., square circles). For example, to both offer and not offer a sacrifice for sin at the same time and in the same sense. But these moral and logical limits notwithstanding, God can and has given noncontradictory, progressive revelations. If taken out of the proper context and juxtaposed, these can look contradictory. But this kind of mistake is just like assuming a parent is self-contradictory for allowing a sixteen-year-old to stay up later at night than a six-year-old.

The Real Problem

After 50 years of careful study of the Bible, I can only conclude that those who have "discovered a mistake" in Scripture do not know too much about the Bible. Rather, they know too little. This does not mean, of course, that we can understand how to resolve all the difficulties in the Scriptures. But we have seen enough problems resolved to know these also admit answers.[4] Mark Twain made a significant point when he concluded that it was not the parts of the Bible he did not understand that bothered him. Rather, it was the parts he did understand!

What Would a Trial Lawyer Say About the Claims of the Gospels?

Christopher P. Burke

The apostle John described the purpose for writing his Gospel when he said, "These are written so that you may believe that Jesus is the Messiah, the Son of God, and that by believing you may have life in his name" (John 20:31 NIV). His bold declaration has eternal implications, challenging the reader to discover the truthfulness of whether Jesus is the Messiah.

In a court of law, the ultimate goal should be the discovery of truth so that just decisions can be rendered. Part of this process deals with discovering what evidence is admissible, discerning the credibility of the witnesses, and determining whether their claims are true. In this chapter we will apply the "evidentiary process" to the Gospels, which contain extraordinary claims written by eyewitnesses and those who consulted them. Can the Gospels pass the test of modern legal scrutiny? To find out, let us first examine the nature of legal proceedings and what constitutes admissible (allowable) evidence.

Sources of the Gospels

The Gospels are the written testimonies of Matthew, Mark, Luke and John. Sometimes they presented their accounts in narrative form (historical stories), and on other occasions they documented their personal experiences. Because Matthew and John were among the original apostles (Mark 3:17-18; Luke 6:14-15), they were in prime positions to record the crucial moments of the life of Christ. In fact, John's Gospel states, "The man who saw it has given testimony, and his testimony is true" (John 19:35 NIV).

As for Mark, a close associate of Peter (1 Peter 5:13), whose mother appeared to own the upper room where the disciples would meet (Acts 12:12), we do not know if he actually knew Jesus. And Luke, a friend of the apostle Paul (Philemon 24), may have seen Jesus, but there is no conclusive evidence of this. Regardless, Luke noted, "Those who from the beginning were eyewitnesses and ministers of the word have delivered them to us" (Luke 1:2). In addition, the book of Acts (the sequel to the Gospel of Luke, also written by Luke) lists at least 84 facts that have since been confirmed by historical and archaeological research without recording a single demonstrable error.[1] This leaves little doubt that Luke was an eyewitness to the events he recorded, or he had access to reliable eyewitnesses, making him a first-rate historian.[2] Thus, both Mark and Luke were either eyewitnesses or consulted others who were.

The Nature of Evidence

When examining the nature and quality of evidence, we must ask ourselves whether the Gospels are believable in terms of what their writers *heard* and *experienced*. To answer this question, we first need to understand the nature of evidence so we know whether it supports their claims.

Evidence is defined as "something (including testimony, documents, and tangible objects) that tends to prove or disprove the existence of an alleged fact."[3] Using this definition, along with the Federal Rule of Evidence (FRE), we will determine the admissibility of the Gospel writings into evidence. Then we will evaluate the witnesses' credibility.

Evidence classifications. Evidence is either direct or indirect. Direct evidence is based on personal knowledge or observation.[4] In contrast, indirect or circumstantial evidence is based on inference and not personal knowledge.[5] The Gospels that contain direct evidence are Matthew and John, for they are eyewitness accounts. Mark and Luke appear to be based on indirect evidence; they appeal to other witnesses.

Forms of evidence. There are three forms of evidence: testimonial, documentary, and real. Testimonial evidence is oral evidence under oath.[6] Documentary evidence consists of writings (i.e., contracts, confessions, and letters).[7] Real evidence includes conveying a firsthand sense impression (i.e., gems, clothing).[8] Thus, the Gospels are documentary evidence, (i.e., writings).

Admissibility and Hearsay

Are the Gospel writings admissible into evidence on their face? No, because their contents are considered *hearsay.* Hearsay is an out-of-court statement, whether oral or written, offered into evidence to prove the *truth* of the matter asserted (cf. FRE 801[c]). Under the hearsay rule, out-of-court assertions need to be open to test by cross-examination and made under oath; otherwise, they are inadmissible (not allowable).[9] Why? Because cross-examination is recognized as the most efficient truth-discovering device. It allows a party to reveal a possible bias or a particular interest someone might have (or may be hiding). If hidden bias or self-interest is discovered, the credibility of the witness may be called into question.

Therefore, hearsay is inadmissible if one cannot cross-examine the individual, unless an "evidentiary exception" applies. Because the Gospels are out-of-court statements used to prove the truthfulness of the events and statements that occurred, they are subject to the hearsay rule. Thus, the Gospel writings would be inadmissible in court unless a hearsay exception applies.

The Gospels and the Ancient Documents Exception. The ancient documents exception allows for statements from documents that are at least 20 years old, free from suspicious alterations, and have been in the proper custody to be admissible into evidence (FRE 803[16]).[10] The reason for this exception is clear: It is unlikely someone would fabricate something in a document and wait 20 years before using it in court. However, the document would also have to be authenticated.

To establish authenticity, the proponent of the evidence must prove that the evidence is what it purports to be (FRE 901[a]). That is to say, when a document is "found in the place where, and under the care of persons with whom, such writings might naturally and reasonably be expected to be found…" To put it another way, appropriate custody contributes to the authenticity of the documents.[11] Because the Gospels "have been used in the church from time immemorial" and they "are found in the place where alone they ought to be looked for," they can be authenticated.[12]

Furthermore, the evidence clearly indicates the early church carefully copied and translated the words and deeds of Jesus without fabrication.[13] In fact, competent scholars have demonstrated that the New Testament has more manuscripts (c. 5,800 Greek copies), earlier manuscripts (ranging within 30-300 years of the original writings), and manuscripts that are more accurately copied than any other book from the ancient world (99+ percent accurate).[14] The late Harvard University professor of law Simon Greenleaf stated that the four Gospels had been "handed down to us in the state in which [they were] originally written, that is, without having been materially corrupted or falsified…are facts which we are entitled to assume as true, until the contrary is shown."[15] To date, the contrary has never been shown. Because the Gospels, although hearsay, are more than 20 years old and can be authenticated, they are admissible into evidence under the ancient document exception.[16]

Claims of the Gospel Writers and Others. Once the Gospels themselves, and their statements, are admitted into evidence, what about the statements made by others within the text? Are they automatically admitted into evidence? Technically, yes. However, some may view this as entering through the back door or on a technicality. If needed, is there another way to admit into evidence the

many accounts of not only the Gospel writers but other individuals[17] and their verbal responses to Jesus's miracles? Yes—as shown below, there are at least two hearsay exceptions that come into play.[18] By forcing these statements to be admitted on their own, the case for their claims is strengthened. This is significant because their claims verify Jesus's teaching and miracles, which Jesus Himself said "bear witness about me" (John 5:36).

The first exception is known as an "excited utterance."[19] This is an unrehearsed, spontaneous statement uttered in response to a startling event while the person was under the stress or excitement it caused (FRE 803[2]). The rationale for this exception is that such statements are given under circumstances that eliminate the possibility of fabrication or coaching. The Gospels are filled with examples of excited utterances that testify to Jesus's deity and the miracles He performed. For example, after Jesus's postresurrection appearance to Thomas, the unsuspecting apostle exclaimed, "My Lord and my God!" (John 20:28).[20] Thus, statements made shortly after Jesus's miracles are excited utterances and are admissible as evidence.

A second exception is known as a "present sense impression." This involves a statement describing a particular event while the individual was viewing the event or immediately thereafter (FRE 803[1]). For instance, upon seeing a dove descend upon Jesus, John the Baptist stated, "I have seen and have borne witness that this is the Son of God" (John 1:34).[21] This exception would include statements made by those who were not followers of Jesus and the reactions from His enemies.[22] Such statements are also admissible under the present sense impression exception.

Claims by Jesus. Would Jesus's claims that

He was the Son of God and the Messiah (John 4:26; 5:25; 17:21; 19:21; Luke 12:8; 22:22,69) be admissible in court? Again, these claims are hearsay unless an exception applies. In this case, these statements could fall under the "person authorized to speak" exception (FRE 801[d][2][c]). That is, Jesus was authorized to speak for God.

There are several other hearsay exceptions that could apply to Jesus's claims. These include the "then existing state of mind" exception of who Jesus believed He was, and the "residual hearsay" exception (FRE 803[3][23] and 807).[24] The then-existing state of mind exception is admissible to show that Jesus considered Himself the Messiah. The residual catchall exception exists in order to allow out-of-court statements that "contain strong circumstantial indicia of reliability, that are highly probative on the material questions at trial, and that are better than other evidence otherwise available."[25] It must be noted that this last exception is completely discretionary with the court.

Admissibility and Non-Hearsay Statements

Some statements are non-hearsay and admissible because there is circumstantial probability of trustworthiness. Two of the most important are (1) admission by a party-opponent; and (2) adoptive admissions (FRE 801[d][2][A] and [B]).

An "admission by a party-opponent" occurs when a party makes a statement that it presents as true when offered against itself, or the party it represents[26] (FRE 801[d][2][A]). This is because the court recognizes that an individual is unlikely to knowingly make a statement against his or her own interest unless it is true. An example of this is seen in the response given by the Roman centurion

who, after Jesus was crucified, stated, "Truly, He was the Son of God"[27] (Mark 15:39).[28]

A second admissible non-hearsay statement is an "adoptive admission." This occurs when a party has adopted a belief in its truth, whether express or implied, and manifests it by any appropriate means, such as language, conduct, or silence (FRE 801[d][2][B]).[29] For instance, Jesus's affirmative response to Pilate, when asked "Are you the King of the Jews?" (Mark 15:2), showed that Jesus expressly accepted this title.[30] Moreover, Jesus never rebuked the disciples when they repeatedly called Him "Lord."[31] His silence is also a non-hearsay admission that would be admitted as evidence.

Competency and Credibility

Greenleaf insightfully observed that when it comes to "oral testimony, the proper inquiry is not whether it is possible that the testimony may be false, but whether there is sufficient probability that it is true."[32]

Competency of the Witnesses. As shown above, there are many ways to admit the Gospels into evidence. But if the witnesses are not competent and credible, how does that help the Gospels' case? Thus we must ask the obvious question: Are the witnesses competent and credible? Witnesses are generally presumed to be competent unless the contrary is demonstrated (FRE 601). Of course, they must pass the basic testimonial qualifications of reliability: (1) the capacity to observe (perception) (FRE 602); (2) the ability to remember (memory); (3) the ability to relate (communicate); and (4) the ability to appreciate the oath obligation to speak truthfully (FRE 603).[33] A breakdown in any of these criteria goes to the weight of their testimony and would only serve to make the witness less persuasive. On this issue, the Gospel writers would all be considered competent to testify in a court of law.

Credibility of the Witnesses. Preacher Haddon Robinson is said to have summed up the credibility issue when he asserted, "Men do not preach a lie, knowing it's a lie, if every time they preach it, they are courting imprisonment, persecution, poverty and death."

A fundamental premise of our legal system, which maintains that a witness should testify as to facts within their personal knowledge, is that the trier of fact (i.e., the jury) should draw any conclusion from a witness's testimony. Once a witness answers a question, his credibility becomes an issue. In fact, the witness's credibility is often the central issue in the case. Usually a trial is a contest of words, with the outcome turning on whom the jurors choose to believe (i.e., credibility).[34] By way of reminder, this is the reason hearsay is excluded in the first place; the inability to cross-examine makes it difficult to determine an individual's credibility.

Greenleaf offered five factors to determine whether the Gospel writers were credible.[35]

First, were they honest? The Gospel writers are entitled to the benefit of the general course of human experience—namely, that individuals normally speak the truth when they have no prevailing motive or inducement to the contrary. An analysis of the Gospels suggests there was no obvious reason for the Gospel writers to lie. In fact, all of Jesus's apostles were willing to die for boldly proclaiming their faith, and with the exception of John, all were martyred.[36] And yes, some people are willing to die for what they *think* is the truth (such as suicide bombers), so martyrdom is not unique to the Christian apostles. However, it is important to keep in mind that no one dies for what they know

to be a lie. The Gospel writers believed their message was true!

Second, they all had the ability to record the truth. It is a uniform presumption of law that individuals are always presumed honest, of sound mind, and of average intelligence until it is shown otherwise. The Gospel writers had the opportunity to observe the facts, the ability to accurately record the facts, and the memory necessary to retain the facts.

Third comes the number and consistency of their testimonies. The Gospel writers had what is termed as "substantial truth under circumstantial variety." In other words, there were enough discrepancies to show that there could not have been any previous collusion among them, and at the same time, they had such a substantial amount of agreement that it was clear they were all independent narrators of the same great events.[37]

Fourth is the conformity of their testimonies. If the Gospels involved ordinary events, individuals would have no problem with their testimonies. Their accounts are questioned only because they involve miracles.[38] However, their descriptions of these miracles are plain and intelligible, and the events transpired in public, so it is unlikely they made mistakes in the course of their observations.

Fifth is the coincidence of their testimonies with collateral and contemporaneous facts and circumstances. False witnesses are not willing to give details of any circumstance in which their testimony might be open to contradiction by a comparison of them with other accounts. Because the Gospel writings match up with facts known at that time, in hindsight, they would not be considered false witnesses. Thus, as Greenleaf discovered, we can conclude that all of the Gospel writers were credible witnesses.[39]

Internal Evidence of the Gospels' Truthfulness

Finally, the Gospels contain the "ring of truth" for many intrinsic reasons. First, even though they were written to different audiences and reveal different aspects of Christ, they verify each other in time, place, date, and substance, but from different points of view. As the late British scholar F.F Bruce said, "The Gospel accounts are *not* intended to be four complete accounts of the same events."[40] The presence of some inconsistencies between their accounts is a sign of truth.[41] If the writers had the exact same testimonies, it would be more likely that collusion was involved.

There are several other reasons we know the New Testament writers told the truth.[42] For example, the presence of counterproductive features (e.g., embarrassing statements and actions) in the Gospels reveals that the authors were more concerned about conveying the truth rather than fabricating details that would make themselves look good. These embarrassing features include (1) Peter's denial of Jesus, (2) an apostle's betrayal of Jesus (Judas), (3) the self-proclaimed Son of God's death on a cross at the hands of His enemies, (4) Jesus appearing to a woman (Mary) first after His resurrection when women had very little legal credibility in the first century, (5) the disciples' fear of death (they were cowards),[43] (6) the admission that Jesus criticized them,[44] (7) the disciples being slow to understand, and (8) the manner in which Jesus appeared helpless in death.[45] With the exception of John stating that he ran faster than Peter to the empty tomb (John 20:4), none of the Gospel writers sought praise. Even in this case, John was merely stating a historical detail that revealed his and Peter's overflowing anticipation of Christ's resurrection. Instead of painting a rosy picture of propaganda, each writer sought to glorify and point others to Jesus in a selfless manner.

What is more, the writers distinguished Jesus's words from their own and included His hard sayings, such as "love your enemies" (Matthew 5:44) and the invitation to "eat the flesh of the Son of Man and drink his blood" (John 6:53). In addition, the Gospels challenge their readers to investigate the facts. Many witnesses were still alive at the time the Gospels were written, and they could have easily refuted Mathew, Mark, Luke and John if their testimonies were not true. Interestingly, early refutations of the Gospels are conspicuously absent in ancient historical records. Instead, a number of non-Christian sources have been found that verify the people, places, dates, and events recorded in the Gospels.[46]

Finally, the role of women in the Gospels is telling. In Jesus's time, women were considered second-class citizens. In fact, according to Graeme Smith, a first-century woman could not give evidence under any circumstances.[47] The early Jewish historian Josephus said, "[F]rom women let no evidence be accepted because of the levity and temerity of their sex" (*Antiquities* 4.219). Yet the Gospel writers portrayed women doing courageous things, such as being the last to leave the cross, the first to visit the tomb, the first (Mary) to carry the good news of Christ's resurrection to the disciples, and the only ones who saw the angels.[48]

Thus, the evidence supporting the truthfulness of the Gospels is overwhelming from both a commonsense and a legal standpoint. Any open-minded seeker can find much of this evidence elsewhere in this excellent handbook.

Credible Sources of Truth

Since the Gospels would be admissible in a court of law, and their witness deemed credible, their contents are easily believable. It is for these reasons the Gospel writers trusted Jesus with both their lives and their eternal destinies. It is also why I, a trial lawyer who gives great weight to the rules of legal evidence, believe Matthew, Mark, Luke, and John are telling the truth about Jesus. What about you?

Can Prophecy Be Used as Evidence That the Bible Is Reliable?

Patty Tunnicliffe

Prophecy is rarely used as evidence for the reliability of the Bible. Normally, those who defend the Bible look to areas where they can back up their points with hard facts—areas such as science, history, or archaeology. In part, this is because people often misunderstand what is meant by a biblical definition of the word *prophecy*. Thus we need to explain what biblical prophecy is. Here are four easy-to-remember criteria:

1. Biblical prophecy is specific and detailed, not vague or generalized.

2. Biblical prophecy must be fulfilled with 100 percent accuracy.

3. Biblical prophecy was spoken in advance of an event, making it impossible for anyone to correctly guess all the details of that event by chance.

4. Biblical prophecy is focused, covering four main areas:

   Focus 1: one people, the Jews

   Focus 2: one nation, Israel

   Focus 3: one city, Jerusalem

   Focus 4: one person, the Messiah Jesus Christ[1]

When ancient biblical prophecies are fulfilled with perfect accuracy, they serve as evidence of the reliability of God's Word.

The Focal Points of Bible Prophecy

Focus 1: One People, the Jews— Predicted About 4,000 Years Ago

From the beginning of the Bible, we see that God spoke to men. Among them was a man named Abraham, to whom God made a series of prophetic statements in the form of a covenant.

In Genesis 12:2; 15:5; 15:18-21; and 17:1-8, God made a series of unilateral *unconditional* promises to Abraham. God guaranteed He would do several specific things for Abraham: (1) Abraham's name would be made great, (2) he would have as many descendants as there are stars in the sky, (3) a great and powerful nation would come from him and his progeny, and (4) all nations would be blessed through him.

When God told Abraham what He was going to do, He did not ask Abraham to do anything in return to earn or ensure these blessings. Future fulfillment depended on God alone. These promises have all been fulfilled, as seen below:

Promise 1: Abraham's name would be made great. Jews, Christians, and Muslims hold Abraham's name in high esteem, even though these religions differ as to how they view him.

Promise 2: Abraham would have many descendants. No one can count the number of offspring that have come from Abraham and his descendants.

Promise 3: A great nation would come from Abraham. During the reigns of David and Solomon, Israel was a powerful nation. And, in 1948, Israel became a nation again after a hiatus of almost 2,000 years.

Promise 4: All nations would be blessed through Abraham. Messiah Jesus, who came from the line of Abraham, has blessed people in every nation. And today, Israel blesses the world with its many advances in a wide variety of areas—advances that enhance the quality of life for people around the earth.

In these ways, prophetic focal point 1 has been fulfilled.

Focus 2: One Nation, Israel— Predicted About 3,500 Years Ago [2]

When a devastating famine hit the Promised Land, Abraham's descendants moved to Egypt. As time passed, the Jews were enslaved by a series of Pharaohs who dealt with them harshly. After some 400 years of slavery, God sent Moses to deliver them. Once the people of Israel left Egypt, God spoke to them and offered them a choice between two different predictive plans. Both plans had prophetic consequences that would affect the future of the nation.

Plan A went like this: God said *if* the people obeyed Him and kept His commands, He would bless all aspects of their lives (Exodus chapters 24–31). Plan B was this: God said *if* the people did not obey His commands, He would bring a series of disasters upon them. He would devastate their land and cities, destroy their temple, and scatter them among all the nations of the world, where they would be persecuted (Exodus 19:5-7; 24:1-4; Leviticus 26; Deuteronomy 4:23-31; 28–30). The predicted blessings or disasters were dependent on whether or not the nation obeyed God.

The predicted consequences of disobedience came to pass. Sadly, the Bible records the fact that over and over again Israel failed to obey God, and turned instead to the worship of idols and pagan gods. After many calls to repentance, God's dire warnings in Plan B were enacted. From AD 66 to 136, the Romans devastated the land and cities of Israel. The temple was destroyed as well. Rome proceeded to turn Judea into a Roman province and drove all but a handful of Jews out of the land. Today, Jews live throughout the entire world. Their exile into the nations and the persecutions that followed was predicted 1,500 years in advance.[3]

The predicted promises to bring them back to their land are fulfilled. Among God's promises to His people was one in which He said there would come a day when He would regather them and bring them back to the land He had promised to Abraham (Deuteronomy 30:1-5). God had spoken of a time when He would call His people out of their graves and bring them home again. This happened as a direct consequence of

Adolf Hitler's attempt to destroy the Jews of Europe in World War II. Here are God's own words as spoken through His prophets some 3,600 years earlier:

> They shall come back from the land of the enemy…your children shall come back to their own country (Jeremiah 31:16-17).

> I [will] open your graves, and raise you from your graves, O my people…and I will place you in your own land (Ezekiel 37:12-14).

The rebirth of the modern state of Israel is one of the most incredible events in history. On November 29, 1947, the newly constituted United Nations voted to divide the territory known as Palestine into two separate nations, one Jewish and the other Arab. While some observers of prophecy had come to believe this would never happen, God had spoken these words through the prophet Isaiah millennia ago: "I will lift up my hand to the nations, and raise my signal to the peoples; and they shall bring your sons in their arms, and your daughters shall be carried on their shoulders. Kings shall be your foster fathers, and their queens your nursing mothers" (Isaiah 49:22-23).

In what was a historical watershed moment, the independent state of Israel was declared on May 14, 1948. God had preserved an ancient people, exiled for almost 2,000 years, and now they claimed this land as their own once again. How could this have happened in one moment, in one day? Listen to what God said about this:

> "Who has ever heard of such a thing? Who has ever seen things like this? Can a country be born in a day or a nation be brought forth in a moment? Yet no sooner is Zion in labor than she gives birth to her children. Do I bring to the moment of birth and not give delivery?" says the LORD. "Do I close up the womb when I bring to delivery?" says your God (Isaiah 66:8-9 NIV).

When Israel became a nation in 1948, its population was approximately 806,000. As of 2017, close to 6.5 million Jews live in Israel, representing about 43 percent of Jewish people worldwide.[4] More continue to come each month, in a steady and unbroken stream.[5] The Jews are back in their land, and they are there to stay.

Prophetic focal point 2 has been fulfilled. The existence of the modern state of Israel is evidence that the Bible is reliable.[6]

Focus 3: One City, Jerusalem

Jerusalem is not merely one of many ancient cities such as Cairo, Athens, or Rome. It is unique because it is the only city where God chose to put His name forever.

> …Jerusalem, the city where I have chosen to put my Name (1 Kings 11:36).

> In Jerusalem…I will put my name forever (2 Chronicles 33:7).

However, in AD 70, as predicted in Scripture, the city was destroyed by Rome. Micah stated, "Zion will be plowed like a field, Jerusalem shall become a heap of rubble, the temple hill a mound overgrown with thickets" (Micah 3:12 NIV).

Yet God had promised that not only would He bring His people back to their land, but He would also restore their ancient capital: "I will bring them back to live in Jerusalem" (Zechariah 8:8 NIV).

In these prophecies, God was not

Detailed Predictions About the Messiah (Jesus)		
Event	Predictions	Fulfillment
His Ancestry	He would be from the line of Abraham, Isaac, Jacob, the tribe of Judah, the family of Jesse and his son David (Genesis 12:3; 17:17-19; 18:18; 21:11; 22:18; 49:10; Numbers 24:17; Isaiah 11:1-10; Jeremiah 23:5).	Matthew 1:1-6
His Birth	He would be born of a virgin in Bethlehem and worshipped by kings (Isaiah 7:14; 60:3; Jeremiah 31:22; Micah 5:2).	Matthew 1:23; 2:1-2 Luke 2:4-11
His Miracles	He would heal the blind, deaf, mute and lame (Isaiah 7:14; 60:3; Jeremiah 31:22; Micah 5:2).	Matthew 15:30-31 Mark 7:32-37 John 5:1-9; 9:1-25
His Death	He would be spat on, struck and scourged. His hands and feet would be pierced. He would be given vinegar to drink. Men would divide His garments and gamble for His clothes. None of His bones would be broken. He would die with transgressors (Psalms 22:14-21; 34:20; Isaiah 50:6; 52:14; 53:7-8; 69:21; Amos 8:9; Zechariah 12:10).	Matthew 27:30,45 Mark 15:19-27 Luke 23:33 John 19
His Resurrection	He would be resurrected without decay (Psalm 16:10-11; Isaiah 25:8; 53:10).	John 20:24-29

speaking about today's modern city of Jerusalem, for it did not exist at that time. Rather, God was speaking about the historic capital just east of today's modern western section.

Even though Israel was reconstituted as a nation in 1948, the ancient walled capital was still controlled by Jordan, making Jerusalem a divided city from 1949 until June of 1967, when what is known as the Six-Day War changed everything. Jewish forces launched a preemptive strike against Egypt, Syria, and Jordan, and within days a Jewish military division found itself occupying the Mount of Olives just east of the old city. In a matter of hours, this division took control of Israel's historic capital.[7]

Prophetic focus 3 was fulfilled. Ancient, detailed promises of a Jewish return to Jerusalem were realized and accurately fulfilled in June 1967.[8]

Focus 4: One Person, Messiah Jesus

So far, each prophetic focus we have examined has had to do with the nation of Israel. Now we come to the final one, which focuses on a unique person, the person of Jesus. The Old Testament contains numerous prophecies about this one specific individual, the Messiah. He is seen in part by the prophecies He fulfilled at the time of His first advent. Again, these prophecies are ancient, dating back thousands of years before Jesus was born. As we will see, they have been fulfilled in detail. The following chart offers a sample of the many detailed prophecies fulfilled by Christ.[9]

A Spectacular Record of Prophetic Fulfillment

From the time of Abraham to today, we have seen many of the prophecies in the Bible fulfilled with perfect precision. These include prophecies about a specific people, nation, city, and person. No other religion, religious text, or prophet can claim such a spectacular record of prophetic fulfillment. Biblical prophecy is unique in the following ways:

1. *A unique purpose.* The sole purpose of the prophets was to speak God's words to people—not to entertain, amaze, or make money. In fact, some were persecuted and faced difficult times.

2. *A unique focus.* Biblical prophecy focuses on the one true God, not a prophet.

3. *A unique scope.* Biblical prophecy covers thousands of years of history, and yet it is a cohesive message spoken by many different men.

4. *A unique track record.* While many prophecies remain to be fulfilled, those that have come to pass have been completed in exacting detail. No other set of prognostications comes remotely close. Prophecy can be used as evidence that the Bible can be trusted as the Word of God.

Part Five

QUESTIONS ABOUT SCIENCE AND FAITH

What Is the Scientific Case for Intelligent Design?

William A. Dembski

In the preface to this volume, Joseph Holden referred to C.S. Lewis's address "Learning in a Time of War." In that address, Lewis had this to say about a key challenge faced by today's Christian leaders:

> To be ignorant and simple now—not to be able to meet the enemies on their own ground—would be to throw down our weapons, and to betray our uneducated brethren who have, under God, no defense but us against the intellectual attacks of the heathen. Good philosophy must exist, if for no other reason, because bad philosophy needs to be answered.[1]

Apologetics, in the end, is always about upholding good philosophy and refuting bad philosophy.

I begin this essay about the scientific case for intelligent design (ID) with this quote from Lewis because the question of ID's scientific status is, in the first instance, a philosophical question, and only then a scientific question. And not until we get the philosophy and science right does ID become a theological question. To expand slightly on the latter point, only after ID is seen to be philosophically sound and scientifically supported, showing that intelligence underlies nature, does the question of the identity of this intelligence arise. Indeed, the identity or nature of the intelligence or designer is a religious question (for the Christian, this question becomes a matter of whether the intelligence behind nature is the triune God revealed in Jesus Christ).

Is Intelligent Design Scientific?

The scientific case for intelligent design thus begins as a philosophical case, showing that ID may indeed legitimately count as science. Only after ID's plausible inclusion within science is recognized can the scientific case for it be fairly considered, such a case showing how theoretical insight and observational evidence do indeed confirm that nature exhibits the effects of intelligence (which is the principal claim of ID).

Philosophy's central role in the scientific case for intelligent design arises precisely because ID's scientific status is challenged. Go to the Wikipedia entry for intelligent design, and you will read in the opening paragraph that ID is "a religious argument," that it is a "pseudoscience," that it "lacks empirical support," and that it "offers no testable hypotheses." All these claims are false, but they gain credence once one embraces bad philosophy and therewith accepts that ID is not science because it cannot be science.

Indeed, whether something is or can count as science is never determined by science, but rather by philosophy. Science is not one thing but rather many special or particular sciences, which may bear little resemblance to each other not only in content but also in method. Inflationary cosmology and string theory, for instance, lack any direct experimental support and are largely exercises in pure mathematics. On the other hand, materials science, which has to do with developing substances with certain properties (e.g., tensile strength), has no overarching theory and is often a matter of trial and error.

Because science is not a monolith but rather a tapestry of diverse specialties, science has no way to police itself and say what does and does not count as science. Such a policing task, if it falls anywhere, falls to philosophy. *It is a philosophical question whether something may or may not count as science.* And even here we have to be careful because bad philosophy, which usually springs from faulty presuppositions, can tell us that something is not science when in actuality it is.

Beware the "Demarcation Criteria"

To be sure, definitions of science abound. Thus we are told that science must be falsifiable, or testable, or supported by empirical evidence, or limited to the study of natural causes, or what have you. But all such definitions arise from philosophical considerations—they are not the result of any scientific inquiry or observation or method. All such definitions constitute demarcation criteria: They are philosophically based meta-scientific criteria that stand outside science and dictate what may and may not count as science. But it has been known for three decades now, notably through the work of philosopher Larry Laudan, that none of these demarcation criteria succeeds. Invariably they exclude things we want to consider as science or include things we do not.

In fact, Laudan argued that it is much healthier intellectually to allow that anything might count as science, but then also to assess whether it constitutes good or bad science. Unlike bad philosophy, which can addle the brain, bad science is simply science that is poorly developed theoretically or unsupported empirically or fails to generate useful insights. There is no way to turn bad philosophy into good philosophy, but bad science might become good science provided its theoretical and empirical understanding improves. For example, alchemy, the enterprise for turning base metals into precious metals, was bad science—it never came close to fulfilling its promises. But alchemy eventually inspired chemistry.

Stephen Meyer, a prominent ID theorist, has taken Laudan's argument against demarcation criteria in science and shown how these criteria cannot legitimately be used to rule out ID's scientific status (see, for instance, his essay "Sauce for the Goose: Intelligent Design, Scientific Methodology, and the Demarcation Problem" in my anthology *The Nature of Nature*). Rather than expand on Meyer's argument here, let us move to ID's scientific status as such.

Science Supports Intelligent Design

I want therefore to turn next to the actual science supporting intelligent design. In other words, on the assumption that good philosophy cannot prejudicially preclude ID's scientific status and that ID may therefore be granted a place at the table of science, what, in broad strokes, is the case for it, not as a matter of philosophy but rather on its own scientific terms?

Intelligent design claims that compelling theoretical grounds and empirical evidence exist to show that nature exhibits the effects of intelligence. Many top cosmologists and physicists, for instance, see the physical universe as giving clear evidence of design. Consider the following quote from Nobel laureate Arno Penzias:

> Astronomy leads us to a unique event, a universe which was created out of nothing, and delicately balanced to provide exactly the conditions required to support life. In the absence of an absurdly improbable accident, the observations of modern science seem to suggest an underlying, one might say, supernatural plan.[2]

ID in physics is widely accepted as scientifically legitimate. Nonetheless, it tends to have a deistic feel, in which design was simply inputted into the fabric of the universe from the start, but played no palpable effect thereafter. By contrast, life arises at some later point in the history of the universe—it is not cotemporal with the universe. Thus, to find design in biology has a more real-time, in-your-face, the-designer-is-active-now feel. That is why, when critics challenge ID's scientific status, they are usually thinking of design in biology.

Showing design in biology. So how do we show that design in biology is real, that it has scientific teeth? The ID movement is now well into its third decade, and many lines of theoretical insight and observational evidence support it. I would cite here my own theoretical work on design detection (*The Design Inference*, Cambridge, 1998), as well as my joint work with Robert Marks on conservation of information (which shows that the information required to build biological systems cannot be produced by unguided material mechanisms such as natural selection; see EvoInfo.org). I would cite here as well the ideas of Michael Behe on irreducible complexity and the edge of evolution and Douglas Axe's research on proteins and the obstacles to their unguided evolution (see Axe's recent book *Undeniable*).

In a short essay like this, I cannot expand on these points; so let me indicate what I regard as the most compelling evidence of design in biology. If you know and understand this example, you will be able to stand your ground against critics of ID. The example is the genetic code.

The smoking gun—the genetic code! The genetic code is, obviously, a code. A code is not merely a way of putting alphanumeric characters into sequences that convey meaning, as I am doing right now in writing this essay. That would simply describe a linguistic convention for organizing alphanumeric characters. What a code does, instead, is relate two such linguistic conventions, mapping one to another. For instance, Morse code takes short strings of dots and dashes and maps them to our alphabet (A through Z) and numbers (0 through 9). Thus, dot dot dot dash dash dash dot dot dot maps to the distress signal SOS ("Save Our Ship").

Now, within every cell, be it the simplest

bacterial cell (which is itself supercomplicated by any technological standards) or the types of cells that make up the human body (which are way more complicated still), there is a genetic code that relates a linguistic convention of four characters (the nucleotides) to a linguistic convention of twenty characters (the amino acids). More specifically, triplets of nucleotides, known as codons, map to amino acids, and sequences of codons map to sequences of amino acids, which are known as proteins if they fold and therefore have biological meaning (the difference between a random amino acid sequence and a protein is the difference between a random string of letters and a word).

But there is more! Not only does every cell operate by such a genetic code to produce proteins from genes, but that code is universal (or almost so). In other words, the same codons map to the same amino acids across all living forms (all of which are composed of cells), except for a handful of variations for some codons. It is like the difference between American versus International Morse Code. The two forms of Morse Code are identical for many letters of the alphabet, but there are a few variations. Thus dash dot dash dot is the letter *j* in American Morse Code, but in International Morse Code it is dot dash dash dash.

Relevance of the genetic code. Why is the genetic code relevant to intelligent design? Because the genetic code is absolutely necessary for living forms to produce proteins, and if a living form is not building proteins, it is dead. Life presupposes this universal genetic code. There is no evolution of the genetic code because for things to evolve they must reproduce, and the only things we know to reproduce are living things made out of cells. Note that even viruses presuppose the genetic code, exploiting it to hijack the inner workings of the cell. Viruses are parasitic on cells—they require cells to exist for them to exist.

The cause of the genetic code. So, what is capable of producing a code? There is only one causal power known to be capable of producing a code—any code—and that is intelligence. It is an eerie coincidence that our understanding of the mathematics underlying codes comes from the work of Claude Shannon as outlined in his 1948 paper "A Mathematical Theory of Communication." But then (drum roll please!) in the 1950s and early 1960s, James Watson and Francis Crick unlocked the structure of DNA (the arrangement of nucleotides in the genetic code), only for Marshall Nirenberg to unlock how codons of nucleotides map to proteins.

Think about this: If humans had not invented codes and understood their mathematics, codes that transmit information and that operate under the control of intelligence, biologists like Crick and Nirenberg would never have discovered that all cells have codes embedded in them (i.e., the genetic code). The entire computer revolution, including the Internet and Web, depend on codes. When you send an email, it starts as an assortment of ordinary letters, but then gets coded according to various protocols that, among other things, introduce error correction so that random electric noise on the communication channels does not disrupt what you are trying to communicate.

Bottom line: We know that intelligence is able to create codes. Moreover, codes are the basis of all electronic communication, and thus the basis of our information economy. Significantly, we have no idea how a code could create itself. Evolution cannot explain the genetic code because evolution presupposes the genetic code. It follows that anyone not infected with bad philosophy will see in the genetic code evidence of intelligent design in biology.

The Value of ID for Christian Apologetics

Granting this conclusion, who is the designer? That is a question for religion to answer. As a Christian theist, I believe the designer is the triune God of Christianity. Persons holding to other religions will interpret the designer as the deity or purposeful power consistent with their faith. So what is the value of ID for Christian apologetics? Its value is not in proving Christianity per se, but in clearing away the bad philosophy and bad science that would keep us from seeing nature as manifesting the wisdom and power of God (see Romans 1:20).

37

How Do We Respond to Objections to Intelligent Design?

Casey Luskin

Hardline Intelligent Design (ID) critics have been effective at spreading misinformation about ID across the Internet, in classrooms, and in the media. As a result, it is not unusual to encounter the same common and often misguided objections to ID whether speaking to a high school biology teacher, an undergraduate humanities major, your next-door neighbor, your plumber, or a Nobel Prize-winning physicist. The good news is that common objections are not only finite in number, but easy to answer—provided that one knows the basic facts about ID and is willing to respond in a loving, patient, and informed manner. With that in mind, let's review the important details about responding to objections to ID.

Is ID Science or Religion?

By far the most common objection to ID is that it is not science but religion. When answering this objection, however, all that matters is the methodology underlying arguments for design.

Intelligent design is a scientific theory that holds that many features of the universe and living things are best explained by an intelligent cause rather than an undirected process like natural selection. ID studies information in nature to discriminate between objects generated by material mechanisms and those caused by intelligence. The type of information that indicates design is generally called *specified complexity*, or known as *complex and specified information* (CSI). (For details, see William Dembski's chapter "What Is the Scientific Case for Intelligent Design?")

We can see that ID is science because it uses the standard scientific method of observation, hypothesis, experiment, and conclusion:

- *Observations:* ID theorists observe that intelligent agents produce high CSI.

- *Hypothesis:* ID theorists hypothesize that if a natural object was designed, it will contain high CSI.

- *Experiment:* Scientists perform experimental tests to determine if natural objects contain high CSI.

For example, as we'll discuss later, mutational sensitivity tests show enzymes contain an unlikely ordering of amino acids that matches a precise sequence necessary for function—high CSI. (More on these experiments later.)

- *Conclusion:* High CSI in DNA, proteins, and molecular machines indicate such structures were designed.

The design argument sketched here is based upon empirical evidence and the scientific method. It offers positive evidence for design by finding in nature the types of information and complexity that we know from experience derive from intelligent causes. One might disagree with the conclusions of ID or disfavor its larger implications, but one cannot reasonably claim this argument is based upon religious premises or faith. It is based upon science.

Ad hominem objections and motive mongering. The most common logical fallacy encountered in the ID debate is the genetic fallacy, which attacks the origin of an argument (i.e., the person or group making the argument) rather than the argument itself. Unfortunately, such ad hominem ("against the man") objections are extremely common among ID critics. A typical example maintains that if a person arguing for ID is a Christian, then he has religious motives which invalidate his arguments for design.

One should always be quick to acknowledge being a Christian, and it is always fair to acknowledge that larger motives are a reality *for everyone,* including the non-Christian. However, one should simultaneously emphasize that in science, motives or personal religious beliefs do not matter; only the evidence matters. Great scientists like Kepler

and Newton were inspired to their scientific work by their religious convictions that God had created an orderly, rational universe with comprehensible physical laws. They turned out to be right because the scientific evidence validated their hypotheses. (For details, see Luskin and Meyer's chapter "Has the Christian Worldview Had a Positive Impact on the Development of Science?")

There are also effective rhetorical responses. For example, there are nonreligious ID proponents, like the philosopher Thomas Nagel, who have no religious motives for supporting ID.[1] Moreover, what's sauce for the goose is sauce for the gander: If religious motives somehow invalidate arguments for design, then what of the many prominent *atheists* who argue for *evolution?* For example, Richard Dawkins—the world's most famous evolutionary biologist—stated, "Darwin made it possible to become an intellectually fulfilled atheist"[2] and asserted "faith is one of the world's great evils, comparable to the smallpox virus but harder to eradicate."[3]

Scientists, whatever their personal beliefs, should have every right to express their views. Their personal religious or antireligious views are irrelevant as long as they are making sound scientific claims.

Dealing with heated critics. Unfortunately, some ID critics will levy ad hominem attacks that are much harsher than merely calling the ID proponent a "religiously motivated Christian." Do not yield to the temptation to respond in kind—it is better to lose the battle and maintain your integrity than to lose your peace of mind. Those who defend ID should emotionally and spiritually prepare to face personal attacks and not be too discouraged when they come. Not only are you in good company, but receiving ad hominem attacks often indicates you have made a good argument!

But how can you reach someone who just wants to heap ridicule on you? By following the Bible, which teaches us to love our enemies (Matthew 5:44), to repay evil with good (Romans 12:14-21), and to not retaliate when insulted (1 Peter 3:9). When we respond in a patient, respectful, and informed manner, malicious critics are often surprised and become more open to hearing our views. Christ's commands aren't just the right thing to do; they can be extremely effective when it comes to reaching people during heated dialogue.

The Kitzmiller v. Dover case and the straw-man definition of ID. Another common fallacious tactic is to attack a straw-man definition of ID: "ID says life is so complex it couldn't have evolved, therefore life was created by a supernatural God." Critics may cite the 2005 *Kitzmiller v. Dover* lawsuit decision, in which federal district court Judge John Jones adopted this incorrect definition and ruled that ID is a form of religion.[4] This straw-man definition is wrong for two reasons.

First, it frames ID as a strictly negative argument against evolution, ignoring the positive case for design discussed in the previous chapter by William Dembski, and in this chapter's answer to the first objection that "ID is not science but religion."

Second, it claims ID appeals to the divine. All ID scientifically detects is the prior action of an intelligent cause. ID respects the limits of scientific inquiry and does not address religious questions about the identity of the designer. (More on this below.)

An accurate definition of ID is this: Intelligent design is a scientific theory that holds that many features of the universe and living things are best explained by an intelligent cause rather than an undirected process like natural selection. And why are these features best explained by intelligent causation? *Because they contain the same kind of information and complexity which, in our experience, come only from intelligence.*

Creationism disguised? One of Judge Jones's central claims was that ID is simply a relabeled version of creationism—another common objection to ID. Is it valid? Again, no. ID is different from creationism in multiple ways.

First, ID theory investigates whether we can scientifically detect design in natural objects; it is not a theory about ages. Thus, ID finds support among both young earth and old earth creationists, as well as among noncreationists who see evidence for design in nature.

Second, ID differs from creationism in substance. In its most general form, creationism is the belief that God created the universe. Even under that broad definition, creationism always entails a religious belief in a supernatural divine Creator,[5] usually the God of the Bible. In contrast, ID does not attempt to engage in religious debates about the identity of the designer.

ID's nonidentification of the designer is not some kind of rhetorical ploy. Rather, it stems from ID's strictly scientific approach, which respects the limits of scientific inquiry. For example, DNA is an information-rich code which is best explained by an intelligent cause—but that code by itself does not tell us who the designer is. To go further and identify the designer would go beyond what the evidence from nature shows.

Some critics may rejoin that ID hides its true belief that the designer is God. Leading ID proponents never hide their personal religious views, and are very open about their beliefs about God. I am intentionally open about my Christian faith whether speaking to religious audiences or secular ones. But I make clear that my belief that the designer is the God of the Bible is not a conclusion of ID; rather, it is a religious belief I hold for separate reasons. Indeed, the ID movement includes people of diverse worldviews, including Christians, Jews, Muslims, people of Eastern religious backgrounds, and even atheists/agnostics. What unites them is not some creationist belief, but a conviction that there is scientific evidence for design.

Are there peer-reviewed pro-ID scientific research publications? Another common objection that received an unfortunate assist from the *Kitzmiller v. Dover* ruling is the assertion that ID research or peer-reviewed pro-ID scientific papers do not exist. These claims are absolutely false, and are easily refuted by citing counterexamples.

As documented at www.discovery.org/id/peer-review, the ID research community has published many (100+) peer-reviewed scientific publications advancing ID. Multiple hubs of ID research are producing these papers.

Biologic Institute, led by protein scientist Douglas Axe, is testing the scientific case for design in biology via experimental research that shows unguided evolutionary mechanisms cannot produce new proteins.

The Evolutionary Informatics Lab, founded by William Dembski and Baylor University engineering professor Robert Marks, has published multiple peer-reviewed articles testing computer simulations to show that evolution works only when it is actively guided by intelligence.

Evidence-Based Rebuttals

Thus far we have mostly reviewed nonevidence-based rebuttals—common objections

that must often be answered in a "ground-clearing operation" before addressing the core question raised by ID: *What is the origin of new biological information?* Let's examine some common substantive objections framed as questions.

Can Darwinian evolution generate new biological information, e.g., novel proteins? A central claim of ID is that only intelligence, rather than unguided natural processes, can produce new features with high CSI. This does not mean that ID denies selection and mutation can do anything. Rather, it means the mechanism cannot do *everything*.

Darwinian evolution can work when one small step (e.g., a single mutation) gives an advantage. ID has no problem with this. But what about cases where many steps, or many mutations, are necessary before gaining some advantage? Natural selection thus breaks down when a feature requires multiple mutations before providing any advantage to select. ID research shows that many structures in biology indeed require many mutations before providing an advantage.

A 2010 study by Douglas Axe calculated that when a multimutation feature requires *more than six* mutations before giving any benefit, even under ideal circumstances of a large population of evolving bacteria, Darwinian evolution could not produce such a trait in the entire history of the Earth.[6] Axe provided empirical backing in two papers he published in *Journal of Molecular Biology*, reporting mutational sensitivity tests on enzymes. His research showed the likelihood of a sequence of 150 amino acids yielding a functional protein fold is less than 1 in 10^{74}.[7] That implies that protein folds are multimutation features, requiring many amino acids to be in the right order before functioning.

Additional empirical confirmation comes

from experimental research published by Axe and biologist Ann Gauger in the journal *BIO-Complexity*.[8] They tried to experimentally convert proteins to perform the functions of closely related proteins—changes that evolutionists claim should be a simple task for natural selection. Yet Axe and Gauger found that 7+ mutations would be required for these protein conversions—exceeding the maximum limit determined by Axe's 2010 study. This suggests many biological features are beyond the reach of mutation selection.

To get around these empirical problems, evolutionists sometimes cite computer simulations of evolution which they claim show complex features can be generated by random mutation and natural selection. ID theorists at the Evolutionary Informatics Lab have analyzed these simulations and have shown, in multiple peer-reviewed papers, that required information is invariably smuggled in by the programmer to yield a predetermined outcome.[9] Rather than showing that unguided evolution can produce new information, evolutionary simulations show that an intelligent programmer is needed.

Collectively, ID research is converging on a consensus: Natural selection and random mutation can produce minor changes, but many information-rich features—like new protein folds—cannot arise by unguided evolutionary mechanisms. They require an intelligent cause.

Can irreducible complexity evolve through co-option? A special type of multimutation feature is an irreducibly complex (IC) system. According to Michael Behe, an IC system has multiple interacting parts, each of which are necessary to perform the function (e.g., a mouse trap).[10] Such systems challenge Darwinian evolution because they require a high

level of complexity before *any* functional advantage is provided and thus cannot evolve in a step-by-step manner.

ID critics often attempt to explain IC by invoking co-option, where biological components are borrowed or co-opted from one system to perform a new function in another during the course of evolution. Co-option explanations, however, suffer many weaknesses.

Primarily, co-option advocates *never* articulate step-by-step Darwinian accounts of how IC systems evolved, so they do not actually explain the evolution of IC. Rather, ID critics typically cite mere sequence similarity between proteins (called *homology*) in an attempt to find possible sources for co-opting parts. Such inadequate explanations ignore that reusage of similar biological parts could reflect common design rather than common descent—and even if they did demonstrate common descent, that is very different from demonstrating a stepwise evolutionary pathway.

Attempts to explain evolution via co-option invariably become teleological—predestined to reach some goal very unlike undirected neo-Darwinian processes. William Dembski and Jonathan Witt thus observe, "What is the one thing in our experience that co-opts irreducibly complex machines and uses their parts to build a new and more intricate machine? Intelligent agents."[11]

Does the multiverse explain fine-tuning? The evidence for design does not just come from biology. There is much evidence for design of the universe from the "fine-tuning" of physics—the exceedingly unlikely values of the laws of nature that yield a life-friendly universe.

Aware that fine-tuning provides powerful evidence for cosmic design, materialists have sought to increase the likelihood of getting a life-friendly universe by postulating a multiverse—a potentially near-infinite number of universes, each with different values for its physical laws. We simply got lucky and occupy the one universe that permits complex life.

The immediate rejoinder to the multiverse argument is that we can observe only one universe. We have no direct evidence that the multiverse exists.

The skeptic may respond that some cosmological models for producing a multiverse make certain testable predictions. That is true, but only superficially. It is impossible to directly test whether there exists the type of multiverse needed to explain fine-tuning—a near-infinite multitude of universes, each with different physical laws.[12]

Last, multiverse advocates fail to appreciate that the mechanisms proposed to generate the multiverse *themselves require fine-tuning!* Whether there is or is not a multiverse, fine-tuning remains a major aspect of nature that materialists can neither explain nor escape.

Multiverse theories are more philosophical speculation than science—in fact multiverse thinking makes it impossible to rule out chance, which eliminates our basis for doing science!

"Even If ID Is Correct" Objections

A final class of objections maintains that even if ID is true, we should reject it. These objections are unreasonable because if science is the empirical search for truth, we should detect design if the evidence warrants, regardless of the larger implications. To do otherwise is to close our minds and restrict the search for truth. Other rebuttals can be made as well.

God of the gaps? Some critics often charge that ID simply inserts God into the gaps in our current knowledge. According to this accusation, for centuries superstitious people would attribute anything they did not understand to the gods. Over time, these gaps were filled with scientific explanations instead of supernatural ones. Thus, it is unwise to ever appeal to God as an explanation. This objection fails as a criticism of ID for multiple reasons:

First, ID does not invoke God, but merely infers intelligent causation.

Second, ID is not a gaps-based argument. ID is not based upon what we do not know, but is rather based upon what we do know. As Stephen Meyer and microbiologist Scott Minnich explain, ID is an "*inference to the best explanation* given what we *know* about the powers of intelligent as opposed to strictly natural or material causes."[13] Thus ID is a rigorous conclusion based upon positively finding in nature the types of information that *we know*, from our prior observation-based experience, derive from intelligent action.

Last, the God-of-the-gaps charge turns out to be a *gaps-based* argument itself: By claiming that all knowledge gaps should be filled with material causes, ID-critics use *materialism of the gaps* reasoning.

Is ID a science stopper? Some critics claim we should not invoke ID because it stops further scientific investigation. This is wrong, as ID makes testable predictions that open up new avenues of investigation and provide a fruitful paradigm for scientific research:

- ID predicts high CSI-like fine-tuning of protein sequences. This has practical implications not just for explaining biological origins but also for engineering enzymes.

- ID has inspired scientists to discover

fine-tuning of physical laws, like the Galactic Habitable Zone.[14] This implies fine-tuning is real, and must be accommodated by proper cosmological models.

- ID identifies limits to Darwinian evolution. This informs efforts to combat antibiotic resistance by creating drug cocktails to which bacteria cannot evolve resistance.

- ID encourages scientists to better understand molecular systems by reverse-engineering them like machines.

- ID inspires scientists to investigate function for noncoding "junk DNA," allowing us to better understand cellular biology.

ID and methodological naturalism. Critics often maintain that even if ID is correct, we cannot bring it into science because that violates methodological naturalism (MN). MN is a requirement that some people impose upon science, which says that whether or not the supernatural exists, we must pretend that it doesn't when practicing science. Philosophers would disagree about whether MN is a requirement of science,[15] but even if it is, there are good reasons why ID offends neither the letter nor the spirit of MN.

ID doesn't violate the letter of MN: ID appeals to intelligence (a cause we understand from studying nature) and does not require supernatural causes.

ID doesn't offend the spirit of MN: Proponents of MN argue that it ensures science uses only testable, predictable, and reliable explanations.[16] However, as we have seen, ID generates testable predictions based upon our knowledge of how the world

works—specifically, our observations of what kind of information is produced when intelligent agents are at work—and can be reliably inferred through the scientific method. Thus, ID does not violate any mandates of predictability, testability, or reliability laid down for science by MN.

ID doesn't go far enough. A common objection from creationists argues that by not identifying the designer, ID doesn't go far enough to demonstrate the designer is Christ. A Christian apologist might respond by saying, "That is a fair point, but this doesn't mean ID lacks value."

The theory of ID doesn't go beyond the data from nature and claim that we can scientifically identify the designer. Creationism does go further and attempts to address religious questions, like how to harmonize the Bible with science, or how to show Christ is God. Those are important questions, but they aren't scientific ones. Because of its scientific approach, the theory of ID doesn't address such questions. But by speaking the language of science, ID can reach scientifically minded skeptics who seek evidence for design in nature.

In his book *How We Believe*, atheist psychologist Michael Shermer recounted a survey of skeptics. *Issues related to scientific evidence for God and design in nature ranked as the number one reason that skeptics doubt God, and also why some believe.*[17]

If one desires to lead a person to Christ on the cross, ID is not enough, and other arguments are needed. But if one seeks convincing scientific arguments to show the skeptic that the universe and life require a designer, then ID is the right tool for the job. As ID's motto says, all we must do is "follow the evidence wherever it leads."

What Are the Top 10 Scientific Problems with Evolution?

Casey Luskin

"There are no weaknesses in the theory of evolution."[1] Such was professed by Eugenie Scott, the de facto head of the Darwin lobby, while speaking to the media in response to the Texas State Board of Education's 2009 vote to require students to learn about both the scientific evidence for and against neo-Darwinian evolution. Nonetheless, when Darwin proposed his theory of evolution in *Origin of Species*, he wisely counseled, "A fair result can be obtained only by fully stating and balancing the facts and arguments on both sides of each question."[2] This chapter will take Darwin's challenge and review the technical literature to show that there are legitimate scientific challenges to core tenets of neo-Darwinian theory and prominent theories of chemical evolution.

Problem 1: No Viable Mechanism to Generate a Primordial Soup

For decades, origin-of-life theorists have hailed the Miller-Urey experiments as a demonstration that the building blocks of life could have arisen under natural, realistic, Earthlike conditions,[3] creating a primordial soup that led to the origin of life. However, these experiments have a problem. The atmosphere used in the Miller-Urey experiments was primarily composed of reducing gasses like methane, ammonia, and high levels of hydrogen. Geochemists now believe that the atmosphere of the early Earth did not contain appreciable amounts of these components, meaning there was no viable mechanism for generating a primordial soup on the early Earth.[4]

Problem 2: Unguided Chemical Processes Cannot Explain the Origin of the Genetic Code

The most prominent hypothesis for the origin of the first life is called the RNA world hypothesis. In living cells, genetic information is carried by DNA, and most cellular functions are carried out by proteins. However, RNA is capable of both carrying genetic information and catalyzing some biochemical reactions. As a result, some theorists postulate that the first life might have used RNA alone to fulfill all these functions. But there are several problems with this hypothesis.

First, RNA is not known to assemble without the help of a skilled laboratory chemist intelligently guiding the process.[5]

Second, while RNA has been shown to perform many roles in the cell, there is no evidence that it could perform all the necessary cellular functions currently carried out by proteins.[6]

Third, the RNA world hypothesis does not explain the origin of genetic information. As origin-of-life theorist Robert Shapiro explains, "The sudden appearance of a large self-copying molecule such as RNA was exceedingly improbable...so vanishingly small that its happening even once anywhere in the visible universe would count as a piece of exceptional good luck."[7]

Fourth, in order to evolve into the DNA/ protein-based life that exists today, the RNA world would need to evolve the ability to convert genetic information into proteins. However, this process of transcription and translation requires a large suite of proteins and molecular machines—which themselves are encoded by genetic information. This poses a chicken-and-egg dilemma, where essential enzymes and molecular machines are needed to perform the very task that constructs them.

Despite decades of work, origin-of-life theorists are still at a loss to explain how this system arose. As Harvard chemist George Whitesides stated, "Most chemists believe, as do I, that life emerged spontaneously from mixtures of molecules in the prebiotic Earth. How? I have no idea."[8]

Problem 3: Random Mutations Cannot Generate Irreducibly Complex Structures

Most everyone agrees that Darwinian evolution works when each small step along an evolutionary pathway provides some survival advantage. However, when multiple mutations must be present simultaneously to gain a functional advantage, Darwinian evolution gets stuck.

Lehigh University biochemist Michael Behe coined the term *irreducible complexity* to describe systems that require many parts—and thus many mutations—to be present before providing any survival advantage to the organism. According to Behe, such systems cannot evolve in the step-by-step fashion required by Darwinian evolution. Thus, he maintains that random mutation and unguided natural selection cannot generate the genetic information required to produce irreducibly complex structures. Too many simultaneous mutations would be required—an event which is highly unlikely to occur.

In his book *Darwin's Black Box*, Behe discusses molecular machines that require multiple parts to be present before they can function and confer any advantage. His most famous example is the bacterial flagellum—a micromolecular rotary engine that functions like an outboard motor on bacteria to propel it through a liquid medium to find food.

The flagellum is irreducibly complex. Genetic knockout experiments have shown that it fails to assemble or function properly if any one of its approximately 35 genes are missing.[9] In this all-or-nothing game, mutations cannot produce the complexity needed to provide a functional flagellar rotary engine one incremental step at a time, and the odds are too daunting for it to assemble in one great leap.

However, it is not just ID proponents who doubt the creative power of mutations. The late biologist Lynn Margulis, a well-respected member of the National Academy of Sciences until her death in 2011, once said that "new mutations don't create new species; they create offspring that are impaired."[10]

Problem 4: Natural Selection Struggles to Fix Advantageous Traits into Populations

Evolutionary biologists often assume that once mutations produce a functionally advantageous trait, it will easily spread (become "fixed") throughout a population by natural selection. However, random forces or events can prevent a trait from spreading through a population, even when it provides an advantage. These random forces are lumped together under the name *genetic drift*.

When biologists run the mathematics of natural selection, they find that unless a trait gives an extremely strong selective advantage, random genetic drift will tend to overwhelm the force of selection and prevent adaptations from gaining a foothold in a population.[11] Some evolutionary biologists are so doubtful of the ability of natural selection to efficiently spread traits through populations that they resort to proposing that random genetic drift should be invoked to explain the origin of complex biological features.[12]

Can a random force explain the appearance of highly complex biological features that are finely tuned to perform useful biological functions? Biologist Ann Gauger observes there is "no explanation of how non-adaptive forces can produce the functional genomic and organismal complexity we observe in modern species."[13] Evolutionary biology now faces a catch-22:

- Natural selection is too inefficient a mechanism to overcome random forces and fix the sort of complex adaptations we observe

in populations because it is easily overpowered by random forces like genetic drift.

- Life is full of highly complex and efficient adaptations, but random genetic drift offers no justifiable reason to believe that such features will have any reason to arise.

Many scientists are skeptical. More than 1,000 PhD scientists have signed a statement agreeing they "are skeptical of claims for the ability of random mutation and natural selection to account for the complexity of life."[14]

Problem 5: Abrupt Appearance of Species in the Fossil Record Contradicts Darwinian Evolution

The fossil record has been long-recognized as a problem for evolutionary theory. The basic pattern is that living organisms appear in a pattern of explosions. As one biology textbook explains:

> Many species remain virtually unchanged for millions of years, then suddenly disappear to be replaced by a quite different, but related, form. Moreover, most major groups of animals appear abruptly in the fossil record, fully formed, and with no fossils yet discovered that form a transition from their parent group.[15]

Probably the most famous instance of abrupt appearance is the Cambrian explosion, where nearly all of the major living animal phyla appear in the Cambrian period. An invertebrate zoology textbook summarizes the problem:

Most of the animal groups that are represented in the fossil record first appear, "fully formed" and identifiable as to their phylum, in the Cambrian, some 550 million years ago...The fossil record is therefore of no help with respect to the origin and early diversification of the various animal phyla...[16]

But the Cambrian explosion is by no means the only explosion of life recorded in the fossil record. We see the same pattern regarding the origin of major fish groups,[17] land plants,[18] flowering plants,[19] mammals,[20] birds,[21] and many marine organisms.[22]

The same problem exists with regard to the origin of humans.[23] Hominid fossils generally fall into one of two groups: apelike species and humanlike species, with a large, unbridged gap between them. In 2004, the famed evolutionary biologist Ernst Mayr recognized the abrupt appearance of humans:

> The earliest fossils of *Homo*, *Homo rudolfensis* and *Homo erectus*, are separated from *Australopithecus* by a large, unbridged gap. How can we explain this seeming saltation? Not having any fossils that can serve as missing links, we have to fall back on the time-honored method of historical science, the construction of a historical narrative.[24]

One commentator even proposed the evidence implies a "big bang theory" of the appearance of our genus *Homo*.[25]

The fossil evidence poses a major challenge to Darwinian evolution, including the view that all animals are related through common ancestry.

Problem 6: Evolutionary Biology Has Failed to Produce a Grand "Tree of Life"

When fossils failed to demonstrate common ancestry, evolutionary scientists turned to another type of evidence—DNA sequence data—to demonstrate a tree of life. Problems arose when molecular biologists sequenced genes from the three basic domains of life—bacteria, archaea, and eukarya—those genes did not yield a treelike pattern. Such data led biochemist W. Ford Doolittle to explain, "Molecular phylogenists will have failed to find the 'true tree,' not because their methods are inadequate or because they have chosen the wrong genes, but because the history of life cannot properly be represented as a tree."[26] The journal *New Scientist* put it this way: "[T]he holy grail was to build a tree of life... But today the project lies in tatters, torn to pieces by an onslaught of negative evidence."[27]

Not all phylogenetic trees are constructed by comparing molecules like DNA or RNA; some are based upon comparing the physical structures of organisms—called *morphology*. But conflicts between molecule-based trees and morphology-based trees are also common. A 2012 paper studying bat relationships stated, "Incongruence between phylogenies derived from morphological versus molecular analyses, and between trees based on different subsets of molecular sequences has become pervasive as data-sets have expanded rapidly in both characters and species."[28] Because of such conflicts, an article in *Nature* reported, "[D]isparities between molecular and morphological trees" lead to "evolution wars" because "[e]volutionary trees constructed by studying biological molecules often don't resemble those drawn up from morphology."[29]

A 2012 paper stated that "phylogenetic conflict is common, and frequently the norm rather than the exception."[30] The dream that DNA sequences and morphology would fit neatly into a tree of life has failed, and with it a key prediction of neo-Darwinian theory.

Problem 7: Differences Between Vertebrate Embryos Contradict Common Ancestry

Another area where evolutionary biologists claim powerful evidence for common ancestry is the patterns of development of vertebrate embryos. Biology textbooks typically portray the embryos of different groups of vertebrate as starting off development in a highly similar fashion, stating that this reflects their common ancestry.[31] However, such claims overstate the degree of similarity between early-stage vertebrate embryos.

Biologists who investigate these questions have found considerable variability among vertebrate embryos from the earliest stages onward, contradicting what we are told to expect from common ancestry.[32] As an article in *Trends in Ecology and Evolution* stated, "[D]espite repeated assertions of the uniformity of early embryos within members of a phylum, development *before* the phylotypic stage is very varied."[33]

Embryologist P.Z. Myers once cited "substantial similarities" between vertebrate embryos as "evidence of common descent,"[34] but later, after conceding that vertebrate embryos "vary greatly,"[35] he wrote that "evolutionary theory predicts differences"[36] too. In other words, when it comes to dealing with the facts of embryology, evolutionary biology cannot predictively explain the data. As the old adage says, "A theory that explains everything explains nothing."

Problem 8: Neo-Darwinism Struggles to Explain the Biogeographical Distribution of Many Species

Biogeography is the study of the distribution of organisms in time and space both in the present and the past here on Earth. According to Darwinian theory, when we find two populations of organisms, if we go back far enough in time and space, we will find links that indicate common descent. But sometimes it is virtually impossible to explain how these populations could have arrived at their respective geographical locations on the globe from some ancestral population.

One of the most severe biogeographical puzzles for neo-Darwinists is the origin of South American monkeys known as *platyrrhines*. New World platyrrhine monkeys are thought to be descended from African Old World or *catarrhine* monkeys. The fossil record shows that monkeys have lived in South America for about the past 30 million years.[37] But plate tectonic history shows that Africa and South America split off from one another between 100 and 120 million years ago (mya), and that South America was an isolated island continent from about 80 to 3.5 mya.[38] If South American monkeys were split off from African monkeys around 30 mya, proponents of neo-Darwinism must somehow account for how the South American monkeys crossed hundreds, if not thousands, of kilometers of open ocean to end up in South America.

For those unfamiliar with the sorts of arguments made by neo-Darwinian biogeographers, responses to these puzzles can be almost too incredible to believe. A HarperCollins textbook explains: "The 'rafting hypothesis' argues that monkeys evolved from prosimians once and only once in Africa, and…made the water-logged trip to South America."[39] And of course, there cannot have been just one seafaring monkey, or that monkey would die leaving no offspring. Thus, at least two monkeys (or perhaps a single pregnant monkey) must have made the rafting voyage.

This is not the only biogeographical conundrum that forces appeals to rafting or other speculative mechanisms of "oceanic dispersal." Other examples include the presence of lizards and large caviomorph rodents in South America;[40] the arrival of bees, lemurs, and other mammals in Madagascar;[41] the appearance of elephant fossils on islands;[42] the appearance of freshwater frogs across isolated oceanic island chains;[43] and numerous similar examples.[44] A paper in *Annals of Geophysics* tried to resolve evolutionary biogeographical problems among fossil organisms on either side of the Pacific Ocean by invoking an "expanding Earth"—a long-discarded geological hypothesis (different from the well-accepted modern theories of plate tectonics).[45]

When evolutionary scientists are forced to appeal to fantastical expanding Earth hypotheses, or unlikely accounts of species rafting across oceans in order to retain common ancestry, clearly their model faces a severe challenge.

Problem 9: Evolutionary Biology Has a Long History of Inaccurate Predictions About Vestigial Organs and "Junk DNA"

For decades, evolutionists have claimed that our bodies and genomes are full of useless parts and genetic material—"vestigial" organs—that show life is the result of eons of unguided evolution. Structures that were previously—and incorrectly—considered to be vestigial include tonsils,[46] the coccyx (tailbone),[47] and the appendix.[48]

Despite the poor track record of claims that certain organs were vestigial, evolutionary biologists have applied this same kind of thinking to our genomes. Many have postulated that the random nature of mutations would fill our genomes with useless genetic garbage, dubbed "junk DNA." But over time, numerous examples of function have been discovered for so-called junk DNA.

In 2012, the journal *Nature* reported the results of a multiyear research project involving more than 400 international scientists who studied the functions of noncoding DNA in humans. Called the ENCODE Project, its set of 30 groundbreaking papers reported that the "vast majority" of the genome has function. The lead paper stated,

> These data enabled us to assign biochemical functions for 80% of the genome, in particular outside of the well-studied protein-coding regions.[49]

Another *Nature* commentary observed that "80% of the genome contains elements linked to biochemical functions, dispatching the widely held view that the human genome is mostly 'junk DNA.'"[50] *Discover Magazine* put it this way: "The key point is: It's not 'junk.'"[51]

Functions for various types of junk DNA have been reported in numerous scientific papers,[52] including functions for many "pseudogenes."[53] While there's still much we do not know about the genome, the trendline of the research is clearly pointing in one direction: The more we study the genome, the more we detect function.

Problem 10: Humans Display Many Behavioral and Cognitive Abilities That Offer No Apparent Survival Advantage

In recent years, evolutionary biologists have tried to explain the origin of human moral, intellectual, and religious abilities in terms of Darwinian evolution. Evolutionary psychologist Marc Hauser promotes the common hypothesis that "people are born with a moral grammar wired into their neural circuits by evolution."[54]

Humans do appear hard-wired for morality—a conclusion that the Christian apologist will find unsurprising. But were we programmed by unguided evolutionary mechanisms? Natural selection cannot explain extreme acts of human kindness. Regardless of background or beliefs, upon finding strangers trapped inside a burning vehicle, people will risk their own lives to help them escape—with no evolutionary benefit to themselves. Francis Collins gives the example of Oskar Schindler, the German businessman who risked his life "to save more than a thousand Jews from the gas chambers," which is "the opposite of saving his genes."[55]

Natural Academy of Sciences member Philip Skell explained why evolutionary psychology does not adequately explain complex human behavior:

> Darwinian explanations for such things are often too supple: Natural selection makes humans self-centered and aggressive—except when it makes them altruistic and peaceable. Or natural selection produces virile men who eagerly spread their seed—except when it prefers men who are faithful protectors and providers. When an explanation is so supple that it can explain any behavior, it is difficult to test it experimentally, much less use it as a catalyst for scientific discovery.[56]

Many of humanity's most impressive charitable, artistic, and intellectual abilities outstrip the basic requirements of natural selection. If life is simply about survival and reproduction, why do humans compose symphonies, investigate quantum mechanics, and build cathedrals? Contrary to neo-Darwinism, the evidence indicates that human life is not about mere survival and reproduction.

What About Darwin's Doubt and the Chances of Information Emerging from Random Mutations?

Stephen C. Meyer

We count on scientists to tell us what they know and do not know—not just what they want us to hear. But when it comes to the contentious issue of the evolution of life on earth, spokespersons for official science are often less forthcoming than we might wish.

When writing in scientific journals, leading biologists candidly discuss the many scientific difficulties facing contemporary versions of Darwin's theory. Yet when scientists take up the public defense of Darwinism—in educational policy statements, textbooks, or public television documentaries—that candor often disappears behind a rhetorical curtain. "There's a feeling in biology that scientists should keep their dirty laundry hidden," says theoretical biologist Danny Hillis, adding that "there's a strong school of thought in biology that one should never question Darwin in public."

Ironically, the reticence that Darwin's present-day defenders feel about openly critiquing evolutionary theory would have likely made Charles Darwin himself uncomfortable.

In *The Origin of Species,* Darwin openly acknowledged important weaknesses in his theory and professed his own doubts about key aspects of it.

In *Origin of Species,* Darwin expressed a key doubt about the ability of his theory to explain one particular event in the history of life—an event known as the Cambrian explosion. I've recently written a book about this doubt and what has become of it. In *Darwin's Doubt,* I argue that the problem Darwin identified not only remains to this day, but that it has grown up to illustrate a more fundamental conceptual difficulty than he could have understood—a problem for all of evolutionary biology that points to the need for entirely different understanding of the origin of animal life on Earth.

The Cambrian Explosion of Animal Life

Darwin was puzzled by a pattern in the fossil record that seemed to document the sudden geological appearance of animal life in a remote period of Earth's history, now known as the Cambrian era. During this geological period, many new and anatomically complex creatures—such as trilobites with their compound eyes and articulated exoskeletons—appeared suddenly in the sedimentary layers without any evidence of simpler ancestral forms in the earlier layers below.

The sudden appearance of animals so early in the fossil record did not easily accord with Darwin's picture of gradual evolutionary change. Indeed, Darwin had depicted the history of life as a *gradually* unfolding branched tree. Thus, as Darwin envisioned the history of life, complex animals such as trilobites, for instance, would have arisen from a series of simpler precursors and intermediate forms over vast stretches of geologic time. Yet Darwin knew that the Precambrian fossil record did not attest to such a rainbow of intermediate forms leading to the Cambrian animals.

In *Origin of Species*, Darwin frankly expressed his puzzlement about this mystery: "The difficulty of assigning any good reason for the absence of vast piles of strata rich in fossils beneath the Cambrian system is very great," he wrote. "The case at present must remain inexplicable; and may be truly urged as a valid argument against the views here entertained."[1]

Of course, Darwin hoped the mystery of the missing ancestral fossils would be solved by the eventual discovery of numerous transitional forms in the Precambrian fossil record. But the opposite of what he expected has happened. In the 150 years since the publication of *Origin*, scientists have combed Precambrian strata worldwide for the alleged precursors to the Cambrian animals, but they haven't found the evolutionary ancestors that Darwin anticipated. Instead, they have made new discoveries that have shown that the Cambrian explosion was

an even more explosive event than Darwin knew. For this and other reasons, the mystery of the missing Precambrian ancestral fossils has only grown more acute.

A Deeper Mystery: How to Build an Animal

There is a second, and arguably deeper, mystery associated with the Cambrian explosion—the mystery of how the neo-Darwinian mechanism of natural selection and random mutation could have *built* all these fundamentally new forms of animal life and done so quickly enough to account for the pattern in the fossil record. That question became acute in the second half of the twentieth century as biologists learned more about what it takes to build an animal.

In 1953, when James Watson and Francis Crick elucidated the structure of the DNA molecule, they made a startling discovery. The structure of DNA allows it to store information in the form of a four-character digital code. Strings of precisely sequenced chemicals called *nucleotide bases* store and transmit the assembly instruction—the information—for building the crucial protein molecules that the cell needs to survive.

Crick later developed this idea with his famous "sequence hypothesis," according to which the chemical constituents in DNA function like alphabetic letters in a written language or digital characters in a computer code. Just as English letters may convey a particular message depending on their arrangement, so too do certain sequences of chemical bases along the spine of a DNA molecule convey precise instructions for building proteins. The DNA molecule carries the same kind of "specified" or "functional" information that characterizes written texts or computer codes. As Richard Dawkins has acknowledged, "the machine code of the genes is uncannily computer-like."[2] Or as Bill Gates has noted, "DNA is like a computer program, but far, far more advanced than any software ever created."[3]

What does all this have to do with the Cambrian explosion? The Cambrian period is marked by an explosion of new animals exemplifying new body plans. But building new animal body plans requires new organs, tissues, and cell types. And new cell types require many kinds of specialized or dedicated proteins. For example, animals with gut cells require new digestive enzymes (proteins). But building new proteins requires genetic information stored on the DNA molecule. Thus, building new animals with distinctive new body plans requires, at the very least, vast amounts of new genetic *information*. (Building a new animal body plan also requires another type of information, not stored in genes, called *epigenetic information*.) Indeed, the Cambrian explosion of animal life not only represented an explosion of new biological *form*, but it also required an explosion of new biological *information*.

What produced the explosion of genetic and other forms of biological information that was necessary to produce these new forms of life? Is it plausible to think that the neo-Darwinian mechanism of natural selection—acting on random mutations in DNA—could produce the highly *specific* arrangements of bases in DNA (the chemicals that function as alphabetic or digital characters) necessary to generate the protein building blocks of new cell types and novel forms of life?

The Combinatorial Inflation Problem

According to neo-Darwinian theory, new genetic information arises first as random mutations occur in the DNA of existing organisms. When mutations arise that confer a survival advantage on the organisms that possess them, the resulting genetic changes are passed on by natural selection to the next generation. As such changes accumulate, the features of a population change over time. Nevertheless, natural selection can only "select" what *random* mutations first generate. Thus, for natural selection to preserve any significant functional or anatomical innovation, random mutations must first produce new genetic information for building novel proteins.

Nevertheless, when it comes to producing new genetic information, the neo-Darwinian mechanism, with its reliance on random mutations, faces a kind of needle-in-the-haystack problem—or what mathematicians call a *combinatorial* problem. In mathematics, the term *combinatorial* refers to the number of possible ways that a set of objects can be arranged or combined. Many simple bike locks, for example, have four *dials* with ten *settings* on each dial. A bike thief encountering one of these locks faces a combinatorial problem because there are 10 × 10 × 10 × 10—or 10,000—possible ways of combining the possible settings on each of the four dials, and only one combination that will open the lock. A random search of possible combinations is unlikely to yield the correct combination unless the thief has plenty of time.

What does this have to do with the origin of biological information? It turns out that it is extremely difficult to assemble a new information-bearing gene or protein by the natural selection/random mutation process because of the sheer number of possible sequences that must be searched in the available time. As the length of the required gene or protein grows, the number of possible base or amino-acid sequences of that length grows exponentially.

Here is an illustration that may help make the problem clear. Imagine that we encounter a truly committed bike thief who is willing to search the "sequence space" of possible bike combinations at a rate of about one new combination every two seconds. If our hypothetical bike thief had three hours and took no breaks, he could generate more than half (about 5,400) of the 10,000 total combinations of a four-dial bike lock. In that case, the probability that he will stumble upon the right combination *exceeds* the probability that he will fail, and it becomes *more likely than not* that he will succeed in opening the lock by chance. Thus, the chance hypothesis—the hypothesis that he will succeed in opening the lock by chance—is also more likely to be *true* than false.

But now consider another case. If that thief with the same limited three-hour time period confronted a lock with ten dials and ten digits per dial (a lock with ten *billion* possible combinations), he would now be able to explore only a small fraction of the possible combinations—5,400 of 10,000,000—far, far fewer than half. In this case, it would be *much more likely* than not that he would *fail* to open the lock by chance. And the chance hypothesis would be much more likely to be *false* than true.

These examples suggest that the ultimate probability of the success of a random search—and the plausibility of any hypothesis that affirms the success of such a search—depends upon both the *size of the space* that needs to be searched and *the number of opportunities* available to search it.

In *Darwin's Doubt*, I show that the number of possible DNA sequences (or amino-

acid sequences) that need to be searched by the evolutionary process dwarfs the time available for such a search—even taking into account evolutionary deep time. Molecular biologists have long understood that the size of the sequence space of possible nucleotide bases and amino acids (the number of possible combinations) is extremely large. Moreover, recent experiments in molecular biology and protein science have established that functional genes and proteins are extremely *rare* within these vast combinatorial spaces of possible arrangements. There are vastly (exponentially!) more ways of arranging nucleotide bases that result in nonfunctional sequences of DNA, and vastly more ways of arranging amino acids that result in nonfunctional amino-acid chains, than there are corresponding *functional* genes or proteins. One recent experimentally derived estimate places that ratio—the size of the haystack in relation to the needle—at 10^{77} nonfunctional sequences for every functional gene or protein.[4] (Note that there are only 10^{65} atoms in our galaxy.)

All this suggests that the mutation and selection mechanism would have enough time in the entire multibillion-year history of life on Earth to generate or "search" only a miniscule fraction (one ten trillion, trillion trillionth, to be exact) of the total number of possible nucleotide base or amino-acid sequences corresponding to a single functional gene or protein. The number of trials available to the evolutionary process turns out to be incredibly small *in relation to* the number of *possible* sequences that need to be searched.

Thus, as with our bike thief, who is confronted with many more combinations than he has time to explore, the mutation and selection mechanism is much *more likely to fail* than to succeed in generating even a single new gene or protein in the known history of life on earth. It follows that the neo-Darwinian mechanism—with its reliance on a random search—is not an adequate mechanism to generate the *information* necessary to produce even a single new protein, let alone a whole new Cambrian animal, in the time available. Or to put the point differently, the neo-Darwinian explanation for the origin of genetic information is *overwhelmingly* more likely to be *false* than true.

Theory of Intelligent Design

Could this *unexplained*—from a materialistic point of view—origin of the information necessary to build the Cambrian animals point instead to the activity of a different type of cause? Do we know of any other kind of entity that has the power to create large amounts of specified information?

We do. As information scientist Henry Quastler recognized, the "creation of new information is habitually associated with conscious activity."[5] Indeed, experience affirms that functionally specified information routinely arises from the activity of intelligent agents. A computer user who traces the information on a screen back to its source invariably comes to the mind of a software engineer or programmer. Similarly, the information in a book or newspaper column ultimately derives from a writer—from a mental rather than a strictly material cause.

Those of us who support the theory of intelligent design advocate a more open approach to scientific investigation. Not only do we believe the public has a right to know about the problems with evolutionary theory, we also believe that the rules of science should allow scientists to "follow the evidence wherever it leads"—even if it leads to conclusions that raise deeper and unwelcome metaphysical questions.

How Should Christians Think About the Origins of the Universe?

J. T. Bridges

The question in the title is directed at Christians and their thoughts. Before we develop an answer, we should be committed to thinking Christianly about the subject of the universe and its origins. Christians should not be shy about noting the theological and supernatural elements in their considerations. There are, broadly speaking, two approaches to the question: faith and reason.

Faith, as a mode of forming beliefs, is a matter of authoritative testimony. Just as one might believe a diagnosis solely on the testimony of a competent physician, one may believe something about physical or spiritual reality solely on the testimony of God. Thomas Aquinas was a Christian thinker who did not believe the origin of the universe could be demonstrated scientifically or philosophically. He believed the universe's supernatural creation in the finite past was a matter of faith and not reason. As Christians, we may follow Aquinas in believing, as a matter of faith, that God is the sole supernatural cause of the universe. The other option is to try to satisfy our intellect by demonstrating that God created the universe.

The Kinds of Explanations

As we move from the realm of faith into the realm of reason, we have several options available to us. We can try to develop a strict scientific explanation; we can use a mixture of science and another discipline, such as philosophy or theology (which we'll call a "science [+] explanation"); or we can develop a strict philosophical explanation. Christian thinkers and trained philosophers typically ignore the first path (strict scientific demonstration) because they tend to recognize the philosophical implications of the question. Some working scientists, however, are good examples of thinking about the universe's origins along strictly scientific lines.

Science-Only Explanation

Lawrence Krauss, for example, says, "*Nothing* is actually a very interesting thing in modern physics…[it is a] boiling, bubbling brew of virtual particles that pop into and out of existence on timescales so short, you never see them."[1] In Krauss's opinion, science has given us a definitive explanation of the origin of the universe: nothing. Similarly, Neil deGrasse Tyson, in a recently posted video interview, was asked if there was a way to combine modern cosmology and the idea of a Creator. The interviewer commented, "From a scientific standpoint, you cannot speak to this because you are speaking about the fact of a Creator or higher power creating this." To which Tyson replied, "Sure you can. If there is a higher power in this universe, there is no reason that should be beyond the ability of science to determine that."[2] For working scientists who follow the line of thinking that Krauss and Tyson have indicated, there is nothing about the universe (even God's causal relationship to it) that science is unable to detect or explain. The universe came into being from nothing, and its nature is whatever modern physics says it is. Physicist George Ellis remarks, "Krauss does not address why the laws of physics exist, why they have the form they have, or in what kind of manifestation they existed before the universe existed...He does not begin to answer these questions."[3]

Science-Plus Explanation

Many in the world of Christian apologetics are used to an approach that incorporates the findings of modern science with elements either of theology (e.g., the Bible) or broader philosophical reasoning to the conclusion that God is the cause of the universe's beginning. Even within this broader distinction of a science-plus approach to the question there are different flavors of response.[4] For an example of the philosophical use of science for Christian apologetics, we turn to the work of William Lane Craig.

Craig's approach to answering the question of the universe's origins is to combine the best cosmology of the day with a tight philosophical argument to conclude God is the universe's origin. Craig is well known

for his defense of the kalam cosmological argument:

1. Whatever begins to exist has a cause.

2. The universe began to exist.

Therefore, the universe has a cause.[5]

To defend the first premise, one must usually debunk assertions about events or effects happening uncaused. Atheist philosopher of science Bradley Monton challenges,

> [Granting the failure of philosophical explanations of causal principles] doesn't mean that we should stop using causal language though; we're still allowed to say that the incoming baseball caused the window to break. It's just that these sorts of causal claims can't be understood as claims of fundamental physics. Instead, they have to be understood as claims of "folk science"...Causal principles are applicable in the domains of folk science, but not in general.
>
> It would follow from all this that a principle like Premise 1, which says that everything that begins to exist has a cause of its existence, is only applicable in the limited domain of folk science.[6]

How should one respond to this challenge? One way is to point out that our metaphysical commitments should be based largely on the world that we *do* experience *directly* and not a world known in a highly indirect manner. Philosopher of science W.A. Wallace explains,

> The possibility of a science of nature, or of a science based on natures, is jeopardized if one begins straightaway with atoms or subatomic particles as

though these were immediately given, and then attempts to construct an entire universe out of them…This is not to prejudice the case against causal explanations that make use of elementary particles [etc.]…The point is rather that entities remote from man's experience, which require elaborate instrumentation and theoretical construction for their very discussion, are prima facie lacking in the intelligibility that enables one to grasp a nature, and are *thus poor candidates with which to begin a study of the natural world.*[7]

We have a more immediate grasp of baseballs breaking windows than we do the causal interactions of the subatomic world. Our notions of causality should therefore be shaped by the interactions of which we are more commonly aware. Monton adopted the strange causal events of microphysics as the standard for our causal principles; this is philosophical bias.

To defend the second premise, Craig has surveyed a host of alternative explanations that seek to avoid a true beginning in the finite past, which follows on the standard interpretation of big bang cosmology. These alternatives include the steady-state model, oscillating models, vacuum fluctuation models, chaotic inflationary models, and quantum gravity models. These seek to avoid a genuine beginning to the universe. Currently, quantum gravity models seem to be popular. About these Craig says, "The use of imaginary quantities for time is an inherent feature of all Quantum Gravity models. This precludes their being construed realistically as accounts of the origin of the space-time universe…"[8]

After defending both premises and the conclusion that the universe was caused, Craig then goes on to summarize the straightforward characteristics of the kind of being responsible for the universe's origins. He states, "If the universe has a cause of its existence, then an uncaused, personal Creator of the universe exists, who sans the universe is beginningless, changeless, immaterial, timeless, spaceless, and enormously powerful."[9] Craig's science-plus approach is compelling and popular. The final approach to the question of the universe's origin will be a strict philosophical demonstration.

Philosophy-Only Explanation

This section, like the science-only section, will necessarily be brief. Just as a scientist delving into the details of a discipline is in danger of losing an audience of laypersons, so too a philosopher presenting a position can make such presentation inaccessible to the laity and therefore practically useless. What follows is a brief sketch of how one might think of the universe in a strictly philosophical way.

In everything that is not God (every finite, contingent thing), *what* that thing is (its essence) is distinct from its act of existing (which accounts for the *fact* that it is). Consider an extinct species of animal. Tyrannosaurus Rex used to exist, but do so no longer. For Aquinas, "It is therefore necessary that everything whose act of existing is other than its nature [essence] have its act of existing from another."[10] This is so for Aquinas because by definition a finite, contingent being is one that comes into existence at a point in time and can pass out of being. If its act of existing were a part of what it was, then it could not cease to exist. Indeed, it would have had to always exist. But if a finite, contingent being does not have its act of existing essentially, then its existence is given to it from another.

This reasoning leads us to a Being who exists essentially and therefore necessarily; further, this Being is responsible for giving existence to all contingent beings every moment of their being. For example, the created universe is like the music of a musician. The music of the musician exists only while it is being played. If God ceased His causal interaction with the universe, it would cease to be. This line of reasoning points to no scientific theory for support; it is purely a metaphysical way of thinking about the nature of the universe.

The Value of the Explanations

What we have seen in this chapter is that, broadly speaking, there are four ways to think about the origins of the universe. One may hold that the universe has a beginning based solely on faith. One may take a reasoned approach that seeks to limit the question to natural science alone. One may take a reasoned approach that seeks to combine the best of contemporary science and philosophical contemplation. Finally, one may take a reasoned approach that rests on a purely philosophical demonstration. Each of these approaches has challenges to it. The faith-alone position is poor ground for apologetics. The science-only position ignores metaphysics. The science-plus position demands familiarity with modern cosmology and its debates. The philosophy-only position requires a technical metaphysics. One must choose which approach is clearest and strongest in terms of its apologetics value.

Do We Have a Privileged Planet?

Guillermo Gonzalez

On August 21, 2017, Americans were privileged to witness one of nature's most awe-inspiring phenomena: a total eclipse of the sun. Tens of millions flocked to a narrow strip of land stretching from the west coast to the east coast to enjoy less than three minutes of totality (i.e., when the moon almost perfectly covers the sun). Watching from within the moon's dark umbral shadow on Earth's surface, people often report feeling a deep personal connection to the broader universe, as if they were participants in a kind of choreographed celestial drama.

Other more common natural phenomena seem to evoke similar feelings of awe and wonder from those who witness them. Have you ever paused to drink in the beauty of a rainbow or of a star-studded dark night sky? There is also mystery about them. While gazing at the night sky, I can remember asking myself, *Who ordered that?* Are these gratuitous displays of beauty for our benefit? I am convinced that they are, and that they point to a profound truth about our existence.

Solar Eclipses, the Start of an Inquiry

There are remarkable coincidences associated with solar eclipses visible from Earth. First, as countless people have noted for millennia, from our perspective on this planet, the sun and moon appear to be the same size. Thus, when the moon covers the sun's bright disk during a total solar eclipse, it permits views of the sun's thin chromosphere as well as its much fainter corona. Even distant stars and planets become visible during totality.

But this situation will not remain indefinitely. The moon is slowly receding from Earth; as a consequence, the Earth's tides will rise. Within about 250 million years, the moon will be too far from Earth to completely cover the sun, and total solar eclipses will cease to be possible. Humans arrived on Earth at just the right time to enjoy solar eclipses at their best!

But wait a minute. Do other planets have moons that help to produce solar eclipses too? Yes, eclipses do occur on other planets, but they are inferior to Earth's eclipses on multiple counts. From the host planet's surface, some moons appear too small compared to the sun, so they cannot produce total eclipses. This is the case for the two moons that orbit Mars. The large Galilean moons of Jupiter, on the other hand, appear much larger than the sun, assuming someone could observe from the planet's cloud tops.

Earth's moon is one of the largest in the Solar System, and is able to form itself into a nearly perfect sphere as a result of its relatively high surface gravity. Such is not the case for the many small moons in the Solar System, which often look like oversized potatoes. The round profile of Earth's moon matches well the sun's round disk. And, as the closest moon-accompanied planet to the sun, Earth provides the most detailed views of the eclipsed sun.

In spite of the close match between the sun and moon in our skies, our total eclipses are relatively long in duration. For the same distance, a moon around a gas giant orbits around it much faster because of the greater mass of the planet.

Finally, as it turns out, the only planet in the Solar System that is inhabited by observers also happens to be the best place to observe solar eclipses! Given all the facts we've just considered, we have to ask: Are these all mere coincidences, or do they point to a deeper truth? To answer this, we need to review a few aspects of planetary habitability.

First, in order to host complex life, a terrestrial planet must be located within the Circumstellar Habitable Zone (CHZ), where it can maintain liquid water on its surface. Second, it needs to orbit a G-spectral type main-sequence star. Third, the presence of a large moon enhances the planet's habitability in several ways: (1) it makes possible the tidal mixing of mineral nutrients from the continents to the oceans, (2) it helps drive the deep ocean currents, and (3) it helps stabilize the planet's rotation axis tilt (leading to a more stable climate). Last, there are additional complex details that set tighter habitability constraints on the mass, distance, and size of the moon.

Did you notice something interesting

about these requirements for life? Satisfying them makes it more likely that total solar eclipses will be visible. A location within the CHZ of a G-type star sets the range of possible angular sizes that the star will appear in the sky. And the lunar habitability factors bring in the final piece. Thus, the actors for a total solar eclipse are on stage while the audience is watching in their comfortable theater.

Not only are total solar eclipses beautiful and awe-inspiring, but they have led to important scientific discoveries. The element helium was discovered in a spectrum of the sun taken during a total solar eclipse in 1868. Observations of the spectrum of the chromosphere gave astronomers important clues about how the spectra of distant stars are produced. And, perhaps most important, a total solar eclipse in 1919 provided the first opportunity to test Albert Einstein's freshly minted general theory of relativity. Empirical confirmation of his predictions resulted in its rapid acceptance.

Because there appears to be a physical basis for the coincidences that make total solar eclipses possible, does this not remove the need for a design explanation? Not at all! It seems surprising that the universe would be set up, by chance, in a way that the most habitable locations would also be the best places to observe total solar eclipses. But this makes sense on the hypothesis that the universe is designed so that observers can learn and enjoy total solar eclipses. The case of solar eclipses was the first example of the *Privileged Planet* thesis[1]—the thesis that the universe is designed for scientific observation and discovery.

Additional Examples of What Makes Earth Unusual

If the solar eclipse coincidences were the only example of the mysterious link between life and scientific discovery, I would not be making this claim. But solar eclipses motivated me to search for other instances. This was a prediction: If the solar eclipses example did not point to a deeper truth about the universe, then my search would end quickly. As it turned out, over a period of several months I found additional examples that pointed to the same eerie pattern found in solar eclipses. I will review them here.

Earth's transparent atmosphere permits relatively clear views not only of solar eclipses, but also of other planets, moons, asteroids, comets, stars, nebulae, and distant galaxies. For millennia, writers have waxed poetic about the starry heavens. A moment's reflection, however, should make it clear that this ability to see so far into space is a surprising situation. German philosopher and historian Hans Blumenberg wrote,

> The combined circumstance that we live on Earth and are able to see stars— that the conditions necessary for life do not exclude those necessary for vision, and vice versa—is a remarkably improbable one. This is because the medium in which we live is, on the one hand, just thick enough to enable us to breathe and to prevent us from being burned up by cosmic rays, while, on the other hand, it is not so opaque as to absorb entirely the light of the stars and block any view of the universe. What a fragile balance between the indispensable and the sublime.[2]

In other words, we do not need to be able to see the stars to exist. A cloud-covered but still-translucent atmosphere would have been just fine for us and for our plant friends. What is more, the information accessible to us in the night sky goes far beyond what we can see with unaided vision. A small telescope reveals millions of stars and thousands of galaxies and nebulae. Astronomers are still building ever-larger ground-based telescopes, evidence that they have not yet exhausted what the night sky has to offer.

Yet an active hydrological cycle is necessary for complex life, resulting in the need for some cloudiness. This is a minor nuisance to astronomers, but the clouds and rain more than make up for it in other ways. For example, the humble rainbow is possible to see only because we have partly cloudy skies and rain. The ingredients for a rainbow are small water droplets suspended in the atmosphere and direct sunlight when the sun is at a low altitude. Most often, rainbows are seen following a rainstorm in the late afternoon. Not only are rainbows beautiful, but they also served to inspire scientists to reproduce them artificially. In the nineteenth century, astronomers attached spectroscopes to telescopes and opened a new window to the universe that continues to unlock its secrets.

As consumers, we are far removed from the mining industries that provide the raw materials that get turned into cars, airplanes, and phones. You cannot just dig up a kilogram of pure aluminum out of the ground. Most of the chemical elements are found in the form of compounds in minerals, and we mine them as ores. Mining is economically feasible only because mineral ores have been concentrated by huge factors compared to the original source material. How did this happen?

Water is not only the elixir of life, but it is also the major agent for quickly moving around the diverse array of chemical elements in the earth. The hydrological cycle, in concert with the plate tectonic cycle, makes possible many economically accessible ores. Fluid-rock interactions occur when hot water containing dissolved minerals courses through the cracks of the earth. As the water encounters cooler temperatures, minerals precipitate out of the water and form crystals. Other mineral concentration processes include evaporation of inland seas, various types of volcanism, and even single-celled organisms.

You read that last item right: Living things have been responsible for concentrating mineral ores. Robert Hazen, a research scientist at the geophysical laboratory at the Carnegie Institution of Washington and a professor of earth science at George Mason University, states that Earth is unique given the vast range of minerals in its crust. Surprisingly, most of the 5,000-plus known mineral species have been formed from the activities of living things. Hazen estimates that, in contrast, the moon has fewer than 300 mineral species, and Mars has no more than a few hundred.[3]

In addition, the rise of oxygen on Earth not only made possible oxygen breathers like people and sheep, but it also allowed for a rapid increase in mineral diversity. This rich diversity of mineral species makes Earth more habitable for complex life. For example, we require some 27 elements in the right concentrations and chemical forms.

Mining and processing mineral ores takes a great deal of energy, as do many activities of modern civilization. Our society runs on fossil fuels: coal, oil, and natural gas. We use them not only to power our machines but also to make a wide variety of products. Although we tend to take them for granted, fossil fuels have not always been available. They come from the remains of millions of generations of swamp and ocean life that have gradually built up and cooked deep within Earth's crust. It's almost as though a stagehand was preparing for our arrival in the next scene.

A Satisfactory Answer

In summary, our planetary home is extravagantly furnished with the tools we need to learn about the cosmos. We certainly do not *need* to be able to see total solar eclipses, rainbows, stars, or galaxies to survive, but the kind of atmosphere that allows us to view these things *is* physically (but not logically) necessary for our existence. People got by just fine before vast reservoirs of oil and gas were discovered, and we can probably do with fewer than 5,000-plus mineral species. Having these resources, however, allows us to build the instruments of scientific discovery. Appealing to chance in combination with Darwinian selection is utterly impotent to explain our situation. Only intelligent design offers a satisfactory answer.

Do Science and the Bible Conflict?

Terry Mortenson

To answer this question, we must define some terms carefully. First, what do we mean by *science*? The English word comes from the Latin *scientia*, which simply means "knowledge." But for the last roughly 400 years of the development of modern science, it has meant a *method* by which humans attempt to discover truth about the physical world. The *New Oxford American Dictionary* defines science as "the intellectual and practical activity encompassing the systematic study of the structure and behavior of the physical and natural world through observation and experiment: *the world of science and technology.*"

Science: A Method of Knowing

Science is a method of knowing that is performed by humans. We must carefully note that science doesn't say or show or prove anything; it is scientists who say, show, or prove things. Furthermore, not all scientists say the same things about the world or some aspect of the physical creation. There is no monolithic view held by all scientists on hardly any scientific question. Scientists with PhDs in the same field of study can and do disagree, for example, about the

benefit or harm of cholesterol, the cause and best treatment for many diseases, the tempo of evolution (gradualism or punctuated equilibrium), or the validity of the big bang theory. What is often called science is actually the scientific consensus view (i.e., what most scientists believe to be true at any given time). But in the history of science, the majority has often been wrong.[1] Therefore, truth should not be determined by majority vote.

The Bible: A Source of Truth

In contrast to science, the Bible is not a *method* for discovering truth. Rather, it is a *source* of propositional truth. Scientific consensus comes from man's efforts to discover truth. But the Bible is God's revelation of truth to mankind. Furthermore, according to the Bible, the natural world we live in is not like the original creation Adam lived in before he sinned. Thus, scientists are studying a cursed creation that is in bondage to corruption (Genesis 3:14-21; Romans 8:18-25) and is waiting to be redeemed and restored after the curse is removed (Acts 3:21; Colossians 1:15-20; Revelation 22:3). In contrast, the Bible is inerrant and infallible propositional truth. It is not cursed.

Another Important Difference

Now, it is true that both the natural world and the Bible must be studied and interpreted by humans. But there is an important difference: Nature communicates to us nonverbally, whereas Scripture speaks to us verbally. The Bible communicates infallibly that the Creator exists and has certain attributes or characteristics (Psalms 19:1; 97:6; Acts 14:15-17; 17:24-29; Romans 1:18-20; 2:14-16): God is eternal, powerful, moral/ righteous, good, sovereign, etc. But nowhere does the Bible teach that the creation infallibly communicates the truth about the origin and history of the creation. Both nature and Scripture must be interpreted. But verbal communication from a truthful person who wants to be understood is always easier to interpret accurately than nonverbal communication. And a person's worldview assumptions will affect how he interprets both nature and Scripture.

Different Kinds of Science

Before we can answer the question of this chapter, we also need to understand the inadequacy of the dictionary definition given above because there are two broad categories of science that are significantly different. I like to call them *operation science* and *origin science* (or experimental/observational science and historical science).

Operation or experimental science includes most of biology, chemistry, and physics, as well as engineering research and medical research. Scientists in these fields use observable, repeatable experiments (usually in a lab) to understand how things operate or function so they can develop new technology, find cures for disease, improve the quality of food, build better bridges, and more.

But operation science won't answer the questions of how and when the Grand Canyon was formed, or how and when Saturn or the first humans came into existence. We can't reproduce those things in a laboratory. These are historical questions for which we need origin or historical science, which includes the fields of historical geology, paleontology, archaeology, and forensic science (used in criminal investigations). Scientists in these fields use eyewitness testimony (if any is available) and observable physical evidence to try to reconstruct the unobservable, unrepeatable event(s) in the past that produced the evidence we see today.

So, for example, how cancer cells function and how we can cure cancer patients is a different kind of question than that of how the Grand Canyon formed. How dogs produce variety is a different question from how the first dog came into existence. How an air conditioner functions is a different kind of question from how the first air conditioner came into existence. The question of operation is different from the question of origin.

Both kinds of science use observation. But operation scientists are observing things as they function or operate repeatedly in the present. Origin scientists observe things in the present that are the result of some event(s) that happened in the unobservable, unrepeatable past. The famous Harvard evolutionary zoologist Ernst Mayr noted this difference when he wrote,

> Darwin introduced historicity into science. Evolutionary biology, in contrast with physics and chemistry, is a historical science—the evolutionist attempts to explain events and processes that have already taken place. Laws and experiments are inappropriate

techniques for the explication of such events and processes. Instead one constructs a historical narrative, consisting of a tentative reconstruction of the particular scenario that led to the events one is trying to explain.[2]

However, it wasn't Darwin who introduced historicity into science. Geologists had already done this decades before Darwin's famous book published in 1859.[3] But Mayr is right that in historical science the scientist constructs a narrative (a story about the past) to explain the evidence we see in the present. Darwin did this to explain the existence of the diverse plants and animals as well as man. He built his evolutionary story of biology on the foundation of the ideas of Charles Lyell, the most influential geologist of the nineteenth century. Similarly, the big bang theory is a story about the past to explain the origin and arrangement of stars, galaxies, planets, and our Solar System.

The Role of Worldview Assumptions

These evolutionary stories about origins are not based on eyewitness accounts but on the worldview assumptions of naturalism. In constructing his scenario of earth history to explain the formation of rock layers and fossils, Lyell said that his goal was to "free the science [of geology] from Moses."[4] Darwin was "freeing" the science of biology from Moses (i.e., Genesis) and big bang theories have done the same in cosmology. The worldview of naturalism took control of geology 200 years ago and became the ruling paradigm in all other sciences, as it is today.[5] Naturalism says everything can be explained by time and chance and the laws of nature working on matter. In contrast, Genesis 1–11

(as part of the inspired Word of God) is the Creator's eyewitness account of His acts of creation and judgment.

No one looks at the world with an empty mind. There is no such thing as a completely objective and unbiased scientist who lets the facts speak for themselves. Every scientist (in fact, every person) has a worldview—a set of philosophical and religious presuppositions or assumptions that affect what a scientist sees and how he interprets what he sees. Worldview assumptions do not influence the work of operation scientists much, if at all, because they rely on observable, repeatable experiments for their data. But worldview assumptions are enormously influential in the minds of origin scientists who are trying to reconstruct the unobservable, unrepeatable past.

Is There a Conflict?

There is no conflict between the study of the natural world (either in operation science or origin science) and the teachings of the Bible. In fact, Scripture commands us to study the creation. Genesis 1:28 implies the scientific enterprise as it commands man to subdue the earth and rule over the fish, birds, and land animals. Job 12:7-10 commands us to study living creatures and the earth itself because in doing so, we will see evidence of the existence and work of God, just as Psalm 19:1, 97:6, Acts 14:15-17, and Romans 1:18-20 also imply. Early man obviously observed and experimented, and mining, metallurgy, and musical instruments were among the results (Genesis 4:21-22). A considerable amount of experimental science produced the skills and technology used to build Noah's ark and the Tower of Babel. And Jacob undoubtedly studied his sheep and goats in a selective breeding program to develop a fruitful flock

(Genesis 30:25-43). So, the conflict is *not* between science and the Bible.

The conflict is between the Bible's account of origins and the evolutionary, naturalistic consensus view of the origins. Both are stories about the unrepeatable and unobservable past. And neither story is the result of experimental observational science.

Most people see this conflict. Those who deny any conflict are not paying careful attention to the Bible or to the claims of evolutionary scientists. Millions of non-Christians, especially young people, see the conflict and have rejected the Bible and the gospel because they believe science has proven Genesis is myth, and therefore the rest of the Bible cannot be trusted either.[6]

The evolutionary story conflicts with the Bible on many important points—for example, the order of creation events in Genesis 1,[7] the timescale of history since the beginning,[8] the fall of man and the curse on what was an originally good creation,[9] the global flood of Noah's day,[10] and Adam being made from dust and Eve made from his rib.[11]

That Christians see a conflict is reflected in the many different interpretations of Genesis and different degrees of acceptance of the evolutionary, naturalistic story. Theistic evolutionists accept virtually the whole evolutionary story from the big bang to the origin of man, although they reject the atheistic elements, believing that God initiated and providentially guided the whole process. Various forms of old-earth creationism reject biological evolution and accept most, or all, of what Genesis says about the supernatural origin of man, plants, and animals. And although they believe God created the matter and energy that exploded in the big bang, they accept what evolutionary cosmologists and geologists claim about the age and development of the universe and Earth over billions of years. Young-earth creationists reject the whole evolutionary story, take Genesis 1–11 as straightforward literal history, and contend that there is compelling scientific evidence for the truth of that history.

Therefore, the Bible itself does not conflict with science. Rather, it is the origins story advocated by most scientists that conflicts with the Bible's history in Genesis. They are irreconcilable accounts of the origin and history of the universe because they are based on fundamentally contradictory worldviews.

43

What Is the Relationship Between Science and Faith?

Terry Mortenson

To discuss what relationship, if any, there is between science and faith, we must be clear about what we mean by the terms *science* and *faith*. As stated in my previous chapter ("Do Science and the Bible Conflict?"), *science* is a method for studying the natural physical world to try to understand how it functions or operates, and determine what its history and origin are. Most people are clear about that, although there is considerable confusion between what I discussed as *operation science* and *origin science*. The question of how things in the present creation function or operate (regularities) is significantly different from the question of how the universe, earth, and the original plants, animals, and people came into existence (singularities).

On the other hand, *faith* is an ambiguous word. It means to trust in or rely upon something or someone. But in this case, the question becomes, Faith in what or whom? Most people would think that this chapter's question refers to religious faith. But again, which religion? Buddhism, Hinduism, Judaism, Islam, Christianity? And if we say the

Christian faith, then which form? A Roman Catholic, an evangelical, a theologically liberal Protestant, and an Eastern Orthodox believer might answer this question differently. That is why we need to think carefully about how to best answer the question about the relationship between science and faith.

Faith-Based Assumptions

Science is possible only by making certain faith commitments—that is, assumptions or beliefs that cannot be proven by any scientific experiment or observation. There are many important questions that have a bearing on one's approach to science. Does God exist? If He does exist, does He interact with His creation in any way, or is He a distant, hands-off kind of God? Do the laws of nature accurately describe physical reality, and do they apply everywhere in the universe? Are the laws of logic valid? Is the Bible the Word of the Creator or not? How a person answers those questions will affect his or her scientific study of the world. Ultimately, scientists cannot do their work without faith. Every scientist must make some faith assumptions.

Biblical Christians, of course, believe that an eternal, self-existent God created the world out of nothing and that the laws of nature, as discovered by scientists, describe how God providentially upholds and sustains His creation. But Christians also believe that from time to time, for divine purposes, God has worked in His creation to suspend, disrupt, or modify some of those laws in supernatural events recorded in the Bible (e.g., the curse on creation when Adam sinned, Noah's flood, Israel's exodus out of Egypt, Jesus walking on water, etc.). But science cannot prove those beliefs.

The atheistic scientist also has faith. He believes that there is no God and that he can explain everything within the parameters of time, chance, and the laws of nature. He also believes either that the universe is eternal or that something came from nothing. Like scientists of other faiths, he also believes that the laws of nature apply to the whole universe at all times, that the laws of logic are valid, and that his five senses (taste, sight, touch, smell, and sound) are basically giving him reliable information about the real world. But he cannot scientifically prove any of those beliefs.

Faith and the History of Science

The ancient Greeks, Chinese, and Muslims made empirical observations, performed experiments, and developed mathematical techniques, all of which contributed to the rise of scientific knowledge and technology. In addition, historians of science generally agree that the Christian worldview has had a significant influence on the development of modern science in Europe. It did not develop within a Hindu or Buddhist or ancient pagan Greek or Roman worldview or within an atheistic worldview.

Many of the most influential thinkers of modern science before the twentieth century operated within a biblical worldview. The English philosopher Francis Bacon, who strongly advocated for the scientific method of gaining knowledge by careful observation, experimentation, and inductive reasoning, believed that "the laws of nature, which now remain and govern inviolably till the end of the world, began to be in force when God first rested from his works, and ceased to create; but received a revocation, in part, by the curse, since which time they change not."[1]

Sir Isaac Newton believed,

> Atheism is so senseless. When I look at the solar system, I see the Earth at the right distance from the sun to receive the proper amounts of heat and light. This did not happen by chance...This most beautiful system of the sun, planets and comets, could only proceed from the counsel and dominion of an intelligent Being.[2]

Copernicus and Galileo were devout Roman Catholics. According to the Lutheran astronomer Johannes Kepler, the astronomers of his day (including himself and Tycho Brahe, the Danish astronomer whose extremely accurate observations Kepler used) sought "to carry out investigations in the heavens for the praise of their Creator."[3]

Many other great scientists embraced a Christian worldview in their work, including Leonardo da Vinci (amazing engineer, architect, and artist), Nicholas Steno (father of geological stratigraphy), Blaise Pascal (mathematician and a founder of hydrostatics and hydrodynamics), and Carolus Linnaeus (father of biological taxonomy). We could add Robert Boyle (father of modern chemistry), William Herschel (outstanding nineteenth-century astronomer), Michael Faraday (pioneer in the sciences of electricity and magnetism), William Kirby (father of entomology), and Louis Pasteur (leading bacteriologist and developer of germ theory of disease and the process of pasteurization). Others were Joseph Lister (father of modern surgery), Lord Kelvin and James Clerk Maxwell (both brilliant nineteenth-century physicists), Matthew Maury (pioneer in oceanography), and Gregor Mendel (father of genetics), to name just a few. Their Christian beliefs did not prevent them from doing science, but rather, were the foundation and motivation of their scientific researches.

Scripture says that the earth is the Lord's (Psalm 24:1), and that He owns the cattle on a thousand hills (Psalm 50:10). God gave Adam and Eve stewardship over the creation (Genesis 1:28), not to pollute it or destroy it but to manage it for the good of mankind and the glory of God. The command to rule over creation implies that we must study the creation so we can rule it well. God is the author of mathematics; He made the world to function in an orderly way, and He gave us minds capable of reasoning and knowing truth. Faith in God, in His sovereign lordship, and in the truth of His Word is the sure foundation for sound experimental science and the right application of that research to cure diseases, produce new technology, fight moral evils, and in other ways benefit human flourishing. Faith in God and the history recorded in His Word (starting in the very first verse of Genesis) is also the sure foundation for the correct interpretation of the evidence, especially as we seek to reconstruct the unobservable and unrepeatable history of the creation through research in the historical sciences.

The Dominant Faith Among Contemporary Scientists

Today, in virtually every country, science is dominated by an atheistic, naturalistic worldview (the belief that only natural causes can explain phenomena). The transition from the biblical worldview (in which modern science arose) to the current atheistic worldview (that controls science today) happened during the late eighteenth and early nineteenth centuries. This transition first took place in geology, especially through the writings of James Hutton and Charles Lyell.[4] Hutton's naturalism is evident in his words, "The past history of our globe must be explained by what can be seen to be happening now…No powers are to be employed that are not natural to the globe, no action to be admitted except those of which we know the principle."[5]

By insisting on present, natural processes *alone* to explain the origin and history of the earth, Hutton ruled out the biblical account of creation and Noah's flood for religious and philosophical reasons before he ever examined the geological evidence. Lyell, following Hutton's ideas, wrote to a friend that he wanted to "free the science [of geology] from Moses."[6] Lyell and Hutton's deistic (or atheistic) faith rejected the Bible's account of the origin and history of creation.

This antibiblical, naturalistic faith first expressed through the science of geology then spread into biology through Charles Darwin, who acknowledged,

I always feel as if my books came half out of Lyell's brains and that I never acknowledge this sufficiently, nor do I know how I can, without saying so in so many words—for I have always thought that the great merit of the *Principles* [*of Geology*], was that it altered the whole tone of one's mind & therefore that when seeing a thing never seen by Lyell, one yet saw it partially through his eyes.[7]

With the apparent triumph of Darwinism, naturalism conquered all the other sciences. George Wald (1906–1997), a professor of biology at Harvard for more than four decades and winner of the Nobel Prize in physiology or medicine 1967, reflected this faith commitment when he wrote about the origin of life:

> Time is in fact the hero of the plot. The time with which we have to deal is of the order of two billion years. What we regard as impossible on the basis of human experience is meaningless here. Given so much time, the "impossible" becomes possible, the possible probable, and the probable virtually certain. One has only to wait: time itself performs the miracles.[8]

More recently, Scott Todd, a professor of biology at Kansas State University, expressed that faith this way: "Even if all the data point to an intelligent designer, such a hypothesis is excluded from science because it is not naturalistic."[9] This modern, science-controlling faith is not derived from any scientific experiment or observation, but is a metaphysical, philosophical, religious choice.

Every Scientist Has Faith

Faith and science are inseparable. Without faith that the laws of nature apply everywhere in the universe, that the laws of logic are valid, and that our five senses are basically reliable, science would be impossible. Furthermore, what we believe about God (His existence or nonexistence), His relationship to the creation (active or inactive), and the truth of His revelation (the Bible) will affect what questions we are permitted to ask in scientific research (and what answers we are permitted to put forth). The same is true for what we observe, how we interpret what we observe, and how we apply the knowledge gained by that research (for good or for evil). The atheist—as well as the Christian, Jew, Muslim, Hindu or Buddhist—has faith commitments that affect his or her scientific endeavor.

It would be a mistake to assume that scientists are totally objective, unbiased, and free from faith commitments. There is no such human. Every scientist has faith, even the most ardent atheist. The only question is this: Are all our beliefs true, especially our beliefs about God and His Word? If our beliefs are contrary to His Word, we can be sure that sooner or later our scientific understanding of the world will be wrong in some ways.

Has the Christian Worldview Had a Positive Impact on the Development of Science?

Casey Luskin and Stephen C. Meyer

In his Pulitzer Prize-winning book *Summer for the Gods*, historian and legal scholar Edward Larson explains that in the decades following the publication of *Origin of Species* (1859), a "warfare model" of science and religion became "ingrained into the received wisdom of many secular Americans."[1] Another historian of science explains that this warfare model is "[d]eeply embedded in the culture of the west and has proven extremely hard to dislodge."[2] Two books in the late nineteenth century played a major role in crystalizing this mindset: John William Draper's *History of the Conflict Between Religion and Science* and Andrew Dickson White's *A History of the Warfare of Science with Theology*.

These books caricatured religion as historically at war with science and "fostered the impression that religious critics of Darwinism threatened to rekindle the Inquisition."[3] Draper himself saw major forms of organized religion as a direct and existential threat to the advancement of science:

> Roman Christianity and Science are recognized by their respective adherents

as being absolutely incompatible; they cannot exist together; one must yield to the other; mankind must make its choice—it cannot have both.[4]

Historian J.B. Russell observed that White's book "is of immense importance, because it was the first instance that an influential figure had explicitly declared that science and religion were at war. It fixed the idea that 'science' stood for freedom and progress against the superstition and repression of 'religion.' Its viewpoint became conventional wisdom."[5] Another expert stated that the "Draper-White thesi[s] has been routinely employed in popular-science writing, by the media, and in a few older histories of science."[6]

Take, for example, the reboot of *Cosmos* that aired on Fox in 2014. The series repeatedly portrayed religion as holding back science. Its host, agnostic physicist Neil deGrasse Tyson, called Isaac Newton a "God-loving man" and "a genius." Then he told viewers that Newton's religious studies "never led anywhere." He charged that

Newton's appealing to God was "the closing of a door. It doesn't lead to other questions." In other words, according to Tyson, it was only when Newton *was not* doing religion, and was doing science, that he made a positive contribution to society. The message that *Cosmos* preached to the masses is simple: The only way to do good science is to throw off the shackles of religion.

Correcting Fake History

But this warfare model between science and religion is fake history. Real history—the view backed by a chorus of modern historians who have studied the history of science and religion—tells a dramatically different story.

These scholars find that the founders of modern science were inspired to their scientific research *precisely because of their religious beliefs*. In fact, the consensus among serious historians is that it was the virtues of the Judeo-Christian religion that caused science to be born in Europe, where that religious worldview had taken deep root.

Exhibit A: Newton

Sir Isaac Newton, probably the greatest founder of modern science, was a monotheist who believed in a loving, truthful, personal God who had created an orderly, intelligible universe that He wanted us to discover and enjoy. It was these theological beliefs that propelled Newton to study the laws of nature.

The secular narrative is that science was able to advance only by casting off religion. Yet the eminent historian of science John Hedley Brooke explains that this narrative is false because Newton and his contemporaries were inspired by belief in God to do science in the first place:

> Any suggestion that what was revolutionary in 17th century thought was the complete separation of science from theology would be disqualified by Newton himself, who once wrote that the study of natural philosophy included a consideration of divine attributes and of God's relationship with the world...

> Isaac Newton saw the study of nature as a religious duty. A knowledge of God's power and wisdom could be inferred from the intelligence seemingly displayed in the designs of nature. Newton affirmed that the natural sciences had prospered only in monotheistic cultures...He believed the universality of his laws was grounded in the omnipresence of a single divine Will...If he is made to symbolize the new canons of scientific rationality, then it cannot be said that the scientific revolution saw a separation of science from theology.[7]

Brooke, who taught at Oxford University and served as president of the British Society for the History of Science and the International Society for Science and Religion, further states: "For Newton, as for Boyle and Descartes, there were laws of nature only because there had been a Legislator."[8] Thus, these early scientists wanted to discover the laws that God had built into the natural world. They searched for those laws because they believed in a divine "Legislator." To wit, religion inspired them to make scientific discoveries.

Another eminent scholar of science and religion worth considering is Ian G. Barbour. He wrote: "Newton himself believed that the world-machine was designed by an intelligent Creator and expressed God's purposes."[9] Barbour explained just how profound an influence religion had on inspiring science in England during the crucial early stages of the scientific revolution:

The English authors whom we would call scientists called themselves "natural philosophers" or "virtuosi." They were mainly from Anglican (Church of England) and Puritan (Calvinist) backgrounds. The charter of the Royal Society instructed its fellows to direct their studies "to the glory of God and the benefits of the human race." Robert Boyle (1627–1691) said that science is a *religious task*, "the disclosure of the admirable workmanship which God displayed in the universe." Newton believed the universe bespeaks an all-powerful Creator. Sprat, the historian of the Royal Society, considered science a valuable aid to religion…

The virtuosi identified themselves with the Christian tradition in which they were nourished, and many of them seem to have experienced a personal response of *reverence* and *awe* toward the marvels they beheld…The sense of the grandeur and wisdom of God was evidently a very positive experience for many of them and not just an abstract intellectual formula or a concession to cultural respectability.[10]

It is not hard to see how the founders of the world's most prestigious and long-lasting scientific society—who believed in a wise and powerful Creator—would then be inspired to investigate the workmanship of that Creator. Religion and the founding of modern science went hand in hand.

Why Christian Europe?

Barbour asked a key question: "Why was it in *Western civilization* alone, among all the cultures of the world, that science in its modern form developed?"[11] Because only the West had what Barbour said are the needed "*intellectual presuppositions* underlying the rise of science." Those presuppositions came directly from the Judeo-Christian worldview, which had uniquely permeated the West. As Barbour explained:

> [T]he medieval legacy also included presuppositions about nature that were congenial to the scientific enterprise. First, the conviction of the *intelligibility of nature* contributed to the rational or theoretical component of science. The medieval scholastics… combined the Greek view of the orderliness and regularity of the universe with the biblical view of God as Lawgiver. Monotheism implies the universality of order and coherence…

> Second, the doctrine of creation implies that *the details of nature can be known only by observing them*. For if the world is the product of God's free act, it did not have to be made as it was made, and we can understand it only by actual observation…

> Third, an *affirmative attitude towards nature* is dominant in the Bible. The goodness of the world is a corollary of the doctrine of creation.[12]

Barbour concluded, "[M]any historians of science have acknowledged the importance of the Western religious tradition in molding assumptions about nature that were congenial to the scientific enterprise."[13]

Holmes Rolston III, Distinguished Professor of Philosophy at Colorado State University and winner of the Templeton Prize, likewise explains:

> [T]o turn the tables, it was monotheism that launched the coming of

physical science, for it promised an intelligible world, sacred but disenchanted, a world with a blueprint, which was therefore open to the searches of the scientists. The great pioneers in physics—Newton, Galileo, Kepler, Copernicus—devoutly believed themselves called to find evidences of God in the physical world. Even Einstein, much later and in a different era, when puzzling over how space and time were made, used to ask himself how God would have arranged the matter. A universe of such beauty, an Earth given over to life and to culture—such phenomena imply a transcending power adequate to account for these productive workings in the world.[14]

Yet another scholar, David C. Lindberg of the University of Wisconsin-Madison, former president of the US History of Science Society, writes:

There was no warfare between science and the church. The story of science and Christianity in the Middle Ages is not a story of suppression nor one of its polar opposite, support and encouragement. What we find is an interaction exhibiting all of the variety and complexity that we are familiar with in other realms of human endeavor: conflict, compromise, understanding, misunderstanding, accommodation, dialogue, alienation, the making of common cause, and the going of separate ways. Out of this complex interaction (rather than by repudiation of it) emerged the science of the Renaissance and the early-modern period.[15]

The End of the Warfare Thesis

Historian of science Michael Keas explains that among serious historians of science, the warfare thesis simply does not hold water:

Are Christianity and science at war with one another? Not according to leading historians. "The greatest myth in the history of science and religion holds that they have been in a state of constant conflict," wrote historian of science Ronald Numbers in 2009. Even though he and other historians of science have documented this conclusion thoroughly, many myths about the alleged warfare between science and religion continue to be promulgated in the popular literature and textbooks.

The truth is that science and biblical religion have been friends for a long time. Judeo-Christian theology has contributed in a friendly manner to such science-promoting ideas as discoverable natural history, experimental inquiry, universal natural laws, mathematical physics, and investigative confidence that is balanced with humility. Christian institutions, especially since the medieval university, have often provided a supportive environment for scientific inquiry and instruction.

Why have we forgotten most of the positive contributions of Christianity to the rise of modern science? This cultural amnesia is largely due to the influence of a number of anti-Christian myths about science and religion. These myths teach that science came of age in the victory of naturalism over Christianity.[16]

Unfortunately, these myths continue to be perpetuated by popularizers of atheistic science who want to rewrite history and scrub religion's positive influence upon science. Thus, when Neil deGrasse Tyson's *Cosmos* claims that Isaac Newton's religious beliefs were like "the closing of a door" that "never led anywhere" or that belief in God "doesn't lead to other questions," that is absolutely historically false. A chorus of modern historians of science and religion agree that Judeo-Christian conceptions of God played an important and positive role in the rise of modern science.

Not only that, but Judeo-Christian religion is crucial in answering a question that has long puzzled historians: *Why did modern science first arise only in the West?* To summarize, it's because the Judeo-Christian worldview that permeated Western culture proposed that a rational, orderly, and moral-lawgiving God created a rational and orderly universe that was governed by predictable physical laws. Simultaneously, the Judeo-Christian worldview taught that nature was not sacred, and thus could be studied and enjoyed as it teaches us about the loving God who created it.

Even more, this worldview encouraged the humility necessary to admit mistakes and abandon wrong ideas so our theories about nature could be improved. In other words, when properly practiced, history shows that Christian virtues helped inspire the scientific method.

Instead of acknowledging historical reality, *Cosmos* and other popularizers of the warfare myth present a shallow revisionist formula: science good, religion bad. If the founders of modern science themselves had thought in such simplistic terms, science would never have been born.

What Is the Scientific
Evidence for Adam and Eve?

J.C. Sanford

Chapter 1 of Genesis describes the creation of mankind in a broad context, chapter 2 describes the creation of Adam and Eve in detail, and chapter 3 describes the fall into sin and its consequences. Collectively, these three chapters are foundational in terms of defining the nature of God, the nature of Scripture, the nature of man, the nature of gender, the nature of marriage, the nature of sin, the nature of redemption, the nature of evil, and the nature of spiritual warfare.

No wonder these foundational chapters have consistently been attacked. However, Scripture has proven to be resilient and has withstood the test of time due to its grounding in history. For example, there exists an unbroken coherent historical narrative that begins in Genesis 1–3 and continues through the rest of the Bible. It leaves no rational way to reject Genesis 1–3 as history and still support the historicity of the rest of the Bible. From beginning to end, Scripture provides a story line that is anchored in history, making it difficult to assail and is a primary reason we can trust it.

The Continuous Attack
on Adam and Eve

From the first century until the Enlightenment period (c. 1688–1800), nearly all Christians held, as a foundational belief, to the doctrine of a literal Adam and Eve. With the Enlightenment came a profound reversal—namely, a transition from a dependency upon Scripture to an unbridled confidence in man's intellect and his study of nature. An early manifestation of this shift was the popularization of "higher criticism," and the infamous "documentary hypothesis" developed by Julius Wellhausen. He speculated that Genesis 1–3 was a chimeric fabrication written by competing groups of priests who worshipped different gods. He declared that chapters 1 and 2 of Genesis were conflicting "creation myths." This was the beginning of ongoing attacks on Scripture emerging from respected Christian institutions, reflecting a growing shift toward naturalism (disbelief in miracles).

Clearly, these attacks were directed against Scripture in general, but they were particularly focused against the biblical accounts of creation and the fall. In addition, antibiblical ideas were being promoted as if they reflected genuine scholarship, affecting nearly every book of the Bible. These criticisms often framed Scripture as invalid fiction authored by unknown persons who lived in later time periods.

Interestingly, the primary leaders of the Enlightenment were not scientists, but philosophers, poets, and theologians. The monumental shifts that characterized the critical attitude toward the Bible were taking place *apart from science*. Fortunately, during this time, genuine scientists were still mostly Christians who would have believed in the biblical Adam and Eve. Naturalism was never a reflection of true science, but was itself a type of metaphysical philosophy that is beyond the realm of scientific investigation. Whether miracles are possible has always been a philosophical question, not a scientific one, because miracles are singularities (one-time events) and cannot be repeated under observation. Unfortunately, naturalists typically either deny God outright (atheism) or embrace a vague "god of nature" that seems to be the worldview fueling the skeptical approach to Scripture. The rapid rise of philosophical naturalism, along with the idolizing of intellectual man, set the scene for the current attempts to rework Adam and Eve.

The recently published book *Adam and the Genome*[1] militantly attacks the idea of a literal creation, a literal Adam and Eve, and a literal fall of mankind. The book conveys hostility and even contempt toward those Christians and scholars who are inclined to be faithful to the biblical perspective and the orthodox Christian tradition. Most importantly, *Adam and the Genome* has the potential to undermine the faith of large numbers of Christians—therefore, a very firm response is necessary.

In *Adam and the Genome*, a scientist and a philosopher/theologian join forces to transform biblical creation (and the fall) into a *vacuous abstraction*. Ever since Darwin, both theistic and atheistic evolutionists have joined ranks in a militant defense of naturalism and evolution. What is more, they have teamed up to oppose the miraculously created first couple. Together, theistic and atheistic evolutionists have successfully conflated *evolutionary theory* with *science*—as if they were synonymous. In reality, evolution is at best a minor aspect of what is called *historical science*—which is not a hard science at all, but is actually a soft and ever-changing science.

Historical and Genealogical Evidences for Adam and Eve

The historical evidences for Adam and Eve include the following: Jewish scripture and tradition, Christian scripture and tradition, and Muslim scripture and tradition. In addition, there are ancient genealogical records of Adam that represent powerful historical evidence that he is mankind's universal ancestor. This includes the biblical genealogies in Genesis 5, 10, 11; 1 Chronicles 1; and Luke 3. Luke provided the unbroken maternal genealogy of Jesus Christ, tracing the lineage back to David, Jacob, Abraham, and finally to Adam, and documents that the "father" (Creator) of Adam was God Himself.

How can sincere Christians deliberately ignore Luke 3? In addition to these biblical genealogies, there are a great many ancient secular genealogies that trace back to Adam. For example, most Arab tribes have genealogies that go back to Ishmael, and from there, back to Adam. The same is true for many

Europeans. A large fraction of the medieval European kings had genealogies that went back to Adam, and many Europeans can now trace their ancestry back to these kings, thus making it possible to trace their own personal genealogies back to Adam. New genetic services like Ancestry.com and 23andMe are giving many people a much deeper and converging lineage record. Many more will soon discover that their own personal genealogical record goes back to Adam.

Genetic Evidence for Adam, Eve, and the Fall

God's perfect creation is not just reflected in the beauty we see around us, it is also seen in the *exquisite design of the world*, the *programming of life*, and the *singular attributes of man*. By God's grace, to complement these intuitively obvious evidences for a miraculous creation, there is now abundant genetic data that supports the existence of a literal Adam and Eve. This material is much too extensive and technical for this brief chapter, but is detailed in several recent publications.[2] However, below are some of the most recent developments.

Genetic Entropy. Not only is there strong genetic evidence for the miraculous creation of a literal Adam and Eve, there is also firm genetic evidence for a literal fall, which affected creation in a profound and tragic way. Evidence for the fall is not just seen in the sin, suffering, and natural evil that has corrupted God's good creation. It is also observed in the genetic degeneration of life, including the continuous degeneration of our own genomes.

The obvious genetic degeneration of life is documented in the book *Genetic Entropy*.[3] Mutations cause the corruption and loss of biological information. The human genome ("the book of life") is the hardware/software that programs us to be human. Mutations are like word-processing errors (or more accurately, programming errors) in that program. This is why mutations are almost always harmful. We know that the human mutation rate is alarmingly high—roughly 100 new mutations per person per generation. So mutations are entering the human population at a rate much faster than natural selection could possibly select away such mutations.

Scientists have recognized that the extremely high human mutation rate is a profound problem. Moreover, it is problematic that most harmful mutations have only a tiny effect on fitness. Therefore, most harmful mutations are essentially invisible to the natural selection process, meaning that the human genome (and apparently all genomes) must be accumulating harmful mutations continuously, such that genomes must slowly "rust out." This inevitable genetic degeneration process has been validated by extensive numerical simulation experiments[4] and by biological test systems.[5]

Furthermore, the Bible appears to record, in a remarkable way, this systematic degeneration of mankind.[6] It seems that everything, including all life, is subject to entropic decay. This strongly indicates three things: (1) the fall was real; (2) creation and the fall had to be quite recent; and (3) Adam and Eve should have initially had zero mutations prior to when degeneration began. Ironically, the painful reality of genetic entropy means that evolution is going in the wrong direction. We are devolving, not evolving. Genetic entropy contradicts evolution in general and human evolution in particular. Looking backward, the sad reality of genetic entropy demands a literal Adam, a literal Eve, and a literal fall.

Mitochondrial Chromosome Eve. Thanks to DNA sequencing technology, we have been able to not only sequence a human genome, we have been able to sequence more than 1,000 individual human genomes. This genetic database can help us understand the history of certain human chromosomes, such as the mitochondrial chromosome. All people have a mitochondrial chromosome, but this chromosome is only inherited from *mother* to child, which makes the historical analysis of this chromosome very straightforward.

As this chromosome is passed down through the generations, new mutations accumulate continuously over time. By looking at many modern mitochondrial sequences, we can look backward in time and see where each mutation entered a given lineage. This has enabled us to reconstruct ancestral sequences of women who are now long dead, including haplogroup ancestors and the primary root sequence (the sequence of Mitochondrial Eve).[7] Interestingly, all the human mitochondrial chromosomes in the world *are nearly identical and trace back to a single woman,* known as "Mitochondrial Eve." In terms of this special chromosome, Mitochondrial Eve is literally the mother of us all. The small number of mutations that separate modern people from the sequence of Mitochondrial Eve indicates that Mitochondrial Eve lived in the recent past (see endnote 7 above). There has not been enough time for very many new mutations to have accumulated on this chromosome. Based upon the actual, empirically observed mutation rate for this human chromosome, studies indicate this Mitochondrial Eve lived recently (just thousands of years ago).

Evolutionists have performed similar analyses, but rather than using the actually observed mutation rate, they have been compelled to use hypothetical mutation rates that are about twentyfold lower than what is actually observed! They justify this based upon certain evolutionary *assumptions.* The most fundamental assumption they make is that evolution is an absolute fact, and so all data must be force-fitted to support that paradigm. They calculate that Mitochondrial Eve is more than 100,000 years old. Regardless of how far back we go in time, there appears to be a singular woman in history who passed on her mitochondrial chromosome to all living humans beings, and in this sense she is the uncontested mother of us all. These significant findings offer support for the historical Eve described in the Bible.[8]

Y-Chromosome Adam. The Y chromosome is similar to the mitochondrial chromosome because it is passed down from generation to generation intact. However, unlike the mitochondrial chromosome (which is only transmitted from mother to child), the Y chromosome is only transmitted from father to son. Remarkably, what is seen is that all of the human Y chromosomes in the world are nearly identical and trace back to a single man, or "Y-Chromosome Adam." Regarding this special chromosome, the historical figure now referred to as Y-Chromosome Adam is recognized as being the father of all living men. The small number of mutations that separate modern men from the sequence of Y-Chromosome Adam indicates that this man lived in the relatively recent past. Based upon the actual observed mutation rate for the human Y chromosome, our studies show that Y-Chromosome Adam lived just thousands of years ago.[9] These findings are strong evidence supporting the literal Adam of the Bible.

Ironically, the terms *Y-Chromosome Adam* and *Mitochondrial Eve* were coined (tongue in cheek) by leading evolutionists. Little did they realize that the history of these two special chromosomes would independently provide strong evidence supporting both a literal Adam and a literal Eve who lived in the same time frame, or at most, tens of thousands of years ago.

Biological Information. A biological revolution is taking place, thanks to advances in genomics and molecular biology.[10] Most of this research is happening at the National Institutes of Health in a host of special programs such as ENCODE.[11] We are now learning that life is very literally programmed! The programming of life is just as essential as the programming that would be required for the operation of a hypothetical robot-operated factory. However, biological programming is much more wonderful than any imagined robotic factory because it is happening on the atomic/molecular level, meaning that a single cell contains as much programming as a *robotic city*!

In a single cell there are many layers of information along with many information networks. Within a single cell there are millions of molecules that are sending and receiving information every second, representing something like a biological Internet. All these bits of information, with information systems as well as software and hardware, are *profoundly integrated*. To better appreciate the detailed integration involved in biological information, we must realize that no information network can become functional until all the essential components are in place. To create a single functional unit, or even a specific short string of nucleotides, requires reaching a *functional threshold*. There is a minimal functional threshold for every biomolecule, and for every byte of information.

That's why it is not even remotely conceivable that largely random, isolated, single-letter changes could alter the programming that specifies "ape" into the programming that specifies "human" That is to say, the biological programming that specifies "human" could never arise by unguided spelling errors in the ape genome—not even given the limited filtration that natural selection can provide. Natural selection cannot favor any new biological function until the hoped-for function has reached its *functional threshold*. Functional threshold for any hoped-for new function cannot normally be achieved until a host of very specific complementary letter changes are established—which takes inordinate *waiting times*.[12]

The only credible way a robotic factory (and its required programming), could arise would be by means of very high levels of intelligent design. The revolution that is happening in our understanding of biological information systems is telling us that complex biological systems can never arise bit by bit, and they can never arise apart from intelligence. The only reasonable way that a human being could ever arise would be by supernatural intelligent design. In light of all this, the miraculous origin of man is not only feasible, it is the only rational explanation for how we could have been so fearfully and wonderfully made.

Debunking Evolutionary Arguments Against Adam and Eve

The recent book *Adam and the Genome* is state of the art in terms of diminishing, dismissing, and denying biblical creation, the biblical Adam and Eve, and the biblical fall. Thus we will turn our attention now to addressing the challenges outlined in that book. Although

Adam and the Genome was coauthored by Dennis R. Venema and Scot McKnight, only Venema addresses the evidence itself, so we will focus on his arguments.

Failing Icons of Evolution. For both atheistic and theistic evolutionists, evolution is a foundational belief. For them, evolution is absolutely true, and nothing can stand in its way. Therefore, in their eyes, human evolution is a foregone conclusion and the debate is over before it even starts. To them, Adam and Eve could only exist as either fiction or allegory. That is why Dr. Venema begins by reciting the popular evolutionary arguments such as the fish-to-amphibian story, the wolf-to-whale story, and the story of the spontaneous nylonase gene. Strangely, these issues seem to be off topic, but according to Venema, they prove evolution, and evolution disproves Adam and Eve.

It is easy for Venema to articulate any of these arguments because he did not have to develop them; they are easily found on any atheistic website. It is quite clear from his writing that he has not critically examined the primary literature behind any of these stories, and so his book does not reflect solid scholarship. He has simply recited the classic atheistic arguments available within the blogosphere. Indeed, Venema's portion of the book is primarily a compilation of his own blog posts. Unlike Venema, for each one of the "evidences" he cites, my colleagues and I have spent months (in some case, years) researching the primary literature on each topic. On this basis, we can confidently assert the following: (1) Tiktaalik is not a credible transitional form between fish and amphibian.[13] (2) There is no credible transitional fossil series from wolf to whale.[14] (3) The outdated story of a spontaneous nylonase gene has been thoroughly debunked.[15] All of these

more recent "icons of evolution" are failing even as earlier icons have fallen short, and even as evolution in general is increasingly failing. In this light, the so-called logic statement "since evolution, therefore no Adam" also fails.

The Ape-to-Man Fossils Are Now Singing a New Tune. Venema quips that there is ever-growing fossil evidence that supports the ape-to-man evolution. Ironically, just the opposite is happening. His statement again reflects poor scholarship. Venema seems to be completely unaware that the field of paleoanthropology is now openly admitting it is in disarray. My colleague Christopher Rupe and I have spent the last four years digging deeply into the literature on hominin fossils, and we have published the book *Contested Bones.*[16] We show that the experts in the field are fiercely contesting every bone (hence the book's title), and they can agree on very little. The fossil evidence shows that there are only two primary types of hominin bones. The genus *Australopithecus* is Latin for "southern ape," and these bones are very distinctly apish. The genus *Homo* is Latin for "man," and these bones are very distinctly human. Therefore, recent claims of bridge species between the two genera (either *Au. sediba* or *H. naledi*), are collapsing.

The crisis is accelerating, and all the new developments are bad for human evolution. In just the last year the age of *Homo sapiens* has been extended to be over 300,000 years.[17] At the same time *Homo naledi* has been dated to be only about 300,000 years old, not 2-3 million years old.[18] So *H. naledi* appears to have coexisted with *Homo sapiens* and is *not* our ancestor. In addition, a human archaeological site in California has been dated to 130,000 years, apparently overturning the Out of Africa Theory.[19]

These reports are remarkable, but pale in

light of the latest news, which suggests that fossil footprints, which are essentially identical to human footprints, have been found on the Island of Crete. These footprints have been dated to be 5.7 million years old.[20] This seems to indicate that creatures with human feet lived 2.3 million years earlier than the reputed ancestor "Lucy." Furthermore, these footprints seem to be much older than any of the candidate pre-human fossils. This suggests that either: (a) man walked upon the earth at least as early as any reputed "pre-human"; (b) the standard hominin dating methods are extremely unreliable; or (c) both are true.

Fatal Flaws of Evolutionary Theory. There is a growing body of profound theoretical problems that are devastating for the Darwinian mechanism. These include classic problems like Haldane's Dilemma, Muller's Ratchet, Kondrashov's Paradox, and the deficiencies of Fisher's Theorem. More recent problems include Genetic Entropy,[21] and "Haldane's Ratchet."[22] In particular, there is a profound Waiting Time Problem,[23] which specifically applies to human evolution. We now recognize that within a pre-human population it requires an inordinately long time to establish, at a given chromosome site, even the shortest string of specific mutations (as would be required for creating a minimal amount of useful information). Advanced numerical simulations show that in a pre-human population of 10,000, the fixation of *just two* specific and adjacent mutations requires a waiting time of at least 84 million years. Waiting times increase exponentially as more mutations are required for reaching the required *functional threshold*. To establish a functional string of just 8 nucleotides requires over 18 billion years. Yet ape-to-man evolution requires millions of very specific sets of mutations of this type. All this has to happen in less than 6 million years!

Genetic Arguments Against Adam and Eve. The subtitle of the book *Adam and the Genome* reads "Reading Scripture after Genetic Science." This is revealing in that it presumes that evolutionary science leads, and Scripture must follow, implying that evolutionary claims demand that Christians rework Scripture. Of course, this reflects an inordinately high view of evolutionary theory and an inordinately low view of the Bible. It is increasingly clear that we can maintain a high view of both science and the Bible. However, contrary to what Dr. Venema's title implies, there is actually much more genetic evidence that supports the notion of Adam, Eve, and a literal Fall, than refutes it.

It is important to note that the primary arguments for *defending* a literal Adam and Eve (as given above) are all related to the data emerging from *genetics*. When we let Scripture lead, we can easily see how the genetic evidence supports Scripture. Dr. Venema, a Christian, seems to be unaware of this. Consequently, he appears to have committed his career to defending strict Darwinism while trying to discredit a miraculous creation, a literal Adam and Eve, and the Fall. Several of his key genetic arguments have been falsified, such as his nylonase argument.[24]

While there are numerous genetic arguments that support a literal Adam and Eve, the genetic arguments against Adam and Eve are collapsing.

Part Six

QUESTIONS FROM CHRISTIANS, SEEKERS, AND SKEPTICS

Is There Any Evidence of Life After Death?

Gary R. Habermas and Benjamin C.F. Shaw

The topic of near-death experiences (NDE) numbers among the most intriguing subjects in the twenty-first century. This essay will explore a particular type of NDE—those presenting various sorts of evidence that something objective is really happening.

Some clarifications precede our launch in an evidential direction. First, we will refer to NDEs as reported events often thought to have occurred during a time when an individual may typically have been clinically dead or close to it. These experiences could occur during a period of unconsciousness, when a person is apparently without pulse or breathing, or other related phenomena, in isolation or together. The individual often reports some sort of experience thought to have happened during this time, though some reportedly occur in the absence of such conditions.[1]

Among the experiences people most commonly report include viewing their body from above, traveling through a dark tunnel toward a light, meeting others whom they knew in the past, or witnessing a life review.

These experiences are often said to take place in a beautiful location, perhaps featuring some sort of boundary, and are accompanied by feelings of joy. After being revived, these people often look forward to returning, and lose their fear of death.

But occasionally the reports are not so pleasant. Sometimes they are more hellish in nature, featuring unpleasant experiences of one sort or another.

What are Christians to make of such claims? Could some objective reality possibly lie behind NDEs? Perhaps these experiences are simply hallucinations? Can any of these claims be tested? Does evidence exist to support them? Do these experiences align with Christianity, or do they stand in conflict?

These questions provide an important backdrop for this chapter. Most NDEs are untestable because we are unable to examine or inspect the claims involved. Hence, we will be less interested in the majority of the testimonies, and they are generally not cited in this study. Rather, the class of evidential NDEs that we describe below are significantly different in that they exhibit criteria that help identify them as either verifiable or unverifiable. In other words, some evidential cases do appear to be corroborated.

Evidence for Near-Death Experiences

As per this distinction, we are not pursuing the general NDE phenomena. Neither are the hellish cases being investigated. Rather, upon inquiring whether NDEs provide confirmation of any sort of initial afterlife, the emphasis must be placed squarely on the evidential cases. What sort of verifiable data have been reported?

Initially, the most noteworthy situations for such data would be particular cardiac arrest cases involving ventricular fibrillation, during which the patients are without any measurable heartbeat. Then, within an average of just ten to twenty seconds, the person's brain would register no observable upper brain activity. A very few minutes after that, measurable brain stem activity also ceases.[2]

Therefore, corroborated reports of verifiable information from these individuals beyond, say, four or five minutes after the initial cardiac arrest would be highly evidential, due to there being a significant lack of measurable heart or brain activity by this time. Sure, these are "near-death" cases from which many people survive. But the point here is that even should there be some noticeable events occurring in their immediate vicinity—in front of their eyes, so to speak—they should not be able to report such events while they are in this state, according to the common view that the brain would not be functioning.

Yet of the hundreds of *evidenced* near-death accounts, dozens of the confirmed reports involved patients who had experienced the cessation of both measurable heart and brain activity. This window of a combined loss of measurable heart and brain inactivity prior to the heart beating again is arguably the closest that a near-death state comes to approximating a real-death state. Therefore, evidence from this time frame presents the best likelihood of reporting what may happen at or even after death. A couple dozen other types of NDEs even purportedly supply evidence far beyond this point too.

Evidential NDEs provide information from this world that could not otherwise have been known by the person, especially since the majority are beyond the NDEr's range of vision. This is especially important because these cases may provide empirical evidence for some sort of life after death and create significant problems for naturalists. The point for the remainder of this chapter is to present a small sampling of cases that provide evidence that measurable consciousness may well exist beyond death and that normal bodily activity does not account for these experiences.

There does not appear to be a viable naturalistic means of accounting for the observed data we are discussing here. Indications are that a person without measurable heart or brain activity should not be able to report real, verifiable experiences, let alone ones that provide information that they could not observe from their location.

Habermas has enumerated at least five categories[3] in which to classify evidential near-death phenomena. Some confirmed cases are reported from the observer's immediate vicinity, often in a hospital (inside patient-care or emergency rooms, or during surgery). In other accounts, the described circumstances are observed a distance away (even miles removed!) from the witnesses' location. Fewer numbers of evidenced near-death accounts are also related in two other situations: by blind persons, or in cases where the NDEs were shared and observed by healthy onlookers as well! Last, a number of accounts concern reported meetings with previously deceased persons, some of whom had died a long time ago, who related information that was otherwise unknown to the patient and was later verified. In fact, dozens of instances from each of these categories could be chosen.

For example, some of the most notable accounts from the immediate vicinity include cardiologist Michael Sabom's half-dozen cases in which the patients reported readings on medical machines, the whereabouts of various objects in the room, and even a scene that occurred down the hall outside the room.[4] Another highly detailed case involved a young girl who "drowned" in a swimming pool and "was without spontaneous heartbeat for 19 minutes and had fixed and dilated pupils." Three days later she recovered completely, recognizing the two physicians who resuscitated her in the emergency room, along with minutely accurate details of her own resuscitation, as well as the locations of various objects and machines in two different rooms, plus a few conversations that took place.[5]

Regarding the second category of reports extending beyond the area where the NDEr was located, we return to the young girl's case mentioned in the previous paragraph. Besides the plethora of details in and around the emergency room, she explained that an angel named Elizabeth had escorted her around heaven, and then allowed her to view some of her family members inside their home. She provided very detailed descriptions of what all four people were doing, and most noticeably she named the meal that her mother had prepared for dinner that night, just a very brief time before.[6] Another case involved a patient who seemingly floated upward through hospital floors and out onto the roof, where she spotted a red tennis shoe that was later retrieved, confirming her testimony.[7]

The third evidential category is that of near-death experiences reported by blind persons. For example, Vicki, because of her blindness, had never seen her best friends, who had died years before. Yet Vicki reported that they were present during a NDE and she gave excellent descriptions of them, including some peculiar physical details. In another notable case, a blind woman reported some embarrassing facts about her own home that she could not see before her NDE—facts that her husband corroborated afterwards. Last, though blind, Nancy properly reported specific details from down the hospital hallway that were later confirmed by the testimonies of those present.[8]

The fourth evidential category is joint observations reported by an NDEr and a healthy person—such as the nurse who seemed to experience accompanying her patient on a peaceful trip through a tunnel, though she returned. However, her patient, who was at the hospital, died at the same time.[9]

Last are the many cases that involve reports of meeting previously deceased friends and loved ones, some of whom had died long before. These people who had died earlier had shared previously unknown but later-verified information with the NDEr.[10]

Conflicting Religious Claims?

What about NDE testimonies that appear to conflict with one another? For example, is there a judgment or hell after death? What about a demonic realm of some sort? Is there only one way to heaven, or many? Does the presence of a religious worldview (or none at all) lead to peace and rest?

It is true that NDE testimonies sometimes conflict. However, these issues cannot be resolved from the NDE perspective alone. The reason for this conclusion is due to our chief research criterion, which is that only *evidenced* NDE accounts will be cited. These corroborated reports almost entirely concern situations in the physical world, militating against the presence of hallucinations, wishful thinking, false memories, or particular medical conditions in the NDEr.

But this is precisely the rub with these conflicting religious claims. Because they reportedly emanated from unverified "otherworldly" testimonies, these conflicting claims cannot be adjudicated. Hence, one conflicting interpretation cannot trump another by assertions or alternative suppositions alone.

Such reported statements, then, without verification, cannot speak authoritatively on topics like the presence or absence of angels, hell, or heaven. Thus, the lack of evidential considerations in these testimonies do not resolve these conflicts. Therefore, NDEs should not be rejected due to the presence of seemingly false religious beliefs.

Benefits of Evidentially Derived NDE Accounts

At least two major benefits emerge from employing the central idea of utilizing only evidentially derived NDE accounts. Succinctly, evidential cases contribute knowable data to a crucial subject—namely, the existence of an afterlife. Natural hypotheses do not seem to come close to explaining this information either. Further, these data allow us to cut through the morass of conflicting religious testimonies regarding these NDErs as well.

Is It Reasonable to Believe in Heaven (and Hell)?

Randy Alcorn

> *"If I find in myself a desire which no experience in this world can satisfy, the most probable explanation is that I was made for another world."*
>
> C.S. Lewis

If there is a supreme being with a will and capacity to create beauty, it is entirely plausible that He would choose to have a central dwelling place from which He governs the universe. That being is God, and that place is Heaven.

Furthermore, it is perfectly reasonable that an eternal God who creates people in His image and loves them would make it possible for those people to live forever where He lives—and that He might go to great lengths to do so.

So what hinders people from believing in Heaven? Even for many Christians, Heaven is a place difficult to envision, and therefore, most do not look forward to going to such a place.

Nonetheless, those who believe there is a spiritual realm sometimes succumb to a naturalistic assumption—that only what we can see is real. Yet the Bible calls upon us to do what, in light of reality, is truly the reasonable thing: adopt an eternal perspective. The apostle Paul wrote, "We fix our eyes not on what is seen, but on what is unseen, since what is seen is temporary, but what is unseen is eternal" (2 Corinthians 4:18 NIV).

How do we fix our eyes on what cannot be seen? First, by recognizing our blindness. The blind must take by faith that there are stars in the sky. If they depend on their ability to see, they will conclude there are no stars. Likewise, many people conclude that God cannot be real because we cannot see Him. And Heaven must not be real because we cannot see it. Through the eyes of faith, we see how wrong those conclusions are.

Is Heaven Just a Fairy Tale?

According to many modern thinkers, yes. According to the Bible, absolutely not. Most people assume that if it exists at all, Heaven is eternity in a disembodied state. After all, no one can jump into a lake, hug a friend, or eat or drink. Many envision strumming harps forever (though I do not know how they could without hands!). With ideas like these, no wonder people dread Heaven.

Bertrand Russell has been called the greatest mind of the twentieth century. Awaiting his death, he said, "There is darkness without, and when I die there will be darkness within. There is no splendor, no vastness anywhere; only triviality for a moment, and then nothing."[1]

Russell failed to recognize what children intuitively know. Heaven is not a fairy tale or a baseless dream. Heaven is an objective reality that exists independently of anyone's belief or disbelief in it. Heaven is real—so real that Earth, in comparison, is what C.S. Lewis called the Shadowlands.

When Stephen faced death because of his faith in Christ, he said, "I see heaven open and the Son of Man standing at the right hand of God" (Acts 7:55-56 NIV). God did not create a mere vision for Stephen. Rather, He allowed Stephen to *see* a Heaven that was absolutely real.

The prophet Elisha asked God to give his servant, Gehazi, a glimpse of the invisible realm. He prayed, "'Open his eyes, LORD, so he may see.' Then the LORD opened the servant's eyes, and he looked and saw the hills full of horses and chariots of fire all around Elisha" (2 Kings 6:17 NIV).

We do not know whether these heavenly horses and chariots and angelic warriors exist in our universe, or live in a universe that opens into ours. But in any case, they are *real*. Acts 7 and 2 Kings 6 are narrative accounts, historical in nature, not apocalyptic or parabolic literature. The text is clear that Stephen and Gehazi saw actual objects, as real as your house, car, or dog.

How Do We Know Heaven Exists?

Some people at a television studio in New York City wanted to interview me about Heaven. They asked my assistant, "Randy's been to Heaven, hasn't he?"

She responded, "If he has, he hasn't mentioned it."

They said, "Oh…we really want to hear from someone who's *actually* been there."

I smiled when I heard about the exchange. All I had done was spend years studying what the Bible says to be true about Heaven and the New Earth, and how God's people throughout the ages have viewed them.

The problem is, near death experiences are not reliable. How can even the most sincere person distinguish between a medication- and trauma-induced dream and reality? Paul, who actually did experience the reality of Heaven, wrote, "I was caught up to paradise and heard things so astounding that they cannot be expressed in words, things no human is allowed to tell" (2 Corinthians 12:2 NLT).

Instead of basing beliefs about Heaven on fallible memories of personal experience, it is better to understand what God's unchanging Word teaches us. It tells us Heaven is the dwelling place of God. It is the actual place Christ came from (John 6:42), where He returned after His resurrection (Acts 1:11), where He now is, and the place from which He will physically return to Earth again to live with His people forever (Acts 1:11; Revelation 19:1-16).

What Do We Know for Sure About Heaven?

We are partly right when we think about Heaven as the place where our Christ-loving grandma goes when she dies, leaving behind her body. Those who have died trusting Jesus for salvation live in the present Heaven, without their current bodies. But resurrection awaits, the day when God will bring back to life our dead bodies just as He did Christ's body.

God does not disdain the physical; He delights in it, as should we. Scripture is emphatic about the resurrection. First Corinthians 15:16-19 makes clear that if there is no resurrection (or if we do not believe in the resurrection), we are most to be pitied.

Jesus's resurrection body is the model for our future resurrection bodies: "Touch me, and see. For a spirit does not have flesh and bones as you see that I have" (Luke 24:39). It is true that the DNA of all who have died becomes a scattered part of the ecosystem. But as the old earth will be made new, so our old bodies will be made new.

A new car is a better version of an old car—but with the same essential components that make it a car (four wheels, engine, transmission, steering wheel, etc.). The New Earth will be a far better version of the old earth, with the same essential components. Heaven will exist in the realm of the New Earth and will therefore be very earthy in its properties.

Physical and spiritual are neither opposite nor contradictory. In fact, the apostle Paul referred to the resurrection body as a "spiritual body" (1 Corinthians 15:44). God is a spirit, and angels are spirit beings, but both can—and on the New Earth will—live in a physical environment.

Understanding and anticipating the final, physical nature of Heaven corrects a multitude of errors in our thinking. It frees us to love the world God has made, while saying no to that world corrupted by our sin. It reminds us that God Himself gave us a love for the earth, and will give us forever the New Earth (the post-resurrection Heaven). Heaven is a physical realm. The Bible describes the New Jerusalem, capital city of the New Earth, using weighty tangible terms such as precious stones and walls and gates, a great river and the tree of life (Revelation 21–22).

Though we do not see the full picture, the Bible tantalizes us with glimpses of life on the New Earth—where God's beloved will live in redeemed, resurrected bodies on a redeemed, resurrected Earth. God's original plan will be fulfilled: men and women ruling Earth as stewards of His creation (see Genesis 1–3).

Will God Satisfy Our Desire for Permanent Happiness?

C.S. Lewis wrote,

> Creatures are not born with desires unless satisfaction for those desires exists. A baby feels hunger: well, there is such a thing as food. A duckling wants to swim: well, there is such a thing as water…Probably earthly pleasures were never meant to satisfy it, but only to arouse it, to suggest the real thing.[2]

Our desires correspond precisely to God's design. It is not that we want something, so we engage in wishful thinking that what we want exists. It is the opposite—the reason we want it is precisely because God has planned for it to exist. That is to say, resurrected people living in a resurrected universe is not our idea—it is *God's*.

Trying to develop an appetite for a disembodied existence in a nonphysical Heaven is like trying to develop an appetite for gravel. It will never happen. And we will never look forward to being ghosts and living somewhere that is not an actual place.

Cultures everywhere, in every age, have recognized the likelihood of life after death. *Life* is an earthly existence in which we work, rest, play, and relate to one another, using our creative gifts to enrich and enjoy culture. Yet many Christians reimagine *eternal life* to mean an off-Earth existence stripped of life's defining properties.

Instead, eternal life means enjoying forever the finest moments of life on the New Earth. Is it rational to believe in Heaven? It is every bit as rational as believing in God Himself. It accounts for what we see around us and sense to be true. God designed us with a deep desire to find our happiness in Him and to be with Him. Where God is, there happiness is (see Psalm 16:11). And Heaven is wherever God makes His home.

Since in Heaven we will finally experience life at its best, it would be more accurate to call our present existence the *beforelife* rather than to call what follows the *afterlife*.

Is It Reasonable to Believe in Hell?

The current trend, even in some evangelical churches, is to answer this question with a resounding *no*. Surely a loving God could not or would not send people to Hell!

But if God is just, and human sinners are unjust, then the existence of Hell makes perfect sense. It is morally good, because a good God must punish evil. Sometimes we cry out for true and lasting justice, then fault God for taking evil too seriously by administering eternal punishment. But we cannot have it both ways. To argue against Hell is to argue against justice and the necessary punishment for evil.

When most people speak of what a terrible concept Hell is, they talk as if it involves the suffering of innocent people. That would

indeed be terribly unjust—but nowhere does the Bible suggest the innocent will spend a single moment in Hell!

Without Hell, justice would never overtake the unrepentant tyrants in world history who have been responsible for murdering millions. Perpetrators of evil throughout the ages would get away with murder, rape, torture, and every evil. If there is no Hell, there is also no justice.

We do not think of ourselves as evildoers. We consider ourselves good people, but we are wrong. Scripture says, "There is no one righteous, not even one" (Romans 3:10 NIV). We each have our preferred ways of sinning, whether as prostitutes, porn addicts, materialists, gossips, or the self-righteous. But we all are sinners who deserve Hell.

If we better understood both God's nature and our own, we would not feel shocked that some people go to Hell. (Where else could sinners go who do not wish to spend eternity with Christ?) Rather, we would feel shocked that any fallen human would be permitted into Heaven. That is what makes God's grace, and Heaven itself, so *amazing*!

How Can We Know Whether We Will Go to Heaven?

The only way we can know that we will get to Heaven is if we believe Jesus when He said, "I am THE way, and THE truth, and THE life…" Not *a* way but *the* way. Jesus finished by saying, "No one comes to the Father except through me" (John 14:6). What do you need to believe?

First, that Jesus took on Himself the wrath of God, wrath that was deserved by us. "God made him who had no sin to be sin for us, so that in him we might become the righteousness of God" (2 Corinthians 5:21 NIV).

Second, that Jesus, the Son of God, died and came back to life. But believing is not mere mental assent. In the Bible, belief leads to a choice. We choose to follow Jesus, seeking to do what He tells us to do.

We were all made for a person and a place. Jesus is the person. Heaven is the place. You do not have to wonder whether you are going to Heaven. *You can know it today.*

John wrote, *"I write these things to you who believe in the name of the Son of God so that you may know that you have eternal life"* (1 John 5:13 NIV, emphasis added).

Heaven is not about wishful thinking, but is about raw, objective truth—reality. We should not believe in Heaven because it makes us feel better. We should believe in Heaven because it is real—as real as the Christ who is even now preparing it for us.

God tells us, "Set your mind on things that are above" (Colossians 3:2). He says, "In keeping with his promise we are looking forward to a new heaven and a new earth, where righteousness dwells" (2 Peter 3:13 NIV).

We are not past our peaks; we have yet to reach them, and we will not reach them until we live as resurrected people on a resurrected Earth, in the presence of the resurrected Jesus. The best is yet to come! Christ's blood-bought promise is that we really *will* live happily ever after. We will live with our King and each other, not in some intangible or imaginary realm, but in a place so real and so enticing that thoughts of it should occupy our minds until the day we experience it. And when that day comes, right when we think, *It can't get any better than this*, it will!

48

Is Jesus the Only Way to God?

Phil Fernandes

Today, many in our culture are repulsed by anyone claiming to be the "only way," convulsing at the notion of intolerant religious exclusivity. Jesus gave the critics much to complain about when He said, "I am the way, and the truth, and the life. No one comes to the Father except through me" (John 14:6). Likewise, concerning Jesus, the early church proclaimed, "There is salvation in no one else, for there is no other name under heaven given among men by which we must be saved" (Acts 4:12).

If we are going to effectively defend the faith once for all delivered to the saints (Jude 3), we should provide good reasons for Jesus's exclusivistic claims to be the only way to God. And because not everyone accepts the Bible as God's inerrant Word, we should not be content with merely a biblical case for Jesus as the *only* Savior; we should present the biblical case with a rational (i.e., philosophical) defense that salvation can be found only in Jesus of Nazareth.

There are four distinct views to consider concerning Jesus and salvation: universalism, pluralism, inclusivism, and exclusivism. If, as the Bible states, salvation is found in Jesus *alone*, we must defend exclusivism.

Will Everyone Be Saved? (Universalism)

Universalism is the false teaching that everyone is or will be saved—there is no hell. This view says everyone eventually goes to heaven or is saved in some sense. This clearly contradicts the teaching of the New Testament, which has been shown throughout this book to be the historically reliable Word of God. Indeed, Jesus unambiguously taught that many have chosen the path that leads to destruction and consequently will not find eternal life (Matthew 7:13-14). Moreover, He said that many would spend eternity in "eternal fire prepared for the devil and his angels" (Matthew 25:41). Jesus used vivid language when He called the place of eternal torment a place where "their worm does not die and the fire is not quenched" (Mark 9:48). What is more, the book of Revelation speaks of a place of eternal torment called "the lake of fire" (Revelation 19:20; 20:11-15). Sadly, those who die without accepting Jesus as their Savior will spend eternity apart from God in conscious torment.

Jesus taught that the only way to escape the coming wrath of eternal torment is to trust in Him alone for salvation (John

3:16-18; 14:6). Clearly, Jesus did not teach that everyone will be saved. Instead, He taught that whoever trusts in Him for salvation will be saved (John 6:35,47; 11:25-26; Romans 10:13).

Do All Religions Lead to God? (Pluralism)

Religious pluralism is the view that all religions lead to God—namely, that a person can be saved regardless of their religious beliefs or affiliation. This approach teaches that there are many different paths to the same God, and that the various world religions all worship the same object, though in different ways. This is the view espoused by many Hindus, New Agers, the Bahai Faith, and liberal "Christians." But, according to Jesus and the Bible, all religions do not teach the same thing; all roads do not lead to God.

Though there are some points of agreement among the world's religions, all disagree at their core, having mutually exclusive beliefs about God. Only Christianity teaches that the one true God is three equal and eternal persons—the Father, Son, and Holy Spirit.

Beliefs also differ regarding the identity of Jesus. Uniquely, Christianity posits that Jesus is God the Son who is the second person of the Trinity—being fully God and fully man (John 1:1-18; Colossians 2:9). All other religions demote Jesus to a status of less than fully and uniquely God.

In addition, all other religious belief systems differ on the issue of salvation. Only Christianity teaches that salvation is by God's grace alone, through faith alone, in Jesus alone—not of works or from human effort (John 3:16-18; Ephesians 2:8-9). Jesus clearly taught that salvation comes only through Him, providing the only way for

us to be saved (John 14:6; 1 Timothy 2:5). Furthermore, He proclaimed that those who believe in Him for salvation receive the free gift of eternal life (John 3:16-17; 6:29,47); alternatively, those who do not trust in Him for salvation remain condemned (John 3:18). The apostle Peter taught that salvation is found in Jesus alone, not in other religions (Acts 4:12).

The apostle Paul clearly proclaimed, "I do not nullify the grace of God; for, if righteousness were through the law, then Christ died for no purpose" (Galatians 2:21). If man could earn his own salvation (which is basically what all other world religions teach), then Jesus died unnecessarily on the cross.

Of course, the truth of the matter is this: We cannot save ourselves by our works; salvation is found only through faith in Christ, the one who died on the cross for our sins (John 1:29; Romans 5:8; Ephesians 2:8-9; 1 Peter 2:24; 3:18).

Many people claim that they are going to heaven because they believe in God the Father, but they do not believe in His Son. Jesus rejected this way of thinking when He said, "The one who rejects me rejects him who sent me" (Luke 10:16). Therefore, no one can have the Father if they reject the Son, for they share the same divine nature (1 John 2:23; cf. Matthew 10:32-33). The only way to receive the Father is to accept the one whom He sent.

The Bible clearly teaches that not all roads lead to God; rather, some paths seem right to mankind but ultimately lead to destruction and death (Proverbs 14:12; 16:25); only Christ has the power to save. Throughout Scripture we see a consistent condemnation of false religion (Joshua 24:14-15; 1 Kings 18:21; Isaiah 45:22). Scripture unequivocally rejects any other view that deviates from

God's prescribed way (Galatians 1:8-9). Jesus is the only way to God (John 14:6).

Philosophically speaking, some fail to realize that pluralism (i.e., many ways to God) is in fact an *exclusive* position! Because pluralism is the logical opposite of exclusivism (i.e., only one way to God), and because it rejects exclusivism outright, it is essentially saying that pluralism is true and exclusivism is false—*making pluralism an exclusive position.* That is to say, any belief that claims to be true always logically rejects its opposite, making the belief an exclusive position itself. To put it another way, if pluralism is true, then all nonpluralism must be false, thus making pluralism just as exclusive as exclusivism.

Most unbelievers and relativists mistakenly respond that exclusivim is narrow-minded and intolerant, forgetting that truth is always narrow and always rejects its opposite. No one would call a math teacher narrow-minded for communicating the truths about mathematics—some things are narrow by nature! Sometimes there is only one road that can take us to our destination. In this case, Jesus is the only road that can take a person to a heavenly destination.

Are Some People Who Don't Believe in Jesus Saved? (Inclusivism)

Some professing Christians believe that even though salvation comes only through Jesus, a person does not have to consciously believe in Jesus as Savior to be saved. This view is called *inclusivism*, and it comes in two distinct forms—extreme and moderate.

The more extreme type of inclusivism teaches that even people of other religions who have heard about Jesus and knowingly reject Him can still be saved if they love God and their neighbors. This extreme

form contradicts Scripture. The Bible clearly teaches that anyone who denies the Son does not have the Father (Matthew 10:32-33; Luke 10:16; 1 John 2:23). Simply put, if you reject the Son, you are not saved.

A moderate form of inclusivism teaches that those who have never heard the gospel can be saved by Jesus without them actually knowing it. According to this view, if one loves God with all their heart and their neighbor as themselves they will be saved. However, even the moderate form of inclusivism is unbiblical (except possibly in cases of infants who die before they reach the age of accountability, or people who are permanently and severely disabled in their mental abilities). For it has been said, "Heaven is for those *who cannot* believe, but not for those who *will not* believe." The Bible declares that those who do not believe in Jesus remain condemned (John 3:18). The only way for a person to be saved is by trusting in the true Jesus of the Bible alone for salvation (John 3:16-18; 6:37-40,47; 11:25-26).

With regard to those who never heard the gospel, the Bible teaches that God draws all people to Himself (John 12:32-33; 16:7-11). He does this through the lesser lights of creation and conscience. Through creation, God reveals to us that the Creator exists (Romans 1:18-22). Through our consciences, God reveals His laws to us and shows us that we are sinners without excuse, and that we are in need of His salvation (Romans 2:14-15).

If a person responds to the lesser lights of creation and conscience, God will reveal the light of Christ to him. From creation, we learn the Creator exists. From our conscience, we learn of right and wrong and that we stand condemned before Him and are in need of salvation. If someone is seeking the true God, that person will find Him (Jeremiah

29:13; Psalm 145:18-19; Acts 17:22-31; 16:6-10; James 4:8). Inevitably, the Holy Spirit will reveal the greatest light, the Lord Jesus Christ, to the person who practices the truth revealed to him through nature (John 3:19-21). God usually reveals Jesus to people by sending missionaries (Romans 10:13-15), but has at times revealed Jesus to people through visions or an appearance of Jesus Himself (Acts 9:1-9; Galatians 3:6-8).

God is sovereign—He is in control. He draws all people to Himself (John 12:32-33). Anyone who seeks to accept Christ will, by the grace of God, receive the opportunity. A biblical example of this is Cornelius (Acts 10–11). He was a Gentile who acknowledged that the God of Israel was the true God. But he did not yet know Jesus as Savior. God gave visions to both Cornelius and Peter, and guided Peter to preach the gospel message to Cornelius. The Bible is clear that Cornelius the God-seeker was not saved until the moment he accepted Jesus while Peter preached (Acts 11:13-14). If inclusivism were true, Cornelius would have already been saved before he met Peter. But Cornelius was not saved until he believed in Jesus for salvation.

Is Jesus the Only Way to God? (Exclusivism)

The true, biblical view of salvation reflects exclusivism. This means that (again, with the possible exceptions of those who die before the age of accountability and those with severe mental disabilities) only those who consciously trust in God's promised Messiah for salvation will be saved (John 3:16-18; 14:6). Those who do not trust in Jesus alone for salvation are excluded from salvation; they remain lost.

The gospel message is exclusive, yet God's love is unlimited (Matthew 5:43-48). He loves all mankind and desires that all be saved (John 3:16-18; 1 Timothy 2:1-6; 2 Peter 3:9; 1 John 2:2). The Bible teaches that we are all sinners and we cannot save ourselves (Romans 3:10,23; 6:23). But God loves us so much that He sent His Son to die for our sins. However, as a God of love, He will not force us to trust in Christ. He will not force us to worship Him. Through the power of the Holy Spirit, God draws all people to Himself; but, in the end, we must make the choice to accept or reject Jesus as our personal Savior. Yet He cries out to us, "Turn to Me and be saved, all the ends of the earth; for I am God, and there is no other" (Isaiah 45:22; see also Matthew 11:28).

If we acknowledge that none of us are perfect, then we will realize that for us to be saved, there must be a substitute who pays the penalty for our sins. And because all sin is rebellion against the ultimately worthy God, the substitute must be God (i.e., ultimately worthy). There is no other way for us to be saved. Jesus (who is fully God and fully man) is the only hope for mankind—He is the sacrificial substitute who paid the penalty for our sins, and who is the only way for us to be saved.

Are Christians Intolerant and Narrow-Minded?

Dillon Burroughs

Questions about whether Christians are intolerant and narrow-minded have been asked with increasing frequency with the rise of skepticism and postmodernism. Skepticism questions Christian truth claims, while postmodernism suggests absolute truth is either nonexistent or unimportant. Answering these questions requires a proper understanding of tolerance and truth.

Clear Definitions Are a Necessary Starting Point

Defining Tolerance

Tolerance has traditionally been defined as a willingness to allow a fair attitude toward beliefs different from one's own. According to this definition, the Bible does teach Christians are to be tolerant. Paul taught in Ephesians 4:15 believers are to "[speak] the truth in love." Jude 1:22 says, "Be merciful to those who doubt."

Recently, however, tolerance has been redefined as accepting the beliefs of all people and all positions as equally valid. For example, one person may claim there are many ways to

heaven, expecting those who are "tolerant" to accept this view. When it comes to matters that are based on opinions, this may be possible. One person can have a different favorite food from another person. However, when two or more views differ regarding claims of truth, then another approach is needed. One may show respect to differing views, but not all views can be considered correct or equal.

For example, if one person claims 2 + 2 = 4 and a second person claims 2 + 2 = 5, both claims cannot be right under the same conditions. One and only one option can be correct. Scripture makes the same claims regarding certain spiritual teachings. For example, Jesus either literally rose from the dead or He did not. Heaven is either real or not. When the Bible makes a truth claim, there are no other options or opinions that the Bible considers possible or equally valid. When Christians uphold the Bible's truth claims, they are not attempting to be intolerant, but to be accurate.

Jesus Himself made absolute claims that are recorded in Scripture. In John 14:6 He claimed to be the way, the truth, and the life, and that no one could come to the Father except through Him. Either Jesus was correct and other views are incorrect, or Jesus was incorrect. Both options are not possible or equally valid. In addition, Jesus's claim was not uttered with the intention of being mean-spirited, but rather, to offer eternal life to those who would receive Him (John 3:16). He clearly showed His love for all people through His life as well as His death—He died for the sins of humanity on the cross.

Finally, from a practical standpoint, it is not possible to be tolerant of all views and practices. D.A. Carson notes, "No culture can be tolerant of everything or intolerant of everything: it is simply not possible. A culture that tolerates, say, genocide (e.g., the Nazis) will not tolerate, say, the Jews it wants to kill or homosexual practice."[1] Every culture exhibits ethical codes of right and wrong, regardless of whether these ethics are the same from one culture to another.

Defining Narrow-Minded

Today, the term *narrow-minded* is generally used in a negative way to say that a person is unwilling to consider other viewpoints. But as with tolerance, it's important to consider the subject matter at issue. For example, from the perspective of some, a case could be made that the teachings of the New Testament are narrow-minded. In Matthew 7:13-14, Jesus taught, "Enter by the narrow gate. For the gate is wide and the way is easy that leads to destruction, and those who enter by it are many. For the gate is narrow and the way is hard that leads to life, and those who find it are few" (Matthew 7:13-14). Some will point to that statement and claim it is narrow-minded, for Jesus clearly allowed for no other options. But if what Jesus said is true and the only way to heaven is in fact

through Him, then it is not a negative statement at all.

Many people assume that holding to an exclusive view on a given matter is negative or bad. However, if a person's view is in fact correct, then it is true regardless of whether anyone considers that view to be narrow-minded.

For example, if a doctor said, "You have a heart blockage. We need to operate immediately to save your life," you would not respond, "Stop being so narrow-minded. You have your view; I have mine. I think I'll be just fine." A person with this attitude could end up in a worse situation. Further, the person who responds in this way is offering his or her own statement of absolute truth—a statement based on personal choice rather than actual evidence.

The same is true about biblical teachings. We can investigate these claims, and if it turns out they are correct, then they are not narrow-minded. They are teachings of great importance for our lives today and for eternity. Josh and Sean McDowell note that we live in a generation in which many "tend to go to the Bible *not to discover the truth* and bend their lives to it accordingly but to use it as sort of a self-help book to help them form their own version of what's true and false, good and evil, right and wrong."[2] In contrast, the Bible claims to be God-inspired (2 Timothy 3:16-17) and authoritative. Christians are not called to pick and choose truth, even from the Bible, but affirm and apply all its principles (Psalm 1).

The Key Issue: What Is Truth?

Pilate asked Jesus, "What is truth?" (John 18:38). Pilate asked this in the context of being unable to resolve the tension between pleasing the people around him and responding appropriately to Jesus. Many people face a similar challenge today. When faced with the truth claims of Christianity, they struggle between determining that which is true and satisfying personal desires. There is also the question of what is true as opposed to what one will accept as true. Bible teacher Erwin Lutzer notes:

> We have bought into the world's values, into its entertainment, its morals, its attitudes. We have also bought into its tolerance, its insistence that we should never challenge the private beliefs of individuals, whether outside the church or within it. In the face of cultural pressures, we have found ourselves confused, hesitant to act, unable to give a loving but convincing witness to the world.[3]

The Bible begins with facts rather than feelings, though both are important. Jesus predicted He would return from the dead, and He did. This truth claim can be evaluated utilizing the Bible, history, archaeology, and other areas of learning. While the decision regarding whether to accept this belief is based on faith (Ephesians 2:8-9), it is a faith based on an analysis of objective reality.

Other claims of absolute truth must be made on some type of basis. For Christians, truth is based on the reality around us. In other words, truth corresponds to reality. Further, there is an unseen spiritual reality revealed through Scripture. Those who say we should not make absolute truth claims end up creating their own form of absolute truth by claiming, "There is no absolute truth." Whether people realize it or not, everyone makes and acts upon various truth claims. The issue is upon what *basis* those truth claims are made.

A related concern is the statement, "That may be true for you, but it's not true for me." This view, known as relativism, holds that "personal truth" may vary from one person to another. In some situations, such differences may be valid. For instance, it is legitimate to say, "My favorite food is pizza, but your favorite food is ice cream." People can vary in their opinions about some things. However, when it comes to issues like God or morality, competing claims cannot both be true. Does God exist? He either does exist or He does not. Is there objective, moral right and wrong? Either there is or there is not. Is Jesus God's Son? Either He is, or He isn't. Jesus cannot be God's Son for one person and then not be God's Son to another person.

What about the claim that all religions are basically the same? A close look at the core teachings of various world religions quickly discredits this claim. For example, Hinduism speaks of many gods, while Christianity affirms one God, and atheism declares there is no God. On this single key issue, multiple religions offer contrasting and contradictory views. Either one of these views is correct, or none of them are correct, but they cannot all be correct.

More specifically, Judaism, Christianity, and Islam all believe there is one God, yet each religion defines God differently. Jewish and Christian teachings affirm the same God, yet Jews reject the Christian view of the Triune God of Father, Son, and Spirit. Islam teaches there is only one God, yet the Allah of the Qur'an is defined and acts in different ways than the views of the God of the Bible.

Objections to the Claim Christians Are Intolerant

There are five responses that can be given to those who claim Christians are intolerant or narrow-minded because of Christianity's exclusive truth claims.

First, truth corresponds to reality. For example, in a test in which an answer is either true or false, there is typically only one correct answer. If a student misses the question by choosing the incorrect answer, it is not intolerant to mark it wrong. To do so is accurate, not intolerant.

Second, claiming intolerance is actually an expression of intolerance. In other words, those who claim absolute truth is wrong or does not exist are making a claim of absolute truth. To claim that someone is intolerant because of his or her view is actually a statement of intolerance toward that someone.

Third, truth is true regardless of how it is presented. There is a difference between the information one presents and the manner in which it is presented. A doctor can say, "You have cancer" in a kind manner or a rude manner. Either way, the words, if true, are still valid.

For the Christian, it is important to note that the way one communicates has an impact on the effectiveness of the message. First Peter 3:15-16 teaches that we are to communicate Christ "with gentleness and respect, having a good conscience, so that, when you are slandered, those who revile your good behavior in Christ may be put to shame."

Fourth, sincerity does not equal truth. Just because a person's belief is sincere doesn't mean that belief is true. An example of sincere truth is to claim, "I really believe one person can make a difference." It is possible for this truth claim to be correct based on ample evidence of individuals having made a difference throughout history. An example of being sincerely wrong is when a person takes a wrong turn while driving: "I thought I was driving the right direction, but now I am five miles from where I'm supposed to be." Sincerity is secondary to the objective trustworthiness of whatever it is a person is trusting.

Fifth, disagreement is different from intolerance. Disagreement means one person simply does not accept another person's view as true. Intolerance includes both a rejection of another person's view and a critical attitude toward that person.

The Call to Stand Firm

No one likes to be called intolerant or narrow-minded. For that reason, many Christians are hesitant to speak the truths affirmed in Scripture. Yet we are called to "stand firm in the faith...be strong" (1 Corinthians 16:13). What's important is that we make sure we are "speaking the truth in love" (Ephesians 4:15). We are called to love our enemies (Matthew 5:44) and to show respect to all people (1 Peter 2:17).

Why Is It Important That Jesus Died on the Cross?

Terry L. Miethe

If Jesus had not died on the cross, our sins would not have been forgiven and we could not have been restored to the Father.[1] These key truths are better understood when we realize who Jesus was and the nature of His mission on Earth.

The humanity of Christ is related to God's love. That the Father would send the Son—in human flesh—to die for us was a remarkable act of love on God's part. And it's vital that we understand the significance of Christ's humanity. His death on the cross was essential to proving His humanity—just as His resurrection was essential to proving His deity!

God Reveals His Humanity

A God who shares existence, communicates with, and gives the free gift of grace is truly related to us! He has a relationship with us in covenant. I realize talking about God's humanity may sound strange, but is it really? I believe our very knowledge of His deity points to His humanity—"It is precisely God's deity which, rightly understood, includes his humanity."[2]

Many people misunderstand what it is to be human. When a person does something wrong or disappoints another individual, oftentimes you'll hear the expression, "After all, they are only human." Used this way, the state of being human is inseparably tied to something base, sinful, or in error. But it is important to realize that it is not our sin or imperfections that make us human. The Bible says are were *created* as human beings—we were made in God's image (Genesis 1:27). Thus our rebellion away from God made us less human, not more!

God is absolute. He is also truly related to us. We may not be able to understand this completely, but that does not make it less true. In history, many philosophers have made the mistake of not realizing this truth. They have destroyed the delicate balance between the two. God is made either totally separate from us, our world, and our knowledge (wholly other, transcendent in an extreme sense) or just a projection of the mind or the collective consciousness of humankind (only immanent).

Yet God is both transcendent and truly related to us! Karl Barth said it well:

In this divinely free volition and election, in this sovereign decision (the ancients said, in His decree), God is *human*. His free affirmation of man, His free concern for him, His free substitution for him—this is God's humanity. We recognize it exactly at the point where we also recognize His deity. Is it not true that in Jesus Christ, as He is attested in the Holy Scripture, genuine deity includes in itself genuine humanity?… In the mirror of this humanity of Jesus Christ the humanity of God enclosed in His deity reveals itself.[3]

It is because we are so related to God that we can know, love, and share Him with each other!

It is in the person of Jesus Christ that we see both true God and true man. (In theology, this is known as His dual nature.) Jesus is both fully God and fully man at the same time. There are various views as to how this mixture was manifest in reality. It is well known that a certain difference exists between the Reformed (Calvinistic) doctrine[4] and the Lutheran doctrine. They both accept what is stated in the Creed of Chalcedon: The two natures were not mingled, but they were united in one person.[5] The certain difference that the Lutherans teach is the *communicatio idiomatum* (i.e., the blending of the two natures in an historic person, Jesus).[6] He was and is the mediator and reconciler between God and man.[7] Jesus could not be a mediator if He had not died on the cross for us! Thus Jesus reveals God and man to each other. In Jesus's becoming fully human, we see God's desire not only to be a compassionate Savior, but also our friend and partner.

This, after all, is the beautiful truth of the story of the Good Samaritan (Luke 10:30-37). The Samaritan not only took pity on the one who was robbed and beaten, but he cared for him personally. He gave of his resources so his patient could recover. The compassion we see here, so unexpected and so undeserved, speaks to us of what God has done for us. Just as the Samaritan freely cared for one who was not his own, so God freely cares for us who are not His own by virtue of our sin. God is truly humane! In His very deity He is human.

Some moderns have come to the point that they say the "complete humanity of the historical personality of Jesus of Nazareth" is a very "great embarrassment for faith."[8] But our faith must preserve and protect both His deity and His humanity. Jesus ate, drank, slept, got tired, was sorrowful, and rejoiced even as we do. He even needed to pray! He was tempted in all points as we are.

The Importance of Christ's Humanity

The humanity of Jesus is important to our faith in at least four ways.

First, Christ's humanity guarantees a truly real incarnation. If He was not man in every point, then He did not truly come down to our level. He would have left some part of our burden untouched. But Jesus became fully man. He truly became flesh and lived among us (John 1:14). The word *flesh* is a very potent, perhaps the strongest word in Scripture referring to man's lowliness. It suggests the completeness of Jesus's humanity. It is used of a condition as far removed from divine glory as is possible. The apostle Paul wrote that Jesus was in the "likeness of sinful flesh" (Romans 8:3). Certainly Paul witnessed powerfully to the deity of Jesus, but he also witnessed to the humanity of Christ.

There is another element of the incarnation that is important to us. God did not force Himself upon us! He did not come as a sovereign king demanding our worship. Rather, He came as a humble servant asking each of us to make our own decision about Him.

Second, the humanity of Christ provides a necessary foundation for the sacrificial death of Jesus (known as the atonement). The only reason Jesus could stand in our stead before God is because He was human. We often take for granted the significance of His death for us. He did not just die for us; He also lived for us. He had so much compassion that He cried and wept for humanity (Luke 19:41; John 11:35)! The fact Jesus came in human flesh and died on the cross is the very cornerstone of our being restored to harmony with God.

Third, Christ's humanity secures the reality of a perfect example. He felt the burden He carried for us so greatly that even He prayed to God about it (Luke 22:39-44). In our times of temptation, it is vital to realize that He too experienced temptation! In Jesus, the Christ (the Word made flesh), perfect righteousness is put within the sphere of our existence. The fruits of the Spirit (Galatians 5:22-23) are but aspects of Jesus's character.

Fourth, Christ's humanity indicates the direction of our destiny after death. Because He died and rose to new life, we too can believe in the life to come (Romans 6:9-12). Because He was triumphant, we too can transcend this mortal experience. As our example, Jesus was also our "test case." If He had not been fully human, we could not expect our humanity to continue into eternal life.

Interestingly, in Jesus of Nazareth we see that divinity and humanity are not mutually exclusive. Though these two natures were distinct, they were not hopelessly separated. Similarly, because of our relationship to Him, spiritual separation is not the case for us. Meaning, our nature (humanity) was created by Him, and in Christ, our humanity is restored! We also have the glorious responsibility to share God's humanity, Christ's humanity, and our humanity with each other. This is why Jesus's death on the cross is so very important to us. May your life be increasingly human—*and* in His image!

Is Christian Belief Just Psychological Wish Fulfillment?

Denise Ostermann

I spent many years searching for the truth about mankind's torn nature in secular education before receiving my invitation to follow Jesus. Only in reading Genesis 3 by the light of the Holy Spirit was I finally able to apprehend and accept the origin of our intrinsic struggles in our alienation from God by sin. At last, I found an answer that truly satisfied, and what a joy it was to be saved!

Of course, not everyone would regard my newfound life in Christ as being grounded in objective reality and truth. Rather, there are many who view Christian belief as a subjective wish fulfillment fantasy. They say that people have conjured God in their minds to fulfill their need for approval and security. Such was the teaching of Sigmund Freud, the founder of psychoanalysis. In endeavoring to provide an answer to the question posed by this chapter's title, we will consider Freud and his 1927 work *The Future of an Illusion*, in which he claimed that religious belief arose from psychological wish fulfillment.

Freud's Early Life

Freud's parents were orthodox, observing Jews, though they were not always consistent in their practice. Through the tutoring of a trusted scholarly mentor, Freud received a religious education grounded in the study of the Bible, probably the Torah. This instruction extended well into his teenage years. Although historical evidence suggests that Freud wrestled with an agnostic position toward God most of his life,[1] at the time he wrote *The Future of an Illusion* he professed a passionate atheism. Thoroughly influenced by the Enlightenment philosophers, he held to determinism, reductionism, materialism, Darwinism, atheism, and scientific empiricism as the only ways to apprehend truth.

Understanding Freud

It is perhaps worth noting that in *The Future of an Illusion*, Freud made no mention of any prior influences upon his thought except for an expression of gratitude to Charles Darwin for his "monumental" discovery of evolution, which, in Freud's view, opened men to the light of reason. In this, as in his other writings, Freud stood largely on his work alone, as influenced by philosophy.[2]

Surprisingly, Freud counted himself a scientist, apparently believing that his methodology for treating patients and the formulation of his "theory of the neuroses" qualified as empirical research. His method combined eliciting his patients' "free associations" with his interpretations of unconscious motives and meanings. I have found no evidence that Freud understood that his anecdotal case studies and theories would not have been amenable to verification by the mathematical measures of validity and reliability required by scientific empiricism. While Freud could base his judgment of effective treatment on the mitigation of his patients' symptoms and their improved functioning, without experimental controls it would be impossible to identify what exactly it was in his treatments that best accounted for his patients' improvement.

The Future of an Illusion was the first in a series of papers by Freud concerned with whether civilization could survive the self-centeredness of man's "animal instincts." Writing in Germany between the World Wars, Freud had good cause for concern! How much more may we today share Freud's concerns about mankind's destructiveness? Yet from the Bible we know this to be the result of fallen man's sin nature, and not our supposed instinctual heritage from animal evolution! And we rejoice that God has provided a way of escape from slavery to sin through faith in Jesus Christ our Savior, as was so boldly laid out by Paul (cf. Romans 6–8). You may enjoy the exercise of further contrasting Freud's view of the problem and its solution with the biblical view as we consider *The Future of an Illusion*.

Freud made a long argument indeed (63 pages!), collecting into the main path of his reasoning many collateral issues we will not address here. He stated the problem to be that man is, by nature, an enemy of civilization's restraints upon his self-centered, destructive, and antisocial instincts. Freud asserted that "civilization's most important psychical asset for achieving the renunciation of instinct *is its religious ideas...in other words, its illusions*" (emphasis added).[3] Our focus here will be to provide an answer to this assertion that religious ideas are *illusions*.

Freud and Religion

I must admit that I found this chapter very difficult to write because Freud's line of reasoning itself can be so erratic! At this point in Freud's work, we are expecting to hear about how our faith makes good citizens of us when, in truth, he shifted gears from what is good for civilization *to what is bad about religion.* With regard to this we will make the reasonable assumption that Freud did not wish to comment upon how the gospel itself, which exhorts Christians to follow Jesus's example in loving one another, is directly related to our positive impact upon a culture.

Freud began by presenting his theory of how people came to believe in God. Finding themselves in peril by the violence of nature, the threat of disease and of attack by animals and each other, and confronted by "the painful riddle of death," people sought to assuage their terror. They made images of humans and animals and sought to influence and appease them. Finally, they gave to these images the character of a father and turned them into gods. Over time, a "store of ideas" was gradually created. Freud wrote,

> Here is the gist of the matter. Life in
> this world serves a higher purpose...a

perfecting of man's nature…Everything that happens is an expression of the intentions of an intelligence superior to us which, in the end, orders everything for the best—that is, to make it enjoyable for us…Death itself is not extinction, but the beginning of a new kind of existence which lies on the path of development to something higher… the superior wisdom which directs this course…the infinite goodness…the justice—these are the attributes of the divine beings who created this world, or rather, of the one divine being into which, in our civilization, all the gods of antiquity have been condensed. The people which first succeeded in thus concentrating the divine attributes was not a little proud of the advance… man's relations to him could recover the intimacy and intensity of the child's relations to his father. But if one had done so much for one's father, one wanted to have a reward, or at least to be his only beloved child, his Chosen People. Very much later, pious America laid claim to being God's own Country.[4]

I have quoted Freud at length because in these words he provided a handy, cogent summary of the main points we are concerned about. Freud in fact drew a picture of the wish-fulfillment god he accused people of creating, especially with regard to the Judeo-Christian worldview, which professes belief in the one true God. I had to stop here and ask myself: Why would faith in the one God so pique Freud's ire? And why did he consider the Jewish and Christian followers of this God to be conceited in their faith?

Freud's sarcastic description of the God of the Bible is a good example of an intellectual "argument from contempt."[5] He, with great personal confidence, assailed both the character of the one God and of the people who put their trust in Him and in His plans for them. What Freud evidently failed to realize is that atheism requires faith too. As Ravi Zacharias points out, quoting David Berlinski (2009), "no one has ever proved that God does not exist!"[6] In fact, on the dust jacket of his book,[7] Berlinski, a philosopher of science, asks a series of provocative questions about scientific atheism. The last one reads: "Is scientific atheism a frivolous exercise in intellectual contempt?" His answer: "Dead on!"[8]

From where did Freud draw his evidence for making the assertions he proclaimed against the God of his fathers and of Christians? Certainly he presented a satirical distortion of the God of the Bible he studied as a child and young man. What we have here in place of the proven *reliable evidence* of Scripture is simply Freud's own theory. How is it that Freud—born into a devout Jewish family and endowed by God with such remarkable gifts of innovative intelligence, insight, and capacity to communicate—came to such disrespectful and demeaning conclusions about the God of the Bible? One possibility is that Freud was well aware of his remarkable gifts and felt obliged to employ them to disentangle people from what he regarded as their harmful religious illusions.

But let us now consider Freud's defense of his position as drawn from his ending dialogue with a challenging alter ego.

Responding to Freud

Freud affirmed that the religious ideas he was concerned about were those that "correspond[ed] to the final form taken by our present day white Christian civilization, usually put forth as divine revelation." Unlike everyday school lessons, these religious teachings about facts of reality "lay claims to one's belief without producing grounds for their claims. Religious teachings we are told deserve to be believed because they were believed by our ancestors, who were far more ignorant than we are. It is forbidden to raise the question of their authentication at all."[9]

Freud continued,

The proofs they have left us are set down in writings which themselves bear every mark of untrustworthiness. They are full of contradictions, revisions and falsifications, and where they speak of factual confirmations they are themselves unconfirmed. It does not help much to have it asserted that their wording, or even their content only, originates from divine revelation; for this assertion is itself one of the doctrines whose authenticity is under examination, and no proposition can be a proof of itself.[10]

He also said,

Thus, religious ideas are illusions, fulfillments of man's urgent wish in the terrifying impression of helplessness in childhood which aroused the need for protection through love by the father...later represented by the benevolent rule of a divine Providence. His provision includes the wished-for establishment of a moral world order ensuring justice, and the prolongation of earthly existence in a future life in which these wish-fulfillments shall take place.[11]

Freud then asserted,

Because illusions are derived from human wishes they come close to psychiatric delusions in which we emphasize their being in contradiction to reality. Whether one classifies the belief that the Messiah will come and found a golden age as an illusion or a delusion will depend upon one's personal attitude. But scientific work is the only road which can lead us to a knowledge of reality outside ourselves.[12]

What a barrage of unfriendly fire! But let's take a closer look at these claims about Christian belief. Is it true that we as Christians are expected to believe Christian history and doctrine without any evidence of their truthfulness? Are we told anywhere to believe because our "less intelligent" ancestors believed? Of course not!

Our answers to Freud's derogations of the legitimacy of our faith rest heavily upon the reliability of the Scriptures, which Freud claims "bear every mark of untrustworthiness...full of contradictions, revisions and falsifications." While Freud would not have had access to all of the convincing evidence we have today that supports the historical reliability of the Bible and its accurate transmission through the centuries, he certainly had access to German translations of both Testaments. If he had judiciously studied these texts as the rigorous scientist he claimed to be, and he had critically challenged the negative biblical criticism of his day, might that have made him more careful about eliciting such strong pessimism?

Today, marshalling the various pieces of evidence to answer Freud's criticisms of Scripture is no problem—especially in light of the numerous biblical manuscripts that attest to biblical accuracy in the transmission process, archaeological research that has shown the Bible to be consistent with history and geography, fulfilled prophecy, and modern discoveries that have supported the Bible's scientific accuracy.

In the main point of his essay, Freud suggested an entirely human origin for Judeo-Christian beliefs. Not surprisingly, this takes us to his own theory of the Oedipus complex and eventually to his own god of the Dutch writer Multatuli.[13] Freud argued that even in present-day man, as opposed to his "primeval ancestors," perhaps people would kill one another without reservation:

> …if it were not that among those murderous acts there was one—the killing of the primitive father—which evoked an irresistible emotional reaction with momentous consequences. From it arose the commandment: Thou shalt not kill! The primal Father was the original image of God, the model on which later generations have shaped the figure of God…Religion would thus be the universal obsessional neurosis of humanity; like the obsessional neurosis of children, it arose out of the Oedipus complex, out of the relation to the Father.[14]

Freud went on to agree with his alter ego that religion cannot be done away with by force without great danger to civilization. He said, "A man who has been taking sleeping draughts for tens of years is naturally unable to sleep if his sleeping draught is taken away from him."[15] Yet he argued that "forward motion" for mankind lies in people coming to admit "the full extent of their helplessness in the machinery of the universe; they can no longer be the center of creation, no longer the object of tender care on the part of a beneficent Providence."[16] In facing "the truth"

in this way, Freud saw himself as something of a noble, humble, heroic figure:

> Take my attempt for what it is: A psychologist who does not deceive himself about the difficulty of finding one's bearings in this world, makes an endeavor to assess the development of man. In so doing, the idea forces itself upon him that religion is comparable to a childhood neurosis, and he is optimistic enough to suppose that mankind will surmount this neurotic phase, just as many children grow out of their similar neurosis. The primacy of the intellect lies, it is true, in a distant, distant future, but probably not an infinitely distant one. Our God, Aoyog, will fulfill whichever of these wishes nature outside us allows, but he will do it very gradually. He promises no compensation for us, who suffer grievously from life. On the way to this distant goal your religious doctrines will have to be discarded. You know why: In the long run nothing can withstand reason and experience, and the contradiction religion offers is all too palpable. Our God, Aoyog, is perhaps not a very almighty one, and he may only be able to fulfill a small part of what his predecessors have promised. But we have the sure support which you lack. We believe that it is possible for scientific work to gain some knowledge about the reality of the world…science has given us evidence by its numerous and important successes that it is no illusion.[17]

And there you have it: The Lord God of all, or Freud? The Word of God, the Bible, for which we now have profound evidence of its truth and reliability; or Freud's 24 volumes revolving around what he considered to be his great discovery of the Oedipus complex, the foundation of his theory of the neuroses? Both claim to hold the key to understanding mankind's conflicted nature and the solution for our discontent.

Though I am jesting when I propose the choice between the two, it truly is a stark choice! Our need to decide between the contrary words of men and the sure Word of God is always vital. Moreover, if Freud was arguing that religion (God) is simply the psychological creation of an illusory father figure to avoid the feeling of helplessness, what do we make of his atheism that sought to deny a heavenly Father? By the same logic employed by Freud against Christianity (i.e., in its "myth" of a longed-for benevolent and protective Father God), one could say that his denial of this Father is a psychologically competitive, murderous desire to eliminate one's father. The motive here would be to avoid deserved punishment. Ironically, it appears no accident that Freud's most treasured "discovery" of the Oedipus complex, ever present in his extensive publications, exactly fits this mold!

In a chapter titled "Freud and the Bible," William Meissner insightfully describes Freud's attempt to impose his views on Scripture within his publications.

> Freud's closest engagement with the biblical texts came at the end of his life in his attempt to rewrite the Moses legend in *Moses and Monotheism* (1939). It is flawed by faulty data selection and lacks appropriate methodology and verification; its conceptual structure is built on the sand of unverifiable hypotheses...Certainly, the Freudian encounter with scripture carries

its own lesson—that the reading and interpretation of the biblical texts may not be divorced from the motives, sometimes hidden, of the reader.[18]

What is more, portraying Christianity as psychological wish fulfillment seems inconsistent with a fallen human nature that seeks loose morals and unrestricted access to all kinds of pleasure. Who would *wish* for a morally restrictive lifestyle, the denial of fleshly appetites, and total faith and obedience while under the watchful eye of a heavenly Father who can and will discipline those who rebel against Him?

It makes more sense to interpret Christianity and Christians according to the explanation provided in Scripture: We were sinners saved by God's grace through faith in Jesus Christ.

Opening the Door for Dialogue

In closing, I want to make it clear that not all people who assume that Christian belief is just too good to be true do so because of intellectual arrogance. For example, many individuals have never experienced the love of God in their personal lives, or they have been so hurt by those who seem to believe in Christianity that they have closed the door to such hope. The good news is that you can communicate that love of Christ to others by coming alongside them as a true Christian friend. Letting others experience the love of Jesus can open the door for you to share about Him with others.

The poem often attributed to Martin Luther said it best when he distinguished the sure Word of God from human feelings: "For feelings come and feelings go, and feelings are deceiving; my warrant is the Word of God, naught else is worth believing."

52

Are Miracles Possible?

Richard G. Howe

The medieval theologian Thomas Aquinas defined a miracle as an event produced by the power of God alone, causing things to act contrary to what they would naturally have a tendency to do.[1] C.S. Lewis defined miracles as "an interference with Nature by supernatural power."[2] Norman Geisler says, "A miracle is a divine intervention into the natural world. It is a supernatural exception to the regular course of the world that would not have occurred otherwise."[3]

As these (and other) definitions say, a miracle is an event to which the term *supernatural* accurately applies. It is an event that only God can perform. The wonders of creation that we observe (a beautiful sunset, the birth of a child, a butterfly emerging from a cocoon) are not, strictly speaking, miracles, for they do not violate the laws according to which God has ordained His creation to operate. When He makes an exception to the normal operations of physical events, then we have a miracle.[4]

How Are Miracles Possible?

Two facts are nested in the definition of miracles.

Miracles and the Existence of God. First, miracles are possible only because God exists.

Miracles presuppose the existence of God, meaning that miracles as events are not themselves evidence for God's existence.[5] This is so because no event could, by definition, even be a miracle unless there is a God. Thus, an atheist, if he is to be consistent, could never interpret an event to be a miracle. If, as the atheist maintains, there is no God, then there could not be an event that is (in his estimation) an act of God. But because God does exist and is the Creator and Sustainer of the universe, then God can suspend any natural law at any time.

Miracles and the Transcendence of God. Second, miracles are possible only because the God who exists is transcendent to (beyond and other than) the creation. Because God is transcendent, He is not subject to the laws of nature. His acts which suspend such laws are miracles. To deny God's transcendence is to deny that God is fundamentally different than the universe.[6] If God is not fundamentally different than the universe, then any act that He does would be, by definition, natural. As such, no act of God could be a miracle. Miracles are possible because God exists and is transcendent.

Miracles and the
Purposes of God

The purpose of miracles is not only to bring glory to God, but to vindicate the messenger of God and confirm the message of God. In John 9:3, when the disciples asked whose sin it was that caused a man's blindness, Jesus, in correcting their misunderstanding of the reason for the man's blindness, stated, "It was not that this man sinned, or his parents, but that the works of God might be displayed in him."[7]

The Bible tells us, in clear language, the purpose of miracles. Hebrews 2:2-4 says,

> Since the message declared by angels proved to be reliable, and every transgression or disobedience received a just retribution, how shall we escape if we neglect such a great salvation? It was declared at first by the Lord, and it was attested to us by those who heard, while God also bore witness by signs and wonders and various miracles and by gifts of the Holy Spirit distributed according to his will.

The apostle John, toward the end of his Gospel (John 20:30-31), tells us that these confirming miracles are for the purpose of leading us to faith:

> Now Jesus did many other signs in the presence of the disciples, which are not written in this book; but these are written so that you may believe that Jesus is the Christ, the Son of God, and that by believing you may have life in his name.

Because miracles could not occur without divine intervention, then miracles show God's approval or vindication of the messengers on whom the miraculous power was bestowed and, therefore, show God's

confirmation of their message. Through the ages, key church leaders and theologians have held this view of the purpose of miracles. For example, Augustine reasoned:

> Men would have laughed [Christ's resurrection and ascension to heaven] out of court; they would have shut their ears and their hearts against the idea, had not the possibility and actuality of these events been demonstrated by the divine power of truth itself or rather by the truth of the divine power, with confirmation by miraculous signs.[8]

Aquinas echoed the same viewpoint:

> Wherefore just as man led by his natural reason is able to arrive at some knowledge of God through His natural effects, so is he brought to a certain degree of supernatural knowledge of the objects of faith by certain supernatural effects which are called miracles.[9]

John Calvin maintained,

> In demanding miracles from us, [our adversaries] act dishonestly; for we have not coined some new gospel, but retain the very one the truth of which is confirmed by all the miracles which Christ and the apostles ever wrought... The deception would perhaps be more specious if Scripture did not admonish us of the legitimate end and use of miracles. Mark tells us (Mark xvi. 20) that the signs which followed the preaching of the apostles were wrought in confirmation of it; so Luke also relates that the Lord "gave testimony to the word of his grace, and granted signs and wonders to be done" by the hand of the apostles (Acts xiv. 3). Very much to the same effect are those words of the

apostle, that salvation by a preached gospel was confirmed, "the Lord bearing witness with signs and wonders, and with divers miracles" (Heb. ii. 4).[10]

This was also the view of James Arminius, who said,

An illustrious evidence of the same divinity is afforded in the miracles, which God has performed by the stewards of his word, his prophets and apostles, and by Christ himself, for the confirmation of *his* doctrine and for the establishment of *their* authority. For these miracles are of such a description as infinitely to exceed the united powers of all the creatures and all the powers of nature itself, when their energies are combined. But the God of truth, burning with zeal for his own glory, could never have afforded such strong testimonies as these to false prophets and their false doctrine; nor could he have borne such witness to any doctrine even when it was true, provided it was not his, that is, provided it was not divine.[11]

This understanding of miracles does not preclude God from performing a miracle as an act of grace, which is different from vindicating a messenger and confirming a message. However, it is important to recognize that the miracles recorded in the Bible are largely for vindication and confirmation.[12]

Objections to Miracles

Miracles and Science. Some have trouble believing that miracles can occur because, by definition, miracles defy the laws of nature. They argue that because science has proven that these laws of nature are "fixed" and

hold invariantly across the universe, then miracles are not possible. What this objection fails to understand is that the laws of nature, as science studies them, are not fixed and invariant. The term *laws* gives rise to this misunderstanding. More specifically, there are no laws that govern nature's behavior. Rather, what we experience are regularities (i.e., natural conditions that occur on a regular basis). The discipline of science seeks to understand these regularities. We are able to manipulate the actions of nature and make predictions based upon nature's regular actions. But there is nothing in nature itself that *requires* that there cannot be exceptions to the way nature normally works. Consequently, because God is the Creator of nature and because He sustains all the forces and principles that give rise to nature acting in a regular fashion, He is able to suspend these laws (also because they are not *prescriptive* laws, like the laws of logic or moral laws). As the Creator, God is above and beyond these laws and is not subject to them.

The Criticism of David Hume. Without a doubt, the most often-touted objections to the possibility (and credibility) of miracles are those from the eighteenth-century Scottish philosopher David Hume.[13] Hume's objection was primarily against the knowability of miracles.[14] He argued not so much that miracles *cannot* occur, but that it would never be reasonable to *believe* that miracles can occur.[15]

A common response to Hume from apologists rests on a misunderstanding of Hume's philosophy. For example, C.S. Lewis accused Hume of being inconsistent when Hume employed the principle of the uniformity of nature (i.e., the idea that the physical laws of nature remain relatively constant and are not changing randomly) to argue against the probability of miracles. As Lewis understood it, Hume could claim that miracles are improbable *only* by assuming the principle of the uniformity of nature. But, as Lewis rightly observed, Hume's own philosophy ruled out the principle of the uniformity of nature.[16] Thus, Lewis concluded, Hume was being inconsistent.

Lewis and others say that Hume was utilizing a philosophical principle that Hume's own philosophy rejected. But, in fact, Hume's argument for the improbability of miracles was quite consistent with Hume's own philosophy. Thus, the response to Hume is *not* to claim Hume was being inconsistent, because he was not. Rather, the response should be that Hume's philosophy *itself* is flawed.

Instead of a principle of the uniformity of nature, Hume employed a principle of the *uniformity of beliefs*, which arose consistently from Hume's philosophy. Hume argued that every belief we come to hold is caused by custom or habit.[17] Primarily for Hume, the uniformity of nature is psychological not philosophical. To put it another way, our expectation that one event will follow another (like our expectation that a certain effect will follow a certain cause) is no different than our expectation that "e-i-e-i-o" will follow the phrase "Old MacDonald had a farm," or that "Who's there?" will follow upon our hearing the phrase "Knock, knock."

Because of this, on account of the fact miracles are (in Hume's understanding) rare occurrences (and *not* customary, regular, or habitual), then no one could ever come to believe in them by habit (which, in Hume's philosophy, is the only way we can come to believe something). If miracles occurred often enough that one could develop the habit of believing in them, then they would no longer be designated as miracles. Instead, they would be thought of as regular acts of nature.

A Response to Hume

If this is Hume's position, what can be said in response? Does this mean it is never reasonable to believe that a miracle has occurred? Not at all. Hume's philosophy entails something deeply incoherent. For Hume, to believe something is to have a feeling or a sentiment of a particular kind. Thus, the difference between a claim being true and a claim being false is only a difference in the feeling one has toward each claim.[18] Hume could not account for the fact that a proposition is true precisely because it corresponds to reality, regardless of how one feels.[19] But if this is what truth was for Hume, then how could he assume, imply, or claim that his own philosophy was true? How could he say that it really is the case that this is how beliefs arise? How could he maintain his claim that beliefs are merely feelings that correspond to how reality is? The fact is, he cannot. As such, there is no reason for anyone to adopt Hume's philosophy.[20] Further, there is no reason why we should think that Hume has posed any challenge to miracles. Besides, if God exists, miracles are possible!

Is It Okay for Christians to Doubt?

Terry L. Miethe

The very short answer is yes! The Bible is full of stories about doubt.[1] How many times have you puzzled over God's silence? Maybe you prayed about something very important to you—even agonized over it—and wondered why nothing happened.[2] You prayed according to all the biblical conditions for putting a request before God, and still did not receive the answer you sought.

If God truly exists, and if Christianity is true, then this complicates the issue of God's silence even further. Did not Jesus say that all the hairs of our heads are numbered (Matthew 10:30, Luke 12:7), and that God is intimately involved with our needs? Then why does it seem that He does not always respond to us? When God does not act in the way that we think He should, it's common for doubt to enter our minds.

The Example of Abraham

We will find it instructive to look at Abraham's struggles with doubts about God. How did this man of faith handle his own conflicts? As we look to his example, a crucially important set of principles emerge—principles that

are helpful for when we ourselves question God's silence.[3]

Abraham wasn't the only major figure in the Bible to deal with doubt. Scripture documents people in both the Old and New Testaments who struggled with uncertainty about God. We see them crying out for assistance, yet God did not answer them in the way they had hoped He would.

We are first introduced to Abraham when he was known as Abram. God spoke to Abram and called him to move his family to a faraway land known as Canaan. God promised that a great nation would come from Abraham, and that this nation, in turn, would become a source of blessing for all the peoples of the earth (Genesis 12:1-3). Eventually, Abram's family settled in Canaan. He and wife Sarah lived and died there. And after a long wait of many years—a wait that was accompanied by doubt—the son promised to them was born, and Abraham became the father of the Israelites through his son Isaac and his grandson Jacob.

The writer of the book of Hebrews noted several of the accomplishments that came from Abraham's trust in God. From the outsct, he responded to God and migrated to Canaan even though he did not know where he was going (Hebrews 11:8-10). He likewise believed God's promise that he and Sarah would have a child, even though both were quite elderly. To make matters worse, Sarah had been childless all along. But in the midst of struggles with doubt, Abraham clung in faith to God's promise, and eventually he became the father of a great nation (Hebrews 11:11-12).

Then came another test for Abraham—perhaps the greatest one of all. He was commanded to sacrifice his son Isaac. He was willing to do this because he believed God's word and trusted His promises. Abraham believed God could raise his son from the dead, if that was to be the way He wanted it (Hebrews 11:17-19).

Abraham lived by faith; God honored that and blessed him (cf. James 2:21-24). Some have asked, How can we ever compare Abraham to ourselves? Why would he ever have reason to question God's leading? After all, didn't Abraham speak directly to God basically whenever he wanted to do so? And wasn't God always there to communicate with Him? It's not the same for us.

The modern conception is that Abraham and God had frequent interaction, but that's not necessarily the case. For example, at the close of Genesis 16, Abraham was 86 years old (verse 16). As far as we know, the next time God spoke to him was 13 years later, when Abraham was 99 years old (Genesis 17:1)!

It is difficult to be dogmatic here, but it is at least possible that God did not communicate with Abraham during that time frame. Neither does it appear that God conversed with Abraham throughout his life on a weekly or even a yearly basis. There may have been sizeable gaps of time during which

no communication took place at all. Many Christians today would probably say that God has communicated with them in some way or other more than once over the last 13 years.

This does not mean that God expected Abraham to believe in the midst of a vacuum. Abraham was given warrant for his trust. God spoke to him, and this communication must have been quite convincing. A particularly good example of this is the time when Abraham asked God how he might *know* that Canaan would be given to him (Genesis 15:8). The Lord responded that Abraham could know this truth *for certain*, utilizing a supernatural manifestation in order to make a covenant with Abraham (Genesis 15:13-21). Faith does not exclude good grounds for belief, and one way we can strengthen our own belief in the midst of doubt is by looking at the many accounts in Scripture that show God fulfilling His promises.

Scripture records for us other times when Abraham experienced troublesome moments of doubt. For example, on at least two occasions, Abraham concealed the true identity of Sarah in order to save his own life (Genesis 12:10-20; 20:1-18). But if he really believed God would raise a great nation from him, why should he be fearful for his life, as we are told he was (Genesis 12:12-13; 20:11)? I don't bring this up to denigrate Abraham's faith—after all, these episodes were spread out over a span of 25 years. No human being lives perfectly free of doubt. On the whole, Abraham regularly acted in faith, never allowing unbelief to master him.[4]

The apostle Paul pointed to Abraham as an example of faith even in the midst of his momentary lapses into doubt. At times when Abraham could have given up and ignored God's call, Abraham chose to believe and persevere. Abraham did not give up or cease to believe; his faith was actually strengthened (Romans 4:18-25). What was his secret? Abraham not only exercised faith, but his faith grew as he trusted God more and more, one step at a time, even after his failures. *Imagine a faith that actually grows even when the pressures of life are at their greatest!* That was Abraham's experience. He trusted God.

Other Biblical Examples of Doubt

Let's look at some other biblical examples of doubt.

Job questioned God about his suffering, and concluded that God was trustworthy. What Job already knew about God was enough to convince him that God could be trusted in the unknown areas of life (see Romans 4:20-21). Believers today can also look to God's faithfulness and let their faith grow during the times when they are under attack.

David realized that one's personal sin keeps an individual's prayers from being answered (Psalm 66:18). Then in Psalm 35:13-14, David spoke of his prayers returning to him unanswered—a complaint also voiced by Christians today. In this instance he was apparently unaware of the reason for God's silence, and it affected him emotionally.

One of the more stunning examples of doubt appears in Psalm 44. There we are told that God stopped giving the people of Israel victories over their enemies. Instead, they were being disgraced before their foes (verses 1-16). In all this, the psalmist claimed that the Jewish people had done nothing to deserve God's judgment (verses 17-22). The writer concluded with this stinging rebuke in verses 23-24: "Awake! Why are you sleeping, O Lord? Rouse yourself! Do not reject

us forever! Why do you hide your face? Why do you forget our affliction and oppression?" Wow—God was accused of breaking promises, sleeping on the job, and forgetting about His people. What serious charges against the sovereign God!

A major example of God's silence occurs in the gap between the Old and New Testaments. We hear little about the so-called 400 silent years between the last of the minor prophets and the birth of Christ. This long silence may have provoked some emotional dilemmas for the Jewish people of that era, and has been the source of confusion for some Christians today. Why had the people not heard from the Lord all through those generations? Had God forgotten them?

The darkest night is often followed by a new morning of rejoicing (Psalm 30:5); the Jews who lived during these "dark ages" did not realize that the coming of the Messiah would be "just around the corner." The central event in history effectively broke the silence of those 400 years. The incarnation revealed God's desire to be personally involved with His people—and it came after a long and intense silence. This stands as a lesson for us today!

In the New Testament, the main instance of God's seeming silence is when Jesus prayed to the Father while in the Garden of Gethsemane. Suffering deep agony to the extent of sweating drops of blood, Jesus requested that His Father allow the coming event to be bypassed. Nonetheless, Jesus prayed that the Father's will be done (Matthew 26:36-43; Mark 14:33-36; Luke 22:39-44). Jesus was tempted like us, suffering distraught emotions, yet was without sin (Hebrews 4:15).

Paul also discovered that God does not always act according to our will. This apostle prayed three times that God would remove an apparent physical problem, but without success. Through this Paul learned the lesson that Jesus already knew—that the Father's will is preferable to ours (2 Corinthians 12:7-10). These biblical cases signify that God does not always answer our prayers or act in the way we think He should. Sometimes we receive what is, from our perspective, a negative answer.

Understanding Doubt and Our Response

Many biblical saints lived their entire lives during one of the silent periods when God did not send revelation. What can we learn from them? Are there any helpful truths that can assist us today? How did the people in Scripture react when God didn't answer their prayers? How did they cope?[5]

For Christians, perhaps one of the best-known cases of extreme suffering and God's silence is what happened to Job. As Job searched for the reasons he was going through such great pain, God was silent for a while. Eventually, however, God confronted Job and challenged his misconceptions about suffering and God's seeming silence. In the process, Job realized several key truths about God's nature, including the fact He could be trusted no matter what. In the end, Job agreed that God was wholly vindicated (not that the Lord needed Job's agreement!).

With all that in mind, what are the biblical conditions for answered prayer? Most of these factors are personal in nature:

confessing one's sin (Psalm 66:18; 1 John 1:9), exercising faith (Mark 11:24; James 1:5-8), being obedient (John 15:7; 1 John 3:22), and praying in Jesus's name (John 14:13-14; 15:16; 16:23). We are also told to pray according to God's will (1 John 5:14-15).

There is no dichotomy between the way God operated in Bible times and how He works today. Sometimes God answers our prayers, and other times, He doesn't. And when He *does* respond, sometimes He does so in spectacular fashion!

In Abraham and Job, we find that our trust in God can grow even during tough times.[6] Perhaps the key principle here is that we know enough about God and His faithfulness such that when we cannot figure things out, we don't succumb to doubt. We might not know why things happen as they do, but this is still a world in which God raised Jesus from the dead and believers have the assurance of eternal life.

Practicing the truth is crucial here: We need to exercise our faith during our times of doubt by directly affirming our belief in God through prayer or meditation.[7] Praising God is another way we can redirect our thoughts toward Him. Still another helpful practice is to list our answers to prayer as they occur, thereby providing a ready record for the times when we experience difficult circumstances. As Abraham and Job discovered, we can witness growth in our own faith and a corresponding lessening of doubt's grip on our lives!

How Do We Reason from the Scriptures with Cultists?

Ron Rhodes

While witnessing to cultists can be challenging, your chances of success greatly increase to the extent that you incorporate the following principles into your witnessing strategy:

Consider Yourself a Missionary. You may have heard the saying, "Every heart with Christ is a missionary; every heart without Christ is a mission field."

Prepare by Prayer. Pray regularly about all your witnessing opportunities. Remember, only God, in His mighty power, has the ability to lift the cultic veil of blindness from the human heart (2 Corinthians 4:4; see also 3:17; John 8:32). Acts 16:14 tells us that when the apostle Paul spoke to a woman named Lydia, "The Lord opened her heart to pay attention to what was said by Paul." Pray that the Lord opens the hearts of the cultists to whom you speak.

Know Your Bible. Build an arsenal of Bible verses relating to issues that come up frequently during witnessing encounters. Store those verses in your mind. Your arsenal should include verses on the inspiration of Scripture, the one true God, the deity of

Christ, Jesus's work on the cross, the deity and personality of the Holy Spirit, the Trinity, and salvation by grace through faith. This arsenal will make your task far easier. My book *Find It Fast in the Bible* (Harvest House Publishers) contains the best verses on such subjects.

Show Love and Respect. Apologetics is more than just "right answers." Apologetics also involves a man or woman who is so committed to Jesus that it shows in the way he or she treats other people. Let the love of Christ shine through you (1 Corinthians 16:14; Ephesians 5:2; 1 Timothy 4:12).

In keeping with this, always be "prepared to make a defense to anyone who asks you for a reason for the hope that is in you; *yet do it with gentleness and respect*" (1 Peter 3:15). The Greek word translated "gentleness" carries the idea of meekness and humility. You should not show even the slightest hint of arrogance. The word "respect" has two important nuances: We are to maintain a reverential awe of God (1 Peter 1:17; 2:17; 3:2), and we are to treat the person to whom we are speaking with respect (Colossians 4:6).

Even if your theological arguments are strong and persuasive, they will have little effect if they are not communicated with gentleness and respect.

Be Patient. Being patient may mean going over the same doctrinal point repeatedly or reviewing the same verse ten times, if necessary (see 2 Timothy 4:1-2). If you should lose your patience and raise your voice at the cultist, the likelihood is that he or she will not be willing to speak with you again. This would be regrettable. After all, it may take multiple exposures to the truth before the cultist finally grasps it.

Beware That Cultists Are Often Warned About Influence from Friends and Relatives. Some cults warn their new followers that Satan may try to dissuade them from remaining with the group through the influence of friends and relatives. As a result, when a friend or relative does try to dissuade a new member from remaining with the group, it makes the cult appear to be prophetic. Emphasize that when it comes to the truth, the Bible is the only thing that really matters. Keep moving the discussion back to the authoritative Word of God.

Beware of Peer Pressure. It is a sad reality that in some cults, members can be disfellowshipped (kicked out) and shunned (given the silent treatment by friends and family) if they dare to question the group. Fear of disfellowshipping and shunning makes it difficult for anyone to leave the cult, for the sacrifice is a heavy one. Even if you convince a cultist that you are right and he is wrong, he may yet stay in the group so he won't lose family and friends. Pray that God moves upon his heart to put God first.

Avoid False Assumptions. Do not assume everyone affiliated with a particular cult believes the same thing. They often don't!

This is sometimes due to varying levels of training among individual members. On one occasion two Jehovah's Witnesses visited me, and I asked them if they believed in two gods. The younger (new) Jehovah's Witness immediately shook her head and affirmed, "Absolutely not." The older Jehovah's Witness (the trainer) corrected her and said, "Yes, we do. Jehovah is God Almighty, and Jesus is a lesser god."

It is best not to tell a cultist what he or she believes. It is better to simply ask. Once they reveal their beliefs, you can move the discussion to the Bible.

Address Issues That Matter. When cultists show up on the doorstep, they may want to chat about any number of possible topics—Christian holidays, saluting the flag, apostate Christendom, or some other topic. Whatever they use as their starting point, it is best for you to move the discussion to spiritually relevant matters as soon as possible. For example, address the true identity of Jesus, what He accomplished at the cross, and speak clearly about the gospel of salvation. If you've got only a short time with the cultist, you want to make your discussion count for eternity.

Beware that Cultists Are Often Trained to Answer Your Objections. Many cultists—the Jehovah's Witnesses and Mormons are good examples—are trained to answer common objections on the doorstep. For example, they are taught how to respond when people say, "I'm not interested," or "I have my own religion," or "We are already Christians here," or "I'm busy." They often seem to have an answer for everything. This can make you feel a bit frazzled. The solution is to not panic, but simply move the discussion to the Bible, where it belongs.

Define Your Terms. Cultists typically use many of the same words and terms Christians do—*revelation, Jesus Christ, God, Holy Spirit, resurrection, ascension, second coming*, and the like. The problem is that they pour their own cultic meanings into those terms. When they use these terms, you may not understand what they mean by what they are saying. Likewise, when you use such terms, they will likely not interpret them in the ways you do. Unless you define your terms biblically and overcome the "terminology block," little true communication will take place. Do all you can to clearly define the words you use in your communication with them.

Always Look Up Bible Verses Cited by Cultists. There's a good chance that any verse cited by a cultist has been taken out of context. For example, Jehovah's Witnesses claim that Matthew 14:6-10 teaches that birthdays are evil. Looking up the passage reveals that Herod, on his birthday, executed John the Baptist. In reality, the passage does not say that birthdays are evil, but only that Herod was evil. Never take a cultist's word for what a verse teaches without looking it up.

Ask Strategic Questions. You cannot shove your theology down the throat of a cultist. But well-placed questions can help force them to rethink their position.

For example, you could ask a Jehovah's Witness, "If the Jehovah's Witnesses are the only true witnesses for God, and if the Jehovah's Witnesses as an organization came into being in the late nineteenth century, does this mean God was without a witness for more than eighteen centuries of church history?"

You could ask a New Age follower, "If human beings are God, then why do we have to buy and read New Age books to discover this fact? Wouldn't we already know it?"

If a Mormon asks you to pray about the Book of Mormon, you could ask, "Which Book of Mormon do you want me to pray about? The 1830 edition? The 1921 edition? Or today's edition, which has more than 4,000 changes from the original 1830 edition?"

My books *Reasoning from the Scriptures with Jehovah's Witnesses* and *Reasoning from the Scriptures with Mormons* (Harvest House Publishers) contain hundreds of such questions.

Address Barriers to Faith. Make every effort to correct a cultist's wrong understanding of Bible verses, for these misunderstandings constitute barriers to faith. For example, a Jehovah's Witness might say: "In Colossians 1:15, Jesus is called the firstborn of all creation. This means he came into being at a point in time and therefore isn't eternal deity." This wrong understanding of Scripture constitutes a barrier to faith in the true Jesus.

You can respond this way: "The word *firstborn* in the Bible can mean 'preeminent one.' That is what happened with David. Even though he was the youngest of Jesse's sons, he was called the 'firstborn' in Psalm 89:27 because he became preeminent as Israel's king. Jesus is the firstborn of creation because He is preeminent over creation. After all, He *created* the creation, as Colossians 1:16 states." Point by point, you must try to dismantle a cultist's barriers to faith in the true Jesus.

Undermine Their Basis of Authority. When possible, it is wise to undermine the cultist's confidence in the cult's leadership and its holy books. For example, you can undermine a Jehovah's Witness's confidence in the Watchtower Society by pointing out its many false prophecies and doctrinal changes. You can undermine a Mormon's confidence in the Book of Mormon by pointing out that it plagiarized heavily from the Bible, has no true archaeological support, and has had thousands of changes introduced through the years. The more you can undermine a cultist's basis of authority, the more he or she will be open to the true basis of authority—*the Bible.*

Talk About the True Jesus. Cultists consistently get the identity of Jesus wrong. An important aspect of witnessing to cultists, therefore, involves not only making a positive case for the absolute deity of Christ, but also answering objections to the deity of Christ. I provide all the scriptural information you need in another chapter in this book, titled, "How Do We Know That Jesus Is God?"

Emphasize the Gospel of Grace. Without exception, cultists always believe in some form of works salvation. Jehovah's Witnesses believe they must obey the countless rules of the Watchtower Society to be saved. Mormons are told they must prove themselves worthy by working toward perfection. In such contexts, the wonderful grace of God is truly good news: "By grace you have been saved through faith. And this is not your own doing; it is the gift of God, not a result of works, so that no one may boast" (Ephesians 2:8-9; see also Romans 5:1-11; 6:23; Ephesians 1:7).

Give a Bible-Based Testimony. Cultists may argue about doctrine, but they cannot argue about your testimony (1 John 1:3; see also Matthew 10:32; Mark 5:19-20; John 4:28-30,39; 2 Timothy 1:8; 1 Peter 3:15). In your testimony, focus heavily on the true Jesus, and how the gospel of grace has set you free from a life of legalism. Sprinkle your testimony with many uplifting verses on the grace of God. Speak joyfully about your assurance of salvation. After giving your testimony, invite the cultist to *right now* trust in Jesus for the free gift of salvation.

I can promise you that when the cultist leaves your house, he or she will remember what you said in your testimony. He or she may forget parts of your discussion about doctrine and various teachings, but your testimony is not likely to be forgotten.

If They Convert, Your Job Is Not Over. A cultist's conversion to Christ comes with a lot of baggage—including the baggage of losing contact with family members and friends who are still in the cult. You need to be there for him or her. Introduce the convert to other Christians—a new family of believers—at your church. Get him or her involved in a good Bible study, and attend the study yourself so you can answer any questions along the way. Keep reiterating God's marvelous love and grace. And after you've done that, remind the person *again and again* of God's marvelous love and grace. Be a steady help in this difficult transitionary period. Help him or her to experience what it really means to be set free in Jesus (John 8:32).

Is the Trinity a Contradiction?

Ed Hindson

The Christian church historically has affirmed the doctrine of the Trinity, which refers to the tri-unity of God. A common objection from skeptics regarding the doctrine of the Trinity is that Christians worship three gods. However, orthodox Christians have never worshipped three gods. Instead, they worship one God in three persons—Father, Son, and Holy Spirit. Norman Geisler observes, "The Trinity goes beyond reason but not against reason...it is complex but not contradictory."[1]

A clear understanding of the roles and relationships of the three persons of the Triune God will demonstrate that the Trinity is not a contradiction, but rather an essential understanding of the biblical data. Brandon Crowe and Carl Trueman refer to the Trinity as a "robustly biblical doctrine with immense relevance for practical living."[2] It is based on three propositional truths of Scripture: (1) There is only one God. (2) Three persons are called God. (3) Each person is distinct from the other two.[3]

God Is One

A central teaching of both Judaism and Christianity is the oneness of God. Deuteronomy 6:4, known as the Shema, declares, "Hear, O Israel: The LORD our God, the LORD is one." The clear message throughout the Old Testament is that God is one. The Ten Commandments include this: "You shall have no other gods before me" (Exodus 20:3). The prophet Malachi taught that one God created us (Malachi 2:10,15). The song of Moses asks, "Who is like you, O LORD, among the gods? Who is like you, majestic in holiness, awesome in glorious deeds, doing wonders?" (Exodus 15:11). Isaiah 45:5 adds God Himself saying, "I am the LORD, and there is no other, besides me there is no God."

In the New Testament, when Jesus was asked about the most important commandment, He began by affirming this same teaching (Mark 12:29). Paul's writings repeatedly note God as "one God and Father of all" (Ephesians 4:6; see also 1 Corinthians 8:6; 1 Timothy 2:5). Romans 3:30 clearly affirms "God is one." He is also called the "only God" (John 1:18; 5:44; 1 Timothy 1:17; Jude 1:25), excluding the possibility of any other god. James 2:19 further argues, "You believe that God is one; you do well. Even the demons believe—and shudder!" Both testaments clearly emphasize the fact that there is only one true God.

341

The Bible Identifies
Three Persons as God

The triune God exists as three *distinct* persons, meaning that the Father is not the Son or the Spirit; each person is a distinct "who." First, the *Father* is called God in Scripture. God is "Our Father in heaven" (Matthew 6:9; see also verse 32) and "the Father of spirits" (Hebrews 12:9). True worshippers worship the Father in spirit and in truth (John 4:23). He is called "our Father" (Romans 1:7), "the Father" (John 5:45; 6:27), and "God and Father" (2 Corinthians 1:3). As noted above, the Father is also called the "one God" (1 Corinthians 8:6). Further, the Father is called the "Father of our Lord Jesus Christ" (Romans 15:6).

Second, *Jesus* the Son is called God. Jesus is distinct from the Father and Spirit in the Great Commission (Matthew 28:18-20). Jesus also heard the Father's voice at His baptism (Matthew 3:17) and the Transfiguration (Matthew 17:5). Jesus spoke to the Father in prayer on multiple occasions, noting communication between Father and Son. Jesus is likewise distinct from the Holy Spirit, who appeared at His baptism and is mentioned separately by Jesus in the Great Commission. Yet Jesus is distinctly worshipped as God (Matthew 8:2; 14:33; 15:25; 20:20; 28:17; Mark 5:6 and others). Thomas called Jesus, "My Lord and my God!" (John 20:28). Paul referred to Jesus as the person in whom "the whole fullness of deity dwells bodily" (Colossians 2:9). In John 8:58 Jesus declared Himself to be the "I am" who was before Abraham, claiming equality and eternality with God the Father. This proclamation led to His opponents' to desire to kill Him.

Third, the *Holy Spirit* is referred to as God. The Spirit is distinct from Father and Son in the Great Commission (Matthew 28:18-20) as well as at the baptism of Jesus (Matthew 3:17). The Spirit of God was involved in creation (Genesis 1:2). The Spirit is also specifically referred to as "God" in Acts 5:3-4. The Spirit has attributes only God has, including omnipresence (Psalm 139:7-12) and omniscience (1 Corinthians 2:10-11). The Spirit is further defined as the third person of the triune Godhead in many of the New Testament's benedictions, such as 2 Corinthians 13:14, and in verses including all three persons of the Trinity (Hebrews 9:14).

The Holy Spirit is a distinct person of the Godhead. He is not a mere emanation of God; He is God.

Each Person of the
Trinity Is Distinct

In addition to revealing the three persons of the Trinity, the Bible also notes the three persons are distinct from one another. Those who reject the concept that the Bible teaches the three persons of the triune God are distinct from one another are called modalists. Modalism believes God is only one person who has presented Himself to us in three distinct modes of Father, Son, and Spirit. This belief is like the concept of one man who serves in three roles, such as a father, a husband, and a friend. Some modalists (Jehovah's Witnesses) reject the deity of Christ and the distinct person and deity of the Holy Spirit, identifying only the Father as God. Others (Oneness Pentecostals) believe God's manifestation is triune but not His essence, insisting that only Jesus is God.

The Bible, however, notes all three persons of the triune God operating at the same time. For example, at the *baptism of Jesus* (Matthew 3:13-17; Mark 1:9-11; Luke 3:21-22; John 1:32-34), Jesus came up from the water, the Holy Spirit descended upon Him in the form of a dove, and the Father spoke with a voice from the sky. This cannot be one person manifest in all three roles at the same time.

In the Great Commission, Jesus told His followers to baptize new believers in "the name of the Father and of the Son and of the Holy Spirit" (Matthew 28:19). Greek scholar A.T. Robertson noted that this baptism was "in the name of the Trinity."[4] This is not one person with three names, but rather three distinct persons. Though distinct, the three persons of the triune God are one God. This is also why Paul could write of "one Lord, one faith, one baptism, one God and Father of all" (Ephesians 4:5-6). References to baptizing in Jesus's name (Acts 2:38; 8:12; 10:48; 19:5) do not exclude the Trinity, but emphasize the uniqueness of Christian baptism—especially for Jewish converts. Grant Osborne observed, "There is a Trinitarian theology in the NT, seen in 1 Corinthians 12:4-6; 2 Corinthians 13:14; Ephesians 4:4-6; and this is in line with each member of the Godhead."[5]

Another argument against modalism and in favor of the distinctiveness of each person of the Godhead is found in Christ's *prayers* to the Father. He often prayed to the Father, yet spoke to Him as a separate person. Otherwise, Jesus would have been praying to Himself, something very different from the presentation of His prayers in the Gospel accounts. Jesus could say, "I and the Father are one" (John 10:30), yet could also pray to Him, noting both a unity and uniqueness between the Father and the Son.

Current Debate Regarding the Trinity

One debate among evangelical scholars regarding the Trinity involves the *authority and submission* between the persons of the triune Godhead. Scholars Bruce Ware and Wayne Grudem have argued God the Father and God the Son have eternally been equal in divinity but that the Son has submitted to the Father eternally, a view known as eternal functional subordination, or sometimes as the eternal roles of authority and submission.

This view emphasizes the Father "always acts in ways that befit who he distinctively is as Father."[6] This includes recognizing the Father elects believers through the Son (Ephesians 1:4-5), created the world through the Son (John 1:2; 1 Corinthians 8:6; Hebrews 1:2), and sent the Son into the world (John 3:16). The great Princeton theologian Charles Hodge espoused this view as well:

> The Nicene doctrine includes…the principle of the subordination of the Son to the Father, and of the Spirit to the Father and the Son. But this subordination does not imply inferiority…The subordination intended is only that which concerns the mode of subsistence and operation…The creeds are nothing more than a well-ordered arrangement of the facts of Scripture which concern the doctrine of the Trinity.[7]

Yet others have argued against the eternal subordination of the Son to the Father. The Athanasian Creed, for example, notes, "In this Trinity none is afore, nor after another; none is greater or less than another." Theologian Albert Mohler argues, "Clearly, there can be no eternal subordination in terms of being. That would deny what the Nicene Creed affirms and affirm what it denies. But describing the social dimensions of the Trinity is far more difficult."[8]

One of the arguments used to support the view of eternal subordination refers to the names *Father* and *Son*. For example, John 5:19 notes, "So Jesus said to them, 'Truly, truly, I say to you, the Son can do nothing of his own accord, but only what he sees the Father doing. For whatever the Father does, that the Son does likewise.'" This verse affirms Father and Son are two distinct persons, with full equality, yet they exhibit different roles within the triune Godhead. While the Son does obey the Father's will in this verse, it is not because of any required subordination. Even if there is subordination implied in this passage, it does not require that it is eternal.

In fact, one of the crucial aspects of this debate involves the role between Father and Son before the creation of the world. Did the Son submit to the Father even in eternity past? The temporary submission view argues He did so only during the period of His incarnation on Earth. Yet John 3:35 says, "The Father loves the Son and has given all things into his hand" (see also Ephesians 1:4). This difficult debate is summarized in this way by Michael Horton, who notes, "…in every external work of the Godhead, the Father is always the source, the Son is always the mediator, and the Spirit is always the perfecting agent."[9] Others have explained the roles of the Godhead: the Father is the *Planner*, the Son the *Accomplisher*, and the Holy Spirit the *Applier*.

One further consideration is whether the sending of Jesus the Son to Earth requires holding to the view of the eternal submission of the Son. For example, Galatians 4:4 says, "When the fullness of time had come, God sent forth his Son, born of woman, born under the law" (see also 1 John 4:9-10).

God clearly sent the Son, and the Son obediently responded. However, is this to be seen as an act of submission? The limitations of human language may be a concern at this point. Though submission is involved, it appears to be a voluntary submission. The Son already wanted to do what the Father had commanded. The act agreed with the wills of both the Father and the Son.

God's Tri-unity on Display

In summary, both the view of the eternal subordination of the Son and the view of the temporary subordination of the Son (limited to His incarnation) can affirm the biblical view of the triune Godhead. However, each view holds different beliefs regarding particular operations between the Father and the Son, and these remain of healthy debate among evangelical scholars.

The New Testament often includes appeals featuring all three persons of the Trinity. For example, 2 Corinthians 1:21-22 states, "It is God who establishes us with you in Christ, and has anointed us, and who has also put his seal on us and given us his Spirit in our hearts as a guarantee." Father, Son, and Spirit all serve vital roles within the life of the church—and in the lives of individual believers. We are called to worship in spirit and in truth (John 4:24), be baptized into the name of the Father, Son, and Spirit (Matthew 28:19), and live for the glory of God the Father through faith in Jesus by the power of the Holy Spirit. In each case, the tri-unity of God is on display—to His glory, and to our benefit.

Part Seven

QUESTIONS ABOUT WORLDVIEWS

What Is Philosophy, and Why Is It Important?

Richard G. Howe

Philosophy is probably one of the most difficult disciplines to define, though it becomes easier after one becomes more familiar with its tenets. The word *philosophy* is a compound word that comes from the Greek *philos*, meaning "beloved" or "friend" (or the verb form *phileo*, meaning "I love"), and the Greek word *sophia*, meaning "skill in arts or crafts or in matters of common life; sound judgment, intelligence, practical wisdom."[1] Philosopher Ed Miller defines philosophy as "the attempt to think rationally and critically about the most important questions."[2] Here, "think[ing] rationally" is in contrast to allowing undue emotions to distort our understanding. In other words, to think critically is to subject our thinking to legitimate critique as opposed to being gullible.

The history of philosophy has seen innumerable ideas, criticisms, and conclusions offered by seemingly countless philosophers. Étienne Gilson, a historian of philosophy, offered a helpful observation when he wrote, "A philosopher talks about things, while a professor of philosophy talks about philosophy."[3] Gilson was not disparaging professors of philosophy when he said this; he had a venerable career as one. Instead, in contradiction to countless dead ends that different paths of philosophy have taken over the past millennia, Gilson was reminding us that philosophy is a human analysis of the real. That is to say, philosophy aims at understanding the things that occupy reality.

As humans, we *know things* (people, trees, rocks, etc.), not merely beliefs, or ideas, or thoughts, or perceptions, or propositions (statements). In both instances (i.e., of knowing things *and* our beliefs, ideas, thoughts, perceptions, and propositions) there is a knowing, but one should distinguish between the knowing and the *things* that we know. To put it more clearly, beliefs are *about* things, thoughts are *about* things, perceptions are *about* things, and propositions are *about* things. However, knowledge is knowledge *of* reality (of the things themselves), not merely the knowing *implied* in the beliefs, ideas, thoughts, perceptions, and propositions. This emphasis is what characterizes the classical tradition in philosophy.

What About Colossians 2:8?

Colossians 2:8 says, "See to it that no one takes you captive by philosophy and empty deceit, according to human tradition, according to the elemental spirits of the world, and not according to Christ." Some Christians might take Paul here to be warning us to avoid philosophy altogether. However, Paul was clearly warning against humanistic, worldly, and anti-Christian philosophy. In fact, from the context it can be argued that Paul is not talking about philosophy the way we use the term today.[4] Instead, Paul was warning the Colossians against an insidious form of legalism (i.e., following rules and regulations for some spiritual benefit), asceticism (i.e., rejecting sensual objects to avoid spiritual contamination or for spiritual gain), and mysticism (i.e., inappropriate worship) (cf. 2:16-23).[5]

But let us suppose that Paul was warning us of the dangers of philosophy. There certainly are such dangers.[6] That is why it is important to gain familiarity with philosophy. C.S. Lewis wisely observed:

> To be ignorant and simple now—not to be able to meet the enemies on their own ground—would be to throw down our weapons, and betray our uneducated brethren who have, under God, no defense but us against the intellectual attacks of the heathen. Good philosophy must exist, if for no other reason, because bad philosophy needs to be answered.[7]

Philosophy in the Service of Christian Thinking

It is my contention, however, that there is more that philosophy can do in service of Christian thinking than merely fending off

error.[8] Many Christian leaders throughout church history have defended philosophy's role in doing theology.[9]

I was once accused of making apologetics and theology elitist by suggesting that there was an indispensable role that philosophy sometimes plays.[10] To answer this charge, let me illustrate the role of philosophy in Christian thinking. Suppose a mother asked her son to bring her a flower. Assuming he knows what the word means, the son knows what a flower is and knows that there is a difference between the flower and his mother. But if one wanted to understand deeper aspects of the physical nature of the flower, one would need to understand botany. To understand at an even deeper level the various physical aspects of the flower and the plant on which it blooms (for example, its photosynthesis), one would need to understand chemistry. Finally, to understand deeper still (e.g., the workings of the plant at the atomic and subatomic levels), one would need to understand physics. All of these levels would certainly be out of reach of the child, but it would be wrong to level the accusation that we were making the understanding of flowers elitist.

By analogy, suppose one wanted to account for a number of other aspects of the flower and the mother. What makes a flower to be the kind of thing it is (namely, a flower) and what makes his mother the kind of thing she is (namely, a human), these are their respective *natures* (or essences). This takes us into *metaphysics*—the philosophical discipline of the study of the nature of reality. In addition, we can *know* from our senses what their natures are and that one is a flower and the other is a human. This takes us into *epistemology*—the philosophical discipline of the study of the nature of the knowledge of reality.

Because of the different kinds of things they are, we *value* the human over the flower. This takes us into *ethics*—the philosophical discipline of the study of value and personal actions toward different kinds of things. Furthermore, we also insist not only that we ourselves, but also others, value the human over the flower and we hold them accountable when they do not. This takes us into *political philosophy*—the philosophical discipline of the study of the organization of and obligations within communities. What is more, we can know that neither the flower nor the human can account for their own existing but are, instead, created by God. This takes us into *philosophy of religion*—the philosophical discipline of the study of the existence, attributes, and actions of God knowable from nature (Romans 1:20).

Why Is Philosophy Important?

Perhaps it is evident by now how important philosophy can be in the service of Christian thinking. One more illustration might press the issue even closer to what we cherish as Christians. In *The Dake Annotated Reference Bible*, Finis Jennings Dake taught that God has numerous "spiritual" body parts, such as "spiritual" lips and "spiritual" hair.[11] Dake referenced a number of scriptural citations to make his case.[12]

During a discussion about this, I asked a friend if he thought that God had legs, for Genesis 3:8 describes God as "walking in the garden in the cool of the day." My friend said that God does not have legs because we know from John 4:24 that God "is spirit." I then asked him what he did with the Genesis passage. He said that he understood it as a figure of speech. My question to him was, "How do you know that Genesis 3:8 is

a figure of speech, but not John 4:24?" How did he conclude that God had not physically walked in the garden? How did he know that the statement about God being spirit was not figurative language?[13]

Let's consider another example. Isaiah 55:12 says, "You shall go out in joy and be led forth in peace; the mountains and the hills before you shall break forth into singing, and all the trees of the field shall clap their hands." It is easy to see that Isaiah was speaking figuratively when he wrote about trees clapping their hands. We can know that this is a figure of speech because we know the nature of trees—we know that trees do not have hands. This principle (i.e., knowing the nature of something sufficiently to discern whether language is literal or figurative) is the same principle we must use when it comes to discerning whether the Bible is speaking literally or figuratively about God.[14]

But this brings us to a problem. It is because we can know the nature of trees that we know they don't have hands. This is true even when we don't know the specific facts about the tree. For example, if someone said, "I have a tree in my backyard," we would instantly know what he meant, even if he did not say whether the tree was deciduous or evergreen, flower-bearing or fruit-bearing or neither, tall or short, young or old, healthy or sick. Because our intellects know what a tree is, we can understand what he meant without knowing any of the particulars that are themselves not part of the nature of a tree.

But how can we come to any understanding about the nature of God? After all, it is impossible for us to see God, who is invisible (1 Timothy 6:15-16). From where, then, are we able to discover God's attributes sufficiently to discern when the Bible is speaking literally about God and when it is speaking figuratively? Romans 1:20 holds the key. There, Paul tells us:

> His invisible attributes, namely, his eternal power and divine nature, have been clearly perceived, ever since the creation of the world, in the things that have been made. So they are without excuse.

I believe that most people, when they encounter God's creation, know that God is beyond the physical world and that He is the all-powerful Creator of the universe's beauty. This is the testimony of Psalm 19:1, which says, "The heavens declare the glory of God, and the sky above proclaims his handiwork." Moreover, Romans 2:14-15 tells us that God's moral requirements for mankind are knowable apart from the oracles of God.

> When Gentiles, who do not have the law, by nature do what the law requires, they are a law to themselves, even though they do not have the law. They show that the work of the law is written on their hearts, while their conscience also bears witness, and their conflicting thoughts accuse or even excuse them.[15]

However, because of the increasing influence of bad philosophies and alternative religions, it can sometimes be necessary to utilize arguments to show how it is that the invisible attributes of God are clearly perceived and seen by the things that are made. For better or worse, the discipline that attends itself to this question is philosophy.[16]

Where Can We Go from Here?

When it comes to gaining a clearer understanding of matters like the attributes of God, philosophy can play an essential role. But what else might philosophy offer to Christian apologetics and theology? Without going into detail here, there are many other issues worthy of discussion that have important philosophical aspects to them. Now, I am not saying that there are no other disciplines beyond philosophy that can help inform us. Nor am I saying that one must be conversant in philosophy to have informed opinions about apologetic or theological issues. Instead, we should recognize that when it comes to an in-depth analysis and defense of certain aspects of the Christian worldview, it may be necessary at times to make use of philosophy.

Philosophy can assist us with several aspects of apologetics and theology, including (1) foundational issues, (2) clarifying the meaning of terms and categories, and (3) safeguarding certain doctrines. The following chart identifies several of these vital areas.

Foundational Issues of Apologetics and Theology				
Truth	Logic	Knowledge	Morality	God
The nature of truth	The nature of logic	The nature of knowledge	The objectivity of morality	His existence
Theories of truth	The laws of logic	The role of the senses in knowledge	Natural Law Theory	His attributes
Tests for truth	Answering objections to logic	Knowledge of immaterial things like metaphysics, logic, ethics, and God	Responding to objections to objective morality	Responding to objections to the existence and attributes of God

Clarifying the Meaning of Certain Terms and Categories		
Flesh v. Spirit	Nature/Essence	Biblical Inerrancy
Flesh v. spirit as material v. immaterial	Its philosophical use v. its theological use	Inerrancy and theories of truth
Flesh v. spirit as godly v. ungodly	The question of the two natures of Christ	Explaining alleged discrepancies in the Bible
Interrelationship between body and spirit/soul	The distinction between nature and function	Responding to objections to inerrancy
	The role of human nature in the question of morality	

Safeguarding Certain Doctrines of Apologetics and Theology			
Doctrine of God	Doctrine of Miracles	Doctrine of Inerrancy	Doctrine of Faith
Responding to the erosion of the classical attributes (immutability, eternality, etc.) of God in contemporary evangelicalism	A philosophy of miracles A theology of miracles An apologetic of miracles	Refuting liberalism Refuting neo-orthodoxy Refuting postmodernism	Defining and defending the nature of a reasonable faith Refuting the heresies of the Word of Faith movement

The Usefulness of Philosophy

It is true that some have been led astray by adopting bad philosophy. However, this should not deter believers who seek to defend the Christian faith and render it intelligible to a world that thinks critically. The fundamental question is not whether one does philosophy or possesses a philosophy—we all do both every day. Clearly, to reject all philosophy is self-defeating because to do so endorses the philosophy of nonphilosophy. Rather, the question is whether you have a good set of ideas and a philosophical framework for engaging in a deeper analysis of the fundamental characteristics of reality. Thomas Aquinas, with elegant simplicity, summed up the apologetic task of "always being prepared to make a defense [*apologia*] to *anyone*" (1 Peter 3:15, emphasis added) when he said, "[S]eeing that a teacher of sacred Scripture must at times oppose the philosophers, it is necessary for him to make use of philosophy."[17]

What Is Agnosticism, and
What Is Its Essential Flaw?

Richard G. Howe

The word *agnosticism* comes from the Greek word *gnosis*, meaning "knowledge," with the negation *a* (*a*-gnosticism) meaning "not" or "no." The word literally means "no knowledge." While one can lack knowledge about practically any subject and thus be said to be "agnostic" about that subject, often when people use the word they mean that they have a lack of knowledge or suspension of judgment on the question of God's existence.

In apologetic literature, one can find a distinction between soft agnosticism and hard agnosticism.[1] Soft agnostics simply acknowledge that they do not know whether God exists. Their lack of knowledge may stem from an ongoing (but not yet complete) examination of the evidence, or from a completed (as they see it) examination of the evidence that nevertheless has left them still agnostic, or from an indifference toward the question.[2]

Alternatively, hard agnostics not only say they do not know, but insist that no one else knows either. Such hard agnosticism usually stems from a skepticism regarding the human ability to know transcendent truths (such as truth claims about God). According to some agnostics, such inability might be a function of language itself[3] or of the nature of philosophy's ability to address the transcendent itself.[4]

The Flaws of Agnosticism

The major criticisms against agnosticism can be directed at the various forms of hard agnosticism that pose the most direct threat to whether one can have knowledge of God. The Christian apologist will try to demonstrate that truths about God and other immaterial aspects of reality can be sufficiently known to overcome any serious agnosticism. The first order of business is to examine the question of knowledge in general. This question is addressed in more detail in the chapter "How Can We Know Truth?" but a summary should suffice here.

When it comes to the different ways philosophers approach issues of knowledge or morality, I sometimes liken the dispute to the differences between engineering and reverse engineering. In engineering, a problem is identified (such as how to build a bridge across a certain expanse) and assessed. The engineer then gathers the relevant tools and materials to accomplish a task that solves the problem. However, in reverse engineering, the activity goes in the opposite direction. In a relevant sense, there is no problem to be solved. Instead, the solution is already present. Many of us probably learned the phrase *reverse engineering* when manufacturers attempted to take a computer chip from one company (the solution) and create another chip that performed the same function. What is needed, then, is not an effort to solve a problem, but an effort to understand the elements of the already-existing solution.

Likewise, different philosophers have endeavored to use philosophy to solve certain human problems. For example, even as far back as the ancient Greeks, the question of whether humans can know reality plagued certain philosophers. To settle the question, numerous assessments were made of the problem of, for example, can we know reality?[5] These philosophers then marshalled the intellectual tools and materials (e.g., categories, arguments) to try to solve the problem and decide whether knowledge (for example) was possible.

In contrast, the Aristotelian/Thomistic tradition (sometimes referred to as the classical tradition, though some classical thinkers might not be sympathetic to some of the philosophy of Aristotle or Thomas Aquinas) would not see philosophy as a method of discovering *whether* we have knowledge of reality. Instead, this tradition starts with the solution (humans have knowledge of reality inasmuch as it would be *self-refuting* to say that we do not) and, with the tools, methods, categories, and data that philosophy can provide, "reverse engineer" knowledge to see

how it is that we have it (instead of *whether* it is that we have it).

This classical tradition employs the view that says all knowledge begins in the senses and is completed in the intellect.[6] What this means is that our senses are able to bring to our intellect both physical and metaphysical truths. But it is the intellect that understands the data.[7] The eyes can deliver to the intellect that there is a brown dog in the yard. But it is the intellect that understands (the human knower understands by means of the intellect) that it is a dog (*what* it is, or essence); that when I say, "That is a brown dog," I am saying something true (truth corresponds to reality); that a dog is not a nondog (distinguishing mutually exclusive ideas by means of logic); that it exists (metaphysics); that there is a distinction between the dog's essence and its existence (metaphysics); that it is brown (a characteristic not essential to its nature is an accident); that it is beautiful (aesthetics); that it is valuable as a living being (value, ethics); that it is caused to exist by a being whose existence *is* its essence (metaphysics, philosophy of religion); and more. This is what Thomas Aquinas meant when he said, "Our knowledge, taking its start from things, proceeds in this order. First, it begins in sense; second, it is completed in the intellect."[8]

The importance of this should not be missed. Empiricism is the view that knowledge arises from the senses. Contemporary empiricism grants that knowledge begins in the senses. But it makes the mistake of thinking that it ends in the senses as well. This sometimes leads to the demonstrably absurd conclusion that there can be no truths about metaphysical issues.[9] The worst version of this misunderstanding of human knowing is called *scientism*. An example would be Richard Dawkins when he claims, "The presence or absence of a creative super-intelligence is unequivocally a scientific question, even if it is not in practice—or not yet—a decided one."[10] Dawkins, neither in his book *The God Delusion* nor in any other work of his with which I am familiar, advances any argument to this end. He merely imperializes over the question as to whether so-called science can, by its own tools and methods, settle the question of God's existence.

The fact is, our knowledge of certain metaphysical truths undeniably arises from our empirical encounter with sensible objects (cf. Romans 1:19-21). This has been done throughout human history. From what we see, hear, taste touch, and smell, philosophers from Aristotle onward through Thomas Aquinas and beyond have come to conclusions about logic, metaphysics, ethics, and God. This is not to say that any given philosopher was right in every detail. But occasional mistakes (even big ones) do not disqualify this classical empiricism.[11]

The bottom line here is that it is self-refuting to say that we cannot truly know reality. But what does this have to do with agnosticism? After all, agnosticism (in this context) does not deny that knowledge of reality is possible. Instead, agnosticism says that knowledge specifically of God is either not possible or at least not actual. Presumably, even Richard Dawkins, while being an atheist, is not a skeptic.

The reason for raising the specter of skepticism is to set the groundwork for knowledge in general to show that once we understand how basic knowledge of reality comes about, we are in a position to see how knowledge of God is possible—indeed, is actual. To see how this is so, let us expand upon an earlier point. Our encounter with sensible objects lets us come to know of

philosophical categories such as causality, natures or essences, teleology and existence. All of these (and more) are metaphysical truths that we come to know upon our apprehension of the physical objects we encounter. As chapter 12 ("What Are the Classical Proofs for God's Existence?") says in more detail, these metaphysical truths are, at the same time, metaphysical truths that even atheistic science cannot do without, and truths that demonstrate that God exists.

Can We Know Everything About God?

I would be remiss if I did not deal with one last important point. When I argue that agnosticism about God's existence is unwarranted, I do not mean that a level of agnosticism about God is completely unwarranted. But the reasons for this (perhaps ironically) bolster the case for the God of classical Christianity. When the classical tradition says that we can know sensible reality, this means that, at a metaphysical level, the knower becomes the thing known. As odd as this sounds, it makes perfect sense once its meaning is made clear. In Aristotle, as well as in Thomas Aquinas, a thing is the kind of thing it is because of its Form. Form is that metaphysical aspect of a thing by virtue of which it is the kind of thing it is. It might help to think of Form as a definition, although it is not merely verbal, but is a real constituent of a thing. The intellect of the knower, upon the encounter with the thing by means of the senses, is able to abstract the Form into itself. The intellect of the knower formally becomes the thing it knows because the same Form that is in the particular object known is also at the same time in the intellect of the knower. Aristotle used the illustration of a signet ring being pressed into wax. The form of the ring remains in the wax without any of the matter from the ring itself. The form is simultaneously in both the ring and the wax.[12]

This might be fine with regard to how we know physical objects, but how does this explain how we know God? The short answer is that it does not—at least not directly. Because God is not a physical object and does not "have" a Form,[13] then this understanding of knowledge cannot account for how we know God. But this does not leave us in complete agnosticism about God.

Our knowledge of God is a process of reasoning from effects to cause. Even with physical objects we sometimes reason this way. For example, we can see a pile of ashes and reason to the previous existence of the fire, even though we did not directly see the fire. Similarly, we can reason from the effects of God in His creation and come to conclude

what the Cause of those effects must be like. Our knowledge of the physical world can demonstrate that there is a Creator of this world that is eternal, simple, omnipotent, omniscient, all-loving, and personal.[14] One need only consult the relevant primary and secondary sources in the classical philosophical tradition for the details of what this demonstration looks like. When one marries (1) what we can know from reason's attendance to the metaphysical truths knowable in sensible objects with (2) the truths about God that God Himself has revealed to us in His Word, the Bible, then we have all the knowledge of God we need or could have in this world.

As the apostle John said in 1 John 3:2, "Beloved, we are God's children now, and what we will be has not yet appeared; but we know that when he appears we shall be like him, because we shall see him as he is."

What Is Materialism, and What Is Its Essential Flaw?

Mark M. Hanna

The philosopher Bertrand Russell attributed the following quip to his grandmother: "What is mind? No matter. What is matter? Never mind."[1] This quip nicely encapsulates the two false worldviews of idealism and materialism. Christian theism, however, recognizes the reality of both mind and matter.

This chapter explains philosophical materialism and shows why it is not rationally tenable. Its fundamental claim is that the whole of reality consists of matter, which is generally understood to be whatever physicists say it is—namely, the fundamental wave-particles of quantum mechanics. But quantum mechanics is not well understood, and many physicists speculate that there is something even more fundamental, such as a quantum vacuum or "strings" in multiple dimensions. In physics, then, the term *matter* does not refer to solid, three-dimensional stuff, but rather to a hidden microworld of subatomic constituents. Yet no one knows how this microworld brings about the macroworld of our everyday lives with all of its qualitative diversity.

What Is Philosophical Materialism?

First, we must distinguish between philosophical materialism and cultural materialism. *Cultural materialism* is the pursuit of money and the things money can buy above all else. *Philosophical materialism* comes in two main versions: eliminative materialism, also known as reductive materialism, and emergent materialism, also known as nonreductive materialism.

Before explaining the differences between these two versions, I would like to list some tenets that generally describe philosophical materialism (henceforth referred to as materialism):

1. As its name indicates, materialism assumes that *all* of reality is *fundamentally* composed of matter.

2. The physical domain is a causally closed system in space and time.

3. The universe is the result of purely physical laws and physical processes having evolved into its present form

from a quantum substrate into atoms, molecules, stars, planets, diverse flora and fauna, and human beings.

4. There are no immaterial or supernatural entities that exist and interfere with physical processes.

5. All genuine and final explanation is from the bottom up, never from the top down.

6. Any features of the world that cannot be satisfactorily explained at present will eventually be explained in purely physical terms, if they can be explained at all.

7. The methods of the natural sciences are the only way to discover the truth and to gain knowledge, and because literally everything depends upon and derives from physics, it is the final arbiter of truth and knowledge.

Assessing the Tenets of Materialism

Because space doesn't allow for detailed rebuttals of each of these seven tenets, I will provide short one-sentence responses below before elaborating on the major flaw of materialism.

1. No one, not scientists nor philosophers nor anyone else, is in a position to know that *all* of reality is composed of matter; furthermore, undeniable nonphysical phenomena show the falsity of such an assumption.

2. No one is in a position to know that the physical domain is a causally closed system; any such assumption results from confusing

methodological naturalism with philosophical naturalism.

3. The laws of physics are not themselves physical, and without the transcendent laws of nature that form the broad context of physical processes, the universe and its specific contents and features could not exist.

4. No one is in a position to know that no immaterial or supernatural realities exist and possess causal power to affect the world.

5. Some explanations are bottom-up, and others are top-down, with a necessary and sufficient explanation being top-down, thereby explaining the possibility of all secondary explanations.

6. This is a promissory note that no one can guarantee to be fulfilled, for it is a wishful hope that raises many questions and fails to satisfactorily answer them.

7. To say that the natural sciences are the only way to gain truth and knowledge is to assert that which is self-refuting, for this claim itself is not a scientific one but a philosophical one.

Not only are there no good reasons to believe any of the materialist's claims, there are very good reasons to reject them.

Distinguishing Emergent Materialism from Eliminative Materialism

First, eliminative materialism is self-refuting, for consciousness and meanings are necessary to make the claim that *everything* is physical, but both consciousness and meanings are nonphysical. Further, the claim itself cannot be known to be true, because it entails that literally everything—including all meanings, claims and beliefs—is predetermined by blind, purposeless physical causes.

Second, eliminative materialism, which asserts the identity of the mind with the brain, cannot explain how a physical entity, the brain, can have nonphysical properties, such as consciousness, a personal point of view, subjectively privileged access, qualia (the qualitative aspects of experiencing, such as the feeling of pain), intentionality (the "aboutness" of most mental states), and free will (the uncoerced ability to decide among various options). No matter how closely the brain is examined, none of these properties can be found in it or in any other physical entity. Yet one cannot deny the reality of these nonphysical properties, for any attempt to deny them implicitly acknowledges them by *necessarily* experiencing and using them.

Eliminative materialists claim that consciousness is an illusion. However, if anything is an illusion, there is always some consciousness for which it is an illusion. There is no way to argue oneself out of mental states without having mental states. The following argument shows the fundamental flaw in eliminative materialism.

1. If eliminative materialism is true, then *consciousness* is an illusion.

2. But there cannot be an illusion without a *conscious* subject to whom it would be an illusion.

3. Therefore, eliminative materialism is false.

No matter how hard they try, materialists

cannot circumvent or solve "the hard problem of consciousness."

These considerations have led many philosophers to adopt a different kind of materialism called *emergent materialism*, which holds that the mind is not the brain, but emerges from the brain and is wholly controlled by the brain even though the mind is nonphysical. Although qualitatively different from the brain, the mind supposedly emerges from the brain when the latter reaches a certain level of complexity.

Accordingly, the mind is called an *epiphenomenon*, for it is a new property that supervenes on the brain from which it has emerged. The causal relation is only from the brain to the mind, not the reverse. One of several cogent arguments against emergent materialism is as follows:

1. If emergent materialism is true, then the mind is an epiphenomenon that has no causal powers.

2. But mutual mind-body causal interaction is an immediate datum of experience that is known better than any theory that would deny it.

3. Therefore, emergent materialism is false.

Two Kinds of Emergence

The following analogy is often used to try to elucidate what is meant by a new property emerging out of a substrate that does not itself exhibit that property. Neither hydrogen nor oxygen has the property of wetness, but when two parts of hydrogen and one part of oxygen are combined to comprise a water molecule, the property of wetness emerges.

However, this analogy is not accurate, for it ignores the profound difference between physical and nonphysical properties. The mind that supposedly emerges from the brain is not anything like a physical property, such as wetness. The mind is *intrinsically* different from anything physical. More correctly, the analogy is one that involves a radical difference in the nature of the source and the epiphenomenon of a supposed emergence, such as the personal from the impersonal, or intelligence from nonintelligence.

But an appeal to the latter kinds of supposed emergence doesn't help the emergent materialist at all; rather, it only exacerbates his problem, for such assumed cases of emergence would be as inexplicable as the claim that the mind emerges from the brain. The emergent materialist first *assumes* that physicality is all there is. Then when he is confronted with the undeniability of consciousness and its nonphysical properties, he has no alternative but to believe that the mind *must* have emerged from the brain. He has painted himself into a corner, leaving himself no other option.

The Uniqueness of the Mind

Moreover, either the mind, which is the allegedly emergent epiphenomenon, must somehow already be in the brain (at least latently), or the mind has emerged from nothing, a new reality intrinsically different from the physical brain. There is no evidence for the former alternative, and there is no possibility of the latter alternative.

Essential to emergentism is the claim that the mind is something nonphysical, and therefore, its nature contrasts fundamentally with the brain, which is physical. The materialist is in a quandary, for he has rejected the view that the mind and brain are two different substances because he thinks it would create the insuperable problem of explaining how

two such intrinsically different things could relate to one another and causally affect one another. But if he claims that the mind must somehow be in the brain and emerges from it, he is faced with the same kind of problem. How can the physical and nonphysical relate to one another in the brain?

There is no evidence whatsoever that the mind, whether viewed as a property or entity, is in the brain. Neither an MRI nor an electron microscope has ever found anything like mental states or qualia in a brain. To think that one could find such phenomena in mere physicality is to commit an egregious category mistake—a fallacy as glaringly wrong as believing that the number 3 tastes like an orange or a thought weighs ten ounces.

The emergent materialist is limited to two unviable options: He must hold that either the mind is somehow in the brain, or that mind is the generation of something out of nothing. Both alternatives are insuperable problems for a materialist, for his fundamental assumptions are (1) that the brain is wholly physical, having no inherent mental properties, and (2) that no event can come from nothing, but must have a physical cause. He can tell us nothing, however, about how a physical cause can produce anything nonphysical, like a mind.

Conclusion

If humans consist of nothing more than physical components, then why is it that physical things do not bring ultimate satisfaction? John Stuart Mill expressed the point in a memorable line: "It is better to be a human being dissatisfied than a pig satisfied."[2] Even philosophers who are materialists want more than the mere satisfaction of their physical needs and desires. They want to be on the right side of every intellectual issue they discuss, they want their views to be self-consistent, they want to be respected, they want to love and to be loved. No electrons or quarks ever envisaged such values or had such longings.

Again, if humans are made of nothing more than atoms, why do we desire things that go far beyond mere physicality and the satisfaction of physical needs and wants? Materialism is incapable of providing a satisfactory answer to this question. The only answer that makes sense of the human condition is that we are more than the physical constituents that compose our bodies.

To come to grips with the "more" beyond the physicality of the body is to be on the path not only to authentic self-understanding but also to a true understanding of the nature of ultimate reality, namely, of the Creator who made us and joined together both body and soul.

Speaking to the philosophers of his day, including Epicureans who were atomistic materialists, the apostle Paul emphasized that humans have not only a body but also a soul, one that is made in the image of God. "The God who made the world and everything in it...gives to all mankind life and breath and everything...Being then God's offspring, we ought not to think that the divine being is like gold or silver or stone, an image formed by the art and imagination of man" (Acts 17:24-29).

59

What Is Rationalism, and What Is Its Essential Flaw?

Richard G. Howe

Rationalism is a model of how human knowledge is acquired, having a venerable history in philosophy. Socrates (470–399 BC), Plato (428–348 BC), Descartes (1596–1650), Spinoza (1632–1677), and Leibniz (1646–1716) were all rationalists.

Generally speaking, rationalism stands in contrast to empiricism. Unlike empiricism, which says that knowledge begins in or is confined to the senses, rationalism maintains that at least some (if not all) knowledge arises from reason. However, the specifics of rationalism are easy to miss given the theory's name, because everyone desires to be rational. Even empiricism acknowledges that reason must play a role in acquiring knowledge. Merely saying that reason has a role in acquiring knowledge is not enough to make a model rationalism. One can be rational without being a rationalist.

Rationalism insists there are certain aspects of reality that are accessible only by reason, and not by the senses alone. In addition, rationalists often regard truths about mathematics, logic, and (for some) ethics as knowable only because the human mind either possesses such truths innately (i.e., naturally present at birth) or has the capacity to grasp these immaterial aspects of the real world, which is external to the mind.

Some Examples of Rationalists

Socrates and Plato

Because there are no extant writings from Socrates, most of what we know about him comes from his student Plato. For our purposes, we can treat their rationalism as being the same. Plato believed that reality was composed of two realms. The first of these is the transcendent world of *being*, where all the Forms reside. For Plato, the Forms were transcendent, eternal, immutable, intelligible, archetypal, and perfect realities.[1] They are the only things that are fully real.

The second realm is below, which is the realm of *becoming*. Here is where all the physical objects reside. They are spatio-temporal, changeable, sensible, copied, and imperfect. Though in Plato's estimation physical objects were not unreal, he considered them less real than the Forms. To make this clearer, Plato used the illustration of how a thing might relate to its shadow. Namely, while the shadow is not unreal, it is less real than the thing of which it is a shadow.

Plato's rationalism maintained that we as humans preexisted with the Forms and subsequently were incarnated on Earth. According to this view, all our knowledge of the Forms was forgotten due to the trauma of being born. Consequently, learning in this life is a process of recollecting our knowledge from our previous lives with the Forms. This recollection is triggered by our encounters with the physical objects of this realm. Though Plato held that sensory experience is the occasion for such recollection, he regarded sensory experience as unreliable and potentially deceptive. In his work *Meno*, Plato (through the mouth of Socrates) took an uneducated slave boy and, through a series of questions, enabled the boy to recite the Pythagorean theorem. According to Plato, because the slave boy had never learned the theorem in this life, the only way he could have recited it is that he was recollecting it from his previous life with the Forms.

Descartes

Rationalism is found not only in ancient Greek thought and in subsequent non-Christian thought (Spinoza), it is also found in Christians like René Descartes. Descartes is regarded as the father of modern philosophy. In certain circles, Descartes is more famous for his contributions to mathematics. He and Pierre de Fermat helped to discover analytic geometry.

Unlike Plato, Descartes's rationalist model of knowing did not include any notion of a transcendent realm of Forms or of preexistence. Instead, Descartes believed

that by the rational act of intuition, humans could grasp—with their reason—basic, undoubtable truths of reality. From those truths, through a process of logical deduction, humans could conclude further truths. He applied the "geometric method" borrowed from his mathematics to try to demonstrate philosophical truths—most importantly the existence of God. The process involved the demonstration of the existence of the self, the existence of God, and the existence of the material world.

The Essential Flaw of Rationalism

Critiques of rationalism can be subtle and complicated. It is unavoidable that critiques of rationalism (a theory of knowledge) spill over into a discussion of metaphysics (theories of the nature of reality itself). This is not necessarily a weakness of rationalism, as classical empiricism will insist that questions about the knowledge of reality must ultimately be framed in terms of the nature of reality as such. Indeed, it would seem that any theory of how we know reality would implicitly or explicitly entail a theory of the nature of reality itself.

Rationalism and the Nature of Reality. The differences between rationalism and empiricism revolve around the nature of those things that we know by means of our intellect. Some rationalists regard logic, numbers, the principles of mathematics, properties, propositions, and (for some) the categories of ethics as abstract objects (sometimes called universals). They maintain that these abstract objects are real, immaterial entities that cannot be grasped by the senses, but rather, by reason. In important respects, they are not unlike Plato's Forms.

Some who believe in the existence of

abstract objects believe that these objects are eternal and self-existing. (In the rationalist's view, it cannot be the case that the number two came into existence a finite amount of time ago.) If there are abstract objects, then they could not have been created by God, or they would be as eternal and self-existent as God is. For some Christians, this is an affront to God's role as the Creator of all things other than Himself (John 1:3; Colossians 1:16-17).[2]

Some rationalists do not explicitly hold that the objects the mind knows are abstract objects co-eternal with God. Descartes did not seem to hold to the notion of abstract objects. Instead, these abstracts (not Descartes's word) were found in immaterial minds—both human minds and God's mind. What is more, Descartes held that these abstracts were created by God such that if He wanted, He could have made 2 + 2 equal 5. But, given that God created 2 + 2 to equal 4, human minds (which are immaterial) are able to know such truths intuitively (apart from sense experience).

Critics of Descartes's rationalism would deny that 2 + 2 = 4 is anything less than an absolute and unchangeable truth of the nature of reality.[3] But how could one protect the inviolate status of mathematics or logic or other seemingly abstract truths and, at the same time, avoid the problem of saying that such abstract truths are objects whose realities are co-eternal with God?

Rationalism and the Classical Tradition of Aristotle and Thomas Aquinas. There have been alternatives to the rationalism of Plato and Descartes.[4] First, there are variations of the theory known as *nominalism*, which denies any reality whatsoever to any abstractions. That is to say, nominalism maintains that such abstractions are nothing more than names we assign to certain ways that the human mind thinks about the world. William of Ockham (1287?–1347?) is the philosopher who first comes to mind when thinking about nominalism.

Unfortunately, in too many situations, philosophers assume the only choices they have are (1) a commitment to the reality of independently existing abstract objects, or (2) nominalism. Fortunately, the classical tradition strikes a middle ground known as *moderate realism* (or *scholastic realism*). This is the view of Aristotle and Thomas Aquinas. It says that abstracts (more often called universals) do exist, but only as abstracted from sensible objects by the intellect. Moderate realism says that universals do not exist independently of intellects, as Plato would have it. But the universal in an intellect is not merely a name we give to our ideas (per nominalism), as William of Ockham would have it. Instead, the universal that exists in an intellect arises from something that is metaphysically real (has being) in the physical object that we know. This reality is known as the Form.

But unlike the Forms of Plato, which are independent, transcendent objects, the Forms of Aristotle and Aquinas are particular, real constituents of individual objects that make the individual object the kind of thing it is. For Aristotle, there would be no universals if there were no human intellects, since human intellects are the only places they reside as universals. For Aquinas, these universals also exist in the mind of God as their Creator. Some of these universals (like logic or goodness) reflect fundamental aspects of being itself and, thus, characterize the nature of God. While others (like redness) reflect aspects of qualified being (like physical) and, thus, do not point to anything in God beside the fact that He is their Creator.

The Data to Know Something About God

To be certain, Christians strive to be sober and rational at all times, but fortunately, one need not adopt rationalism to do so. For Christian apologists and theologians, it is important to recognize that our model for acquiring knowledge must be grounded in reality. The reasons for this should be obvious, because leaving reality in one's quest for knowledge provides no anchor or ground of correspondence to test the veracity of the ideas themselves. Moreover, it also appears that once an empirical approach (or moderate realism) is abandoned, we would find it difficult to discover any objective reason for why others should embrace Christ.

Thankfully, God has created a world that is intelligible, a world that has been situated in the best possible way to promote discovery, which, in turn, provides our senses with the data to know something about God. The apostle Paul affirmed that knowledge of God can be clearly understood by the human mind: "What can be known about God is plain to them, because God has shown it to them. For his invisible attributes, namely, his eternal power and divine nature, have been clearly perceived, ever since the creation of the world, in the things that have been made. So they are without excuse" (Romans 1:19-21).

What Is Scientism, and What Is Its Essential Flaw?

Douglas E. Potter

Scientism is the view that says something is true only if it is proved through modern scientific methodology. In general, the scientific method involves careful observation of phenomena, the forming of hypotheses based on those observations, experiments to test the hypotheses, and the use of results to establish a theory.

John Wellmuth, in his 1944 lecture critiquing scientism, said it is thought to "afford the only reliable natural means of acquiring such knowledge as may be available about whatever is real."[1] According to scientism, anything that is not able to incorporate scientific methods cannot be considered true or rational. In effect, it is saying this: That which cannot be observed and tested does not exist. Essentially, it is a commitment to a way of knowing that leads to materialism. If this view is correct, it leaves subjects such as theology out of the marketplace of truth.

Historical Background

Scientism is historically rooted in positivism, which began with the French atheistic philosopher Auguste Comte (1798–1857). He wrote a series of books titled *Discourse on the Positive Spirit* (1830). It was here that he argued for positivism in science and a humanistic sociology. Comte confessed to losing belief in God early in his life. He was influenced by atheism and materialism, and saw the possibility of positivism in the world formed by our minds. This he called the absolutizing of the relative, or the method of the positive sciences. Comte rejected all supernatural claims and embraced the world in terms of a regulated system of general forces. That which is real, he said, attaches to the positivistic view by the law that says, If a proposition cannot be reduced to a fact, it is unable to give any real or intelligible meaning.[2] Even in his own day, Comte's ideas did not escape critique.[3]

Following in the footsteps of Comte was A.J. Ayer (1910–1989), a British humanist and member of the Vienna Circle. In his book *Language, Truth and Logic* (1936), he put forward what he called the principle of verification. Ayer also saw theology and metaphysics as meaningless. Therefore, science and its overlapping fields are the only means to arrive at truth. His principle of verification rested on two points:

First, that things must be verifiable in practice or in principle. If in practice, it means something can be verified now—for example, "We can study life on earth." If in principle, it means it might be verified in the future—for example, "There is life on other planets."

Second, only weak verification is possible, which is at best probable and subject to future correction. Early positivists suggested certitude in science as possible, but this was quickly abandoned. In fact, Ayer had to make several qualifications to his principle of verification. This ultimately led to its abandonment. It was the teaching and influence of Ayer that C.S. Lewis had in mind when he penned *The Abolition of Man*.[4]

Scientism Today

As a philosophical movement, positivism is dead.[5] However, the threat of scientism today is its power and appeal to the populace—what C.S. Lewis called "the sweet poison of the false infinite."[6] Many today still believe science is king when it comes to knowing, and nothing else compares.

J.P. Moreland and William Lane Craig identify both a strong and weak version of scientism that still emanates with many.[7] Strong scientism says knowledge must be established by the scientific method. There is no real or solid truth apart from scientific truths. Weak scientism says knowledge established by the scientific method is the most authoritative kind of knowledge. Strong scientism holds that the truths contained in metaphysics and theology are unknowable. For weak scientism, areas such as theology or philosophy must look for science to ultimately provide any legitimacy to their

pursuit. Apart from this, there is no rational or true knowledge.

Evaluation of Scientism

There is no reason to think that the scientific method is the only road to truth. The scientific method deals only with observable phenomena in the world, and therefore, is limited. Science as a subject of study is based on inductive reasoning and evidence. It must form a hypothesis, and then test the hypothesis to see if any revision or correction is necessary. At best, it can give us only a strong probability that something is true. As the history of science has shown, the scientific method does not always arrive at the correct conclusion. Time and again, subsequent generations of scientists have come along and refuted the research of earlier scientists.[8] Without a doubt, some scientific discoveries are more certain than others. That the earth is round, a certain size, weight, and astronomical location may be as certain as possible, as far as our knowledge goes. Even what a human being is, biologically speaking, is at least accepted as certain. But it is not *ultimate* in the sense that science has discovered the purpose or meaning of human life on earth—which it hasn't.[9]

Further, not everything scientists study is able to be subjected to the scientific method. When the natural sciences investigate past singularities (i.e., things that occurred once in the past), such as the origin of the universe or first life, it is not using the scientific method. Singular events that are unrepeatable require a more forensic type of investigation. This is especially true with regard to the debate over biological evolution.[10]

No one has shown that other disciplines are unable to arrive at truth. Indeed, as Wellmuth said in his lecture,

The scientific method, as employed in modern science, admittedly rests on many assumptions regarding the nature of truth and criteria for distinguishing between truth and error, as well as on a more or less definite aggregate of useful beliefs which are explicitly referred to nowadays as "the faith of the scientists."[11]

The Fatal Flaw of Scientism

The logical argument against scientism can be put like this:

1. All self–defeating statements are necessarily false.

2. The affirmation of scientism is self–defeating.

3. Therefore, scientism is false.

The fundamental flaw that haunts scientism is the fact that it is self-defeating. Self-defeating statements explicitly claim one thing is true and implicitly claim its opposite is true at the same time. Hence, it is necessarily false. Scientism puts forward a statement or principle that says, "Only what can be established by science is true." The truthfulness of this statement, however, is not something established by science; therefore, the statement itself cannot be true. That's why it is self-defeating or false. What is more, neither is the scientific method established by the scientific method. Science presupposes many truths that it is unable to establish.

Some Truth Not Established by Science

As others have shown,[12] science is dependent upon many truths discovered outside the domain of science. Some of these include

(1) the knowability of the world, (2) the absolute nature of truth, (3) the uniformity of nature, (4) the laws of logic, (5) mathematics, and (6) ethics.

Knowing the World. The answer to the question about the world being knowable is unable to be established by science. To say we must prove or justify that we know the world is to follow in the footsteps of the French mathematician René Descartes, who began with doubt and questioned the reliability of our senses. *That* we know, however, is undeniable. Saying, "No one knows reality" is self–defeating, for you must at least know *that* reality. It may indeed be that "knowing," because it is undeniable that we do know, is something that happens to be evident to us and is not subject to philosophical justification. At least such a justification could never be more convincing than the actual *act* of knowing reality. As such, intellectual "knowing" may only be open to philosophical description rather than in need of justification.[13]

The Absolute Nature of Truth. The definition of truth, as affirmed by Aristotle, is that which corresponds to reality, or the way things really are. As such, truth must be absolute as opposed to relative. Relative truth is self-defeating—for someone to be able to say, "All truth is relative" depends on an absolute truth. To put it another way, the statement itself is an absolute truth claim. In addition, if truth was relative, science as a discipline would be impossible, for something affirmed as true in one place or time could be affirmed as false at another place or time. There would be no sense of reliable or firm laws for science to lean on. Truth being absolute does not mean our grasp of truth is absolute. We may, as some scientists say, be able to do nothing more than approximate some truths.

But even this understanding of truth is not established science. Science may change, and finite minds will always be limited. But truth itself does not change.

Uniformity of Nature. Scientific methodology is dependent upon the uniformity of nature. The principle of uniformity states that causes and effects observed in the present are at least similar to causes and effects in the past. This affects science's ability to describe reality by various laws. But nothing in science can establish the truth of this principle. Nor does anything in science decide which paradigm or philosophy is the correct one to account for the principle itself.

Laws of Logic. The basic laws of logic are undeniable and govern our thinking correctly about reality. This is a material logic as opposed to a symbolic logic.[14] Science depends upon the laws of logic, such as the law of noncontradiction (A is not non-A), the law of identity (A is A), and the law of excluded middle (either A or non–A). Without these laws and the ability to detect formal and informal fallacies, all correct human thinking, not to mention science, would be impossible.

Mathematics. Like logic, math deals with nonmaterial realities science cannot touch. Science and math are deeply interconnected. Science may help verify the application of math to reality, but science as a method does not establish the proofs and theorems related to mathematical abstract thinking. Further, any debate about the nature of math or numbers would not concern math or science, but a philosophy of mathematics.

Ethics. Finally, science does not establish moral values or ethics—that is, what is right or wrong. Rather, ethical truths should guide what is done with scientific knowledge. Even if the technology resulting from scientific knowledge is morally neutral, there are moral implications. Science may have given us the atomic bomb, but it does not give us the morality that governs its use. This moral truth is beyond the discovery of scientific inquiry.

Metaphysics and Theology

Nothing has shown metaphysics, as a branch of philosophy, to be impossible. Indeed, metaphysics is the most fundamental of all studies. It studies reality and existence, also called *being.* It explores the nature of existence and the kinds of existence things can have. In short, it studies being as *being.* And it is a great mistake to force the methodology of science, math, or any other discipline into metaphysics to legitimize it.[15] All other subjects study existence as some *thing.* Physics studies the motion of things, biology studies living things, chemistry studies the matter of things, etc. Therefore, because the things that science studies are different than what metaphysics studies, the methodology is different.

Metaphysics identifies and uses undeniable first principles. For example, "something exists" is an undeniable statement about reality. If I say, "Nothing exists," I am affirming my own existence (for I would have to exist to make the statement), which makes my statement self-defeating. These principles are exhaustively known and demonstrate their own truthfulness. Such first principles undergird all other subjects, such as science, even if they do not acknowledge it.

Sound and valid arguments for the existence of God can be reducible to such intuitive and certain first principles. Therefore, these kinds of arguments for the existence of God show that science is not the only road to certain realities.[16] All this reasoning is done outside and independent of science.

Such reasoning is involved in the defense and construction of a theistic worldview, through which all facts, including scientific ones, are interpreted. None of this needs to involve the scientific method or needs scientific justification. Even the scientist will adopt or reject such a theistic worldview. But if the theistic worldview is true, then miracles and revelation from God are possible and defensible. Truth can indeed be found outside of science.

Summary of Scientism

Scientism, the belief that only science can give us truth about what is real, is still evidenced widely in our culture. A key reason for this is society's enormous emphasis on scientific discoveries and technological advancements. However, scientism is ultimately self-defeating and assumes many truths established by nonscientific means. Metaphysics, theology, and many other nonscientific fields of study can help establish truths appropriate to their objects of study and proportionate to their methods and reasoning.

What Is Moral Relativism, and What Is Its Essential Flaw?

Sean McDowell

A few years ago, when I was teaching Bible full-time at a Christian high school, I moderated a public debate between three of my Christian students and three atheist/agnostic students from a local freethinking club. Topics included the merits of intelligent design and Darwinian evolution, the evidence for the historical Jesus, and whether God or atheism best explains the origin of morality.

During the discussion on morality, one of my students argued that God is the best explanation for objective moral values. In other words, she argued that there are objective moral values and duties that human behavior universally reveals, so there must be a "Moral Lawgiver." In response, one of the freethinking students argued that there is no objective morality, that values are relative to the individual, and thus there is no need for God.[1]

But when it was time for the closing speeches, the same freethinking student took the opportunity to use the church setting to criticize Christians for being homophobic, bigoted, and intolerant. His goal was to shame Christians for their supposed intolerance.

Initially my students didn't realize it, but his closing speech highlighted the essential flaw of moral relativism: *the impossibility of living it out with consistency.* After all, during the debate, he defended individual moral relativism, but then during his closing speech, he criticized Christians for violating moral norms that he felt they *should* have known and followed.

Do you see the inconsistency? In two separate utterances, he contradicted himself by proclaiming two contrary ideas. He essentially said, "Moral values are relative to the individual. But you bigoted Christians have violated universal moral norms and should have known differently." He defended moral relativism in the debate, but because he was made in the image of God and he possessed a moral conscience that allowed him to know objective morality (see Romans 2:14-16), he failed to live his relativist beliefs with consistency.

My point is not to pick on this high school student. After all, he was still a teenager, and of course he was still developing his worldview. However, in his classic book *Mere Christianity*, C.S. Lewis observed that this same mistake is a common one. There are many who claim to believe morality is relative, but their lives betray them:

> Whenever you find a man who says he does not believe in a real Right and Wrong, you will find that same man going back on this a moment later. He may break his promise to you, but if you try breaking one to him he will be complaining, "It's not fair" before you can say Jack Robinson.[2]

My father shared with me a principle that makes this same point. He once told me, "We can know what people believe not by what they say or do, but by how they want to be treated." In other words, as C.S. Lewis observed, people will violate moral principles when it is convenient for them to do so. But when *others* violate moral principles in a way that affects them, they cry foul. It is not someone's *actions* that reveal their views on morality, but his or her *reactions*.

Moral Relativism: Individual and Cultural

Before we consider specific flaws of moral relativism, it is important to clarify our terms. There are two kinds of moral relativism: cultural relativism and individual relativism. *Cultural relativism* is the belief that the rightness or wrongness of an action is determined by the culture. What is wrong in one culture, therefore, may be right in another. *Individual relativism* is the belief that the individual person determines moral values. Thus, there is no objective standard beyond what a person believes is morally right or wrong for himself or herself.

Moral relativism is different from religious or historical relativism. According to religious relativism, there is no one religion that is true for all individuals or cultures. Religions may be true for some people but not others. And according to historical relativism, historical "facts" are relative to the person or group who believes them. By contrast, moral relativism is a distinctly *ethical* claim about the source of right and wrong. Simply put, moral relativism is the rejection of objective morality and the belief that morals are relative to the individual or society.

What About Moral Differences?

Perhaps the most common argument for moral relativism stems from the observation that morality seems to vary across cultures and time. After all, penalties for stealing are quite different in the West than in the Middle East. And people are quite divided over moral issues like abortion and race. Don't such differences prove morality is relative?

Those who ask this question are confusing moral *practices* and moral *principles*. Yes, moral practices do vary across cultures, but the underlying moral principles do not. Take the issue of abortion. Opposing sides are certainly divided over the moral status of abortion. Yet despite their differences, both sides believe in mercy and justice. Those who are pro-choice tend to emphasize justice and mercy for the mother, whereas those who are pro-life emphasize justice and mercy for the mother *and* the unborn. Both sides believe in objective morality, but they differ over how they apply moral principles. In fact, both sides believe (for the most part) that human persons have the right to life. But they differ over whether or not the unborn qualify as human persons.

My point is not to argue that both sides are morally equivalent. I am firmly pro-life and believe abortion involves the unjustified ending of a precious human life. But we should not assume that everyone who is pro-choice is also a relativist. Rather, there are some who are simply deeply mistaken about the relevant scientific and philosophical facts, and thus they come to the wrong moral conclusions.

As C.S. Lewis has observed, what is most striking about the moral codes of various cultures throughout history is not their differences, but their similarities:

> Think of a country where people were admired for running away in battle, or where a man felt proud of double-crossing all the people who had been kindest to him. You might just as well try to imagine a country where two and two made five.[3]

Cultures often vary on moral practices, but the underlying principles of courage, selflessness, and faithfulness are universal.

Nevertheless, even if morals *did* differ across cultures, moral relativism would not necessarily follow. Here's why: *nothing follows logically from disagreement.* After all, people differ on historical, scientific, and mathematical claims, and relativism does not necessarily follow for these disciplines. Differences of opinion and belief do not imply the absence of objective truth. It may simply indicate that people differ over what is true.

Three Flaws with Cultural Relativism

As we saw earlier, the core problem with moral relativism is those who adhere to it are not consistent about how they practice it. Even for those who claim to be relativists,

a deep commitment to objective morality will eventually bubble to the surface. Let's consider three specific flaws that make this reality evident.

First, cultural relativists cannot consistently embrace moral reformers. A moral reformer is someone who criticizes the moral code of a society (typically from within) and proclaims it in need of transformation. Well-known moral reformers include Dietrich Bonhoeffer, Gandhi, Martin Luther King Jr., and Jesus Christ. Yet if cultural relativism is true, and everyone ought to act consistently with the rest of society, then by definition the moral reformer is the one who is mistaken, because he or she is condemning the moral code of a given society. Yet this is absurd. Consider the fact that moral reformers who have condemned slavery, bigotry, Nazism, and other evils are viewed as being heroic.

Second, cultural relativists cannot consistently critique other cultures as immoral. If cultural relativism were true, then no one could rightfully condemn the actions of another culture since, by definition, whatever a culture believes is morally right for that culture. If a society's standards were the basis of morality, then we would be in the awkward position of justifying slavery, the practice of Sati, cannibalism, genocide, and ultimately *any* moral behavior adopted by a given society. Yet our deepest intuitions reveal that some things are wrong regardless of societal standards. If there is at least one universally wrong action (e.g., slavery), then cultural relativism is false.

Third, cultural relativists cannot consistently promote tolerance as a virtue. Years ago I was in a conversation with an Ivy League professor who embraced cultural relativism. After arguing that there was no objective moral standard beyond culture, he concluded that we should therefore be tolerant of various cultural norms. By tolerance, he meant that we should recognize and respect that every culture's values, truth claims, beliefs, and practices are equally valid.[4]

Did you notice the inconsistency? He argued for cultural relativism, but then he turned around and promoted tolerance as a *meta*cultural standard. Here's the rub: If morals are relative to culture, as he proclaimed, then tolerance is merely relative to *his* culture and he should not try to force it on others. But, if we truly ought to be tolerant, as he *also* proclaimed, then cultural relativism is false. Either way, he fell victim to the essential flaw in relativism: the inability to live it out with consistency.

Three Flaws with Individual Relativism

People who hold to individual relativism also fail to live it out with consistency. Here are three ways this inconsistency becomes evident.

First, relativists cannot consistently raise the problem of evil. The problem of evil is perhaps the most commonly raised objection against the existence and goodness of God. People raise the issue because they are struck with horror in response to many of the atrocities in our world, such as murder, racism, and rape. And yet the recognition that there is such a thing as evil implies the existence of an objective moral standard. Properly understood, evil is a *corruption* of good. There can be good without evil, but there cannot be evil without good. Consequently, the objector who raises the problem of evil unwittingly presupposes an objective moral standard, which reveals the vacuity of moral relativism and the impossibility of living it out with consistency.

Second, relativists cannot consistently claim

they have improved their morality. According to individual relativism, an individual's beliefs about morality determine right and wrong. There is no objective standard of conduct beyond one's personal ethics. But if there is no external standard, then there can be no moral improvement. Individual relativists can change their morality, but they cannot improve it. On the other hand, if there is moral improvement, which individual relativists often proclaim, then relativism is false.

Third, relativists cannot consistently accept praise or offer blame. If relativism is true, then no act is immoral as long as an individual embraces it. There is no external standard for how an individual *should* behave beyond his or her own moral whims. Yet this guts the meaning of moral praise and blame. After all, the concept of praiseworthy behavior implies a standard of how human beings are *supposed* to act. And the concept of blame implies that there is an objective standard someone has *violated.* Yet according to individual relativism, there is no such standard beyond the self. Individual relativism thus makes the concepts of praise and blame meaningless. Moral relativists act inconsistently whenever they accept praise or place blame for moral behavior.

The Reality About Relativism

Because of the seriousness of the criticisms we have considered, most philosophers and theologians reject moral relativism. And yet many laypeople claim to embrace it. The reality, however, is that no one is truly a relativist.

People are made in the image of God and thus know that some things are right, and others are wrong. But even when people claim to be relativists, their lives will betray them. As we have seen, the essential flaw of relativism is that people simply cannot live it out with consistency.

What Is Postmodernism, and What Is Its Essential Flaw?

Mark M. Hanna

In its philosophical expression, postmodernism can be dismissed in one sentence. Because it asserts relativism across the board, it is self-referential and therefore self-refuting. Case closed. End of postmodern philosophy.

This chapter could end here—except for the fact that postmodern philosophy persists despite its incoherence. Moreover, postmodernism is not confined to philosophy. It is a very broad movement that encompasses art, architecture, music, literature—in fact, all aspects of a culture, including a distinctive attitude and way of life. Four of its most prominent spokesmen are Jacques Derrida (1930–2004), Michel Foucault (1926–1984), Jean-Francois Lyotard (1924–1998), and Richard Rorty (1931–2007).

Postmodernism's Roots

The postmodernist movement began in France in the 1960s as a radical rejection of modernism. The term *postmodernism* is attributed to the French philosopher Lyotard, who first used the term in his 1979 book *The Postmodern Condition*.

To gain an understanding of postmodernist claims, we should have some understanding of the basic features of modernism, against which postmodernists rebelled. Modernism reigned in Western intellectual circles from the eighteenth century until the middle of the twentieth century. In fact, modernism itself arose in opposition to the prevailing paradigm of the Middle Ages. The pervasive influence of the Middle Ages was eventually undermined by two circumstances: a growing discontent that culminated in the Renaissance, a version of humanism that flourished from the fourteenth to the seventeenth centuries, and a schism within Roman Catholicism that developed into widespread dissent and the Protestant Reformation (sixteenth century), resulting in the establishment of separate Christian movements. Both these events led to a new cultural paradigm, which found full expression in the Enlightenment (eighteenth century) and in the Industrial Revolution (1760–1840).

Briefly traced, then, the paradigm shifted from the theological and ecclesiological hegemony of the premodern period to the literary and humanistic predominance of the Renaissance, and from the individualism and factionalism of the Reformation to the idolization of autonomous reason in the period of the Enlightenment.

Although postmodernism arose as a rejection of modernism, it would be wrong to think that postmodernism displaced modernism, for both have continued to exist side by side and are even often intermingled. Postmodernists daily employ many concepts and methods of modernism despite claiming that they have abandoned them.

Differences Between Modernism and Postmodernism

What are the specific views of modernism that postmodernism repudiates? As both possess a wide-ranging perspective and a movement, consisting of more than philosophical assumptions and exhibiting themselves in virtually every aspect of Western culture, postmodernism resists all neat and simple definitions. Nevertheless, its philosophical claims are at the root of virtually all other expressions. Given the limited compass of this chapter, I will briefly mention four closely related issues that are at the heart of its philosophical claims, make some general comments regarding these issues, elaborate on postmodernism's essential flaw, and conclude with evaluating truth claims.

Postmodernism rejects the following modernist beliefs: (1) absolute and universal truths, and objective knowledge, (2) sufficiency of reason and science for achieving all knowledge, (3) the inevitably of progress by means of reason and science, and (4) metanarratives.

Postmodernism and Truth

Postmodernism's denial of absolute and universal truth is at the root of its perspective.

Nevertheless, its radical relativism is self-defeating, for its denial of all absolute and universal truth implicitly affirms that there is at least one absolute and universal truth: that there is no absolute and universal truth. To affirm and deny the very same thing is the definition of logical contradiction.

Postmodernists seek to nullify this criticism by saying that they do not acknowledge the objectivity and absoluteness of logical principles. They may think this gets them off the hook, but their maneuver merely deepens their incoherence. One cannot reject the objectivity, absoluteness, and universality of basic logical principles without using them in the act of conceiving and stating the rejection. To put it another way, the statement of denial itself is an objective, absolute, universal, and logical claim.

Postmodernists have no alternative but to use the very logical principles they seek to deny. Otherwise, the string of words that comprise the sentence by which they assert their rejection of logical principles is nothing but meaningless gibberish. If the principle of noncontradiction is jettisoned, then every word of a sentence—and the sentence itself—has no fixed meaning. And if it can mean anything, it means nothing. The absoluteness of the law of noncontradiction is a necessary condition for understanding and expressing anything meaningful.

Every theory of truth, such as the coherence theory or the pragmatic theory, or the relativity theory advocated by postmodernists, depends, in the final analysis, on the *correspondence* view of truth. Every theory that purports to be something other than the correspondence theory of truth implicitly claims that its view of truth is the one that *corresponds* to the way things really are.

To understand the correspondence theory,

one must be clear about what is the *bearer* of truth and what is the *maker* of truth. Simply defined, a proposition is the meaning (not the sentences that may be used to express a meaning) that affirms or denies that a certain "state of affairs" exists or has certain properties. Truth is a property of a proposition that correctly refers to any state of affairs that can be specified—whether it is an object or situation, small or large, simple or complex, material or immaterial, visible or invisible. It is the state of affairs that makes a proposition that refers to it either true or false. Many sentences, whether in the same language or in a different one, can express the same unitary meaning that affirms or denies something to be the case.

Postmodernism and Skepticism

Postmodernists claim that skepticism about reason, like skepticism about truth, is necessitated by our inability to rise above our linguistically and socially circumscribed situation. Our concepts come from our language, and our language comes from our culture, and because there are multiple cultures and subcultures, there are no universal concepts that enable us to discover reality. Our relativistic concepts always intervene and interfere with our attempts to achieve objective and universal knowledge. No one can perceive anything or even think about anything apart from the conceptual grid that fully conditions his mind. In contrast to the philosopher Immanuel Kant (1724–1804), who held that all human beings have the same conceptual grid, postmodernists aver that there are diverse, multiple conceptual grids, each shaped by a social group, and none having priority over any other.

Moreover, Derrida claimed that *everything is a text*, by which he seemed to mean

that everything is subject to an indefinite variety of interpretations. According to his claim, no sentences in any book have a fixed meaning, for meanings are as diverse as the individuals who read the sentences. This notion entails that there is no single author, for every reader becomes the author, and there is no way to determine whether any one of them is right. In fact, according to Derrida, there is no right interpretation.

Derrida's claim that everything is a text creates a dilemma, for to see everything as a text necessitates viewing his claim itself as a text that lacks any fixed meaning. Further, postmodernism itself is nothing more than a relative interpretation bound to a social group, having no more claim on reality or truth than any other social group's perspective. As a text, postmodernism has as many interpretations as readers who hear or read the words of its spokesmen. Consequently, postmodernism dies the death of endless interpretations that can mean anything, and therefore mean nothing.

According to postmodernism there is no universal and objective knowledge. Consequently, that which is termed "knowledge" is primarily useful for a particular social group according to the group's own perceptions and needs. Even scientific knowledge is said to lack objectivity and universality, and is considered no better than any other method of inquiry.

The American postmodernist philosopher Richard Rorty contended that none of our so-called knowledge "mirrors" reality as it is. Thus, neither scientists, nor philosophers, nor theologians can appeal to a mind-independent or language-independent reality to justify any of their claims.

However, postmodernism's claim that our knowledge can never be a correct representation of reality is incoherent, for one must know something about reality in order to know that our knowledge does not represent it. No one could possibly know this without being able to compare our mental representations with the way extra-mental things really are.

How ironic it is, then, that Rorty's entire philosophical edifice is based squarely on representationalism! He *represents* what he takes to be the *real* cognitive situation of human beings. But he cannot have it both ways—that is, not unless he abandons the law of noncontradiction. But if he does that, then nothing he says makes sense; and there is never any reason for paying attention to nonsense.

Postmodernism's Opposition to Metanarratives

The main target of the postmodernist critique is metanarratives, which is basically another term for worldviews. Lyotard asserted the following in his book *The Postmodern Condition: A Report on Knowledge*: "Simplifying to the extreme, I define postmodernism as incredulity toward metanarratives."[1]

For postmodernists, metanarratives include all religions, philosophical systems, nationalism, and even science. A metanarrative is an overarching narrative about other narratives, a grand story to justify other stories. Postmodernists insist that there are only local and individual stories, none of which is superior to others. Because all stories are social constructions embedded in different cultural niches, none can be taken as an all-encompassing truth about the world. However, in view of the sweeping, universal claims made by postmodernism about the way things really are, it is also a metanarrative—one that falls under its own censure and collapses under its own incoherence.

Postmodernism's Essential Flaw

That postmodernism's pronouncements about truth are self-defeating is the most basic flaw in its entire web of mistaken notions. This fundamental error is at the root of many other errors that make postmodernist claims untenable. When postmodernists claim that *all* truths are social constructions, meaning that they derive from, or depend upon, power status, gender, class, race, or the consensus of a social group, their so-called truths themselves cannot be anything other than social constructions, none of which is privileged over any other. This means, therefore, that their claim that all truths are social constructions is itself a social construction, thereby relativizing itself.

That is the price to be paid when one assumes that the semantic content of every claim is completely embedded in some socially limited point of view. Therefore, postmodernism itself cannot be universal, or true, or even superior. It should be evident now why the first paragraph of this chapter gave postmodernism such short shrift; it not only relativizes itself, but it completely implodes by self-referential contradiction.

Rightly Evaluating Truth Claims

The core belief of postmodernism can be summed up in one sentence: It assumes that truth, reason, morality, and all narratives have no universal or fixed meaning, but rather are social constructions deriving from and limited to each social group. It is untenable due to the self-referential incoherence of its fundamental assumption, which is stated as an absolute, universal truth—a metanarrative encompassing all other narratives.

Contrary to postmodernism's fallacious

assumption that truth has no fixed meaning but is determined by the consensus of diverse social groups, truth is actually determined by facts, which are the states of affairs to which propositions refer. Because the correspondence theory is the correct and inescapable view of truth, it is possible to show that the objective credentials of biblical Christianity not only make it credible but also true and universally relevant to every human being.

One final caveat is in order: It would be a serious mistake to think that a Christian should identify with either the premodern paradigm or the modern paradigm in opposition to postmodernism. The biblically informed and discerning Christian will find many fallacious assumptions in each one, for in numerous ways and to varying degrees, each of the paradigms is fundamentally incompatible with the divine revelation of the Bible, which is the only completely trustworthy touchstone for evaluating any and all claims to final truth.

The Roman philosopher Cicero (106–43 BC) once lamented, "There is nothing so absurd that some philosopher has not already said it."[2] Unfortunately, since his time there have been many instances in which philosophers have equaled, if not surpassed, the absurdities of their predecessors. Indeed, it would be hard to find any contemporary philosophy more absurd than postmodernism.

What Is Atheism, and What Is Its Essential Flaw?

David R.C. Deane

Atheism has a long and complex history. As conceptions of God have changed across time and culture, so the meaning of atheism has changed, and as a result, it has become notoriously difficult to define. In both ancient and medieval times atheism was scarcely advocated in public, except when used as an indictment against those who held beliefs contrary to the establishment of their day. The seriousness of such an indictment was not only considered a capital offense, but was even punishable by death in some instances, as observed, for example, in the infamous trial and enforced suicide of Socrates in 399 BC. As strange as it may seem to our contemporary understanding, even Christians in the early church were persecuted for being "atheists"[1] given their singular belief in Jesus Christ as "the way" (John 14:6), which deviated from the prevailing "many ways" of polytheism throughout the ancient Roman Empire.

These older conceptions of atheism began to change, however, during the great transition from medieval to modern times. The religious, social, and intellectual upheavals between the fifteenth and seventeenth centuries saw atheism gain popular currency and a new measure of respect amongst intellectuals of the modern world. Motivated by an impulse to see humanity liberated from the fetters of conventional religion, atheism began to consolidate its newfound status by leveraging itself from the advances and methods of modern science, as well as the humanities, and progressively enclosing itself within the confines of nature and terrestrial values while devaluing and eliminating God from the domains of speculative inquiry as well as the practicalities of daily affairs.

Atheism as we know it today was thus established not as a sterile philosophical belief, but as the convergent effect of a number of philosophies across a broad spectrum of disciplines, each finding agreement in their common appeal to naturalistic-humanistic explanations for the totality of life and existence.[2] Today, its persistence and vitality as a worldview is evidenced by the unprecedented number of professing atheists among Western nations, a trend which is on the rise.[3]

In this chapter, we will examine the

foundations of atheistic belief by considering the nature of its reasoning and the
fundamental misconceptions of God that
materialize as a result. I will adopt the definition of atheism offered by Lee and Bullivant
in their 2016 publication *The Oxford Dictionary of Atheism*:

> Atheism: [Derived from the classical
> Greek *a-* (normally "not" or "without")
> and *theos* ("god"), it first appeared in
> English in the mid-1500s as a transla-
> tion of Plutarch's *atheotēs*.] A belief in
> the non-existence of a God or gods, or
> (more broadly) an absence of belief in
> their existence.[4]

Note, however, that I will only consider this
definition as it relates to Christian theism—
that is, a belief in the nonexistence of God
(singular).

The Building of Belief and Foundations of Reason

From the preceding definition, we can see
that atheism is a statement of "belief" about
the nature of reality. But as Plato identified
long ago, a belief can only be considered
knowledge if it is a "justified true belief,"[5]
and for something to be justified, there must
be *reasons* for its justification. Accordingly,
whether a belief is true or not will depend
upon its reasons, for they are the structural
foundations upon which the building of a
belief is based. These foundations are themselves held up by an underlying substratum
or ground, and it is at this ground level where
we must begin our examination of atheism,
irrespective of whether we agree with it or
not.[6] "The issue between the atheist and the
believer," wrote Austin Farrer, "is not whether
it makes sense to question ultimate fact [the
ground level], it is rather the question: what

fact is ultimate? The atheist's ultimate fact is
the universe [i.e., nature is all there is]; the
theist's ultimate fact is God."[7]

Granting this, the question we must ask
is, How does the ground of atheism anchor
the foundational reasons that hold up the
building of atheistic belief? To begin with,
it's important that we recognize that even
some of the most ardent atheists are willing to admit the *logical* possibility of God's
existence given the inherent difficulties—nay,
impossibility—of trying to prove an absolute
negative such as the nonexistence of God.[8]
However, they are forced to make this reluc-
tant admission (which is essentially a retreat
into agnosticism) only when pressed to offer
a *positive* case for their view.[9] For all intents
and practical purposes, they do not mean
to positively assert the nonexistence of God
inasmuch as they simply mean that they do
not identify as theists.[10]

Yet this is a redefinition of atheism,
because where one places the point of
negation matters. For example, there is a
significant logical difference between the
propositions "I don't believe his name is
Michael" and "I believe his name is not
Michael." Conventionally, the former is an
opinion that expresses a measure of uncertainty, while the latter, which accords with
the definition of atheism, uses the term
believe in the strongest possible sense to
express a psychological awareness that seems
so overwhelmingly probable that any doubts
to the contrary are excluded, even if they cannot be logically excluded.[11]

Playing semantic games like this may
offer atheism a convenient escape from the
burden of proof which it must, by definition,
shoulder. However, if it is to be a properly
held view at all, and not just a trivialized
"catch-all" label for anything that shares in

a nonprofession of theism (dogs, cats, and trees included!), then it must indeed shoulder its burden of proof by way of reasons to uphold its belief in the nonexistence of God. But can it?

Digging at the Ground Level

If there are no positive proofs for the *belief that* God does not exist, then what reasons are there for the *belief in* the nonexistence of God? Surely we cannot dismiss this by simply saying that there are just no good reasons to believe God exists. For not only does that precipitate the need to ground the idea of "good," but it is almost immediately confronted by the irritating fact of history that there has simply never been a time or place where people have not beheld some sort of innate proclivity to live for something beyond themselves—irrespective of whether or not this yet undefined "thing" is known by "God" or some other name. Indeed, the very persistence and vitality of atheism itself invites us to reason why human nature tends towards that for which it has no precise model in material existence. As G.K. Chesterton noted, "If there were no God, there would be no atheists."[12]

By digging at the ground level with the shovel of such questions, we begin to expose the rational flaws in the foundations of atheism. For if atheism, by definition, implies a notion of God which it denies, then what, exactly, is this notion? Because if God does not exist in the first place, then surely old Protagoras had at least this much right: "Man is the measure of all things."[13] But what this means in the broadest possible sense is that every "thing" is essentially an object of human knowledge—*including the very notion of God.*

With this realization, we begin to expose the essential flaw of atheism:

Atheism is a commitment, first and foremost, to a *belief in* the nonexistence of God, which subsequently enslaves all reason to the domain of nature in order to perpetuate the *belief that* God does not exist.[14] That is to say, its *belief in* the nonexistence of God is both prior to and independent of any reasons for the *belief that* God does not exist. Chesterton creatively exposed this faulty logic when he wrote: "if I say 'a peasant saw a ghost,' I am told, 'but peasants are so credulous.' If I ask, 'why credulous?' the only answer is—'that they see ghosts.'"[15] By this unhinged circularity, atheism thus discredits reason itself, including that which it employs in the criticism of beliefs contrary to its own. One cannot help but look upon the naked irony here; the emperor of atheism—which is so often masqueraded in the dress of rationality—has no clothes.[16] As John Lennox quips, "It therefore doesn't simply shoot itself in the foot, which is painful; it shoots itself in the brain, which is fatal."[17]

The Corrosive Effect

It is this kind of deficient reasoning that has a corrosive effect upon the entire building of atheistic belief, from the ground up. Books such as *The God Delusion, God Is Not Great, The End of God, God: The Failed Hypothesis* are, by their cataract of antisupernaturalism, little more than rhetorical diatribes against a caricatured God. For all too often they vilify the God of Abraham, Isaac and Jacob as though He were any other dead mythological deity akin to Homer's Zeus, Odin of the Norsemen, or a "Flying Spaghetti Monster."[18] And when He is entertained as a cosmic designer, then it is asked: Well, "who designed the designer?"[19]

But here we must protest. This is precisely what the Christian understanding of God *is not*. Because atheism enslaves all reason to the domain of nature, it thus follows that the atheistic notions of God and all such deities or mythological creatures are nothing more than the mental abstractions of a natural mind with no recourse to anything beyond its own sense-perception of the universe. The legend of Santa Claus finds recourse to a fourth-century bishop of Greece; the folkloric Easter Bunny finds recourse to eighteenth-century Lutherans from Germany; even the infantile notion of a Tooth Fairy has analogical recourse to a calcified structure we call a tooth. None of these are categorical comparisons to what Christians mean by God.

Similarly, the dilemma of "Who created the creator?" is a problem only for one who has a prior notion of a created god that is subject to the same conceptual domain of nature that we access through science. But God cannot be put into a test tube. If atheism is present in the sciences, it is not owing to the results of science but to the "existential want" of *scientists* who yet remain haunted by a presupposed altar "to an unknown god" (Acts 17:23 NASB).

In contrast to all such representations, the triune essence of the Christian God—as revealed in the created order by His Word and the person of Jesus Christ—is *theistic*. That means that He is not only operative *within* creation but also *beyond* it, and thus He is not bound by the material constraints of space and time. God, according to the Bible, just *is*. "I AM WHO I AM" (Exodus 3:14) declared the Lord to Moses. This profound, eternally present declaration means, amongst other things, that God's essence *is* existence. And so, it is not as simple as merely holding "A belief in the nonexistence of God" as though God were a "thing" to not exist.

For He is the very source of existence itself. His *Being* is the ground of all existing *beings* (including any "Flying Spaghetti Monster" we might find!).

Christian Theism v. Atheism

Thus, it is here, at the ground level concerning the very nature of God that the proverbial fork in the road emerges and atheists and Christians part ways. What atheism calls *god*, Christian theism calls an idol;[20] and what Christian theism calls *God*, atheism truncates as a mere object of speculative imagination. It is my conviction that if Christians are to engage in sincere dialogue with atheists concerning either worldview, then they must determine to begin here, with a concerted effort to understand the nature of God as it has been disclosed in revelation. By failing to do so, Christians only enable their detractors by allowing them to persist in their essentially flawed presuppositions of God.[21]

It is important to note that nothing I have stated here is decisive in rendering atheism false and Christianity true. All we have considered is the flawed logic (invalid reasoning) of atheistic belief so that we can begin to think rightly on this question in our pursuit of truth. Of course, there is room for doubts and uncertainties along the way, but the very fact that there is a truth to pursue by which we can measure our doubts presupposes, once again, the very possibility that there is, indeed, a God to be found.[22]

In closing, atheists and all unbelievers alike should keep in mind what is at the heart of the Christian gospel when considering it for themselves: God is not just a theory to be reasoned from a book; He is a Person who offers relationship. Whereas atheism maintains disunity with God and self-prescribed individuality, Christian theism offers community with God and the restoration of individuality through the person and work of Jesus Christ. Reason is not a substitute for faith, which is the ground of human salvation, because Reason—with a capital *R*—is the very embodiment of salvation in "the Word became flesh" (John 1:14).[23] This, therefore, is the crux of the issue: If Jesus Christ is who He claims to be, then Christian theism is true and atheism is false.

It would be appropriate to allow Etienne Gilson the final word:

The mere fact that men still go to the trouble of declaring themselves atheists, and of justifying their disbelief by means of such arguments as the existence of evil, clearly shows that the issue is still a living one…God will really be dead when no one will still think of denying his existence. Until then, the death of God remains an unconfirmed rumor.[24]

What Is Pantheism, and What Is Its Essential Flaw?

Patrick Zukeran

The worldview of pantheism undergirds many of the Eastern religions, including Hinduism, several schools of Buddhism, and Taoism (along with their Western offshoots), New Age religions, Christian Science, and Unity.

Blockbuster movies such as *Star Wars* and *Avatar* present pantheism in an intriguing, entertaining, and attractive manner. With its emphasis on our unity with all things, it dominates the environmental movement. The popularity of Eastern practices such as yoga, alternative medicine, transcendental meditation, and mystical forms of martial arts, pantheism is now mainstream. With its rising impact, every Christian should understand this worldview and how to effectively engage those who embrace it, as well as recognize its fatal flaws. Because there are different forms of pantheism, I will present the more basic doctrines of this worldview.

What Is Pantheism?

Pan means "all" and *theism* means "God," meaning all *is* God and God *is* all. That is to say,

God and the universe are viewed as one. Pantheism is the worldview that teaches God is the impersonal force or cosmic energy of the universe. James Sire explains pantheism this way: "God is the one, infinite-impersonal, ultimate reality. That is, God is the cosmos. God is all that exists; nothing exists that is not God."[1]

According to pantheism, God should not be understood as a personal being as in the theistic worldview, but rather as an impersonal force. God may reveal Himself in lower forms such as gods, avatars, or spiritual beings. However, personality, consciousness, and intellect are characteristics of lower manifestations of God, but they are not to be confused with God in His being.[2]

In pantheism God is viewed as being beyond comprehension, and He cannot be described. Brahman is the title used of God in Hinduism. *The Rider Encyclopedia of Eastern Philosophy and Religion* states, "Brahman is an abstract concept that is not accessible to the thinking mind…Brahman is a state of pure transcendence that cannot be grasped by thought or speech."[3]

Nature of the Universe (Reality)

In pantheism, God is viewed as the one and only true reality. Pantheists teach that the universe flows out of God (*ex deo*) like a web from a spider, but not out of nothing (*ex nihilo*) as taught in theism. Everything then is viewed as being part of God or the single divine reality.[4]

The Upanishads states, "Everything in this ephemeral [transient] world belongs to the Lord, because the whole universe came out of Him. He pervades everything in the universe."[5]

Absolute pantheism, as taught in Buddhism, believes that the physical universe is "maya" or an illusion. The world around us is a shadow of reality. Whatever changes is considered an illusion, for true reality is permanent.

By contrast, theism teaches that God created the universe and is separate from the universe. He is active in the universe but is not identical to the universe. In other words, God is distinct from the universe as a painting is from the painter.

Nature of Man

The pantheistic understanding of human nature can be summed up in the Hindu phrase "Atman is Brahman." *Atman* refers to the real individual or life force known in the West as the soul. It is in essence identical with Brahman, the impersonal absolute.[6]

In essence, a person is one with Brahman, thus a human's true self is not personal but impersonal. The belief that we are distinct individuals is an illusion. Because all things flow from God, each person is one with God and the universe. Unenlightened individuals fail to attain this knowledge, and it may take many reincarnations for them to attain enlightenment to this view of reality.

Biblical theism, by contrast, teaches that man is a finite creature made in the image of God but fallen in sin. Man reflects the character of God and is a distinct being from God, and can have a relationship with Him.

Human Destiny

Pantheism is typically connected to the doctrine of reincarnation, which means "to come again in the flesh." It is the belief that at death the soul or life force migrates into another body—human or other form. Only the impersonal self will reincarnate, accompanied by its debt of karma. Everything is in a birth-and-rebirth cycle. One could endure endless reincarnations, either evolving into a higher or lower form of life as one works off the debt of karma.

The law of karma is the universal law of cause and effect. Each person's thoughts, words, and deeds have ethical consequences experienced in this lifetime or in future existences. Our present state is the result of actions and intentions performed in a previous life. The amount of good or bad karma attained in our present life will determine our form of existence in the next life.

Biblical theism, by contrast, teaches resurrection (change *in* body that is *immortal*) not reincarnation (change *of* body that is *mortal*). At death, a person's eternal destiny is determined (Hebrews 9:27). The soul goes to heaven or hell, awaiting the resurrection of the body to stand before the final judgment.

Salvation

According to pantheism, individuals are trapped in an endless cycle of reincarnation or rebirth. The soul is imprisoned in the body. The problem is ignorance of true reality and one's identity, with ignorance and karmic debt keeping one in the cycle. When one attains enlightenment, one may break free and unite or be absorbed into God (Brahman). Hindu scholar Shyam Shukla states,

> …when a man identifies himself with his body, with all its limitations, then he is a tiny, weak and mortal creature in this vast universe. On the other hand, when he identifies himself with his inner self, the Atman, which is limitless, immortal and blissful, he achieves divinity in this very life.[7]

Just as a drop of rainwater journeys to the ocean, so the soul must find its way to union with the divine. This enlightenment and mystical union is achieved through various means in the different pantheistic religions.

Pantheism teaches salvation is found in the self through self-effort, while biblical theism teaches that salvation is found in a Savior (Jesus). The sinless Savior pays for the sins of mankind, and He offers salvation as a free gift to all who trust in Him.

Pluralism

Because all is said to be one, all religions are viewed as essentially the same, with each one offering an alternate path to God. Jesus is simply one of many enlightened figures who taught others how to attain enlightenment.

By contrast, the Bible teaches that Jesus is the unique Son of God. He is the only one who could be the perfect sacrifice for sin, and therefore He is the only way to eternal life (John 14:6).

Ethics

Pantheistic literature is filled with exhortations to moral living. However, these apply to those who have *not* attained true enlightenment. Once one has attained enlightenment and union with God "he has no further concern for moral laws. God is beyond good and evil and man must transcend these as God

has. Ultimate reality is beyond good and evil so good and evil as absolute categories are an illusion. Morality is a step toward enlightenment. Therefore, there is no absolute basis for right and wrong."[8]

Theism, however, teaches that moral law comes from the Moral Lawgiver of the universe. God has given mankind a moral standard, which is made known in our conscience (Romans 2:14-15) and in divine revelation.

Essential Flaws of Pantheism

There are numerous criticisms of the pantheist worldview.

First, it is a self-defeating philosophy. Norman Geisler points out a major contradictory premise. Pantheism teaches that every individual is, in essence, God. God, by definition, is eternal and immutable. However, humans forget they are divine and must become enlightened to their true self. This means they undergo change. If God is unchanging, how can man be God if man progresses and changes?[9]

Second, pantheists are inconsistent and incoherent in defining the nature of God. Pantheist literature describes God, or the ultimate reality, as unknowable or indescribable with words, yet volumes have been written that describe God!

What is more, how does the infinite forget it is infinite? If I am God, why do I need to learn this? If we are deceived about our very nature of divinity, how would a pantheist know he is not deceived when he claims to be divine? Pantheists have no real answer to this. Swami Vivekananda writes, "How can the perfect become quasi-perfect; how can the pure, the absolute, change even a microscopic particle of its nature?…I do not know how the perfect being, the soul, came to think of itself as imperfect, as joined to and conditioned by matter."[10]

Third, pantheism fails the test of livability. Pantheism teaches that the world is an illusion. However, no pantheist consistently lives out this belief. I have yet to see a pantheist who does not jump out of the path of an oncoming vehicle.

Pantheism teaches that our individual personhood is an illusion because we are all one with God. However, we are well aware of beings distinct from us, and this is the basis for I-thou relationships. Relationships are possible only with other distinct conscious beings. Emotions such as love can only be experienced between two separate individuals: a lover and the one who is loved.

Fourth, pantheism fails to provide an adequate answer to the problem of evil. One of the greatest challenges for pantheism is defining evil. If God is all and all is God, then there are only four possibilities regarding good and evil. Geisler describes them as follows.

1. If God is all good, then evil must exist apart from God. But this is impossible since God is all—nothing can exist apart from It.

2. If God is all evil, then good must exist apart from God. This is not possible either, since God is all.

3. God is both all good and all evil. This cannot be, for it is self-contradictory to affirm that the same being is both all good and all evil at the same time. Further, most pantheists agree that God is beyond good and evil. Therefore God is neither good nor evil.

4. Good and evil are illusory. They are not real categories.[11]

It is irrational to suppose evil is an illusion. Pantheists cry when they lose a child and protest injustice. To say the pain is not real is an insult. Pantheism only offers attempts to *escape* from pain and suffering. According to pantheism, pain and suffering are the result of the unenlightened mind attaching itself to this illusory world. One must realize true reality, that their individuality and this world are an illusion. When this occurs, one will "rise above" pain and suffering. However, this proves to be a cruel answer because the person is asked to deny the truth about their humanity and reality.

Fifth, the evidence points to a personal Creator who is distinct from the universe. The universe is not eternal, as pantheism teaches, but has a beginning. Many scientific discoveries confirm this—among them are Einstein's theory of relativity, the red shift, the radiation echo, and the laws of thermodynamics. These support the premise that the universe exploded into existence from nothing. Because the law of causality says every effect needs a cause, the universe came into being as the result of a cause with a will. Whatever created the universe has a free will to act independently of the universe. This cause (whom we call God) chose to create the universe, and it came into being.[12]

Sixth, the universe displays design. Scientific study continues to reveal the complexity and design of the universe. We have discovered that the nucleus of a cell is as complex as a metropolitan city. DNA is more complex than any computer program. Design points to an intelligent cause (mind).

Seventh, there is a universal moral law. Morality is connected to personhood. A moral law comes from a Moral Lawgiver. The sum total of these arguments all point to a personal Creator. This Creator we call God!

Conclusion

The West is entrenched in postmodern ideologies such as the relativism of truth, moral relativism, and pluralism (all these views have some element of truth). These dogmas synthesize well with the worldview of pantheism, which provides the spiritual component to one's view of reality. We can expect pantheism to continue to spread in the West, especially because progressive activists are popularizing environmental issues as their primary moral concern. It is therefore, imperative that Christians understand this worldview and engage it with compelling arguments that enlighten people to the truth of Christ and His glorious gospel.

What Is Monism, and
What Is Its Essential Flaw?

Dillon Burroughs

Monism is the belief that all is one. *Monism* comes from the Greek word *monos*, which means "one," and it argues that all reality is ultimately one. It differs from dualism (two realities) as well as pluralism (the belief in multiple gods). A monist believes reality is ultimately unified. The term *monism* came into use in Christian von Wolff's book *Logic* (1728) to distinguish the types of philosophical thought that eliminated the dichotomy of the body and mind.

Various types of monism exist, with the most common of these views being materialistic monism, neutral monism, idealistic monism, and priority monism.

Types of Monism

Materialistic monism is the belief that only the physical world is real (sometimes also called *existence monism*). Mental realities or abstractions are considered part of the same physical realm. According to this view, nonmaterial realities such as God, Satan, angels, demons, heaven, hell, and human souls do not exist. So-called spiritual thoughts are attributed to physical interactions or brain activity, making

them an outcome of material causes. Many contemporary atheists subscribe to this view that all reality is limited to the natural world.

In the first half of the nineteenth century, materialism gained strength with the theories of natural selection and Marxism. Darwin emphasized biological studies to champion the view of life based on materialism,[1] and Karl Marx emphasized economics, utilizing aspects of both materialistic monism and atheism.

Parmenides is considered the father of Western monism (b. 515 BC). He argued there cannot be two realities or beings because all things share similar being and are derived from a single source. Any seeming differences were regarded as an illusion. Parmenides explained monism as follows:

> There cannot be two realities or beings, for if this were so, one would have to differ from the other. If there were no difference, then they would be one identical reality and not two. In order for there to be really different things, there must be some real difference. On the one hand, everything that differs

must differ either by being or by non-being, since there are no other ways to differ. However, two beings cannot differ by nothing or nonbeing. To differ by nothing is not to differ at all.[2]

A second type of monism, called *neutral monism*, suggests the one reality is neither mental nor physical but can be expressed through its attributes. As the name suggests, neutral monism attempts to provide a middle ground between materialistic and idealistic monism. Both physical realities and the mind are therefore one and belong to the same single reality. An adherent of this view was Dutch philosopher Baruch Spinoza (1632–1677). He viewed humans as manifestations of the one absolute substance. People are neither purely spiritual nor material nor a combination of two substances. Instead, people are single finite entities that include both material and nonmaterial aspects. Body and soul are simply modes of being, not distinct things, a view referred to as dual-aspect monism.[3] His view, also called substance monism, is so named due to his emphasis on the idea that one infinite substance (God or nature) is the only substance that exists.

Idealistic monism believes the nonmaterial mind is all that exists. The physical world is merely a mental projection or illusion created by the mind. The Greek philosopher Anaxagoras (c. 510–428 BC) taught all things were created by the mind. He further argued the mind held the "cosmos" together. Two types of idealistic monism exist: absolute idealism and pluralistic idealism.

Absolute idealism (also known as substance monism) specifically believes there is one and only one thing. Everything either flows from the one or is part of the one. This teaching is rooted in Indian philosophy.

Vedanta Hinduism teaches our experiences are illusions and cannot be trusted. Though many view Hinduism as consisting of many gods, according to the *New World Encyclopedia*,

[o]ther parts of the Vedas also provide numerous suggestions as to what this monistic essence actually is, such as hiranya-garbha (the golden germ), Agni (the Vedic deity who represents fire, seen to be present within all things), purusha (the cosmic being) and the idea of Brahmaspiti (sacred utterance), which evolved into the central concept of Brahman (monistic Oneness) in the Upanishads and became the universally accepted monistic principle for the Hindu tradition. Brahman is considered to be the sum total of all that ever is, was, or ever will be, including the human soul, or Atman. Even the individual personal gods that have become so identifiable in both ancient and modern Hinduism are considered to be manifestations of this decidedly monistic concept.[4]

Also known as pantheism (meaning all is God), the goal of Vedanta Hinduism is to empty the mind to become one with God to complete reality. Parmenides presented a Western form of this belief system. Other Western thinkers who have held this view include Plotinus (b. AD 205), as well as German philosopher Georg Hegel (1770–1831). Pluralistic monism believes reality is spiritual, yet there are many different individual spirit entities.

In addition, some have noted *priority monism*, the view that all existing things derived from a source distinct from them. Neoplatonism, which says that everything is derived from the one (see Plotinus's work on this subject, titled *The Enneads*), is also associated with this view.

Christian Monism

Can a Bible-believing Christian hold to monism? A small number of writers have suggested this possibility, often citing Acts 17:28: "In him we live and move and have our being." To justify this belief, it has been noted that the Hebrew word translated "soul" (*nephesh*) does not refer to a separate entity or immortal soul, but rather a living essence also shared by animals that is capable of death. Despite this concern, Christian monism suggests a meaningful afterlife with God as perfected beings. However, such a view stands opposed to other Bible passages, such as Philippians 1:23, where Paul noted his desire is to depart and be with Christ. This affirms a distinction between body and spirit or soul, as well as a distinction between God and created beings (humans). This appears more than a metaphorical discussion of life on Earth contrasted with heaven, and represents two different realities.

A Christian Response to Monism

There are a variety of Christian responses that confront the weaknesses of monism.

The first response points to the first verse of the Bible, which serves as a contrast to the monistic worldview. Genesis 1:1 presents a single God who existed before time and created a time-space universe. The creation account continues with a diverse array of created aspects that differ in their time and type of creation. God already existed, and He created other beings separate from Himself. There is a clear distinction between Creator and creation. The transcendent God created

ex nihilo (out of nothing), not from his own substance (*ex Deo*), and is not to be confused with His creation.

A second response is based on the theological view of the triune God. God is one, yet exists in three persons (Matthew 28:19-20). All three persons of the triune Godhead appear distinctly at the baptism of Jesus (Matthew 3:16-17), yet in Scripture, all are referred to as God.

A third response to monism addresses the assumption that God is all and that there is no distinction between Creator and creation. To hold to this view assumes the creation knows everything the Creator God could know. But if people were created by God, then God would know much more than His creation, including that which is beyond the visible realm. One cannot assume there are unseen realities or nonmaterial entities and claim they are not real or do not really exist outside of the mind without having a knowledge that exists beyond the human mind.

A fourth response to monism (particularly to Parmenides's monism) sees a difference in being itself. Unlike Parmenides, who viewed all being as one (univocal), Thomas Aquinas (c. 1225–1274) argued that there is a real difference in being itself. That is to say, there are different *kinds* of being. For example, God *is* pure being without limitation, whereas humans *have acquired* being with limitation. To put it another way, God is an uncreated *infinite* being and humans are created *finite* beings. These are different *modes* of being, which provides a principle of differentiation between the two kinds. To see being in this way reveals a plurality of being and reflects a real distinction between the infinite Creator and the finite creation.

The fifth response looks to the biblical teaching regarding the human soul. Jesus said that spirits do not have flesh (Luke 24:39). There is clearly a nonphysical or nonmaterial reality belonging to each individual person. This contrasts with materialistic monism, which believes there is no such nonmaterial soul, as well as idealistic monism, which argues against the real existence of the physical body and world.

The sixth response considers the problem of evil. From a biblical perspective, sin has entered the world and will persist in it until the time when Jesus returns and makes all things new (Revelation 21–22). However, for the monist, all things are one. There is no distinction between good and evil, eliminating the problem of evil. Good and evil do not exist as in dualism or in biblical Christianity, eliminating the need for God to provide salvation through Jesus Christ (John 3:16; 14:6; Ephesians 2:8-9).

The seventh response addresses the hopeless conclusions of monism. Monism provides a life filled with illusion, in which a person's purpose is either only in the present state (materialism) or through becoming one with an impersonal ultimate reality (pantheistic monism). At best, this view offers only temporary pleasure and lacks any sense of ultimate value, hope, or meaning. In contrast, the Bible speaks of the joy associated with knowing Jesus (1 Peter 1:8-9) as well as the ultimate pleasure of Christ's followers dwelling with him for eternity (Revelation 22).

Philosopher, William Lane Craig, offers an eighth response from a biblical perspective: If the monistic view were true, the incarnation would be impossible. He notes,

> If human beings are purely physical material entities, how could the second person of the Trinity become

a man? The doctrine of the incarnation is not that the second person of the Trinity turned himself into a human being. It is not like the ancient stories of Zeus where he would turn himself into a bull or a swan. If there is an immaterial part of man then we could understand how the incarnation could make sense—if the second person of the Trinity took on a human body, took on flesh. But how he could become flesh or have a human nature becomes very difficult to understand on a materialistic anthropology.[5]

A Viewpoint with Logical Concerns

In conclusion, monism suggests no ultimate distinction between beings. Others make distinctions between being and nonbeing, both philosophically and based on biblical examples. Monism assumes all things are identical without the ability to prove the case. Reason and human experience point toward various kinds of beings, including distinctions between the Creator and His creation, as well as fundamental distinctions between various types of beings (including between one person and another, person and animal, person and various things). Monism is a philosophical viewpoint, yet as we have seen, it has multiple logical concerns. "How does anyone know for sure that the universe is one substance? What exactly is that one substance that is proposed? What is the essence of it? If properties reflect substance, then why is it that radically different properties exist from one substance?"[6] Scripture and reason both offer better conclusions regarding the Creator and His creation.

What Is Panentheism,
and What Is Its Essential Flaw?

Christopher Travis Haun

Among the great worldviews, panentheism is perhaps the most misunderstood, despite its significant influence over how some individuals understand God and the world. *Panentheism* is a compound word coming from the Greek language meaning "all in God," conveying the idea that the world is inside of God (W→G) and God is inside the world (G→W). By also insisting that God exists beyond the world and is more than the world is (G≥W), panentheism steers a course between pantheism, which views God and the world as identical (G=W), and theism, which views God as totally distinct from the world (G | W).

History

The term *panentheism* was coined in 1828 by Karl Krause to distinguish his view from the views of Friedrich W.J. Schelling, Georg Hegel, and Baruch Spinoza. Previously, the term *pantheism*, coined over 120 years earlier, covered both pantheistic and panentheistic notions. This is why Schelling and Friedrich Schleiermacher, for example, famously identified themselves as pantheists despite quite clearly being what would later be called panentheists. As Krause's term only began to gain wider acceptance in the 1950s, it is still quite common today for panentheists to be mislabeled as pantheists.[1]

While panentheism is relatively new as a classification, as a worldview it is ancient. Some hear panentheistic undertones in the monotheistic reforms of the Egyptian Pharaoh Akhenaton (d. c. 1336/34 BC) and in some of India's most ancient holy books—the Rig Veda (1100 BC), the Bhagavad Gita (500–200 BC), and the Upanishads (100 BC–AD 400). Certainly a few Hindu schools of thought have been more panentheistic than pantheistic, and some modern Buddhist thinkers prefer their metaphysical model to be classified as panentheistic rather than atheistic. Panentheism also echoes in the writings of several thinkers from Islamic Sufism, Kabbalistic Judaism, and some other mystical traditions of the world.[2]

Its development, however, took place in ancient Greece. Both Platonism and Neoplatonism had seminal roles in the formation of the many variations of panentheistic

God-world models in the West. While it may be too great of a stretch to say that Plato himself was a panentheist, he should at least qualify as a proto-panentheist.[3] After all, one of Plato's ideas would go on to inspire the highly contagious panentheistic tradition that flows through Schelling, Schleiermacher (the father of theologically liberal Christianity), German Romanticism, English Idealism, English Romanticism, Jonathan Edwards, C.S. Pierce, and Transcendentalists like Ralph Waldo Emerson and Henry David Thoreau. Through his Neoplatonic interpreters, some of Plato's other ideas would inspire another panentheist stream that can be traced through Plotinus, Pseudo-Dionysius, Meister Eckhart, Jakob Böhme, Georg Hegel, Henri Bergson, and A.N. Whitehead.[4] Whitehead is famous for exaggerating the entire sweep of European philosophy as nothing more than "a series of footnotes to Plato."[5] His pronouncement may not be so exaggerated when applied to his own panentheistic philosophy and its sources.

Varieties

Precisely which way or ways is God in the world? There are differences of opinion about the degree to which God permeates, animates, sustains, influences, and experiences the world. Some see God's energies working in the world to redeem it and gradually turn it into something more indistinguishable from God. Others see God expressing Itself into the world and returning back to God. Some suggest God suffers along with the world, and others say God evolves as the world evolves. In all variations, the line between Creator and creation becomes blurred.

Is the world a necessary part of God? Or is it a voluntary extension of God? Does God determine everything that happens in the world? Or is there cooperation between creatures and Creator? Is God personal or nonpersonal? Not all panentheists answer the same way.[6] Many assume God to be non-personal, while some argue that It is personal. Most say God produced the world out of Itself, while some say God created the world out of nothing.[7] The former may tend to analogize the relationship between God and the world to the relationship between our minds and bodies. The latter may prefer to liken the God-world relationship to that of an adult mother carrying a developing infant inside her womb.

Some panentheistic God-world models are influenced more by the Plato-Schelling stream, while others take their cue from the Plotinus-Hegel stream of thought; some are intoxicated by both. Some may be more influenced by Gnosticism, Hermeticism, Kaballism, Swedenborgism, or Theosophy, while others may be more influenced by Spinoza, Stoicism, Hinduism, or Buddhism. Some variations adapt parts of Christianity to their framework, while others are antagonistic to it. Similarly, some lean more toward the pantheistic end of the spectrum, while others try to stay closer to theism.

Panentheism's Appeal

The panentheistic God-world model has some curb appeal. For some, it can shine like the new model on the block that sits between two dusty, dented, worn-out antiques. Attempting to find a happy medium between extremes, this adaptable view capitalizes on some of the strengths of pantheism and theism while distancing itself from some of their perceived weaknesses. In affirming God's radical immanence without denying Its transcendence, it appeals to those who think the God of pantheism too impersonal and the theistic God uncomfortably personal.[8] It also may provide a framework through which traditional religions like Christianity and Buddhism can be reinterpreted and thereby enhanced. Perhaps someday a panentheistic God-world model will become the ecumenical bridge between the great religious traditions of East and West.[9]

The most modern panentheistic models offer tantalizing fusions and compromises. They try to blend some of the latest trends in science with benign notions of spirituality.[10] This is attractive to those who believe that life evolved basically as Darwin imagined, but with a little help here and there from an intelligent designer who is intertwined with the world. By selectively confusing the supernatural world with the natural, those who feel the need for some type of unobtrusive God can embrace most of the naturalism (and antisupernaturalism) that dominates scientific academia today without totally rejecting some notion of the divine.

The problem of evil and suffering can also incline some people toward adopting the God of panentheism. Such a dynamic God may somehow seem exempt from accusations of blame for the problem of evil.[11] Others find solace in the idea that God's nexus with our world implies that It suffers when we suffer. The idea that God also suffers when the world itself is harmed is helping panentheism grow in popularity among those who are concerned with the ecological health of the earth. These are some of the main reasons that the panentheistic model of God has quietly replaced the traditional view of God in many divinity schools, pulpits, and universities.

Problems with "Christian Panentheism"

The biggest problem with all the attempts to reinterpret Christianity into a panentheistic framework is that the biblical data does not ultimately favor it. The Scripture passages panentheists offer as proof texts are few and are heavily outnumbered by many unambiguous passages that stress God's transcendence, otherness, and separateness from the world. Also, their proof texts may be interpreted better in theistic ways.

Acts 17, for example, contains what may be the most powerful proof text Christian panentheists can cite. While reasoning with Stoic philosophers (verse 18), the apostle Paul quoted the Stoic poet Epimenides, saying, "In him [the highest God] we live and move and have our being" (verse 28). Because Paul seems to quote this favorably, we are left wondering if Paul was sympathetic to pantheistic and panentheistic views of God. But when the verse is viewed in its larger context, it becomes clear that Paul was not sympathetic to Stoicism at all. Rather, he was correcting their misguided metaphysic. He said that they did not know God at all (verse 23), that they were ignorant (verse 30), and that they needed to learn the basics of the proper Hebraic God-worldview.

The points Paul proceeded to make oppose pantheistic, panentheistic, and polytheistic God-world models: God made the world and does not live in any part of it (verse 24); humans do not contribute anything to God or satisfy any of God's needs (verse 25); humans are not part of God (verses 26-27); God is nothing like the things we form from created matter (verse 29). This is in harmony with the rest of the Scriptures, which never depict Earth as an emanation of, extension of, or dwelling place of God—it is never His temple. The Bible depicts heaven[12] as the throne which God sits upon and the earth as His "footstool" (Isaiah 66:1; Matthew 5:35; Acts 7:49).

The attempts by panentheists to discredit classical theism's view of God as being "the God of the philosophers" (in contrast with the God of the Bible) deserve to be discredited.[13] It is true that both Augustine and Aquinas were extremely familiar with Neoplatonism and influenced by it in some significant ways. But they rejected all of its parts that were not reconcilable with the writings of the Old Testament prophets, the New Testament apostles, and the early church fathers.[14]

Meanwhile, every panentheistic model has been built mainly of blocks from many pagan philosophers. Panentheism then is, to understate it, "the other God of the philosophers."[15] No theology can develop in a philosophical vacuum. Rejecting one philosophical trend simply entails the adoption of another. The choice here is not between a pure theology that is wholly uninfluenced by the philosophizing of the ancient Greeks and a theology tainted by it. The choice, rather, is whether philosophy will serve theology, in harmony with divine revelation, or theology will be forced to fit a pagan philosophy that is at odds with revelation. At the risk of oversimplification, the choice is between Aquinas and Plotinus.

The Fatal Flaw of Panentheism

Our world is limited in size, limited in age, caused, and changing. God is not. At the outset, it seems like a fool's errand to try to mix these mutually exclusive characteristics together. But this is what the hard-core panentheists so audaciously attempt to accomplish. Whitehead, for example, concluded that God and the world are somehow both permanent and fluent, one and many, immanent in one another, transcendent to

one another, and created by the other.[16] The God imagined by John Cobb is constantly being destroyed and recreated in every moment of world history.[17] What powerful philosophical arguments can they marshal to commend and defend such credulity-straining Gods?

They assume incorrectly that the traditional reasons given for theism were overturned long ago and, therefore, they don't really need to compete in that arena.[18] Doubting that reason should play a heavy role in faith about a God who exists outside of our universe might help explain their shift toward a more world-centered and scientifically trendy God. Even so, some arguments have been advanced. Some, for example, have argued that because God is absolutely infinite in every possible way, it must be impossible for anything else to exist outside of God.[19] But the insistence that an infinite God is somehow too limited to create a world that fits in the palm of His hand (Psalm 95:3-5), so to speak, while not being confusable with His hand, seems a little presumptuous.

Given that Whitehead's God-world model is acclaimed as one of the most brilliant panentheistic models to date, we might expect to find persuasive arguments in his writings. Cobb, one of the foremost experts on Whitehead, concludes that "Whiteheadian theology is not for those who seek certainty" because our understanding of the world is constantly changing.[20] Commending a changing worldview about a changing God based on our changing understanding of our changing world would be a challenge for anyone.

Not surprisingly then, both Cobb and Whitehead wrote and taught "as though there were no philosophical reason for affirming [their view] of God other than the demand of a coherent completion of the idea of God as actual entity." Only twice did Whitehead begin to make a halfhearted and "obscure" argument for his God.[21] "Has Whitehead 'proved' the existence of God?" Cobb asks. "Obviously the answer to these questions is no," he answers. "Nothing is proved in this sense…Whitehead's argument for the existence of God, insofar as there is an argument at all, is primarily the traditional one from the order of the universe to a ground of order."[22] But because it is impossible for the panentheist to even know where to draw the line between Artist and artwork, the argument for God from order fits better with classical theism. For those seeking a logical and intellectually satisfying God-world model, panentheism may dazzle then disappoint. By contrast, the case for the Christian God, who is entirely different from everything else in the universe, proves far more logically compelling.

Part Eight

QUESTIONS ABOUT APOLOGISTS OF THE PAST

Who Was Justin Martyr?

William E. Nix

During the second century AD, a new genre of literature appeared in the Christian church and flourished from about AD 130–180. It was the "apology" (*apologia*, "a speech for the defense"). "Apologists of the early church faced two distinct fronts, the Jewish and the Greco-Roman, and thus created two discrete bodies of apologetic literature."[1] Harry Y. Gamble offers insight into the interaction between Christianity and Judaism when he writes,

> Christianity was a form of Judaism, and the dialogue between Christianity and Judaism was as old as Christianity itself. Christians used Jewish Scripture to argue their claim to Judaism's ancient revelation, to their continuity with Jewish history, and to the fulfillment of divine promises. Mutual antagonism was commonplace between Judaism and Christianity both theologically and demographically.[2]

Through "missionary efforts among non-Jews outside Palestine, Christianity came increasingly into contact with the Greco-Roman world as it gained visibility in the larger society. Although many Gentiles were drawn to Christianity, many others perceived it as politically dangerous, socially offensive, or intellectually absurd."[3] The earliest apologists were Quadratus (117–138), Aristides (138–147), Melito of Sardis (fl. 169–180), Athenagoras (late second century), Bishop Theophilus of Antioch (late second-century), and Justin Martyr[4] (c. 100–c. 165). Justin Martyr, arguably the most famous apologist, was a lay Christian philosopher who operated a school in Rome around the middle of the second century.

Life

Justin was "the son of Priscus and grandson of Bacchius, natives of Flavia Neapolis ('new city of Flavius') in *Palestine*."[5] Flavia Neapolis was built (AD 72) near the former city of Shechem, by order and in honor of the new Roman emperor, Titus Flavius Caesar Vespasianus Augustus (ruled AD 69–79). It was populated with veterans of Vespasian's legions, imported captives from conquered territories, and native Samaritans. In *Dialogue of Justin with a Jew*,[6] Justin told of his early studies in the various schools of philosophy as a quest for truth and God.[7]

Instead of philosophical unity, he found a many-headed collection of Sophists, Stoics, Peripatetics, Aristotelians, Pythagoreans, and Platonists (he favored Plato for a time).[8]

The Bar Kokhba revolt (AD 132–135) marked the complete separation of Christians from their Jewish roots. Justin related that following this war, Christians were persecuted and threatened with punishment if they did not deny Jesus as the Messiah and blaspheme Him. Justin's conversion to Christianity came at about this time.[9]

Eusebius wrote that Justin's "conversion from Greek philosophy to true religion was an act of deliberate judgment" (*Dial.* 8). It occurred when he encountered an old man in a Grecian covered portico (Xystus) near the sea (at Neapolis or at Ephesus). Using the Socratic method, he raised questions that only the "Christian philosophy" could answer.[10] Justin related his conversion with "Trypho...called a Hebrew of the circumcision, and having escaped from the war lately carried on there... spending [his] days in Greece, and chiefly at Corinth..." So Justin asked, "And in what... would you be profited by philosophy so much as by your own lawgiver and the prophets?" "Why not?" he replied. "Do not the philosophers turn every discourse on God? And do not questions continually arise to them about His unity and providence? Is not this truly the duty of philosophy, to investigate the Deity?"[11] This became Justin's personal quest.

The Jewish background gave Justin ideas of the preexistent Law, preexistent Wisdom, preexistent Messiah, and preexistent Spirit. "For the term *Logos,* there was the possible background in the Old Testament 'word of the Lord' and in the Jewish Targums (paraphrases of Scripture) of the *memra* ('Word') of the Lord as an intermediary between God and his world."[12]

For Justin, God the Father was the ultimate authority who revealed His truth to the Hebrew prophets, who preceded the Greek philosophers and historians by centuries. The Greeks had failed as a result of their personal greed and self-aggrandizement. Their gods were the evil spirits (Aeons) described in the Hebrew Scriptures. According to Justin, the Greeks had lost sight of the object of their investigation and speculation. They were unable to find either God or His truth, or to lead others to their goal.

Justin moved to Rome, where he resided for a long time and opened a school. While in Rome, "at the height of his fame, in the garb of philosopher, [he] served as ambassador of the word of God and contended in his writings for the faith."[13] His church "had orderly arrangements for instructing converts in Christian doctrine and for satisfying itself that they had properly absorbed it."[14]

Writings

Justin was a voluminous writer, but unfortunately, some of his works have not survived. In a letter to Irenaeus (second century), he identified a "*Treatise against all the Heresies that have existed* already composed..."[15] Irenaeus quoted Justin's *Treatise against Marcion*, the heretic "of Pontus who [Marcion] is even at this day alive, and teaching his disciples to believe in some other god greater than the Creator."[16]

Justin's *First Apology* (written at Rome AD 150–155), was addressed "To the Emperor..."[17] His work *Dialogue of Justin with a Jew*[18] contained 152 chapters and is more personal than are his Apologies.

The *Dialogue* expounded on many passages from the Septuagint translation, especially the Psalms, Moses, and the Prophets. Nine chapters are an exposition of Psalm 22, depicting the crucifixion of Christ.[19] He also cited the Gospels as "memoirs" of the apostles.

Justin's eschatology held that "Christ will reign [at Jerusalem] a thousand years. This millenarian, or 'chiliastic,' doctrine was widely popular at this time."[20] One of his followers was Tatian, who traveled to Rome, where he met Justin and may have become a Christian there. He was the author of a combination and collection of the Gospels named *The Diatessaron*.[21] "After Justin's martyrdom, Tatian left the church, being exalted by the idea of becoming a teacher and puffed up as superior to others,"[22] and he followed the way of Valentinus, Marcion, and Saturnius.

Theology

The doctrines of the divinity of Christ and of the Holy Spirit were imperfectly developed in logical precision prior to AD 325, and the doctrine of the Trinity, founded on them, was not made any clearer as a result. "Because of their Jewish background and opposition to paganism, early Christians, stressed the oneness of God, but they knew the Messiah and the experience of the Holy Spirit as the working of God."[23] The trinitarian formula, in its simplest biblical and practical shape, appeared in all the creeds of the first three centuries. It was based on the baptismal order (Matthew 28:19). Trinitarian doxologies were used at Smyrna on the martyrdom of Polycarp, and by Clement of Rome. Justin repeatedly placed Father, Son, and Spirit together as objects of divine worship among the Christians (though not being altogether equal in dignity).

Moreover, Athenagoras wrote *A Plea for the Christians* (c. AD 177) and *On the Resurrection of the Dead*.[24] In *A Plea*, he confessed "his well-developed doctrine about the Trinity"[25] as faith in Father, Son, and Spirit, who were one as to the idea and energizing power (κατὰ δύναμιν, *kata dynamin*), but whom he distinguished as to order or dignity (τάξις, *taxis*) in subordination style.[26]

What is more, Theophilus of Antioch "wrote three books *To Autolycus* (c. AD 180) that attacked pagan idolatry and emperor worship, contrasted the pagan description of their gods with sayings from Old Testament prophets, and compared Christian morality with the immorality of paganism."[27] He was the first to denote the relation of the three divine persons by the term *Triad*,[28] whereas Origen (c. AD 185–c. AD 251) authored the term *God–man*.

As ardent monotheists, "the Apologists were the first try to frame an intellectually satisfying explanation of the relation of Christ to God the Father...They were determined at all costs not to compromise this fundamental truth."[29] Reduced to its essentials, they proposed that "as pre-existent, Christ was the Father's thought or mind, and that, as manifested in creation and revelation, He was its extrapolation or expression."[30] They had recourse to the imagery of the divine *Logos*, or Word, familiar to later Judaism as well as to Stoicism, which had become fashionable through the influence of Philo, and to the fourth Gospel (John 1:1-14).[31]

Regarding the *Logos* before creation, Justin wrote,

...the Logos existed in the Father as His rationality and then, by an act of His will, being generated, He emphasized the Word's essential unity with the Father...The birth of the Logos involves a distribution, but no severance. Whatever is severed is cut off from its original, but that which is distributed undergoes division in the economy without impoverishing the source from which it is derived. The Word issues forth from the Father's power without depriving His begetter of His Word (*Dial.* 61; 128).[32]

The *Logos* served as the Father's instrument in creating and governing the universe and, in particular, making men in the divine image. Justin continued,

> Reason was that which united men to God and gave them knowledge of Him. Before Christ's coming men had possessed, as it were, in a sense, seeds of the Logos and had thus been enabled to arrive at fragmentary facets of truth...The Logos had now become incarnate in His entirety in Jesus Christ, and is now conceived of as the Father's intelligence or rational thought...He was not only in name distinct from the Father, as the light is from the sun, but was "numerically distinct too."[33]

J.N.D. Kelly described Justin's proof:

> ...particularly concerned to develop against Jewish monotheism, was threefold. The Word's otherness, he thought, was implied (a) by the alleged appearances of God in the Old Testament... (b) by the frequent Old Testament passages...which represent God as conversing with another, who is presumable a rational being like Himself... and (c) by the great Wisdom texts... since everyone must agree that the offspring is other than its begetter.[34]

Justin accused the Jews of cutting out portions of the Old Testament and of rejecting the Septuagint (the Greek translation of the Hebrew Scriptures) interpretations, and otherwise rejecting their own Scriptures.[35] Ferguson says, "The Apologists more explicitly state a pre-existent Trinity of God, the *Logos* (Word), and the Holy Spirit, but it is especially in regard to Christ as the Logos of God that they made their most significant contribution."[36]

The majority of Justin's confessions "exhibit the familiar three-clause groundplan...the pattern was imprinted on his mind."[37]

In addition, Justin was among the first to furnish a complete description of the celebration of the Eucharist.[38] He reproduced an accepted baptismal form in *Apology.* I, 46 and again in *Apology.* I, 61.[39] His Christological kerygma (i.e., the core message of Christ) followed the type seen from the preaching of the apostles and in his *Dialogue.*[40] Ferguson said this about the significance of Justin's contribution to Christology:

> The Logos Christology of the second-century Greek Apologists became the basis for later orthodox speculations on the Trinity...[and] Justin pioneered the doctrine that was most fully expressed by Athenagoras and Theophilus... [They] represent the confluence of ideas from both the pagan and the Jewish sides that could be used to support the preexistence of Jesus Christ.[41]

Martyrdom

The fact of Justin's martyrdom is beyond dispute.[42] Irenaeus bore witness to it, and from the time of Tertullian, Justin has always been known as "the martyr." Eusebius wrote,

> Justin...after delivering to the rulers mentioned in a second book in behalf of our opinions, was adorned with

divine martyrdom when the philosopher Crescens, who strove in life and behavior of cynic which he bore, instigated the plot against him, for Justin had often defeated him in debate in the presence of hearers, and finally bound on himself the trophies of victory by his martyrdom for the truth of which he was an ambassador.[43]

Marcus Dods also translated the story of Justin's trial and martyrdom in "The Martyrdom of the Holy Martyrs, Justin, Chariton, Charites, Paeon, and Liberianus, who Suffered at Rome."[44] The *Acts of the Martyrdom of St. Justin and His Companions* is one of the oldest surviving records of trials of Christians.

Who Was Augustine?

William E. Nix

The Nicene (referring to the time of the Council of Nicaea in AD 325) and Post-Nicene (after the Council of Nicaea until the second Council of Nicaea in AD 787) periods of church history have been called the golden age of patristic literature in terms of the quantity and quality of writings available to us.[1] The most dominant Christian writer of this time was Aurelius Augustine, or Austin (354–430).[2] His life, writings, controversies, and influence dominated the period and generations thereafter.

Augustine was born at the Numidian city of Tagaste (Thagaste), a Roman-Berber commercial center located in what is now Algeria. His mother Monica (or Monnica), was a devout Christian, and his father, Patricius, was a pagan who converted to Christianity on his deathbed. Patricius's family were upper-class citizens known as "honorable" people. Augustine's family name, *Aurelius*, suggests that his father's ancestors were *freedmen* of the *gens Aurelia*, who were given full Roman citizenship by the Caracalla in AD 212. From a legal standpoint, Augustine's family had been Roman for at least a century by the time he was born, and his first language was likely to have been Latin.

Augustine, repelled by the grammar and style of the old Latin versions of the Bible, became enamored with classical Latin. After studies at Madaura and Carthage, he taught at Tagaste and Carthage. In the meantime, he acquired a concubine, to whom he was faithful and by whom a son was born, Adeodatus (meaning "gift from God"). His mother, Monica, had urged him throughout his adult life to be rid of her.

Augustine the Manichæan Philosopher

"During his student days, Augustine was converted to philosophy in general, but not to any particular philosophy. Cicero's now lost work, *Hortensius*, was his first intellectual turning point."[3] "Like many Christians, Augustine was attracted by the radical dualism and rational piety of Manichæism, which presented itself as Christianity for intellectuals."[4]

In AD 384, Augustine was appointed professor of rhetoric at Milan, partly due to the influence of his Manichæan students in Rome. While in Milan he heard Bishop Ambrose, who gave the most intellectually respectable interpretation of Scripture he had heard. While there, the presbyter Simplicianus took on Augustine as his personal project. Augustine read the commentary on Paul written by Marius Victorinus, who had been converted in AD 355 from Neoplatonism (the philosophy of Plotinus) to Christianity. Augustine underwent an *intellectual conversion* but not yet a *moral conversion*. It took him some time to get his relationship with his concubine worked out.[5]

...After this failure of sexual self-control, Augustine heard about the austere lives of uneducated monks, who could control themselves in a way the intellectual Augustine could not. Conversion for him, as for many in this period, meant a decision for the highest type of Christianity, asceticism. The problem became now not so much one of belief as of action.[6]

Augustine's moral conversion occurred in AD 386, while he was agonizing in his garden over his moral failures.

He heard...a sing-song the refrain, *Tolle, lege* ("Pick up and read"). There was a book of the letters of Paul on a bench, and Augustine picked it up and read, "Let us behave decently, as in the daytime, not in orgies and drunkenness, not in sexual immorality and debauchery, not in dissension and jealousy. Rather, clothe yourselves with the Lord Jesus Christ, and do not think about how to gratify the desires of the sinful nature" (Romans 13:13-14).[7]

Augustine took this as the Lord speaking directly to him, and he retired to a country estate to reflect seriously about Christianity

before enrolling for baptism from Ambrose on Easter Sunday AD 387. He turned away from his rhetorical career and, with Adeodatus and Monica, started back to North Africa. Monica died at Ostia while awaiting passage. Following her death, Augustine ended his 15-year relationship with his concubine, and shortly after "he decided to become a celibate priest."[8] Having found peace, Augustine returned to Tagaste and gathered some friends to join him in a monastic community.

Augustine's Turning Point

By AD 391, Augustine was ordained presbyter for the Catholic church at Hippo (north Africa). A largely Donatist city, it presented him with a most pressing problem. He began preaching for the Greek bishop, who was not fluent in either Latin or Punic. In AD 395, Augustine became cobishop, and within a year after that he became sole bishop of Hippo. He continued a monastic community life with his clergy and for whom he wrote the *Augustinian Rule*.[9] He spent many hours daily judging and counseling disputes and problems as well as producing an enormous literary output.[10]

Augustine's successive ordinations marked a turning point in his life. No longer was he the philosopher-Christian concerned with the dialectic of the interior search for God. Now he was also a pastor, who had to turn his attention increasingly to the Scriptures and their exposition and to the practical problems of the churches in North Africa. This crucial juncture in his life was marked by the writing of his *Confessions*...[11]

Confessions (c. 397-401) is perhaps Augustine's most influential work and is considered one of the classics of Western literature and spirituality. After praising God for His greatness, Augustine declared, "Thou movest us to delight in praising Thee; for Thou hast formed us for Thyself, and our hearts are restless till they find rest in Thee."[12] *Confessions* is a "penetrating analysis of sin, human nature, and psychology of religion. Books 1-9 are autobiographical, praising God for His graces earlier in Augustine's life despite his own sins; Book 10 is epistemological (on knowledge, time, memory, and the church); Books 11-13 are an allegorical exegesis of Genesis 1."[13]

Walker observes, "In this remarkable work, as he sums up his past and turns to the future, Augustine sounds a theme which will permeate his thinking about every major problem he would face."[14]

The City of God

Written AD 413–426, Augustine's *The City of God* was a response to the sacking of Rome in AD 410. The city was attacked by King Alaric and the Visigoths, and although at this time it was no longer the capital of the empire, Rome was still important as a symbol of the empire. Pagans charged that Rome was being punished by the gods of the Republic for forsaking their worship. Christians, known as "atheists" at the time, were blamed for these misfortunes. Augustine responded to the accusations and addressed the relationship of God's providence to the Roman Empire. This scope "proved too narrow a frame of reference for Augustine, who undertook to study the providential action of God with regard to the whole of human history."[15]

Books 1-10, the negative and apologetic part, are an attack on paganism. They deal with such questions as, Was Christianity responsible for the fall of Rome? What spiritual power presided over the rise of Rome?

Has any pagan system a serious claim against Christianity, the true spiritual religion? Books 11-22, the positive philosophy of history part, explain the origin, progress, and end of the two cities. Here Augustine broadened the term *city* to mean "society." There are two cities—of the just (of God, the celestial city) and of the wicked (of the devil, the self, the terrestrial city). Through their love, human beings adhere to either one or the other—to God or to self. The two cities are confused always and everywhere in this world, and they are in constant strife. God, by His providence, prepares for the victory of the celestial city, which will be consummated in the fullness of time. God's judgment consists of giving people what they love most—life with Him or separation from Him. For Augustine, humans receive the object of their desire.[16]

In *The City of God*, Augustine elaborated a view of history that involved a nonmillennial eschatology (no literal 1,000-year reign of Christ). Instead of taking a literal view of Revelation 20:3,7, he viewed the text as figurative. This was a radical departure from what had been customary among the church fathers prior to him. Another innovation by Augustine was his linear rather than cyclical view of the flow of history. "As the *Confessions* was theology experienced in a soul—God's action in the individual, the *City of God* was theology lived in the historical framework of humanity—God's action in the world. Augustine treated current questions from such a noble standpoint that the work remains a classic statement of Christian philosophy, offering profound and original views on common problems of the human mind. He covers concerns that still present moral dilemmas—rape, abortion, suicide."[17]

On the Holy Trinity

Between AD 399-419, as Arians (followers of the bishop Arius, who rejected the deity of Christ) were entering north Africa, Augustine published *The Fifteen Books of Aurelius Augustinus, Bishop of Hippo, On the Trinity*, as his major doctrinal work. Books 1-7 seek to establish the doctrine according to Scripture, and to answer objections. Books 8-15 explore analogies to the Trinity in human nature.

"Since human beings are made in the image of God, the trinitarian nature of God is imprinted on human beings; for instance, the mind consists of three aspects: memory, intellect, and will. Developing the biblical revelation that 'God is love,' Augustine hypothesizes love as the eternal relation (the Holy Spirit) between the Father (the Lover) and the Son (the Beloved)."[18] Moving beyond the Eastern formulations of the Trinity in a significant way, Augustine gave special content to the third person, and provided the basis for the procession of the Holy Spirit as coming from *both* the Father *and* the Son, not simply from the Father *through* the Son. This would later become critical in the *filioque* controversy (Latin word referring to the controversy over whether the Holy Spirit proceeded from the Father "and [from] the Son") leading to the Third Council of Toledo (589).[19]

Augustine Versus the Manichæans

Augustine had to deal with three heresies, all of which were confronting the Church with problems of the greatest moment...[it was] through struggles with these systems that his own theology was formulated. The least dangerous was Manichaeism, for its doctrines were too obviously remote from historic Christianity to have any real hope of success at that period.[20]

This extreme form of dualism followed the teachings of Manes (or Mani, or Manichæus). Manes (c. AD 216–276) had "transformed the cramped ritualistic views of the Judeo-Christian sect...into a coherent body of Gnostic dogma, uncompromisingly dualistic, consequential, and deeply conscious of having 'unveiled' truths of universal validity."[21]

Manichænism spread from Egypt in the late third century to Rome in the early fourth century and into north Africa during the fourth century. A radical offshoot of the Gnostic traditions of East Persia, Manichænism struck Christians as a "Pauline heresy."[22] It was particularly alluring because it offered an easy solution to the problem of good and evil.

Augustine's anti-Manichæan writings spanned the course of his career.[23] He had been a lector of the Manichæans over a period of nine years before his intellectual conversion.[24] Skepticism led him away from Manichæan dualism, but he did not break with it completely when he moved to Rome.[25] He seems to have retained some elements from his Manichæan experience,[26] including doctrines about the origin of sin, the sin of Adam and Eve being placed in the use of marriage (founded in concupiscence), the transmission of the sin nature both in the body and in the soul (known as traducianism), and election.

Traducianism is a theory that the human soul is transmitted by parents to their children in a way similar to the generation of individual bodies. It was preferred to theories that individual souls "preexist in an immaterial condition [as Origen speculated] and are subsequently joined to bodies by their own choice or God's decree."[27] Early Christians considered two different forms of traducianism: the materialist form following Tertullian (fl. AD 200), and the form developed by Augustine, who rejected Tertullian's theory.

> Augustine proposed…that God creates the soul of the offspring by working on the spiritual substrate drawn from the souls of the generating parents. Such an origin of the human soul could explain the inheritance of the guilt and punishment of original sin and provide a mechanism for the transmission of its consequences, particularly mortality and concupiscence.[28]

Ultimately, however, Augustine was unwilling to endorse either the traducianist theory (soul generated through the parents) or the alternative creationist theory (God creates each new soul) of the origin of the soul. He judged that Scripture simply did not provide an answer to the question.

Augustine Versus Donatists

When Augustine was ordained and began his Christian ministry at Hippo, the most urgent problem he faced on the practical side was the Donatist controversy. "The underlying problem was the old issue of laxism versus rigorism in the treatment of those who were thought to have compromised in some way with the governing authorities during the persecution."[29] Donatists took the line of rigorism; they taught that the validity of the sacraments depended on the worthiness of the minister. By its laxism the church had ceased to be holy and forfeited its claim to be Christ's body because it tolerated unworthy bishops and officers. The infection resulted in the contamination of everyone who maintained communion with them in Africa and throughout the whole world.[30] This controversy "forced Augustine to carry the doctrines of the Church, the Sacraments,

and Sacramental grace to a stage beyond that reached by any of his predecessors, and thereby to influence all subsequent Western theology."[31]

Donatus, a young Numidian deacon, had already caused a schism when he rebaptized Orthodox clergy who had lapsed during the Great Persecution of Diocletian (AD 303– 305). Donatists also claimed that Catholic ordinations to the priesthood were traceable to bishops who had collaborated with persecutors by handing over holy books to them during that persecution.[32] Under Miltiades, Bishop of Rome, a commission investigated the dispute (AD 313). "It decided against the Donatists, who appealed unsuccessfully, to the Synod of Arles (314) and then to the Emperor [Constantine] (316), who complicated the issue by imposing his decision in the matter. The Emperor began to apply coercion in 316, but abandoned it in 321."[33]

Relying on African regional feeling, the theological authority of Cyprian, Numidian jealousy of Carthage, and economic unrest, Donatism prospered. "When later Donatist leaders associated themselves with violent bands of marauders, called *circumcelliones*, state repression began again (347) under Constans, but was relaxed under Julian (361-3)."[34]

The immediate response to the Donatists was written by Optatus, bishop of Milevis (AD 366 or 367), who argued three basic points: First, sacraments derive their validity from God, not from the priest who administers them. Second, he challenged the Donatist doctrine of the church's holiness and their insistence that membership be limited to people who are in a state of goodness. Third, he suggested that catholicity and unity are at least as decisive tokens of the church as holiness. "To Optatus, as with Cyprian, schism is tantamount to apostasy."[35]

Augustine developed and deepened Optatus's thoughts during his prolonged controversy with the Donatists. In *On Baptism, Against the Donatists*, he asserted that "baptism can be conferred outside the Catholic communion by heretics or schismatics, but that it ought not to be received from them; and that it is of no avail to any while in a state of heresy or schism."[36] Augustine also wrote *Answer to Letters of Petilian, Bishop of Cirta*, and *On the Correction of the Donatists* in support of the Catholic position of an open church membership as opposed to the Donatist closed church emphasis.[37] He accepted the civil power as part of God's providence and came to accept the aid of the state to punish and suppress heresy and schism. Augustine argued that the Lord of the harvest would separate the wheat from the tares at His second coming and the judgment of the world.

Augustine Against the Pelagians

Pelagianism was a religious reform movement that was spread from Rome through southern Italy and Sicily into north Africa.[38] "Pelagius was born (c. 350) in Britain. His father was a physician who had accompanied the bureaucrats there and had married a Celt. Both were Christians and had high ambitions for their son, who was a commanding figure."[39]

Pelagius arrived in Rome about AD 390 to study law, be baptized, and to become a moral reformer and spiritual leader.[40] He moved and taught in the same aristocratic circles where Jerome had once proclaimed the virtues of the ascetic life, and Pelagius acquired in the process an enthusiastic and dedicated body of followers. His message called for a rigorous standard of moral

perfection for Christians; he insisted that perfection was truly within the reach of everyone of natural capacity with freedom of choice.[41]

The Pelagian controversy was occasioned by certain teachings that originated with Celestius and not Pelagius. Celestius had remained in Carthage, where he applied for ordination as a presbyter. He had involved himself in discussions about sin, the fall of Adam, and baptism. His discussions were presumed to be the views of Pelagius.

Paulinus, a Milanese deacon, brought six accusations against Celestius as contradicting a standing tradition of African Christian teaching, which "justified the baptism of infants on the ground that from conception they were alienated from God because of their involvement in the original sin of Adam."[42] Celestius's teachings were condemned, and his application for ordination was denied by a local synod (AD 411).[43]

> Augustine was not present at this synod, and he knew of Celestius's teaching only by report...In *On the Reward and Remission of Sins* (412) and *On the Spirit and the Letter* (412) Augustine agreed with his fellow African bishops that the baptism of infants was necessary, which presupposed their implication in Adam's original sin. Pelagius felt no necessity for infant baptism, but was willing to conform to the custom of the church.[44]

Pelagius also wrote a brilliant *Exposition of Paul's Epistle to the Romans*, the text of which is available in Augustine's *Anti-Pelagian Writings*.[45] "More than fourth-century commentators on Paul, Augustine explored the conflict between law and grace, and plumbed the depth of sin as not just wrong acts but as something in human nature."[46]

Augustine also indicated that, for him, the central matter was the necessity of grace. "Grace for Augustine was more than a soteriological concept. It was also important for epistemology. Human beings are unable to see and know God, not only because of their sinfulness, but also because of their created condition and the limitations of time. Hence revelation is necessary for knowledge of God, and grace's effect on the reason is primarily revelatory."[47] He thought both Pelagius and Celestius called into question the truth that it is by the grace of Christ that human beings are saved—"that is, by the Holy Spirit, who sheds the love of God abroad in our hearts."[48]

At Jerusalem, and later at a synod at Diospolis (Lydda), Pelagius disclaimed the teachings of Celestius and assured the assembled bishops that his own views had none of the implications the Africans had seen in them. The synod thus received him into full communion in the church.

In response, Augustine and his colleagues assembled two councils: one at Carthage for the province of Africa, and one at Mileve for the province of Numidia. These unanimously condemned the Pelagian position and appealed for confirmation of their view to Pope Innocent I (AD 402–417). In vague and rather general terms the pope concurred. His successor, Pope Zosimus (AD 417–418), however, was of a different mind. Having received a confession of faith, *Libellus fidei* ("Book of Faith"), from Pelagius himself, and an appeal in person from Celestius, Zosimus declared that he could find no fault in them.

Two developments, however, led the pope to change his position. Celestius's teachings created serious public disturbances among the Christians in Rome. Encouraged by pressure from the leaders of the African church, including Augustine, Emperor Honorius issued a rescript condemning Pelagianism and ordered the exile of its adherents. This caused Zosimus to issue a circular letter, the so-called *Epistola tractatoria*, which approved the African position related to the Council at Carthage (AD 418).

These decisions did not end the theological controversy, however, because many of Augustine's followers sensed that his position against Pelagianism had shifted. Due to the corruption of human nature itself, humans are incapable of turning by their own strength from self-love and "concupiscence" to love for God. His stress of the sole efficacy of divine grace evolved into a strong doctrine of predestination, and he sought to allay the implications of his teaching in the treatise *On Grace and Free Will* (427). "Augustine came under attack by the new leader of the Pelagian cause—the brilliant and acerbic opponent in Julian, bishop of Eclanum. His manner of combining argument, ridicule, and personal attack greatly troubled Augustine's last years, evoked from him uncharacteristically bitter replies, and caused him to adopt more "extreme positions."[49] The debate between these two protagonists was cut short by Augustine's death (432) and the Vandal conquest of Rome's north African provinces.[50]

Augustine's theology survived in a modified form, and has spread far and wide even to this day. It is nearly impossible to do theology or engage in apologetics without drawing upon Augustinian thought at some point. This has earned Augustine the well-respected name of "the Medieval Monolith."

Who Was Anselm?

Ralph MacKenzie

Anselm (AD 1033–1109), Archbishop of Canterbury and Benedictine monk, was born in Italy. He was the son of a Lombard landowner and a native of Aosta. After several years of undisciplined life, he crossed the Alps into France in AD 1056, and by AD 1059, Anselm entered the monastic school in Normandy. His strong character and remarkable intellectual skills gained him a high reputation as a teacher and spiritual director. He paid several visits to England, where he won the respect of William I and many barons. In March of 1093, King William II appointed Anselm to become the Archbishop of Canterbury. Anselm reluctantly agreed and was consecrated.

Anselm was the most penetrating Christian thinker between Augustine and Thomas Aquinas. Like Aquinas, Anselm owed much to Augustine, whose guiding principle "faith seeking understanding" he adopted for his own.

Anselm's practical and devotional writings abound with passages of sincere evangelical warmth. Following is an example that Anselm constructed to be delivered by clerics for those who were close to death:

Does thou believe that thou canst not be saved but by the death of Christ?

The sick man answers, Yes. Then let it be said to him: Go to, then and whilst thy soul abideth in thee, put all your confidence in this death alone…

Lord, I place the death of our Lord Jesus Christ between me and thy judgment; and with thee. And if He shall say unto thee, that thou art a sinner, say, I place the death of our Lord Jesus Christ between me and my sins…

These are welcome words of comfort to those who are dying.

Anselm also wrote *Cure Deus Homo*—a Latin title that translates to *Why God Became Man*. In this famous work, he answered the critical charge, mostly coming from Jews and Muslims, that it was beneath God's nature and unnecessary for God to become a man and die for our sins. Here, Anselm demonstrated that God cannot abandon humanity and that the incarnation was the most reasonable way to solve the sin problem. He essentially redirected people's thinking on the nature and purpose of the atonement, which had been in place since the apostolic era. The view held at the time was the "ransom theory." Like Augustine's view, this position stated that the atonement was an antidote over the forces of sin and evil, a deliverance of humanity from the clutches of Satan.

Anselm's contribution is called the "satisfaction theory." It understands the atonement as compensation to the Father; sin is perceived as robbing God of the honor that is due to Him. Our case seems hopeless; hence, the God-Man. The Reformers would form their view of salvation based on Anselm's model.

Anselm was not only a deep thinker, he was also interested in Christian social work. In 1102, in his capacity as Archbishop of Canterbury, he delivered one of the first and strongest attacks on the slave trade in England. Slavery would not end in England for more than 700 years. In 1720, Pope Clement XI declared Anselm a Doctor of the Church.

Anselm's Apologetic

For Anselm, divine revelation conveyed the content of the Christian faith. However, he allowed a limited role for reason and philosophy, for they could aid in pursuing a fuller understanding or justification of the biblical content. What is more, philosophy can help show the inner consistency of the Christian faith. Because of this, most view Anselm as an early representative of scholasticism, which opened the door for Aristotelian philosophy to have a greater role in the thinking of theologians of the Middle Ages as represented by Thomas Aquinas (c. 1225–1274).

By 1077, Anselm sought a deeper understanding of his faith when he wrote the *Monologion,* in which he offered his

argument for the existence of God based on degrees of goodness. Namely, because we can understand that there are degrees of goodness, there must be a supreme goodness by which to measure the degrees. This supreme goodness is also the greatest good; hence, we know this greatest good as God.

The following year, Anselm wrote the *Proslogion,* in which he set out his ontological argument for the existence of God. Again, arguing from the Augustinian principle of faith seeking understanding, Anselm defined God as the greatest conceivable being. Because this being cannot be conceived not to exist, He is greater than any being than can be conceived not to exist. Therefore, God is identified as the greatest conceivable being who cannot be conceived not to exist. Though not the first to emphasize this, Anselm forcefully advanced in the *Proslogion* the notion that God is a perfect being and exists without lack.

A Faith That Can Stand Scrutiny

Though the merits of Anselm's ontological argument have been debated from the beginning, often with good reason, at the very least it reveals confidence in the role of reason to help the believer understand the Christian faith. It would be incorrect to view Anselm as a fideist; rather, he sought to show the reasonable nature and inner consistency of Christian doctrine. That is to say, for Anselm, any objections from unbelievers could be answered rationally and could stand the scrutiny of the most ardent critic.

Who Was Thomas Aquinas?

Norman L. Geisler

Thomas Aquinas (c. 1225–1274) was a theologian, philosopher, and the premier Christian apologist of the medieval church. Born in Italy, he joined the Dominican Order. He studied at Naples and Paris, then started a school at Cologne and taught at Paris throughout his career except for eight years at the papal Curia at Rome. He died around the age of 49 and was canonized by the Roman Church in 1326.

Aquinas's writings are extensive and include *On the Soul*, *On Being and Essence*, *On Truth*, and *On the Power of God*. His most important work on Christian apologetics is the *Summa contra Gentiles*, which was written as a positive affirmation of Christianity against Islam and paganism. By far his most important and influential writing is his systematic theology, *Summa Theologica*, which was still unfinished at his death.

Aquinas's mind was intensely analytical and his writing was steeped in scholastic vocabulary, thus making his arguments difficult for modern readers to follow. His writing style is sometimes dialectical and highly complex, especially in the *Summa Theologica*. This is less so in *Summa contra Gentiles*.

Relevance to Theology and Apologetics

The most important topics Aquinas addressed in relation to apologetics include revelation, faith and reason, knowledge, reality, God, analogy (of religious language), creation, human beings, the problem of evil, and ethics. On these issues, Aquinas added significantly to a deeper understanding and better defense of the evangelical faith.

Revelation

Aquinas held that God reveals Himself in both nature and Scripture. His natural revelation (Romans 1:19-20) is available to all and is the basis for natural theology. The creation reveals one God and His essential attributes, but not the Trinity or the unique doctrines of the Christian faith, such as the incarnation of Christ or the way of salvation. God's natural revelation also includes a moral law that is binding on all people (Romans 2:12-15).

Although written by humans with differing literary styles,[1] the Bible is the only divinely authoritative book ever written.[2] For Aquinas, the Bible was inspired and inerrant, even in matters not essential to redemption.[3] No other Christian writing, neither those of the fathers nor the creeds, are inspired or revelatory. Instead, they are mere human interpretations of God's revelation in Scripture.[4]

Faith and Reason

Aquinas's answer to the relation of faith and reason is a surprising synthesis of the best elements of rationalism and existentialism. It preserves the sanctity of faith without sacrificing the necessity of reason. His answer stresses the need for faith without diminishing the importance of reason.

Following Augustine, Aquinas understood that faith is based on God's revelation in Scripture. Support for faith, however, is found in miracles and probable arguments.[5] Although God's existence is provable by reason, sin obscures our ability to know,[6] so belief (not proof) *that* God exists is necessary for most people.[7] Human reason, however, is never the basis for faith *in* God. According to Aquinas, demanding reasons for belief in God actually lessens the merit of faith.[8] Nonetheless, believers should reason about and for their faith.

Aquinas acknowledged that there are mysteries of the Christian faith, such as the Trinity and the incarnation, which can be known only by faith in God's revelation in Scripture.[9] These go beyond reason, but are not contrary to reason.

Knowledge

Aquinas made major contributions in epistemology, which examines the crucial elements and process by which we know something. His answer to the age-old question of which elements in the knowing process are innate and which are acquired is both insightful and enduring. Without sacrificing its contact with the real world through the senses, he shows how it is possible to know eternal truths by human reason.

Aquinas said knowledge comes either by supernatural revelation (in Scripture) or by natural means. Though all natural knowledge begins in experience and is gathered through the senses, everyone is born with the capacity to know.[10] That is to say, God has endowed everyone with a mind prior to any life experience, making the mind itself the only thing that was not gathered through sensory experience. For us to know something for certain is in fact possible by means of self-evident and undeniable first principles.[11] These include (1) the principle of identity (being is being), (2) the principle of noncontradiction (being is not nonbeing), (3) the principle of the excluded middle (either being or nonbeing), (4) the principle of causality (nonbeing cannot cause being), and (5) the principle of finality (every being acts for an end). By these and other first principles, the mind can attain knowledge of reality—even some certain knowledge.

Reality

Like Aristotle, order was important to Aquinas, who believed the proper goal of thinking individuals is to understand. The order that reason produces through various means is called logic, ethics, and art. What is more, Aquinas believed that nature was the order that reason contemplates, though Aquinas engaged in metaphysics when nature was studied in terms of reality as being.[12]

The heart of Aquinas's metaphysics is the real distinction between *essence* (*what* something is) and *existence* (*that* which is) in all finite beings.[13] Aquinas argued that only God is uncomposed Pure Being, which was known to him as Pure Actuality, with no "potentiality" whatsoever (i.e., no potential to gain, lose, or change His being in any way).[14]

Humankind is a composition of soul and body, which is composed of act (i.e., being) and potency (i.e., the finite potential to change, something that all creation possess).

God

Aquinas can help us build a solid theistic basis for doing historical apologetics. For him, it made no sense to speak of miracles or interventions of God (e.g., the resurrection) that prove that Christ was the Son of God unless we have first established that there is a God. That is to say, it makes no sense to speak of the Son of God if there is no God. Further, it is absurd to believe in acts of God (miracles) if there is no God who can act. Only God makes it possible to count the resurrection as a miracle. Theistic apologetics is the logical prerequisite of historical apologetics. Aquinas helped us do this foundational theistic work.

According to Aquinas, there are five ways we can demonstrate God's existence. We can argue (1) from motion to an Unmoved Mover, (2) from effects to a First Cause; (3) from contingent being to a Necessary Being, (4) from degrees of perfection to a Most Perfect Being; and (5) from designed purpose in nature to a Designer of nature.[15] Behind each of these arguments is the premise that all finite, changing beings need a cause outside themselves.

Unlike all of creation, which merely *has* being, God *is* Being. The former has *acquired* its being and is therefore dependent upon God for its coming to be and continued being. The latter is independent, for it is of God's essence to exist without dependence upon another (cf. Exodus 3:14, "I AM"). To put it simply, God is a unique Being in that His essence is identical to His existence, whereas there is a real distinction between essence and existence in all of creation.

From this Aquinas deduced the metaphysical attributes of God. For him, this made God a uniquely Necessary Being, which means He cannot *not* exist because it is of His essence to exist. Furthermore, because God has no potential to be anything other than what He is, He cannot change, since change either acquires something new or loses something. Therefore, any change in God would be for the worse, for to acquire being or lose being are both negative. For God to *acquire* being would make Him no different from dependent creation. For Him to *lose* being would mean He no longer exists.

According to Aquinas, if God has no "potential," He must also be unchanging (no potential to gain or lose, or no before or after), infinite (no limiting potential), indivisible (no potential to divide, thus no parts), and eternal (no potential to change, thus no experience of sequence of moments).[16]

Aquinas provided a philosophical answer to the growing influence of the "finite god" of process theology (or its modern evangelical offspring, known as open theism), which is the belief that God changes and develops over time in a similar manner as human beings. There is no better philosophical system capable of answering the threat raised by process theology and defending the traditional theistic and biblical view of God as an eternal, unchanging, and absolutely perfect Being.

Analogy

Thomistic analogy seems to be the only adequate answer to the problem of religious language—that is, how we make and understand meaningful statements about God.[17] Natural knowledge of God is derived from His creation in the same way that an efficient cause (source) is known from its effects. To put it another way, because God made the world, His creation resembles Him much like a painting resembles its painter. It is not the *same* as him (univocal), but it is *like* him (analogical). Our natural knowledge of God is based on that resemblance or analogy. Neither can our natural knowledge be totally different from Him (equivocal), since the cause (God) communicates something of itself to its effects (creation), and if our knowledge is totally different from Him we could know nothing.

On the other hand, univocal (totally the same) knowledge of God is impossible because our knowledge is *limited* and God is *unlimited*. Equivocal (totally different) knowledge of God is impossible because creation resembles the Creator; the effect resembles its efficient cause (source). Of course, there are great differences between God and creatures. Hence, the *via negativa* (i.e., the way of negation) is necessary. That is, *we must negate all limitations from our concepts before we apply them to God.* This means we must apply to God only the perfection signified (e.g., goodness, truth, strength, etc.), but not the finite mode of signification. This is crucial because there is a real difference between God's *infinite* attributes and man's *finite* attributes. Failing to employ the *via negativa* may either elevate man to infinite status or demote God to finite status.

What is more, the same attribute (e.g., goodness) will have the same *definition* for creatures and Creator, but a different *application* when it is applied to God. The reason for this is that creatures are only *finitely* good, while God is *infinitely* good. So before we can appropriately apply the term *good* to God, we must negate the finite mode (how) in which we find good among creatures and apply the meaning (what) to God in an infinite way.[18]

Creation

God did not create the world out of Himself (*ex Deo*) or out of preexisting matter (*ex materia*). Rather, He created it out of nothing (*ex nihilo*). Although an eternal creation is theoretically possible, Scripture teaches that the universe had a beginning; thus, God created a *temporal* universe. Because time did not exist before God created—only eternity—God did not create *in* time; rather, with the world, there was the creation *of* time. There was no time before time began.[19]

Further, the universe is dependent on God for its existence. He not only caused it to come into being (efficient cause), but He also causes it to continue to be (conserving cause). That is to say, God is both the Cause of the origination of the whole of creation and the Cause of its continuation. The universe is absolutely dependent on God; it is contingent. Only God is independent and necessary.

Human Beings

For Aquinas, a human being is a matter/form unity of soul and body.[20] Despite this unity, there is no identity between soul and body—they are distinct. The soul survives death and awaits reunion with the physical body at the final resurrection.[21] According to Aquinas, Adam was directly created by God at the beginning, and God directly creates each new soul in the womb of its mother.[22]

Problem of Evil

Aquinas answered the objection that evil disproves God.[23] He showed how evil came about given that God can only create good creatures.[24] God endowed humans with the good power of free will. But with that freedom came the possibility of evil.[25]

Unfortunately, the good power of free

will was used to bring evil into the world by rebellion against the Creator. Evil is not a substance (tangible thing or being), but a corruption of the good substance God made. It exists only in another, not in itself. It is a deprivation of some good that ought to be present.[26] Moral privations are in things and relations between things. God only indirectly caused physical evil.[27] That is to say, God indirectly made evil *possible* by giving free choice, but man directly made evil *actual* through the misuse of his free will. Evil cannot be totally *destroyed* without destroying good, but evil can be *defeated* without destroying good. Thus, God can and will bring good out of evil.

Ethics

Aquinas distinguished four kinds of law: *Eternal law* is the plan by which God governs creation. *Natural law* is the participation of rational creatures in this eternal law (cf. Romans 2:15). *Human law* is a particular application of natural law to local communities. *Divine law* is the revelation of God's law through Scripture to believers.[28]

Aquinas divided virtues into two classes—natural and supernatural. Prudence, justice, courage, and temperance are natural virtues. These are revealed through natural revelation and are applicable to all human beings. Supernatural virtues consist of faith, hope, and love. They are known from supernatural revelation in Scripture and are binding on believers.[29]

Should Old Aquinas Be Forgotten?

Aquinas's philosophy has undergone a renaissance in recent years, particularly among evangelicals. Some have been more influenced by him or have come closer to his views than they are likely to admit.[30] Although not without his critics, given the breadth and depth of his writing, Thomas Aquinas should not be forgotten. At least not by any Christian who speaks to today's apologetic issues.

Who Was Blaise Pascal?

Terry Glaspey

Blaise Pascal (AD 1623–1662) was arguably one of the greatest geniuses of the modern world. A child prodigy, he became an important scientist and mathematician who invented a machine for making calculations (a precursor of the modern calculator), wrote influential studies of geometry (one of which was published at age 16), and broke new ground in various areas of physics, including critical contributions to the concepts of pressure and vacuum. Although he identified with Jansenism as early as 1646, it was a powerful spiritual experience in late 1654 that caused him to turn much of his attention to explaining and defending the Christian faith.

Pascal's Pensées

Pascal's most important work of apologetics is the *Pensées*, a book which remained unfinished at his early death at age 39. *Pensées* is the French word for "thoughts," which explains the construction of this book. Intended to be a comprehensive examination and defense of the Christian faith, it existed only as a multitude of scraps of paper on which Pascal had scribbled his thoughts. There was little organization to these papers, but they were filled with profound and original aphorisms and arguments that challenged the reigning philosophies of rationalism, skepticism, and empiricism, all of which had a profound influence on the thinking of his day. In their place he urged a faith that was rational without being rationalist, and a faith that made sense of the world around us.

Laying out the strategy of his arguments in *Pensées*, Pascal wrote,

> Men despise religion. They hate it and are afraid it may be true. The cure for this is first to show that religion is not contrary to reason, but worthy of reverence and respect. Next, make it attractive, make good men wish it were true, and then show that it is. Worthy of reverence because it really understands human nature. Attractive because it promises true good.[1]

Apologetics

While a full understanding of Pascal demands a careful reading of *Pensées*, we can trace several lines of thought that are particularly important for understanding his argument for the truthfulness of the Christian faith.

These are the human condition, the limits of human reason, the knowledge of the heart, and the wager of faith. All of these are part of his program of convincing the reader of the veracity of the Christian message.

The condition of the human heart was the starting point for Pascal's apologetics. He saw human beings as caught between their glory as the pinnacle of God's creation and their fallen state:

> Man is only a reed, the weakest in nature, but he is a thinking reed. There is no need for the whole universe to take up arms to crush him: a vapour, a drop of water is enough to kill him. But even if the universe were to crush him, man would still be nobler than his slayer, because he knows that he is dying and the advantage the universe has over him. The universe knows none of this. Thus all our dignity consists in thought.[2]

But what do human beings do with their God-given reason? Sadly, their reasoning does not always lead them to the truth. In fact, sometimes it leads them away from the truth. "What kind of freak then is man! How novel, how monstrous, how chaotic, how paradoxical, how prodigious. Judge of all things, feeble earthworm, repository of truth, sink of doubt and error, glory and refuse of the universe."[3]

Part of human greatness is that we recognize our wretchedness and how far we are from what God intends for us. But our wretchedness is demonstrated in that we don't want to give much attention to this fallen state. Instead, we find all kinds of diversions to keep us from seriously considering our true state. We waste our lives in a ceaseless quest for pleasures that distract us from the uncomfortable realities of our fallenness. Or we simply become indifferent to the big questions.

Pascal lived at the dawn of the Enlightenment, a time when self-confidence and pride in human reason reached new heights due to important scientific discoveries and achievements. An unswerving reliance on reason was at the heart of Enlightenment philosophy, so Pascal made rationalism one of the targets of his book. He countered the skepticism and exaltation of human reason by showing its limits. Although himself a brilliant thinker, as well as a scientist and mathematician, Pascal saw that the advance of rational knowledge only demonstrated how little human beings actually know. Therefore, he wrote, "Reason's last step is the recognition that there are an infinite number of things which are beyond it."[4]

The truth is, we live in a state somewhere between absolute certainty and complete ignorance, and we are reliant on knowledge from outside ourselves to move us closer to the truth. And our passions and emotions often obstruct the search for the truth, leading us astray and causing us to be convinced by false ways of thinking. Our powers of reasoning can be easily derailed by the problems that arise from our fallen state.

Therefore, we cannot trust in reason alone to get to the truth about ourselves and how we stand with God. We need to listen to our heart. "The heart has its reasons of which reason knows nothing."[5] In other words, Pascal argued that there is a type of knowing other than deductive reasoning. There is a reason of the heart. It does not replace the kind of knowing arrived at by reason, but it gives us a further way of accessing truth. It is a reason based upon what we know through intuition. It is not antilogical, but it takes us beyond what rational argument can discover.

Pascal believed that while it is a mistake to exclude reason when asking the big questions, it also a mistake to admit only reason in the undertaking. What cannot be grasped by reason alone can be better accessed through the heart—self-evident truths resident within the fabric of the created world. And such a kind of knowing becomes absolutely essential when we discuss matters that are supernatural. Referring to Isaiah 8:17 and 45:15, which speak of the hiddenness of God, Pascal maintained that God's reality is not immediately apparent to human beings. He can be known only as He reveals Himself in Jesus Christ.

Pascal believed that the knowledge of Christ, as He is revealed in the Scriptures, is the key to knowing God.

> All who have claimed to know God and to prove his existence without Jesus Christ have done so ineffectively…Apart from him, and without Scripture, without original sin, without the necessary Mediator who was promised and who came, it is impossible to prove absolutely that God exists or to teach sound doctrine and sound morality. But through and in Jesus Christ we can prove God's existence, and teach both doctrine and morality.[6]

Clearly one of Pascal's targets was the kind of Deism that was so prevalent among European philosophers of the Enlightenment era. Reason alone could not get a person any further than a belief in some sort of abstract divine being. Faith was necessary to bridge the gap between that divine being and the God of the Scriptures, And such faith was a function of the reason of the heart. "It is the heart which perceives God and not the reason."[7]

When Pascal made his case, he was more interested in using evidences from fulfilled prophecy and miracles than arguments from nature for the existence of God. He realized that abstract arguments have little appeal to the common person, and he therefore based his apologetic on what is more concrete: the unattractive truths about the human condition, and the historical evidence of how God worked among the Jewish people and in the person of Jesus Christ. A good deal of space is given in his book for discussing the Old Testament record, the miracles of Jesus, and the evidence of fulfilled prophecies. And at every turn he used his psychological insight into human motivations to delve into the truth, as in this example: "The Apostles were either deceived or deceivers. Either supposition is difficult, for it is not possible to imagine that a man has risen from the dead. While Jesus was with them He could sustain them, but afterwards if He did not appear to them, who did make them act?"[8]

Pascal carried this same kind of commonsense argument into his famous "wager" argument. We must all choose, he wrote, whether we believe that God exists or that He does not exist. The choice we make is the wager that determines everything. We cannot avoid making a decision, and reason alone cannot make the decision for us. If we wager that God exists and we are right, then we have won eternal life. If we are wrong, we have lost nothing.

However, if we wager against God, then there are two possible outcomes. If we are right, we have won nothing. But if we are wrong, we will lose everything. So which decision is the best bet? Is it not to stake your life on God's reality? While of questionable value as a proof for God's existence, this elegantly simple argument can be seen as an invitation for the nonbeliever to seek God, because Pascal believed that anyone who honestly seeks Him would find Him. Pascal concluded that there are only two classes of people who can be considered rational— "those who serve God with all their heart because they know Him and those who seek Him with all their heart because they do not know Him."[9]

A Key Balance

Pascal's legacy helps us understand both the necessity of the apologetic task as well as its limitations. Although he believed so strongly in the importance of apologetics that he spent years working on a book to argue why a rational person could—and should—believe in the truth of the Christian faith, he ultimately was convinced that such reasoning could only take a person to the doorstep of faith. To cross that threshold would require the risk of faith. We all must make decisions about our lives, but these decisions are never purely rational. Our hearts and our minds must work together to discover the deepest of truths. Such a balance can bring greater effectiveness to the apologetic task.

Who Was William Paley?

Terry L. Miethe

illiam Paley was born in July 1743, in Peterborough, Northampton-shire (now in Cambridgeshire), England. Paley's most important works were *The Principles of Moral and Political Philosophy* (1785), the subject of lectures at the University of Cambridge; and *A View of the Evidence of Christianity* (1794), which was required reading for entrance to Cambridge until the twentieth century and was based on John Ray's *Wisdom of God Manifested in the Works of the Creation* (1691).

Paley was an English minister, apologist, philosopher, and utilitarian best known for his natural theology exposition of the teleological argument for the existence of God. Paley was educated at Giggleswick School, where his father was headmaster. He then went to Christ's College, the University of Cambridge, where he graduated in 1763. His argument was developed in his book *Natural Theology; or, Evidences of the Existence and Attributes of the Deity* (1802), which he finished three years before he died, and in which he stated his famous watchmaker analogy.[1]

Paley's Teleological Argument

The teleological argument is an argument for God's existence based on the premise that an undeniable relationship exists between the order and regularity of the universe and an intelligent Architect, a Designer of the world. One of the oldest attempts to demonstrate God's existence, the teleological argument is again gaining popularity among certain scientists, many of whom are relatively new Christians. In summary, it states that it is hard to deny that the universe seems intricately designed in ways that are necessary to support intelligent life. This purposeful order exists either by the intent of a Designer or by a chance process, such as evolution. The universe, in other words, is either a plan or an accident. Since it cannot be an accident, it must be planned.

Paley, Archdeacon of Carlisle, framed the most popular form of the argument.[2] He said that if he were to find a watch in an empty field, he would rightly conclude from its obvious design that there was a watchmaker.

Similarly, when we look at the exceedingly more complex design of the world, we cannot help but conclude a great designer is behind it. Paley's argument can be summarized:

1. A watch shows that it was put together for an intelligent purpose (to keep time).

   a. It has a spring to give it motion.

   b. It has a series of wheels to transmit this motion.

   c. The wheels are made of brass, so that they do not rust.

   d. The spring is made of steel, because of the resilience of that metal.

   e. The front cover is of glass so that one can see through it.

2. The world shows an even greater evidence of design than a watch.

   a. The world is a greater work of art than a watch.

   b. The world has more subtle and complex design than a watch.

   c. The world has an endless variety of means adapted to ends.

3. Therefore, if a watch calls for a watchmaker, then the world demands an even greater intelligent designer (namely, God).

After Paley

In general, most philosophers have objected to Paley's argument. There have been several standard criticisms of the argument. Yet Hume and Kant seem to have granted some weight to the teleological argument. The general objections made against the teleological argument are as follows: (1) the argument makes it probable but not absolutely certain that there is some kind of intelligence behind the design in the world. Chance is possible, though not probable. (2) The argument does not demand that the designer be absolutely perfect, as must be the case with the Christian God. (3) The argument does not explain the existence of disorder, or evil, in the world. (4) It is based on the cosmological argument because it claims that there must be a cause for the design in the universe. (5) At best, it proves only a design, not the designer.

Paley was widely acknowledged during his life. For his services in defense of the faith with the publication of *A View of the Evidences of Christianity*, the bishop of London gave him a stall in St. Paul's Cathedral; the bishop of Lincoln made him subdean of that cathedral, and the bishop of Durham conferred upon him the rectory of Bishopwearmouth.

During the remainder of Paley's life, his time was divided between that rectory and Lincoln, during which time he wrote *Natural Theology: or, Evidences of the Existence and Attributes of the Deity*, despite his increasingly debilitating illness. He died on May 25, 1805, in Bishopwearmouth, Sunderland, and is buried in Carlisle Cathedral. His second son was the architect Edward Graham Paley, and his grandson was the classical scholar Frederick Apthorp Paley.

The question of order in the universe continues to intrigue. As we continue to advance in our scientific knowledge, instead of our view getting simpler, or the universe being more easily understood, we are finding that it is even more complex than we could have imagined. It is not uncommon for scientists themselves to say the universe is so ordered that one must opt for the existence of God to explain it. In some ways, this "new" development is truly amazing!

This old teleological argument—the design argument—has long been one of the traditional philosophical arguments for the existence of God. And now it seems stronger than ever and is being used not merely by preachers, but by scientists themselves. In fact, some scientists have become Christians, in part, because the incredible design or order in the universe is, to them, overwhelming evidence for a divine plan and the existence of a divine planner.

The interesting fact is this: Instead of there being less need for God to be the explanation for the existence of the physical universe as our knowledge of its intricacies grows and grows (the old ruse, or decoy), just the opposite has happened. Carl Sagan's (1934–1996) (the "high priest of the New Atheism") vision of a self-contained material cosmos blurs as science itself begins to fine-tune a new image. The more we learn, the more it looks as if the only way to explain the complexity that surrounds us is to look beyond the physical universe itself! Maybe old Archdeacon Paley was not so far off after all (see the chapters in this volume on arguments for God by William Dembski and Richard Howe).

73

Who Was C.S. Lewis?

Terry Glaspey

Clive Staples Lewis (1898–1963) was a highly respected tutor and professor at Oxford and Cambridge universities who specialized in medieval and early modern English literature, and the author of numerous influential books on literature, popular theology, and apologetics, as well as fiction for both adults and children. A convinced atheist as a young man, Lewis converted to Christianity and became one of its most effective defenders. He came to see Christianity as the most reasonable explanation for the big questions of life and is still considered one of the clearest explainers of the meaning of faith. Through his careful reasoning, his wit, his creativity, his deep spiritual insight, and his desire to write for the common reader, Lewis reached well beyond the ranks of those who normally read theology and apologetics. Even today his books continue to be very popular and influential among readers.

His Apologetic Approach

In an essay titled "Christian Apologetics," Lewis explained his vision for apologetic work: "You must translate every bit of your theology into the vernacular...I have come to the conclusion that if you cannot translate your thoughts into uneducated language, then your thoughts were confused. Power to translate is the test of having really understood one's own meaning."[1]

This work of "translation" is what Lewis accomplished so well in books such as *The Problem of Pain* (1940), *The Screwtape Letters* (1942), *The Abolition of Man* (1943), *Miracles* (1947), *Mere Christianity* (1952), and *God in the Dock* (1970). All these books are marked by clear, reasonable, and logical thinking, as well as an imaginative use of analogies and word pictures. Lewis argued his case with a beautifully expressive writing style, a respectful tone toward those who disagreed with him, and a conviction of the importance of the issues under discussion.

Lewis referred to such books as his "frontal attacks," but he came to believe that he could just as effectively make the case for Christianity through the power of stories, which can move hearts and minds in a different way than reasoned argument. He believed that the straightforward approach is not always the most effective one, and so he also embedded the truth in a series of fictional works for adults and for children, including his Space Trilogy (1938–1945), *The Great Divorce* (1945), The Chronicles of Narnia (1950–1956), and *Till We Have Faces* (1956). Such books were Lewis's attempt to show that Christianity is not only a set of beliefs, but also provides a vision for seeing this world and the world to come. And tucked away in these pages are many compelling apologetic arguments for the Christian faith. Lewis's own journey toward faith began when books by George MacDonald and G.K. Chesterton (both Christian writers) fired his imagination and demonstrated that a Christian perspective of the world could be both beautiful and sensible. We see both the logic and the beauty of Christianity in Lewis's own entertaining works of fiction, books that continue to enjoy a wide readership.

Lewis's own study of philosophy led him to see the logical inadequacy of some of the most prevalent modern ideas, such as subjectivism (the belief that objective truths about values and ethics either do not exist or cannot be found) and relativism (the conviction that we cannot make universal statements about such issues). As Lewis pointed out, those who espouse such ideas cannot be consistent. In reality, we are all making judgments about value all the time. Otherwise, how can we, for example, be critical of the atrocities of the Nazi regime if we believe that right and wrong are simply a matter of preference?

Lewis's book *The Abolition of Man* effectively reminds readers that we cannot make any such judgments without an innate sense of right and wrong, and that we constantly appeal to standards of behavior that we take for granted when someone steals from us, cuts us off in traffic, or hurts us. We feel that a code of conduct has been transgressed. Where, Lewis asks, did such a code originate if there is not a universal moral law

that ultimately is sourced in God? "We have," wrote Lewis, "only two alternatives: Either the maxims of traditional morality must be accepted as axioms of practical reason which neither require argument to support them and not to 'see' which is to have lost human status; or else there are no values at all, what we mistook for values being 'projections' of irrational emotions."[2] Instead, "every moral rule is there to prevent a breakdown, or a strain, or a friction in the running of that [human] machine."[3]

Another pair of logically deficient modern beliefs can be found in naturalism (the belief that only nature exists and the supernatural is an illusion) and scientism (the conviction that science presents the only option for understanding the world and the only dependable answer for answering human questions). Lewis pointed out that when it comes to the search for meaning, science has largely taken the place of religion. This is a role, however, it cannot adequately fill. Such a philosophy, asserts Lewis, is reductionist, and ultimately dehumanizing. It reduces our human experience to *facts* while ignoring *meanings*, as illustrated in this marvelous exchange from *The Voyage of the Dawn Treader*:

"In our world," said Eustace, "a star is a huge ball of flaming gas."

"Even in your world, my son," replied the old man, "that is not what a star is but only what it is made of."[4]

Or, as Lewis concludes in *Miracles*, "In science we are only reading the notes to a poem; in Christianity we find the poem itself."[5]

His Arguments for Faith

How can we be sure that Christianity presents a more accurate vision of reality than the dominant modern philosophies? How do we know if the "poem" is true? Lewis insisted that he was not making the case that faith is only a matter of the heart. He had come to accept it because he believed it was the truth. "I am not asking anyone to accept Christianity if his best reasoning is against it."[6] Therefore, Lewis was not hesitant about providing reasoned arguments from logic and human experience that confirm Christianity's veracity.

Lewis knew he could not *prove* that Christianity is true, but he set out to show that it is *reasonable* and *plausible*. And that it offers the best explanation for reality as we know it. We find three key arguments for faith that he revisited throughout his works.

As discussed above, the first is the *moral argument*. This argument begins with the observation that there appears to be a set of universal moral absolutes in operation in the universe—a Moral Law. Even those who deny the existence of these absolutes will complain when they are violated, and the search for a "better" rational basis for values always ends up drawing its force from the fundamental Moral Law that already exists. The existence of this Law suggests that there is a divine source for that Law—a Moral Lawgiver who gives a meaning and direction to human life that would not be available from any other source. Lewis worked out the finer points of this argument in elegant detail in *The Abolition of Man*.

The second key argument is the *trilemma*, which aims specifically at answering the question, What is unique about Jesus Christ? In this argument he attempted to counter those who acknowledge Jesus as a great moral teacher but reject the idea that He is part of the Godhead. Lewis stressed, however, that based upon the statements Jesus made about

Himself, we cannot think of Him as merely a great teacher. He is either a liar, a lunatic, or He is the Lord.[7] These, asserts Lewis, are the only options open to us. While not an airtight argument in itself (as it relies upon the presupposition that the scriptural record is both authoritative and accurate), it does focus nicely upon the question of what we are to think about the person of Christ, who is the central figure around which the Christian worldview revolves. As Lewis writes in *Miracles*, "The Central miracle asserted by Christians is the Incarnation."[8]

Lewis's third key argument is the *argument from desire*, where he makes his most unique and original contribution to the field of apologetics. Here, Lewis stressed that our lives are "haunted" by realities beyond ourselves and that there is a universal human desire—a longing—for something beyond our grasp. In his autobiography *Surprised by Joy* (1955), Lewis wrote of how even his childhood experiences pointed him toward something beyond this world. These longings, experienced as nostalgia, awe, and wonder, are often triggered by nature, art, music, literature, and other forms of beauty. But all these merely point toward something they cannot fulfill in themselves. Lewis was likely harkening back to Augustine's prayer, "You have made us for Yourself, and our heart is restless until it finds rest in You."

"Do fish complain of the sea for being wet?" asked Lewis. "Or if they did would that fact itself not strongly suggest that they had not always been, or would always be, purely aquatic creatures? If you really are a product of a materialistic universe, how is it that you don't feel at home there?"[9] The deepest thirsts within us are not adapted to the deepest nature of the world. This argument is summed up memorably in a phrase from

Mere Christianity: "If I find in myself desires which nothing in this world can satisfy, the only logical explanation is that I was made for another world."[10]

At its heart, this is not a purely intellectual argument, but one from shared human experience. In his fiction and nonfiction, Lewis suggested what these signposts of transcendent experiences are pointing toward. The longings that such experiences evoke are not ends in themselves, but pointers toward something beyond. God has created a universe that speaks of Him (Psalm 19), and the syntax of that language can be found in some of our universal human desires.

The Interconnectedness of Everything

Ultimately, what Lewis offered is more than a set of arguments. It is a theology of vision, a way of seeing. Perhaps that is why C.S. Lewis, in all his writings, appealed not only to logic and reason, but also to the imagination. The Christian vision he unfolded allows us to see the interconnectedness of everything in God's grand story. Lewis's methodology was fundamentally nonconfrontational, an invitation to think and imagine alongside him. He wanted us to try on the spectacles that he had found valuable for seeing more clearly. They had worked for him, and he invited his readers to consider whether they might also work for them. Through these lenses we find the Christian vision embodied imaginatively in a sphere where truth and reason, as well as beauty and wonder, exist and flourish hand in hand.

Who Was Cornelius Van Til?

David Haines

Cornelius Van Til (1895–1987) was born the sixth child of Ite and Klazina Van Til on May 3, 1895, in Grootegast, Holland.[1] His family moved to Highland, Indiana, in 1905, joining a community of Dutch Reformed farmers.[2] Young Cornelius received his childhood education in a Dutch Reformed Christian school, and in 1914, he began his theological studies at Calvin Preparatory School, which was associated with Calvin College and Seminary. During these formative years he studied languages and Reformed theology. He was also introduced to philosophy under the teaching of W.H. Jellema (who had been trained in transcendental idealism[3] by the celebrated Josiah Royce, and who was influenced by the British idealists F.H. Bradley, T.H. Green, and Bernard Bosquet).[4] It was also during these years that Van Til developed a great admiration for the work of Abraham Kuyper and Herman Bavinck.[5]

After completing his bachelor's studies in theology at Calvin College, Van Til began pursuing a master's degree in theology in 1921. In 1922, he transferred from Calvin College to Princeton Theological Seminary, where he completed a master's degree in theology (1925) and a doctorate in philosophy, with the doctorate under the direction of Archibald Allen Bowman (1927). His master's thesis was titled *Reformed Epistemology*, and his doctoral dissertation, *God and the Absolute*.

After Van Til finished his studies, he and his wife Rena Klooster (married in 1925) took a year to travel to Holland and Germany. Upon their return from Europe, Van Til accepted a pastoral position in a Reformed church in Michigan. The following year he went to Princeton to teach a course in Christian apologetics (1928–1929), and then he returned to his church in Michigan. Around the same time, J. Gresham Machen was in the process of founding Westminster Theological Seminary. Machen, partly for the purpose of maintaining that Westminster was a continuation of the Old Princetonian tradition, invited Van Til to join the teaching staff.[6] Machen personally travelled to Michigan to recruit Van Til, who eventually accepted the offer and became the first professor of Christian apologetics at Westminster (1929), which has become a bastion of presuppositionalist thought. Van Til remained in this position until his retirement in 1972.

Some major Christian thinkers who have been influenced by Van Til include Francis Schaeffer, John Frame, Greg Bahnsen, K. Scott Oliphint, Vern Poythress, and William Edgar. Van Til's most important works are *The Defense of the Faith*, *An Introduction to Systematic Theology*, *A Christian Theory of Knowledge*, *Christian Apologetics*, and the exchanges between Van Til and a number of important evangelical thinkers, which can be found, along with his *My Credo*, in *Jerusalem and Athens: Critical Discussion on the Philosophy and Apologetics of Cornelius Van Til.*

The Method of Presuppositional Apologetics

Cornelius Van Til always emphasized the importance of a Christian apologetics that gives absolute priority to the Bible and to the total sovereignty of God, and rejected the modern rationalist approach to Christian apologetics (often offering no more than probabilistic arguments in favor of Christianity), which he equated with what is commonly called classical apologetics. Christian apologetics, for Van Til, was "the vindication of the Christian philosophy of life against the various forms of the non-Christian philosophy of life."[7] Van Til described apologetics as a discipline that touches every other discipline in the complete system of Christian knowledge, and as being both offensive and defensive at once. As to the importance of apologetics, Van Til stated, "Apologetics, like systematics, is valuable to the precise extent that it presses the truth upon the attention of the natural man."[8] Let us now turn to an exposition of the major elements of Van Til's approach to apologetics.

To properly understand Van Til's method, we must understand two key claims that are found throughout his works: (1) Every rational being is always, without ceasing, interpreting the world which presents itself to them. (2) Because of the first claim, there is no epistemological or ethical common ground[9] (a) between the regenerate and unregenerate interpretations, which would allow for dialogue,[10] and (b) from which one can examine the truth of these interpretations.[11] Note that both of these claims are epistemological[12] in nature, and concern the way in which man knows things and the limits of this knowledge. Van Til illustrated these two claims in *Christian Apologetics*, where he said, "The sinner has cemented colored glasses to his eyes, which he cannot remove."[13]

From these epistemological claims flow the many statements by which Van Til said that for a person to *truly* know or think about anything (including God,[14] man,[15] this world,[16] science,[17] ethics,[18] history,[19] etc.),[20] to rationally demonstrate the existence of God,[21] to create any work of art,[22] for logic to touch reality,[23] to properly interpret and describe the universe,[24] to distinguish facts from one another,[25] to avoid ultimate irrationalism and skepticism,[26] he must presuppose the existence of the triune God of the Christian Bible and the inspired Scriptures in which He is revealed. By *presupposition* Van Til meant, essentially, that which guaranteed the truthfulness or falsity of any proposition (or statement about something), being both that which is known (objective states of reality) and propositional knowledge (any knowledge that can be expressed in statements).[27] These presuppositions, according to Van Til, are the states of being, and the propositions that comprise the interpretational paradigm of each individual.[28]

According to Van Til, there are four interpretational paradigms (though the first is held by God alone, and the second is no longer held by anyone):[29] (1) the interpretational paradigm of God (which alone is entirely true),[30] and the paradigms of (2) prefall humanity,[31] (3) fallen humanity,[32] and (4) regenerate humanity.[33] In Van Til's system, *the fallen paradigm* is characterized by univocal reasoning (not to be confused with univocal predication),[34] by which fallen man (a) takes himself and the world as the ultimate ground for all thinking about God,[35] (b) sees himself as entirely independent of God—as autonomous,[36] (c) sees God and himself as equals,[37] and (d) sees time and eternity as aspects of each other.[38]

The regenerate paradigm is the exact opposite of the fallen paradigm, for via analogical reasoning (not to be confused with analogical predication),[39] man sees himself, in the light of the triune Creator, as entirely dependent on God (ontologically and epistemologically)—as He reveals Himself in Holy Scriptures, and in Christ; and man sees God as the ultimate point of reference for all knowledge and predication.[40] Analogical reasoning is only possible by presupposing the triune God of the Bible and is the only way to obtain true knowledge of anything. It is impossible, without the regeneration of the Holy Spirit (unsolicited by the human person), for a fallen human to see the world through the interpretative paradigm of regenerate humanity.[41]

In light of the above, the question becomes this: How do we defend, and recommend for belief, the truths of Christianity? Our *purpose*, first of all, as K. Scott Oliphint notes in *Covenantal Apologetics*, cannot be the conversion of our interlocutor (the person with whom we are talking or sharing the gospel);[42] this is the work of the Holy Spirit alone. Christian apologetics

is based, according to Oliphint, upon the fact that the Bible is the ground of all human knowledge,[43] upon the reality of innate human knowledge of God,[44] and upon common grace.[45]

Second, the presuppositional *method* is composed of two volleys.[46] We *first* use the transcendental argument,[47] a form of *Reductio Ad Absurdum*,[48] to demonstrate the incoherence of unregenerate interpretations of reality.[49] This is done by drawing our attention to any fact or experience in reality,[50] and showing that (1) to make sense of this fact or experience one must presuppose the existence of the triune God;[51] and, (2) that any interpretative paradigm that denies the existence of the triune God is incapable of truly explaining that fact or experience. Now, though this argument may demonstrate monotheism, it does not demonstrate the existence of the triune God of the Bible. We *then* invite our interlocutor to try the interpretative paradigm of biblical Christianity, to look at the world and themselves in the light of Christ.[52]

The Outcomes of Presuppositional Apologetics

It might be noted, in conclusion, that the only thing about Van Til's transcendental argument that is unique to Van Til is the name.[53] Furthermore, he cannot be credited with having revived the transcendental argument.[54] Indeed, for hundreds (if not thousands) of years prior to the birth of Van Til, Christian apologists had been using similar arguments to demonstrate the incoherence of denying the existence of God.

Also, the two key claims of presuppositionalism (namely, that everyone always interprets the world through one of two interpretative schemas, and that there is no neutral ground from which we can see the world without interpreting it in this way), held together, seem to force us into undesirable outcomes. One in particular is absolute skepticism about the possibility of knowing for certain that any one "interpretation" of the world is true. Other negative outcomes include absolute relativism of the belief systems of the interpretative paradigms,[55] or, along with the claim that we can know that Christianity is true, dogmatic self-contradiction.[56] In light of these difficulties, and many others which have been raised,[57] it is probably best to learn what we can from Van Til without adopting his presuppositional method of apologetics.

Who Was Francis Schaeffer?

Terry L. Miethe

Francis August Schaeffer was born on January 30, 1912, in Germantown, Philadelphia. He was known as an evangelist, a Presbyterian minister, and a prolific writer on Christian life issues and culture. He and his wife, Edith, founded the L'Abri Fellowship in Switzerland, an international discipleship center.

Schaeffer's Early Life

In 1931, Francis went to Hampden-Sydney College in Virginia to study for the ministry. He graduated in 1935, then entered Westminster Theological Seminary, where he studied under the famous scholars Cornelius Van Til (presuppositional apologetics) and J. Gresham Machen (doctrine of biblical inerrancy).

In 1937, Schaeffer transferred to Faith Theological Seminary, graduating in 1938. This seminary was newly formed as a result of a split between the Presbyterian Church of America (now the Orthodox Presbyterian Church) and the Bible Presbyterian Church. Schaeffer was the first student to graduate and the first to be ordained in the Bible Presbyterian Church. He served pastorates in Pennsylvania and St. Louis. Schaeffer

eventually sided with the Bible Presbyterian Church Columbus Synod and became a member of the Reformed Presbyterian Church, Evangelical Synod, while maintaining a presuppositional approach to Christian apologetics.[1]

In 1947, Francis traveled throughout Europe for three months to evaluate the state of the church there as a representative of the Independent Board for Presbyterian Foreign Missions and the American secretary for the foreign relations department of the American Council of Christian Churches.

By 1948, the Schaeffer family moved to Lausanne, Switzerland, with their three daughters to be missionaries in Europe working for Children for Christ ministry and helping with the formation of the International Council of Christian Churches.

In 1955, Francis established the community called L'Abri (French for "the shelter"). Serving as both a philosophy seminar and a spiritual community, L'Abri attracted thousands of young people, and was later expanded into Sweden, France, the Netherlands, the United Kingdom, and the United States.[2]

Son Francis August Schaeffer IV—popularly known as Franky—was born on August

3, 1952. In 1953, the family returned to the United States on furlough. During this time, Schaeffer traveled across the United States, "speaking 246 times during 515 days about the deeper spiritual life."

Schaeffer's Publications

Francis's talks during his travels later became the basis for his book *True Spirituality* (published in 1971). In 1965, Schaeffer gave lectures at Wheaton College titled "Speaking Historic Christianity into the Twentieth Century." These lectures became the basis for his book *The God Who Is There* and other early works.

In 1968, Schaeffer's book *Escape from Reason* was published. In this work he traced trends in twentieth-century thought and some of the key ideas that have shaped society. He examined philosophy, science, art, and popular culture to identify dualism, fragmentation, and the decline of reason. Three more books were published in 1970: *Pollution and the Death of Man*, *The Church at the End of the Twentieth Century*, and *The Mark of a Christian*. In 1972, *He Is There and He Is Not Silent* was published along with four other books.

Francis's *How Should We Then Live? The Rise and Decline of Western Thought and Culture* was published in 1976 and followed by a film series in 1977 and a subsequent tour. In 1979, *Whatever Happened to the Human Race?* was published along with a film series by the same title. *A Christian Manifesto* came out in 1981, with *The Complete Works of Francis Schaeffer* one year later.

The complete list of resources that the Schaeffers produced under the title *How Should We Then Live?* include the book itself, a study guide for the book, the ten-episode film series, and study aids for the films.[3] Schaeffer died on May 15, 1984, in Rochester, Minnesota, at 72 years of age.

Wife Edith later ran L'Abri and became a well-known prolific writer as well. Her first book was *L'Abri: Death in the City*, published in 1969. Son Franky has had a varied career and has rejected much of his upbringing.[4]

Schaeffer's Apologetics

The focus of Schaeffer's apologetic work was, in his own words, to "take the roof off" of the philosophical positions of those who reject Christianity. By this phrase he meant pursuing the logic of their presuppositions all the way to their unsatisfactory conclusions and what they mean pragmatically for how we live our lives. Bad philosophy, he believed, will have negative consequences for a human life and for the life of a society. But secularists do not want to accept these logical conclusions, so they often try to smuggle Christian values into their system—values that have no place in their intellectual framework. Schaeffer called for the Christian apologist to counter such attempts with firmness, yet with love and compassion as well. This strategy of exposure and redirection is at the heart of his apologetics.

We can see this methodology at work, for example, in *How Should We Then Live?* Francis takes the reader on a selective journey through the history of Western thought to demonstrate that ultimately, modern secular philosophy leads to dehumanization and moral decadence. Though specialists will quibble with his sometimes inadequate summaries and oversimplifications of the complex thoughts of his intellectual adversaries, Schaeffer was more interested in showing the general flow of history than in recording it in detail.

Schaeffer's Focus

Schaeffer was always more concerned with the practice of apologetics than in its theory.

His approach involved authentic discussions with unbelievers rather than in-your-face argumentation. He tried to understand the language and the context of his conversation partners so he could more effectively relate the promises of the gospel to their lives. He founded L'Abri Fellowship to reach sincere seekers and give them honest answers to honest questions. This involved not only engaging in meaningful conversations, but also the demonstration of God's reality through love and hospitality. Christian love, he believed, was the ultimate apologetic.

Bibliography

Ajijola, Alhaj A.D. *The Essence of Faith in Islam*. Lahore, Pakistan: Islamic Publications, 1978.

Ankerberg, John, and Dillon Burroughs. *What's the Big Deal About Other Religions? Answering the Questions About Their Beliefs and Practices*. Eugene, OR: Harvest House, 2008.

Anselm. *Basic Writings*. Ed. and trans. Thomas Williams. Indianapolis, IN: Hackett Publishing, 2007.

Aquinas, Thomas. *Summa contra Gentiles*. Trans. Fathers of the English Dominican Province. London, UK: Burns Oates & Washbourne, 1924.

———. *The Summa Theologica of St. Thomas Aquinas*. Trans. Fathers of the English Dominican Province. Notre Dame: Christian Classics, 1981.

Archer, Gleason. *Encyclopedia of Bible Difficulties*. Grand Rapids, MI: Zondervan, 1982.

Aristotle. *Rhetoric*, W. Rhys Roberts, trans. *The Basic Works of Aristotle*, Richard McKeon, ed. New York: Random House, 1941.

Attridge, Harold W., and Robert A. Oden, eds. *De Dea Syria*. Missoula, MT: Scholars Press, 1976.

Augustine. *Confessions*, trans. Henry Chadwick. New York: Oxford University Press, 1991.

Bacon, Francis. *The Works of Francis Bacon*. London, UK: C. Baldwin, 1819.

Baker, D.L. *Two Testaments: One Bible*. Grand Rapids, MI: Baker, 1976, 1993.

Barker, Dan. *Losing Faith in Faith*. Madison, WI: FFRF, 1992.

Beckwith, Francis J., and Gregory Koukl. *Relativism: Feet Firmly Planted in Mid-Air*. Grand Rapids, MI: Baker, 1998.

Behe, Michael. *Darwin's Black Box: The Biochemical Challenge to Evolution*. New York: Free Press, 1996.

Black, David Alan, and David S. Dockery, eds. *New Testament Criticism and Interpretation*. Grand Rapids, MI: Zondervan, 1991.

Block, Daniel, ed. *Israel—Ancient Kingdom or Late Invention?* Nashville, TN: B&H Academic, 2008.

Blomberg, Craig L. *The Historical Reliability of the Gospel*. Downers Grove, IL: InterVarsity, 1987.

Bowman, Robert M. *Why You Should Believe in the Trinity*. Grand Rapids, MI: Baker, 1989.

Brown, Peter. *Augustine of Hippo: A Biography*. Berkeley, CA: University of California Press, 1970.

Bruce, F.F. *The Canon of Scripture*. Downers Grove, IL: InterVarsity, 1988.

———. *The Defence of the Gospel in the New Testament*. Grand Rapids, MI: Eerdmans, 1959.

———. *The New Testament Documents Are They Reliable?* Grand Rapids, MI: Eerdmans, 1981.

Budziszewski, J. *Written on the Heart: The Case for Natural Law*. Downers Grove, IL: InterVarsity, 1997.

Bultmann, Rudolf. *Theology of the New Testament*. London, UK: SCM Press, 1950.

Burroughs, Dillon, and Jimmy Turner. *Faith Acts: A Provocative Call to Living What You Believe*. Birmingham, AL: New Hope, 2016.

Campbell-Jack, W.C., Gavin J. McGrath, and C. Stephen Evans, eds. *New Dictionary of Christian Apologetics* (Downers Grove, IL: IVP Academic, 2006.

Carson, D.A. *The Intolerance of Tolerance*. Grand Rapids, MI: Eerdmans, 2013.

Carson, D.A., ed. *Telling the Truth: Evangelizing Postmoderns*. Grand Rapids, MI: Zondervan, 2000.

———, and John D. Woodbridge, eds. *Hermeneutics, Authority, and Canon*. Grand Rapids, MI: Zondervan, 1986.

———, eds. *Scripture and Truth*. Grand Rapids, MI: Zondervan, 1984.

Charlesworth, James H., ed. *Jesus and the Dead Sea Scrolls*. The Anchor Bible Reference Library. New York: Doubleday, 1992.

Clarke, Andrew D., and Bruce W. Winter, eds. *One God, One Lord: Christianity in a World of Religious Pluralism*. Grand Rapids, MI: Baker Book House, 1992.

449

Clauss, M. *The Roman Cult of Mithras.* New York: Routledge, 2000.

Clayton, Philip, and Arthur Peacocke, eds. *In Whom We Live and Move and Have Our Being: Panentheistic Reflections on God's Presence in a Scientific World.* Grand Rapids, MI: Eerdmans, 2004.

Cobb, John B. *A Christian Natural Theology: Based on the Thought of Alfred North Whitehead.* 2d ed. Louisville, KY: Westminster John Knox Press, 2007.

Collins, Francis. *The Language of God: A Scientist Presents Evidence for Belief.* New York: Free Press, 2006.

Collins, James. *God in Modern Philosophy* (London, UK: Routledge & Kegan Paul, 1960.

Collins, Steven, C.M. Kobs, and M.C. Luddeni. *The Tall al-Hammam Excavations,* vol. 1. Winona Lake, IN: Eisenbrauns, 2015.

———, and Latayne C. Scott. *Discovering the City of Sodom.* New York: Simon & Schuster, 2013.

Coogan, Michel D., ed. and trans. *Stories from Ancient Canaan.* Philadelphia, PA: Westminster Press, 1978.

Cook, John W. *Body, Soul, and Life Everlasting: Biblical Anthropology and the Monism-Dualism Debate.* Grand Rapids, MI: Eerdmans, 1989.

Cooper, John W. *Panentheism: The Other God of the Philosophers: From Plato to the Present.* Grand Rapids, MI: Baker Academic, 2006.

Copan, Paul. *Is God a Moral Monster?* Grand Rapids, MI: Baker, 2011.

———. *True for You, but Not for Me.* Minneapolis, MN: Bethany House, 1998.

Corduan, Winfried. *Handmaid to Theology: An Essay in Philosophical Prolegomena.* Grand Rapids, MI: Baker, 1981. Republished Eugene, OR: Wipf & Stock, 2009.

Craig, William L. *Reasonable Faith,* 3d ed. Wheaton, IL: Crossway, 2008.

———, and J.P. Moreland, eds. *Naturalism: A Critical Analysis.* New York: Routledge, 2000.

Crain, Natasha. *Talking to Your Kids About God: 30 Conversations Every Christian Parent Must Have.* Grand Rapids, MI: Baker, 2017.

Criswell, W.A. *Why I Preach the Bible Is Literally True.* Nashville, TN: Broadman & Holman, 1969.

Cross, F.L., and E.A. Livingstone, eds. *The Oxford Dictionary of the Christian Church,* 2d. ed. New York: Oxford University Press, 1974.

Crowe, Brandon D., and Carl R. Trueman, eds. *The Essential Trinity.* Phillipsburg, NJ: Presbyterian & Reformed, 2017.

Cumont, Franz. *The Mysteries of Mithra.* New York: Dover, 1945.

Darwin, Charles. *The Correspondence of Charles Darwin.* Cambridge, UK: Cambridge University Press, 1987.

Dawkins, Richard. *River Out of Eden: A Darwinian View of Life.* New York: Basic Books, 1995.

———. *The God Delusion,* 10th ed. London, UK: Penguin Random House, 2016.

Dembski, William A. *The Design Inference: Eliminating Chance Through Small Probabilities.* Cambridge, UK: Cambridge University Press, 2006.

———, and Michael Behe. *Intelligent Design: The Bridge Between Science and Theology.* Downers Grove, IL: IVP Academic, 2002.

Detienne, Marcel. *The Gardens of Adonis.* Princeton, NJ: Princeton University, 1994.

Dever, W.G. *What Did the Biblical Writers Know and When Did They Know It?—What Archaeology Can Tell Us About the Reality of Ancient Israel.* Grand Rapids, MI: Eerdmans, 2001.

Dockery, D.S. *Christian Scripture: An Evangelical Perspective on Inspiration, Authority and Interpretation.* Nashville, TN: Broadman & Holman, 1995.

Dolezal, James E. *All That Is in God: Evangelical Theology and the Challenge of Classical Christian Theism.* Grand Rapids, MI: Reformation Heritage, 2017.

Driver, G.R., trans. *Canaanite Myths and Legends.* Edinburgh, Scotland: T. & T. Clark, 1956.

Dungan, David L. *Constantine's Bible.* Minneapolis, MN: Fortress, 2007.

Duthoy, R. *Taurobolium: Its Evolution and Terminology.* Leiden, Netherlands: Brill, 1963.

Eddy, Paul Rhodes, and Gregory A. Boyd. *The Jesus Legend: A Case for the Historical Reliability of the Synoptic Jesus Tradition.* Grand Rapids, MI: Baker Academic, 2007.

Eusebius. *Ecclesiastical History*, vol. II. Loeb Series. Trans. J.E.L. Oulton. Cambridge, MA: Harvard University, 1926.

Evans, Craig A. *Fabricating Jesus: How Modern Scholars Distort the Gospels*. Downers Grove, IL: InterVarsity, 2006.

———. *Noncanonical Writings and New Testament Interpretation*. Peabody, MA: Hendrickson, 1992.

Farnell, F. David, and Norman L. Geisler, eds. *The Jesus Quest: The Danger from Within*. Maitland, FL: Xulon, 2014.

Farnell, F. David, gen. ed., and Norman L. Geisler, Joseph M. Holden, William C. Roach, and Phil Fernandes, assoc. eds. *Vital Issues in the Inerrancy Debate*. Eugene, OR: Wipf & Stock, 2016.

Farrer, Austin. *A Science of God*. London, UK: Geoffrey Bles, 1966.

Ferguson, Everett. *Church History Volume One: From Christ to the Pre-Reformation: The Rise and Growth of the Church in Its Cultural, Intellectual, and Political Context*. Grand Rapids, MI: Zondervan, 2005.

Feser, Edward. *Aquinas: A Beginner's Guide*. Oxford, UK: Oneword, 2010.

———. *Five Proofs for the Existence of God*. San Francisco, CA: Ignatius Press, 2017.

Finegan Jack. *Myth & Mystery: An Introduction to the Pagan Religion of the Biblical World*. Grand Rapids, MI: Baker, 1989.

Finkelstein, I., and A. Mazar. *The Quest for the Historical Israel: Debating Archaeology and the History of Early Israel*, ed. B.B. Schmidt. Atlanta, GA: Society of Biblical Literature, 2007.

———, and N.A. Silberman. *The Bible Unearthed: Archaeology's New Vision of Ancient Israel and the Origin of Its Sacred Texts*. New York: Touchstone, 2001.

Flew, Antony. *There Is a God: How the World's Most Notorious Atheist Changed His Mind*. New York: Harper Collins, 2007.

———. *A Dictionary of Philosophy*, 2d ed. New York: Gramercy Books, 1979.

Flint, Peter W., ed. *The Bible at Qumran: Text, Shape and Interpretation*. Grand Rapids, MI: Eerdmans, 2001.

Frazer, James. *Adonis, Attis, Osiris*. New York: Macmillan, 1906.

Freke, Timothy, and Peter Gandy. *The Jesus Mysteries: Was the "Original Jesus" a Pagan God?* New York: Harmony Books, 1999.

Freud, Sigmund. *The Future of an Illusion* (*The Standard Edition of the Complete Psychological Works of Sigmund Freud*), vol. 21, gen. ed. James Strachey. London, UK: The Hogarth Press and The Institute of Psycho-Analysis, 1927–1931.

Garner, Bryan A., ed. *Black's Law Dictionary*, 3d Pocket ed. Saint Paul, MN: ThomsonWest, 2006.

Gauger, Ann, Douglas Axe, and Casey Luskin. *Science and Human Origins*. Seattle, WA: Discovery Institute Press, 2012.

Geisler, Norman L. *A History of Western Philosophy, Volume II: Modern and Post-Modern: From Descartes to Derrida*. Matthews, NC: Bastion Books, 2012.

———. *Baker Encyclopedia of Christian Apologetics*. Grand Rapids, MI: Baker Academic, 1999.

———. *Christian Apologetics*, 2d ed. Grand Rapids, MI: Baker Academic, 2013.

———. *Christian Ethics*, 2d ed. Grand Rapids, MI: Baker, 2012.

———. *Miracles and Modern Thought: A Defense of Biblical Miracles*. Grand Rapids, MI: Baker, 1992. Republished Eugene: Wipf & Stock, 2004.

———. *Preserving Orthodoxy Maintaining Continuity with the Historic Christian Faith on Scripture*. Matthews, NC: Bastion, 2017.

———. *Systematic Theology: Sin, Salvation*, vol. 3. Minneapolis, MN: Bethany House, 2004.

———. *The Big Book of Christian Apologetics: An A to Z Guide*. Grand Rapids, MI: Baker, 2012.

———. *Twelve Points that Show Christianity Is True: A Handbook on Defending the Christian Faith*. Charlotte, NC: Norm Geisler International Ministries, 2016.

———, and Paul D. Feinberg. *Introduction to Philosophy: A Christian Perspective*. Grand Rapids, MI: Baker, 1980.

———, and David Geisler. *Conversational Evangelism: Connecting with People to Share Jesus*. Eugene, OR: Harvest House, 2014.

———, and Joseph M. Holden. *Living Loud: Defending Your Faith*. Nashville, TN: Broadman & Holman, 2002.

———, and Thomas Howe. *The Big Book of Bible Difficulties*. Grand Rapids, MI: Baker, 2008.

———, and William E. Nix. *A General Introduction to the Bible*, rev. and exp. Chicago, IL: Moody, 1986.

———, and William C. Roach. *Defending Inerrancy: Affirming the Accuracy of Scripture for a New Generation*. Grand Rapids, MI: Baker, 2012.

———, and Ron Rhodes. *Correcting the Cults*. Grand Rapids, MI: Baker, 2005.

———, and Patty Tunnicliffe. *Reasons for Belief*. Minneapolis, MN: Bethany House, 2013.

———, and Frank Turek. *I Don't Have Enough Faith to Be an Atheist*. Wheaton, IL: Crossway, 2004.

———. *Legislating Morality*. Eugene, OR: Wipf & Stock, 1998.

———, and William D. Watkins. *Worlds Apart: A Handbook on World Views*. 2d ed. Grand Rapids, MI: Baker, 1989.

———, and Patrick Zuckeran. *The Apologetics of Jesus: A Caring Approach to Dealing with Doubters*. Grand Rapids, MI: Baker, 2009.

Geivett, R. Douglas, and Gary R. Habermas, eds. *In Defense of Miracles: A Comprehensive Case for God's Action in History*. Downers Grove, IL: InterVarsity, 1997.

Gibbons, Charles B. *Federal Rules of Evidence with Trial Objections*. Saint Paul, MN: ThomsonWest, 2003.

Gilson, Etienne. *Being and Some Philosophers*. 2d ed. Toronto, Canada: Pontifical Institute of Mediaeval Studies, 1952.

Godwin, Joscelyn. *Mystery Religions in the Ancient World*. San Francisco, CA: Harper & Row, 1981.

Gonzalez, Guillermo, and Jay Wesley Richards. *The Privileged Planet: How Our Place in the Cosmos Is Designed for Discovery*. Washington, DC: Regnery, 2004.

Graves, David E. *Biblical Archaeology: An Introduction with Recent Discoveries That Support the Reliability of the Bible*. Toronto, Ontario: Electronic Christian Media, 2017.

Greenlee, J. Harold. *Introduction to New Testament Textual Criticism*. Grand Rapids, MI: Eerdmans, 1964.

Griffin, David Ray. *Two Great Truths: A New Synthesis of Naturalism and Christian Faith*. Louisville, KY: Westminster John Knox Press, 2004.

Griffiths, J. Gwyn. *The Origins of Osiris and His Cult*. Leiden, Netherlands: Brill, 1980.

Groll, Sarah Israel, ed. *Pharaonic Egypt: The Bible and Christianity*. Jerusalem, Israel: Magnes Press, 1985.

Groothuis, Douglas. *Truth Decay: Defending Christianity Against the Challenges of Postmodernism*. Downers Grove, IL: InterVarsity, 2000.

Grudem, Wayne. *Systematic Theology*. Grand Rapids, MI: Zondervan, 1994.

Gulen, Fethullah. *Questions and Answers About Islam*, vol. 1. Clifton, NJ: Tughra Books, 2010.

Habermas, Gary R. *The Historical Jesus: Ancient Evidence for the Life of Christ*. Joplin, MO: College Press, 1996.

———. *The Risen Jesus and Future Hope*. Lanham, MD: Rowan & Littlefield, 2003.

———, and Michael Licona. *The Case for the Resurrection of Jesus*. Grand Rapids, MI: Kregel, 2004.

Hackett, Stuart. *Resurrection of Theism: Prolegomena to Christian Apology*. 2d ed. Grand Rapids, MI: Baker, 1982.

Hallo, William W., and K. Lawson Younger Jr., eds. *The Context of Scripture I*, Leiden, Netherlands: Brill, 1997.

Halsberghe, Gaston H. *The Cult of Sol Invictus*. Leiden, Netherlands: Brill, 1972.

Haneef, Suzanne. *What Everyone Should Know About Islam and Muslims*. Chicago, IL: Kazi Publications, 1979.

Hanna, Mark M. *Biblical Christianity: Truth or Delusion?* Maitland, FL: Xulon Press, 2011.

Harpur, Tom. *The Pagan Christ*. New York: Walker & Company, 2004.

Heeren, Fred. *Show Me God: What the Message from Space Is Telling Us About God*. 2d rev. ed. Olathe, KS: Day Star Publications, 2004.

Hemer, Colin J. *The Book of Acts in the Setting of Hellenistic History*. Winona Lake, IN: Eisenbrauns, 1990.

Henry, Carl F.H. *God, Revelation and Authority*. 6 vols. Waco, TX: Word, 1976.

Herrick, James A. *The Making of the New Spirituality: The Eclipse of Western Religious Tradition*. Downers Grove, IL: InterVarsity, 2003.

Hicks, Stephen R.C. *Explaining Postmodernism.* Loves Park, IL: Ockham's Razor Publisher, 2011.

Hindson, Ed, ed., et al. *The Popular Encyclopedia of Apologetics.* Eugene, OR: Harvest House, 2008.

————, and Thomas Ice. *Charting the Bible Chronologically.* Eugene, OR: Harvest House, 2017.

Hodge, Charles. *Systematic Theology.* Peabody, MA: Hendrickson, 2013.

Hoffner, H., ed. *Orient and Occident.* Kevelaer, Germany: Butzon und Bercker, l973.

Holden, Joseph M., and Norman Geisler. *The Popular Handbook of Archaeology and the Bible: Discoveries that Confirm the Reliability of Scripture.* Eugene, OR: Harvest House, 2013.

Horton, Michael. *The Christian Faith.* Grand Rapids, MI: Zondervan, 2010.

House, H. Wayne, and Joseph M. Holden. *Charts of Apologetics and Christian Evidences.* Grand Rapids, MI: Zondervan, 2006.

————, and Dennis W. Jowers. *Reasons for Our Hope: An Introduction to Christian Apologetics.* Nashville, TN: B&H Academic, 2011.

Howe, Richard G. "In Defense of the Supernatural," in *The Jesus Quest: The Danger from Within.* Maitland, FL: Xulon, 2014: 621-672.

Howe Thomas. *Objectivity in Biblical Interpretation.* Altamonte Spring, FL: Advantage Books, 2004.

Jacobs, Jim, Esq. *A Lawyer's Case for God.* Brandon, FL: Yaakov Press, 2016.

Jacobsen, Thorkild, and William L. Moran, eds. *Toward the Image of Tammuz and Other Essays on Mesopotamian History and Culture*, Cambridge, MA: Harvard University Press, 1970.

Jenkins, Philip. *Hidden Gospels: How the Search for Jesus Lost Its Way.* New York: Oxford University Press, 2001.

Jones, Clay. *Why Does God Allow Evil? Compelling Answers for Life's Toughest Questions.* Eugene, OR: Harvest House, 2017.

Kaiser Jr., Walter C., ed. *Classical Evangelical Essays in Old Testament Interpretation.* Grand Rapids, MI: Baker, 1972.

————. *The History of Israel: From the Bronze Age Through the Jewish Wars.* Nashville, TN: Broadman & Holman, 1998.

————. *The Old Testament Documents: Are They Reliable and Relevant?* Downers Grove, IL: InterVarsity, 2001.

Keener, Craig S. *Miracles: The Credibility of the New Testament Accounts.* 2 vols. Grand Rapids, MI: Baker, 2011.

Kennedy, H.A.A. *St. Paul and the Mystery Religions.* London, UK: Hodder & Stoughton, 1913.

Kepler, Johannes. *New Astronomy* (1609), trans. by William H. Donahue. Cambridge, UK: Cambridge University Press, 1992.

Kerr, Gaven. *Aquinas's Way to God: The Proof in* De Ente et Essentia. New York: Oxford University Press, 2015.

Kitchen, K.A. *On the Reliability of the Old Testament.* Grand Rapids, MI: Eerdmans, 2003.

————. and P.J.N. Lawrence, eds. *Treaty, Law and Covenant in the Ancient Near East*, 3 vols. Wiesbaden, Germany: Harrassowitz Verlag, 2012.

Koons, Robert C., and George Bealer, eds. *The Waning of Materialism.* Oxford, UK: Oxford University Press, 2010.

Kramer, Samuel N. *The Sacred Marriage Rite.* Bloomington, IN: Indiana University Press, 1969.

————. *The Sumerians: Their History, Culture, and Character.* Chicago, IL: University of Chicago, 1963.

Laeuchli, Samuel. *Mithraism in Ostia.* Evanston, IL: Northwestern University, 1967.

Lane, Eugene N., ed. *Cybele, Attis and Related Cults.* Leiden, Netherlands: Brill, 1996.

Lanier, W. Mark. *Christianity on Trial: A Lawyer Examines the Christian Faith.* Downers Grove, IL: InterVarsity, 2014.

Lewis, C.S. *Mere Christianity.* New York: Macmillan, 1960.

————. *Miracles: How God Intervenes in Nature and Human Affairs.* New York: Macmillan, 1947.

————. *The Weight of Glory.* New York: Macmillan, 1949.

Lichtheim, Miriam, trans. *Ancient Egyptian Literature II: The New Kingdom.* Berkeley, CA: University of California, 1976.

Limbaugh, David. *Jesus on Trial: A Lawyer Affirms the Truth of the Gospel.* Washington, DC: Regnery Publishing, 2014.

Lindsell, Harold. *The Bible in the Balance*. Grand Rapids, MI: Eerdmans, 1979.

Linnemann, Eta. *Historical Criticism of the Bible Methodology or Ideology? Reflections of a Bultmannian Turned Evangelical*. Grand Rapids, MI: Kregel, 1990.

Longenecker, Richard N., ed. *Life in the Face of Death: The Resurrection Message of the New Testament*. Grand Rapids, MI: Eerdmans, 1998.

Lutzer, Erwin. *Who Are You to Judge?* Chicago, IL: Moody, 2016.

MacKenzie, Ralph E. *Revealing Snapshots: People and Events That Shaped Christianity*. San Diego, CA: Clairemont Bookworks, 2014.

Margenau, Henry, and Roy A. Varghese, eds. *Cosmos, Bios and Theos*. La Salle, IL: Open Court, 1992.

Martin, Ralph P., and Peter H. Davids, eds. *Dictionary of the Later New Testament and Its Developments*. Downers Grove, IL: InterVarsity, 1997.

McDowell, Josh, and Sean McDowell. *The Beauty of Intolerance*. Uhrichsville, OH: Shiloh Run Press, 2016.

———. *The New Evidence that Demands a Verdict*. Upd. and exp. Nashville, TN: Thomas Nelson, 2017.

———. *The Unshakable Truth*. Eugene, OR: Harvest House, 2010.

McDowell, Sean, gen. ed., and Dillon Burroughs, Joseph M. Holden, et al., assoc. eds. *The Apologetic Study Bible for Students*. Nashville, TN: Broadman & Holman, 2010, 2017.

McGrath, Alister E. *An Introduction to Christianity*. Cambridge, UK: Blackwell, 1997.

McGrath, Gavin, et al., eds. *New Dictionary of Christian Apologetics*. Downers Grove, IL: Intervarsity, 2006.

Mettinger, Tryggve N.D. *The Riddle of Resurrection: "Dying and Rising Gods" in the Ancient Near East*. Stockholm, Sweden: Almqvist & Wiksell, 2001.

Metzger, Bruce M. *Historical and Literary Studies: Pagan, Jewish and Christian*. Leiden, Netherlands: Brill, 1968.

———, and Michael D. Coogan, gen. eds. *The Oxford Companion to the Bible*. New York: The Oxford University Press, 1993.

Meyer, Stephen C. *Darwin's Doubts: The Explosive Origin of Animal Life and the Case for Intelligent Design*. Rev. ed. New York: HarperOne, 2013.

———. *Signature in the Cell: DNA and the Evidence for Intelligent Design*. Rep. ed. New York: HarperOne, 2010.

Miethe, Beverly, and Terry L Miethe. *Serving Christ: A Family Affair*. Joplin, MO: College Press, 1995.

Miethe, Terry L. *Back to the Future: Postmodernism and the Christian*. Juliet, TN: Winged Lion, 2014.

———. *C.S. Lewis: His Legacy Fifty Years On*. Juliet, TN: Winged Lion, 2014.

———, ed. *Did Jesus Rise from the Dead? The Resurrection Debate, with Gary R. Habermas and A.G.N. Flew*. New York: Harper & Row, 1987; 2d ed., Eugene, OR: Wipf & Stock Publishers, 2004.

———, gen. ed. *I Am Put Here for the Defense of the Gospel: Dr. Norman L. Geisler: A Festschrift in His Honor*. Eugene, OR: Pickwick, 2016.

———. *The Compact Dictionary of Doctrinal Words*. Minneapolis, MN: Bethany House, 1988.

———. *Soul-Making & Virtue*. Juliet, TN: Winged Lion, 2017.

———. *Why Believe? God Exists! Rethinking the Case for God and Christianity*. Joplin, MO: College Press, 1993.

———, and Antony G.N. Flew. *Does God Exist? A Believer and An Atheist Debate*. San Francisco, CA: HarperSanFrancisco, 1991.

Monton, Bradley. *Seeking God in Science: An Atheist Defends Intelligent Design*. Peterborough, Ontario: Broadview Press, 2009.

Moreland, J.P. *Love Your God with All Your Mind*. 2d. ed. Colorado Springs, CO: NavPress, 2014.

———. *Scaling the Secular City*. Grand Rapids, MI: Baker, 1987.

———, and Scott B. Rae. *Body & Soul*. Downers Grove, IL: InterVarsity, 2000.

Mortenson, Terry. *The Great Turning Point*. Green Forest, AR: Master Books, 2004.

———, ed. *Searching for Adam*. Green Forest, AR: Master Books, 2016.

Nash, Ronald H. *Christianity & the Hellenistic World*. Grand Rapids, MI: Zondervan, 1984.

———. *Worldviews in Conflict: Choosing Christianity in a World of Ideas*. Grand Rapids: Zondervan, 1992.

Newton, Isaac. *The Principia: Mathematical Principles of Natural Philosophy: The Authoritative Translation*. Trans. I. Bernard Cohen and Anne Whitman, assisted by Julia Budenz. Oakland, CA: University of California Press, 1999, Kindle.

Plantinga, Alvin. *Warranted Christian Belief*. New York: Oxford University, 2000.

Price, Randall. *Secrets of the Dead Sea Scrolls*. Eugene, OR: Harvest House, 1996.

———. *The Temple and Bible Prophecy*. Eugene, OR: Harvest House, 2005.

———, and H. Wayne House. *Zondervan Handbook of Biblical Archaeology*. Grand Rapids, MI: Zondervan, 2017.

Quastler, Henry. *The Emergence of Biological Organization*. New Haven, CT: Yale University Press, 1964.

Quinn, Philip, and Charles Taliaferro, eds. *A Companion to Philosophy of Religion*. Oxford, UK: Blackwell, 1997.

Rainey, A.F., and R.S. Notley. *The Sacred Bridge*. Jerusalem, Israel: Carta, 2015.

Randall, John H. *Hellenistic Ways of Deliverance and the Making of the Christian Synthesis*. New York: Columbia University Press, 1970.

Reitzenstein, Richard. *Hellenistic Mystery-Religions*. Pittsburgh, PA: Pickwick Press, 1978.

Rhodes, Ron. *Christ Before the Manger: The Life and Times of the Preincarnate Christ*. Eugene, OR: Wipf & Stock, 2002.

———. *The Challenge of the Cults*. Grand Rapids, MI: Zondervan, 2001.

Ritmeyer, Leen. *The Quest: Revealing the Temple Mount in Jerusalem*. Jerusalem, Israel: Carta, 2012.

Ryle, H.E. *The Canon of the Old Testament*. New York: Macmillan, 1892.

S, Acharya. *The Christ Conspiracy*. Kempton, IL: Adventure Unlimited, 1999.

Sanford, J.C. *Genetic Entropy*. 4th ed. Waterloo, NY: FMS Publications, 2014.

Scalf, Foy, ed. *The Book of the Dead: Becoming God in Ancient Egypt*. Chicago, IL: The Oriental Institute of the University of Chicago, 2017.

Schonfield, Hugh. *Those Incredible Christians*. New York: Bernard Geis, 1968.

Sherlock, Thomas. *The Trial of the Witnesses of the Resurrection of Jesus Christ*. CreateSpace, 2015.

Smith, Graeme. *Was the Tomb Empty? A Lawyer Weighs the Evidence for the Resurrection*. Grand Rapids, MI: Monarch Books, 2014.

Smith, Jonathan Z. *Drudgery Divine: On the Comparison of Early Christianity and the Religions of Late Antiquity*. Chicago, IL: University of Chicago, 1999.

Smith, Mark. *Following Osiris*. Oxford, UK: Oxford University, 2017.

Sproul, R.C., John Gerstner, and Arthur Lindsley. *Classical Apologetics: A Rational Defense of the Christian Faith and a Critique of Presuppositional Apologetics*. Grand Rapids, MI: Zondervan, 1984.

Surgy, Paul de, ed. *The Resurrection and Modern Biblical Thought*. New York: Corpus Books, 1970.

Swinburne, Richard. *Faith and Reason*, 2d ed. Oxford, UK: Clarendon Press, 2005.

Thayer, H.S., ed. *Newton's Philosophy of Nature: Selections from His Writings*. New York: Hafner Library of Classics, 1953.

Thomas, Robert L., and F. David Farnell. *The Jesus Crisis*. Grand Rapids, MI: Kregel, 1998.

Turek, Frank. *Stealing from God: Why Atheists Need God to Make Their Case*. Colorado Springs, CO: NavPress, 2014.

VanderKam, James, and Peter Flint. *The Meaning of the Dead Sea Scrolls: Their Significance for Understanding the Bible, Judaism, Jesus, and Christianity*. San Francisco, CA: HarperCollins, 2002.

Vandier, Jacques. *La Religion Égyptienne*. Paris, France: Presses Universitaires de France, 1949.

Van Til, Cornelius. *A Christian Theory of Knowledge*. Phillipsburg, NJ: Presbyterian & Reformed, 1969.

———. *An Introduction to Systematic Theology*, vol. 5 of *In Defense of the Faith*. Phillipsburg, NJ: Presbyterian & Reformed, 1982.

———. *Christian Apologetics*, 2d ed., ed. William Edgar. Phillipsburg, NJ: Presbyterian & Reformed, 2003.

———. *The Defense of the Faith*, 4th ed., ed. K. Scott Oliphint. Phillipsburg, NJ: Presbyterian & Reformed, 2008.

Vermaseren, M.J., ed. *Corpus Inscriptionum et Monumentorum Religionis Mithriacae*, 2 vols. The Hague, Netherlands: Martin Nijhoff, 1956, 1960.

———. *Cybele and Attis: The Myth and the Cult*. London, UK: Thames & Hudson, 1977.

———. *Mithras: The Secret God*. London, UK: Chatto & Windus, 1963.

Wagner, Günter. *Pauline Baptism and the Pagan Mysteries*. Edinburgh, Scotland: Oliver & Boyd, 1967.

Wallace, J. Warner. *Cold Case Christianity: A Homicide Detective Investigates the Claims of the Gospels*. Colorado Springs, CO: David C. Cook, 2013.

———. *God's Crime Scene: A Cold-Case Detective Examines the Evidence for a Divinely Created Universe*. Colorado Springs, CO: David C. Cook, 2015.

Ware, Bruce A. *Father, Son, and Holy Spirit: Relationships, Roles, and Relevance*. Wheaton, IL: Crossway, 2005.

Wielenberg, Erik J. *Robust Ethics*. New York: Oxford University Press, 2014.

Wilhelmsen, Frederick D. *Man's Knowledge of Reality: An Introduction to Thomistic Epistemology*. Englewood Cliffs, NJ: Prentice-Hall, 1956.

Wilkins, Steve, ed. *Faith and Reason: Three Views*. Downers Grove, IL: IVP Academic, 2014.

Williams, Jacqueline A. *Biblical Interpretation in the Gnostic Gospel of Truth from Nag Hammadi*. Atlanta, GA: Scholars Press, 1988.

Woodbridge, John D. *Biblical Authority: A Critique of the Rogers/McKim Proposal*. Grand Rapids, MI: Zondervan, 1982.

Yamauchi, Edwin M. *Persia and the Bible*. Grand Rapids, MA: Baker, 1990.

———. *Pre-Christian Gnosticism: A Survey of the Proposed Evidences*. Eugene, OR: Wipf & Stock, 2003.

———. *The Scriptures and Archaeology: Abraham to Daniel*. Eugene, OR: Wipf & Stock, 2013.

———, and Marvin R. Wilson, eds. *Dictionary of Daily Life in Biblical & Post-biblical Antiquity*. Peabody, MA: Hendrickson, 2017.

Endnotes

Preface

1. C.S. Lewis, "Learning in War-Time" in *The Weight of Glory and Other Addresses*, rev. and exp. ed. (New York: Macmillan, 1980), 28.

Chapter 1—What Is Apologetics and Why Do We Need It?

1. For a basic book that follows these points, see Norman L. Geisler, *Twelve Points that Show Christianity Is True* (Matthews, NC: Norm Geisler International Ministries, 2016), or for an advanced treatment, see Norman L. Geisler, *Christian Apologetics*, 2d ed. (Grand Rapids, MI: Baker, 2013).

2. For detailed archaeological and textual support, see Joseph M. Holden and Norman L. Geisler, *The Popular Handbook of Archaeology and the Bible: Discoveries that Confirm the Reliability of the Scripture* (Eugene, OR: Harvest House, 2013).

3. For books that answer objections and questions, see Norman L. Geisler, *The Big Book of Christian Apologetics: An A to Z Guide* (Grand Rapids, MI: Baker, 2012); Norman L. Geisler and Thomas Howe, *The Big Book of Bible Difficulties* (Grand Rapids, MI: Baker, 2008); Norman L. Geisler and Ron Rhodes, *Correcting the Cults* (Grand Rapids, MI: Baker, 2005).

4. Saint Augustine, *Confessions*, trans. Henry Chadwick (New York: Oxford University Press, 1991).

5. Simon Greenleaf, *The Testimony of the Evangelists* (Grand Rapids, MI: Kregel Classics, 1995).

6. Frank Morrison, *Who Moved the Stone?* (Grand Rapids, MI: Zondervan, 1958).

7. Antony Flew, *There Is a God: How the World's Most Notorious Atheist Changed His Mind* (New York: HarperCollins, 2007), 93.

8. Francis Collins, *The Language of God: A Scientist Presents Evidence for Belief* (New York: Free Press, 2006), 218.

9. Norman L. Geisler and Frank Turek, *I Don't Have Enough Faith to Be an Atheist* (Wheaton, IL: Crossway, 2004).

10. C.S. Lewis, *The Weight of Glory* (New York: Macmillan, 1949), 50.

Chapter 2—What About a Short History of Apologetics?

1. This chapter was originally published by John Warwick Montgomery under the title *A Short History of Apologetics*. Readers interested in the history of apologetics may wish to consult Bernard Ramm, *Varieties of Christian Apologetics*, rev. ed. (Grand Rapids, MI: Baker, 1961 [evangelical]); Joseph H. Crehan, "Apologetics," *A Catholic Dictionary of Theology*, vol. I (London: Thomas Nelson, 1962); Avery Dulles, *A History of Apologetics* (Philadelphia: Westminster Press, 1971) (Roman Catholic bias—as with Crehan); L. Russ Bush, ed., *Classical Readings in Christian Apologetics A.D. 100–1800* (Grand Rapids, MI: Zondervan, 1983) (evangelical); William Edgar and K. Scott Oliphint, eds., *Christian Apologetics Past and Present: A Primary Source Reader*, 2 vols. (Wheaton, IL: Crossway, 2009-2010) (presuppositionist bias). It should be noted that these works treat inadequately, or not at all, the 21st-century scene.

2. See Montgomery, *Faith Founded on Fact* (Nashville, TN: Thomas Nelson, 1978), 119-121.

3. For the author's latest take on the ontological argument, see Montgomery, "God and Gödel," *Philosophia Christi*, vol. 20, no. 1 (2018), 199-206.

4. Cf. Montgomery, *Where Is History Going?* (Minneapolis, MN: Bethany, 1969), 109-110.

5. See Montgomery, "Computer Origins and the Defence of the Faith," 56/3 *Perspectives on Science and Christian Faith* (Sep 2004), 189-203; and reprinted (Part Two, chap. 2).

6. In an otherwise very useful handbook, Boa and Bowman's classification of Luther as an apologetic "fideist"—and the placing of him in the same bed with Kierkegaard, Karl Barth, and Donald Bloesch—would be ludicrous if it were not so factually wide of the mark: Kenneth D. Boa and Robert M. Bowman, Jr., *Faith Has Its Reasons,* 2d ed. (Milton Keynes, UK: Paternoster, 2005).

7. Boa and Bowman also incorrectly classify Pascal as a "fideist"! For a proper understanding of Pascal, see the writings of Emile Cailliet; also, Montgomery, "Computer Origins..." (loc. cit.).

8. Cf. Montgomery, *The Shaping of America* (Minneapolis, MN: Bethany, 1976).

9. Paley's continuing relevance is evidenced by the fact that atheist Richard Dawkins makes him his foil in arguing for biological evolutionism (*The Blind Watchmaker*). Paley, incidentally, was a barrister and wrote as a lawyer with Christ as his client; he was roundly (and unfairly) criticised for doing apologetics "in the spirit of the advocate rather than of the judge" by the great classicist Benjamin Jowett: *The Interpretation of Scripture and Other Essays* (London: George Routledge and Sons, n.d.), 129.

10. Sherlock's *Tryal* is photolithographically reprinted in Montgomery, ed., *Jurisprudence: A Book of Readings*, rev. ed. (Strasbourg, France: International Scholarly Publishers, 1980), available from http://www.ciltpp.com.

11. Montgomery, *Tractatus Logico-Theologicus*, 4th ed. (Bonn, Germany: Verlag für Kultur und Wissenschaft, 2009), *passim*. Available from http://www.ciltpp.com.

12. Cf. more recent—and systematic—decimations of Hume: philosopher (and non-Christian) John Earman, *Hume's Abject Failure: The Argument Against Miracles* (New York: Oxford University Press, 2000); and David Johnson, *Hume, Holism and Miracles* (Ithaca, NY: Cornell University Press, 1999).

13. Cf. Montgomery, ed., *Myth, Allegory and Gospel* (Minneapolis, MN: Bethany, 1974).

14. E.g., Jason Colwell, "The Historical Argument for the Christian Faith: A Response to Alvin Plantinga," 53/3 *International Journal for Philosophy of Religion* (2003), 147-161.

15. E.g., K. Scott Oliphint, "Plantinga on Warrant," 57/2 *Westminster Theological Journal* (1995), 415-435, and "Epistemology and Christian Belief," 63/1 *Westminster Theological Journal* (2001), 151-182.

16. In England, respect for the philosophical defence of Christian faith has not needed rehabilitation; see, for example, the valuable apologetic work of Richard Swinburne.

17. See Montgomery, "Neglected Apologetic Styles: The Juridical and the Literary," *Evangelical Apologetics*, eds. Michael Bauman, David Hall, and Robert Newman (Camp Hill, PA: Christian Publications, 1996), 119-133.

18. Reprinted in Montgomery, *The Law Above the Law* (Minneapolis, MN: Bethany, 1975).

19. Xulon Press, 2009.

20. For an interesting critique of this approach, by Canadian judge Dallas Miller, see 4/3 *Global Journal of Classical Theology*, Oct 2004: http://phc.edu/gj_1_toc_v4n3.php.

21. Cf. Montgomery, "Apologetics for the 21st Century," *Reasons for Faith*, eds. Norman L. Geisler and Chad V. Meister (Wheaton, IL: Crossway, 2007), 41-52.

Chapter 3—What Are Some Apologetic Approaches?

1. Some have suggested other methods, such as Reformed epistemology method, and the cumulative case method. It is not my intent to cover newer views, but the major three that have garnished support over the years, and the lesser but historic alternative of fideism. For more discussion of these newer perspectives, see Steven B. Cowan, ed., *Five Views on Apologetics* (Grand Rapids, MI: Zondervan, 2000), 15-20, and the review on *Five Views on Apologetics* at Apologetics Index, http://www.apologeticsindex.org/a108.html (last accessed January 25, 2007).

2. Norman L. Geisler, *The Big Book of Christian Apologetics: An A to Z Guide* (Grand Rapids, MI: Baker, 2012), Kindle loc. 29.

3. The 12-point argument is as follows: (1) truth about reality is knowable; (2) opposites cannot both be true; (3) the theistic God exists; (4) miracles are possible; (5) miracles performed in connection with a truth claim are acts of God to confirm the truth of God through a messenger of God; (6) the New Testament documents are reliable; (7) as witnessed in the New Testament, Jesus claimed to be God; (8) Jesus's claim to divinity was proven by a unique convergence of miracles (e.g., resurrection); (9) therefore, Jesus was God in human flesh; (10) whatever Jesus (who is God) affirmed as true is true; (11) Jesus affirmed that the Bible is the Word of God; (12) therefore, it is true that the Bible is the Word of God, and whatever is opposed to any biblical truth is false.

   See Norman Geisler, "Argument of Apologetics" in *Baker Encyclopedia of Christian Apologetics*, Baker Reference Library (Grand Rapids, MI: Baker, 1999), 36. I have omitted the verses included by the author in the quote.

4. For further description of evidential apologetics, see Geisler, *Baker Encyclopedia of Christian Apologetics*, 42; John Warwick Montgomery, "The Holy Spirit and the Defense of the Faith" in *Bibliotheca Sacra* 154:616 (Oct 1997):

387-395; for a presuppositional response to the value of evidences, see John C. Whitcomb Jr., "Contemporary Apologetics and the Christian Faith, Part IV: The Limitations and Values of Christian Evidences," *Bibliotheca Sacra* 135:537 (Jan 1978): 25-33.

5. Bernard Ramm, *Protestant Christian Evidences: A Textbook of the Evidences of the Truthfulness of the Christian Faith for Conservative Protestants* (Chicago, IL: Moody, 1953), 16-32.

6. Cornelius Van Til, *The Defense of the Faith* (Philadelphia, PA: Presbyterian & Reformed, 1955).

7. Ronald B. Mayers, "Both/And: A Biblical Alternative to the Presuppositional/Evidential Debate" in Michael Bauman, David W. Hall, and Robert C. Newman, eds., *Evangelical Apologetics* (Camp Hill, PA: Christian Publications, 1996), 35.

8. Classical apologist William Lane Craig says, "…what about the role of the Holy Spirit in the life of the unbeliever? Since the Holy Spirit does not indwell him does this mean he must rely only upon arguments to convince him that Christianity is true? No, not at all. According to the Scripture, God has a different ministry of the Holy Spirit especially geared to the needs of the unbeliever." William Lane Craig, *Apologetics: An Introduction* (Chicago: Moody, 1984); John Warwick Montgomery says, "Ultimately a non-Christian must make a moral choice as to what he will do with the objectively sound case for Christianity. If he exercises his will to accept the Christ of the Scriptures, that act must be attributed to the Spirit alone as a pure gift of grace. But the monergistic event of conversion no more denigrates or renders superfluous the work of the apologist than it does the work of the preacher or evangelist who presented the saving message to the individual in the first place. The Holy Spirit does not create the gospel or the evidence for it; He applies what is preached and defended to produce salvation." John Warwick Montgomery, "The Holy Spirit and the Defense of the Faith" in *Bibliotheca Sacra* 154:616 (Oct 1997): 392.

9. Mayers, "Both/And: A Biblical Alternative to the Presuppositional/Evidential Debate," quoting John Calvin, *The Institutes of the Christian Religion*, J.T. McNeill, ed. (Philadelphia, PA: Westminster Press, 1960), 1.1.1.

10. See my work on this subject in H. Wayne House, "A Biblical Argument for Balanced Apologetics: How the Apostle Paul Practiced Apologetics in the Acts (Acts 14:8-18, 17:16-34)," in Norman L. Geisler and Chad V. Meister, eds., *Reasons for Faith: Making a Case for the Christian Faith* (Wheaton, IL: Crossway, 2007), 53-75.

11. House, "A Biblical Argument for Balanced Apologetics: How the Apostle Paul Practiced Apologetics in the Acts (Acts 14:8-18, 17:16-34)" in *Reasons for Faith*, 71.

Chapter 4—What Is the Overall Apologetic Task?

1. Norman L. Geisler, *Baker Encyclopedia of Christian Apologetics* (Grand Rapids, MI: Baker, 1999), 458.

2. There are several well-known modern apologists, who are contributors to this book, who have written extensively on these subjects, such as John Warwick Montgomery, Josh McDowell, Gary Habermas, H. Wayne House, and Norman Geisler, to name a few.

3. More recently, Daniel Wallace of the Center for the Study of New Testament Manuscripts announced that his team had discovered a fragment from Mark's Gospel, which a paleographer dated to the first century. If this discovery and analysis survive additional research, it will erase any significant gap between the original document and the oldest existing copy. See https://voice.dts.edu/article/wallace-new-testament-manscript-first-century/.

4. For more details, see the chapter in this book by Don Stewart and Joseph M. Holden, "Were the New Testament Manuscripts Copied Accurately?"

5. See Joseph M. Holden and Norman Geisler, *The Popular Handbook of Archaeology and the Bible: Discoveries that Confirm the Reliability of Scripture* (Eugene, OR: Harvest House, 2013), 261-264, 283-289, 295-305.

6. For a detailed description and case for the authenticity of the James Ossuary inscription, see Holden and Geisler, *The Popular Handbook of Archaeology and the Bible*, 310-315, 389-393.

7. For many more interesting finds, see Holden and Geisler, *The Popular Handbook of Archaeology and the Bible*.

8. Many important attributes of God listed in the Old Testament are used of Jesus in the New Testament.

Attribute:	Old Testament	New Testament
Shepherd	Psalm 23:1	John 10:11
First and last	Isaiah 44:6	Revelation 1:17

Judge	Joel 3:12	Matthew 35:31f.
Bridegroom	Isaiah 62:5	Matthew 25:1
Light	Psalm 27:1	John 8:12
Savior	Isaiah 43:11	John 4:42
God's glory	Isaiah 42:8	John 17:5
Giver of life	1 Samuel 2:6	John 5:21

Also, see Ron Rhodes's chapter in this volume on the deity of Christ (chapter 21).

9. See at https://raychoi.org/2012/06/01/what-happened-to-the-12-disciples-after-the-resurrection-and-ascension/.

10. See Gary Habermas and Benjamin C.F. Shaw's chapter on the resurrection (chapter 22). Also see his work *The Case for the Resurrection of Jesus* (Grand Rapids, MI: Kregel, 2004).

11. For more details, see Josh McDowell and Sean McDowell, *The New Evidence that Demands a Verdict,* upd. and exp. (Nashville, TN: Thomas Nelson, 2017).

Chapter 5—What Is the Relationship Between Faith and Reason?

1. Richard Dawkins, "A Scientist's Case Against God," a speech at the Edinburgh International Science Festival on April 15, 1992 (reported in *The Independent,* April 20, 1992).

Chapter 6—What Is Truth?

1. Aristotle, *Metaphysics,* IV, 7, 1011b26-29, translation by W.D. Ross, in Richard McKeon, *The Basic Works of Aristotle* (New York: Random House, 1941), 749. Other philosophers holding a correspondence theory of truth are Plato (*Sophist,* 240d; 263b); Augustine *(Soliloquia* I, 28); Thomas Aquinas (*Truth,* Question 1, Article 1); René Descartes *(Meditations on First Philosophy: Third Meditation; Objections and Replies: Fifth Set of Objection*s (see John Cottingham, Robert Stoothoff, Dugald Murdoch, trans. *The Philosophical Writings of Descartes,* vol. II (Cambridge, UK: Cambridge University Press, 1984): 26, 196; David Hume (*A Treatise of Human Nature,* II, 3, §X, III, 1, §1 (see L.A. Selby-Bigge, 2d ed. [Oxford, UK: Clarendon Press, 448, 458]); John Locke (*An Essay Concerning Human Understandin*g II, II, §2-§5); Immanuel Kant (*Critique of Pure Reason,* I, Second Part, First Div., Bk. II, Chap. II, §3, 3 (Norman Kemp Smith, trans. [New York: St. Martin's Press, 1965]: 220); Bertrand Russell, "On the Nature of Truth" in *Proceedings of the Aristotelian Society* (1906–1907), 28-49, as cited in *The Encyclopedia of Philosophy,* Paul Edwards, ed., (New York: Macmillan, 1967), s.v. "Correspondence Theory of Truth," 232); and the early Ludwig Wittgenstein (*Tractatus Logico-Philosophicus* 2.0211-2.0212, 2.21, 3.01). Philosophers who hold the correspondence theory of truth differ as to exactly where the "correspondence" obtains. Positions include that it obtains between a proposition (or belief) and external reality (naïve realism), that it obtains in the metaphysical formal conformity of the intellect and the thing in external reality (moderate or scholastic realism), or that it obtains only between the idea of reality in the mind and the thing in reality outside the mind (representationalism).

2. Sometimes critics of the Bible charge the Bible with error because they miss these different ways that a statement can truly correspond to reality. Examples include Mark 1:16: Jesus *literally* walked by the sea and the disciples were *literally* casting their nets. Galatians 4:23-24: Paul showed that the story of the bondwoman (Genesis 16) vs. the free woman (Genesis 21) namely, Hagar and Sarah, is an *allegory* of the relationship of the old covenant (law) to the new covenant (grace). Though some English translations use the term *symbolic,* it translates the Greek word *allegoroumena,* from which we get the English word *allegory.* Isaiah 55:12: Isaiah attributing hands to trees is a use of *metaphor.* Isaiah 7:2: Isaiah likening the moving heart of a person to the way the wind moves a tree is a use of *simile.* Second Corinthians 5:7: Paul draws the *analogy* between physical walking and spiritual walking. Hebrews 9:7-9: The writer of Hebrews explains how in the first temple the fact that the priest could only enter the Holy of Holies under strict conditions was *symbolic*—that the way of full access to the presence of God had not yet been made manifest. Judges 7:12: The narrative appropriately exaggerating (for the sake of emphasis) the military might of the Midianites and Amalekites is a use of *hyperbole.* Matthew 5:45: The Bible describing things according to their appearance (like the sun rising) is the use of *phenomenological* language, sometimes called the language of appearance. Joel 2:31 is perhaps even a better example when it says that the moon will be turned into blood. This is clearly a reference to the fact that the moon will have the appearance of blood because it will turn red. Numbers 2:32 compared with Numbers 11:21: To round off numbers is to speak *informally.* Matthew 6:11: The use of a part for the whole is a *synecdoche,* like saying that he "put a roof over our heads." Presumably he provided an entire

house and not just the roof. Matthew 8:8 compared with Luke 7:6: To substitute the agent for the instrument (or vice versa) is a *metonymy*. As emissaries of the centurion, when the friends spoke to Jesus on the centurion's behalf, that was the same as the centurion speaking to Jesus Himself. It is the same thing that happens when the president speaks to a head of state of another country by means of his diplomats. It is metonymically to say that the president spoke to that head of state.

3. For an in-depth discussion of how theories of truth affect one's ability to maintain a proper understanding of biblical inerrancy, see Norman L. Geisler, "The Concept of Truth in the Inerrancy Debate" in *Bibliotheca Sacra* (Oct-Dec 1980): 327-339.

4. Daniel P. Fuller, "Benjamin B. Warfield's View of Faith and History," *Bulletin of the Evangelical Theological Society* 11 (Spring 1968): 81-82.

5. Elsewhere, Fuller says, "This can only mean that all the Biblical assertions which teach or rightly imply knowledge that makes men wise unto salvation are absolutely inerrant" (Fuller, p. 80). His reasoning is evident when he asks why it is not reasonable to infer that "God who lovingly willed to communicate revelational truth to men deliberately accommodated his language in non-revelational matters to the way the original readers viewed the world about them, so as to enhance the communication of revelational truth, by which alone men could be saved?" (Fuller, p. 81).

6. Fuller's thinking here anticipated, by about a decade, the influential work of Jack Rogers and Donald McKim. They argue, "The foundation of the doctrine of Scripture in the early church needs to be recovered. For early Christian teachers, Scripture was wholly authoritative as a means of bringing people to salvation and guiding them in the life of faith…The interpretation of the Bible was influenced by the understanding of its saving purpose… Early theologians accepted God's accommodated style of communication." Jack B. Rogers and Donald K. McKim, *The Authority and Interpretation of the Bible: An Historical Approach* (New York: Harper & Row, 1979), 457-458. Seeing the Bible's authority as arising from it as a "means" of bringing people to salvation or understanding the Bible's "purpose" as somehow influencing interpretation in light of God's "accommodated style of communication" is to employ the functional or intentional theory of truth. One problem with this is that contrasting the supposed purpose of the Bible with an alleged factual error (i.e., an accommodation in the Bible—that is, affirming that the Bible is "true" though it has errors) is also to tacitly acknowledge the correspondence theory of truth. What is more, just as we saw with the pragmatic theory, anyone who would contend for the functional or intentional theory of truth cannot even state what this theory is without utilizing the correspondence theory of truth to do so. Last, one could never know what the intention of a statement is without (1) looking to other statements either within the text itself or from the author, or (2) getting into the mind of the author. The latter is impossible. The former leads to an infinite regress because any statement in the text or from the author that supposedly conveyed the intention of the text or author would itself need to show its intention in order to be understood. For a deft refutation of Rogers and McKim, see John D. Woodbridge, *Biblical Authority: A Critique of the Rogers/McKim Proposal* (Grand Rapids, MI: Zondervan, 1982).

Chapter 7—How Can We Know Truth?

1. For example, we observe that all dogs are mammals and that some trees are deciduous. The study of the relationships of such statements is categorical (or Aristotelian) logic. The four forms are: All S is P; No S is P; Some S is P; and Some S is not P. For a helpful introduction to logic, see Norman L. Geisler and Ronald M. Brooks, *Come Let Us Reason: An Introduction to Logical Thinking* (Grand Rapids, MI: Baker, 1990). For a more in-depth study that deals with the metaphysical grounding for logic, see Peter Kreeft, *Socratic Logic: A Logic Text Using Socratic Method, Platonic Questions, and Aristotelian Principles* (South Bend, IN: St. Augustine's Press, 2008). For a technical exploration of the philosophy of logic according to the classical tradition, see Henry Babcock Veatch, *Intentional Logic: A Logic Based on Philosophical Realism* (New Haven: Yale University Press, 1952; republished, New Haven, CT: Archon Books, 1970).

2. It should come as no surprise that how one regards such issues will have a direct bearing on how one reads and interprets the Bible. For an important reading on how language relates to reality, especially as it relates to biblical interpretation, see Thomas Howe, *Objectivity in Biblical Interpretation* (Altamonte Springs, FL: Advantage Books, 2004).

3. This is often challenged by postmodernists who resist the constraints of logic and, consequently, resist the classical

method of apologetics. See, for example, Robert E. Webber, *The Younger Evangelicals: Facing the Challenges of the New World* (Grand Rapids, MI: Baker, 2002). Likely influenced (if only indirectly) by Jack Rogers and Donald McKim's *The Authority and Interpretation of the Bible: An Historical Approach* (New York: Harper & Row, 1979), Webber's defense of postmodernism exhibits a very common misunderstanding of the history of ideas, particularly regarding the notion of truth and logic, and their bearing on proclaiming and defending the message of Christianity.

4. We can see this law in Genesis 3:1-5, where God said that Adam and Eve would die the day they ate of the tree of the knowledge of good and evil. Satan contradicted God and said they would not die. These statements cannot both be true at the same time and in the same sense.

5. For helps on logic, see the works cited in note 1.

6. For a quick summary of the arguments for Isaiah being the author, see Normal Geisler and Thomas Howe, *When Critics Ask: A Popular Handbook of Bible Difficulties* (Wheaton, IL: Victor Books, 1992), 265-267. For a more in-depth analysis and defense of the single authorship of Isaiah, see Oswald T. Allis, *The Unity of Isaiah: A Study in Prophecy* (Phillipsburg, NJ: Presbyterian & Reformed, 1980).

7. For a helpful summary of the philosophy of Aquinas, see Edward Feser, *Aquinas: A Beginner's Guide* (Oxford, UK: Oneword, 2010). Feser has also written a more in-depth treatment of Aquinas's philosophy in *Scholastic Metaphysics: A Contemporary Introduction* (Piscataway, NJ: Transaction Publishers, 2014). For a good treatment of Aquinas's philosophy in the context of defending it against other interpretations of Aquinas in contemporary philosophy, see John Knasas, *Being and Some 20th Century Thomists* (New York: Fordham University Press, 2003). For a treatment of Aristotle (the philosopher who influenced Aquinas) by contemporary philosophers, see Edward Feser, ed., *Aristotle on Method and Metaphysics* (London, UK: Palgrave Macmillan, 2013).

8. Aquinas wrote, "Sensible things [are that] from which human reason takes the origin of its knowledge." See *Summa contra Gentiles*, I, 9, §2., trans. Anton C. Pegis (Notre Dame, IN: University of Notre Dame Press, 1975), I, 77. Elsewhere he says "Our knowledge, taking its start from things, proceeds in this order. First, it begins in sense; second, it is completed in the intellect." See *Truth*, I, 11, trans. Mulligan, 48, in *Truth* (3 vols.), vol. 1 trans. Robert W. Mulligan (Chicago, IL: Henry Regnery, 1952); vol. 2 trans. James V. McGlynn (Chicago, IL: Henry Regnery, 1953); vol. 3 trans. Robert W. Schmidt (Chicago, IL: Henry Regnery, 1954). The three volumes were reprinted as *Truth* (Indianapolis, IN: Hackett, 1994). Other comments by Aquinas in this regard include: "Our senses give rise to memories, and from these we obtain experiential knowledge of things, which in turn is the means through which we come to an understanding of the universal principles of sciences and art." See *Summa contra Gentiles*, II, 83, §26. Trans. James F. Anderson, II, 279; "Our knowledge of principles themselves is derived from sensible things." See *Summa contra Gentiles*, II, 83, §32., trans. James F. Anderson, II, 282.

9. The Bible demonstrates that empiricism can give us knowledge even about God. Repeatedly, both in the Old Testament and the New Testament, God and His prophets and apostles appealed to what we experience with our senses to demonstrate His truths. For example, see Deuteronomy 29:2-3; Luke 1:1-4; Acts 10:37-41; and 1 John 1:1-3. Romans 1:20 tells us that the invisible attributes of God are clearly seen, being understood by the things that are made. Jesus appeared to His disciples and showed Himself physically to their senses (to Mary and other women—Matthew 28:1-10; to the two disciples on the way to Emmaus—Luke 24:13-35; to the ten disciples—Luke 24:36-49; to Mary Magdalene—John 20:10-18; and to the eleven disciples—John 20:24-31).

10. In its earliest manifestation in contemporary thinking, this philosophy was known as logical positivism. It was exemplified in the thinking of A.J. Ayer in his work *Language, Truth, and Logic* (New York: Dover, 1952). Ayer was famous for formulating (and then soon thereafter repudiating) the verificationist principle, which said that only those statements that are true by definition or empirically verifiable are meaningful. It was quickly recognized that the verificationist principle did not meet its own standard of being a meaningful statement. For a critique of other aspects of Ayer's philosophy, see Richard G. Howe, "On the Function of Philosophy," *Christian Apologetics Journal* 7, no. 2 (Fall 2008): 57-82. Today, such erroneous thinking (known disparagingly by its detractors as *scientism*) is not uncommon among scientists. Regarding the question of God's existence, Richard Dawkins asserts, "The presence or absence of a creative super-intelligence is unequivocally a scientific question, even if it is not in practice—or not yet—a decided one." See Richard Dawkins, *The God Delusion* (Boston, MA: Houghton Mifflin, 2006), 58-59. Marcia McNutt, president of the National Academy of Sciences, said, "Science is not a body of

facts. Science is a method for deciding whether what we choose to believe has a basis in the laws of nature or not." See in Joel Achenbach, "The Age of Disbelief," *National Geographic* (March 2015): 40.

11. Such is the philosophy of John Locke (1623–1704), who said, "Since the Mind, in all its Thought and Reasonings, hath no other immediate Object but its own Ideas, which it alone does or can contemplate, it is evident, that our Knowledge is only conversant about them…'Tis evident, the Mind knows not Things immediately, but only by the intervention of the *Ideas* it has of them. *Our Knowledge* therefore is *real*, only so far as there is a conformity between our *Ideas* and the reality of Things." See John Locke, *An Essay Concerning Human Understanding*, IV, I, 1, §1 and IV, I, 4, §3, ed. Peter H. Nidditch (Oxford, UK: Clarendon Press, 1975), 525, 563.

12. For an excellent treatment of how representationalism (as this philosophy is known in some of the literature) lies at the heart of much contemporary skepticism, see the Howe work cited in note 2. See also Étienne Gilson, *The Unity of Philosophical Experience* (San Francisco, CA: Ignatius Press, 1999).

Chapter 8—What Is Conversational Apologetics?

1. Ravi Zacharias, "An Ancient Message, Through Modern Means to the Postmodern Mind" in D.A. Carson, ed. *Telling the Truth: Evangelizing Postmoderns* (Grand Rapids, MI: Zondervan, 2000), 27.

2. See Matthew 4:23; John 5:36; 10:37-38; 20:30-31; Acts 2:22; 9:22; 14:1; 17:2-3; 26:28-29; 28:23. I remember reading through the whole New Testament specifically looking for the connection between apologetics and evangelism. I was surprised at how many passages implied the important link between the two.

3. In the 1970s and even in the 1980s, it was easy to share a simple gospel message with many different kinds of people in the United States and still see people respond positively to our message.

4. In Matthew 13:19-23 we have the parable of the four soils. Jesus pointed out some things that keep the seed from getting into the good soil. In verse 19, Jesus pointed out that one of those things is a person's lack of understanding. Some may not understand because of their own distortions of the truth.

5. This is especially true of those of us living in the West, and is a growing concern in the East.

6. See J.P. Moreland's excellent book *Love Your God with All Your Mind* (Colorado Springs, CO: Navpress, 1997). He points out that our crisis is a shift from a Judeo-Christian understanding to a post-Christian one.

7. See the video of how I do this with a college student at www.conversationalevangelism.com. Go to C.E. in Action.

8. The sobering truth is that we now live in a world where direct persuasion is frowned upon, and even ranting has becoming the rage.

9. One way to determine how best to do this is by keeping in mind the three *d*s of a conversational evangelism approach (doubt, defensiveness, desire). See our book *Conversational Evangelism: Connecting with People to Share Jesus* (Eugene, OR: Harvest House, 2014), 42-43, 98-102.

10. See our discussion about the five planks approach in our book *Conversational Evangelism*, 139-143. See also Norman L. Geisler, *Twelve Points that Show Christianity Is True: A Handbook on Defending the Christian Faith* (Charlotte, NC: Norm Geisler International Ministries, 2016).

11. David Reed, *Jehovah's Witnesses Answered Verse by Verse* (Grand Rapids, MI: Baker, 1986), 113.

Chapter 9—How Can We Make Apologetics Culturally Relevant?

1. In general and for this article, we may understand the term *progressive* as referring to the political view of those who favor the implementation of social reforms that dislodge many traditional moral values. On the other hand, *conservative* refers to the political view of those who are more cautious concerning social reforms, lest these overturn traditional values.

2. Aristotle, *Rhetoric*, trans. W. Rhys Roberts, in *The Basic Works of Aristotle*, Richard McKeon, ed. (New York: Random House, 1941), 1327.

3. Jonathan Haidt, *The Righteous Mind: Why Good People Are Divided by Politics and Religion* (New York: Pantheon, 2012). Though I recommend the results of Haidt's research to create persuasive apologetic appeals, it does not mean that I agree with his explanations for the results of his research.

4. Haidt, *The Righteous Mind*, 123-127.

5. Haidt, *The Righteous Mind*, 305-306.

6. Haidt, *The Righteous Mind*, 295-296.

7. I realize that some do not agree that the apostle Paul began on common ground in Acts 17. However, given that the Apostle was educated in a major intellectual Hellenistic city, Tarsus, and that he seemed to be well versed in Hellenistic philosophy, it seems at least possible that he would have known about and maybe even employed the technique of beginning on common ground.

Chapter 10—What Is the Holy Spirit's Role in Apologetics?

1. Norman L. Geisler, *Baker Encyclopedia of Christian Apologetics* (Grand Rapids, MI: Baker, 1999), 330. Geisler discusses this issue at length, examining and comparing both presuppositional and evidential apologetics.

2. As quoted in Michael A. Milton, *Oh, the Deep, Deep Love of Jesus* (Eugene, OR: Wipf & Stock, 2007), 16.

Chapter 11—Why Does God Seem "Hidden"?

1. Dan Barker, *Losing Faith in Faith* (Madison, WI: Freedom from Religion Foundation, 1992), 87.

2. A lecture by Richard Dawkins extracted from *The Nullifidian* (December 1994).

3. Greta Christina, "6 (Unlikely) Developments that Could Convince This Atheist to Believe in God," Alternet, July 4, 2010, www.alternet.org/story/147424/6_%28unlikely%29_developments_that_could_convince_this_athe ist_to_believe-in_god.

4. Friedrich Nietzsche, *Daybreak*, trans. R.J. Hollingsdale (Cambridge, MA: Cambridge University Press, 1982), 89-90.

5. Blaise Pascal, *Pensées* (New York: E.P. Dutton, 1958), 118.

Chapter 12—What Are the Classical Proofs for God's Existence?

1. Regarding the legitimacy and value of utilizing philosophy in arguing for God's existence: While there certainly have been (and continue to be) those who think that the Christian faith ought not utilize the tools, methods, categories, and claims arising from philosophy, there have been (and continue to be) those who recognize the proper role that philosophy can play in Christian theology in general and Christian apologetics in particular.

   Christians who repudiate philosophy to some degree or another do so for different reasons. Fideism rejects any dominant role of reason in Christian thinking. Colin Brown maintains that "the existence of God is not a matter of rational deduction. Rather it is a *profound inner intuition* that makes us aware of God and of the relation of the created order to him." See Colin Brown, *Philosophy and the Christian Faith* (Downers Grove, IL: InterVarsity, 1968), 250, emphasis added. Presuppositionalists, while utilizing philosophy at points, nevertheless reject natural theology, that body of data about God discovered by human reason in its assessment of creation. An example of the presuppositionalist view would be Greg Bahnsen, who said (regarding Herman Dooyeweerd's position that the Bible does not provide us with philosophical ideas), "This is a troublesome conception of Christian philosophy... The philosopher is placed in the privileged position of laying down for the exegete how the Bible may and may not be used, how its teaching must be broadly conceived, and what the Bible can and cannot say. ...Philosophy is thereby rendered rationally autonomous..." See Greg L. Bahnsen, *Van Til's Apologetic: Readings and Analysis* (Phillipsburg, NJ: Presbyterian & Reformed, 1998), 50. For a brief summary of the view that philosophy can play in Christian theology in general and Christian apologetics in particular, see Richard G. Howe, "Defending the Handmaid: How Theology Needs Philosophy" in Terry L. Miethe, ed., *I Am Put Here for the Defense of the Gospel: Dr. Norman L. Geisler: A Festschrift in His Honor* (Eugene, OR: Pickwick, 2016), 233-256.

2. Examples of excellent treatments of the popular, contemporary arguments include Frank Turek, *Stealing from God: Why Atheists Need God to Make Their Case* (Colorado Springs, CO: NavPress, 2014) and J. Warner Wallace, *God's Crime Scene: A Cold-Case Detective Examines the Evidence for a Divinely Created Universe* (Colorado Springs, CO: David C. Cook, 2015). In saying that these works are popular, I do not mean to imply that they lack sophistication in their own right. Nor do I mean to imply that they are entirely free of any of the categories of ancient Greek philosophy. They certainly utilize such categories as truth and causality. Instead, I mean that they (1) avoid relying heavily upon these ancient categories; (2) are largely free of the technicalities of academic philosophy (even versions of the classical arguments sometimes try to do this); and (3) traffic often in the data of contemporary science.

3. While this might prove to be a practical strength for the popular, contemporary arguments, one should note well the words of philosopher Joseph Owens in contrasting the classical proofs with the popular, contemporary arguments when he said, "Other arguments may vividly suggest the existence of God, press it home eloquently to human consideration, and for most people provide much greater spiritual and religious aid than difficult metaphysical demonstrations. But on the philosophical level these arguments are open to rebuttal and refutation, for they are not philosophically cogent." Joseph Owens, "Aquinas and the Five Ways," *Monist* 58 (Jan 1974), 33.

4. This version is known as the Kalam cosmological argument. It arose prominently in the Middle Ages. It was revived in contemporary thinking largely due to the work of Christian philosopher and apologist William Lane Craig in *The Kalam Cosmological Argument* (London, UK: Macmillan, 1979; republished Eugene, OR: Wipf & Stock, 2000). According to Craig, the term *kalam* literally means "speech" in Arabic. For a defense of the argument against objections raised after Craig published his work, see Richard G. Howe, *An Analysis of William Lane Craig's Kalam Cosmological Argument*, unpublished master's thesis (Oxford, MS: University of Mississippi, 1990). For a more succinct treatment and defense of the argument, see J.P. Moreland, *Scaling the Secular City: A Defense of Christianity* (Grand Rapids, MI: Baker, 1987), 18-33.

5. It is interesting to note that Aquinas's argument is indifferent as to whether the universe came into existence a finite time ago or if it has existed from all eternity. As a Christian, Aquinas certainly believed that the universe began a finite time ago in creation, just as Genesis says. But the nature of his argument does not play off of this aspect of the universe.

6. In its medieval version and in its contemporary academic version, the Kalam cosmological argument involves the notion of the impossibility of infinite temporal regression. Appealing to the mathematical nature of infinite sets, it argues that the past cannot be infinitely long; therefore, the universe must have had a beginning. If it had a beginning, then it must have had a cause. This cause is God.

7. For philosophical treatments (primary and secondary) of the notion of being (existence) in Aquinas, see Thomas Aquinas, *On Being and Essence*, trans. Armand Maurer, 2d rev. ed. (Toronto, Canada: Pontifical Institute of Mediaeval Studies, 1983); *Commentary on Aristotle's Metaphysics*, trans. John P. Rowan (Notre Dame, IN: Dumb Ox Books, 1961); Dominic Báñez, *The Primacy of Existence in Thomas Aquinas*, trans. Benjamin S. Llamzon (Chicago, IL: Henry Regnery, 1966); Étienne Gilson, *Being and Some Philosophers* (Toronto, Canada: Pontifical Institute of Mediaeval Studies, 1952); and Joseph Owens, *An Interpretation of Existence* (Houston, TX: Center for Thomistic Studies, 1968). For an analytic philosophical perspective on existence that stands in contrast to Aquinas's, see William Lane Craig and J.P. Moreland, *Philosophical Foundations for a Christian Worldview* (Downers Grove, IL: InterVarsity, 2003), 187-193. For a broader exploration of the notion of existence in ancient and medieval philosophy, see Parviz Morewedge, ed. *Philosophies of Existence: Ancient and Medieval* (New York: Fordham University Press, 1982).

8. A thing's essence is that aspect of the thing by virtue of which it is the kind of thing it is. Thus, a human being is a human being precisely because it possesses a human essence. A dog is a dog precisely because it possesses a dog essence. Another word for essence is *nature*.

9. What is more, there are things that have the essence of human but do not have existence, such as Sherlock Holmes or Aragorn. They are conceptual beings or beings of reason, otherwise known as fictional beings. But if it was of the essence of humans to have existence, then Sherlock Holmes and Aragorn could not fail to really exist.

10. Thomas Aquinas, *St. Thomas Aquinas Summa Theologica: Complete English Edition in Five Volumes*, trans. Fathers of the English Dominican Province (Westminster, MD: Christian Classics, 1981), I, Q2. What is an added strength of the classical argument over the popular, contemporary arguments is that in exploring more of what is entailed by seeing that God's essence is existence itself, one discovers that this God has all the superlative attributes of classical theism. For a treatment of these classical attributes, see James E. Dolezal, *All That Is in God: Evangelical Theology and the Challenge of Classical Christian Theism* (Grand Rapids, MI: Reformation Heritage, 2017).

11. Philosopher Robin Collins describes the fine-tuning argument this way: "When scientists talk about the fine-tuning of the universe they're generally referring to the extraordinary balancing of the fundamental laws and parameters of physics and the initial conditions of the universe. Our minds can't comprehend the precision of some of them. The result is a universe that has just the right conditions to sustain life. The coincidences are simply too amazing to have been the result of happenstance." See Robin Collins, "The Evidence of Physics: The Cosmos

on a Razor's Edge" in Lee Strobel, *The Case for a Creator: A Journalist Investigates Scientific Evidence That Points Toward God* (Grand Rapids, MI: Zondervan, 2004), 130.

12. Irreducible complexity refers to the fact that there are systems in biological life that consist of several interlocking parts that must be in place before they can function at all. The argument demonstrates that this irreducibly complex system could not have come about by gradual, incremental changes, but must have been given all at once. Even Charles Darwin himself admitted, "If it could be demonstrated that any complex organ existed which could not possibly have been formed by numerous, successive, slight modifications, my theory would absolutely break down." See Charles Darwin, *Origin of Species*, chapter 6, "Difficulties of the Theory" section "Modes of Transition" in Robert Maynard Hutchins, ed. in chief, *Great Books of the Western World*, vol. 49 (Chicago, IL: Encyclopedia Britannica, Inc.), 87. The definitive work on irreducible complexity is Michael J. Behe, *Darwin's Black Box: The Biochemical Challenge to Evolution* (New York: The Free Press, 1996).

13. Information theory, sometimes referred to as intelligent design, refers to the fact that the DNA of biological life forms contains information encoded at the molecular level. Because information always arises from intelligence, there must be an intelligent source of the DNA's information. Mechanical engineer Walter Bradley and biochemist Charles Thaxton explain, "Proponents of an intelligent origin of life note that molecular biology has uncovered an analogy between DNA and language…The genetic code functions exactly like a language code—indeed it is a code. It is a molecular communications system: a sequence of chemical 'letters' stores and transmits the communication in each living cell." See Walter L. Bradley and Charles B. Thaxton, "Information and the Origin of Life," in J.P. Moreland, ed., *The Creation Hypothesis: Scientific Evidence for an Intelligent Designer* (Downers Grove, IL: InterVarsity Press, 1994), 205.

14. Most contemporary design arguments follow in the tradition of William Paley (1743–1805) and his famous watchmaker argument from his work *Natural Theology: or Evidences of the Existence and Attributes of the Deity, Collected from the Appearances of Nature* (Philadelphia, PA: John Morgan, 1802).

15. Edward Feser describes the difference this way: "One key difference between the design argument and the Fifth Way…is that whereas the former takes for granted a 'mechanical' conception of the natural world…Aquinas's argument crucially presupposes that final causes are as real and objective a feature of the natural world as gravity or electro-magnetism." See Edward Feser, *Aquinas: A Beginner's Guide* (Oxford, UK: Oneword, 2010), 112.

16. The classical understanding of the four causes is from Aristotle. He discusses the four causes in *Metaphysics* D (V), 2, 1013^a24-1013^b3.

17. Aquinas says it this way: "We see that things which lack intelligence, such as natural bodies, act for an end, and this is evident from their acting always, or nearly always, in the same way, so as to obtain the best result. Hence it is plain that not fortuitously, but designedly, do they achieve their end. Now whatever lacks intelligence cannot move towards an end, unless it be directed by some being endowed with knowledge and intelligence; as the arrow is shot to its mark by the archer. Therefore some intelligent being exists by whom all natural things are directed to their end; and this being we call God." See Aquinas, *Summa Theologica*, I, Q2, Art. 3.

18. Examples of this kind of moral argument for God's existence include William Lane Craig, *Reasonable Faith: Christian Truth and Apologetics*, 3d ed. (Wheaton, IL: Crossway, 2008), 172-183; and Chad V. Meister, *Building Belief: Constructing Faith from the Ground Up* (Grand Rapids, MI: Baker, 2006), 110-121. Among other things, the argument aims to show that without a transcendent, objective moral standard for right and wrong, there is no way to account for that which everyone knows to be the case—that such objective moral values do exist. It is challenging to find this argument in the classical tradition. This is not to say that the classical tradition sees no connection between morality and God. Rather, that connection is somewhat more complex and hinges on a commitment to specific philosophical (i.e., metaphysical) doctrines.

19. An excellent reading on being and goodness is Jan A. Aertsen, "The Convertibility of Being and Good in St. Thomas Aquinas," *New Scholasticism* 59 (1985), 449-470.

20. The "good" of a plant seed is its growing toward the perfection of being the kind of plant God intends it to be. The "good" for a newborn puppy is its growing toward the perfection of being the kind of dog God intends for it to be. To be sure, this "good" is not a moral good. Instead, it is good as such. *Good* means the end goal toward which a thing's potentials aim in accordance to its nature, which is to say, in accordance to the kind of thing God has created it to be. When humans study these aspects of God's creation, this gives rise to what we call the

sciences (e.g., physics, geology, biology, etc.). These laws or regularities can never be violated except by miraculous intervention from the Creator.

21. By analogy, a knife "ought" to have a sharp blade because that is what it means to *be* a knife. It would not make any sense for someone to object by saying, "Who are you to say that a knife ought to have a sharp blade!"

22. This is why virtually all the world's religions and philosophies have the same general views about how humans ought to act—obligations such as do not kill another human, respect others' property, keep your promises, nurture the children, respect the elders, and more are found throughout all times and places. There are, of course, exceptions. There are also instances when, even knowing what we ought to do, we still fall short. Yet the history of ideas shows a remarkable pattern to human behavior. Romans 2:14-15 tells us, "When Gentiles, who do not have the law, by nature do what the law requires, they are a law to themselves, even though they do not have the law. They show that the work of the law is written on their hearts, while their conscience also bears witness, and their conflicting thoughts accuse or even excuse them." See C.S. Lewis, *Mere Christianity* (New York: Macmillan, 1960) and *The Abolition of Man* (New York: Macmillan, 1955).

Chapter 13—What Are Some Other Arguments for God's Existence?

1. Thomas Aquinas, *The Summa Theologica of St. Thomas Aquinas*, trans. Fathers of the English Dominican Province (Notre Dame, IN: Christian Classics, 1981), Ia.2.3. Thomas Aquinas, *Summa contra Gentiles*, trans. Fathers of the English Dominican Province (London, UK: Burns Oates & Washbourne, 1924), I.13.

2. Isaac Newton, *The Principia: Mathematical Principles of Natural Philosophy: The Authoritative Translation*, trans. I. Bernard Cohen and Anne Whitman, assisted by Julia Budenz (Oakland, CA: University of California Press, 1999), Kindle loc. 76.

3. Norman L. Geisler, *Systematic Theology*, vol. 1 (Minneapolis, MN: Bethany House, 2002), 30.

4. Anselm, *Basic Writings*, ed. and trans. Thomas Williams (Indianapolis, IN: Hackett Publishing, 2007).

5. Aquinas, *Summa Theologica*, Ia.2.3

Chapter 14—If God Exists, Why Is There Evil?

1. See Clay Jones, *Why Does God Allow Evil? Compelling Answers for Life's Toughest Questions* (Eugene, OR: Harvest House, 2017).

2. Some might wonder about John 9:1 and the man born blind, of whom Jesus said, "'Neither this man nor his parents sinned…but this happened so that the works of God might be displayed in him'" (NIV). But would the man have been born blind if Adam and Eve had never sinned?

3. Christopher R. Browning, *Ordinary Men: Reserve Police Battalion 101 and the Final Solution in Poland* (New York: HarperCollins, 1992), xx.

4. Harald Welzer, "On Killing and Morality: How Normal People Become Mass Murderers," *Ordinary People as Mass Murderers: Perpetrators in Comparative Perspective*, eds. Olaf Jensen and Claus-Christian W. Szejnmann (New York: Macmillan, 2008), 148-149.

5. Hannah Arendt, *Eichmann in Jerusalem: A Report on the Banality of Evil* (New York: Penguin, 1994, reprint 1963), 277.

6. Elie Wiesel, *The Town Beyond the Wall*, trans. Stephen Barker (New York, NY: Avon, 1970), 174.

7. Alvin Plantinga, *Warranted Christian Belief* (Oxford, UK: Oxford University, 2000), 207.

8. Michael Ruse, "Darwinism and Christianity Redux: A Response to My Critics," *Philosophia Christi* 4 (2002), 192.

9. Romans 3:12-15 (NIV).

Chapter 15—Canaanites, Crusades, and Catastrophes—Is God a Moral Monster?

1. Deuteronomy 7:1 adds a seventh nation to the list in Deuteronomy 20:16-17, cf. Acts 13:19.

2. See Clay Jones, "We Don't Hate Sin So We Don't Understand What Happened to the Canaanites," *Philosophia Christi*, 11, no. 1 (2009): 53-72.

3. John W. Wenham, "Christ's View of Scripture" in *Inerrancy*, ed. Norman L. Geisler (Grand Rapids, MI: Zondervan, 1980), chapter 1.

4. Paul Copan, *Is God a Moral Monster?* (Grand Rapids, MI: Baker, 2011), 170-173.

5. The ban (*hērem*) commands of God can be taken literally as are other similar commands, like Abraham did concerning God's command to sacrifice his son Issac (Genesis 22), and this does not prevent acknowledging the failure of Israel to fulfill God's command or the use of hyperbole regarding post-military success.

6. The apostle Paul seemed to take this position when he answered the question about whether God was unjust (Romans 9:14-18).

7. An argument for the universal salvation of infants is found in Norman L. Geisler, *Systematic Theology*, vol. 3 (Minneapolis, MN: Bethany House, 2004), chapter 15.

8. Gleason Archer, *Encyclopedia of Bible Difficulties* (Grand Rapids, MI: Zondervan, 1982), 158-159.

9. For a defense of graded absolutism, see Norman L. Geiser, *Christian Ethics*, 2d ed. (Grand Rapids: Baker, 2012), chapter 7.

10. William Brenton Greene Jr., "The Ethics of the Old Testament," in Walter C. Kaiser Jr., ed., *Classical Evangelical Essays in Old Testament Interpretation* (Grand Rapids, MI: Baker, 1972), 221.

11. Geisler, *Christian Ethics*, chapter 13.

12. Rodney Stark, *God's Battalions: The Case for the Crusades* (New York: HarperOne, 2009), 8.

13. Stark, *God's Battalions*, 125-127.

14. Stark, *God's Battalions*, 157, 171.

15. Paul Copan & Matthew Flannagan, *Did God Really Command Genocide?* (Grand Rapids, MI: Baker, 2014), chapter 20.

16. Alvin J. Schmidt, *How Christianity Changed the World* (Grand Rapids, MI: Zondervan, 2004).

17. Norman L. Geisler, *If God, Why Evil?* (Bloomington, MN: Bethany House, 2011), 23; emphasis in original.

18. C.S. Lewis, *The Problem of Pain* (New York: Macmillan, 1962), 93.

19. Geisler, *Systematic Theology*, vol. 3, 158; emphasis in original.

20. See Norman L. Geisler and Douglas E. Potter, *The Doctrine of God*, vol. 2 (Matthews, NC: Norm Geisler International Ministries, 2016).

Chapter 16—How Can a Loving God Send People to Hell?

1. Robert E. Egner and Lester E. Denonn, eds., *The Basic Writings of Bertrand Russell* (New York: Touchstone, 1961), 593.

2. Norman L. Geisler, *Systematic Theology, Church Last Things,* vol. 4 (Minneapolis, MN: Bethany House, 2005), 337.

3. Douglas F. Moo, "Paul on Hell," in Christopher W. Morgan and Robert A. Peterson, eds., *Hell Under Fire* (Grand Rapids, MI: Zondervan, 2004), 105-106.

4. Matthew 5:29-30; 10:28; 11:23; 13:40-41,49-50; 22:13; 23:15-33; 25:41; Mark 9:43-48; Luke 6:19-31; 12:5.

5. Charles Ryrie, *Basic Theology: A Popular Systematic Guide to Understanding Biblical Truth* (Chicago, IL: Moody, 1999), 606.

6. Norman L. Geisler, *Chosen but Free* (Minneapolis, MN: Bethany House, 1999), 49.

7. C.S. Lewis, *Screwtape Letters* (New York: HarperCollins, 1996), 39.

8. C.S. Lewis, *The Great Divorce* (New York: Macmillan, 1943), 72.

9. Norman L. Geisler and Douglas E. Potter, *A Popular Survey of Bible Doctrine* (Matthews, NC: Norm Geisler International Ministries, 2016), 166. See Matthew 8:12; Mark 9:44-48; Luke 16:28; 1 Peter 3:19; Jude 13; Revelation 20:1,3.

10. See especially the parallelism between Matthew 25:41 and 25:46.

11. C.S. Lewis, *The Problem of Pain* (New York: Macmillan, 1962), 127.

12. C.S. Lewis, *God in the Dock* (Grand Rapids, MI: Eerdmans, 1970), 292.

13. Robert W. Yarbrough, "Jesus on Hell," in *Hell Under Fire*, 76.

14. See Robert A. Peterson "A Traditionalist Response to Conditionalism" in *Two Views of Hell* (Downers Grove, IL: IVP Academic, 2000).

Chapter 17—Who Is Jesus?

NOTE: This article was drawn from Josh McDowell and Sean McDowell, *The Unshakable Truth* (Eugene, OR: Harvest House, 2010), excerpts from chapters 16, 17, and 21.

1. Peter W. Stoner and Robert C. Newman, *Science Speaks* (Chicago, IL: Moody, 1976), 107.

2. Stoner and Newman, *Science Speaks*.

3. C.S. Lewis, *Mere Christianity* (New York: Macmillan, 1960), 40-41.

4. Diagram drawn from Josh McDowell, *The New Evidence That Demands a Verdict* (Nashville, TN: Thomas Nelson, 1999), 158.

5. William E. Lecky, *History of European Morals from Augustus to Charlemagne* (New York: D. Appleton, 1903), 2:8-9.

6. Clark H. Pinnock, *Set Forth Your Case* (Nutley, NJ: Craig Press, 1967), 62.

7. Gary R. Collins, quoted in Lee Strobel, *The Case for Christ* (Grand Rapids, MI: Zondervan, 1998), 147.

8. Dan Brown, *The Da Vinci Code* (New York: Doubleday, 2003), 233.

9. James A. Kliest, "To the Ephesians," *The Epistles of St. Clement of Rome and St. Ignatius of Antioch* (Ramsey, NJ: Paulist Press, 1978).

10. Alexander Roberts, *First Apology, the Ante-Nicene Fathers,* vol. 1 (Grand Rapids, MI: Eerdmans, 1993), 184.

11. Joseph P. Smith, *St. Irenaeus: Proof of the Apostolic Preaching* (Ramsey, NJ: Paulist Press, 1978), chapter 47.

Chapter 18—Is There Evidence That Jesus Really Existed?

1. For further information on this topic, see Robert E. Van Voorst, *Jesus Outside the New Testament: An Introduction to the Ancient Evidence* (Grand Rapids, MI: Eerdmans, 2000); Gary R. Habermas, *The Historical Jesus: Ancient Evidence for the Life of Christ* (Joplin, MO: College Press, 1996).

2. Bart D. Ehrman, *Did Jesus Exist? The Historical Argument for Jesus of Nazareth* (New York: HarperOne, 2012), 74 (emphasis added).

3. Tacitus, *Annals*, 15.44. Another Roman historian, Suetonius, also made a brief mention of Christians suffering under Nero after the great fire in Rome. Suetonius, *Nero*, 16.

4. Josephus, *Antiquities*, 18.3.

5. Origen, *Contra Celsum*, 1.47. However, when Eusebius quoted Josephus, he included the disputed sections (Eusebius, *Ecclesiastical History*, 1.11).

6. Edwin M. Yamauchi, "Jesus Outside the New Testament: What Is the Evidence?" in *Jesus Under Fire*, ed. Michael J. Wilkins and J.P. Moreland (Grand Rapids, MI: Zondervan, 1995), 212.

7. James Charlesworth, *Jesus Within Judaism* (Garden City, NY: Doubleday, 1988), 93-94.

8. Josephus, *Antiquities*, 20.9.

9. Clement of Rome, *Corinthians*, 42.

10. Ignatius, *Trallians*, 9.

11. Bart D. Ehrman, *The New Testament: A Historical Introduction to the Early Christian Writings*, 2d ed. (New York: Oxford University Press, 2000), 262, 290, 44.

12. Gary R. Habermas and Michael R. Licona, *The Case for the Resurrection of Jesus* (Grand Rapids, MI: Kregel, 2004). See also chapter 22 in this book.

Chapter 19—Are the Gospel Accounts Reliable?

1. For example, see Thucydides's comments on his writing of history in *History of the Peloponnesian War*, 1.22.1. Charles Fornara lamented that ancient historians "invented speeches" and "unintentional perjury" into their works. Charles William Fornara, *The Nature of History in Ancient Greece and Rome* (Berkeley, CA: University of California, 1983), 167-168. Another example is Plutarch, who displayed imperfect understanding and faulty memory as "historically inaccurate" and "sacrificing the truth" many times in works; see Christopher Pelling, *Plutarch and History: Eighteen Studies* (London, UK: Gerald Duckworth, 2002), 156.

2. Read the thrilling account of David Laird Dungan's "Eusebius's Defense of Catholic Scripture" in his *Constantine's Bible* (Minneapolis, MN: Fortress Press, 2007), 54-93.

3. Eusebius, *Ecclesiastical History*, 3.25.1.

4. Eusebius, *Ecclesiastical History*, 3.36.15-16.

5. E.g., Irenaeus, *Against Heresies*, 3.1.

6. E.g., Irenaeus, *Against Heresies*, 2.2.5; 3.1.1.

7. Eusebius, *Ecclesiastical History*, 6:14.5-7.

8. Eusebius, *Ecclesiastical History*, 6.14.7.

Chapter 20—What About the Alternative "Gospels"?

1. Craig Evans examines the matter of the literacy of Jesus, but the same type of argument may apply to His disciples. His third consideration, that of the need to know the law in Judaism, caused parents to take care to teach their children to read. Craig A. Evans, *Fabricating Jesus: How Modern Scholars Distort the Gospels* (Downers Grove, IL: InterVarsity, 2006), 35-38. This is something that has been a consistent characteristic of the Jewish people to the present day.

2. Smith argues that Egypt is the likely location of the birth of Gnosticism, and that disaffected Jews, upon their loss of identity after the time of Hadrian, and even some Jewish Christians, who could not embrace the entirety of the Christian message, were responsible for its birth and growth from the ideas of several sources. Carl B. Smith II, *No Longer Jews: The Search for Gnostic Origins* (Peabody, MA: Hendrickson, 2004).

3. See Edwin M. Yamauchi, *Pre-Christian Gnosticism: A Survey of the Proposed Evidences* (Eugene, OR: Wipf & Stock, 2003).

4. See Evans, *Fabricating Jesus*, for further discussion.

5. Helmut Koester, "Gospel of Thomas" in James M. Robinson, *The Coptic Gnostic Library: A Complete Edition of the Nag Hammadi Codices* (Leiden, Netherlands: Brill, 2000), vol. 2, tractate 2, 38.

6. Bertie Gärtner, *The Theology of the Gospel According to Thomas*, trans. by Eric J. Sharpe (New York: Harper & Brothers, 1961), 271.

7. Evans, *Fabricating Jesus*, 55.

8. Philip Jenkins, *Hidden Gospels: How the Search for Jesus Lost Its Way* (New York: Oxford University Press, 2001), 71; Evans, *Fabricating Jesus*, 62-77.

9. Philip Jenkins, *Hidden Gospels*, 70; see Bart D. Ehrman, *Lost Scriptures: Books that Did Not Make It into the New Testament* (New York: Oxford University Press, 2003), 20; also see Craig A. Evans, *Noncanonical Writings and New Testament Interpretation* (Peabody, MA: Hendrickson, 1992), 162-168.

10. Wesley W. Isenberg, "Gospel According to Philip," and James M. Robinson, "Gospel of Thomas," *The Coptic Gnostic Library: A Complete Edition of the Nag Hammadi Codices*, vol. 2, tractate 3, p. 131.

11. Evans, *Fabricating Jesus*, 211.

12. Evans, *Fabricating Jesus*.

13. Evans, *Fabricating Jesus*, 212.

14. Harold W. Attridge and George W. MacRae, S.J., "The Gospel of Truth" in Ames M. Robinson, *The Coptic Gnostic Library: A Complete Edition of the Nag Hammadi Codices* (Leiden, Netherlands: Brill, 2000), vol. 2, tractate 2, 63.

15. Attridge and MacRae, "The Gospel of Truth," 65-66.

16. Jacqueline A. Williams, *Biblical Interpretation in the Gnostic Gospel of Truth from Nag Hammadi* (Atlanta, GA: Scholars Press, 1988), 3.

17. W.W. Isenberg, "The Gospel of Truth" in Robert M. Grant, ed., *Gnosticism: A Source Book of Heretical Writings from the Early Christian Period* (New York: Harper & Brothers, 1917), 146-161.

18. Attridge and MacRae, "The Gospel of Truth," 71-72.

Chapter 22—Is There Evidence That Jesus Rose from the Dead?

1. Raymond Brown, *An Introduction to New Testament Christology* (New York: Paulist, 1994), 14-15, 102.

2. Cf. Gary R. Habermas, "Mapping the Recent Trend Toward the Bodily Resurrection Appearances of Jesus in Light of Other Prominent Critical Positions" in *The Resurrection of Jesus: John Dominic Crossan and N.T. Wright in Dialogue*, ed. by Robert B. Stewart (Minneapolis, MN: Fortress, 2006), 78-92.

3. Ben F. Meyer, *The Aims of Jesus* (London, UK: SCM, 1979), 131; cf. also 141.

4. Although there are differences among these terms, these creeds are sometimes referred to similarly by the terms *traditions, confessions,* or *hymns.*

5. Also Luke 24:34; Romans 1:3-4; 10:9-10; 1 Corinthians 8:6; 11:23-26; 1 Peter 1:21; 2:21, along with the sermon summaries in Acts.

6. V.H. Neufeld, *The Earliest Christian Confessions* (Leiden, Netherlands: Brill, 1963), 140-146.

7. Darrell L. Bock, *Studying the Historical Jesus: A Guide to Sources and Methods* (Grand Rapids, MI: Baker Academic, 2002), 182.

8. Bart D. Ehrman, *How Jesus Became God: The Exaltation of a Jewish Preacher from Galilee* (New York: Harper One, 2014), 216 (emphasis in original).

9. Pinchas Lapide, *The Resurrection of Jesus: A Jewish Perspective* (Eugene, OR: Wipf & Stock, 2002), 99.

10. Bock, *Studying the Historical Jesus,* 182-183.

11. Lydia McGrew, *Hidden in Plain View: Undesigned Coincidences in the Gospels and Acts* (Chillicothe, OH: DeWard, 2017), 220-221.

12. For details, see Gary R. Habermas, "The Minimal Facts Approach to the Resurrection of Jesus: The Role of Methodology as a Crucial Component in Establishing Historicity," *Southeastern Theological Review,* vol. 3 (Summer 2012), 15-26.

13. McGrew, *Hidden in Plain View,* 220.

14. Gary R. Habermas, *The Risen Jesus and Future Hope* (Lanham, MD: Rowman & Littlefield, 2003).

Chapter 23—Did Christianity Copy Earlier Pagan Resurrection Stories?

1. Marvin R. Wilson, "Death and the Afterlife," in *Dictionary of Daily Life in Biblical and Postbiblical Antiquity*, eds. Edwin M. Yamauchi and Marvin R. Wilson (Peabody, MA: Hendrickson, 2017), 389-409.

2. A number of scholars have assumed that the belief in a resurrection among the Jews arose from the influence of Zoroastrianism, but this is a dubious thesis in the light of the lateness of the Persian sources on eschatology. See Edwin M. Yamauchi, "Did Persian Zoroastrianism Influence Judaism?" in *Israel—Ancient Kingdom or Late Invention?,* ed. Daniel Block (Nashville, TN: B & H Academic, 2008), 282-297. Mark S. Smith, "The Death of 'Dying and Rising Gods' in the Biblical World," *Scandinavian Journal of the Old Testament* 12 (1998), 312, comments: "Frazer's driving motivation to 'explain' Jesus' death and resurrection against the background of 'dying and rising gods' entirely misses the background of Jewish resurrection."

3. Mystery religions involved initiations and secret rites that were more personally appealing than the Roman state religion. See Joscelyn Godwin, *Mystery Religions in the Ancient World* (San Francisco, CA: Harper & Row, 1981). The scholarly literature on mystery religions is enormous. Bruce M. Metzger, "A Classified Bibliography of the Graeco-Roman Mystery Religions, 1924-1973; with a Supplement, 1974-1977," *Aufstieg und Niedergang der römische Welt* II.17.3 (1984), 1259-1423, lists 3647 items. For early responses to such allegations, see H.A.A. Kennedy, *St. Paul and the Mystery Religions* (London, UK: Hodder & Stoughton, 1913) and George C. Ring, "Christ's Resurrection and the Dying and Rising Gods," *Catholic Biblical Quarterly* 6 (1944), 216-29. For more recent

responses, see Bruce M. Metzger, "Considerations of Methodology in the Study of the Mystery Religions and Early Christianity," *Harvard Theological Review* 48 (1955), 1-20; Ronald H. Nash, *Christianity and the Hellenistic World* (Grand Rapids, MI: Zondervan, 1984); and Gary R. Habermas, "Resurrection Claims in Non-Christian Religions," *Religious Studies* 25 (1989), 167-177.

4. For details of Frazer's various editions, see Jonathan Z. Smith, *Drudgery Divine: On the Comparison of Early Christianity and the Religions of Late Antiquity* (Chicago, IL: University of Chicago, 1999), 92.

5. Richard Reitzenstein, *Hellenistic Mystery-Religions*, trans. John E. Steely (Pittsburgh, PA: Pickwick Press, 1978).

6. Rudolf Bultmann, *Theology of the New Testament* (London, UK: SCM, 1950), 140.

7. A. Loisy, "The Christian Mystery," *Hibbert Journal*, 10 (1911), 51. Alfred Loisy was a Catholic modernist, who was excommunicated by Pope Pius X in 1908. See Jeffrey L. Morrow, "*Études Assyriologie* and 19th and 20th Century French Historical-Biblical Criticism," *Near East Archaeological Society Bulletin* 59 (2014), 9-12.

8. Hugh Schonfield, *Those Incredible Christians* (New York: Bernard Geiss, 1968), xii.

9. John H. Randall, *Hellenistic Ways of Deliverance and the Making of the Christian Synthesis* (New York: Columbia University, 1970), 154.

10. Timothy Freke and Peter Gandy, *The Jesus Mysteries* (New York: Harmony Books, 1999), 206. Cf. Tom Harpur, *The Pagan Christ* (New York: Walker & Company, 2004), 84-85, claims that the figure of Christ is based on Horus.

11. Roland Guy Bonnel and Vincent Arieh Tobin, "Christ and Osiris: A Comparative Study," *Pharaonic Egypt: The Bible and Christianity*, ed. Sarah Israel Groll (Jerusalem, Israel: Magnes Press, 1985), 1.

12. Bonnell and Tobin, "Christ and Osiris," 28.

13. Paul de Surgy, ed., *The Resurrection and Modern Biblical Thought* (New York: Corpus Books, 1970), 1, 131.

14. Samuel N. Kramer, *The Sacred Marriage Rite* (Bloomington, IN: Indiana University Press, 1969). Cf. Edwin M. Yamauchi, "Cultic Prostitution—a Case Study in Cultural Diffusion," *Orient and Occident*, ed. H. Hoffner (Kevelaer: Butzon und Bercker, l973), 213-222.

15. Thorkild Jacobsen, *Toward the Image of Tammuz and Other Essays on Mesopotamian History and Culture*, ed. William L. Moran (Cambridge, MA: Harvard University, 1970).

16. Though Dumuzi/Tammuz had a major role in literary texts, the god played only a minor role in cult practice. Only two Mesopotamian temples were dedicated to him. See Rafael Kutscher, "The Cult of Dumuzi/Tammuz," *Bar-Ilan Studies in Assyriology*, eds. Jacob Klein and Aaron Skaist (Ramat Gan, Israel: Bar-Ilan University, 1990), 29-44.

17. Edwin M. Yamauchi, "Descent of Ishtar," *The Biblical World: A Dictionary of Biblical Archaeology*, ed. C. Pfeiffer (Grand Rapids, MI: Baker, l966), l96-200.

18. Samuel N. Kramer, *The Sumerians: Their History, Culture, and Character* (Chicago, IL: University of Chicago Press, 1963), 155-157. See Edwin M. Yamauchi, "Tammuz and the Bible," *Journal of Biblical Literature*, 84 (1965), 283-290.

19. Bendt Alster, "Tammuz," *Dictionary of Deities and Demons in the Bible*, eds. Karel van der Toorn, Bob Becking, and Pieter W. van der Horst (Leiden, Netherlands: Brill, 1999), 833. Günter Wagner, *Pauline Baptism and the Pagan Mysteries* (Edinburgh, Scotland: Oliver & Boyd, 1967) observes: "As a general rule Tammuz is regarded as a dying and rising god, but his 'resurrection' is nowhere directly mentioned or attested."

20. Stephanie Dalley, trans, "The Descent of Ishtar to the Underworld," *The Context of Scripture I*, eds. William W. Hallo and K. Lawson Younger, Jr. (Leiden, Netherlands: Brill, 1997), 384. See Edwin M. Yamauchi, "Additional Notes on Tammuz," *Journal of Semitic Studies* 11 (1966), 10-15.

21. Samuel N. Kramer, "Dumuzi's Annual Resurrection: An Important Correction to Inanna's Descent," *Bulletin of the American Schools of Oriental Research* 183 (1966), 31.

22. Marcel Detienne, *The Gardens of Adonis* (Princeton, NJ: Princeton University, 1994).

23. Tryggve N.D. Mettinger, *The Riddle of Resurrection: "Dying and Rising Gods" in the Ancient Near East* (Stockholm, Sweden: Almqvist & Wiksell, 2001), 149.

24. P. Lambrechts, "La 'résurrection' d'Adonis," *Mélanges Isidore Lévy* (Bruxelles, Belgium: Éditions de l'Institut, 1955), 207-240.

25. Harold W. Attridge and Robert A. Oden, eds. *De Dea Syria* (Missoula, MT: Scholars Press, 1976), 13.

26. Attridge and Oden, *De Dea Syria*, 15.

27. G.R. Driver, trans., *Canaanite Myths and Legends* (Edinburgh, Scotland: T. & T. Clark, 1956), 73-121; Michael David Coogan, ed. and trans., *Stories from Ancient Canaan* (Philadelphia, PA: Westminster Press, 1978), 75-115.

28. Mark S. Smith, "The Death of 'Dying and Rising Gods' in the Biblical World," 290.

29. M.J. Vermaseren, *Cybele and Attis* (London, UK: Thames and Hudson, 1977).

30. P. Lambrechts, "Les Fêtes 'phrygiennes' de Cybèle et d'Attis," *Bulletin de l'Institut Historique Belge de Rome*, 27 (1952), 141-170. Cf. A.T. Fear, "Christ and Cybele," *Cybele, Attis and Related Cults*, ed. Eugene N. Lane (Leiden, Netherlands: Brill, 1996), 41.

31. Günter Wagner, *Pauline Baptism and the Pagan Mysteries* (Edinburgh, Scotland: Oliver & Boyd, 1963), 266. Robert Duthoy, *The Taurobolium: Its Evolution and Terminology* (Leiden, Netherlands: Brill, 1969), 127, notes that "there are no *taurobolium* inscriptions from Rome dated before AD 295."

32. Bruce M. Metzger, *Historical and Literary Studies: Pagan, Jewish and Christian* (Leiden, Netherlands: Brill, 1968), 11.

33. J. Gwyn Griffiths, *The Origins of Osiris and His Cult* (Leiden, Netherlands: Brill, 1980).

34. Jacques Vandier, *La Religion Égyptienne* (Paris, France: Presses Universitaires de France, 1949). 44-47.

35. Jan Assmann, *Death and Salvation in Ancient Egypt* (Ithaca, NY: Cornell University Press, 2005), 59-60.

36. Foy Scalf, ed., *The Book of the Dead: Becoming God in Ancient Egypt* (Chicago, IL: The Oriental Institute of the University of Chicago, 2017). One example, the Papyrus of Ani, in the British Museum, is nearly 80 feet long.

37. Miriam Lichtheim, trans., *Ancient Egyptian Literature II: The New Kingdom* (Berkeley, CA: University of California, 1976), 81-86.

38. J. Gwyn Griffiths. *Plutarch's De Iside et Osiride* (Cardiff, Wales: University of Wales Press, 1970).

39. See Andrea Kucharek, "The Mysteries of Osiris," in Scalf, *The Book of the Dead*, 117-126.

40. Mark S. Smith, "The Death of 'Dying and Rising Gods' in the Biblical World," 271.

41. For the transmission of magical spells over two millennia from the Pyramid Texts, the Coffin Texts, the Book of the Dead to the Demotic Book of Breathings, see Foy Scalf, "From the Beginning to the End: How to Generate and Transmit Funerary Texts in Ancient Egypt," *Journal of the Ancient Near Eastern Religions* 15 (2015), 202-223.

42. For details, see Edwin M. Yamauchi, "Life, Death, and the Afterlife in the Ancient Near East," in *Life in the Face of Death: The Resurrection Message of the New Testament*, ed. by Richard N. Longenecker (Grand Rapids, MI: Eerdmans, 1998), 21-29.

43. Most Egyptologists, such as Foy Scalf, believe that the Osiris + personal name indicated an identification with the god. However, Mark Smith, *Following Osiris* (Oxford, UK: Oxford University Press, 2017), 159-161, argues that it meant that the person was a follower of Osiris. In either case, the name expressed the hope of an afterlife like Osiris's, and in his company.

44. See Edwin M. Yamauchi, *Persia and the Bible* (Grand Rapids, MI: Baker, 1990), chapter 14, "Mithraism."

45. Jonathan David, "The Exclusion of Women in Mithraic Mysteries: Ancient or Modern?" *Numen* 47 (2000), 121-141.

46. M.J. Vermaseren, ed., *Corpus Inscriptionum et Monumentorum Religionis Mithriacae*, 2 vols. (The Hague, Netherlands: Martin Nijhoff, 1956, 1960).

47. In 1997, excavators from the University of Münster discovered a cave at Doliche, in Commagene, which contained two mithraea. They believe that these may date to the first century AD or even the first century BC, but the only inscription from the cave dates to the third century AD. See Roger Beck, "Postscript," *Journal of Roman Studies* 88 (1998), 128.

48. E.D. Francis, "Plutarch's Mithraic Pirates," in *Mithraic Studies* I, ed. John R. Hinnells (Manchester, UK: Manchester University Press, 1975), 207-210.

49. E.D. Francis, "Franz Cumont and the Doctrines of Mithraism," in Hinnells, *Mithraic Studies*, 215-247. Cf. Roger Beck, "Mithraism Since Cumont," *Aufstieg und Niedergang der römischen Welt* II.17.4 (1984), 2002-2115.

50. See Samuel Laleuchli, *Mithraism in Ostia* (Evanston, IL: Northwestern University, 1967).

51. Roger Beck, "The Mysteries of Mithras: A New Account of Their Genesis," *Journal of Roman Studies* 88 (1998), 126.

52. Manfred Clauss, *The Roman Cult of Mithras* (New York: Routledge, 2000), 21.

53. Gary Lease, "Mithraism and Christianity: Borrowings and Transformations," *Aufstieg und Niedergang der römischen Welt* II.23.2 (1980), 1328.

54. Tom Harpur, *The Pagan Christ*, 82. Cf. Acharya S., *The Christ Conspiracy* (Kempton, IL: Adventure Unlimited, 1999), 119.

55. Gaston H. Halsberghe, *The Cult of Sol Invictus* (Leiden, Netherlands: Brill, 1972).

56. See Edwin M. Yamauchi, "*The Apocalypse of Adam*, Mithraism and Pre-Christian Gnosticism," *Études Mithriaques*, ed. J. Duchesne-Guillemin (Teheran-Liège: Bibliothèque Pahlavi, 1978), IV, 557-562.

57. See M.J. Vermaseren, *Mithras: The Secret God* (London, UK: Chatto & Windus, 1963). For the origin of these wild claims, see the excellent website The Mithras Project, maintained by Roger Pearse.

58. Robert M. Price, "Is There a Place for Historical Criticism?" *Religious Studies* 27 (1991), 383.

59. Mettinger, *The Riddle of Resurrection*, 221.

Chapter 24—Why Is It Important That Jesus Rose from the Dead?

1. Blaise Pascal, *Pensees*, trans. A.J. Krailsheimer (London, UK: Penguin Books, 1966), 434.

2. Gary R. Habermas, *The Risen Jesus and Future Hope* (Lanham, MD: Rowan & Littlefield, 2003), 182-183, 187-197.

Chapter 25—How Did Jesus Use Apologetics?

1. Dallas Willard, "Jesus the Logician," Dallas Willard, http://www.dwillard.org/articles/individual/jesus-the-logician.

2. Ralph P. Martin and Peter H. Davids, eds., *Dictionary of the Later New Testament and Its Developments* (Downers Grove, IL: InterVarsity, 1997), 845.

3. Norman Geisler and Frank Turek, *I Don't Have Enough Faith to Be an Atheist* (Wheaton, IL: Crossway, 2004), 201-202.

4. Norman Geisler, *Baker Encyclopedia of Apologetics* (Grand Rapids, MI: Baker, 1999), 53.

5. J. Barton Payne, *The Encyclopedia of Biblical Prophecy* (Grand Rapids, MI.: Baker, 1987), 511.

Chapter 26—Are the Old Testament Manuscripts Reliable?

1. For a similar treatment of this same topic, see Bruce Waltke, "How We Got the Old Testament," *Cruce* 30 (December 1994), 14.

2. See the article by the head archaeologist of the cave excavation, Gabriel Barkay, "The Priestly Benediction on the Ketef-Hinnom Plaques," *Cathedra* 52 (1989), 37-76.

3. The best scholarly work on this question was done in a doctoral dissertation and eventually an article by Jack P. Lewis, "What Do We Mean by Jabneh?" *Journal of Biblical Literature* 32 (1964), 125-130.

4. Lewis, "What Do We Mean by Jabneh?" 130.

5. I am beholden to my teacher R. Laird Harris for setting forth this concept in his book *Inspiration and Canonicity in the Bible: An Historical and Exegetical Study* (Grand Rapids, MI: Zondervan, 1957), 166-79. This series of prophets and their work is continued in verses such as 2 Chronicles 20:34; 32:32; 33:18-19.

Chapter 27—How Do the Dead Sea Scrolls Show the Reliability of the Old Testament Text?

1. For a justification of this protracted period of research and publication, see my *Secrets of the Dead Sea Scrolls* (Eugene, OR: Harvest House, 1996), 51-72.

2. See "Why Are the Scrolls Important for Understanding Second Temple Judaism?" in C.D. Elledge, *The Bible and the Dead Sea Scrolls*, SBL Archaeology and Biblical Studies 14 (Atlanta, GA: Society of Biblical Literature, 2005), 97-114.

3. See James H. Charlesworth, ed., *Jesus and the Dead Sea Scrolls,* The Anchor Bible Reference Library (New York: Doubleday, 1992).

4. See Murphy O'Connor and James H. Charlesworth, eds., *Paul and the Dead Sea Scrolls* (New York: Crossroad, 1990).

5. See Lawrence H. Schiffman, *Qumran and Jerusalem: Studies in the Dead Sea Scrolls and the History of Judaism* (Grand Rapids, MI: Eerdmans, 2010), 270-320.

6. From 2006–2015, a number of new manuscript fragments were sold by the Kando family to US institutions (Princeton University, Azuza Pacific University, Southwestern Baptist Theological Seminary) and domestic and foreign private collectors (the Green family/Museum of the Bible, Mark Lanier, Martin Schøyen of Norway, David Sutherland of New Zealand). I have also seen unpublished fragments of the Temple Scroll and a number of Old Testament books that remain with the Kando family, including a three-column fragment of Genesis 41.

7. Operation Scroll was initiated in 1993 to survey the caves in the Judean Desert with the intention of excavating caves with high potential in order to recover more scrolls before the area, then in negotiation, was given over to Palestinian control. These surveys were published in *'Atiqot* 41:1-2 (Jerusalem: Israel Antiquity Authority, Civil Administration for Judea and Samaria, 2002). Politics in the region prevented systematic exploration and excavation of these caves until 2017, when Randall Price (Liberty University) and Oren Gutfeld (Hebrew University) codirected the excavation of Cave 53 at Qumran. The discovery there of some seven scroll jars hidden in rock-hewn niches in the recesses of the cave, although without scrolls, but with scroll fragments and scroll wrappings, proved that many of the caves are scroll caves and may yield future manuscript finds. For further information, see O. Gutfeld and R. Price, "The Excavation of a Dead Sea Scroll Cave (Cave 53) at Qumran," paper presented to the Qumran section of the Society of Biblical Literature, Boston, MA, November 19, 2017, and Marcello Fidanzio, *The Caves of Qumran: Proceedings of the International Conference, Lugano 2014*, Studies on the Texts of the Desert of Judah 118 (Leiden, Netherlands: Brill, 2016).

8. James VanderKam and Peter Flint, *The Meaning of the Dead Sea Scrolls: Their Significance for Understanding the Bible, Judaism, Jesus, and Christianity* (San Francisco, CA: HarperCollins, 2002), 152.

9. Both the Aleppo Codex and the Leningrad Codex (AD 1008) represent the Ben-Asher tradition. However, because of the incomplete condition of the Aleppo Codex, most versions of the Masoretic Text are based on the Leningrad Codex.

10. M. Martin, *The Scribal Character of the Dead Sea Scrolls* (Louvain, Belgium: Publications Universitaires, 1958), 44-45.

11. For further evidence to support this conclusion, see Bruce K. Waltke, "The Reliability of the OT Text" in "How We Got the Hebrew Bible: The Text and Canon of the Old Testament," in Peter W. Flint, ed., *The Bible at Qumran: Text, Shape and Interpretation* (Grand Rapids, MI: Eerdmans, 2001), 47-50.

12. For these variants see Eugene Ulrich and Peter Flint, "Qumran Cave 1: The Isaiah Scrolls," *Discoveries in the Judean Desert* 32 (Oxford: Clarendon Press, 2010), Part 2: Introductions, Commentary, and Textual Variants.

13. See James D.G. Dunn, "Paul and the Dead Sea Scrolls" in James H. Charlesworth, ed., *Caves of Enlightenment: Proceedings of the American Schools of Oriental Research, Dead Sea Scrolls Jubilee Symposium: 1947–1997* (North Richard Hills, TX: Bibal Press, 1998), 105-127.

14. See Craig A. Evans, "Jesus and the Dead Sea Scrolls from Cave 4" in Craig A. Evans and Peter W. Flint, eds., *Eschatology, Messianism, and the Dead Sea Scrolls* (Grand Rapids, MI: Eerdmans, 1997): 91-100.

15. Harold P. Scanlin, *The Dead Sea Scrolls and Modern Translations of the Old Testament* (Wheaton, IL: Tyndale House, 1993), 27, 107.

16. For a study of these apologetic issues, see my *Secrets of the Dead Sea Scrolls*, 154-163.

17. Price, *Secrets of the Dead Sea Scrolls*, 154-163.

Chapter 28—Does Archaeology Confirm the Historical Reliability of the Old Testament?

1. With more than 25 seasons of excavation in Israel and Jordan to his credit, field archaeologist Steven Collins, PhD, is the director and chief archaeologist of the historic Tall el-Hammam Excavation Project in Jordan, the site of biblical Sodom, now in its second decade. He served for 18 years as Dean of the Trinity Southwest University

College of Archaeology, and currently directs the Veritas International University Archaeology Institute (ves.edu). He is also head curator of the TSU Museum of Archaeology.

2. This was the end result of so-called "higher critical theory" claiming that the OT was "pious fiction," written by Israelite and Judahite priests between the ninth and fifth centuries BC in order to justify Israel's claims to the "promised land."

3. I. Finkelstein and N. Na'aman, eds., *From Nomadism to Monarchy* (Jerusalem, Israel: Israel Exploration Society, 1994), 13.

4. N.P. Lemche, *Prelude to Israel's Past* (Peabody, MA: Hendrickson, 1998), 39.

5. The following contain good examples of the "minimalist" approach to the Old Testament: I. Finkelstein and N.A. Silberman, *The Bible Unearthed: Archaeology's New Vision of Ancient Israel and the Origin of Its Sacred Texts* (New York: Touchstone, 2001); I. Finkelstein and N.A. Silberman, *David and Solomon: In Search of the Bible's Sacred Kings and the Roots of the Western Tradition* (New York: Free Press, 2006); I. Finkelstein and A. Mazar, *The Quest for the Historical Israel: Debating Archaeology and the History of Early Israel*, ed. B.B. Schmidt (Atlanta, GA: Society of Biblical Literature, 2007).

6. Joseph M. Holden and Norman L. Geisler, *The Popular Handbook of Archaeology and the Bible: Discoveries that Confirm the Reliability of the Scriptures* (Eugene, OR: Harvest House, 2013), 183.

7. While Dever does not hold to the historicity of Genesis through Judges, he does admit a considerable amount of historical credibility for the stories of Israel's United and Divided Monarchy Periods. The following are good examples of his middle-of-the-road approach to much of the Old Testament: W.G. Dever, *What Did the Biblical Writers Know and When Did They Know It?—What Archaeology Can Tell Us About the Reality of Ancient Israel* (Grand Rapids, MI: Eerdmans, 2001); W.G. Dever, *Who Were the Early Israelites and Where Did They Come From?* (Grand Rapids, MI: Eerdmans, 2003); W.G. Dever, *Did God Have a Wife?—Archaeology and Folk Religion in Ancient Israel* (Grand Rapids, MI: Eerdmans, 2005); W.G. Dever, *Beyond the Texts: An Archaeological Portrait of Ancient Israel and Judah* (Grand Rapids, MI: Eerdmans, 2017).

8. A. Rainey, "The 'House of David' and the House of the Deconstructionists," *Biblical Archaeology Review* 20:6 (1994), 24-36; cf. K.A. Kitchen, *On the Reliability of the Old Testament* (Grand Rapids, MI: Eerdmans, 2003), 81-158.

9. Kenneth A. Kitchen is a formidable Ancient Near East historian, Egyptologist, and Bible scholar. He is Personal and Brunner Professor Emeritus of Egyptology and Honorary Research Fellow in the School of Archaeology, Classics, and Egyptology at the University of Liverpool, England. He is a leading expert on the Ramesside Period (Dynasties 19–20), the Third Intermediate Period, and Egyptian chronology. Since the mid-1950s he has written more than 250 books and journal articles. Professor Kitchen has been a strong opponent of Old Testament higher critical theory for his entire academic career.

10. Kitchen, *On the Reliability of the Old Testament*.

11. Kitchen, *On the Reliability of the Old Testament*, xiv.

12. These are instances of *historical synchronisms* and *cultural specificity*. Cultural specificity refers to elements of social and material culture existing exclusively in specific times and places. Historical synchronisms are elements of biblical and Near Eastern history with close correspondence.

13. A.F. Rainey and R.S. Notley, *The Sacred Bridge* (Jerusalem: Carta, 2015), 9-42.

14. K.A. Kitchen, "The Patriarchal Age: Myth or History?" *Biblical Archaeology Review* 21:2 (1995), 48-57, 88-95; Kitchen, *On the Reliability of the Old Testament*, 283ff; K.A. Kitchen and P.J.N. Lawrence, eds., *Treaty, Law and Covenant in the Ancient Near East*, 3 vols. (Wiesbaden, Germany: Harrassowitz Verlag, 2012), vol. 2, particularly 231-268; cf. G.E. Mendenhall, "Law and Covenant in Israel and the Ancient Near East" (1955), as reprinted in *Biblical Archaeologist* 17 (1954).

15. Kitchen, *On the Reliability of the Old Testament*, 283ff; K.A. Kitchen and P.J.N. Lawrence, eds., *Treaty, Law and Covenant in the Ancient Near East*, 3 vols. (Wiesbaden, Germany: Harrassowitz Verlag, 2012), vol. 3, particularly 93-213, see also vol. 2, 231-268.

16. Kitchen, *On the Reliability of the Old Testament*, 283ff; K.A. Kitchen, "The Patriarchal Age: Myth or History?" *Biblical Archaeology Review* 21:2 (1995), 48-57, 88-95.

17. Steven Collins, *Let My People Go: Using Historical Synchronisms to Identify the Pharaoh of the Exodus* (Albuquerque, NM: Trinity Southwest University Press, 2005), 49-85.

18. C.R. Krahmalkov, "Exodus Itinerary Confirmed by Egyptian Evidence," *Biblical Archaeology Review* 20.5 (1994), 55-62; cf. J.B. Pritchard, *Ancient Near Eastern Texts Relating to the Old Testament* (Princeton, NJ: Princeton University, 1955), 242-243; J. Simons, *Handbook for the Study of Topographical Lists Relating to Western Asia* (Leiden, Netherlands: Brill, 1937).

19. K.A. Kitchen, "The Patriarchal Age: Myth or History?," 48-57, 88-95; Kitchen, *On the Reliability of the Old Testament,* 344ff.

20. A. Mazar, *Archaeology and the Land of the Bible 10,000–586 BCE* (New York: Doubleday, 1990), 275-276; J. Naveh, *Early History of the Alphabet* (Jerusalem, Israel: Magnes Press, 1987), 23-28; J.C. Darnell and D. Darnell, "1994–95 Annual Report," *The Luxor-Farshut Desert Road Project* (Chicago, IL: Oriental Institute, University of Chicago, 1997); C. Rico and C. Attucci, *Origins of the Alphabet: Proceedings of the First Polis Institute Interdisciplinary Conference* (Cambridge, UK: Cambridge Scholars Publishing, 2015).

21. W.F. Albright, *Yahweh and the Gods of Canaan* (Winona Lake, IN: Eisenbrauns, 1994); Steven Collins, "Tell Tales: History, Archaeology, and the Bible," in Steven Collins, *The Defendable Faith* (Albuquerque, NM: Trinity Southwest University Press, 2012), 221; O. Kee and C. Uehlinger, *Gods, Goddesses, and Images of God in Ancient Israel* (Minneapolis, MN: Fortress Press, 1998); W.W. Hallo and K.L. Younger, Jr., eds., *The Context of Scripture: Monumental Inscriptions from the Biblical World,* vol. 2 (Leiden, Netherlands: Brill, 2003), 171-173.

22. C. Herzog and M. Gichon, *Battles of the Bible* (London, UK: Greenhill Books, 2002), 49; Collins, *Let My People Go,* 67-85.

23. Collins, *Let My People Go.* K.M. Kenyon's reports on her Jericho excavations in the 1950s identify a gap of occupation during the Late Bronze Age. However, dedicated conference and professional society sessions held jointly by the Tall el-Hammam/Sodom and Tell es-Sultan/Jericho excavation teams confirm the recent discovery of a walled LB2a phase at Jericho, destroyed in the mid-fourteenth century BC (publication pending). This new data synchronizes perfectly with Tuthmosis IV as Pharaoh of the Exodus, as does the collapse of the eighteenth dynasty following his death.

24. A. Ben-Tor, *The Archaeology of Ancient Israel* (New Haven, CT: Yale University Press, 1992), 258-301; I. Shaw and P. Nicholson, eds., *The Dictionary of Ancient Egypt* (London, UK: British Museum, 1995), 203; J.K. Hoffmeier, "The (Israel) Stela of Merneptah," in *The Context of Scripture: Monumental Inscriptions from the Biblical World,* vol. 2, eds. Hallo and Younger, Jr., 40-41; cf. J.E.M. White, *Ancient Egypt: Its Culture and History* (New York: Dover, 1970), 170-180.

25. B. Severs, *Warfare in the Old Testament: The Organization, Weapons, and Tactics of Ancient Near Eastern Armies* (Grand Rapids, MI: Kregel, 2013); cf. Y. Yadin, *The Art of Warfare in Biblical Lands,* 2 vols. (New York: McGraw-Hill, 1963), vol. 1, 79.

26. N. Bierling, *Giving Goliath His Due: New Archaeological Light on the Philistines* (Grand Rapids, MI: Eerdmans, 1992), 71-76.

27. Kitchen, *On the Reliability of the Old Testament,* 81-158.

28. A. Lemaire, "'House of David' Restored in Moabite Inscription," *Biblical Archaeology Review* (May-June 1994, w/ reply Nov-Dec 1994), 30-31; A. Rainey, "The 'House of David' and the House of the Deconstructionists," *Biblical Archaeology Review* 20:6 (1994); A. Biran, interview (1996) in *The Stones Cry Out* by Randall Price (Eugene, OR: Harvest House, 1997), 165-170; K.A. Kitchen, "A Possible Mention of David in the Late Tenth Century BCE, and Deity 'Dod' as Dead as the Dodo?" *Journal for the Study of the Old Testament* 76 (1997), 3-27; K.A. Kitchen, *On the Reliability of the Old Testament,* 81-158.

29. K.A. Kitchen, "Shishak's Military Campaign in Israel Confirmed," *Biblical Archaeology Review* 15:3 (1989), 32-34; K.A. Kitchen, "Where Did Solomon's Gold Go?" *Biblical Archaeology Review* 15:3 (1989), 30-31, 34; Kitchen, *On the Reliability of the Old Testament,* 24, 81-158; cf. J.B. Pritchard, *Ancient Near Eastern Texts Relating to the Old Testament* (Princeton, NJ: Princeton University, 1955), 118, 263-264.

30. D.D. Luckenbill, *The Annals of Sennacherib,* Oriental Institute Publications, vol. II (Chicago: University of Chicago Press, 1924); C.K. Telfer, "Toward a Historical Reconstruction of Sennacherib's Invasion of Judah in

701 B.C.—with Special Attention to the Hezekiah Narratives of Isaiah 36–39," *Mid-America Journal of Theology* 22 (2011), 7-17.

31. L.L. Grabbe, "The Belshazzar of Daniel and the Belshazzar of History," *Andrews University Seminary Studies*, 26.1 (1988), 59-66; R.P. Dougherty, *Nabonidus and Belshazzar: A Study of the Closing Events of the Neo-Babylonian Empire* (Eugene, OR: Wipf & Stock, 2008).

32. Steven Collins, *The Search for Sodom and Gomorrah*; Steven Collins and L.C. Scott, *Discovering the City of Sodom* (New York: Simon & Schuster, 2013); Steven Collins, C.M. Kobs, and M.C. Luddeni, *The Tall al-Hammam Excavations*, vol. 1 (Winona Lake, IN: Eisenbrauns. 2015); Steven Collins and P.J. Silvia, eds., *Tall al-Hammam, Jordan: Exploration, Survey, Excavation, Interpretations, and Insights from Seasons One Through Twelve*, 2 vols. (Albuquerque, NM: Trinity Southwest University Press, 2017).

33. Steven Collins, "Where Is Sodom?—the Case for Tall el-Hammam," *Biblical Archaeology Review* 39.2 (Mar-Apr 2013), 32-41; cf. D.E. Graves, *Key Facts for the Location of Sodom, Student Edition: Navigating the Maze of Arguments* (Moncton, New Brunswick: D.E. Graves, 2014); D.E. Graves, *Biblical Archaeology: An Introduction with Recent Discoveries that Support the Reliability of the Bible* (Toronto, Ontario: Electronic Christian Media, 2017), 121-134;

34. Collins and Scott, *Discovering the City of Sodom*, 200-230; Collins, Byers, and Kobs, "The Tall al-Hammam Excavation Project, Season Twelve 2017 Report: Excavation, Interpretations, and Insights," in *Tall al-Hammam, Jordan: Exploration, Survey, Excavation, Interpretations, and Insights from Seasons One Through Twelve*, vol. 1, ed. Steven Collins (Albuquerque, NM: Trinity Southwest University Press, 2017), 443-498.

35. K.A. Kitchen, *Ancient Orient and Old Testament* (Chicago, IL: InterVarsity, 1966), 172.

Chapter 29—Were the New Testament Manuscripts Copied Accurately?

1. See the tally by The Institute for New Testament Textual Research at http://www.uni-muenster.de/INTF/KgLS GII2010_02_04.pdf. To keep updated on the ever-growing tally, see the searchable database at http://ntvmr .uni-muenster.de/liste.

2. See Martin L. West, *Studies in the Text and Transmission of the Iliad* (Munchen, Germany: K.G. Saur Verlag, 2001), 86ff, and the more recent work by Graeme D. Bird, *Multitextuality in the Homeric Iliad: The Witness of the Ptolemaic Papyri* (Washington, DC: Center for Hellenic Studies, 2010).

3. John Warwick Montgomery, *History and Christianity* (Downers Grove, IL: InterVarsity, 1971), 29.

4. Daniel B. Wallace, *The Number of Textual Variants: An Evangelical Miscalculation* at https://danielbwallace .com/2013/09/09/the-number-of-textual-variants-an-evangelical-miscalculation/, accessed on July 27, 2017.

5. J. Harold Greenlee, *Introduction to New Testament Textual Criticism* (Grand Rapids, MI: Eerdmans, 1964), 66.

6. Bruce Metzger, *A Textual Commentary on the Greek New Testament,* 2d ed. (Stuttgart, Germany: German Bible Society, 1994), 3-4.

7. David Alan Black and David S. Dockery, eds., *New Testament Criticism and Interpretation* (Grand Rapids, MI: Zondervan, 1991), 103.

8. B.F. Westcott and F.J.A. Hort, *The New Testament in Greek* (New York: MacMillan, 1957), 565.

9. Benjamin B. Warfield, *Introduction to the Textual Criticism of the New Testament*, 7th ed. (London, UK: Hodder & Stoughton, 1907), 14.

10. Maurice A. Robinson and William G. Pierpont, *The New Testament in the Original Greek According to the Byzantine/Majority Text Form* (Atlanta, GA: Original Word Publications, 1991), xvi-xvii.

11. Phillip Schaff, *A Companion to the Greek Testament and the English Version* (New York: Macmillan, 1877), 177.

12. Kurt Aland and Barbara Aland, *The Text of the New Testament* (Grand Rapids, MI: Eerdmans, 1987), 28.

13. Joseph M. Holden and Norman Geisler, *The Popular Handbook of Archaeology and the Bible: Discoveries that Confirm the Reliability of Scripture* (Eugene, OR: Harvest House, 2013), 128.

14. Bruce Metzger, *Chapters in the History of New Testament Textual Criticism* (Grand Rapids, MI: Eerdmans, 1963), 146.

15. B.B. Warfield, *An Introduction to Textual Criticism of the New Testament* (London, UK: Hodder & Stoughton, 1886), 13-14.

16. Brooke Foss Westcott, Fenton John Anthony Hort, and W.J. Hickie, *The New Testament in the Original Greek* (New York: Macmillan, 1951), 2.2.

17. A.T. Robertson, *An Introduction to the Textual Criticism of the New Testament* (London, UK: Hodder & Stoughton, 1925), 22.

18. Bart Ehrman, *Misquoting Jesus: The Story Behind Who Changed the Bible and Why* (New York: HarperSanFrancisco, 2005), 55.

Chapter 30—Is the Qur'an's Text More Reliable Than the Biblical Text?

1. *Sahih Al-Bukhari Hadith*, 1.3.

2. Suzanne Haneef, *What Everyone Should Know About Islam and Muslims* (Chicago, IL: Kazi Publications, 1979), 18-19.

3. Fethullah Gulen, *Questions and Answers About Islam*, vol. 1 (Clifton, NJ: Tughra Books, 2010).

4. Abdullah Yusuf Ali, *The Holy Qur'an: English Translation of Meaning and Commentary* (Saudi Arabia: King Fahd Holy Qur'an Print Complex, 1413 AI I).

5. Malvi Muhammad Ali, *Muhammad and Christ* (The Ahmadiyya Anjuman-i-ishaat-i-Islam, 1921), 7.

6. *Basic Principles of Islam* (Abu Dhabi, UAE: The Zayed Bin Sultan Al Nahayan Charitable Foundation, 1996), 4.

7. Alhaj A.D. Ajijola, *The Essence of Faith in Islam* (Lahore, Pakistan: Islamic Publications, 1978), 79.

8. These include the Topkapi Manuscript (Istanbul, Turkey), the Sammarqand Manuscript (Tashkent, Uzbekistan), the Ma'il Manuscript (London, England), the Petropolitanus Manuscript (Paris, France), the Husaini Manuscript (Cairo, Egypt), and the Sana'a Manuscript (Sana'a, Yemen); see Altıkulaç, Tayyar, Ekmeleddin Ihsanoglu, and Salih Sadawi. *Al-Mushaf Al-Sharif Attributed to Uthman Bin Affan (the Copy at the Topkapi Palace Museum)*. (Istanbul, Turkey: Organisation of the Islamic Conference/Research Centre for Islamic History, Art and Culture, 2007).

9. Altıkulaç and İhsanoğlu, *Al-Mushaf Al-Sharif*, 23, 35, 36—footnote, 14a, 67, 70, 80-81; Francois Deroche, *Qur'ans of the Umayyads* (Leiden, Netherlands: Brill, 2014), 54.

10. Altıkulaç and İhsanoğlu, *Al-Mushaf Al-Sharif*, 10-13, 23.

11. Altıkulaç and İhsanoğlu, *Al-Mushaf Al-Sharif*, 67, 70, 81.

12. Deroche, *Qur'ans of the Umayyads*, 52.

13. Altıkulaç and İhsanoğlu, *Al-Mushaf Al-Sharif*, 41f, 65, 71-72 (for instance, the favorite manuscript among Muslims today, the Topkapi, contains 2,270 manuscript variants, Altıkulaç and İhsanoğlu, *Al-Mushaf Al-Sharif*, 81); Gerd Puin, "Observations on Early Qur'an Manuscripts in Şan'ā'," in Stefan Wild, *The Qur'an as Text* (Leiden, Netherlands: Brill, 1997), 107-111.

14. Yet unpublished.

15. Up to 2,200 at last count.

16. The dots added to Arabic letters either above or below the letters.

17. The *Dhamma*, *Kasra*, and *Fatah* vowels added to the letters.

18. Note: You will notice that the videos Pfanderfilms published on this subject in July 2017 claim there are 26 different Qur'ans (see https://www.youtube.com/watch?v=wmVocNyeFEk). As of this printing, five more have been discovered by Hatun, making a total of 31 different Arabic Qur'ans.

19. See the videos taken at Speaker's Corner in July 2017 (https://www.youtube.com/watch?v=wmVocNyeFEk and https://www.youtube.com/watch?v=1y-SAF2-otw). Note: at the end of this video, at 1 hour and 38 minutes, there are 70 slides comparing the differences between various renditions of the 26 Qur'ans. Watch also the more sedate studio film videotaped in August 2016 (https://www.youtube.com/watch?v=msY5IHtXxS8).

20. As an example, in the earlier Kufan Hafs version (d. AD 805) of Surah 6:115, the word *Kalimatu* ("the word"), which is singular, does not agree with the plural form at the end of the verse. This problem is corrected in the later Medinan Warsh version (d. AD 812).

21. For instance, notice the differences between the Hafs version of Surah 3:146, which says "many prophets fought" *(Qaatala)*, and the Warsh version, which says "many prophets were killed" *(Qutila)*. This is significant, because if I were a prophet, I would rather fight than be killed, as the former survives.

22. Examples of these can be found in (1) Surah 2:58, between the Hafs (*Naghfiru* = "we shall forgive"), and Qalun's (*Yughfaru* = "it shall be forgiven"). Thus, who is it that forgives: God, or are one's sins arbitrarily forgiven? (2) Surah 98:6, between the Hafs (*al bareiyyati* = "creatures"), and Warsh's (*al bare'ati* = "the innocent"). If the Warsh version is correct, then what are innocent Christians, Jews, and polytheists doing in hell?

Chapter 31—Does Archaeology Confirm the Historical Reliability of the New Testament?

1. See the recent book by Joseph M. Holden and Norman L. Geisler, *The Popular Handbook of Archaeology and the Bible: Discoveries that Confirm the Reliability of the Scripture* (Eugene, OR: Harvest House, 2013).

2. See Lawrence Mykytiuk, "New Testament Political Figures Confirmed," *Biblical Archaeology Review* 43/5 (Sept-Oct 2017), 50-55f.

3. Lino Concina, Guido Cremonini, and Giovanni Leonardi, *L'Evangelista Luca A Padova: La Tomba Dell'Evangelista Nella Basilica Di Santa Guistina* (Padova, Italy: Edizioni Messaggero Padova, 2010), 30-31.

4. Nicholas Wade, "'Body of St. Luke' Gains Credibility," *New York Times* (Oct 16, 2001), http://www.nytimes.com/2001/10/16/world/body-of-st-luke-gains-credibility.html.

5. Renzo Allegri, "St. Luke's Bones," *The Messenger of Saint Anthony* (Mar 2005), convention of Franciscan friars of the Basilica of Saint Anthony in Padua, Italy. http://www.messengersaintanthony.com/content/saint-lukes-bones.

6. Olga Craig, "DNA Test Pinpoints St Luke the Apostle's Remains to Padua," *The UK Telegraph* (Oct 21, 2001), http://www.telegraph.co.uk/news/worldnews/europe/italy/1360095/DNA-test-pinpoints-St-Luke-the-apostles-remains-to-Padua.html.

7. Cristiano Vernesi, et. al., "Genetic characterization of the body attributed to the evangelist Luke," *Proceedings of the National Academy of Science* 98.23 (Nov 6, 2001), 13460–13463, www.pnas.org_cgi_doi_10.1073_pnas.211540498.

8. Renzo Allegri, "St. Luke's Bones," http://www.messengersaintanthony.com/content/saint-lukes-bones.

9. See http://www.biblearchaeology.org/post/2009/10/08/New-Discoveries-Relating-to-the-Apostle-Paul.aspx# Article; http://www.biblearchaeology.org/post/2011/08/04/Martyrium-of-Apostle-Philip-Found.aspx#id_69289 ae1-76fd-4d86-b6bc-07702d99db24.

10. See John McRay, *Archaeology and the New Testament* (Grand Rapids, MI: Baker Academic, 1991); Holden and Geisler, *The Popular Handbook of Archaeology and the Bible.*

11. For additional discoveries, see Holden and Geisler, *The Popular Handbook of Archaeology and the Bible.*

12. Hershel Shanks, "The Siloam Pool: Where Jesus Healed the Blind Man," *Bible History Daily* (7-2-17), https://www.biblicalarchaeology.org/daily/biblical-sites-places/biblical-archaeology-sites/the-siloam-pool-where-jesus-healed-the-blind-man/. See also H. Shanks, "Where Jesus Cured the Blind Man," *Biblical Archaeology Review* 31/5.

13. Shimon Gibson, "The Pool of Bethesda in Jerusalem and Jewish Purification Practices of the Second Temple Period," in *Proche-Orient-Chrétien* 55 (2005), 270-293.

14. Urban C. von Wahlde, "The Puzzling Pool of Bethesda," *Biblical Archaeology Review* 37/5 (Sept-Oct 2011), https://members.bib-arch.org/biblical-archaeology-review/37/5/4.

15. Hershel Shanks, "The Siloam Pool," https://www.biblicalarchaeology.org/daily/biblical-sites-places/biblical-archaeology-sites/the-siloam-pool-where-jesus-healed-the-blind-man/.

16. Yori Yalon, "Study: Jerusalem Reservoirs Used by Pilgrims 2,000 Years Ago," *Israel Hayom Newsletter* (May 23, 2017), http://www.israelhayom.com/2017/05/23/study-jerusalem-reservoirs-used-by-pilgrims-2000-years-ago/.

Chapter 32—What Is the Internal Evidence for the Historical Reliability of the New Testament?

1. Norman L. Geisler and William E. Nix, *A General Introduction to the Bible*, rev. and exp. ed. (Chicago, IL: Moody, 1986), 91.

2. See Colin J. Hemer, *The Book of Acts in the Setting of Hellenistic History* (Winona Lake, IN: Eisenbrauns, 1990).

3. Richard Bauckham, *Jesus and the Eyewitnesses: The Gospels as Eyewitness Testimony* (Grand Rapids, MI: Eerdman's, 2006), 12-92; see also Paul Rhodes Eddy and Gregory A. Boyd, *The Jesus Legend: A Case for the Historical Reliability of the Synoptic Jesus Tradition* (Grand Rapids, MI: Baker Academic, 2007).

4. For the discussion on contradictions, lies, and myths, as well as several other matters about the various evidences regarding the New Testament writings, see the work in the website "Know What You Believe," http://www.knowwhatyoubelieve.com/believe/evidence/index.html, last visited September 14, 2017.

Chapter 33—Are There Contradictions in the Bible?

1. Augustine, *Reply to Faustus the Manichaean* 11.5, in Philip Schaff, ed., *A Select Library of the Nicene and Ante–Nicene Fathers of the Christian Church*, vol. 4 (Grand Rapids, MI: Eerdmans, 1956).

2. See Norman L. Geisler, ed. *Inerrancy* (Grand Rapids, MI: Zondervan, 1980) and Norman L. Geisler and William C. Roach, *Defending Inerrancy: Affirming the Accuracy of Scripture for a New Generation* (Grand Rapids, MI: Baker, 2012).

3. For more on how inerrancy applies to the Bible, see the complete statements of the International Council on Biblical Inerrancy (ICBI) and official commentary in R.C. Sproul, *Explaining Biblical Inerrancy* (Matthews, NC: Bastion Books, 2012).

4. See Norman L. Geisler and Thomas Howe, *The Big Book of Bible Difficulties* (Grand Rapids, MI: Baker, 2008) and Gleason Archer, *Encyclopedia of Bible Difficulties* (Grand Rapids, MI: Zondervan, 1982).

Chapter 34—What Would a Trial Lawyer Say About the Claims of the Gospels?

1. Norman Geisler, L. and Frank Turek, *I Don't Have Enough Faith to Be an Atheist* (Wheaton, IL: Crossway, 2004), 256-259.

2. See Colin J. Hemer, *The Book of Acts in the Setting of Hellenistic History* (Winona Lake, IN: Eisenbrauns, 1990).

3. Bryan A. Garner, gen. ed., *Black's Law Dictionary* (3d Pocket Edition) (Saint Paul, MN: ThomsonWest, 2006), 255.

4. Garner, *Black's Law Dictionary*, 257.

5. Garner, *Black's Law Dictionary*, 256.

6. Garner, *Black's Law Dictionary*, 261.

7. Garner, *Black's Law Dictionary*, 257.

8. Garner, *Black's Law Dictionary*, 259.

9. Garner, *Black's Law Dictionary*, 337.

10. Charles B. Gibbons, *Federal Rules of Evidence with Trial Objections* (Saint Paul, MN: Thomson West, 2003), 82.

11. Simon Greenleaf, *The Testimony of the Evangelists: The Gospels Examined by the Rules of Evidence* (Grand Rapids, MI: Kregel, 1995), 16.

12. Greenleaf, *The Testimony of the Evangelists*, 16-17.

13. David Limbaugh, *Jesus on Trial: A Lawyer Affirms the Truth of the Gospel* (Washington, DC: Regnery Publishing, 2014), 212.

14. Limbaugh, *Jesus on Trial*, 212. Also see Joseph M. Holden and Norman L. Geisler, *The Popular Handbook of Archaeology and the Bible: Discoveries That Confirm the Reliability of Scripture* (Eugene, OR: Harvest House, 2013).

15. Greenleaf, *The Testimony of the Evangelists*, 16.

16. For that matter, the entire Bible would be admissible into evidence.

17. Although the statements of others are known as hearsay-within-hearsay, or *double hearsay*. This just means their statements have to be admitted on their own after the Gospel writers' statements are admitted into evidence.

18. Another hearsay exception is when the statement is *not* used to prove truth, but offered to show the effect on the hearer. (See Luke 5:8.)

19. *Idaho v. Wright*, 497 US 805, 827 (1990).

20. For other examples, see Matthew 14:33; John 9:38.

21. For other examples, see Matthew 14:33; John 1:48-49; 3:2; 4:19; 9:38; 20:28.

22. For examples of each, see Matthew 8:29; Mark 1:24; 5:6; Luke 4:34; 8:28 and Matthew 12:24; Mark 3:22; Luke 11:15; John 7:20.

23. "Father, forgive them..." (Luke 23:34).

24. Another exception would be a "prior consistent statement" FRE 801(d)(1)(B). See Graeme Smith, *Was the Tomb Empty? A Lawyer Weighs the Evidence for the Resurrection* (Grand Rapids, MI: Monarch, 2014), 157. (Jesus had prophesied about His resurrection a number of times before it happened. So His statements would come in to rebut a charge by others of recent fabrication after His resurrection had occurred.)

25. *See Tome v. Untited States,* 513 US 150, 166 (1995).

26. Garner, *Black's Law Dictionary*, 20.

27. This statement could also come in as an excited utterance.

28. For other examples, see Matthew 8:5-13; Luke 7:6; John 1:45-49; 3:2.

29. *Schering Corp. v. Pfizer Inc.*, 189 F.3d 218, 239 (2nd Cir. 1999).

30. This exchange would also fall under the "declaration against interest" exception because, at the time it was made, Jesus was being physically persecuted for who He claimed to be. Thus, unless true, it would not be in His best interest to admit to that.

31. See Matthew 8:25; 16:22; 17:4; 18:21; Mark 8:29; Luke 9:20.

32. Greenleaf, *The Testimony of the Evangelists*, 28.

33. In the past, individuals were deemed incompetent to testify if they had a financial interest in the matter, if they lacked mental capacity, had been convicted of a crime, or lacked religious belief. However, in modern times, these have all been removed. On January 2, 1972 (Pub. L. 93-595, p.1), FRE 610 was amended to exclude evidence of religious belief to imply someone is not truthful. See *Malek v. Federal Ins. Co.*, 994 F.2d 49 (2nd Cir.1993) (error to permit questions attempting to show witness's truthfulness was affected by his religious beliefs); *U.S. v. Sampol*, 636 F.2d 621 (D.C. Cir. 1980) (Lucerne); *Government of Virgin Islands v. Petersen*, 553 F.2d 324 (3rd Cir. 1977) (Rastafarian); see *also Bains v. Cambra*, 204 F.3d 964 (9th Cir. 2000) (Sikh).

34. Edward J. Imwinkelried, *Evidentiary Foundation* (Charlottesville, VA: The Michie Company, 1980), 29.

35. Greenleaf, *The Testimony of the Evangelists*, 31-44.

36. Smith, *Was the Tomb Empty?* 91.

37. Greenleaf, *The Testimony of the Evangelists*, 34.

38. The Gospels contain 37 miracles, with 20 in Matthew alone. Some examples include Matthew 8:3,8,13; 9:25-27; 12:13; Mark 1:25,31,34; Luke 2:26-28; 3:22; 4:39; 5:12-13; John 2:9; 4:51; 5:9; 6:11,19.

39. Greenleaf, *The Testimony of the Evangelists*, 39-40.

40. Smith, *Was the Tomb Empty?* 109.

41. Smith, *Was the Tomb Empty?* 127.

42. Geisler, *I Don't Have Enough Faith to Be an Atheist*, 275-290 (top ten reasons).

43. See Matthew 26:56; Mark 14:50; John 18:15-18,25-26.

44. See Mark 9:32; Luke 18:34.

45. See Matthew 27:27-44; Mark 15:16-37; Luke 23:26-39; John 19:28-30.

46. Geisler, *I Don't Have Enough Faith to Be an Atheist*, 223. See Holden and Geisler, *The Popular Handbook of Archaeology and the Bible*.

47. Smith, *Was the Tomb Empty?* 126.

48. See Matthew 28:1-2; Mark 16:1-4; Luke 24:1-3.

Chapter 35—Can Prophecy Be Used as Evidence That the Bible Is Reliable?

1. Resources for three other areas of prophecy are noted below in endnotes 6, 7, and 8. They deal with the predicted restoration of the devastated land of Israel, the Temple Mount, and the seemingly irreconcilable problem of Jerusalem.

2. Bryant G. Wood, "Recent Research on the Date and Setting of the Exodus," *Associates for Biblical Research* (Oct 19, 2009), accessed June 21, 2017, http://www.biblearchaeology.org/post/2009/10/19/Recent-Research-on-the -Date-and-Setting-of-the-Exodus.aspx#Article.

3. The Holocaust of WWII was just a larger example of the horrific persecution the Jews have endured throughout history.

4. "Vital Statistics: Latest Population Statistics for Israel Updated May 2017," *Jewish Virtual Library* (May 2017), accessed June 21, 2017, http://www.jewishvirtuallibrary.org/latest-population-statistics-for-israel.

5. Randall Price, *The Temple and Bible Prophecy* (Eugene, OR: Harvest House, 2005), 608-609. This also includes an interesting discussion on the two regatherings of Israel in Scripture.

6. God had also promised to restore the devastated land when His people returned. You can read the details in the following prophetic passages: Isaiah 27:6; 35:1-2; 41:18-20; Jeremiah 31:5; Ezekiel 36:29-30. Here are several Internet sites with articles, among many, where you can read about biblical prophecy being fulfilled on a regular basis in Israel:

   Abigail Klein Leichman, "12 top ways Israel feeds the world," *Israel 21c* (May 10, 2012), accessed June 23, 2017, https://www.israel21c.org/the-top-12-ways-israel-feeds-the-world/.

   "Crops in Israel," *IsraelAgri*, accessed June 23, 2017, http://www.israelagri.com/?CategoryID=522.

   Israel Ministry of Foreign Affairs, "The Israel Briefing Book: Israel Overview— Agriculture," *Jewish Virtual Library*, accessed June 21, 2017, http://www.jewishvirtuallibrary.org/the-israel-briefing-book-agriculture.

   Oishimaya Sen Nag, "Global Leaders in Cut Flowers, *World Atlas* (March 1, 2017), accessed July 3, 2017, https://www.worldatlas.com/articles/global-leaders-in-cut-flower-exports.html.

   Ty Haqqi, "Ten Countries That Export the Most Cut Flowers in the World," *Insider Monkey* (May 23, 2016), accessed June 21, 2017, http://www.insidermonkey.com/blog/10-countries-that-export-the-most-cut-flowers-in -the-world-447851/?singlepage=1.

   The Gale Group, "Israel Environment and Nature: Olive," *Jewish Virtual Library*, accessed June 21, 2017, https://www.jewishvirtuallibrary.org/olive.

   Israel Wine Producers Association, "The Israel Wine Producers Association, Rich History of Israel Wines," *Israel Wine Producers Association*, accessed July 3, 2017, http://iwpa.com.

   See this site for a list of Israeli wineries and their wines: https://secure.jnf.org/site/Donation2?df_id=1980&1980 .donation=form1&printer_friendly=1.

   "Israel's Remarkable Reforestation," *American Associates Ben-Gurion University of the Negev* (January 15, 2014), accessed June 23, 2017, https://aabgu.org/israels-remarkable-reforestation/. Note in particular the following quote from that site: "In 1948, …forests covered two percent of Israel's territory. Today, trees cover eight and a half percent of the land—approximately 247,000 acres—in a country that is 97 percent drylands…"

   "Forestry & Green Innovations," *Jewish National Fund*, accessed June 21, 2017, http://usa.jnf.org/jnf-tree-plant ing-center/. This page will also direct you to the following site if you want to plant a tree in Israel: http://usa.jnf .org/jnf-tree-planting-center/.

7. One other prophecy connected to the Temple Mount and Jerusalem is witnessing an ongoing fulfillment. The prophet Zechariah recorded these words of God about Jerusalem: "I am going to make Jerusalem a cup that sends all the surrounding peoples reeling…I will make Jerusalem an immovable rock for all the nations" (Zechariah 12:2-3, NIV). Of all the problem areas in the world for the past 70 years, the status of Jerusalem has proven to be the most intractable. The Palestinians demand a state with Eastern Jerusalem as its capital, which would include all of the Old City and Temple Mount. Israel has repeatedly and clearly stated that they will never relinquish the eastern portion of the city. One world leader after another has tried without success to solve the "immovable rock" of Jerusalem.

8. Another fascinating area of prophecy deals with the ongoing question of Israel's full control over the Temple Mount in the Old City as promised by God. For a comprehensive look at the topic of the temple and Temple Mount, Randall Price's book *The Temple and Bible Prophecy* (Eugene, OR: Harvest House, 1999, 2005) is excellent. See in particular pages 425-448, along with chapter 20, "The Coming War."

   For more current information on the increasing Israeli activity on the Temple Mount, see the following sites (accessed on June 21, 2017): http://www.ir-amim.org.il/en/print/1731, https://www.breakingisraelnews.com/88691/1000-jews-ascend-temple-mount-jerusalems-jubilee, and https://www.youtube.com/watch?v=gzqjcIWIKPg. For excellent, up-to-date information on this topic as well as others coming out of Israel, visit the following site, where you can subscribe to an online magazine about current events in Israel and can also receive daily updates: http://www.israeltoday.co.il.

9. For anyone who argues that prophecies, such as the ones we listed about Jesus, could have been fulfilled by chance under the guise that "anything is possible," see the following refutations: Dr. Peter Stoner's study in *Science Speaks*, chapter 3, "The Christ of Prophecy." The book is available online at http://sciencespeaks.dstoner.net/#c0 and http://sciencespeaks.dstoner.net/Christ_of_Prophecy.html#c9. Also, see Marvin Bittinger's study in *The Faith Equation*, chapter 4, "The Probability of Prophecy" (Advantage Inspirational, 2010).

Chapter 36—What Is the Scientific Case for Intelligent Design?

1. C.S. Lewis, "Learning in War-Time" in *The Weight of Glory and Other Addresses*, rev. and exp. ed. (New York: Macmillan, 1980), 28.

2. Henry Margenau and Roy A. Varghese, eds., *Cosmos, Bios and Theos* (La Salle, IL: Open Court, 1992), 83.

Chapter 37—How Do We Respond to Objections to Intelligent Design?

1. Bradley Monton, *Seeking God in Science: An Atheist Defends Intelligent Design* (Peterborough, Ontario, Canada: Broadview Press, 2009), 7.

2. Richard Dawkins, *The Blind Watchmaker* (New York: W.W. Norton, 1986), 6.

3. Richard Dawkins, "Is Science a Religion?" *Humanist* (Jan-Feb 1997), 57, http://www.thehumanist.org/humanist/articles/dawkins.html.

4. See *Kitzmiller v. Dover*, 400 F. Supp. 2d 707 (M.D. Pa. 2005). For rebuttals to the *Dover* ruling, see "The Truth About the Dover Intelligent Design Trial," http://www.traipsingintoevolution.com. For a detailed legal rebuttal, see David K. DeWolf, John G. West, and Casey Luskin, "Intelligent Design Will Survive *Kitzmiller v. Dover*," *Montana Law Review* (2007), 68: 7-57.

5. *Edwards v. Aguillard*, 482 U.S. 578, 592 (1987); National Academy of Sciences, *Science and Creationism: A View from the National Academy of Sciences*. 2d ed. (Washington, DC: National Academy Press, 1999), 7; Phillip Johnson, *Darwin on Trial* (Washington, DC: Regnery Gateway, 1991), 4; Eugenie Scott, "Antievolutionism and Creationism in the United States," *Annual Review of Anthropology* (1997), 26: 266; *Intelligent Design Creationism and Its Critics: Philosophical, Theological & Scientific Perspectives*, ed. Robert Pennock (Cambridge, MA: MIT Press, 2001), 646; William A. Dembski, *The Design Revolution* (Downers Grove, IL: InterVarsity Press, 2004), 40; Barbara Forrest and Paul Gross, *Creationism's Trojan Horse* (New York: Oxford University Press, 2004), 283.

6. Douglas Axe, "The Limits of Complex Adaptation: An Analysis Based on a Simple Model of Structured Bacterial Populations," *BIO-Complexity* (2010) (4).

7. Douglas Axe, "Estimating the Prevalence of Protein Sequences Adopting Functional Enzyme Folds," *Journal of Molecular Biology* (2004), 341: 1295-1315; Douglas Axe, "Extreme Functional Sensitivity to Conservative Amino Acid Changes on Enzyme Exteriors," *Journal of Molecular Biology* (2000), 301: 585-595.

8. Ann Gauger and Douglas Axe, "The Evolutionary Accessibility of New Enzyme Functions: A Case Study from the Biotin Pathway," *BIO-Complexity* (2011) (1); Mariclair A. Reeves, Ann K. Gauger, and Douglas D. Axe, "Enzyme Families—Shared Evolutionary History or Shared Design? A Study of the GABA-Aminotransferase Family," *BIO-Complexity* (2014) (4).

9. See Winston Ewert, William A. Dembski, Robert J. Marks II, "Measuring meaningful information in images: algorithmic specified complexity," *IET Computer Vision* (Dec 2015), 9 (6): 884-894; Winston Ewert, W.A. Dembski, and Robert J. Marks II, "Algorithmic Specified Complexity in the Game of Life," *Systems, Man, and Cybernetics:*

Systems, IEEE Transactions (Apr 2015), 45(4): 584-594; Winston Ewert, "Complexity in Computer Simulations," *BIO-Complexity* (2014) (1); Winston Ewert, William A. Dembski and Robert J. Marks II, "On the Improbability of Algorithmically Specified Complexity," *Proceedings of the 2013 IEEE 45th Southeastern Symposium on Systems Theory (SSST),* Baylor University (Mar 11, 2013), 68-70; Winston Ewert, William A. Dembski, Robert J. Marks II, "Active Information in Metabiology," *BIO-Complexity* (2013) (4); Winston Ewert, W.A. Dembski, and Robert J. Marks II, "Conservation of Information in Relative Search Performance," *Proceedings of the 2013 IEEE 45th Southeastern Symposium on Systems Theory,* Baylor University (Mar 11, 2013), 41-50; Winston Ewert, William A. Dembski, Ann K. Gauger, Robert J. Marks II, "Time and Information in Evolution," *BIO-Complexity* (2012) (4); Winston Ewert, W.A. Dembski, and Robert J. Marks II, "Climbing the Steiner Tree—Sources of Active Information in a Genetic Algorithm for Solving the Euclidean Steiner Tree Problem," *BIO-Complexity* (2012) (1); George Montañez, Winston Ewert, W.A. Dembski, and Robert J. Marks II, "A Vivisection of the ev Computer Organism: Identifying Sources of Active Information," *BIO-Complexity* (2010) (3); William A. Dembski and Robert J. Marks II, "The Search for a Search: Measuring the Information Cost of Higher Level Search," *Journal of Advanced Computational Intelligence and Intelligent Informatics* (2010), 14 (5): 475-486; Winston Ewert, George Montañez, William A. Dembski, and Robert J. Marks II, "Efficient Per Query Information Extraction from a Hamming Oracle," *42nd South Eastern Symposium on System Theory* (Mar 2010), 290-297; Winston Ewert, William A. Dembski and Robert J. Marks II, "Evolutionary Synthesis of Nand Logic: Dissecting a Digital Organism," *Proceedings of the 2009 IEEE International Conference on Systems, Man, and Cybernetics* (Oct 2009), 3047-3053; William A. Dembski and Robert J. Marks II, "Bernoulli's Principle of Insufficient Reason and Conservation of Information in Computer Search," *Proceedings of the 2009 IEEE International Conference on Systems, Man, and Cybernetics* (Oct 2009), 2647-2652; William A. Dembski and Robert J. Marks II, "Conservation of Information in Search: Measuring the Cost of Success," *IEEE Transactions on Systems, Man, and Cybernetics-Part A: Systems and Humans* (2009), 39(5): 1051-1061.

10. Michael Behe, *Darwin's Black Box: The Biochemical Challenge to Evolution* (New York: Free Press, 1996), 39.

11. William Dembski and Jonathan Witt, *Intelligent Design Uncensored: An Easy-to-Understand Guide to the Controversy* (Downers Grove, IL: InterVarsity, 2010), 54.

12. George F.R. Ellis, "Does the Multiverse Really Exist?" *Scientific American* (Aug 2011).

13. Scott A. Minnich and Stephen C. Meyer, "Genetic analysis of coordinate flagellar and type III regulatory circuits in pathogenic bacteria," *Proceedings of the Second International Conference on Design & Nature, Rhodes, Greece* (2004), 8, http://www.discovery.org/f/389.

14. Guillermo Gonzalez, Donald Brownlee, and Peter D. Ward, "Refuges for Life in a Hostile Universe," *Scientific American* (Oct 2001), 62-67.

15. "[T]here is no demarcation line between science and nonscience, or between science and pseudoscience, which would win assent from a majority of philosophers." Larry Laudan, *Beyond Positivism and Relativism: Theory, Method, and Evidence* (Boulder, CO: Westview Press 1996), 210.

16. For example, see John A. Moore, *Science as a Way of Knowing* (Cambridge, MA: Harvard University Press, 1993); Eugenie C. Scott, "Monkey Business," *New York Academy of Sciences* (Jan-Feb 1996), 36(1): 20-25.

17. See Michael Shermer, *How We Believe: The Search for God in an Age of Science* (New York: W.H. Freeman, 2000), 77-78.

Chapter 38—What Are the Top 10 Scientific Problems with Evolution?

NOTE: This chapter is an abridged version of Casey Luskin, "The Top Ten Scientific Problems with Biological and Chemical Evolution," in Paul D. Brown and Robert Stackpole, eds., *More Than Myth: Seeking the Full Truth About Creation, Genesis, and Evolution* (British Columbia, Canada: The Chartwell Press, 2014), 8ff. Used by permission.

1. Eugenie Scott, quoted in Terrence Stutz, "State Board of Education debates evolution curriculum," *Dallas Morning News* (January 22, 2009), also requoted in Ed Stoddard, "Evolution gets added boost in Texas schools," Reuters .com, http://blogs.reuters.com/faithworld/2009/01/23/evolution-gets-added-boost-in-texas-schools/.

2. Charles Darwin, *The Origin of Species*, ed. J.W. Burrow (London, UK: Penguin Group, 1985; 1859), 66.

3. See Jonathan Wells, *Icons of Evolution: Why Much of What We Teach About Evolution Is Wrong* (Washington, DC:

Regnery, 2000); Casey Luskin, "Not Making the Grade: An Evaluation of 19 Recent Biology Textbooks and Their Use of Selected Icons of Evolution," Discovery Institute (September 26, 2011), http://www.discovery.org/f/12081.

4. David W. Deamer, "The First Living Systems: a Bioenergetic Perspective," *Microbiology & Molecular Biology Reviews* (1997), 61: 239; Jon Cohen, "Novel Center Seeks to Add Spark to Origins of Life," *Science* (Dec 22, 1995) 270: 1925-1926.

5. Richard Van Noorden, "RNA world easier to make," *Nature* (May 13, 2009), http://www.nature.com/news/2009/090513/full/news.2009.471.html.

6. See Stephen C. Meyer, *Signature in the Cell: DNA and the Evidence for Intelligent Design* (New York: HarperOne, 2009), 304.

7. Robert Shapiro, "A Simpler Origin for Life," *Scientific American* (June 2007), 46-53.

8. George M. Whitesides, "Revolutions in Chemistry: Priestley Medalist George M. Whitesides' Address," *Chemical and Engineering News* (Mar 26, 2007), 85: 12-17.

9. See Transcript of Testimony of Scott Minnich, pp. 103-112, *Kitzmiller et al. v. Dover Area School Board*, No. 4:04-CV-2688 (M.D. Pa., Nov 3, 2005); Robert M. Macnab, "Flagella," in *Escheria Coli and Salmonella Typhimurium: Cellular and Molecular Biology*, vol. 1, eds. Frederick C. Neidhart, John L. Ingraham, K. Brooks Low, Boris Magasanik, Moselio Schaechter, and H. Edwin Umbarger (Washington, DC: American Society for Microbiology, 1987), 73-74.

10. Lynn Margulis, quoted in Darry Madden, "UMass Scientist to Lead Debate on Evolutionary Theory," *Reformer* (Feb 3, 2006).

11. Michael Lynch, "The frailty of adaptive hypotheses for the origins of organismal complexity," *Proceedings of the U.S. National Academy of Sciences* (May 15, 2007), 104: 8597-8604.

12. Michael Lynch, "The evolution of genetic networks by non-adaptive processes," *Nature Reviews Genetics* (2007), 8: 803-813.

13. Ann Gauger, "The Frailty of the Darwinian Hypothesis, Part 2," *Evolution News & Science Today* (Jul 14, 2009), http://www.evolutionnews.org/2009/07/the_frailty_of_the_darwinian_h_1022911.html.

14. See "A Scientific Dissent from Darwinism," http://www.dissentfromdarwin.org/.

15. C.P. Hickman, L.S. Roberts, and F.M. Hickman, *Integrated Principles of Zoology*, 8th ed. (St. Louis, MO: Times Mirror/Moseby College Publishing, 1988), 866.

16. R.S.K. Barnes, P. Calow, and P.J.W. Olive, *The Invertebrates: A New Synthesis*. 3d ed. (Malden, MA: Blackwell Science Publications, 2001), 9-10.

17. Arthur N. Strahler, *Science and Earth History: The Evolution/Creation Controversy* (New York: Prometheus Books, 1987), 408-409.

18. Richard M. Bateman, Peter R. Crane, William A. DiMichele, Paul R. Kenrick, Nick P. Rowe, Thomas Speck, and William E. Stein, "Early Evolution of Land Plants: Phylogeny, Physiology, and Ecology of the Primary Terrestrial Radiation," *Annual Review of Ecology and Systematics* (1998), 29: 263-292.

19. Stefanie De Bodt, Steven Maere, and Yves Van de Peer, "Genome duplication and the origin of angiosperms," *Trends in Ecology and Evolution* (2005), 20: 591-597.

20. Niles Eldredge, *The Monkey Business: A Scientist Looks at Creationism* (New York: Washington Square Press, 1982), 65.

21. Frank Gill, *Ornithology*, 3d ed. (New York: W.H. Freeman, 2007), 42.

22. Walter Etter, "Patterns of Diversification and Extinction," *Handbook of Paleoanthropology: Principles, Methods, and Approaches*, eds. Winfried Henke and Ian Tattersall, 2d ed. (Heidelberg, Germany: Springer-Verlag, 2015), 351-415.

23. For a more detailed discussion of the fossil evidence and human origins, see Casey Luskin, "Human Origins and the Fossil Record," in Douglas Axe, Ann Gauger, and Casey Luskin, *Science and Human Origins* (Seattle, WA: Discovery Institute Press, 2012), 45-83.

24. Ernst Mayr, *What Makes Biology Unique?* (New York: Cambridge University Press, 2004), 198.

25. "New study suggests big bang theory of human evolution," (Jan 10, 2000), http://www.umich.edu/~newsinfo/Releases/2000/Jan00/r011000b.html.

26. W. Ford Doolittle, "Phylogenetic Classification and the Universal Tree," *Science* (Jun 25, 1999), 284: 2124-2128.

27. Partly quoting Eric Bapteste, in Lawton, "Why Darwin was wrong about the tree of life" (internal quotations omitted), *New Scientific* (Jan 21, 2009). Cited in *More Than Myth: Seeking the Full Truth About Genesis, Creation, and Evolution*, eds. Paul D. Brown and Robert Stackpole (Leicester UK: Chartwell Press, 2014), 32.

28. Liliana M. Dávalos, Andrea L. Cirranello, Jonathan H. Geisler, and Nancy B. Simmons, "Understanding phylogenetic incongruence: lessons from phyllostomid bats," *Biological Reviews of the Cambridge Philosophical Society* (2012), 87: 991-1024.

29. Trisha Gura, "Bones, Molecules or Both?" *Nature* (Jul 20, 2000), 406: 230-233.

30. Dávalos et al., "Understanding phylogenetic incongruence."

31. For example, see Colleen Belk and Virginia Borden Maier, *Biology: Science for Life* (San Francisco, CA: Benjamin Cummings, 2010), 234 ("Similarity among chordate embryos. These diverse organisms appear very similar in the first stages of development [shown in the top row], evidence that they share a common ancestor that developed along the same pathway"); Neil. A. Campbell and Jane B. Reece, *Biology* (San Francisco, CA: Benjamin Cummings, 7th ed., 2005), 449 ("Anatomical similarities in vertebrate embryos. At some stage in their embryonic development, all vertebrates have a tail located posterior to the anus, as well as pharyngeal [throat] pouches. Descent from a common ancestor can explain such similarities"); Holt Science & Technology, *Life Science* (New York: Holt, Rinehart, and Winston, 2001), 183 ("Early in development, the human embryos and the embryos of all other vertebrates are similar. These early similarities are evidence that all vertebrates share a common ancestor... The embryos of different vertebrates are very similar during the earliest stages of development").

32. See Andres Collazo, "Developmental Variation, Homology, and the Pharyngula Stage," *Systematic Biology* (2000), 49:3 (internal citations omitted); Kalinka et al., "Gene expression divergence recapitulates the developmental hourglass model," *Nature* (Dec 9, 2010), 468:811 (internal citations removed).

33. Brian K. Hall, "Phylotypic stage or phantom: is there a highly conserved embryonic stage in vertebrates?" *Trends in Ecology and Evolution"* (Dec 1997), 12(12): 461-463.

34. PZ Myers, "Casey Luskin, smirking liar," *Pharyngula* (May 8, 2009), http://scienceblogs.com/pharyngula/2009/05/08/casey-luskin-smirking-liar/.

35. PZ Myers, "Jonathan MacLatchie collides with reality again," *Pharyngula* (June 17, 2011), http://scienceblogs.com/pharyngula/2011/06/17/jonathan-maclatchie-collides-w/.

36. Myers, "Jonathan MacLatchie."

37. Alfred L Rosenberger and Walter Carl Hartwig, "New World Monkeys," *Encyclopedia of Life Sciences* (New York: Nature Publishing Group, 2001).

38. Carlos G. Schrago and Claudia A. M. Russo, "Timing the origin of New World monkeys," *Molecular Biology and Evolution* (2003), 20(10): 1620-1625; John J. Flynn and A.R. Wyss, "Recent advances in South American mammalian paleontology," *Trends in Ecology and Evolution* (Nov 1998), 13(11): 449-454; C. Barry Cox and Peter D. Moore, *Biogeography: An Ecological and Evolutionary Approach*, 5th ed. (Oxford, UK: Blackwell Science, 1993), 185.

39. Adrienne L. Zihlman, *The Human Evolution Coloring Book* (Napa, CA: HarperCollins, 2000), 4-11.

40. John C. Briggs, *Global Biogeography* (Amsterdam: Elsevier Science, 1995), 93.

41. Susan Fuller, Michael Schwarz, and Simon Tierney, "Phylogenetics of the allodapine bee genus Braunsapis: historical biogeography and long-range dispersal over water," *Journal of Biogeography* (2005), 32: 2135-2144; Anne D. Yoder, Matt Cartmill, Maryellen Ruvolo, Kathleen Smith, and Rytas Vilgalys, "Ancient single origin of Malagasy primates," *Proceedings of the National Academy of Sciences USA* (May 1996), 93: 5122-5126; Peter M. Kappeler, "Lemur Origins: Rafting by Groups of Hibernators?" *Folia Primatol* (2000), 71: 422-425; Christian Roos, Jürgen Schmitz, and Hans Zischler, "Primate jumping genes elucidate strepsirrhine phylogeny," *Proceedings of the National Academy of Sciences USA* (Jul 20, 2004), 101: 10650-10654; Philip D. Rabinowitz and Stephen Woods, "The Africa-Madagascar connection and mammalian migrations," *Journal of African Earth Sciences*, 44 (2006): 270-276; Anne D. Yoder, Melissa M. Burns, Sarah Zehr, Thomas Delefosse, Geraldine Veron, Steven

M. Goodman, and John J. Flynn, "Single origin of Malagasy Carnivora from an African ancestor," *Nature* (Feb 13, 2003), 421: 734-777.

42. Richard John Huggett, *Fundamentals of Biogeography* (New York: Routledge, 1998), 60.

43. G. John Measey, Miguel Vences, Robert C. Drewes, Ylenia Chiari, Martim Melo, and Bernard Bourles, "Freshwater paths across the ocean: molecular phylogeny of the frog *Ptychadena newtoni* gives insights into amphibian colonization of oceanic islands," *Journal of Biogeography* (2007), 34: 7-20.

44. Alan de Queiroz, "The resurrection of oceanic dispersal in historical biogeography," *Trends in Ecology and Evolution* (Feb 2005), 20(2): 68-73.

45. Giancarlo Scalera, "Fossils, frogs, floating islands and expanding Earth in changing-radius cartography—a comment to a discussion on *Journal of Biogeography*," *Annals of Geophysics* (Dec 2007), 50(6): 789-798.

46. Sylvia S. Mader, *Inquiry into Life*, 10th ed. (New York: McGraw Hill, 2003), 293.

47. See Casey Luskin, "From the Steadily Shrinking Catalogue of 'Functionless,' 'Vestigial' Organs: Now, the Tailbone," *Evolution News & Science Today* (Feb 18, 2015), https://evolutionnews.org/2015/02/from_the_steadi/.

48. See Loren G. Martin, "What is the function of the human appendix? Did it once have a purpose that has since been lost?" *Scientific American* (Oct 21, 1999), https://www.scientificamerican.com/article/what-is-the-function-of-the-human-appendix-did-it-once-have-a-purpose-that-has-since-been-lost/; William Parker quoted in Charles Q. Choi, "The Appendix: Useful and in Fact Promising," *LiveScience* (Aug 24, 2009).

49. The ENCODE Project Consortium, "An integrated encyclopedia of DNA elements in the human genome," *Nature*, 489 (Sep 6, 2012): 57-74.

50. Joseph R. Ecker, "Serving up a genome feast," *Nature* (September 6, 2012), 489: 52-55.

51. Yong, "ENCODE: the rough guide to the human genome," *Discover Magazine* (Sep 5, 2012).

52. See Jonathan Wells, *The Myth of Junk DNA* (Seattle, WA: Discovery Institute Press, 2011).

53. See Casey Luskin, "Pseudogenes," in *Dictionary of Christianity and Science*, eds. Paul Copan, Tremper Longman III, Christopher L. Reese, Michael G. Strauss (Grand Rapids, MI: Zondervan, 2017), 535-537.

54. Nicholas Wade, "An Evolutionary Theory of Right and Wrong," *The New York Times* (Oct 31, 2006), http://www.nytimes.com/2006/10/31/health/psychology/31book.html.

55. Francis Collins quoted in Dan Cray, "God vs. Science," *Time* (Nov 5, 2006), http://www.time.com/time/printout/0,8816,1555132,00.html.

56. Philip S. Skell, "Why do we invoke Darwin?" *The Scientist* (Aug 29, 2005), 19:10.

Chapter 39—What About Darwin's Doubt and the Chances of Information Emerging from Random Mutations?

1. Charles Darwin, *On the Origin of Species by Means of Natural Selection* (a facsimile of the first edition, published by John Murray, London, 1859. Reprint, Cambridge, MA: Harvard University Press, 1964), 308.

2. Richard Dawkins, *River Out of Eden: A Darwinian View of Life* (New York: Basic Books/Harper Collins, 1995), 17.

3. Bill Gates, *The Road Ahead* (New York: Viking, Penguin Group, 1995), 188.

4. Douglas Axe, "Estimating the Prevalence of Protein Sequences Adopting Functional Enzyme Folds," *Journal of Molecular Biology* 341 (2004), 1295-1315.

5. Henry Quastler, *The Emergence of Biological Organization* (New Haven, CT: Yale University Press, 1964), 16.

Chapter 40—How Should Christians Think About the Origins of the Universe?

1. Lawrence M. Krauss, "A Universe from Nothing," a lecture given on April 18, 2013 at the Radcliffe Institute for Advanced Study, Harvard University, https://www.radcliffe.harvard.edu/event/2013-lawrence-krauss-lecture (accessed Aug 1, 2017).

2. Neil deGrasse Tyson, "On God and the Big Bang," https://www.youtube.com/watch?v=9AC3FCEHZoc (accessed Aug 1, 2017).

3. John Horgan, "Physicist George Ellis Knocks Physicists for Knocking Philosophy, Falsification, Free Will," *Scientific American* (July 22, 2014), https://blogs.scientificamerican.com/cross-check/physicist-george-ellis -knocks-physicists-for-knocking-philosophy-falsification-free-will/ (accessed August 11, 2017).

4. Astrophysicist and Christian apologist Hugh Ross, for example, favors a way of showing how detailed scientific data are coherent with elements of the biblical text. Ross's coherence approach attempts to give a straightforward and unadorned reading of the data and only then to bring out its interesting coordination with biblical claims. Space prohibits us from exposing his views more fully. See his *Why the Universe Is the Way It Is* (Grand Rapids: MI, Baker, 2008).

5. See the wonderful video produced by Reasonable Faith that summarizes Craig's approach, "The Kalam Cosmological Argument," https://www.youtube.com/watch?v=6CulBuMCLg0.

6. Bradley Monton, *Seeking God in Science: An Atheist Defends Intelligent Design* (Peterborough, Ontario, Canada: Broadview Press, 2009), 92.

7. William A. Wallace, *The Modeling of Nature: Philosophy of Science and Philosophy of Nature in Synthesis* (Washington, DC: The Catholic University of America Press, 1996), 12 (emphasis added).

8. William Lane Craig, "Naturalism and Cosmology," *Naturalism: A Critical Analysis*, eds. William Lane Craig and J.P. Moreland (New York: Routledge, 2000), 228.

9. Craig, "Naturalism and Cosmology," 244.

10. Thomas Aquinas, *De Ente Et Essentia*, quoted in Edward Feser, *Aquinas: A Beginner's Guide* (Oxford, UK: Oneworld Publications, 2009), 85.

Chapter 41—Do We Have a Privileged Planet?

1. Guillermo Gonzalez and Jay W. Richards, *The Privileged Planet: How Our Place in the Cosmos Is Designed for Discovery* (Washington, DC: Regnery, 2004).

2. Hans Blumenberg, *The Genesis of the Copernican Revolution*, trans. Robert M. Wallace (Cambridge, MA: MIT Press, 1987), 3.

3. Robert M. Hazen, *The Story of Earth: The First 4.5 Billion Years, from Stardust to Living Planet* (New York: Viking-Penguin, 2012), https://aeon.co/essays/how-life-made-the-earth-into-a-cosmic-marvel.

Chapter 42—Do Science and the Bible Conflict?

1. For example, building on the work of Francesco Redi (1626–1697), Louis Pasteur (1822–1895) proved that the majority view of spontaneous generation was wrong and that life only comes from life (the law of biogenesis). For many years, most biologists asserted that junk DNA and vestigial organs in humans were useless leftovers from alleged animal ancestry. Both ideas are now demonstrably false.

2. Ernst Mayr, "Darwin's Influence on Modern Thought" (Nov 24, 2009), http://www.scientificamerican.com/ article/darwins-influence-on-modern-thought/.

3. Terry Mortenson, *The Great Turning Point* (Green Forest, AR: Master Books, 2004).

4. Katherine Lyell, *Life, Letters and Journals of Sir Charles Lyell, Bart.*, vol. 1 (London: John Murray, 1881), 268.

5. Terry Mortenson, "The Religion of Naturalism" (May 5, 2017), https://answersingenesis.org/world-religions/ religion-of-naturalism/.

6. That the ideas of evolution and millions of years have caused many to reject the Bible is shown in the national survey reported and analyzed by Ken Ham and Britt Beemer, *Already Gone* (Green Forest, AR: Master Books, 2009).

7. Terry Mortenson, "Evolution vs. Creation: The Order of Events Matters!" (Apr 4, 2006), https://answersingenesis .org/why-does-creation-matter/evolution-vs-creation-the-order-of-events-matters/.

8. Terry Mortenson, "When was Adam Created?" (Jan 11, 2017), https://answersingenesis.org/bible-characters/ adam-and-eve/when-was-adam-created/.

9. Terry Mortenson, "The Fall and the Problem of Millions of Years of Natural Evil" (Jul 18, 2012), https://answers ingenesis.org/theory-of-evolution/millions-of-years/the-fall-and-the-problem-of-millions-of-years-of-natural-evil/.

10. Terry Mortenson, "The Biblical Necessity of the Global Flood," https://answersingenesis.org/the-flood/global/biblical-necessity-global-flood/, Jul 2, 2018.

11. Terry Mortenson, ed. *Searching for Adam* (Green Forest, AR: Master Books, 2016).

Chapter 43—What Is the Relationship Between Science and Faith?

1. Francis Bacon, *The Works of Francis Bacon* (London, UK: C. Baldwin, 1819), 482-484.

2. Cited in H.S. Thayer, ed., *Newton's Philosophy of Nature: Selections from His Writings* (New York: Hafner Library of Classics, 1953), 42, 65.

3. Johannes Kepler, *New Astronomy* (1609), trans. by William H. Donahue (Cambridge, UK: Cambridge University Press, 1992), 32.

4. Terry Mortenson, *The Great Turning Point: The Church's Catastrophic Mistake on Geology—Before Darwin* (Green Forest, AR: Master Books, 2004). See also Terry Mortenson, "The Religion of Naturalism" (May 5, 2017), https://answersingenesis.org/world-religions/religion-of-naturalism/; Terry Mortenson and H. Thane Ury, eds., *Coming to Grips with Genesis* (Green Forest, AR: Master Books, 2008), 79-104; and Terry Mortenson, "Millions of Years: Where Did the Idea Come From?" DVD, https://answersingenesis.org/store/product/millions-of-years/?sku=30-9-500.

5. James Hutton, "Theory of the Earth," *Transactions of the Royal Society of Edinburgh*, 1785, quoted in Arthur Holmes, *Principles of Physical Geology* (UK: Thomas Nelson and Sons, 1965), 43-44.

6. Katherine Lyell, *Life, Letters and Journals of Sir Charles Lyell, Bart.*, vol. 1 (London, UK: John Murray, 1881), 268.

7. Charles Darwin, *The Correspondence of Charles Darwin* (Cambridge, UK: Cambridge University Press, 1987), III:55.

8. George Wald, "The Origin of Life," *Scientific American* 191:2 (August 1954), 48.

9. Scott Todd, "A View from Kansas on that Evolution Debate," *Nature* 401 (Sep 30, 1999), 423.

Chapter 44—Has the Christian Worldview Had a Positive Impact on the Development of Science?

1. Edward J. Larson, *Summer for the Gods* 22 (Cambridge, MA: Harvard University Press, 1997).

2. Colin A. Russell, "The Conflict of Science and Religion," in Gary B. Ferngren, ed., *The History of Science and Religion in the Western Tradition: An Encyclopedia* 12 (New York: Garland Publishing, 2000).

3. *Id.* at 21-22. *See also* Claude Welch, *Dispelling Some Myths About the Split Between Theology and Science in the Nineteenth Century*, in W. Mark Richardson and Wesley J. Wildman, eds., *Religion and Science History, Method, Dialogue* 73 (New York: Routledge, 1996).

4. See John William Draper, *History of Conflict Between Science and Religion* (New York: Cosimo, 2005; originally published by D. Appleton and Co. in 1874), 363.

5. Jeffrey Burton Russell, *Inventing the Flat Earth* (Westport, CT: Praeger, 1991).

6. Russell, "The Conflict of Science and Religion."

7. Russell, "The Conflict of Science and Religion," 8.

8. Russell, "The Conflict of Science and Religion," 9.

9. Ian G. Barbour, *Religion and Science: Historical and Contemporary Issues* (San Francisco, CA: HarperSanFrancisco, 1997), 18.

10. Barbour, *Religion and Science*, 19-20.

11. Barbour, *Religion and Science*, 27, emphasis in original.

12. Barbour, *Religion and Science*, 28.

13. Barbour, *Religion and Science*, 29.

14. Holmes Rolston, III, *Science and Religion: A Critical Survey* (Philadelphia, PA: Temple University Press, 1987), 39.

15. David C. Lindberg, "Medieval Science and Religion," in Gary B. Ferngren, ed., *The History of Science and Religion in the Western Tradition: An Encyclopedia* (New York: Garland Publishing, 2000), 266.

16. Michael Keas, "In the Beginning," *Salvo* (Fall 2013), http://salvomag.com/new/articles/salvo26-science-faith/in-the-beginning.php.

Chapter 45—What Is the Scientific Evidence for Adam and Eve?

1. D.R. Venema, and S. McKnight, *Adam and the Genome* (Grand Rapids, MI: Brazos Press, 2017), 1-225.

2. Terry Mortenson, et al. *Searching for Adam* (Green Forest, AR: Master Books, 2016), 1-524; J.C. Sanford and R. Carter, "In Light of Genetics…Adam, Eve, and the Creation/Fall," *Christian Apologetics Journal*, vol. 12, no. 2, Fall 2014, Southern Evangelical Seminary; J.C. Sanford and R. Carter, *"God, Family, and Genetics—a Biblical Perspective, Part 1,"* in *Genetic Evidences Supporting the Divine Origin of Man and Family* (2016); published in Proceedings of the Symposium at Rome: "The Two Shall Become One" at The Creation of Adam and Eve as the Foundation of the Church's Teaching on Holy Marriage. Human Life International; and J.C. Sanford and R. Carter, "God, Family, and Genetics—a Biblical Perspective," Part 2 in *Genetic Evidences Refuting the Evolution of Man and Family* (2016); published in Proceedings of the symposium at Rome: "The Two Shall Become One" at The Creation of Adam and Eve as the Foundation of the Church's Teaching on Holy Marriage. Human Life International.

3. J.C. Sanford, *Genetic Entropy* (Waterloo, NY: FMS Publications, 2014), 1-271.

4. C. Nelson, and J.C. Sanford, "Computational Evolution Experiments Reveal a Net Loss of Genetic Information Despite Selection," *Biological Information—New Perspectives* (2013), 338-368; J.C. Sanford, J. Baumgardner, P. Gibson, W. Brewer, and W. ReMine, "Using Computer Simulation to Understand Mutation Accumulation Dynamics and Genetic Load," Shi, et al., eds., ICCS 2007, Part II, LNCS 4488 (Berlin-Heidelberg, Germany: Springer-Verlag, 2007), 386-392; P. Gibson, J. Baumgardner, W. Brewer, and J.C. Sanford, "Can Biological Information Be Sustained by Purifying Natural Selection?" *Biological Information—New Perspectives*, 232-263.

5. R.C. Carter and J.C. Sanford, "A New Look at an Old Virus: Patterns of Mutation Accumulation in the Human H1N1 Influenza Virus Since 1918," *Theoretical Biology and Medical Modeling* (2012), 9:42doi:10.1186/1742-4682-9-42.

6. See at https://www.logosra.org/genetic-entropy.

7. Robert W. Carter, "Mitochondrial Diversity Within Modern Human Populations," *Nucleic Acids Research* 35, no. 9 (May 2007): 3039-3045; R. Carter, D. Criswell, and J.C. Sanford, "The 'Eve' Mitochondrial Consensus Sequence," A.A. Snelling, ed., *Proceedings of the Sixth International Conference on Creationism* (Pittsburgh, PA and Dallas, TX: Creation Science Fellowship and Institute for Creation Research, 2008), 111-116; Sanford and Carter, "In Light of Genetics…Adam, Eve, and the Creation/Fall; R. Carter, S.S. Lee, and J.C. Sanford (in review), "An Overview of the Histories of the Human Y Chromosome and the Human Mitochondrial Chromosome."

8. Space does not allow further elaboration, but evolutionists make the counterargument of "coalescence," which is not valid when there is not random mating (i.e., when there are dispersed subpopulations).

9. Sanford and Carter, "In Light of Genetics…Adam, Eve, and the Creation/Fall; R. Carter, S.S. Lee, and J.C. Sanford (in review), "An Overview of the Histories of the Human Y Chromosome and the Human Mitochondrial Chromosome."

10. R.J. Marks, M.J. Behe, W.A. Dembski, B.L. Gordon, and J.C. Sanford, *Biological Information—New Perspectives* (Singapore: World Scientific Publishing, 2013), 1-559.

11. E. Pennisi, "ENCODE Project Writes Eulogy for Junk DNA," *Science*, Sep 7, 2012, vol. 337, issue 6099, 1159-1161 DOI: 10.1126/science.337.6099.1159.

12. J.C. Sanford, W. Brewer, F. Smith, and J. Baumgardner, "The Waiting Time Problem in a Model Hominin Population," *Theoretical Biology and Medical Modelling* 12 (2015), 18.

13. See at https://www.logosra.org/tiktaalik.

14. See at https://www.logosra.org/whale-evolution.

15. S.T. Cordova and J.C. Sanford, *Nylonase Genes and Proteins—Distribution, Conservation, and Possible Origins* (forthcoming), download available at http://vixra.org/pdf/1708.0370v1.pdf.

16. C. Rupe and J.C. Sanford, *Contested Bones* (Waterloo, NY: FMS Publications, 2017).

17. J. Hublin, et al., "New Fossils from Jebel Iroud, Morocco and the Pan-African Origin of *Homo Sapiens*," *Nature*, 546:289-292 (2017). DOI:10.1038/nature22336.

18. P. Dirks, et al., "The Age of *Homo naledi* and Associated Sediments in the Rising Star Cave, South Africa," *eLife*, (2017), DOI: 10.7554/elife.24231.

19. S.R. Holen, et al., "A 130,000-Year-Old Archaeological Site in Southern California, USA," *Nature*, 544:479-483, 2017, DOI: 10.1038/nature22065.

20. G.D. Gierlinski, et al., "Possible Hominin Footprints from the Late Miocene (c. 5.7 Ma) of Crete?" *Proceedings of the Geologists' Association*, 621:1-14, (2017), DOI: 10.1016/j.pgeola.2017.07.006.

21. J.C. Sanford, *Genetic Entropy* (Waterloo, NY: FMS Publications, 2014), 1-271.

22. C.L. Rupe and J.C. Sanford, "Using Numerical Simulation to Better Understand Fixation Rates, and Establishment of a New Principle: Haldane's Ratchet," ICC Proceedings (2013), http://media.wix.com/ugd/a704d4_47b cf08eda0e4926a44a8ac9cbfa9c20.pdf.

23. J.C. Sanford, W. Brewer, F. Smith, and J. Baumgardner, "The Waiting Time Problem in a Model Hominin Population," *Theoretical Biology and Medical Modelling* 12 (2015), 18.

24. Dr. Venema raises several arguments: First, he raises the old argument that since apes and man have many biological and genetic similarities, therefore this proves evolution. However, this is clearly false because similarities can arise either by common ancestry or by *common design*. Furthermore, the ape/human similarities have been greatly exaggerated, especially the genetic similarities. See J. Tomkins, "Documented Anomaly in Recent Versions of the BLASTN Algorithm and a Complete Reanalysis of Chimpanzee and Human Genome-Wide DNA Similarity Using Nucmer and LASTZ," *Answers Research Journal* 8 (2015), 379-390. In addition, Venema's counterargument to common design is the typical claim that "shared genetic mistakes" prove common ancestry. Unfortunately, this response is false since it incorrectly assumes that any shared DNA sequences that do not encode protein (i.e., most of the genome), are necessarily junk DNA (and so cannot be attributed to common design). The NIH research program named ENCODE is an international consortium of scientists which has clearly shown that most of the genome is *not* junk, but has many functions apart from protein synthesis (see https://evolutionnews.org/2017/02/encode_team_con/). Every day, new NIH discoveries are reinforcing this fact. Dr. Venema fails to mention this, even though this new information is pivotal to his argument. This again reflects poor scholarship. He does not mention the most famous proof of a shared mistake, which was the B-globin pseudogene. The famous example of a shared mistake was fully overturned several years ago, with high profile papers showing that the B-globin pseudogene is not only highly functional, it is in fact essential (see J. Tomkins, "The Human Beta-Globin Pseudogene Is Non-Variable and Functional," *Answers Research Journal* 6 [2013], 293-301). Therefore, the same gene that was the very best proof of a shared mistake (thus proving common ancestry) turns out to be a perfect illustration of similarity by design. Regardless of whether Dr. Venema was simply not aware of this, or chose not to mention it, again reflects poor scholarship. Dr. Venema also cites shared Alu-elements as part of his proof. Perhaps Dr. Venema is not aware of the great deal of scientific literature that shows that many Alu elements are functional. Numerous high-profile papers now show that Alu-elements typically have (multiple) functions, and so they are not all junk DNA, and cannot be assumed to be shared mistakes. See David L. Nelson and Michael M. Cox, *Lehninger Principles of Biochemistry*, 6th ed. (New York: W.H. Freeman, 2013), 1113. Again, failure to even include this current literature reflects poor scholarship.

In another argument, Dr. Venema says there is irrefutable proof that long ago, two chimpanzee chromosomes fused to generate human chromosome 2 (chr2). He does not seem to be aware of recent work that strongly refutes that very old claim. Regardless of whether he deliberately decided not to cite this information or was simply not aware of it, this again reflects poor scholarship. Dr. Jeff Tomkins has spent his career as the director of a university genomics sequencing center, and has published many research papers relating to genomics. He has recently published a very compelling paper which shows that the reputed chromosome 2 "fusion site" is not a telomeric fusion site at all, but is a functional transcription factor binding site, and is embedded in a very active pseudogene. This appears to completely invalidate the chr2 fusion hypothesis. In the same paper, Dr. Tomkins shows that the reputed "pseudo-centromere" sequence (said to support the fusion hypothesis) is too small, too divergent, and is (like the reputed fusion site), actually internal to a functional gene. At best, the chr2 fusion hypothesis is now highly questionable. Each of the genetic arguments that Dr. Venema cites in his book are easily available from anti-Christian, anti-ID, and anti-creation blog sites. It appears that his only original contribution to the Adam and Eve debate is the argument that Adam and Eve could not have given rise to the large amount of genetic diversity, as is now seen within the modern human population. My colleagues and I have researched this topic for several years, and have a publication in progress (see in review article by J.C. Sanford, W. Brewer, R. Carter, and J. Baumgardner, "Adam and Eve—Testing the Designed Diversity Model"). On a superficial level, the topic is very simple: Adam and Eve could easily have been heterozygous at any number of nucleotide sites. Thus Adam and Eve could account for any number of single nucleotide variants (polymorphisms). On a more advanced level, one can examine human diversity in more detail. For example, one can examine the actual allele frequency distributions and observed linkage patterns. Even at this higher level, we can readily account for any pattern of human diversity, given a created Adam and Eve, and assuming that their countless reproductive cells were simultaneously created with the gametogonia carrying their own specified alleles and linkages. Last, our numerical simulations show that even without invoking created gametes, various parameter settings can generate the same type of allele frequency distribution as is seen in the modern human population today.

Chapter 46—Is There Any Evidence of Life After Death?

1. We note the distinction between clinical death, which may be reversible after medical efforts like CPR, and biological death, which, by definition, is irreversible. For details, see Michael B. Sabom, *Recollections of Death: A Medical Investigation* (New York: Harper & Row, 1982), 6-12.

2. Jaap W. de Vries, et al., "Changes in Cerebral Oxygen Uptake and Cerebral Electrical Activity During Defibrillation Threshold Testing," *Anesthesia and Analgesia*, vol. 87 (1998), 16-20; Pim van Lommel, "Near-Death Experience, Consciousness, and the Brain: A New Concept about the Continuity of our Consciousness Based on Recent Scientific Research on Near-Death Experience in Survivors of Cardiac Arrest," *World Futures*, vol. 62 (2006): 134-151.

3. In the 1998 volume coauthored with J.P. Moreland, *Beyond Death: Exploring the Evidence for Immortality* (Wheaton, IL: Crossway), chiefly 157-164, Habermas divided about a dozen and a half evidenced near-death reports into four different evidential categories: where the individual was close to death without formal medical measurements; accounts beyond heart stoppage; several other examples involving the absence of measurable brain activity; and a category of evidential details seemingly drawn from seeing deceased friends and family, similar to the fifth category above.

4. Sabom, *Recollections of Death,* 87-115.

5. Melvin L. Morse, "Near-Death Experiences and Death-Related Visions in Children: Implications for the Clinician," *Current Problems in Pediatrics*, vol. 24 (1994), 61; cf. Morse with Paul Perry, *Closer to the Light: Learning from Children's Near-Death Experiences* (New York: Random House [Villard], 1990), especially 3-9.

6. Morse, "Near Death Experiences and Death-Related Visions in Children," 61; Morse, *Closer to the Light*, 6-9.

7. Kenneth Ring and Madelaine Lawrence, "Further Evidence for Veridical Perception During Near-Death Experiences," *Journal of Near-Death Studies*, vol. 11 (1993), especially 226-227.

8. Kenneth Ring and Sharon Cooper, *Mindsight* (Palo Alto, CA: William James Center for Consciousness Studies, Institute for Transpersonal Psychology, 1999), 22-28, 108-120. For a medical perspective on such cases, see Jeffrey Long with Paul Perry, *Evidence of the Afterlife: The Science of Near-Death Experiences* (New York: HarperOne, 2010), 83-92.

9. L. Houlberg, "Coming Out of the Dark," *Nursing* (Feb 1992), 43.

10. Examples can be found in Janice Miner Holden, Bruce Greyson, and Debbie James, eds., *The Handbook of Near-Death Experiences: Thirty Years of Investigation* (Santa Barbara, CA: Praeger, 2009), 100 (in Cherie Sutherland's chapter), 231-232 (in the chapter by Bruce Greyson, Emily and Edward Kelly).

Chapter 47—Is It Reasonable to Believe in Heaven (and Hell)?

1. Bertrand Russell, *Autobiography*, vol. 2 (London, UK: George Allen and Unwin, 1968), 159.

2. C.S. Lewis, *Mere Christianity* (New York: Macmillan, 1960), 120.

Chapter 49—Are Christians Intolerant and Narrow-Minded?

1. D.A. Carson, *The Intolerance of Tolerance* (Grand Rapids, MI: Eerdmans, 2013), 47.

2. Josh McDowell and Sean McDowell, *The Beauty of Intolerance* (Uhrichsville, OH: Shiloh Run Press, 2016), 72.

3. Erwin Lutzer, *Who Are You to Judge?* (Chicago, IL: Moody, 2016), 11-12.

Chapter 50—Why Is It Important That Jesus Died on the Cross?

1. See "Cross" in Terry L. Miethe, *The Compact Dictionary of Doctrinal Words* (Minneapolis, MN: Bethany House, 1988), 66.

2. Karl Barth, *The Humanity of God* (Richmond, VA: John Knox Press, 1960), 46.

3. Barth, *The Humanity of God*, 51.

4. See "Reformed Theology" in Terry L. Miethe, *The Compact Dictionary of Doctrinal Words*, 175.

5. See "Chalcedon, Council of" in Terry L. Miethe, *The Compact Dictionary of Doctrinal Words*, 55.

6. See "Lutheran" in Terry L. Miethe, *The Compact Dictionary of Doctrinal Words*, 132-134.

7. See Emil Brunner's *The Mediator: A Study of the Central Doctrine of the Christian Faith* (Philadelphia, PA: Westminster Press, 1962). This is a formidable theological treatise.

8. Brunner, *The Mediator*, 328.

Chapter 51—Is Christian Belief Just Psychological Wish Fulfillment?

1. William W. Meissner, S.J., "Freud and the Bible," *The Oxford Companion to the Bible,* gen. eds. Bruce M. Metzger and Michael D. Coogan (New York: The Oxford University Press, 1993), 232-236.

2. For a clear and concise discussion of the philosophers and their ideas that influenced Freud, see Norman Geisler, "The History of Destructive Biblical Criticism," *Systematic Theology*, vol. 1 (Minneapolis, MN: Bethany House, 2002), 315-349.

3. Sigmund Freud, *The Future of an Illusion*, The Standard Edition of the Complete Psychological Works of Sigmund Freud, vol. 21, gen. ed. James Strachey (London, UK: The Hogarth Press and The Institute of Psycho-Analysis, 1927–1931), 14.

4. Freud, *The Future of an Illusion*, 18-19.

5. James Bishop, "Atheism Was an Error: English Professor and Atheist Mark Bauerlein Converts to Christianity" (March 8, 2017), in *Reasons for Jesus*, http://reasonsforjesus.com/atheism-was-an-error-english-professor-atheist-mark -bauerlein-converts-to-christianity/.

6. Ravi Zacharias, "The Case for God," *Truth in the Balance: The Case for Christianity,* DVD/MP3 (Costa Mesa, CA: Veritas International University, 2009).

7. David Berlinski, *The Devil's Delusion*, rep. ed. (New York: Basic Books, 2009).

8. For more on the argument from contempt or ad hominem argument, see Richard Dawkins vs. John Lennox, *The God Delusion Debate* (2009), DVD/Video (Fixed Point Foundation, www.fixed-point.org).

9. Freud, *The Future of an Illusion,* 19-24.

10. Freud, *The Future of an Illusion,* 25.

11. Freud, *The Future of an Illusion,* 28-29.

12. Freud, *The Future of an Illusion,* 29.

13. See the editor's footnote to *The Economic Problem of Masochism* (1924), standard edition.

14. Freud, *The Future of an Illusion,* 39-40.

15. Freud, *The Future of an Illusion,* 45.

16. Freud, *The Future of an Illusion.*

17. Freud, *The Future of an Illusion,* 50.

18. William W. Meissner, "Freud and the Bible," *The Oxford Companion to the Bible*, gen. eds. Bruce M. Metzger and Michael D. Coogan (New York: Oxford University Press, 1993), 234-236.

Chapter 52—Are Miracles Possible?

1. He says, "Those effects are properly called miracles, which are produced by God's power alone on things which have a natural tendency to the opposite effect or to a contrary mode of operation; whereas effects produced by

nature, the cause of which is unknown to us or to some of us, as also those effects, produced by God, that are of a nature to be produced by none but God, cannot be called miraculous but only marvelous or wonderful." See Thomas Aquinas, *On the Power of God: quæstiones disputatæ de potential dei*, trans. English Dominican Fathers, II, vi, 2 (Eugene, OR: Wipf & Stock, 2004), 164-165. I take Aquinas to mean that not every act of God is a miracle. The act of creation itself is not miraculous because God was not acting "on things which have a natural tendency to the opposite effect or to a contrary mode of operation." This is because, since creation was from nothing, there was not anything there (before creation) upon which God acted and which could be said to have any natural tendency.

2. C.S. Lewis, *Miracles: How God Intervenes in Nature and Human Affairs* (New York: Macmillan, 1947), 5. Lewis's footnote reflecting on his own definition is interesting: "This definition is not that which would be given by many theologians. I am adopting it not because I think it an improvement upon theirs but precisely because, being crude and 'popular,' it enables me most easily to treat those questions which 'the common reader' probably has in mind when he takes up a book on Miracles."

3. Norman L. Geisler, *Miracles and the Modern Mind* (Grand Rapids, MI: Baker, 1992), 14.

4. I encourage Christians to guard the proper use of the term *supernatural*. It is common in our culture to refer to the activities of angels and demons as supernatural. There is even a genre of literature and movies that goes by this term. The term *paranormal* is better for such activities (though, admittedly, *paranormal* frequently has an evil connotation).

5. I am not suggesting that no one could go from atheism to theism upon witnessing a miracle. Instead, I am stating a principled point that any true miracle should always (if one is to be philosophically consistent) be interpreted by the atheist as an anomaly that might be explained with further scientific knowledge. Kai Nielsen, in his debate with J.P. Moreland, illustrated this when he said, "Suppose that it were the case that Jesus was raised from the dead. Suppose you collected the bones, and they went together in some way reconstituting the living Jesus…This wouldn't show there was an infinite intelligible being. It wouldn't give you any way of being able to detect if there is a God. It would be just that a very strange happening happened…It would just be a very peculiar fact we hadn't explained and indeed lacked the scientific resources to explain." See J.P. Moreland and Kai Nielsen, *Does God Exist? The Great Debate* (Nashville, TN: Thomas Nelson, 1990), 64; republished *Does God Exist? The Debate Between Theists and Atheists* (Amherst, NJ: Prometheus, 1993), 64.

   Atheist Peter Atkins, in his debate with William Lane Craig, made the same point. In discussing his take on the reported miracles at Lourdes, he said, "I believe that anything that has been reported reliably—anything—can be interpreted scientifically within the framework of modern science." The debate can be viewed at http://www.reasonablefaith.org/debate-transcript-what-is-the-evidence-for-against-the-existence-of-god (accessed Sep 11, 2017).

6. Pantheism says that God just *is* the universe. Panentheism says that God is to the universe as a soul is to a body. Both of these deny God's transcendence.

7. Other miracles wrought by Christ were clearly done to demonstrate who Jesus was. Jesus calming the storm in Matthew 8:27 prompted the disciples to marvel and ask, "What sort of man is this, that even winds and sea obey him?" Jesus walking on water in Matthew 14 climaxes in the reaction of the witnesses, who, according to verse 33, "worshiped him, saying, 'Truly you are the Son of God.'" The account of Jesus healing the paralytic man in Matthew 9:2-7 demonstrated that Jesus had the authority to forgive sins. This same purpose of miracles was also seen with the apostles. Norman Geisler observes, "Not every follower of Christ was an apostle…Apostles had a special task. They were the foundation of the Christian church…Paul declared that the church is 'built on the foundation of the apostles and prophets, with Christ himself as the chief cornerstone' (Ephesians 2:20). Indeed, the early church 'devoted themselves to the apostles' teaching' (Acts 2:42). Their special divine authority was exercised in both doctrine (Acts 15) and in discipline (Acts 5)." See Norman Geisler, *Signs and Wonders* (Wheaton, IL: Tyndale House, 1988), 134-135.

8. Augustine, *City of God*, XXII:8, 1033.

9. Thomas Aquinas, *St. Thomas Aquinas Summa Theologica: Complete English Edition in Five Volumes*, trans. Fathers of the English Dominican Province (Westminster, MD: Christian Classics, 1981), I-II, 178, i.

10. John Calvin, "Prefatory Address by John Calvin to Francis I., King of France," *Institutes of the Christian Religion*, 2 vols., trans. Henry Beveridge (Grand Rapids, MI: Eerdmans, 1975), I, I, 8-9.

11. James Arminius, *The Writings of James Arminius*, 3 vols., trans. James Nichols and W. R. Bagnall (Grand Rapids, MI: Baker, 1977), I, 129-130. Other theologians on miracles include: "A miracle is (1) an event occurring in the physical world, capable of being discerned and discriminated by the bodily senses of human witnesses, (2) of such a character that it can be rationally referred to no other cause than the immediate volition of God, (3) accompanying a religious teacher, and designed to authenticate his divine commission and the truth of his message." See A.A. Hodge, *Outlines of Theology for Students and Laymen* (Grand Rapids, MI: Zondervan, 1972), 275; "From this view [of the Duke of Argyle] I wholly dissent. It is inconsistent with the prime end for which God has introduced miracles, to be attestations to man of God's messages." See Robert Lewis Dabney, *Systematic Theology* (Grand Rapids, MI: Zondervan, 1972), 283; "Though miracles are wonders (Acts 2:19) in the eyes of men and display the power of God, their true purpose is that of a 'sign' (Matthew 12:38; John 2:18). They certify and authenticate a teacher or his doctrine." See Lewis Sperry Chafer, *Systematic Theology*, 8 vols. (Dallas, TX: Dallas Seminary Press, 1947), I, 256-257. "Biblical miracles are extraordinary events (*ergon*) which capture public notice, producing amazement (*teras, thaumadzō*) and which have meaning (*sēmeion*). This meaning is the special presence of God in some special way usually declared by a prophet (Aaron, Elijah, Moses, Jeremiah). Finally a biblical miracle is *dunamis*, the product of and evidence of divine power and authority, not only in the event itself but of delegated power in the divinely authorized person at whose word the miracle took place." See Robert Duncan Culver, *Systematic Theology: Biblical & Historical* (Geanies House, Fearn, Ross-shire, UK: Christian Focus, 2005), 206.

12. This explains why Jesus did not heal everyone; the purpose of a healing miracle was not merely to make someone well.

13. For Hume's arguments against miracles, see chapter X of his *An Enquiry Concerning Human Understanding and Concerning the Principles of Morals*, ed. L.A. Selby-Bigge, 3d ed., revised by P.H. Nidditch (Oxford, UK: Clarendon Press, 1975). The chapter is reprinted in R. Douglas Geivett and Gary R. Habermas, *In Defense of Miracles: A Comprehensive Case for God's Action in History* (Downers Grove, IL: InterVarsity, 1997), 29-44.

14. Hume defined a miracle as "a violation of the laws of nature…Nothing is esteemed a miracle, if it ever happened in the common course of nature…There must, therefore, be a uniform experience against every miraculous event, otherwise the event would not merit that appellation." See Hume, *Enquiry*, §X, Pt. 1, SelbyBigge, 114-115. He claimed that he could "establish it as a maxim, that no human testimony can have such force as to prove a miracle, and make it a just foundation for any such system of religion." See Hume, *Enquiry*, §X, Pt. 2, SelbyBigge, 127.

15. For Hume, because a miracle is a violation of the law of nature, then "as a firm and unalterable experience has established these laws, the proof against a miracle, from the very nature of the fact, is as entire as any argument from experience can possibly be imagined." See Hume, *Enquiry*, §X, Pt. 1, SelbyBigge, 114.

16. Lewis says, "The question, 'Do miracles occur?' and the question, 'Is the course of Nature absolutely uniform?' are the same question asked in two different ways. Hume, by sleight of hand, treats them as two different questions. He first answers 'Yes,' to the question whether Nature is absolutely uniform: and then uses this 'Yes' as a ground for answering, 'No,' to the question, 'Do miracles occur?' The single real question which he set out to answer is never discussed at all. He gets the answer to one form of the question by assuming the answer to another form of the same question." See C.S. Lewis, *Miracles: How God Intervenes in Nature and Human Affairs* (New York: Macmillan, 1947), 103.

17. Hume, *Enquiry*, §V, Pt. 1, Selby-Bigge, 42-43.

18. Hume, *Enquiry*, §V, 2, Selby-Bigge, 48.

19. The classical definition of truth is the correspondence theory of truth. See the chapter titled, "What Is Truth?"

20. In contrast to Hume's philosophy that human thinking is comprised of nothing more than the barest of perceptions together with the feelings they produce and the habits accruing therefrom. Instead, the classical tradition affirms the human faculties of sense can give us knowledge, not only of real sensible objects, but also of the real metaphysical constituents, characteristics, and principles of those objects. Thomas Aquinas said, "Our knowledge, taking its start from things, proceeds in this order. First, it begins in sense; second, it is completed in the intellect." See Aquinas, *Truth*, 3 vols., vol. 1 trans. Robert W. Mulligan (Chicago, IL: Henry Regnery, 1952); vol. 2 trans. James V. McGlynn (Chicago, IL: Henry Regnery, 1953); vol. 3. trans. Robert W. Schmidt (Chicago: Henry Regnery, 1954). The three volumes were reprinted as *Truth* (Indianapolis, IN: Hackett, 1994), I, 11.

Aquinas went on to say, "For according to its [the human intellect's] manner of knowing in the present life, the intellect depends on the sense for the origin of knowledge; and so those things that do not fall under the senses cannot be grasped by the human intellect except insofar as the knowledge of them is gathered from sensible things." See Aquinas, *Summa contra Gentiles*, 5 vols., I, 3, §3, trans. Anton Pegis (Notre Dame, IN: University of Notre Dame Press, 1975), 64.

For a succinct treatment of how we can know the real (particularly in light of the challenges from Locke onward through Hume and culminating with Kant), see Étienne Gilson, *Methodical Realism*, trans. Philip Trower (Front Royal, VA: Christendom Press, 1990), reprinted *Methodical Realism: A Handbook for Beginning Realists*, trans. Philip Trower (San Francisco, CA: Ignatius Press, 2011). For a more in-depth account and defense of empiricism, see Frederick D. Wilhelmsen, *Man's Knowledge of Reality: An Introduction to Thomistic Epistemology* (Englewood Cliffs, NJ: Prentice-Hall, 1956).

Chapter 53—Is It Okay for Christians to Doubt?

1. Bible Verses About Doubt: 20 Scripture Quotes: whatchristianswanttoknow.com/bible-verses-about-doubt-20-scripture-quotes/.

2. Terry L. Miethe, *Soul-Making & Virtue* (Mt. Juliet, TN: Winged Lion, 2017). This is available from wingedlion@tds.net.

3. See Michael Novak, *Belief and Unbelief: A Philosophy of Self-Knowledge*, 3d ed. (New York: Routledge, 1994), 266; Eton Trueblood, *A Place to Stand* (New York: Harper & Row, 1969), 128; Peter Berger and Anton Zijderveld, *In Praise of Doubt: How to Have Convictions Without Becoming Fanatic* (San Francisco, CA: HarperOne); Jennifer Michael Hecht, *Doubt: A History: The Great Doubters and Their Legacy of Innovation from Socrates and Jesus to Thomas Jefferson and Emily Dickinson* (San Francisco, CA: HarperOne, 2004), 576; Dallas Willard, *Knowing Christ Today: Why We Can Trust Spiritual Knowledge* (San Francisco, CA: HarperOne, 2014), 256.

4. Lynn Anderson, *If I Really Believe, Why Do I Have These Doubts?* (Grand Rapids, MI: Bethany House, 1992), 72-80.

5. See Terry L. Miethe, *Why Believe? God Exists! Rethinking the Case for God and Christianity* (Joplin, MO: College Press, 1993), ch. 22, "When All Else Fails," for a more complete look at Job.

6. See Miethe, *Soul-Making & Virtue*.

7. Martin Laird, *Into the Silent Land: A Guide to the Christian Practice of Contemplation* (New York: Oxford University Press, 2006), 154.

Chapter 55—Is the Trinity a Contradiction?

1. Norman L. Geisler, "Trinity," in *Baker Encyclopedia of Christian Apologetics* (Grand Rapids, MI: Baker, 1999), 730-737.

2. Brandon D. Crowe and Carl R. Trueman, eds., *The Essential Trinity* (Phillipsburg, NJ: Presbyterian & Reformed, 2017), 19. They emphasize the "triadic contours of the text that lead—inexorably—to the doctrine of the Trinity."

3. "Trinity," in Ed Hindson and Ergun Caner, eds., *The Popular Encyclopedia of Apologetics* (Eugene, OR: Harvest House, 2008), 473-477.

4. A.T. Robertson, *Word Pictures in the New Testament* (Grand Rapids, MI: Baker, 1930), 1: 245.

5. Grant R. Osborne, *Matthew* (Grand Rapids, MI: Zondervan, 2010), 1081.

6. Bruce A. Ware, "God the Son—at Once Eternally God with His Father, and Eternally Son of the Father," Reformation21.org, June 9, 2016, http://www.reformation21.org/blog/2016/06/god-the-sonat-once-eternally-g.php.

7. Charles Hodge, *Systematic Theology* (Peabody, MA: Hendrickson, 2013), 460-462.

8. Albert Mohler, "Heresy and Humility—Lessons from a Recent Controversy," AlbertMohler.com, June 28, 2016, http://www.albertmohler.com/2016/06/28/heresy/.

9. Michael Horton, *The Christian Faith* (Grand Rapids, MI: Zondervan, 2010), 381.

Chapter 56—What Is Philosophy, and Why Is It Important?

1. Variations in ancient literature include *philosopheo*, meaning "discuss, investigate, study"; *philosophos*, meaning "lover of wisdom" and used of all men of education and learning; and *philosophia*, used only once in the New

Testament in Colossians 2:8, in a bad sense to speak of an insidious legalism and Gnosticism that was plaguing the Colossian Christians. For definitions of Greek words in the New Testament, see Walter Bauer, William F. Arndt, and F. Wilber Gingrich, *A Greek-English Lexicon of the New Testament and Other Early Christian Literature* 2d ed. (Chicago, IL: University of Chicago Press, 1979) (or a later edition).

2. Ed. L. Miller, *Questions That Matter: An Invitation to Philosophy* (New York: McGraw-Hill, 1987), 14.

3. Étienne Gilson, *Methodical Realism*, trans. Philip Trower (Front Royal, VA: Christendom, 1990), 129.

4. Regarding the grammar of Colossians 2:8, Greek scholar Henry Alford notes, "The absence of the article before [kenēs] shews the [kai] to be epexegetical, and the same thing to be meant by the two." This suggests the translation "the philosophy that is vain deceit." Alford continues, "This being so, it may be better to give the [tēs] the possessive sense, the better to mark that it is not all philosophy which the Apostle is here blaming." See Henry Alford, *Alford's Greek Testament: An Exegetical and Critical Commentary, Galatians–Philemon*, vol. 3 (Grand Rapids, MI: Guardian Press, 1976), 218.

5. Arthur Samuel Peake concludes, "There is no condemnation of philosophy in itself, but simply of the empty but plausible sham that went by that name at Colossae." See A.S. Peake, "The Epistle to the Colossians" in W. Robertson Nicoll, ed., *The Expositor's Greek Testament, Second Corinthians, Galatians, Ephesians, Philippians, Colossians*, vol. 3 (Grand Rapids, MI: Eerdmans, 1974), 521-522. Peake argues to the above conclusion: "The second noun [deceit] is explanatory of the first, as is shown by the absence of the article and preposition before it and the lack of any indication that Paul had two evils to attack. The meaning is 'his philosophy, which is vain deceit.' The word has, of course, no reference to Greek philosophy, and probably none to the allegorical method of Scripture exegesis that the false teachers may have employed. Philo uses it of the law of Judaism, and Josephus of the three Jewish sects. Here, no doubt, it means just the false teaching that threatened to undermine the faith of the Church."

6. For a treatment of the dangers of philosophy for biblical scholarship, see Norman L. Geisler, "Beware of Philosophy: A Warning to Biblical Scholars," in *Journal of the Evangelical Theological Society* (March 1999): 3-19.

7. C.S. Lewis, "Learning in War-Time," *The Weight of Glory: A Collection of Lewis's Most Moving Addresses* (London, UK: HarperCollins, 2013), 59. Lewis echoes the thinking of Thomas Aquinas, who observed, "But seeing that a teacher of sacred Scripture must at times oppose the philosophers, it is necessary for him to make use of philosophy." See Thomas Aquinas, *Commentary on the* De Trinitate *of Boethius*, Q. 2, art. 3.6, published as *Faith, Reason and Theology: Questions I-IV of His Commentary on the* De Trinitate *of Boethius*, trans. Armand Maurer (Toronto, Canada: Pontifical Institute of Medieval Studies, 1987), 48.

8. For a brief summary (in anticipation of a forthcoming book) of the role that philosophy can play in Christian theology in general and Christian apologetics in particular, see Richard G. Howe, "Defending the Handmaid: How Theology Needs Philosophy" in Terry L. Miethe, ed., *I Am Put Here for the Defense of the Gospel: Dr. Norman L. Geisler: A Festschrift in His Honor* (Eugene, OR: Pickwick, 2016): 233-256.

9. Augustine maintained, "Moreover, if those who are called philosophers, and especially the Platonists, have said aught that is true and in harmony with our faith, we are not only not to shrink from it, but to claim it for our own use from those who have unlawful possession of it." See Augustine, *On Christian Doctrine*, trans. from *Select Library of Nicene and Post-Nicene Fathers*, Book 2, Chap. 40, §60. From http://www9.georgetown.edu/faculty/jod/augustine/ddc2.html (accessed Oct 9, 2017).

In the same vein, John Calvin observed, "Therefore in reading the profane authors, the admirable light of truth displayed in them should remind us, that the human mind, however much fallen and perverted from its original integrity, is still adorned and invested with admirable gifts from its Creator." John Calvin, *Institutes of the Christian Religion*, 2 vols., trans. Henry Beveridge (Grand Rapids: Eerdmans, 1975), 2.2.15, vol. 1, 236. Calvin goes on, "But if the Lord has been pleased to assist us by the works and ministry of the ungodly in physics, dialectics [i.e., the method of philosophy], mathematics, and other similar sciences, let us avail ourselves of it, lest, by neglecting the gifts of God spontaneously offered to us, we be justly punished for our sloth." Calvin, *Institutes*, 2.2.16, vol. 1, 236-237.

The Puritan theologian Francis Turretin observed, "Philosophy...has many and various uses in theology which must be accurately distinguished from its many abuses." Francis Turretin, *Institutes of Elenctic Theology*, First Topic: Theology, Q. XIII, trans. by George Musgrave Giger (Phillipsburg, NJ: Presbyterian & Reformed, 1992), vol. 1,

44. He then claimed "they sin in defect who hold that philosophy is opposed to theology and should therefore be altogether separated from it, not only as useless, but also as positively hurtful." See Turretin, *Institutes*, vol. 1, 44.

To be sure, this view of the place of philosophy in the Christian life and of philosophy's role in doing theology was not the unanimous opinion from the early writers. But these and others are brought forth to disprove the contrary, namely, that no voices recognized a proper role for it. It is no different today. There are those who either give too much or too little place to philosophy. While I acknowledge that philosophy cannot demonstrate every truth of the Christian faith, I do think that it nevertheless is necessary in certain circumstances for much of what apologetics and theology has to say and do.

10. Apologist K. Scott Oliphint from Westminster Theological Seminary said, "What Howe's…apologetic methodology does, therefore, is establish an elite group of academics and intellectuals who alone can protect the rest of us from the challenges and objections that are brought against our faith." K. Scott Oliphint, "Covenantal Response" in *Christian Apologetics Journal* 11, no. 2 (Fall 2013): 50.

11. Finis Jennings Dake, *The Dake Annotated Reference Bible* (Lawrenceville, NJ: Dake Bible Sales, 1991). On page 97 Dake says, "God has a personal spirit body (Dan. 7:9-14; 10:5-19); shape (Jn. 5:37); form (Phil. 2:5-7); image and likeness of a man (Gen. 1:26; 9:6; Ezek. 1:26-28; 1 Cor. 11:7; Jas. 3:9). He has bodily parts such as, back parts (Ex. 33:23), heart (Gen. 6:6; 8:21), hands and fingers (Ps. 8:3-6; Heb. 1:10; Rev. 5:1-7), mouth (Num. 12:8), lips and tongue (Isa. 30:27), feet (Ezek. 1:27; Ex. 24:10), eyes (Ps. 11:4; 18:24; 33:18), ears (Ps. 18:6), hair, head, face, arms (Dan. 7:9-14; 10:5-19; Rev. 5:1-7; 22:4-6), and other bodily parts."

12. There is no doubt that the Bible talks this way about God. But despite Dake's numerous references to Bible verses, I suspect that even he does not believe that God has wings and feathers, as Psalm 91:4 says.

13. After all, Galatians 6:1 says, "Brothers, if anyone is caught in any transgression, you who are spiritual should restore him in a spirit of gentleness. Keep watch on yourself, lest you too be tempted." I know of no one who would argue that Paul was addressing immaterial church leaders to restore the sinner despite the fact that "spiritual" is the adjective form of the noun "spirit."

14. One often hears the expression "Scripture interprets Scripture" sometimes incorrectly labeled as the "analogy of faith." For a brief but helpful discussion of the principle, see Thomas A. Howe, "The Analogy of Faith: Does Scripture Interpret Scripture?" *Christian Research Journal* 29, no. 2 (2006): 50-51. The article is available for downloading at http://www.equip.org/articles/the-analogy-of-faith (accessed October 9, 2017).

15. Note how Paul contrasts the Gentiles in Romans 2 with the Jews in Romans 3:1-2, who received the oracles of God. The contrast shows that these oracles (e.g., the law of Moses) were something the Gentiles had not received.

16. For an excellent read on the classical attributes of God, see James E. Dolezal, *All That Is in God: Evangelical Theology and the Challenge of Classical Christian Theism* (Grand Rapids, MI: Reformation Heritage, 2017).

17. See Thomas Aquinas, *Commentary on the* De Trinitate *of Boethius*, Q. 2, art. 3.6, published as *Faith, Reason and Theology: Questions I-IV of His Commentary on the* De Trinitate *of Boethius*, trans. Armand Maurer (Toronto, Canada: Pontifical Institute of Medieval Studies, 1987), 48.

Chapter 57—What Is Agnosticism, and What Is Its Essential Flaw?

1. Winfried Corduan uses the terms *benign* and *malignant* to make a similar point. Winfried Corduan, *No Doubt About It: The Case for Christianity* (Nashville, TN: Broadman & Holman, 1997), 88.

2. For an interesting read by an admitted agnostic who nevertheless was interested in following where the evidence led, see Robert Jastrow, *God and the Astronomers* (New York: W.W. Norton, 1978). For an account of an atheist who followed the evidence and came to theism, see Antony Flew, *There Is a God: How the World's Most Notorious Atheist Changed His Mind* (New York: HarperOne, 2007).

In contrast, atheist Kai Nielsen, in his debate with J.P. Moreland on the evidence for the resurrection of Jesus during his debate on the existence of God, said he was "not much interested in it." See J.P. Moreland and Kai Nielsen, *Does God Exist? The Great Debate* (Nashville, TN: Thomas Nelson, 1990), 66, republished as *Does God Exist? The Debate between Theists and Atheists* (Amherst, MA: Prometheus, 1993), 66.

3. Examples of philosophers who would be linguistic agnostics include Ludwig Wittgenstein, A.J. Ayer, and Kai Nielsen. They generally regard the subject of God as linguistically meaningless (as opposed to being false). For a

critique of Ayer, see Richard G. Howe, "On the Function of Philosophy," *Christian Apologetics Journal* 7, no. 2 (Fall 2008): 57-82.

4. Examples of philosophers who would deny philosophy's ability to address the question of God's existence include David Hume and Immanuel Kant.

5. The skepticism among the ancient Greeks took several forms. Heraclitus maintained that the nature of reality itself prevented humans from knowing truths about reality. For many of the ancient Greeks, knowledge of a thing was possible only inasmuch as that thing was unchanging. Heraclitus, however, believed that reality was in a constant state of fluctuation, thus knowledge of reality was impossible. Pyrrho maintained that the nature of the human knowing apparatus precluded any possibility of knowledge. The contemporary philosopher Keith Leher opts for skepticism arising from the impossibility of meeting the criteria for knowledge as widely defined in contemporary analytic philosophy as true, justified belief. Since, in Leher's estimation, justification was never possible, then, by definition, knowledge was not possible.

Philosopher Étienne Gilson put his finger on the problem of skepticism. "If metaphysical speculation is a shooting at the moon, philosophers have always begun by shooting at it; only after missing it have they said that there was no moon, and that it was a waste of time to shoot at it. Scepticism [sic] is defeatism in philosophy, and all defeatisms are born of previous defeats. When one has repeatedly failed in a certain undertaking, one naturally concludes that it was an impossible undertaking. I say naturally, but not logically, for a repeated failure in dealing with a given problem may point to a repeated error in discussing the problem rather than to its intrinsic insolubility." See Étienne Gilson, *The Unity of Philosophical Experience* (San Francisco, CA: Ignatius Press, 1999), 309.

6. Thomas Aquinas said, "Sensible things [are that] from which human reason takes the origin of its knowledge." *Summa contra Gentiles*, I, 9, §2., trans. Anton C. Pegis (Notre Dame: University of Notre Dame Press, 1975), I, 77. Elsewhere he said, "Our knowledge, taking its start from things, proceeds in this order. First, it begins in sense; second, it is completed in the intellect." Other comments by Aquinas in this regard include: "Our senses give rise to memories, and from these we obtain experiential knowledge of things, which in turn is the means through which we come to an understanding of the universal principles of sciences and art." *Summa contra Gentiles*, II, 83, §26, trans. James F. Anderson, II, 279. "Our knowledge of principles themselves is derived from sensible things." *Summa contra Gentiles*, II, 83, §32, trans. James F. Anderson, II, 282.

7. Gilson said, "The senses are only the bearers of a message which they are incapable of reading, for only the intellect can decipher it." See Etienne Gilson, *Thomist Realism and the Critique of Knowledge* (San Francisco, CA: Ignatius Press, 1983), 199. While in context Gilson was referring to the act of existing, I believe his point can be extended to other metaphysical aspects of things.

8. Thomas Aquinas, *Truth*, I, 11, trans. Mulligan, 48, in *Truth* (3 vols), vol. 1 trans. Robert W. Mulligan (Chicago, IL: Henry Regnery, 1952); vol. 2 trans. James V. McGlynn (Chicago, IL: Henry Regnery, 1953); vol. 3. trans. Robert W. Schmidt (Chicago, IL: Henry Regnery, 1954). The three volumes were reprinted as *Truth* (Indianapolis, IN: Hackett, 1994).

9. For a deft refutation of scientism, see Edward Feser, *The Last Superstition: A Refutation of the New Atheism* (South Bend, IN: St. Augustine's Press, 2008). Feser demonstrates that the very science that supposedly disproves the existence of God is only possible because certain metaphysical truths that science cannot fail to employ (like universals, natures, causality, teleology), when properly assembled in an argument, give us the cosmological proof of God's existence.

10. Richard Dawkins, *The God Delusion* (Boston, MA: Houghton Mifflin, 2006), 58-59.

11. For an in-depth treatment of classical empiricism in the vein of Thomas Aquinas, see Frederick D. Wilhelmsen, *Man's Knowledge of Reality: An Introduction to Thomistic Epistemology* (Eaglewood Cliffs, NJ: Prentice-Hall, 1956). Other helpful readings include Joseph Owens, *Cognition: An Epistemological Inquiry* (Houston, TX: Center for Thomistic Studies, 1992) and George P. Klubertanz, *Philosophy of Human Nature* (New York: Appleton-Century-Crofts, 1953).

12. Aristotle, *De Anima*, II, 12, 424^{a}17-21.

13. Thomas Aquinas said that "God is absolute form, or rather absolute being." This means the same thing as saying that "God is His own essence," or "His own substance," or "His own being." See *Summa Theologiae*, I, 3, 2-4 and I, 3, 7. The translation is *St. Thomas Aquinas Summa Theologica: Complete English Edition in Five Volumes*, trans.

Fathers of the English Dominican Province (Westminster, MD: Christian Classics, 1981). This being so, strictly speaking, God does not have form that is *conjoined* with His being, as if to say that God's form and God's being were really distinct as they are in creatures. See chapter 12, "What Are the Classical Proofs for God's Existence?"

14. The Westminster Confession of Faith (1646) says, "I. There is but one only living and true God, who is infinite in being and perfection, a most pure spirit, invisible, without body, parts, or passions, immutable, immense, eternal, incomprehensible, almighty, most wise, most holy, most free, most absolute, working all things according to the counsel of his own immutable and most righteous will, for his own glory, most loving, gracious, merciful, long-suffering, abundant in goodness and truth, forgiving iniquity, transgression, and sin; the rewarder of them that diligently seek him; and withal most just and terrible in his judgments; hating all sin; and who will by no means clear the guilty. II. God hath all life, glory, goodness, blessedness, in and of himself; and is alone in and unto himself all-sufficient, not standing in need of any creatures which he hath made, nor deriving any glory from them, but only manifesting his own glory in, by, unto, and upon them; he is the alone foundation of all being, of whom, through whom, and to whom, are all things; and hath most sovereign dominion over them, to do by them, for them, or upon them, whatsoever himself pleaseth. In his sight all things are open and manifest; his knowledge is infinite, infallible, and independent upon the creature; so as nothing is to him contingent or uncertain. He is most holy in all his counsels, in all his works, and in all his commands. To him is due from angels and men, and every other creature, whatsoever worship, service, or obedience he is pleased to require of them."

Chapter 58—What Is Materialism, and What Is Its Essential Flaw?

1. Bertrand Russell, *The Autobiography of Bertrand Russell 1914–44* (New York: Routledge, 1975), 40.

2. John Stuart Mill, *Utilitarianism*, chapter 2, paragraph 6, Gutenberg.org.

Chapter 59—What Is Rationalism, and What Is Its Essential Flaw?

1. *Transcendent* means that the Forms are beyond this world, akin to a heavenly realm. Since they are transcendent, they are not subject to time or space, and thus are eternal. Because they are timeless and spaceless, they cannot change, otherwise known as immutable. Because they are not physical objects, they are intelligible, meaning that they cannot be grasped by the senses but only by the intellect. Being archetypal means that they are the models of every kind of thing that does or could exist. For example, the Form "human" is the model for the individual humans in this realm. Being perfect means that they include absolutely and perfectly all the features of the things of which they are the models. This description of Plato's rationalism is a summary of the treatment in Ed. L. Miller, *Questions that Matter: An Invitation to Philosophy* (New York: McGraw-Hill, 1987), 78-79.

2. A panel discussion between three Christians, each defending a different view of the nature of abstract objects and their relationship to God, can be viewed at https://www.youtube.com/watch?v=eFU1BKxJf1k.

3. For a technical treatment of Thomas Aquinas's view of the nature of mathematics, see Armand Maurer, "Thomists and Thomas Aquinas on the Foundation of Mathematics," *Review of Metaphysics* 47 (Sep 1993): 43-61.

4. For a helpful reading on the various options, see Edward Feser, "Teleology: A Shopper's Guide" *Neo-Scholastic Essays* (South Bend, IN: St. Augustine's Press, 2015), 28-48.

Chapter 60—What Is Scientism, and What Is Its Essential Flaw?

1. John Wellmuth, *The Nature and Origins of Scientism, The Aquinas Lecture, 1944* (Milwaukee, WI: Marquette University Press, 1944), 1-2.

2. James Collins, *A History of Modern European Philosophy* (Milwaukee, WI: Bruce Publishing, 1954), chapter 16.

3. See John Stewart Mill, *The Positive Philosophy of Auguste Comte* (New York: Henry Holt, 1873).

4. See Michael D. Aeschliman, *The Restitution of Man: C.S. Lewis and the Case Against Scientism* (Grand Rapids, MI: Eerdmans, 1983).

5. Herbert Feigl, "Logical Positivism After Thirty-Five Years," *Philosophy Today*, 8, no. 4 (Winter 1964).

6. C.S. Lewis, *Perelandra* (New York: Macmillan, 1965), 81, as quoted in Aeschliman, *The Restitution of Man*, 20.

7. J.P. Moreland and William Lane Craig, *Philosophical Foundations for a Christian Worldview* (Downers Grove, IL: InterVarsity Press, 2003), 346-350.

8. See Nigel Brush, *The Limitations of Scientific Truth* (Grand Rapids, MI: Kregel, 2005).

9. I am indebted to professor J.T. Bridges for this and other insightful observation he provided.

10. Norman L. Geisler and J. Kerby Anderson, *Origin Science: A Proposal for the Creation Evolution Controversy* (Grand Rapids, MI: Baker, 1987).

11. Wellmuth, *The Nature and Origins of Scientism*, 11.

12. List adapted from Moreland, *Philosophical Foundations*, 348, and Norman L. Geisler, *Baker Encyclopedia of Christian Apologetics* (Grand Rapids, MI: Baker, 1999), 66.

13. This is not a naive realism, but moderate realism—see Fredrick D. Wilhelmsen, *Man's Knowledge of Reality: An Introduction to Thomistic Epistemology* (Englewood Cliffs, NJ: Prentice-Hall, 1956).

14. Peter Kreeft, *Socratic Logic* (South Bend, IN: St. Augustine's Press, 2010), section 3.

15. See Etienne Gilson, *The Unity of Philosophical Experience* (San Francisco, CA: Ignatius Press, 1964).

16. Norman L. Geisler, *Christian Apologetics*, 2d ed. (Grand Rapids, MI: Baker Academic, 2013), chapter 15.

Chapter 61—What Is Moral Relativism, and What Is Its Essential Flaw?

1. While moral relativism is arguably the most consistent atheistic position, there are some atheistic defenses of objective morality. For instance, see Erik J. Wielenberg, *Robust Ethics* (New York: Oxford University Press, 2014).

2. C.S. Lewis, *Mere Christianity* (New York: Touchstone, 1960, first published 1943 by Macmillan), 19.

3. Lewis, *Mere Christianity*.

4. See Sean and Josh McDowell, *The Beauty of Intolerance: Setting a Generation Free to Know Truth and Love* (Uhrichsville, OH: Barbour, 2016), 21.

Chapter 62—What Is Postmodernism, and What Is Its Essential Flaw?

1. Jean-Francois Lyotard, *The Postmodern Condition: A Report on Knowledge*, English translation (Minneapolis, MN: University of Minnesota, 1984), xxiv.

2. Marcus Tullius Cicero, *On Divination* (44 BC), Book II, Chapter LVIII, Section 119.

Chapter 63—What Is Atheism, and What Is Its Essential Flaw?

1. See early church father Justin Martyr (ca. 100–165), who wrote, "Hence are we called atheists. And we confess that we are atheists, so far as gods of this sort are concerned, but not with respect to the most true God." Martyr, "The First Apology," in Philip Schaff, *The Apostolic Fathers with Justyn Martyr and Irenaeus* (Edinburgh: T&T Clark, n.d.). Available online at http://www.ccel.org/ccel/schaff/anf01.

2. James Collins, *God in Modern Philosophy* (London, UK: Routledge, 1960), 239.

3. Professor of sociology and secular studies at Pitzer College Phil Zuckerman observes that "irreligion is on the rise throughout Europe, Australia, New Zealand, Canada, and the USA—in some countries, dramatically so—and also in Japan. It is also growing slowly in parts of South America. However, religion is rising in many former USSR states, and it is rising in poor countries with high birth rates, such as Africa and many Muslim-majority societies. China remains a huge question mark." Personal e-mail correspondence, June 23, 2017. Used with permission.

4. Lois Lee and Stephen Bullivant, *A Dictionary of Atheism* (New York: Oxford University Press), Kindle edition.

5. Plato, *Theætetus*, 201c-d.

6. This analogy is like the parable of the wise and foolish builders whom Jesus speaks about in Matthew 7:24-27. The strong foundation is "the rock" of Jesus Christ and His Word (verse 24), while the weak foundation is "the sand" (verse 26). Jesus calls the person who builds their life upon the sand (i.e., anything other than Jesus Christ and His Word) a "foolish" builder, echoing back to the "fool" of Psalm 14:1 and Psalm 53:1 who "says in his heart, 'There is no God.'"

7. Austin Farrer, *A Science of God* (London: Geoffrey Bles, 1966), 33-34.

8. Richard Dawkins, *The God Delusion* (London, UK: Penguin Random House, 2016), 54.

9. In a televised discussion between Bishop Rowan Williams and Richard Dawkins at the Sheldonian Theatre,

Oxford University, Dawkins identified himself as a "six" on his seven-point scale of belief laid out in his book *The God Delusion* (where 1 is strong agreement and 7 is strong disagreement to the proposition of God's existence). In response, moderator Sir Anthony Kenny asked, "Why don't you call yourself an agnostic?" to which Dawkins replied "I do." Kenny: "You are described as the world's most famous atheist." Dawkins: "Not by me. Not by me." Shortly thereafter, Dawkins clarified, "I'm a 6.9." Richard Dawkins, "Dialogue with Richard Dawkins, Rowan Williams and Anthony Kenny," filmed 23 February, 2012, YouTube video, from 1:11:40. https://www.youtube.com/watch?v=bow4nnh1Wv0 (accessed August 16, 2017).

10. Antony Flew, "The Presumption of Atheism," *A Companion to Philosophy of Religion,* eds. Philip Quinn and Charles Taliaferro (Oxford, UK: Blackwell, 1997), 451.

11. C.S. Lewis in *C.S. Lewis Essay Collection and Other Short Pieces*, ed. Lesley Walmsley (London, UK: HarperCollins, 2000), Kindle edition.

12. G.K. Chesterton, "Where All Roads Lead," *The Collected Works of G.K. Chesterton*, vol. 3, eds. George J. Marlin, Richard P. Rabatin, and John L. Swan (San Francisco, CA: Ignatius Press, 1990), 38.

13. Protagoras, *DK* 80B1.

14. A qualification is needed here. Atheism, as defined by Lee and Bullivant, comes in many different forms. What I am considering here is naturalistic atheism, the type of atheism that seems most prevalent today. But while all naturalists are atheists, not all atheists are necessarily naturalists. Stephen Jay Gould, for example, is at pains to qualitatively distinguish between the scientific and religious modes of thinking as being relative to two separate dimensions of reality or "Non-Overlapping Magisteria" (NOMA) in his book *Rocks of Ages: Science and Religion in the Fullness of Life*. But even then, at best, Gould's atheism is treading on the toes of deism, similar to an Antony Flew or Albert Einstein.

15. Chesterton, *Orthodoxy* (Mineola, NY: Dover, 2012), 144.

16. I accept that one could very well turn this argument around and charge Christianity as being a circular commitment to the *belief in* God. For those familiar with the ontological proof for God's existence put forward by Anselm of Canterbury (ca. 1033–1109), this may indeed appear to be just another supporting argument to that proof. However, unlike Anselm, my intention is not to offer a proof for God's existence. Nor am I concerned with the notion of God as an unfounded *a priori* idea in the human mind. To the contrary, it seems that the notion of God is *a posteriori* in that human beings, "made in the image of God" (Genesis 1:26), have been endowed with cognitive faculties capable of abstracting the notion of God as an empirical fact from nature. We come to an awareness of this notion via means of general revelation (see Psalm 19:1-6; Romans 1:18-20; 2:14-15), and with the complement of scriptural revelation, receive (salvific) clarity by which we can make a *positive case* for the existence of God (something which atheism cannot do for its own belief).

17. John Lennox, "Intellectually Fulfilling Faith: Lessons from C.S. Lewis," *Broadcast Talks*, vol. 1 no. 3, 2016. Available online at http://www.cslewisinstitute.org.

18. Dawkins, *The God Delusion*, 76.

19. Dawkins, *The God Delusion*, 188.

20. Exodus 20:3-5 describes an idol as an image made by human hands, which is precisely what atheism constructs when it reduces God into an object of human knowledge.

21. See Romans 1:18-32 for examples.

22. Étienne Gilson, "The Idea of God and the Difficulties of Atheism," *The Great Ideas Today: 1969*, eds. Robert M. Hutchins & Mortimer J. Adler (Chicago, IL: Encyclopedia Britannica, 1969): 201. Available online at https://philpapers.org/rec/GILTIO-13. I am indebted to Gilson for this excellent work, which, owing to my unreserved agreement, has shaped much of the thought in this chapter.

23. In the original Greek text of John 1:14, "Word" is *logos*. While the semantic range of *logos* is wide and varied, it connotes elements of reason, intelligence, and logic. Amongst other things, therefore, John is declaring the embodiment of divine reason within the mortal "flesh" (verse 14) of the God-man, "Jesus Christ" (verse 17).

24. Gilson, "The Idea of God and the Difficulties of Atheism," 174-205.

Chapter 64—What Is Pantheism, and What Is Its Essential Flaw?

1. James Sire, *The Universe Next Door* (Downers Grove, IL: InterVarsity Press, 1988), 140.

2. Norman L. Geisler, "Pantheism," *Baker Encyclopedia of Christian Apologetics* (Grand Rapids, MI: Baker, 1999), 580.

3. Stephan Schumaker and Gert Woerner, eds., *The Rider Encyclopedia of Eastern Philosophy and Religion* (Boston, MA: Shambala Publications, 1994), 44.

4. Shyam Shukla, *The Upanishads* (Fremont, CA: Asian Humanities Press, 1999), 58.

5. Shukla, *The Upanishads*, 2.

6. Schumaker and Woerner, eds., *The Rider Encyclopedia of Eastern Philosophy and Religion,* 22.

7. Shukla, *The Upanishads*, xiii.

8. Norman L. Geisler and William D. Watkins, *Worlds Apart: A Handbook on World Views*, 2d ed. (Grand Rapids, MI: Baker, 1989), 100.

9. Geisler and Watkins, *Worlds Apart*, 102.

10. Swami Vivekananda, quoted in Abdu Murray, *Grand Central Question* (Downers Grove, IL: InterVarsity Press, 2014), 144.

11. Norman L. Geisler, "Pantheism," *Baker Encyclopedia of Christian Apologetics*, 582.

12. William Lane Craig, *On Guard* (Colorado Springs, CO: David C. Cook, 2010), 74.

Chapter 65—What Is Monism, and What Is Its Essential Flaw?

1. "Monism," *New Dictionary of the History of Ideas* (Farmington Hills, MI: Gale Group, 2005). Accessed at http://www.encyclopedia.com/philosophy-and-religion/philosophy/philosophy-terms-and-concepts/monism.

2. Norman L. Geisler, *Christian Apologetics* (Grand Rapids, MI: Baker, 2013), elec. ed.

3. John W. Cook, *Body, Soul, and Life Everlasting: Biblical Anthropology and the Monism-Dualism Debate* (Grand Rapids, MI: Eerdmans, 1989), 18.

4. "Monism," *New World Encyclopedia*, http://www.newworldencyclopedia.org/entry/Monism (accessed Sep 17, 2017).

5. William Lane Craig, "Doctrine of Man (Part 7)," *Reasonable Faith*, http://www.reasonablefaith.org/defenders-2-podcast/transcript/s10-07#ixzz4sTnAmuMt.

6. Matt Slick, "What Is Monism?" *CARM*, August 19, 2009, https://carm.org/what-is-monism.

Chapter 66—What Is Panentheism, and What Is Its Essential Flaw?

1. Hegel is often labeled pantheist when panentheist is more accurate. Spinoza, whose writings influenced Schelling, Hegel, and countless other panentheists and pantheists alike, is normally classified as a pantheist. However, based on a few of his writings, a case can be made that he may have occasionally thought as a panentheist.

2. Loriliai Biernacki and Philip Clayton, eds., *Panentheism Across the World's Traditions* (New York: Oxford University Press, 2013).

3. James W. Cooper, *Panentheism: The Other God of the Philosophers* (Grand Rapids, MI: Baker Academic, 2006), 32-38.

4. James Cooper's *Panentheism* provides the most extensive overview of philosophic influences upon panentheism. Geisler provides a more intensive effort in explaining process thought, one of the more prominent forms of panentheism. Norman L. Geisler, *The History of Western Philosophy: Modern and Post-Modern*, vol. 2 (Matthews, NC: Bastion Books, 2012), 404-435. Although he does not distinguish between pantheism and panentheism, Herrick provides a very helpful historical survey. James A. Herrick, *The Making of the New Spirituality: The Eclipse of Western Religious Tradition* (Downers Grove, IL: InterVarsity Press, 2003).

5. Alfred North Whitehead, *Process and Reality* (New York: Free Press, 1978), 39.

6. Most of these distinctions are taken from J. Cooper, *Panentheism*, 27-30, and Niels Henrick Gregersen, "Three Varieties of Panentheism," *In Whom We Live and Move and Have Our Being*, eds. Philip Clayton and Arthur Peacocke (Grand Rapids, MI: Eerdmans, 2004), 21.

7. Griffin posits, "[M]ost of the problems of Christian theology, I have emphasized, have been due to, or at least aggravated by the doctrine of creation *ex nihilo*, which was introduced at the end of the second Christian century." David Griffin, *Two Great Truths* (Louisville, KY: Westminster John Knox Press, 2004), 83. The term creation *ex nihilo* (out of nothing) may have been coined in the second century, but the underlying concept is implied in many passages in books of the Bible that date back many centuries prior.

8. Albert Einstein, a believer in the nonpersonal "God" of Spinoza, asserted, "The main source of the present-day conflicts between the spheres of religion and science lies in the concept of a personal God." Philipp Frank, *Einstein: His Life and Times* (Boston, MA: Da Capo Press, 2002), 285-286.

9. John B. Cobb, Jr., *A Christian Natural Theology* (Louisville, KY: Westminster John Knox Press, 2007), 119-120, 167, 188.

10. A survey of a few of the titles and subtitles of panentheistic books from the early twenty-first century show the importance of this fusion to the movement: *Two Great Truths: A New Synthesis of Scientific Naturalism and Christian Faith; Panentheism and Scientific Naturalism: Rethinking Evil, Morality, Religious Experience, Religious Pluralism, and the Academic Study of Religion; All That Is: A Naturalistic Faith for the Twenty-First Century; Theology for a Scientific Age: Being and Becoming-Natural, Divine and Human; Paths from Science Towards God: The End of All Our Exploring; The Cyclic God Hypothesis: Why and How God Experiences the Universe Through You: A Brief Introduction to General and Special Scientific Panentheism; When Science Meets Religion: Enemies, Strangers, or Partners?*

11. Whitehead argued that "traditional theism, by regarding God as having created the world out of absolute nothingness, left no alternative except to discern in [God] the origin of all evil as well as of all good." Griffin, *Two Great Truths*, 88. One possible answer to this objection is that evil is a privation of something good rather than a created thing. God created the conditions where evil became possible, but did not create evil itself.

12. It is important to clarify which of the three senses the Hebrew concept of "heaven" is in focus here. First, heaven may refer to the sky immediately above us, where birds fly and clouds float—the troposphere. Second, it may refer to the larger area where the moon, planets, and stars can be found—the "outer space" beyond the earth's atmosphere. Third, it may be a place entirely outside of our universe. This third sense is the one I am using here. In 2 Corinthians 12:2, Paul refers to the realm where God lives as "the third heaven." This corresponds with the third sense. Similarly, Solomon gave no room for a panentheistic view of the world when he prayed, "But will God indeed dwell with man on the earth? Behold, *heaven and the highest heaven* cannot contain you, how much less this house [temple] I have built…for your name, then hear from heaven *your dwelling place* their prayer and their pleas" (2 Chronicles 6:18,38-39, emphasis added). Although God is fully able to reach into our universe and can even manifest Himself in some localized way at any time He chooses, He does not, contrary to the panentheistic models, dwell inside of our universe.

13. See Elenore Stump, *The God of the Bible and the God of the Philosophers* (Milwaukee, WI: Marquette University Press, 2016).

14. Gilson, for example, says, "There is a great deal of Neoplatonism in Augustine, but there is a point, and it is a decisive one, at which he parts company with Plotinus: there is nothing above God in the Christian world of Augustine, and, since God is being, there is nothing above being…he parted from Plotinus on this fundamental principle of the primacy of Being." Etienne Gilson, *Being and Some Philosophers* (Toronto, Canada: Pontifical Institute of Mediaeval Studies, 1952), 31.

15. Cooper summarizes, "Most contemporary alternatives to classical theism are branches of a single family tree with roots in Plato and Neoplatonism. Broadly speaking, this is the ancient tradition of panentheism…it is not, however, possible simply to equate Neoplatonism and panentheism…" Cooper, *Panentheism*, 17-19.

16. Cobb, *A Christian Natural Theology*, 104. Cobb points out that these "antitheses" which Whitehead is famous for are not in violation of the law of noncontradiction because God has two "natures" and therefore these propositions are true in slightly different ways.

17. That this god that is constantly being recreated every moment was made clear in a public debate between classical theist Norm Geisler and process panentheist John Cobb ("Process Theism versus Classical Theism," April 1988, http://normangeisler.com/listen). Like Whitehead, his god has an infinite pole beyond the world and a finite pole in the world. It is easier to imagine their view as two separate gods—one great, unchanging, uncreated, and infinite god in the metaphysical world, and a lesser, changing, created, dying, recreated, temporal god inside our physical world. But then the two have to be cobbled back together into one internally inconsistent and impossible god.

18. Panentheists generally assume that the five ways Thomas Aquinas used to argue logically for the existence of God were discredited by modern philosophers like Hume and Kant. Feser, however, argues that they did not understand Aquinas properly and only succeeded in knocking over straw men. Edward Feser, *Aquinas: A Beginner's Guide* (London, UK: OneWorld, 2009), 8-9; Edward Feser, "Taking Aquinas Seriously," *First Things*, June 30, 2017, https://www.firstthings.com/web-exclusives/2017/06/taking-aquinas-seriously; Edward Feser, *Five Proofs for the Existence of God* (San Francisco, CA: Ignatius Press, 2017).

19. Cooper, *Panentheism*, 339.

20. Cooper, *Panentheism*, 138.

21. Cobb, *A Christian Natural Theology*, 104-105.

22. Cobb, *A Christian Natural Theology*, 106-107.

Chapter 67—Who Was Justin Martyr?

1. Harry Y. Gamble, "Apologetics," *Encyclopedia of Early Christianity*, ed. Everett Ferguson, 2d ed. (New York: Garland Publishing, 1998), 81-86.

2. Gamble, "Apologetics," 82.

3. Gamble, "Apologetics," 84.

4. Justin Martyr is identified as "St. Justin the Philosopher, M" in Rev. Alban Butler, *The Lives of the Saints* (New York: Catholic Way Publishing, 2015, republished edition of New York: P.J. Kenny, 1903).

5. *The First Apology of Justin, the Martyr*, 242, https://www.ccel.org/ccel/richardson/fathers.x.ii.iii.html.

6. J.N.D. Kelly, *Early Christian Creeds*, 3d ed. (London, UK: Continuum, reprint of Longman Group Limited, 1972), *passim*, and most modern publications use the title *Dialogue with Trypho the Jew*, although the title used in the text is as it appears in Saint Justin Martyr, *Saint Justin Martyr Collection* (New York: Aeterna Press, 2016), Kindle edition.

7. Saint Justin Martyr, *Saint Justin Martyr Collection, Dialogue* (ch. 2-8). Also see Philip Schaff, ed., *The Apostolic Fathers with Justin Martyr and Irenaeus* (Grand Rapids, MI: Eerdmans, rep. 2001). Also see Kirsopp Lake, trans., *Eusebius: The Ecclesiastical History, with an English Translation* (London: William Heinemann, 1926), Book IV.4-5, vol. 1, 322-323.

8. Everett Ferguson, *Church History: From Christ to Pre-Reformation, the Rise and Growth of the Church in Its Cultural, Intellectual, and Political Context*, vol. 1 (Grand Rapids, MI: Zondervan, 2005), 75.

9. Lake, *Eusebius: The Ecclesiastical History*, Book IV.4-5, vol. 1, 322-323.

10. Ferguson, *Church History*, 73.

11. Saint Justin Martyr. *Saint Justin Martyr Collection*, "Chapter I, Introduction," where the Jew's name is revealed as Trypho. See also Philip Schaff, *The Apostolic Fathers*, Saint Justin Martyr, *Saint Justin Martyr Collection*, and Justin Martyr, *Dialogue with Trypho* (The Fig Classic Series, elec. ed., 2012).

12. Ferguson, *Church History*, 76.

13. Lake, *Eusebius: The Ecclesiastical History*, Book IV.11.1-11, vol. 1, 330-331.

14. Kelly, *Early Christian Creeds*, 43.

15. B.L. Gildersleve provides background information in his "Preface to the Apologies of Justin Martyr" in Saint Justin Martyr, *Saint Justin Martyr Collection*, Justin, *Apology I*, XXVI.8; discusses Marcion's heresy in *Apology I*, Chapter 58. Also see Lake, *Eusebius: The Ecclesiastical History*, Book IV.11.1-11, vol. 1, 330-331.

16. Irenaeus, *Against Heresies*, Book I, XXVIII, in the American edition of *The Apostolic Fathers: The Apostolic Fathers, Justin Martyr, Irenaeus*, vol. 1 (Buffalo, NY: Christian Literature Publishing, 1885; republication by Varitatis Splendor Publications, 2012). Also see Lake, *Eusebius: The Ecclesiastical History*, IV,11.8-10, vol. 1, 396-397.

17. *Apol.* I.1 is addressed "To the Emperor, Titus Ælius Adrianus Antoninus Pius Caesar [138-161], Verisimus the philosopher, and to Lucius the philosopher, the natural son of Caesar, and the adopted son of Pius, a lover of learning, and to the Senate, with the whole people of the Romans. For an extensive list of Justin's writings see Lake, *Eusebius: The Ecclesiastical History*, IV.18.1-10, vol. 1, 368-373.

18. Justin Martyr, "Introduction to *Justin's Dialogue with a Jew*" in Saint Justin Martyr, *Saint Justin Martyr Collection*.

This treatise is also seen in Lake, *Eusebius: The Ecclesiastical History*, Book IV.11.1-11, vol. 1, 330-331. The identification *Dialogue of Trypho* or *Dialogue of Trypho the Jew* is commonplace as in the eBook edition of Justin Martyr, *Dialogue with Trypho* (The Fig Classic Series, elec. ed., 2012).

19. See, for example, Justin's *Dialogue with a Jew*, Chapters XCVIII–CVI, an exposition of Psalm 22.

20. J.N.D. Kelly, *Early Christian Doctrines*, rev. ed. (Peabody, MA: Prince Press, reprint of New York: HarperCollins, 1976), 465.

21. Lake, *Eusebius: The Ecclesiastical History*, vol. 1, 394-397.

22. Irenaeus, *Against Heresies*, Book I, XXVIII. See aso Lake, *Eusebius: The Ecclesiastical History*, vol. 1, 396-397.

23. Clement of Rome, *The First Epistle of Clement to the Corinthians*, LVIII, Rev. John Kieth, D.D., *The Epistles of Clement*, reprinted from the translation given in the first volume of *The Ante-Nicene Fathers*. Completed and revised from a manuscript discovered after the publication of that volume as cited in *The Church Fathers: The Complete Ante-Nicene and Nicene and Post-Nicene Church Fathers Collection* (London, UK: Catholic Way Publishing, 2015) Kindle ed.

24. Athenagoras, *A Plea for the Christians* in *Fathers of the Second Century: Hermas, Tatian, Athenagoras, Theophilus, and Clement of Alexandria*, eds. A. Roberts, J. Donaldson, and A.C. Coxe; trans. B.P. Pratten, vol. 2 (Buffalo, NY: Christian Literature Company, 1885), 140-148. *On the Resurrection of the Dead* in *Fathers of the Second Century: Hermas, Tatian, Athenagoras, Theophilus, and Clement of Alexandria*, eds. A. Roberts, J. Donaldson, and A.C. Coxe; trans. B.P. Pratten, vol. 2 (Buffalo, NY: Christian Literature Company, 1885), 149-162.

25. Hendrick F. Stander, "Athenagoras (latter half of second century)" *Encyclopedia*, ed. Ferguson, 140-141.

26. Athenagoras, *A Plea for Christians*, chapter 10.

27. Frederick W. Norris, "Theophilus of Antioch (second century)" in *Encyclopedia*, ed. Ferguson, 1122. Also see William E. Nix, "Historical Theology: Period I, Notes" (Santa Ana, CA: Veritas International University, 2009).

28. θεός, Λόγος and Σοφία. By Σοφία, like Irenæus, he means the Holy Spirit.

29. Kelly, *Doctrines*, 95.

30. Kelly, *Doctrines*.

31. Kelly, *Doctrines*, 96.

32. Kelly, *Doctrines*, 98.

33. Kelly, *Doctrines*, 96.

34. Justin, *Dialogue with a Jew* (*Dial.* 56; 60) (*Dial.* 62) (*Dial.* 129). See Kelly, *Early Christian Doctrines*, 96-97. Also see Ferguson, *Church History*, 78, for a schematized rendering of their thought as reflecting five stages in the Apologists' career of the *Logos*.

35. Justin, *Dialogue with a Jew*, especially chapters 71-87.

36. Ferguson, *Church History*, 75.

37. Justin, in *Apol.* I.6.2; *Apol.* I.65.3; *Apol.* I.67.2; and the longest and most elaborate comes in *Apol.* I.13. Kelly, *Early Christian Creeds*, 71.

38. Justin, *First Apology*, 61-67 begins the conclusion of the Apology and provides the locus classicus concerning baptism, eucharist, and meetings of Christians. See also Charles Belmonte's statement in *First Apology* (Manila, Philippines: Studium Theologiae Foundation, 2006), 458-459.

39. Kelly, *Early Christian Creeds*, 72-73.

40. Justin *Apol.* I, 21, 1; *Apol.* I, 31, 7; *Apol.* I, 42, 4; *Apol.* I, 46, 5. Throughout the *Dialogue with a Jew*, *Dial.* 63.1; *Dial.* 85.2; *Dial.* 126.1 *Dial.* 132, Justin refers to the Gospels, frequently calling them the "memoirs" of the apostles. See above note 15. Also see Kelly, *Early Christian Creeds*, 73-75.

41. Ferguson, *Church History*, 75.

42. Justin, *Saint Justin Martyr Collection*.

43. Lake, *Eusebius: The Ecclesiastical History*, Book IV.16.1, vol. 1, 358-361. Extended treatment of Justin's end is

provided by Basil L. Gildersleve. He has an extended analysis of Justin's martyrdom and influence in "Introduction and Notes" of Saint Justin Martyr, *Saint Justin Martyr Collection*.

44. M. Dods, trans., "The Martyrdom of the Holy Martyrs, Justin, Chariton, Charites, Pæon, and Liberianus, Who Suffered at Rome," eds. A. Roberts, J. Donaldson, and A.C. Coxe; trans. M. Dods, *The Apostolic Fathers with Justin Martyr and Irenaeus*, vol. 1 (Buffalo, NY: Christian Literature Company, 1885), 305-306.

Chapter 68—Who Was Augustine?

1. Everett Ferguson, *Church History: From Christ to the Pre-Reformation: The Rise and Growth of the Church in Its Cultural, Intellectual, and Political Context*, vol. 1 (Grand Rapids, MI: Zondervan, 2005), 212.

2. Reverend Alban Butler, "St. Augustine, Bishop, C," *The Lives of the Saints* (New York: P.J. Kenedy, 1903; republished Catholic Way Publishing, Kindle ed., 2015). Butler's subtitle reads, "And Doctor of the Church."

3. Ferguson, *Church History*, 269.

4. Ferguson, *Church History*.

5. Ferguson, *Church History*, 270 (emphasis added). This Victorinus was "by birth an African," according to E.B. Pusey, *Confessions of Saint Augustine*, Book VIII, Chapter II (trans. and annotated by J.G. Pilkington, 1892). *The Confessions of Saint Augustine; The Complete Works of Saint Augustine: The Confessions, On Grace and Free Will; The City of God; On Christian Doctrine; Expositions on the Book of Psalms...* (50 books with active table of contents, Kindle ed.). Also see Philip Schaff, ed., *The Church Fathers: The Complete Ante-Nicene & Nicene and Post-Nicene Church Fathers Collection*, Kindle ed., 2014.

6. Ferguson, *Church History*, 270.

7. Ferguson, *Church History*.

8. For Augustine's conversion, see Augustine, *Confessions of Saint Augustine*, Book VIII, Chapter XIII (trans. and annotated by J.G. Pilkington, 1892). For Augustine's separation from his mistress and decision on a celibate life, see Peter Brown, *Augustine of Hippo: A Biography* (Berkeley, CA: University of California Press, 1970), 63.

9. Augustine, *Rule of Saint Augustine,* trans. Robert Russell, O.S.A., is based on the critical text of Luc Verheijen, O.S.A. (La regle de saint Augustin, Etudes Augustiniennes, Paris, 1967). Two sentences not contained in the critical text have been included to conform with the official text published with the Constitutiones Ordinis Fratrum S. Augustini (Rome, Italy: 1968; reprinted by Brothers of the Order of Hermits of Saint Augustine, 1976). See also Philip Schaff, ed., *The Church Fathers*.

10. Ferguson, *Church History*, 271, states, "One authority cites 113 books and treatises by Augustine, close to 250 letters (some are equal in length to treatises), and more than 500 sermons."

11. Williston Walker, Richard A. Norris, David W. Lotz, and Robert T. Handy, *A History of the Christian Church*, 4th ed. (New York: Charles Scribner's Sons, 1985), 200-201.

12. Augustine, *Confessions of Saint Augustine*, I.I. See also Philip Schaff, ed., *The Church Fathers*.

13. This observation is expanded in Ferguson, *Church History*, 268-269.

14. Walker, *History*, 201.

15. Ferguson, *Church History*, 272.

16. Ferguson, *Church History*, 272-273.

17. Ferguson, *Church History*, 273.

18. Ferguson, *Church History*, 273-274. Saint Augustine, *On the Holy Trinity*, trans. Rev. Arthur West Haddan, revised and annotated with an introductory essay by William G.T. Shedd (New York: Christian Literature Company, 1887).

19. See Walter H. Principe, C.S.B., "Filioque," in Everett Ferguson, *Encyclopedia of Early Christianity* (New York: Garland Publishing, 1990), 426-429.

20. F.L. Cross and E.A. Livingstone, eds., s.v. "Augustine, St., of Hippo (354–430)," *The Oxford Dictionary of the Christian Church*, 2d ed. (New York: Oxford University Press, 1974, 1978), 109.

21. Cross, s.v. "Manes (or Mani) and Manichæism," *Oxford Dictionary of the Christian Church*, 864.

22. Cross, *Oxford Dictionary of the Christian Church*, 864-865.

23. Cross, *Oxford Dictionary of the Christian Church*. Augustine, *The Complete Works of Saint Augustine*. See also Philip Schaff, ed., *The Church Fathers*.

24. Ferguson, *Church History*, 269.

25. Butler, "St. Augustine, Bishop, C," *The Lives of the Saints*. Butler's endnote 3086 has an extensive discussion of Augustine's relationship and interaction with Manicheism as well as a thorough evaluation of the teachings of Mani and his followers.

26. Cross, s.v. "Augustine," *Oxford Dictionary of the Christian Church*, 108.

27. See Robert J. Daly, S.J., "Origen," in Ferguson, ed., *Encyclopedia of Early Cristianity*, 836; also see J. Patout Burns, "Traducianism," in Ferguson, ed., *Encyclopedia of Early Christianity*, 1141.

28. Burns, "Traducianism," 1141. Burns cites Augustine, *The Literal Meaning of Genesis* 10, letters 166 and 190, and *On the Nature and Origin of the Soul*.

29. Ferguson, *Church History*, 188.

30. J.N.D. Kelly, *Early Christian Doctrines* (Peabody, MA: Hendrickson reprint of HarperCollins, 1978), discussion follows Kelly, 410-411.

31. Cross, s.v. "Augustine," *Oxford Dictionary of the Christian Church*, 109.

32. Margaret R. Miles, s.v. "Augustine (354–430)," in Ferguson, ed., *Encyclopedia of Early Christianity*, 148-154.

33. Cross, s.v. "Donatism," *Oxford Dictionary of the Christian Church*, 419.

34. Cross, *Oxford Dictionary of the Christian Church*. Called circumcelliones by Catholics, they called themselves Agonistici, "soldiers (of Christ)."

35. Kelly, *Early Christian Doctrines*, 411-412.

36. Augustine, *Retractiones*, Book II. XVIII, in Augustine, *The Complete Works of Saint Augustine*. See also Philip Schaff, ed., *The Church Fathers*. See also Cross, s.v. "Augustine," *Oxford Dictionary of the Christian Church*, 109.

37. Kelly, *Early Christian Doctrines*, 412.

38. Walker, *Church History*, 206. Also see Cross, s.v. "Pelagianism," *Oxford Dictionary of the Christian Church*, 1058-1059, and "Augustine," 109. The following discussion is drawn from these sources.

39. Ferguson, *Church History*, 279.

40. Ferguson, *Church History*, 280.

41. Ferguson, *Church History*, 206.

42. Ferguson, *Church History*, 207.

43. Ferguson, *Church History*.

44. Ferguson, *Church History*, 279.

45. Augustine, "Anti-Pelagian Writings," *The Complete Works of Saint Augustine*. See also Philip Schaff, ed., *The Church Fathers*.

46. Ferguson, *Church History*, 277.

47. *Ferguson, Church History*, 279.

48. Walker, *Church History*, 207-208, where he cites Romans 5:5, and On the Spirit and the Letter, 5.

49. Walker, *Church History*, 209.

50. Walker, *Church History*.

Chapter 70—Who Was Thomas Aquinas?

1. Thomas Aquinas, *Summa Theologica*, 2a2ae. 173, 3, ad1.

2. Aquinas, *Summa Theologica*, 1a.1, 2, ad2.

3. Aquinas, *Summa Theologica*, 1a.1, 10, ad3.

4. Aquinas, *Summa Theologica*, 2a2ae. 1, 9.

5. Thomas Aquinas, *On Truth*, 10, 2.

6. Aquinas, *Summa Theologica*, 2a2ae. 2, 4.

7. Thomas Aquinas, *Summa contra Gentiles*, 1.4, 3–5.

8. Aquinas, *Summa Theologica*, 2a2ae. 2, 10.

9. Aquinas, *Summa contra Gentiles*, 1.3, 2.

10. Aquinas, *On the Soul*, 3.4.; *Summa Theologica*, 1a2ae. 17, 7.

11. First principles are known by way of inclination before they are known by cognition; *Summa Theologica*, 1a. 17, 3, ad2.

12. Metaphysics, then, is the study of the real as real or being, insofar as it is being.

13. See Aquinas, *On Being and Essence*. Aristotle had distinguished between actuality and potentiality but applied this only to things composed of form and matter, not to the order of being. Aquinas took Aristotle's distinction between act and potency and applied it to form (being).

14. Hence, the central premise of the Thomistic view of reality is that actuality in the order in which it is actuality is unlimited and unique, unless it is conjoined with passive potency.

15. Aquinas, *Summa Theologica*, 1a, 2, 3.

16. Aquinas, *Summa Theologica*, 1a. 3; 1a. 7-11. Besides these metaphysical attributes, God is also morally perfect and infinitely wise—*Summa Theologica*, 1a. 4, 5.

17. Without analogy, there appears to be no way to avoid the sheer equivocation of skepticism or the linguistic idolatry of a univocal one-to-one correspondence between our finite ideas and the infinite mind of God. The middle road of analogy still appears to be the best option.

18. Aquinas, *Summa contra Gentiles*, I, 29-34; *Summa Theologica*, 1a. 13.

19. Aquinas, *Summa Theologica*, 1a. 44-46.

20. The human soul is the formal cause, while the body is the material cause of a human being. God, of course, is the efficient cause (source). Parents are only the instrumental cause (instrument) of the body. The final cause (purpose) is to glorify God, who created us.

21. Aquinas, *Summa Theologica*, 1a. 75-76.

22. Aquinas, *Summa Theologica*, 1a. 90-93.

23. Aquinas, *Summa Theologica*, 1a. 2, 3, ad 1.

24. Aquinas, *Summa Theologica*, 1a. 82, 1.

25. Aquinas, *Summa Theologica*, 1a. 19, 10, ad 3.

26. Aquinas, *Summa Theologica*, 1a. 48, 3.

27. Aquinas, *Summa Theologica*, 1a.49, 2.

28. Aquinas, *Summa Theologica*, 1a2ae. 91.

29. Aquinas, *Summa Theologica*, 1a. 60-61.

30. For more on Aquinas, see Norman L. Geisler, *Should Old Aquinas Be Forgotten?* 2d ed. (Matthews, NC: Bastion Books, 2013).

Chapter 71—Who Was Blaise Pascal?

1. Blaise Pascal, *Pensées*, trans. A.J. Krailsheimer (London, UK: Penguin Books, 1966), 12. All references will use the numbering system within the original manuscript rather than the page number so that you can refer to any translation of this work.

2. Pascal, *Pensées*, 200.

3. Pascal, *Pensées*, 131.

4. Pascal, *Pensées*, 188.

5. Pascal, *Pensées*, 423.

6. Pascal, *Pensées*, 547.

7. Pascal, *Pensées*, 424.

8. Pascal, *Pensées*, 322.

9. Pascal, *Pensées*, 427.

Chapter 72—Who Was William Paley?

1. Abridged edition by F. Ferré, *Natural Theology or Evidences of the Existence and Attributes of the Deity* (Indianapolis, IN: Bobbs-Merrill, 1963).

2. Terry L. Miethe, *The Compact Dictionary of Doctrinal Words* (Minneapolis, MN: Bethany House, 1988), 202.

Chapter 73—Who Was C.S. Lewis?

1. C.S. Lewis, *God in the Dock* (Grand Rapids, MI: Eerdmans, 1970), 98.

2. C.S. Lewis, *Christian Reflections* (Grand Rapids, MI: Eerdmans, 1967), 75.

3. C.S. Lewis, *Mere Christianity* (New York: Macmillan, 1952), 69.

4. C.S. Lewis, *The Voyage of the Dawn Treader* (New York: Macmillan, 1952), 180.

5. C.S. Lewis, *Miracles* (New York: Macmillan, 1947), 135.

6. Lewis, *Mere Christianity*, 123.

7. Lewis, *Mere Christianity*, 60.

8. Lewis, *Miracles*, 143.

9. Quoted in Clyde Kilby, *A Mind Awake* (New York: Harcourt Brace Jovanovich, 1968), 23.

10. Lewis, *Mere Christianity*, 120.

Chapter 74—Who Was Cornelius Van Til?

1. Timothy I. McConnel, *The Historical Origins of the Presuppositional Apologetics of Cornelius Van Til*, dissertation (Milwaukee, WI: Marquette University, 1999), 12. Cf. Raymond Perron, *Plaidoyer pour la Foi Chrétienne: L'apologétique selon Cornelius Van Til* (Montréal, QC: Publications de la FTÉ, 1996), 25. Norman Geisler, *Baker Encyclopedia of Christian Apologetics* (Grand Rapids, MI: Baker Academic, 2010), s.v. "Van Til, Cornelius." Robert den Dulk, *The Van Til Family: Humble Beginnings*, https://presupp101.wordpress.com/category/about-cornelius-van-til/ (accessed on Apr 21, 2016). John Frame, "Van Til, Cornelius," in Walter Elwell, ed., *Handbook of Evangelical Theologians* (Grand Rapids, MI: Baker, 1993), 156-167, downloaded from http://frame-poythress.org/cornelius-van-til/ (May 16, 2012, accessed on Apr 21, 2016).

2. McConnel, *The Historial Origins*, 13. Cf. Den Dulk, *The Van Til Family: Humble Beginnings*. Harriet A. Harris, *Fundamentalism and Evangelicals* (New York: Oxford University Press, 2016), 242. Frame, "Van Til, Cornelius." Perron says that the Van Til family settled in Hammond, Indiana (Perron, PFCASCV, 25). McConnel, Den Dulk, and Frame all agree that the Van Tils settled in Highland. Highland and Hammond are neighbouring towns in Indiana, so the confusion may be due to the fact that the Van Tils arrived by train in Hammond, where, according to Den Dulk, they were met by Reinder (Cornelius's uncle), who took them to Highland to find an apartment (Den Dulk, *The Van Til Family: Humble Beginnings*).

3. *Transcendental idealism* is what we call the approach of Immanuel Kant to human knowledge of the world. Kant proposed that humans participate actively in the knowledge process by imposing the universal categories of the intellect upon the empty forms that were received by the senses.

4. McConnel, *The Historical Origins*, 13.

5. McConnel, *The Historical Origins*. Cf. Den Dulk, *The Van Til Family: Humble Beginnings*. Perron, *Plaidoyer pour la Foi Chrétienne*, 26. Cornelius Van Til, "My Credo" in *Jerusalem and Athens: Critical Discussions on the Philosophy and Apologetics of Cornelius Van Til*, ed. E.R. Geehan (Phillipsburg, NJ: Presbyterian & Reformed, 1980), 8.

6. D.G. Hart and John R. Muether, "Why Machen Hired Van Til," *Ordained Servant* (vol. 6, no. 3), 65. It should

be noted that Machen did not hire Van Til due to any agreement with Van Til's approach to apologetics. Rather, as even a cursory reading of Machen's works will show, he did not agree with Van Til's approach to the traditional theistic arguments (cf. J. Gresham Machen, *The Christian Faith in the Modern World* (Grand Rapids, MI: Eerdmans, 1965), 15-17.

7. Cornelius Van Til, *Christian Apologetics*, 2d ed., ed. William Edgar (Phillipsburg, NJ: Presbyterian & Reformed, 2003), 17.

8. Van Til, *Christian Apologetics*, 135. Cf. Cornelius Van Til, *The Defense of the Faith*, 4th ed., ed. K. Scott Oliphint (Phillipsburg, NJ: Presbyterian & Reformed, 2008), 127. (Note that most of the content of *Christian Apologetics* is found, verbatim, in *The Defense of the Faith*.)

9. Van Til distinguishes between what he calls "metaphysical and psychological facts" (MPFs) and "epistemological and ethical facts" (EEFs) (see Van Til, *The Defense of the Faith*, 190.). Both MPFs and EEFs are seen as "presuppositions" by Van Til. According to Van Til, MPFs are common to all men (all humans are created by God, and thus dependent on God for their being, knowing, and willing), but are not known (nor knowable) by unregenerate men (*The Defense of the Faith*, 191.). Regenerate and unregenerate men do not have EEFs in common (*The Defense of the Faith*, 191, 257); thus, no epistemological or ethical common ground. According to Van Til, unregenerate thinkers can contribute to scientific discoveries, philosophy, and other areas of general human knowledge about the world—not because they "presuppose" (as in actually and actively holding to be true, without evidence, and as a starting point) that the triune God of the Bible exists, but because of the fact that MPFs apply just as much to them as to regenerate persons (*The Defense of the Faith*, 196.). This being said, unregenerate humans, due to their false EEFs, cannot really understand their contributions to true human knowledge.

10. Van Til, *The Defense of the Faith*, 10, 15, 82, 90fn2, 91, 105, 116-117, 120, 121. This means that we cannot reason with them in order to recommend Christianity as both true and verifiable. The only possibility could be the *sensus divinitatus*, which is deeply rooted in the hearts of all men.

11. Van Til, *An Introduction to Systematic Theology* (Phillipsburg, NJ: Presbyterian & Reformed), 3. Van Til, *The Defense of the Faith*, 57, 122, 180, 191, 193, 198, 199, 258, 288, 294.

12. *Epistemology* is the branch of philosophy that has to do with the study of knowledge (How do we know what we know? What are the limits of our knowledge? What does it mean to know?). An epistemological statement is a statement which is a declaration having to do with knowledge.

13. Van Til, *Christian Apologetics*, 98. Cf. Cornelius Van Til, *A Christian Theory of Knowledge* (Phillipsburg, NJ: Presbyterian & Reformed, 1969), 295.

14. Cf. Cornelius Van Til, *An Introduction to Systematic Theology*, vol. 5 of *In Defense of the Faith* (1974; Phillipsburg, NJ: Presbyterian & Reformed, 1982), 102.

15. Cf. Van Til, *An Introduction to Systematic Theology*, 37, 81-82, 85, 105, 108, 113. Van Til, *The Defense of the Faith*, 58, 66, 96, 118, 128.

16. Van Til, *An Introduction to Systematic Theology*.

17. Van Til, *Christian Apologetics*, 81. Cf. Van Til, *An Introduction to Systematic Theology*, 85.

18. Cf. Van Til, *The Defense of the Faith*, 82-83.

19. Van Til, *The Defense of the Faith*, 118, 137.

20. Cf. Van Til, *An Introduction to Systematic Theology*, 14, 17, 18, 22, 23, 37, 39, 63, 87, 102, 105, 108. Van Til, *The Defense of the Faith*, 16, 56-57, 66. Van Til, *Christian Apologetics*, 20.

21. Cf. Van Til, *An Introduction to Systematic Theology*, 17, 102. Van Til, *The Defense of the Faith*, 96.

22. Van Til, *An Introduction to Systematic Theology*, 67.

23. Van Til, *An Introduction to Systematic Theology*, 39. Van Til, *The Defense of the Faith*, 18.

24. Van Til, *An Introduction to Systematic Theology*, 102, 105. Van Til, *The Defense of the Faith*, 16, 18, 58, 67, 118.

25. Cf. Van Til, *The Defense of the Faith*, 137.

26. Van Til, *The Defense of the Faith*, 142.

27. Cf. Van Til, *The Defense of the Faith*, 121fn5. Oliphint explains that, for Van Til, a *presupposition* is "that which is

true and provides for the truth or falsity of another proposition. A presupposition in the way that Van Til uses it need not be confined to propositions, but includes the objective 'state of affairs' as well" (Van Til, *DF*, 121fn5).

28. The resemblance to Kant's categories of the understanding is striking.

29. It is important to note that when we talk of interpretational paradigms, we are not speaking of simple pre-suppositions (beliefs which must be believed prior to believing some other proposition) that might taint our understanding of the phenomena of the world in which we find ourselves; nor are we speaking of what has become known as worldviews—different religions and philosophies that could be said to have stock interpretations of the world; but, rather, to what Van Til refers to as a "life-and-world view" (Van Til, *The Defense of the Faith*, 103, 118), an interpretational system (*The Defense of the Faith*, 137-142), a consciousness (*The Defense of the Faith*, 72-73), etc. The general idea that Van Til expresses through these, and many other terms, is summed up by the term we use above—*interpretational paradigm,* or *schema.* Keep in mind that there are only two interpretational paradigms: The Fallen and the Regenerate. The idea of an interpretational paradigm can be illustrated, as we noted earlier, with the idea of a pair of "colored glasses [which] are cemented to his [the sinner's] face" (Van Til, *Christian Apologetics*, 98. Cf. Van Til, *A Christian Theory of Knowledge*, 295). It is also worth noting that there may be many "Belief systems/ worldviews" in one of the two interpretational paradigms. For example, all non-Christian religions (different belief systems/worldviews) would fall under the "interpretational paradigm" of fallen man.

30. Van Til, *Christian Apologetics*, 27, 77. Cf. Van Til, *An Introduction to Systematic Theology*, 24.

31. Van Til, *The Defense of the Faith*, 72.

32. Van Til, *The Defense of the Faith.*

33. Van Til, *The Defense of the Faith.*

34. Van Til, *An Introduction to Systematic Theology*, 11, 61, 101, 103. Cf. Van Til, *The Defense of the Faith*, 71.

35. Van Til, *An Introduction to Systematic Theology*, 101.

36. Van Til, *An Introduction to Systematic Theology*, 15, 23. For Van Til, any reasoning that does not begin with the triune God of Christianity, and His divinely inspired and inerrant Scriptures, understanding all of humanity to be fully dependent on the triune God of Christianity, is autonomous reasoning or a compromise with autonomous reasoning. Thus, Van Til accuses just about every reputable partisan of classical apologetics (including, thinkers such as Charles Hodge, C.S. Lewis, Thomas Aquinas, etc.) of compromising with autonomous reasoning, or of assuming that human reasoning is autonomous. For Van Til, autonomous reasoning necessarily understands everything, even the truths it discovers, wrongly. It should be noted that the notion of autonomy with which Van Til is dealing seems to be the Kantian notion of the autonomous will, which Van Til then reads into many pre-Kantian thinkers (such as Aquinas). Not only is this anachronistic, it is also wrong, at least when it comes to thinkers such as Aquinas, who boldly proclaimed that all of creation, humans included, are entirely dependent on God not only for their capacity to know, think, or will, but for their very being (cf. R.P. Sertillanges, *La Philosophie Morale de St. Thomas d'Aquin*, 2e ed. (Paris: Éditions Montaigne, 1946), 95-96.

37. Van Til, *An Introduction to Systematic Theology*, 11, 16.

38. Van Til, *An Introduction to Systematic Theology.*

39. Van Til, *An Introduction to Systematic Theology*, 11, 25, 61, 72, 101. Cf. Van Til, *The Defense of the Faith*, 62-63, 67, 70, 71. It should be noted that Van Til's understanding of *analogical* thinking/reasoning and predication is not at all related to the views of Aristotle and Aquinas, and their respective schools, on analogy. As is obvious from even a superficial lecture of both views. Oliphint says as much in a commentary in a footnote to Van Til's *Defense of the Faith* (Van Til, *The Defense of the Faith*, 62fn25). It should be noted, however, that Van Til does use the term analogy, on occasion, in the same way that Thomistic scholars use it (cf. Van Til, *The Defense of the Faith*, 60). For Van Til, *analogical knowledge* signifies that man's knowledge is dependent on God's knowledge (cf. Van Til, *The Defense of the Faith*, 62-63, 67, 70, 71). Van Til explains that analogical thinking or reasoning is "the form of reasoning employed by the Christian who recognizes that God is the ultimate reference point of predication" (Van Til, *An Introduction to Systematic Theology*, 101fn1. Cf. Ibid., 18, 257). Oliphint notes that "for Van Til, the notion of analogy was meant to communicate the ontological and epistemological difference between God and man. This difference has been expressed historically in terms of an archetypal/ectypal relationship" (Van Til, *The Defense of the Faith*, 62fn25). A general definition of *analogical predication*, from a well-known Thomistic scholar, would be as follows: "The property of a concept or linguistic term (not a real being) by which a concept or term is

predicated of several different subjects according to a meaning partly the same, partly different in each case: *strength of muscles - strength of will*" (W. Norris Clarke, *The One and the Many: A Contemporary Thomistic Metaphysics* (Notre Dame, IN: University of Notre Dame Press, 2001), 315).

40. Van Til, *An Introduction to Systematic Theology*, 101fn1. Cf. Ibid., 18, 257. Van Til, *Christian Apologetics*, 77.

41. Van Til, *The Defense of the Faith*, 73, 78, 87, 99, 105, 112, 127. Cf. Van Til, *Christian Apologetics*, 80, 135.

42. K. Scott Oliphint, *Covenantal Apologetics: Principles & Practice in Defense of Our Faith* (Wheaton, IL: Crossway, 2013), 159.

43. Oliphint, *Covenantal Apologetics*, 128.

44. Oliphint, *Covenantal Apologetics*, 129. It should be noted, in passing, that presuppositional apologetics depends upon a Platonic-Augustinian epistemology, in which we find the claim that there are innate ideas in the human intellect. The theory of innate ideas is, however, far from evident, highly debatable, and is certainly not clearly taught in Scripture.

45. Oliphint, *Covenantal Apologetics*, 130-135.

46. Cf. Van Til, *The Defense of the Faith*, 121-127, 135, 139, etc.

47. A *transcendental argument* is any attempt to prove some conclusion by showing that this conclusion follows from some other truth, or state of being, which can be taken for granted. It is sometimes said that Van Til never really explained the transcendental argument. One place where he did mention something that resembles the transcendental argument is in *Christian Apologetics*, 39. Here he showed that unless God exists, language is meaningless: "Christians are interested in showing to those who believe in *no* god or in *a* god, *a* beyond, *some* ultimate or absolute, that it is *this* God in whom they must believe lest all meaning should disappear from human words."

48. A *Reductio Ad Absurdity* is what we do when we reduce some position (A) to absurdity—when we show that some position entails obviously absurd conclusions. For example, based upon beliefs x, y, and z of position A, some absurdity follows (such as the negation of x, y, or z; the negation of position A; or some other belief that is untenable for those who hold to position A).

49. By showing both (a) that if they are coherent with their presuppositions, then they will necessarily arrive at the falsity of Christianity, and (b) that if they are coherent with their presuppositions, then they will also necessarily arrive at the falsity of their own position. (cf. Van Til, *The Defense of the Faith*, 121-127.)

50. For example, the existence of objective morals, the faculty of human reasoning, meaning, language, logic, art, etc.

51. Van Til, *Christian Apologetics*, 133-134. Cf. Van Til, *The Defense of the Faith*, 126.

52. Oliphint, *Covenental Apologetics*, 191, 192.

53. And this only by the addition of the word *argument*, for Immanuel Kant (a major influence on Van Til) frequently spoke of Transcendental deductions, and proofs, and used the same essential argument, for the same basic purposes, as Van Til (cf. Immanuel Kant, "The Only Possible Argument for the Demonstration of the Existence of God," in *Theoretical Philosophy, 1755-1770*, ed. David Walford (Cambridge, UK: Cambridge University Press, 1992), 107-201. This type of argument was also used by many idealists prior to Van Til.

54. For while Van Til did not elaborate on this argument, a contemporary of Van Til, C.S. Lewis, popularized both the argument from reason and the moral argument, which argue, based upon the facts of reasoning and objective morality, both (1) that God must exist, and (2) that any position denying the existence of God is incoherent (Cf. C.S. Lewis, *Mere Christianity*, ch. 1, and C.S. Lewis, *Miracles*, chs. 1-5).

55. The two key claims are (1) that all rational beings are always, and without ceasing, interpreting the world which presents itself to us, and (2) that there is no neutral point/ground from which we can see the world without interpreting it through one of the two interpretative schemas. If (1) and (2) are both true, then there is no way to know that our interpretative schema is true (unless something from outside of our schema tells us it is; but, then how would we know that this "something" was truly outside our schema, and not just another presupposition of our schema? Thus, we are left with the same consequence. Thus, absolute skepticism (we cannot know which belief system or interpretative schema is true) or absolute relativism (all belief systems or interpretative schemas are true) must be accepted.

56. Based on the above, we cannot know that our interpretation is true; we know that we cannot know that it is true;

but we dogmatically claim that it is. Cf. David Haines, "A Potential Problem with Presuppositional Apologetics," *Journal of the International Society of Christian Apologetics*, vol. 10, no. 1 (Mar 2017): 44-66. For other critiques of Van Til's approach to Christian Apologetics, see E.R. Geehan, ed., *Jerusalem and Athens: Critical Discussions on the Philosophy and Apologetics of Cornelius Van Til* (Phillipsburg, NJ: Presbyterian & Reformed, 1980), and R.C. Sproul, John Gerstner, and Arthur Lindsley, *Classical Apologetics: A Rational Defense of the Christian Faith and a Critique of Presuppositional Apologetics* (Grand Rapids, MI: Zondervan, 1984).

For further defenses of Presuppositionalism, aside from the works of Van Til and K. Scott Oliphint, which have already been mentioned, see Scott Oliphint, *The Consistency of Van Til's Methodology* (Scarsdale, NY: Westminster Discount Book Service, 1990), and Greg L. Bahnsen, *Van Til's Apologetic: Readings and Analysis* (Phillipsburg, NJ: Presbyterian & Reformed, 1998).

57. Some have suggested that Van Til confuses ontology with epistemology (and, indeed, he does). For example, he seems to suggest that states of affairs, or beings, are presuppositions (cf. Oliphint, *The Consistency of Van Til's Methodology*, 10fn26). Others have suggested that Van Til is incapable of coherently maintaining the doctrine of God (the classical doctrine of God) to which they so adamantly claim to adhere, for they jettison the very thing which allows them to maintain it (natural theology). One might also suggest that because he denies that unregenerate humans can obtain true knowledge of the true God through their reasoned observations of nature (cf. Van Til, *An Introduction to Systematic Theology*, 101, 104), he is, therefore, unorthodox on this point (cf. David Haines, "Natural Theology and Protestant Orthodoxy," *Ad Fontes*, 1, 9 (May 2017), 1-3.

Chapter 75—Who Was Francis Schaeffer?

1. See "Evidentialism" in Terry L. Miethe, *Compact Dictionary of Doctrinal Words* (Minneapolis, MN: Bethany House, 1988), 87; "Fideism," 92-93; "Presuppositionalism," 164-165.

2. See William Edgar, "10 Things You Should Know about Francis Schaeffer," https://www.crossway.org/articles/10-things-you-should-know-about-francis-schaeffer/.

3. See *The Francis A. Schaeffer Trilogy: Three Essential Books in One Volume* (Wheaton, IL: Crossway, 1990), with the understanding that Schaeffer viewed these three works as foundational to all the rest.

4. See "Frank Schaeffer, Son of Evangelical Royalty, Turns His Back, and Tells the Tale," https://www.nytimes.com/2011/08/20/us/20beliefs.html.

Index

To learn more about Harvest House books and
to read sample chapters, visit our website:

www.harvesthousepublishers.com

HARVEST HOUSE PUBLISHERS
EUGENE, OREGON